CW00926017

THE HISTORY OF HERODOTUS,

LITERALLY TRANSLATED INTO ENGLISH;

ILLUSTRATED

WITH NOTES,

EXPLANATORY AND CRITICAL,

FROM

LARCHER, RENNELL, MITFORD, SCHWEIGHÆUSER,

MODERN BOOKS OF TRAVELS, &c. &c.

TO WHICH IS ADDED

LARCHER'S TABLE

OF THE CHRONOLOGY OF HERODOTUS.

BY

A GRADUATE OF THE UNIVERSITY.

IN TWO VOLUMES.

VOL. I.

OXFORD:

PRINTED AND PUBLISHED BY TALBOYS AND WHEELER.

SOLD BY MESSRS. LONGMAN, HURST, REES, ORME, BROWN, AND GREEN; G. AND W. B. WHITTAKER; AND J. DUNCAN, LONDON.

1824.

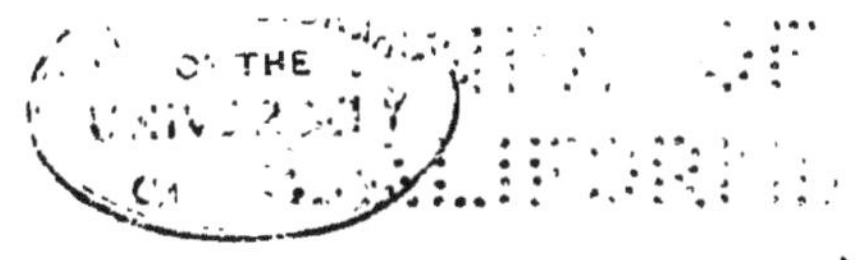

THE HISTORY OF HERODOTUS.

BOOK I.

CLIO.

HERODOTUS of Halicarnassus publishes these historical researches[a] in order that the actions of men may not be obliterated by length of time, and that the great and wonderful deeds which have been displayed both by Greeks and Barbarians[b] may not become destitute of glory, and also that other things[c], and the reason for which they carried on war with each other, *may not be forgotten.*

CHAP. I. Those of the Persians that are celebrated for their knowledge[d] in the history of their country affirm, that the Phœnicians were the original cause of the contention; for that this nation having migrated from the coast of that which is called the Red Sea[e] to the shores of our sea[f], and having settled in that country which they inhabit at the present day,

[a] Ἱστορίη does not signify history, but researches made with careful and accurate inquiry; the word ἱστορέω signifying to inquire minutely.

[b] This name was given by the ancient Greeks and Romans, to all who were not of their country, or not initiated in their language, manners and customs. In this sense, the word signified with them no more than foreigner; not as with us, a wild, rude, and uncivilized person.

[c] This last part of the introduction cannot evidently be referred to what immediately precedes, but either to μὴ ἐξίτηλα γένηται, or as Schweighæuser wishes to the first line. See his note.

[d] Λόγος in Herodotus and other authors often signifies a history; λογοποιός, a writer of history; λόγιος, a man skilled in the history and antiquities of a country. *Larcher.*

[e] Herodotus denominates Erythræan or Red, the whole of that sea which lies between India, Persia, and Arabia, (our sea of Omman,) together with its gulfs and bays. But he, notwithstanding, distinguishes the Arabian gulf very pointedly. *Rennel*, p. 197.

It is evident from book vii. chap. 89. that the Phœnicians, when they changed their place of residence, passed over by land. *Larcher.*

[f] The Greeks always distinguished the Mediterranean by this name.

presently applied themselves *to make* long voyages, and making it their practice to export the merchandizes of Egypt and Assyria[g], visited divers countries, and among others Argos. Now Argos at that time was superior in every point to the cities[h] in the country which is now called Greece[i]. *They add*, that the Phœnicians on their arrival began to expose their merchandize for sale; and on the fifth or sixth day, when nearly every thing had been disposed of, many other women, and the king's daughter in particular, came down to the shore; (the Persians and Greeks agree in calling her Io the daughter of Inachus;) that while these women standing about the stern of the ship were buying what they most had a mind to, the Phœnicians, having mutually encouraged one another, rushed upon them: now *they state* that the greater part of them escaped by flight, but that Io with some others was carried off; and the Phœnicians having secured them on board sailed away for Egypt.

II. In this manner the Persians, differing from the Greeks, relate that Io passed into Egypt, and that this was the commencement of the acts of injustice *which they committed against each other*. *They affirm also*, that after this event, certain Greeks (for they cannot tell the *name of their country*, but they most probably were Cretans) having touched at Tyre in Phœnicia, carried away Europa the king's daughter; now this *they say* was only a fair retaliation, but the Greeks afterwards became guilty of a second injustice, for having sailed in a ship of war[k] to Aia, a town of Colchis, and to the river Phasis, and having dispatched the affairs which were the immediate object of their voyage, carried off from thence Medea the daughter of the king; the Colchian king sent a herald into Greece to demand satisfaction for the violence, and the restitution of his daughter; the Greeks returned for answer, that as they had not given any satisfaction for the violence offered to Io[l] the Argive, so they would give none to the Colchians.

[g] This probably includes not only that of Assyria, but of Persia and Arabia also; transmitted through Assyria. *Rennel*, p. 249.

[h] προέχειν, in this sense, governs a genitive of the person excelled, and a dative of the thing in which the superiority consists; the passage is interpreted in this way in the Latin to Schweighæuser's edition, but Larcher translates it, "superior to all the cities, &c." See his note.

[i] The country which in the time of Herodotus was called Hellas or Greece, was not known by any one name in the times of the Trojan war, and for some considerable time after, but by the names of its several nations. This is positively affirmed by Thucydides, book i. chap. 3.

[k] Literally, in a long ship. The long vessels were vessels of war; the round, merchantmen and transports. *Larcher*.

[l] It may be urged that the king of Colchis had nothing to do with the violence offered to Io; she was carried off by the Phœnicians. But, according to the Persians, all the nations of Asia composed but one body, of which they were the head. An injury, therefore, offered to one of the members, was considered as an hostility against the whole. Thus, as

III. They relate that, in the next succeeding age, Alexander the son of Priam, having heard of this, was desirous of obtaining a wife from Greece by the same means, being fully persuaded that he should not have to make any reparation, since they had made none; that when with this persuasion he had carried off Helen, the Greeks determined in the first place to send ambassadors to demand her restitution, and to require satisfaction for the violence offered her; the Trojans, when the ambassadors had explained their instructions, objected to them the rape of Medea; that they, when they had themselves neither given satisfaction, nor restored Medea when they demanded her, desired to obtain satisfaction from others.

IV. *The Persians continue to relate*, that hitherto rapes alone were reciprocally committed; but after this period, the Greeks beyond all doubt were peculiarly culpable; for they entered Asia with an army before the Persians had entered Europe[m]. To commit rapes, the Persians considered the part of unjust men, but to take such pains to revenge, the part of fools, as of wise men to pay no regard to such women; for it was obvious that they would never have been carried off, unless they had themselves been willing. For this reason, the Persians assert, that they of Asia had paid no attention to the women that had been carried off, whereas the Greeks, for the sake of a Lacedæmonian woman collected a large armament, and then having passed over to Asia overthrew the power of Priam[n]. From this event they have always consi-

we see in the fourth chapter, the Persians considered the Greeks as their enemies, from the time of the destruction of Troy. *Larcher.*

[m] Mr. Larcher asks, whether the Persians did not know that the Strymonian Thracians, who were afterwards called Bythinians, had been carried from Europe to Asia by the Teucrians and Mysians? (Herod. lib. vii. chap. 75.) and that Cadmus had come from Phœnicia, (Herod. lib. ii. chap. 49.) and established himself in Bœotia, and Pelops from Phrygia in the Peloponnese? (Herod. lib. vii. chap. 9.)

But Asia, however, is to be understood in a limited sense, for the parts beyond India and Turkestan were unknown. *Rennel*, p. 231.

[n] Perhaps it may not be an improper digression here, to bring to the reader's recollection a passage in the history of the British island. Exploits like that of Paris were not uncommon in Ireland, in the twelfth century. In a lower line, they have been frequent there still in our days; but in that age popular opinion was so favourable to them, that even princes, like Jason and Paris, gloried in such proofs of their gallantry and spirit. Dermot, king of Leinster, accordingly formed a design on Dervorghal, a celebrated beauty, wife of O'Ruark, king of Leitrim, and, between force and fraud, succeeded in carrying her off. O'Ruark resented the affront, as might be expected. He procured a confederacy of neighbouring chieftains, with the king of Connaught, the most powerful prince of Ireland at their head. Leinster was invaded, the princess recovered, and, after hostilities continued with various success during many years, Dermot was expelled from his kingdom. Thus far the resemblance holds with much exactness. The sequel differs; for the rape of Dervorghal, beyond comparison inferior in celebrity, had yet consequences far more important than the rape of Helen. The fugitive Dermot, deprived of other hope,

dered the Greeks as their enemies; for the Persians lay claim to Asia and all the barbarian tribes that inhabit it, but they consider Europe and the Greeks as totally distinct.

V. Thus the Persians relate the events that took place, and attribute to the taking of Troy the cause of their enmity towards the Greeks. The Phœnicians however do not agree with them with regard to Io, for they affirm that they did not carry her away by force to Egypt, but that she had an illicit connection with the master of the ship while at Argos, and that, when she discovered herself to be pregnant, she voluntarily embarked and departed with them, through fear of her parents, and in order that she might not be detected. Such then are the relations of the Persians and Phœnicians, and I will not attempt to say in which way these things happened; but after I have given an account of him whom I know to have been the first to commit injustice towards the Greeks, I will proceed to the rest of my narration, and will alike describe both the smaller and larger states; for many of those which were formerly powerful, have become inconsiderable, and those which flourish in our days, were formerly obscure. As I am convinced therefore that human felicity never continues in the same state, I will make mention of both in like manner.

VI. Crœsus, by birth a Lydian, and son to Alyattes, was king of those nations that are situate on this side the river Halys[o], which flowing from the south between the Syrians[p] and Paphlagonians, discharges itself towards the north into the sea called the Euxine. He was the first of all the barbarians we know, who rendered some of the Grecians tributary to him, and received others into his alliance; for he subdued the Ionians and Æolians, with the Dorians that inhabit in Asia, and made the Lacedæmonians his friends: whereas before his reign, all the Greeks were free. For the irruption of the Cimmerians[q] into Ionia with an army, which happened

applied to the powerful monarch of the neighbouring island, Henry the Second; and in return for assistance to restore him to his dominions, offered to hold them in vassalage of the crown of England. The English conquest of Ireland followed. Mr. Hume, in his History of England, has written the name of the heroine of this story, Omach. Dr. Leland's History of Ireland is here followed, with which Mr. Hume's more abridged account, in all material circumstances sufficiently tallies. Lord Lyttleton, in his History of Henry the Second, both relates the facts and writes the names nearly as Dr. Leland. *Mitford's Hist. Greece*, chap. i.

[o] The Halys had two branches, one flowed from the south, the other from the east. Herodotus speaks only of the first, Arrian of the second. See M. D'Anville's Geograph. Ancienne, Abreg. vol. ii. p. 7.

[p] By the Syrians, Herodotus here means the Cappadocians, called by the Greeks Leuco-Syrians; the Σύριοι properly mean the Cappadocians; the Σύροι, the inhabitants of Syria, from the Mediterranean to the Euphrates. *Gronovius.*

[q] Strabo dates this incursion of the Cimmerians about the time of Homer, or somewhat before. Wesseling thinks, and with reason, the authority of the geographer of less weight than that of

before the time of Crœsus, ended not in the destruction of cities; but only in ravages, incident to a sudden invasion.

VII. This kingdom belonged to the Heraclidæ, and passed into the family of Crœsus, called Mermnadæ, in the following manner: Candaules, by the Greeks named Myrsilus, being descended from Alcæus the son of Hercules, was king of Sardis; for Agron the son of Ninus, grandson to Belus, and great grandson to Alcæus, was the first of the Heraclidæ that reigned in Sardis, and Candaules the son of Myrsus was the last. Those who had been kings of this country before Agron, were descended from Lydus the son of Atys, who gave his name to the whole nation, which before his time were called Mæones. The Heraclidæ descended from Hercules, and a slave of Jardanus, to whom the administration of the government had been entrusted[r] by these princes, obtained the supreme power from the declaration of an oracle; and held it five hundred and five years, during two and twenty generations[s] of men, the son always succeeding the father, to the time of Candaules the son of Myrsus.

VIII. This Candaules[t] so passionately loved his wife, that he thought her by far the most beautiful of all women; and in this persuasion extolled her beauties above measure to Gyges the son of Dascylus, who was one of his guard, a particular favourite, to whom he used to communicate his most important affairs. Not long after, being marked out by fate

our historian, who supposes it to have been in the reign of Ardys. See chapter fifteen of this book, and chapter twelve of book four. For my own part, I am of opinion that the two authors speak of two distinct incursions. Herodotus refers to the last. At the time of the first there were no Greek cities in Asia Minor; and it was his intention to intimate, that the last had no operation injurious to the liberties of Greece. *Larcher.*

Many learned men are of opinion that the Cimmerians were the descendants of the Gomer of Scripture. The reasons alleged are of this nature: in the genealogical table of Moses, we are told that Gomer was the son of Japhet. The Scholiasts, and those of them too who are most authentic, say that Cimmeris was the son of Japetus. Japetus is by Apollodorus said to be the son of Cœlum and Terra, that is of Noah, who was called Vir Terræ. *Beloe.*

r Ἐπιτραφθεὶς is the part. aor. 1. pass. from ἐπιτρέπομαι, it is entrusted to my care. Homer uses the word in this sense, Il. lib. ii. v. 25. ᾧ λαοί ἐπιτετράφαται, to whose care the people have been committed. Compare book iii. chap. 142, 155, and 157. *Larcher.*

s For this number Larcher, contrary to all authority, puts fifteen, without any sufficient reason; and is corrected by Volney Chron. Herod. Paris, 1808. *Schweighæuser.*

t The story of Rosamond, queen of the Lombards, as related by Mr. Gibbon, bears an exact resemblance to this of Candaules. "The queen of Italy had "stooped from her throne to the arms of "a subject; and Helmichis, the king's "armour-bearer, was the secret minister "of her pleasure and revenge. Against "the proposal of murder he could no "longer urge the scruples of fidelity or "ingratitude; but Helmichis trembled "when he revolved the danger, as well "as the guilt. He pressed, and obtain-"ed, that one of the bravest champions "of the Lombards should be associated "to the enterprise; but no more than a "promise of secrecy could be drawn "from the gallant Peredeus. The mode "of seduction employed by Rosamond, "betrays her shameless insensibility both "to honour and to love. She supplied the

for destruction[u], he addressed Gyges to this effect: "Since "you seem to me not to believe the things I have said con- "cerning the beauty of my wife, (for the ear is less easily "convinced than the eye[x],) you must contrive to see her "naked." But he exclaimed aloud, and said, "What disor- "dered words are you uttering, when you command me to "view the queen my mistress naked? a woman puts off her "modesty with her garments[y]. Many excellent precepts "have been discovered by men of former ages for our in- "struction, and this one among the rest, *That every man* "*should look into his own affairs*. As for me, I believe the "queen to be the most beautiful of all women; but I earnest- "ly desire you would not make an unlawful request."

IX. Thus Gyges, dreading lest any harm might result from it, combated *his proposal*. But he replied in these words; "Be confident, Gyges, and neither fear, that I address you "thus in order to make experiment of your fidelity, nor lest "any mischief befal you from my wife; for I will so contrive "the matter, that she shall never know she was seen by you. "To this end I will place you behind the open door of the "apartment in which we sleep; after I have entered, my wife "will make her appearance, and as she undresses herself, she "will lay her garments, one by one, on a seat near the door, "and will give you time to take a full view of her at leisure; "when she approaches the bed with her back turned towards "you, be careful that she may not discover you afterwards "repassing through the doors."

"place of one of her female attendants, "who was beloved by Peredeus, and "contrived some excuse for darkness "and silence, till she could inform her "companion, that he enjoyed the queen "of the Lombards, and that his own "death, or the death of the king, must "be the consequence of such treasonable "adultery. In this alternative he chose "rather to be the accomplice than the "victim of Rosamond, whose undaunted "spirit was incapable of fear or re- "morse." *Gibbon*, chap. 45.

u Herodotus frequently uses this kind of expression. See book ii. chap. 161. iv. 79. v. 92, 94. ix. 109.

x Dionysius of Halicarnassus remarks, that Herodotus has here made use of an expression appropriate to Barbarians, since he substitutes the ears and eyes for the discourse and sight of objects;

Segnius irritant animos demissa per aurem,
Quam quæ sunt oculis subjecta fidelibus.
Hor. Ars. Poet. 180.

So also Polyb. Excerpta e libro xii. 15. and Sophocles Fragm. 77. ex edit. Brunck. Theophrastus, according to Plutarch, affirms that of all the senses, by the ear, the passions are most easily excited. *Larcher.*

For acquiring a knowledge of many things, or any science, (ἐπιστήμη,) the ear is most fitted. *Wesseling.*

y Plutarch in his Conjugal Precepts, (tom. ii. p. 139.) denies the truth of this; but he applies it to a woman with regard to her husband. Timæus (Athen. Deipnosoph. xii. 3.) states, that the Tyrrhenians are waited upon by naked women; and Theopompus (Id. ibid.) adds, that it was not held disgraceful in that nation for women to appear naked in the presence of men. Ennius when speaking of men says,

Flagiti principium est nudare inter civis corpora. Fragm. p. 300.

Larcher.

X. Gyges, being unable to avoid it, held himself in readiness, and at the usual hour the king took Gyges to his apartment. The queen came immediately after, and Gyges saw her enter and lay aside her garments. But as she turned her back to go towards the bed, he endeavoured at the same time to escape unnoticed, but she observed him as he went out. And though she plainly perceived that this was her husband's contrivance, shame restrained her from making the least exclamation, and she pretended not to have perceived him, being resolved within herself to be revenged upon Candaules: for among the Lydians, and almost all barbarous nations, it is a great dishonour even for a man to be seen naked[z].

XI. In this manner then, without making any disclosure, she preserved silence, but as soon as the day arrived, after having prepared those, whom she knew to be most faithful among her servants, she summoned Gyges to her presence. He, not suspecting the queen[a] to be acquainted with what had passed, and being accustomed to go to her as often as she sent for him, failed not to obey her order. When he was come, she said to him, "Gyges, of two ways which are "open before you, I permit you to choose which you will "take; either kill Candaules, and take possession of me, toge"ther with the kingdom of Lydia; or you must yourself thus[b] "die immediately: that by obeying Candaules without re"serve, you may not hereafter behold what ought not to "be seen by you; for either the contriver of this thing must "perish, or you, who have seen me naked, and have done "what is contrary to custom. Gyges at first stood amazed at these words; and afterwards earnestly begged her, that she would not bind him to the necessity of making so hard a

[z] Plato tells us, (Polit. lib. v.) that the Greeks had not long considered it disgraceful and ridiculous for a man to be seen naked; an opinion, he adds, which still exists even among the greater part of the Barbarians. *Larcher.*

It may also be remarked that Lycurgus ordered the young women of Sparta, to dance naked at their solemn festivals, in the midst of the young men. This practice, as we learn from Plato de Leg. v. p. 452. was not peculiar to Sparta, having been before established at Crete. The omission of subligacula in the Grecian games, and the practice of wearing them among the Barbarians, see Thucydides, book i. chap. 6.

[a] This wife of Candaules was called Nyssia, according to Hephaestion. Plato makes Gyges a shepherd in the service of the king of Lydia, who having entered into a chasm of the earth, discovered a dead man enclosed within a brazen horse, and took a ring from his finger. He soon discovered that this ring had the property of making him invisible, when he turned the seal or stone set in it to the inside of his hand, and by the assistance of it he seduced the queen, and assassinated Candaules, (de Rep. lib. ii.) Xenophon (Cyrop. vii. 2.) says, he was a slave. Plutarch (Quæst. Græc. p. 302.) says, that Gyges took up arms against Candaules, and by the assistance of the Milesians defeated that prince, who died in the field of battle. The opinion of Herodotus appears preferable, as he was born in a city contiguous to Lydia. *Larcher.*

[b] The word *οὕτω* shews that she pointed to the servants who were prepared to put him to death if he disobeyed. *Schweigh.*

choice. But when he saw he could not prevail, and that he must either kill his master, or die himself by the hands of others, he chose to save his own life. "Since then," said he to the queen, "you compel me against my will to kill my "master, let me know how we shall execute this enterprise." "From that very place," replied she, "where he exposed me "naked to your view, you shall fall upon him as he sleeps."

XII. When they had thus concerted their measures, on the approach of night he followed the queen to the chamber, (for he was not permitted to return home, nor was there any possibility of escape, but it was necessary that either he or Candaules should perish,) where she gave him a dagger, and placed him behind the door, as Candaules had done. After some time he went softly to the bed, killed the king as he slept, and possessed himself of his wife and kingdom. He is mentioned in the Iambic verses of Archilochus[c] the Parian, who lived at the same time.

XIII. In this manner Gyges obtained the kingdom, and was confirmed in his acquisition by the oracle of Delphi. For when the Lydians, highly resenting the death of Candaules, had assembled together in arms, an agreement was at last concluded between them and the soldiers of Gyges, that if the oracle should pronounce him king of Lydia, he should be permitted to reign; if not, he should restore the kingdom to the Heraclidæ. The oracle gave an answer, and thus Gyges became king. But the Pythian added this clause; "that the "Heraclidæ should be avenged, in the time of the fifth de-"scendant of Gyges[d];" though neither the Lydians nor their kings had any regard to this prediction, before it was actually accomplished.

XIV. Thus the Mermnadæ having excluded the Heraclidæ obtained the supreme power. After Gyges had obtained the kingdom, he sent many presents to Delphi; for he not only dedicated the greatest part[e] of the silver seen in that place, but also made an offering of a vast quantity of gold; among all which nothing better deserves to be remembered, than six bowls of gold[f] weighing thirty talents; these now stand in

[c] He was one of the first writers of Iambics. All that remain of his writings are carefully collected in Brunck's Analecta.

Larcher has a note of considerable length to ascertain the precise period in which he flourished.

[d] This was fulfilled on Crœsus; see chapter XCI.

[e] Ὅσα must be joined with πλεῖστα. This kind of expression occurs very frequently in Greek writers. They say, πλεῖστον ὅσον, ἀμήχανον ὅσον, θαυμαστὸν ὅσον, &c. Cicero and other Latins have imitated; Sales in dicendo *mirum quantum* valent. Orat. 26. See Viger. ch. iii. 7. The construction however may be, ἀλλ' ὅσα μέν ἐστιν ἀναθήματα ἀργύρου ἐν Δελφοῖς, τούτων τὰ πλεῖστα ἐστὶν οἱ. *Larcher*.

[f] Gyges, Alyattes and Crœsus, according to Strabo, derived their wealth

the treasury of the Corinthians[g]; though to say the truth, that treasury was not founded by the people of Corinth, but by Cypselus the son of Aetion. This Gyges is the first of all the barbarians we know, who dedicated donations at Delphi; except Midas the son of Gordius[h] king of Phrygia, who presented the royal tribunal, on which he used to sit in public and administer justice, which is a piece of workmanship that deserves to be considered, and stands in the same place as the cups of Gyges. The gold and silver, of which these dedications consist, is called Gygian, from the name of the donor. He made war against Miletus and Smyrna, and took Colophon by force; but as he performed no other memorable action during all the time of his reign, which was eight and thirty years, we will pass on from him after having said so much.

XV. I will proceed to mention Ardys, his son and successor; who took the city of Priene, and invaded the territories of Miletus. In his time the Cimmerians[i], who had been dispossessed of their own country by the Scythian Nomades, passed into Asia, and possessed themselves of all Sardis, with the exception of the citadel.

XVI. He reigned forty-nine years, and his son Sadyattes succeeded him, and reigned twelve years. Alyattes succeeding Sadyattes, made war upon Cyaxares[k] grandson of Deioces, and upon the Medes. He expelled the Cimmerians out of Asia; and having taken the city of Smyrna founded by the Colophonians, he invaded the territories of the Clazomenians. But not finding the event answerable to his desires[l], he was obliged to return with considerable loss. He also performed in the course of his reign the following actions which fully deserve mention.

from some mines in Lydia, situated between Atarnæ and Pergamos. The riches of Gyges became proverbial, as this verse of Archilochus shews,

Ού μοι τὰ Γύγεω τοῦ πολυχρύσου μέλει.

Those of Crœsus surpassed them;

Divitis audita est cui non opulentia Crœsi?
Ovid. Epist. Pont. lib. iv. ep. 3. 37. *Larcher.*

g In the temple of Delphi there were different apartments or chapels, which belonged to different cities, princes, or opulent individuals. The offerings which these respectively made to the Deity were here deposited. *Larcher.*

In aftertimes we find that the most venerated temples were resorted to as banks, where the sanctity of the place afforded security for treasures deposited which could not be procured elsewhere. The insecurity which prevailed is evident from Herod. book viii. ch. 86.

h There were in Phrygia a number of princes called after this name, as is proved by Bouhier in his Researches on Herodotus, p. 78. *Larcher.*

i See note on chapter VI.

k This is perfectly consistent; Phraortes, the father of Cyaxares, reigned in Media during the time that Ardys, grandfather of Alyattes, sat on the throne of Sardis. Phraortes began to reign B.C. 677. and died 628. *Larcher.*

l Literally: From these he retired not as he wished, but having met with a considerable check. The Greeks frequently soften any calamity by such an expression. So in chapter XXXII. and Eurip. Androm. 1168. *Larcher.*

XVII. He continued the war which his father had begun against the Milesians, and entering their country, attacked them in the following manner. When their corn and fruits were ripe, he took the field with his army, attended in his march with pipes, harps, and flutes masculine and feminine[m]. On his arrival in the territory of the Milesians, he neither demolished nor burnt their country houses, nor forced off the doors, but when he had destroyed their trees and the produce of the land, he returned home; for he knew it was in vain to sit down before the city, because they were masters of the sea. He would not destroy their houses, to the end that the Milesians having those habitations, might apply themselves to sow and cultivate their lands, and by that means he might have something to ravage, when he should invade them with his army.

XVIII. In this manner he carried on the war eleven years, during which the Milesians received two great blows, one at Limeneion within their own territories, and the other in the plains of the Mæander. Six of these eleven years Sadyattes the son of Ardys was still king of the Lydians, and during those he made incursions into the Milesian territory, (for this Sadyattes was the person that began the war.) But during the five succeeding years Alyattes the son of Sadyattes, who (as I have before mentioned) received it from his father, earnestly applied himself to it. The Milesians had no support all that time from any of the Ionians, except the Chians only; who came to their assistance, in requital for the succour they had received, for formerly the Milesians had assisted the Chians in prosecuting the war against the Erythræans.

XIX. In the twelfth year, when the corn had been set on fire by the army, an accident of the following nature occurred. As soon as the corn had caught fire, the flames were carried by the force of the wind to the temple of Minerva, called Assesian[n]; the temple being thus set on fire was burnt to the ground. No notice was taken of this at the time; but afterwards, when the army had returned to Sardis, Alyattes fell sick. When the disease continued a considerable time he sent to Delphi messengers to consult the oracle, either from the advice of some friend, or because it appeared right to his own mind to make inquiries of the God concerning his disorder. The Pythian refused to give any answer to the messengers when they arrived at Delphi, until they had rebuilt

m Aulus Gellius finds fault with the luxury of Alyattes in having female flute players in his army; but Larcher and Schweigh. are of opinion that it alludes to the different sounds of the flutes.

n Assesus was a small town dependent on Miletus. Minerva had a temple there, and hence took the name of the Assesian Minerva. *Larcher*.

the temple of Minerva which they had burnt at Assesus in the country of Miletus.

XX. This relation I had from the Delphians: and the Milesians add; that Periander the son of Cypselus, who was at that time very intimately connected with Thrasybulus, king of Miletus, having heard of the answer that had been delivered to Alyattes, dispatched a messenger to inform him of it, in order that by being aware of it beforehand[o], he might form his plans on the present circumstance. This is the Milesian account.

XXI. When Alyattes had received information of what had passed at Delphi, he immediately sent ambassadors to Miletus, being desirous of making a truce with Thrasybulus and the Milesians, for all the time the temple should be rebuilding. The messenger[p] accordingly set out for Miletus. But Thrasybulus having had the preceding intelligence, and perceiving the design of Alyattes, had recourse to the following artifice: having collected in the market-place all the corn which was in the city, either of his own or belonging to private persons, he made a proclamation, that all the inhabitants should eat and drink cheerfully together, upon a signal to be given by him.

XXII. This was done and ordered by Thrasybulus, to the end that the Sardian ambassadors, seeing so great a quantity of corn, and the people feasting and enjoying themselves, might make their report accordingly; which happened as he designed. For when the ambassador had seen these things, and delivered this message to Thrasybulus, he returned to Sardis; and for no other reason, as I am informed, did a cessation of hostilities ensue. For Alyattes expecting that there was a great scarcity of corn in Miletus, and that the people were reduced to extreme distress, received a quite contrary account from his ambassador at his return; by which means an agreement was made between them, that for the future they should be friends and confederates; and Alyattes, instead of one, having built two temples at Assesus, dedicated to Minerva, recovered his health. The events of the war, which Alyattes made against Thrasybulus and the Milesians, were such.

[o] Τι is not governed by *προειδὼς*, but by *βουλεύηται*. *Χρηστήριον* is understood with *προειδὼς*. See the Memoirs of the Academy of Inscriptions, tom. xxiii. Hist. p. 111. *Larcher*.

[p] The word in the Greek is *ἀπόστολος*, which signifies a vessel for carrying passengers or merchandize, &c. In that case *ναῦς* is either expressed or understood; for *ἀπόστολος* in that sense is an adjective. But it most commonly signifies a naval expedition, which has induced Gronovius to suppose that the herald went by sea. *Στόλος* signifies a body or troop of men who go either by sea or land to execute any enterprise. Compare Xenoph. Anab. lib. iii. ch. 1. Eurip. Phœn. v. 1072. *Larcher*.

XXIII. Periander the son of Cypselus, who acquainted Thrasybulus with the answer of the oracle, was king of Corinth: and the Corinthians say, that a most astonishing thing happened there in his time, which is also confirmed by the Lesbians. Those people give out, that Arion of Methymna, who was second to none of his time in playing on the harp[q], and who was the first, that we are acquainted with, who composed, named and taught the Dithyrambic measure[r] at Corinth, was brought on shore at Tænarus upon the back of a dolphin.

XXIV. They say, that Arion having continued long with Periander, was desirous of making a voyage to Italy and Sicily, where when he had acquired great riches, determining to return to Corinth, he went to Tarentum, and hired a ship of certain Corinthians, because he put more confidence in them than in any other nation. But these men, when they were in the open sea, conspired together to throw him overboard and seize his money, which he no sooner understood, than offering them all his treasure, he only begged they would spare his life. But the seamen being inflexible, commanded him either to kill himself, that he might be buried ashore, or to leap immediately into the sea. Arion, reduced to this hard choice, most earnestly desired, that having determined his death, they would permit him to dress in his richest apparel, and to sing to them, standing on the poop of the ship, promising to make away with himself when he had done. The seamen, pleased that they should hear a song from the best singer in the world, granted his request, and went from the stern to the middle of the vessel. In the mean time Arion, having put on all his robes, took up his harp, and performed the Orthian[s] strain; at the end of the air he leaped into the sea as he was, and the Corinthians continued their voyage homeward. They say, a dolphin received him on his back[t], and carried him

[q] Κιθαρῳδὸς differs from Κιθαριστής. In order to understand the difference we must observe that the ancients called the lyre not only λύρη but κίθαρις, and that κιθάρα is the cithara or harp, from which we have formed the word guittar, although the cithara and guittar are very different instruments. Apollo invented the lyre, Mercury the cithara. The κιθαριστής then strikes the lyre, the κιθαρῳδὸς accompanies his cithara with his voice. *Larcher.*

[r] This was a kind of verse or hymn in honour of Bacchus, or in praise of drinking; it was a rude and perplexed composition, replete with figurative and obscure expressions. *Bellanger.*

[s] The Orthian air was performed on a flute or cithara, in an elevated key and a quick time, and was therefore particularly adapted to animate combatants. Timotheus played this air before Alexander. *Larcher.* See Dryden's Ode on St. Cecilia's day.

[t] In all probability Arion threw himself into the sea in or near the harbour of Tarentum. The Corinthians, without troubling themselves any farther, set sail. He gained the shore, and if the remainder of the tale has any foundation, he probably met with a vessel ready to sail, which outstript the Corinthians. There are on the head of vessels, figures from which they often are named, as the Centaur and

to Tænarus; where he went on shore, and thence proceeded to Corinth without changing his clothes, and upon his arrival there, he related the whole of what had happened to him; but that Periander, giving no credit to his relation, put him under a close confinement, and took especial care to find out the seamen: that when they appeared before him, he inquired if they could give any information concerning Arion; and they answering, that they had left him with great riches at Tarentum, and that he was undoubtedly safe in some part of Italy, Arion in that instant appeared before them in the very dress he had on when he leaped into the sea; at which they were so astonished, that being fully convicted, they could no longer deny the fact. These things are reported by the Corinthians and Lesbians; in confirmation of which, a statue of Arion, made of brass, and of a moderate size, representing a man sitting upon a dolphin, is seen at Tænarus.

XXV. Alyattes the Lydian, having put an end to the Milesian war, died, after he had reigned fifty-seven years. He was the second of his family that made offerings at Delphi; which he did upon the recovery of his health, dedicating a large silver goblet, with a saucer made of iron, inlaid; which deserves attention above all the offerings that are at Delphi. It was made by Glaucus the Chian, who first invented the art of inlaying iron.

XXVI. After the death of Alyattes, his son Crœsus, having attained the age of thirty-five years, succeeded him in the kingdom, and made war upon the Ephesians, before any other Grecian people. The Ephesians being besieged by him consecrated their city to Diana, by tying a rope[u] from the temple to the walls. The distance between the old town, which was then besieged, and the temple, is seven stadia. When Crœsus had reduced the Ephesians, he attacked the several cities of the Ionians and Æolians one after another, alledging different pretences against different people, important when they could be found, but in some instances only frivolous pretexts.

XXVII. And after he had compelled all the Grecians of

Pristis of Virgil. The vessel in which Arion embarked the second time, had doubtless a dolphin at the head; and this circumstance might occasion the story of Arion's being saved by a dolphin. I also think that Helle embarked in a vessel having a ram on its prow, which gave rise to the tradition that she passed, on a ram, the sea which bears her name. Pliny, after citing a number of facts to prove the friendship of dolphins for man, concludes, that the story of Arion is credible. *Larcher.*

[u] The object of the ancients in thus consecrating their towns was to retain their gods by force. It was believed, that when a city was on the point of being taken, the deities abandoned it. See Æsch. Sept. Theb. 219, 220.—It was by similar means that Polycrates, king of Samos, consecrated the island of Rhenæa, by joining it with a chain to Delos. *Larcher.*

Asia to be tributary to him, he formed a design to build a fleet, and by that means to invade the Islanders. But when all things were prepared for the building of ships, Bias[x] of Priene, (or, as others say, Pittacus[y] of Mitylene,) arriving at Sardis, put a stop to his intended project, by making this reply, when Crœsus inquired what news he had from Greece: "O king," said he, "the Islanders have bought up ten thousand horses, with intention to make war upon you, and to "attack Sardis." Crœsus thinking he had spoken the truth, "May the gods," replied he, "inspire the Grecians with a "resolution to attack the Lydians with horse." "It seems, "then," said Bias, "you would wish above all things to see "the Islanders on horseback upon the continent; and not "without reason. But what can you imagine the Islanders "will more earnestly desire, after having heard of your resolution to build a fleet in order to attack their islands, than to "meet the Lydians by sea, that they may revenge the cause "of those Greeks who dwell on the continent, whom you "hold in subjection?" It is related that Crœsus was very much pleased with this conclusion, and was so influenced, (for he appeared to speak to the purpose,) that he left off building a fleet, and then made an alliance with all the Ionians who inhabit the islands.

XXVIII. In the course of some years he became master of all the nations that lie within the river Halys, except only the Cilicians and the Lycians: that is to say, of the Lydians, the Phrygians, the Mysians, the Mariandynians, the Chalybians, the Paphlagonians, the Thracians[z], the Thynians and the Bithynians, the Carians, the Ionians, the Dorians, the Æolians, and the Pamphylians.

XXIX. When these nations were subdued, and the power of the Lydians was thus augmented by Crœsus, all the other wise men of that time went from Greece to Sardis, which had then attained to the highest degree of prosperity; and Solon of Athens in particular, who having made laws for the Athenians at their request, absented himself from his country, under colour of seeing the world for the space of ten years, that he might not be driven to the necessity of abrogating any of the laws he had established. For the Athethians of themselves could make no alteration, having taken

[x] Bias surpassed all men in the force of his eloquence. He made use of his powers in defending the cause of the oppressed poor. *Bellanger*.

[y] Pittacus was a philosopher and politician superior to every one else that Lesbos has produced. He delivered his country from three great evils—tyranny, sedition and war. *Bellanger*.

[z] Larcher has in his translation, "Thra-"cians of Asia;" that is to say, Thynians and Bithynians. These people were originally European. See his note.

a solemn oath to observe whatever laws Solon might enact for them, during ten years.

XXX. With this intention therefore, and to see the state of things abroad, Solon went first to the court of Amasis king of Egypt, and afterwards to that of Crœsus[a] at Sardis. He was hospitably entertained by Crœsus on his arrival in the palace, and on the third or fourth day, in obedience to the orders of the king, the attendants conducted him round the treasury, and shewed him all their grand and costly contents; which when Solon had seen and examined sufficiently, Crœsus said to him, "My Athenian guest, having heard much "discourse of your person, of your wisdom, and of the "voyages you have undertaken, as a philosopher, to see "many things in various countries, I am very desirous to "ask you, who is the most happy man you have seen?" This question he asked, because he thought himself the most happy of all men. But Solon, speaking the truth freely, without any flattery, answered, "Tellus the Athenian[b]." Crœsus, astonished at his answer, eagerly[c] asked him, "On what ac-"count do you think Tellus the happiest of all men?" "Be-"cause," replied Solon, "Tellus lived in a well-governed "commonwealth; had several sons who were virtuous and "good; his sons had children like to themselves, and all "these survived him; and also, when he had lived as hap-"pily as the condition of human affairs will permit, he ended "his life in a glorious manner. For coming to the assistance "of his countrymen in a battle they fought at Eleusis against "some of their neighbours, he put the enemy to flight, and "died in the field of victory. He was buried by the Athe-"nians at the public charge in the place where he fell, and "was magnificently honoured at his funeral."

XXXI. When Solon had turned the attention of Crœsus to what related to Tellus, by mentioning many happy circumstances, Crœsus, hoping at least to obtain the second place,

[a] Some authors have rejected this interview, and have conceived it to be a fable of Herodotus. See Larcher's long note on the subject. And Pindar Pyth. I. v. 184.

[b] We should not be led away by the censures and applauses of men, but consider the figure that every person will make at that time when wisdom shall be justified of her children, and nothing pass for great and illustrious, which is not an ornament and perfection to human nature.

The story of Gyges, the rich Lydian monarch, is a memorable instance to our present purpose. The oracle being asked by Gyges, who was the happiest man, replied, Aglaus. Gyges, who expected to have heard himself named on this occasion, was much surprised, and very curious to know who this Aglaus should be. After much inquiry he was found to be an obscure countryman, who employed all his time in cultivating a garden and a few acres of land about his house. Spectator, No. 610.

[c] Ἐπιστρεφέως. Herod. in the 8th book, ch. 62. has the phrase *λέγων μᾶλλον ἐπεστραμμένα*, speaking with greater vehemence.

asked, who of those he had seen might be accounted next to him. "Cleobis, said he, and Biton, natives of Argos, possessed of a plentiful fortune, and withal so strong and vigorous of body, that they were both equally victorious in the Olympian exercises. And more particularly it is reported, that when the Argives were celebrating a festival of Juno, it was absolutely necessary that their mother should be drawn to the temple by a pair of oxen[d]; which happened not to be brought up in time from the field, the young men being pressed for time[e], put themselves under the yoke, drew the chariot in which their mother sate forty-five stades, and brought her in that manner to the temple. After they had done this in the view of a great concourse of people met together to celebrate the festival, a most happy termination was put to their lives; and the Deity clearly shewed by this event, that it is better for a man to die than to live. For when the men of Argos, who stood round, commended the strength of the youths, and the women magnified the happiness of the mother of such sons, the mother herself, transported with joy by the action and the honours she received on that account, made it her petition as she stood before the image of the goddess, that she would bestow on Cleobis and Biton, who had so highly honoured her, the greatest blessing man could receive. When she had finished her prayer, and her sons had sacrificed and feasted with her, they fell asleep in the temple, and awaked no more, but met with a such a termination of life. Upon which the Argives, in commemoration of their piety, caused their statues[f] to be made and dedicated at Delphi."

XXXII. Thus Solon adjudged the second place of felicity to Cleobis and Biton. Crœsus, roused to indignation, said to him, "Is my happiness then so completely rejected by you, Athenian friend, that you do not think me of so much value as private men?" "Crœsus," replied Solon, "do you inquire of me concerning human affairs—of me, who know that the divinity is always jealous, and delights

[d] Servius says, that the want of oxen, on this occasion, was on account of a pestilential malady which had destroyed all the cattle belonging to Argos.

[e] Ἐκκληϊόμενοι τῇ ὥρῃ. The Latins also use the phrase *exclusi tempore*. Sic illi a negotiis publicis, tanquam ab opere aut *temporibus exclusi*, aut voluntate conferiati, &c. Cicero de Orat. III. 15. So also Cæsar de Bello Gallico, vii. 9. The author of the book of Maccabees, lib. ii. cap. 8. v. 25, 26. uses συγκλείεσθαι in the same sense. *Coray.*

[f] There was at Argos, in the temple of Apollo Lysius, a statue of Biton bearing a bull on his shoulders. And in the same temple a representation in marble of Cleobis and Biton drawing their mother in a chariot to the temple of Juno. Pausan. Corinth. lib. ii. cap. 19, 20. The verb ἀνατίθημι after ἐς Δελφοὺς, shews that these statues were consecrated in the temple of Delphi. *Larcher.*

"in confounding mankind?[g] For in the course of a long life, men are constrained to see many things they would not willingly see, and to suffer many things they would not willingly suffer. Let us suppose the term of man's life to be seventy years, which consist of twenty-five thousand and two hundred days, without including the intercalary month; and if we add that month[h] to every other year, in order that the seasons arriving at the proper time may agree, we shall find thirty-five months more in the seventy years[i], which make one thousand and fifty days. Yet in all this number of twenty-six thousand two hundred and fifty days, that compose these seventy years, one day will bring before us nothing entirely like another. So that thus, O Crœsus, man is entirely vicissitude. You appear to me to be master of immense treasures, and king of many nations; but I cannot say that of you which you demand, till I hear you have ended your life happily. For the richest of men is not more happy[k] than he that has a bare sufficiency for a day, unless his good fortune attend him to the grave, and he finish his life in happiness. Many men, who abound in wealth, are unhappy; and many, who have only a moderate competency, are fortunate. He that abounds in riches, and is yet unhappy, exceeds the other only in two things; but the other surpasses him in many more. The wealthy man indeed is better furnished with means to gratify his passions, and to bear the blow of adversity. But the other surpasses him in this; although he is not equally able to bear misfortune or satisfy his desires, yet his good fortune wards off those things, and he enjoys the full use of his limbs; he is free from diseases and misfortunes, he is blessed with a fine form and virtuous children: and if all these things come at last to be crowned by a decent end, such a one is the man you seek, and may justly be called happy. For to that time we ought to suspend[l] our judgment, and not to pronounce him happy, but

[g] We find in Herodotus, iii. 40. vii. 10 and 46. similar complaints against the deity; as also in Homer and the tragedians. Herodotus probably expresses the opinion of the times in which he lived.

[h] If the first number 25,200 is correct, it follows that the year was 360 days; if the number of intercalary days 1050 in 70 years, there will be altogether 26,250, which will give 375 days to the year; so that in spite of the precaution the seasons will be confused.—Wyttenbach alters the number of intercalary months and days to make it agree with truth. *Larcher.*

[i] "The days of our age are threescore years and ten; and though men be so strong, that they come to fourscore years: yet is their strength then but labour and sorrow; so soon passeth it away, and we are gone." Psal. xc. 10.

[k] The word ὄλβιος signifies one who is happy during his whole life—ὁ διὰ τοῦ ὅλου βίου μακαριστός. Hesych. The word happy does not properly express its meaning. *Larcher.*

[l] The same sentiment is expressed by

"only fortunate. Now because no man can possibly attain "to this perfection of happiness; as no one region yields all "good things, but produces some and wants others, that "country being ever esteemed best, which affords the great- "est plenty; and farther, because no human body is in all "respects self-sufficient, but possessing some advantages, is "destitute of others; he therefore, who, after he has most "constantly enjoyed the greatest part of these, finishes the "last scene of life with a decent serenity of mind, in my "judgment, O king, justly deserves the name of happy. We "ought therefore to consider the end of every thing; for the "Deity having displayed felicity to many, has afterwards en- "tirely overthrown them."

XXXIII. When he had made this reply, Crœsus did not bestow on him any present, but dismissed without holding him in any estimation[m]; since he considered him a very ignorant man, because he overlooked present prosperity, and bid men look to the end of all things.

XXXIV. After the departure of Solon, the indignation of the gods fell heavy upon Crœsus, probably because he thought himself the most happy of all men. A dream soon after visited him while sleeping, which pointed out to him the truth of the misfortune that was ready to befal him in the person of one of his sons. For Crœsus had two sons, of whom one was afflicted by a natural defect, for he was dumb[n]; but the other, whose name was Atys, far surpassed all the young men of his age in rare endowments. His dream represented to him that he would lose this same Atys by a wound inflicted by the point of an iron weapon: when he awoke, and had considered the thing, dreading the consequence of the vision, he provided a wife for his son; and though he was accustomed to command the Lydian troops, he did not ever after send him out any where for that purpose; and caused all the spears, lances, and other weapons of war,

Sophocles at the conclusion of the Œdip. Tyrannus. See also Eurip. Androm. v. 99. and Ovid Metamorph. III. v. 135.

Ultima semper
Expectanda dies homini, dicique beatus
Ante obitum nemo supremaque funera debet.

This opinion is combatted by Aristot. Nic. Eth. book i. cap. 10. Compare also Ecclesiasticus, chap. xi. v. 28. "Judge "no man blessed before his death."

m This is according to Schweighæuser's emendation. According to the common reading it is interpreted, *when he said this to Crœsus he is dismissed, since he neither gratified him by flattery, nor held him in any high estimation.*

n The Greek word κωφὸς, properly signifies dumb, and in that sense it is used by the ancients. The sense of deaf is added by more modern writers. Herodotus was an ancient, and uses it only in the first sense. One might however conclude from the end of the twenty-eighth chapter, διεφθαρμένον τὴν ἀκοὴν, that he used it as deaf; but the words τὴν ἀκοὴν were, I think, added by some copyist who was ignorant of the proper meaning of κωφός. *Larcher.*

to be removed from the apartments of the men, and laid up in private chambers, that none of them might fall upon his son, as they were suspended.

XXXV. While Crœsus was engaged with the nuptials of his son, a man oppressed by misfortune, and whose hands were polluted, a Phrygian by birth, and of royal family, arrived at Sardis. This man, having come to the palace of Crœsus, was desirous of obtaining purification according to the custom of the country. (Now the manner of expiation[o] is nearly the same among the Lydians and the Greeks.) Crœsus purified him; and, having performed the usual ceremonies, asked him whence he came, and who he was; speaking to him in the following terms: "Stranger, who art thou, and from what "part of Phrygia hast thou come as a suppliant[p]? and what "man or woman hast thou killed?" The stranger made answer; "I am the son of Gordius, grandson to Midas, and "my name is Adrastus. I involuntarily killed my brother, "and being banished by my father and deprived of every "thing, am come hither." "I perceive," replied Crœsus, "you are born of parents who are our friends, and you are "come to friends, among whom, if you will stay, you shall "want nothing, and if you can bear your misfortune with "courage, you will be a great gainer." So Adrastus lived in the palace of Crœsus.

XXXVI. At this time a boar of enormous size appeared in Mysia, which used to issue from mount Olympus, and destroy the labours of the inhabitants. The Mysians had often attacked him, but always came off with loss, and could not hurt him. At last deputies having come to Crœsus, delivered their message in these words: "There is, O king, a mon- "strous boar in Mysia, that ravages all the country; and

[o] The Scholiast on the 480th line of the last book of the Iliad remarks, that it was customary among the ancients, for the person who had committed an involuntary murder to leave his country, and betake himself to the house of some powerful individual, where covering himself he sate down, and entreated to be purified. No writer has given a more full and correct account of the ceremonies of expiation than Apollonius Rhodius in his 4th book. The suppliant takes his seat in silence at the hearth, with his eyes fixed on the ground, and sticks the instrument of the murder in the earth. The person, whose protection he implores, discovers by these signs, that he desires to be purified of a murder. He accordingly takes a sucking pig, cuts its throat, and smears with its blood the hands of the suppliant. He then uses lustral water, at the same time invoking Jupiter the expiator. Every thing which is used in the expiation, is carried without the house. They then burn some cakes, and sprinkle them with water, and invoke the Gods, in order to appease the anger of the Furies, and to render Jupiter propitious. See also Eurip. Orest. 511. Iphig, Taur. 950. *Larcher*.

[p] The Greek word is *ἐπίστιος*, Ionicè for *ἐφεστίος*, one who sits at the hearth. Ulysses having implored the succour of Alcinous, seated himself at the hearth; (Homer Odyss. lib. vii. v. 153.) and also Themistocles in the same manner supplicated Adrastus, king of the Molossians. (Thucyd. lib. c. 136. *Larcher*.

" though we have often endeavoured to take him, yet all our " attempts have been unsuccessful. We therefore earnestly " beg, that you would send your son and some other chosen " young men with dogs, that we may drive him from the " country." When they had spoken in this manner, Crœsus remembering his dream answered, " Make no farther men- " tion of my son; for I shall not send him, because he is " lately married, and that now occupies his attention: but I " will send the most skilful of the Lydians, with dogs and all " things necessary for hunting, and order them to assist you " with their best endeavours, to free your country from the " boar."

XXXVII. This was the reply of Crœsus; and when the Mysians were expressing their satisfaction[q], his son, who had heard of their request, came in, and when Crœsus refused to send him, he addressed him in this manner: " Father," said he, " in time past, I was permitted to signalize myself " in the two most noble and becoming exercises of war and " hunting; but now you keep me excluded from both, with- " out having observed in me either cowardice or incapacity. " How will men look on me when I go or return from the " forum? What kind of man shall I appear to my fellow- " citizens? What to my newly married wife? What kind of " man will she think she has for a partner? Either suffer me " to go to this enterprise, or convince me that you have " better reason to detain me at home."

XXXVIII. " My son," answered Crœsus, " the resolu- " tion I have taken proceeds not from any doubt of your " courage, or from any thing I have observed in you dis- " pleasing to me; but I have been admonished in a dream " that you shall not live long, and must die by the wound of " a spear. For that reason I hastened your marriage, and " now refuse to send you to this expedition; taking every " precaution to preserve you as long as I live, for you are " my only son; the other, who is deprived of his hearing, I " consider as lost."

XXXIX. " Indeed," replied the youth, " I cannot " blame you, if after such a dream you take so much care of " me; but it is right for me to explain that which you do not " comprehend, and in which the dream has escaped your " notice. You say the dream signified that I should die by " an iron lance. But what hand or what lance has a boar, to " create such fears in you? Had your dream foretold I

[q] This is translated, quum non essent contenti, by Valla, Henry Stephens, and Gronovius. The Abbé Geinoz has rightly observed, that the negative particle must not be expressed. See the Memoirs of the Acad. des Belles Lettres, vol. xxxiii. p. 113. He has been followed by Wesseling and Larcher.

"should lose my life by a tusk, or something of like nature, "you ought then to have done as you now do; whereas *it* "*said* by the point of a weapon, let me go therefore, since "our attempt is not to be made against men."

XL. "You have surpassed me," replied Crœsus, "in ex-"plaining the import of the dream; and therefore, changing "my resolution, I permit you to go to the chase."

XLI. Thus Crœsus, having given his consent, sent for Adrastus the Phrygian, and, when he came into his presence, spoke to him in this manner: "Adrastus, I purified you "when you were oppressed by a disagreeable misfortune[r], "which I do not upbraid you with, and have received you "into my house, and supplied you with every thing neces-"sary. Now, therefore, (for it is your duty to requite me "with kindness, since I have before conferred a kindness on "you,) I beg you would be my son's guard in this hunt, and "take care that no assassins surprise and fall upon you by "the way. Besides, you ought to go for your own sake, in "order to signalize yourself; for this was the glory of your "ancestors, and you are besides in full vigour."

XLII. Adrastus answered, "No other reasons, sir, could "induce me to take part in this enterprise; for one in my un-"fortunate circumstances ought not to appear, nor desire to "appear among those of his own years, who are innocent and "unblemished; and therefore I have often restrained myself. "Now, however, since you desire it, and because I ought to "shew my gratitude for the benefits I have received from your "hand, I am ready to obey your order; and rest assured, "that your son, whom you bid me take care of, shall, as far "as his guardian is concerned, return to you uninjured."

XLIII. After Adrastus had made this answer to Crœsus, they went away, well provided with a chosen company of young Lydians, and with dogs. When they arrived at mount Olympus they sought the boar, and having found him, drew into the form of a circle, and from all sides lanced their jave-lins at him. Among the rest the stranger, the same that had been purified of murder, named Adrastus, throwing his jave-lin at the boar, missed him, and struck the son of Crœsus; thus he being wounded by the point of the lance, fulfilled the prediction of the dream. Upon this a messenger ran back to Crœsus, and having arrived at Sardis, gave him an account of the action, and of his son's fate.

XLIV. Crœsus, violently disturbed for the death of his

[r] Ἀχάριτι. Herodotus frequently uses this kind of expression to signify a very great misfortune. See note to chapter XVI. This figure is called Litotes, in Rhetoric.

son, bore the disaster with less patience, because he fell by the hand of one, whom he himself had purified from blood; and bitterly lamenting his misfortune, he addressed himself to Jupiter[s], the God of expiation, attesting the calamity brought upon him by this stranger. He invoked the same deity again, by the name of the God of hospitality, and private friendship: as the God of hospitality, because, by receiving a stranger into his house, he had, without being aware of it, supported the murderer of his son; as the God of private friendship, because he had entrusted the care of his son to one, whom he now found to be his greatest enemy.

XLV. After this, the Lydians approached, bearing the corpse, and after it followed the murderer. He, *when he arrived*, having advanced in front of the body, and delivered himself up to Crœsus, begged of him to kill him upon it, relating his former misfortune, and how in addition to that he had destroyed his purifier[t], and that it was impossible for him to live. When Crœsus heard this, though his own affliction was above measure great, he pitied Adrastus, and said to him, "You have made me full satisfaction by condemning yourself "to die[u]. But no, Adrastus, you were not the author[x] of this "disaster, except as far as you were the involuntary agent. "But that God, whoever he was, that foretold my misfortune, "it was he that brought it upon me." Crœsus celebrated the funeral of his son, as the dignity of his birth required; but Adrastus, who had been the murderer of his brother, and the murderer of his purifier, when all was silent round the tomb, judging himself the most miserable of all men, killed himself upon the grave.

XLVI. Crœsus continued disconsolate for the loss of his son during two years; after which, the overthrow of the kingdom of Astyages the son of Cyaxares by Cyrus, the son of Cambyses, and the growing greatness of the Persians, interrupted the course of his grief; and it entered into his

[s] Jupiter was adored under different names, according to the place and circumstances of the worshippers. *Larcher.*

[t] It was Crœsus we have seen that expiated Adrastus; but he might have appointed his son to the office as a compliment of his marriage. *Larcher.* But may we not suppose Crœsus considered life as scarcely worth preserving after his son's death and therefore, in that sense Adrastus might be considered the destroyer of Crœsus.

[u] Crœsus threatened at first to burn Adrastus alive, but when he saw the young man voluntarily offering himself up to be put to death, he pardoned him. *Diodor. Sic. Excerpt. de Virtut. et Vitiis.* tom. ii. p. 553.

[x] The confession of faults appeases a man's anger. Arist. Rhet. book ii. chap. 3. So Helen was the cause of all the ills that befel Troy, but when she confessed her fault, Priam, touched with compassion, thus addressed her:

No crime of thine our present suff'ring draws
Not thou, but Heav'n's disposing will, the cause. Pope's Il. iii.

thoughts to check, if it were any way possible, their increasing power, before it should become formidable. After these thoughts he immediately determined to make trial of the oracles of Greece and Lybia[y]; and sent some persons to Delphi, and to Abæ a city of Phocis; others to Amphiaraus and Trophonius; and some to the Branchidæ in the territories of the Milesians. These were the Grecian oracles, to which Crœsus sent to consult; and at the same time he dispatched other men to consult that of Ammon in Lybia; designing to try the several oracles, and if they should be found to give a true answer, in that case to send again, to inquire whether he should make war against the Persians.

XLVII. He dismissed them to make a trial of the oracle with the following orders, that computing the days from the time of their departure from Sardis, they should on the hundredth day make trial of all the oracles, by asking, what was Crœsus the son of Alyattes king of Lydia now doing? commanding moreover, that they should bring him the answer of each oracle in writing. What were the answers given by the other oracles, is mentioned by none: but the Lydians no sooner entered the temple of Delphi to consult the God, and asked the question they had in charge, than the Pythian thus spoke in heroic verse:

> I know the number[z] of the Libyan sands;
> The ocean's measure: I can penetrate
> The secrets of the silent, or the dumb.
> I smell th' ascending odour of a lamb
> And tortoise, in a brazen cauldron boil'd:
> Brass lies beneath, and brass above the flesh.

[y] For a description of the oracles of Abæ and Trophonius, see note on chap. 134. book viii. For the oracle of Dodona, see Herod. book ii. chap. 52, 54, 55, &c. and the note. For that of the Branchidæ, book v. chap. 36. note. The oracle of Apollo at Delphi was, to use Mr. Bayle's words, the judge without appeal, and is very well known. For a complete description, see Mitford's History of Greece, chap. iii. sect. 2.

Amphiaraus was son of Oïcleus, and married Eriphyle, the sister of Adrastus, king of Argos. By his knowledge of futurity, he foresaw that he must perish if he accompanied Adrastus against Thebes. He therefore hid himself, but was betrayed by Eriphyle, who was bribed by Polyneices with a golden chain. Being thus discovered, he went to the war, where, as he had foretold, the earth opened and swallowed him up, together with his chariot and horses. Pausanias says, that this happened about twelve stadia from Oropus; but other accounts are given. The Oropians, however, were the first who paid him divine honours, and they erected a temple to him, with a statue of white marble. They who came to consult were to fast twenty-four hours, and abstain three days from wine, according to Philostratus. A ram was then sacrificed, and the person laid down on the skin to sleep in the vestibule, and the answers of the Deity were delivered in dreams. His son Amphilochus was associated with him. For an account of the oracle of the Lybian Ammon, see book ii. chap. 55.

[z] I cannot believe with M. Rollin, (Hist. Anc. vol. i. p. 387.) "That God, "in order to punish the blindness of the "Pagans, suffered the Demons some-"times to utter answers agreeable to the

XLVIII. The Lydians having written down this answer of the Pythian, returned to Sardis. And when the rest, who had been sent to other places, were arrived, Crœsus opened and viewed the answers they brought, without being satisfied with any[a]. But when he heard the words of the Delphian oracle, he adored the God, and acknowledged the truth of it, being convinced that that alone was a real oracle, because it had discovered the thing he did at Sardis. For when he had sent in different directions people to consult the oracles, bearing in mind the time that had been fixed, he contrived the following thing; having carefully devised what he thought it was impossible to discover or guess at, he cut up a tortoise and a lamb, and boiled them himself together in a brazen cauldron, and put on it a brazen cover.

XLIX. I can say nothing certain touching the answer given to the Lydians by Amphiaraus, after they had performed the ceremonies required by the custom of the place; nothing else is mentioned but that he considered it a true oracle.

L. After this he endeavoured to conciliate the God by magnificent sacrifices, for he offered three thousand head of cattle of every kind[b], and having made a great pile, he burnt beds of gold and silver, vials of gold, with robes of purple, and other rich apparel, hoping by that means more completely to gain the favour of the God; he also ordered all the Lydians to offer to the God whatever he was able. In this offering so great a quantity of gold was melted down, that one hundred and seventeen tiles were made out of it; of which the longest[c] were six palms in length, the shortest three; and both sorts one palm in thickness. Four of these

"truth." Cicero appears to speak more wisely, "Cur autem hoc credam unquam "editum Crœso? aut Herodotum cur "veraciorem ducam Ennio? num minus "potuit ille de Crœso, quam de Pyrrho "fingere Ennius?" I do not however think that Herodotus invented this answer. He found it established by report, and believed it, because it was conformable with the superstition of his country. This history of Crœsus is either entirely false, or in part true, and the other circumstances have been added to render it marvellous; or it is probable that Crœsus may have entrusted his secret to somebody, from whom the priests contrived to learn it. *Larcher.*

[a] Literally; Of these answers none came home to him. The phrase is put by Hypallage, *τῶν μὲν δὴ οὐδὲν αὐτὸς προσίετο.*

[b] This is the meaning of *πάντα*. A similar phrase occurs in the fourth book, chapter eighty-eight, and in the ninth book, chapter eighty. This immense number appears to some incredible. See the account of Solomon's sacrifice, 2 Chron. vii. 5. "Then the king and all "the people offered sacrifices unto the "Lord. And king Solomon offered a "sacrifice of twenty-two thousand oxen, "and an hundred and twenty thousand "sheep."

[c] The Abbé Barthelemy translates this passage, six palms in length, three in breadth, and one in thickness. See Larcher's refutation, which is too long to transcribe.

were of pure gold, each weighing two talents and a half; the rest were of a paler gold, and weighed two talents each. He also caused the figure of a lion to be made of fine gold, weighing ten talents; but while the temple of Delphi was burning, the lion fell down from the tiles, on which it stood to that time, and lies now in the treasury of the Corinthians, reduced to the weight of six talents and a half[d], the rest having been melted off by the fire.

LI. When these things were finished, Crœsus sent them to Delphi, accompanied with many other donations, among which were two large bowls, one of gold and the other of silver. That of gold was placed on the right hand as men go into the temple, and that of silver on the left; but they were both removed when the temple was burnt; and the golden bowl, weighing eight talents and a half and twelve mines, is laid up in the treasury of Clazomenæ; the other of silver, containing six hundred amphoræ, lies in a corner of the portico, and is used at Delphi for mixing the wine on the Theophanian festival[e]. The Delphians say it was made by Theodorus the Samian; which I think probable, because to me it appears to be a work that we do not every day meet with. He also presented four vessels of silver, which are placed in the treasury of the Corinthians; and gave two round basons to contain the holy water[f] used in the temple, one of gold and the other of silver. On the bason of gold is an inscription, OF THE LACEDÆMONIANS, and they say that it was their donation, but wrongfully, for it was given by Crœsus; though a certain Delphian, whose name I know[g], and am not willing to mention, engraved those words in order to please the Lacedæmonians. They gave indeed the boy, through whose hand the water runs; but neither the one nor the other of the basons. At the same time Crœsus sent many other presents which are marked with no title[h], and several round plates of silver; and more particulaly an image of a woman in gold three cubits high, which the Delphians say represents the person that prepared his bread[i]: and to all these things he added the necklaces and girdles of his wife.

[d] There is a great difference between *ἕβδομον ἡμιτάλαντον*, and *ἕπτα ἡμιτάλαντα*. The first signifies six talents and a half, the other only three talents and a half.

[e] The festival of the appearance of the God. The day on which it was reported that Apollo first appeared to them, was held sacred by the Delphians.

[f] *Περιῤῥαντήρια*. These vessels were filled with water, with which all those that were admitted to the sacrifices were sprinkled, and beyond which no profane person was allowed to pass.

[g] If Ptolemæus in Photius may be believed, his name was Æthus.

[h] *Οὐκ ἐπίσημα*. Larcher follows the Latin interpreter, and translates this, *presents of less value*. A golden statue three cubits high, is not of so very little value. *Schweighæauser*.

[i] Crœsus, says Plutarch, honoured the

LII. These were the donations he dedicated at Delphi; and to Amphiaraus, having learnt by inquiry his virtue and sufferings, he sent a shield of gold, and a lance of solid gold; the shaft as well as the points being of gold[j], which remain to this day at Thebes in the temple of Ismenian Apollo.

LIII. When the Lydians were upon their departure, charged with these presents for the two oracles, Crœsus commanded them to inquire of both, if he should undertake a war against the Persians, and if he should unite any other nation as an ally. Accordingly, when the Lydians had arrived at the places to which they were sent, they consulted the oracles in these words: "Crœsus, king of the Lydians "and of other nations, esteeming these to be the only ora-"cles among men, sends these presents in acknowledgment "of the thing you have discovered; and now asks, whether "he shall lead an army against the Persians, and whether he "shall join any auxiliary forces with his own?" The opinions of both oracles tended to the same purpose, and foretold, "That if Crœsus would make war upon the Persians, he "should destroy a great empire[k];" counselling him at the same time to engage the most powerful of the Grecians in his alliance.

LIV. When Crœsus learnt the answers that were brought, he was beyond all bounds delighed with the oracles; and being sanguine in his expectations of overthrowing the kingdom of Cyrus, he again sent to Delphi, and caused two staters of gold to be distributed to each of the inhabitants, whose number he had already learnt. In consideration of which, the Delphians granted to Crœsus and the Lydians a right to consult the oracle before any others, and certain immunities[l], together with the first place in the temple, and the privilege of being made citizens of Delphi, to as many as should desire it in all future time.

LV. Crœsus having made these presents at Delphi, sent a third time to consult the oracle. For after he had satisfied

woman who made his bread with a statue of gold from emotions of gratitude. Alyattes, his father, married a second wife, by whom he had other children. This woman wished to remove Crœsus, and gave the female baker a dose of poison to put in the bread she made for Crœsus. The woman informed Crœsus, and gave the poisoned bread to the queen's children.

[j] Herodotus must here allude to a spear which had a head like our halberds. *Larcher.*

[k] This is quoted by Arist. Rhet. book iii. as an instance of the general way in which soothsayers express themselves. Horace ridicules it in the 2d book of Sat. v. 59.

O Laërtiade, quicquid dicam, aut erit, aut non.

See also Cicero de Div. book ii. ch. 54.

[l] It was established by the Amphictyons, that all strangers who came to consult the oracle should pay a stated sum. Crœsus and the Lydians were probably exempted from paying this.

himself of the oracle's veracity, he indulged himself in often consulting it. His demand now was, whether he should long enjoy the kingdom? to which the Pythian gave this answer,

When o'er the Medes a mule shall reign as king,
Learn thou the name of coward to despise;
And on thy tender feet, O Lydian, fly
O'er pebbly Hermus, and his fury shun.

LVI. With this answer, when reported to him, Crœsus was pleased more than with all the others. For he presumed that a mule should never be king of the Medes, and consequently that neither he nor his posterity, should ever be deprived of the kingdom. In the next place he began to inquire carefully who were the most powerful of the Greeks whom he might gain over as allies; and upon inquiry found that the Lacedæmonians and Athenians were the principal nations of Greece, the first being of Dorian and the other of Ionian descent. For these were in ancient time the most distinguished, the latter being a Pelasgian[m], the other an Hellenic nation; the latter had constantly continued in one country[n], while the former had very often changed their seat; for under the reign of Deucalion they inhabited the country of Pthiotis; and in the time of Dorus, the son of Hellen, possessed that region which is called Istiæotis, lying at the foot of the mountains Ossa and Olympus. From thence being expelled by the Cadmæans, they betook themselves to Macednum on mount Pidnus; which place they afterwards abandoned for another settlement in Dryopis; and again changing their country, came to the Peloponnesus, where they were called Dorians.

LVII. What language the Pelasgians used I cannot certainly affirm; but if I may form a conjecture from those Pelasgians who now exist, and who are now settled at Crestona beyond the Tyrrhenians[o], but were formerly neighbours to

[m] Although Herodotus says so, the Athenians were never Pelasgians, as I have proved in my Essay on Chronology, ch. viii. sect. 9. *Larcher.*

Herodotus, however, again alludes to the Pelasgian origin of the Athenians, II. 51. VII. 94. VIII. 44.

[n] The Athenians prided themselves on being *αὐτόχθονες*, and boasted of it before Gelon, in the 7th book, ch. 161. Thucydides, in his 1st book, ch. 2. attributes the circumstance of their not having often changed their residence to the barrenness of the soil. It appears evident that this must refer to the *τοὺς δὲ, τοῦ Ἰωνικοῦ*, although expressed by *τὸ μέν*: Herodotus, perhaps, changed the order, that he might bring the description of the Dorian migrations last, lest the length of it might break the connection between the first and last mention of the other race.

[o] Crestona, or Crestonia, lay between Mygdonia and Sintica, and may be reckoned the eastern frontier of Macedonia towards Thrace. The river Chidoms, which discharges itself into the Axius near Pella, rises in Crestona, and flows through Mygdonia. It may be suspected that Tyrrhenians is a mistake, and that Thermæans should be substituted for it; as Therma, afterwards Thessalonia, agrees

those called at this day Dorians, and at that time occupied the country called Thessaliotis; and if I may conjecture from those Pelasgians who founded Placia and Scylace in the Hellespont, and once dwelt with the Athenians[p], and whatever other cities, which though really Pelasgian, have changed their name; if, I say, I may be permitted to give my conjecture, the Pelasgians spoke a barbarous language. And if the whole Pelasgian body did so, the people of Attica, who are descended from them, must at the time they changed into Hellenes, have altered their language. For neither do the Crestonæans use the same language with any of their neighbours, nor yet do the people of Placia, but they both use the same language; by which it appears they have taken care to preserve the character of the language they brought with them into those places.

LVIII. But the Hellenes, as I think, have from the time they became a people used the same language as they now speak: and though, when separated from the Pelasgians, they were at first of no considerable force; yet from a small beginning they advanced to a mighty power, by the conjunction of many nations, as well barbarians as others. Whereas, on the other hand, the Pelasgians being a barbarous nation, seem to me never to have risen to any considerable grandeur.

LIX. Of these nations Crœsus learnt by inquiry that the Attic was oppressed and distracted by Pisistratus the son of Hippocrates, then reigning in Athens; to this Hippocrates a strange prodigy happened, while as a private man he was present at the Olympian exercises. For having killed a victim, the cauldrons, which were full of flesh and water, bubbled up without any fire and boiled over. Chilon the Lacedæmonian, who was accidentally there, and saw the prodigy, advised Hippocrates not to marry any woman by whom he might have children; or, if he was already married, to divorce his wife; and if he had a son, to disown him. But Hippocrates, not persuaded by the counsel of Chilon, had afterwards this same Pisistratus; who, when a sedition happening between those who dwelt on the sea-coast, led by Megacles the son of Alcmæon, and those of the plains, headed by Lycurgus the son of Aristolaides, Pisistratus, having cherished[q] designs on the sovereign power, formed a third

to the situation. We have heard of no Tyrrhenians but those of Italy. *Rennel*, p. 45.

If the reading of Tyrrhenians is correct, it shews that there was once a nation called Tyrrhenians in Thrace. This is also confirmed by Thucydides, book iv. ch. 109. See Larcher's elaborate note.

p The reason of their separation is given in book vi. ch. 137.

q The verb καταφρονεῖν implies, according to Valckenaer, a great idea of one's own power, and a contempt for that of the adversary. A similar expression occurs in chap. 66.; also in Thucydides, book ii. ch. 62.

party, and having assembled his partizans under colour of protecting those of the mountains, contrived this stratagem. He wounded himself and his mules[r], he drove his chariot into the public place, as if he had escaped from enemies that designed to murder him in his way to the country, and besought the people to grant him a guard, having before acquired renown in the expedition against Megara[s], by taking Nisæa[t], and displaying other illustrious deeds. With these pretences the people of Athens were deluded, and appointed some chosen men of the city for his guard, who were to attend him armed with clubs and not with javelins. By the help of this guard Pisistratus seized the Acropolis, and then possessed himself of the whole power; yet he neither disturbed the ancient magistracies, nor altered the laws; but leaving things as they were, administered the government with order and moderation[u].

LX. Not long after the parties of Megacles and Lycurgus being reconciled, drove him out. In this manner Pisistratus first made himself master of Athens, and was dispossessed before his power was very firmly rooted. But new dissensions arising between those who expelled him, Megacles, harassed by the sedition, dispatched a herald to Pisistratus, and offered him his daugher in marriage, with the sovereignty. Pisistratus accepted the proposition; and in order to his restitution, they contrived the most ridiculous project, that, I think, was ever imagined; especially if we consider, that the Greeks have from old been distinguished from the barbarians as being more acute and free from all foolish simplicity, and more particularly as they played this trick upon the Athenians, who are esteemed among the wisest of the Grecians. Phya, a woman of the Pæanean tribe, was four cubits high,

[r] Ulysses, Zopyrus, and others, availed themselves of similar artifices for the good of their country; but Pisistratus employed this to enslave his. Solon, therefore, thus addressed him: "Son "of Hippocrates, you ill apply the stra"tagem of Ulysses; he wounded his "body to delude the public enemies; "you wound your's to deceive your "countrymen." Dionysius employed a similar artifice, and was alike successful in obtaining a body-guard, and by that means the kingdom of Syracuse. *Larcher.*

Mitford, in his History of Greece, (ch. v. sect. 5.) thinks it probable that the attempt upon the life of Pisistratus was real.

[s] Different accounts of this expedition are given by Æneas Poliorcet, Plutarch, and Diodorus Siculus.

[t] Nisæa was the port of the Megarians, about two miles from the city; it was to Megara what the Piræus were to Athens. We find several instances of cities built a short distance from the shore. This, as Thucydides informs us, book i. ch. 7. was on account of the system of piracy. Thus Argos was about two miles from the shore, and Nauplia was its port.

[u] Pisistratus (says Plutarch in Solon) was not only observant of the laws of Solon, but compelled others to be so also. Whilst in the enjoyment of supreme power, he was summoned before the Areopagus on a charge of murder. He appeared modestly to plead his cause, but his accuser did not appear. Aristot. de Repub. V. 12. relates the same fact. *Larcher.*

wanting three digits, and in other respects beautiful: this person they dressed in a complete suit of armour, placed her on a chariot, and having disposed all things in such a manner as might make her appear with all possible advantage, they conducted her towards the city, having sent heralds before, who upon their arrival in the city proclaimed what was ordered in these terms: "O Athenians, receive with kind "wishes Pisistratus, who is so much honoured by Minerva "above all other men, that she herself condescends to bring "him back to her Acropolis." When the heralds had published this in several places, the report was presently spread through the adjoining parts, that Minerva was bringing home Pisistratus; and in the city the multitude, believing this woman to be the goddess, addressed with prayers a human being, and readily received Pisistratus.

LXI. Pisistratus having thus recovered the sovereignty, married the daughter of Megacles in performance of his agreement. But because he had sons already, and knew besides, that the Alcmæonidæ were reported to be guilty of an unexpiated[x] crime, he resolved to have no children of this marriage, and therefore used the company of his new wife contrary to custom. The woman for some time concealed the thing; but afterwards, either moved by her mother's solicitation, or other reasons, discovered it to her, and she to her husband. Megacles felt highly indignant at being dishonoured by Pisistratus, and in his anger he immediately reconciled himself to the adverse party; which Pisistratus understanding to be done in enmity to him, he withdrew quite out of the country, and arriving in Eretria[y], consulted with his sons about the state of their affairs. The opinion of Hippias prevailing, viz. to recover the kingdom, they immediately began to collect contributions from those cities where they had an interest[z]; and many gave great sums; but the Thebans surpassed the rest in liberality. To be short, after an interval, when all things were ready for the expedition, they were joined by some Argive troops which they had hired in Peloponnesus; and a Naxian named Lygdamis, who having come

[x] The origin of this crime is related by Thucydides, book i. ch. 126. Cylon had formed a conspiracy, and got possession of the citadel. His party being reduced by famine took refuge at the altars, from which they removed, upon condition that they should receive no hurt. Megacles, however, who was archon at the time, caused them to be put to death, and some of them were murdered even within the sacred places; from that time the family was considered ἐναγεῖς. It is briefly mentioned also by Herodotus, book v. ch. 71.

[y] There were two places of this name, one in Thessaly and another in Eubæa. Pisistratus retired to this last. *Larcher.*

[z] Literally; who felt any gratitude for benefits which had been before conferred on them by the Pisistratids. The word is used in the same sense in the 40th chapter of the 3d book.

voluntarily, and brought both men and money, shewed great eagerness in the cause.

LXII. In the eleventh year of their exile, departing from Eretria, they arrived in Attica, and in the first place possessed themselves of Marathon; where, while they lay encamped, they were joined not only by their seditious partizans of the city, but by great numbers from the adjoining parts, who were more fond of tyranny[a] than of liberty. On the other hand, the Athenians had shewn very little concern all the time Pisistratus was soliciting for money, or even when he made himself master of Marathon. But when they heard he was marching directly for Athens, they assembled all their forces to defend themselves, and to repel the invader. In the mean time Pisistratus, advancing with his army from Marathon, arrived at the temple of the Pallenian[b] Minerva; and after they had encamped before the temple, Amphilytus a prophet of Acarnania, by divine impulse[c], went to him, and pronounced this oracle in hexameter verse:

> The net is spread, and dexterously thrown;
> By the clear moonlight shall the tunnies come.

LXIII. When the prophet had delivered these words, Pisistratus, comprehending the oracle, and saying he accepted the omen, led his army against the enemy. At that time the Athenians of the city were engaged at their dinner, and some had betaken themselves afterwards to dice or sleep[d]; so that the army of Pisistratus falling upon them by surprise, soon put them to flight; and as they were endeavouring to make their escape, Pisistratus contrived an artful stratagem, in order to disperse them so entirely, that they might not rally again. He mounted his sons on horseback and sent them on; and when they had overtaken the fugitives, as they were ordered by Pisistratus, they bid them be confident, and every man to depart to his own habitation.

LXIV. The Athenians readily embracing the opportunity, Pisistratus took a third time possession of Athens[e]; and esta-

[a] For the proper meaning of τύραννος, see note on book iii. ch. 50.

[b] Pallene was the name of one of the boroughs of Attica, belonging to the tribe Antiochides, on the road from Marathon to Athens.

[c] Πομπὴ comes from πέμπω mitto, deduco. Hence it signifies *missio*, or the act of sending; *impulsus, instinctus*, impulse or inspiration; *deductio*, or the act of accompanying. Mr. Bryant derives it from the oriental languages. *Larcher.*

[d] In all the warmer climates of the globe, the custom of sleeping at noon is invariably preserved. It appears from modern travellers, that many of the present inhabitants of Athens have their houses flat-roofed, and decorated with arbours where they sleep at noon. Horace shews that the custom existed at Rome;

Lusum it Mæcenas, dormitum ego Virgilique. 1 Serm. V. 48.

[e] Pisistratus, although a tyrant, culti-

blished himself more firmly in the tyranny, partly by the assistance of auxiliary forces, and partly by revenues collected at home, or brought from the river Strymon[f]. He compelled those who resisted in the battle, and had not presently fled out of the field, to deliver up their sons to him as hostages, and sent them to Naxus; which island he had formerly conquered, and put into the hands of Lygdamis. He likewise purified the island of Delos[g], as he had been admonished by an oracle; causing the dead bodies to be taken up, and removed from all places that lay within the prospect from the temple. In this manner Pisistratus recovered the dominion of Athens; many of the Athenians had been killed in the fight, and many left the country with the Alcmæonidæ.

LXV. Crœsus received information that this was the present condition of the Athenians; and that the Lacedæmonians, having extricated themselves out of great difficulties, had been at last victorious against the Tegeans. For in the time of Leon and Hegesicles, kings of Sparta, they were successful in all other wars except only against that people. But before their reign they had been governed by almost the worst laws of any people in Greece with regard to their dealings with one another, and were intolerable towards strangers. They thus changed into good order. Lycurgus[h], who was a man much esteemed in Sparta, arriving at Delphi to consult the oracle, no sooner entered the temple, than the Pythian spoke these words:

> Welcome Lycurgus to this happy place;
> Thou favourite of heav'n: I doubting stand,
> Whether I shall pronounce thee God or man:
> Inclining yet to think thou art a God.

Some men say, that besides this, the Pythian at the same

vated letters. He collected all Homer's works, and presented the public with the Iliad and Odyssey, in their present form. *Bellanger.*

[f] There were silver mines in Attica, at Laurium, and Thoricus. The country between the Strymon, and the Nessus, was celebrated for its mines. The mines of that coast of Thrace are particularly mentioned in book vi. ch. 46, 47. The Athenians possessed several places on this river, and among others Amphipolis. *Larcher.*

[g] This perfectly agrees with Thucydides, who says, (book iii. ch. 104.) that Pisistratus purified Delos, but not the whole of it, only the space that could be seen from the temple. This the Athenians afterwards completed; they removed all the bodies from the island, and ordered that all pregnant women, and sick people, should be removed to the island Rhenæa, that no one might die in Delos. To the neglect of this the Athenians attributed the plague that ravaged Attica, at the commencement of the Peloponnesian war. *Larcher.*

[h] The most judicious writers of antiquity have contributed to the perplexity about the age of Lycurgus. See Thucyd. i. 18. Plato on Minos, Xenophon on the Government of Sparta, Aristot. Polit. Eratosthenes, and Apollodorus; the chronologers, undertook to decide upon it, but Plutarch in his Life tells us what credit is due to them. Perhaps the best modern attempt to reconcile the disagreement of ancient authors is by Wesseling. *Mitford*, ch. iv. sect. 3. note.

time communicated[i] to him that form of good government, which is now observed in Sparta. But the Lacedæmonians themselves affirm, that Lycurgus, being both uncle and tutor to Leobotas[k] king of Sparta, brought those institutions from Crete. For as soon as he had taken the guardianship, he altered all their customs, and took care that men should not transgress them[l]. Afterwards he arranged the military laws the Enomotiæ[m], the Triecades[n], and the Syssitia[o], and instituted the Ephori[p] and the Senate[q].

[i] Minos also pretended that he received his laws from Jupiter; and Numa Pompilius from the nymph Egeria; Zoraster, Pythagoras, and others, thought it necessary to profess some intercourse with heaven, in order to give the greater sanction to their laws and institutions. So also Mahammed with the angel Gabriel.

[k] Authors unanimously agree that the name of the nephew of Lycurgus was Charilaüs; it also appears that Leobotas could not be the nephew of Lycurgus, as Lycurgus was descended from Procleus, but Leobotes from Eurysthenes: Larcher therefore thinks it ought to be; who was guardian to his nephew, under the reign of Leobotas.

[l] There were some Lacedæmonians who, deeming the laws of Lycurgus too severe, chose rather to leave their country than to submit to them. These passed over to the Sabines in Italy; and when these people were incorporated with the Romans, communicated to them a portion of Lacedæmonian manners. *Larcher.*

[m] The Enomotiæ was one of the divisions of the Lacedæmonian army. This, according to Thucydides was formed with the utmost simplicity, from the file of eight men, by an arithmetical progression of fours; and probably for some purposes the file itself was divided into four quarter files. Four files then, made the Enomoty; four Enomoties the Pentycostyes; four Pentycostyes the Lochus; and according to Xenophon, four Lochi the Mora; which was thus analogous to the modern brigade of four battalions. *Mitford*, ch. iv. sect. 3.

[n] This appears to have been a division made for conveniency in taking their repast, and to have consisted of thirty men. *Larcher.*

[o] Lycurgus strictly ordained that all, even the kings, should eat at public tables only; where the strictest frugality should be observed. Larcher thinks, that Herodotus in this place merely alludes to the Syssitia in war, and that he added the word to explain the Triecades, lest it might be supposed that it was a regular division of the Lacedæmonian army, and not one that had no existence except at time of eating.

[p] Authors are not agreed about the institution of the Ephori. Plutarch, in his life of Lycurgus, (p. 43.) says that they were instituted about 130 years after his death, by Theopompus king of Sparta; Aristotle was of the same opinion, (Politic. v. 11.) Herodotus, Xenophon, Plato, and Satyrus, are of a contrary opinion. Barthelemy has endeavoured to reconcile the two opinions in his Voyage du jeune Anacharsis, tom. ii. p. 527, &c.

The Ephori were five in number according to the generality of authors; others say that there were nine. They were originally instituted as a balance to the regal power. Their authority gradually became very great; they sometimes expelled, and even put to death the kings; and abolished or suspended other magistrates, calling them to account at pleasure. They presided at public shows, festivals, &c. They were the sole managers of the public treasures. Every one rose up when they entered, but they did not rise up even to the kings. Their office was annual, and they were elected from the class of the people. Cleomenes put an end to them about 226 years B. C. by causing them to be massacred.

[q] Lycurgus having remarked that the princes of his family who reigned at Argos and Messene, had degenerated into tyrants, and that they had ruined themselves and their states; to prevent the same at Sparta, instituted the Senate and the Ephori, as a salutary remedy to the royal authority. He also instituted knights at Sparta upon the model of the Equestrian order at Crete, with this difference, that the knights of Crete had horses, those of Sparta, none. *Larcher.*

LXVI. The Lacedæmonians built a temple to Lycurgus after his death[r], and paid him divine honours. In a short time, assisted by the natural goodness of their country and increase of their people, they sprang up, and attained to a great degree of power. And now they could no longer be contented to live in peace; but proudly considering themselves superior to the Arcadians, sent to consult the oracle of Delphi touching the conquest of all the conntry, and received this answer:

To ask Arcadia is a high demand:
A hardy race of men defend that land.
But against Tegea if thou wilt advance,
Upon her plains thy sounding feet shall dance;
And with a line thou shalt trace out the soil.

When the Lacedæmonians heard the report of their messengers, they laid aside their design against all Arcadia; and, relying on this equivocal oracle, led an army against Tegea only; carrying fetters with them in their march, as if they had been sure of making all the Tegeans prisoners. But coming to a battle, they themselves were defeated[s], and all that were taken alive, being bound with the same fetters they brought, were compelled to measure the lands of the country, and thus to labour. Those fetters were afterwards hung up by the Tegeans in the temple of Alean[t] Minerva, and continued there to my time.

LXVII. In this first war, which the Lacedæmonians made against Tegea, they were always unprosperous; but in the time of Crœsus, and during the reign of Anaxandrides and Ariston kings of Sparta, they had at length become superior in the following manner; when they had always been beaten by the Tegeans, they sent to inquire of the oracle at

Lycurgus committed the executive power of the state to a senate composed of thirty persons, twenty-eight selected from among those leading men in whom he could most confide, with the two kings, as presidents. To this body he gave also the most important part of the legislative authority; for laws were to originate there only. To the assembly of the people he entrusted merely the power of confirming or annulling what the senate proposed, forbidding them all debate; the members only gave a simple affirmative or negative, without being allowed to speak even so far as to declare why they gave either. To the people however he committed the future election of senators, confining only their choice to persons who had passed their sixtieth year. *Mitford's Greece*, ch. iv. sect. 3.

[r] The Lacedæmonians having bound themselves by an oath not to abrogate any of the laws of Lycurgus before his return to Sparta; he went to consult the oracle at Delphi, and was told that Sparta would be happy as long as it observed his laws. Upon this he resolved to return no more, but went to Crisa and killed himself. *Larcher.*

[s] This happened under the reign of Charilaüs, and was effected by the women of Tegea, who placed themselves in ambush at the foot of mount Phylactris, and fell upon the Lacedæmonians while they were engaged with the Tegeans. *Larcher.*

[t] Minerva was so called by many people of Grecce, from ἀλέα, a refuge. This, however, must not be confounded with another called Alea, because she was worshipped at a town of Arcadia of that name. *Larcher.*

Delphi, what God they should appease, in order to be victorious against that people. The Pythian answered, they should then be successful, when they should carry back the bones of Orestes the son of Agamemnon to Sparta. The Lacedæmonians not knowing where to find the sepulchre of Orestes, sent again to inquire of the God in what country he lay interred, and received this answer from the Pythian:

In the Arcadian plains lies Tegea,
Where two impetuous winds are forc'd to blow:
Form resists form: mischief on mischief strikes.
Here mother Earth keeps Agamemnon's son;
Carry him off, and be victorious[u].

The Lacedæmonians having heard this answer, were not at all nearer finding it, though they searched every where: till Lichas, one of those Spartans who are called Agathoergi[v], found it by an accident. These Agathoergi consist of citizens who have served in the cavalry till they attain a considerable age; and then five of the eldest are yearly exempted from that duty, who are expected during the year of their dismissal to go about from place to place; being sent to different parts by the commonwealth. Lichas, one of these persons, by good fortune and sagacity discovered it. For as the Lacedæmonians had at that time an intercourse with the Tegeans, Lichas having one day entered into a smith's shop, attentively observed the process of working iron, and was struck with wonder when he saw what was done. The smith having observed his astonishment desisted from his work, and said: "O "Laconian stranger, you would certainly be astonished if you "had seen what I have, since you so admire the working of "iron. For as I was sinking a well in this inclosure, I found a "coffin seven cubits long; and because I could not think that "men were ever of a higher stature than in our time[x], I "opened the coffin, which I saw exactly fitted to the body: "and after I had taken the just measure, I covered all again "with earth."

LXVIII. Lichas reflecting on this discourse, conjec-

[u] Ἐπιτάῤῥοθος, is derived from ἐπιῤῥοθεῖν, which signifies to approach clamorously, and hence in the same manner as βοηθεῖν, signifies to come with a noise to one's assistance, to bring succour; the word ἐπιτάῤῥοθος, as Beloe remarks, is singularly used here—you shall become the defender of Tegea, having by victory become the proprietor.

[v] Those who have done well: Suidas says, that they were chosen from the Ephori. Hesychius however agrees with Herodotus. It may however be remarked, that the knights or ἱππεῖς of Sparta had no horses.

[x] Several traditions are found of a pretended race of giants in every country, even among the savages of Canada. Bones of an extraordinary size, found in different regions, have obtained such opinions credit. In 1613, was shewn through Europe, the bones of the giant Teutobachus; unluckily, a naturalist proved them to be the bones of an elephant. *Larcher*.

They shew at present in the Museum

tured from the words of the oracle, that this was the body of Orestes; not doubting that the smith's bellows he saw were the two winds; the anvil and hammer the two contending forms; and that the shaping of iron was signified by the redoubled mischiefs mentioned in the oracle; because he imagined that the invention of iron had been destructive to men. Having made this conjecture, he returned to Sparta, and gave the Lacedæmonians an account of the whole matter; they having brought against him a false accusation from a plot which had been formed, sent him into banishment. The Spartan arriving in Tegea[y], related his misfortune to the smith, and wished to hire the inclosure of him, because he would not sell it. But after he had persuaded him, he inhabited it, and having opened the sepulchre, collected all the bones, and carried them away with him to Sparta. From that time the Lacedæmonians were always superior in war to the Tegeans whenever they made trial of their power; and besides, they had already subdued many countries of Peloponnesus.

LXIX. Crœsus being informed of all these things, sent ambassadors to the Spartans, with presents, and orders to desire their alliance; who, when they were arrived, delivered their message, as they were instructed, in these words: "Crœsus, king of the Lydians and of other nations, has sent "us with this message. Since the Deity has directed me by "an oracle to unite myself to a Grecian friend, in obedience "to the oracle I invite you, O Lacedæmonians, (for I have "learnt that you are pre-eminent in Greece,) being desirous "of becoming your ally and confederate, without fraud or "artifice." The Lacedæmonians, who had notice of this oracle before, were pleased with the coming of the Lydians, and readily entered into a league of amity and mutual assistance with Crœsus; from whom they had formerly received some kindness. For when they had sent to Sardis to purchase gold[z], in order to erect that statue to Apollo which now stands on mount Thomax in Laconia, Crœsus gave it as a present to them, when they were desirous of purchasing it.

LXX. For which cause, and because he had selected them from all the Greeks and desired their friendship, they accepted

at Oxford, a large thigh-bone, which some pretend to be the thigh-bone of a man; it is, however, nothing more than the thigh-bone of an elephant.

[y] It may be asked how Orestes, who neither reigned nor resided at Tegea, could possibly be buried there? Strabo merely informs us, that he died in Arcadia, whilst conducting an Æolian colony. Stephen of Byzantium says, that he died at a place called Orestium, from the bite of a viper. His body was doubtless carried to Tegea, which was at no great distance, as he was descended, by his grandmother Aërope, from Tegeates, the founder of Tegea. *Larcher.*

[z] Literally; they wished to purchase gold, for that is the force of the imperfect *ὠνέοντο*; so in the last chapter *ἐμισθοῦτο*, he wished to hire.

the offer of his alliance; engaging to be ready with their forces, whenever he should desire their assistance. And also being desirous of making some return, they caused a vessel to be made of brass, capable of containing three hundred amphoras, and wrought all over the exterior part with the figures of various things[a]. But this vessel never reached Sardis, for one of these two reasons: the Lacedæmonians on their part say, that the Samians being informed of their design, fitted out divers long ships, and falling upon them in the road of Samos, robbed them of the present. On the other hand the Samians affirm, that when the Lacedæmonians, who were charged with the vessel, came too late, and heard that Sardis was taken, and Crœsus himself made prisoner, they sold the intended present at Samos to some private persons, who dedicated it in the temple of Juno; and that possibly when they were returned to Sparta, they might say the Samians had taken it away.

LXXI. In the mean time Crœsus, mistaking the oracle, prepared to invade Cappadocia with an army, in hope to destroy the power of Cyrus and of the Persians; and whilst he was preparing all things for this expedition, a Lydian named Sandanis, who before that time was esteemed a wise man, and on this occasion acquired a very great name in Lydia, gave him advice in these words: "O king, you are preparing to make war "against a people, who have no other clothing than skins; who "inhabit a barren country and eat not the things they would "choose, but such as they can get. They use water for drink[b], "and have neither wine nor figs, nor any delicious thing "among them. In the first place, if you conquer, what will you "take from them, since they have nothing? but on the other "hand, if you are conquered, consider what good things you "will lose. When they come to taste of our voluptuous way "of living, they will establish themselves in this country, and "we shall never be able to drive them out. As for me, I "thank the Gods, that they have not inspired the Persians "with thoughts of attacking us." But all this was not sufficient to dissuade Crœsus from making war against the Persians, who before they conquered the Lydians possessed nothing either delicious or commodious.

LXXII. The Cappadocians are by the Greeks called Syrians; these Syrians were subject to the Medes before the

[a] The ζώδια implies the figures not only of animals, but also of fruits, flowers, &c.; ζῶα is used in the same sense, book i. ch. 203. and elsewhere. *Wesseling.*

[b] Xenophon (Cyrop. i. 2.) also informs us, that the Persians drank only water; yet Herodotus (ch. 133.) says, that they were addicted to wine. In this there is no contradiction; when the Persians were poor, a little satisfied them; when they became rich by the conquests of Cyrus, and his successors, luxury and all its attendant vices were introduced. *Larcher.*

establishment of the Persian power; and in the time this of war were under the dominion of Cyrus. For the kingdoms of Media and Lydia are separated by the river Halys, which descending from the mountains of Armenia, passes through Cilicia; and leaving the Matienians[c] on the right and the Phrygians on the left hand, tends to the northward, and divides the Syrians of Cappadocia from the Paphlagonians; the former inhabiting on the right, and the latter on the left of that stream. In this manner the river Halys divides almost all the lower Asia, from the sea which is opposite Cyprus to the Euxine; the whole of which country forms a neck of land, over which an *active man*[d] may travel in five days[e].

LXXIII. Crœsus marched against Cappadocia from a desire of adding it to his dominions, and more particularly from his confidence in the oracle, and a wish to punish Cyrus on account of Astyages. For Cyrus the son of Cambyses had defeated and taken Astyages the son of Cyaxares, who was king of the Medes, and nearly related to Crœsus, in the following manner. Upon a sedition which happened among the Scythian Nomades, a party of them escaped into Media, where Cyaxares the son of Phraortes, and grandson to Deioces, was then king; who considering their distress, received them at first with great humanity; and having entertained a good opinion of them, entrusted to their care divers youths, to learn the use of the bow[f], and the Scythian tongue. These strangers exercised themselves with frequent hunting, and were ever accustomed to return with prey. But one day, when they had taken nothing, and came back with empty hands, Cyaxares, who, as plainly appeared, was of a violent temper, treated them with most opprobrious language. The Scythians having met with this treatment from Cyaxares, and

[c] Strabo makes mention of these people, and calls them Morimenians. They probably came from the original Matiene, being compelled to move thither by some king; or a colony might have been left there after some successful incursion. *Larcher.*

[d] Literally; a well-girt man, the long flowing dresses of the ancients making it necessary to gird them up when they wished to move expeditiously. So the Latins said succinctus.

[e] Scymnus of Chius, who upbraids Herodotus with ignorance in this passage, estimated the journey at probably 150 furlongs, whilst Herodotus makes it 200. *Larcher.*

It appears from the late observations of M. Beauchamp, that this Isthmus is not less than 240 Gr. miles. This would require a rate of 55½ Brit. miles in direct distance, and more than 60 by the road, for each day; a rate of travelling on foot which our author certainly had not in contemplation. Allowing 33 miles for each day, Herodotus supposed the Isthmus to be no more than 125 Gr. miles in breadth; that is 115 short of the truth. *Rennell*, p. 189.

[f] The Scythians were esteemed excellent archers. The Scholiast on Theocritus says, that according to Herodotus and Callimachus, Hercules learned to use the bow from the Scythian Tentarus. Theocritus himself says, that Hercules learnt it from Eurytus, one of the Argonauts. The Athenians had Scythian archers among their troops, as had probably the other Greeks. *Larcher.*

considering it undeserved by them, determined to kill one of the youths that were educated under their care, to prepare his flesh as they used to dress venison, and serve it up to Cyaxares as if it were game; and then to make their escape immediately to Alyattes the son of Sadyattes, king of Lydia. These things they executed as they designed: Cyaxares and those who sat with him at the table tasted of the flesh; and the Scythians, flying to Sardis, implored the protection of Alyattes.

LXXIV. After this, (for Alyattes refused to deliver up the Scythians to Cyaxares who demanded them,) war continued between the Medes and Lydians for five years; the Medes sometimes defeating the Lydians, and sometimes being defeated by them; during which time they had a kind of nocturnal combat[g]. In the sixth year, when they were carrying on the war nearly equally on both sides, they came to battle, and whilst they were contending for victory, the day was suddenly turned into night; which alteration Thales the Milesian[h] had foretold to the Ionians, and named the year when it should happen. The Lydians and Medes seeing darkness succeeding in the place of light, desisted from fighting, and shewed a great inclination on both sides to make peace. Syennesis[i] of Cilicia, and Labynetus[j] the Babylonian, were the mediators of their reconciliation; and these persons recommended them to strengthen the treaty by an oath, and made a matrimonial connection, for they persuaded Alyattes to give his daughter Aryenis in marriage to Astyages the son of Cyaxares. For without strong necessity, agreements are not wont to remain firm. These nations in their federal contracts observe the same ceremonies as in Greece; and besides this, both parties cut themselves on the arm till the blood gushes out[k], and then mutually lick it from the wounds.

[g] It is this battle which he proceeds to describe. Astronomers have affirmed from calculation, that this eclipse must have happened in the 7th year of Astyages, and not in the reign of Cyaxares. Volney shews that it happened on the 3rd of February, B. C. 625. See Larcher's long note.

[h] The life of Thales is given by Diodorus Siculus. He was born at Miletus, but his ancestors were Phœnicians. He learnt Geometry of the Egyptians, and was the first of the Greeks who studied that science. He was also a good astronomer and physician. Dodwell will not allow Thales to have been astronomer enough to have calculated an eclipse, but supposes that the darkness was occasioned by a tempest or exhalation, which he foresaw. On which Larcher observes, that it is much easier to calculate an eclipse, than the rising of any exhalation, &c.

[i] It appears that the name of Syennesis was common to the kings of Cilicia, at least we are certain that it was given to four princes. The first lived in the time of Cyaxares, the second was cotemporary with Darius, (Herod. v. 118.) the third with Xerxes, (Herod. vii. 98.) the the fourth with Artaxerxes. *Bellanger.*

[j] The same, says Prideaux, with the Nebuchadnezzar of Scripture.

[k] The Scythians have a custom nearly similar, (see book iv. ch. 70.) If the Siamese wish to vow an eternal friendship, they pierce some part of the body,

LXXV. Cyrus had conquered and confined this same Astyages, his grandfather by the mother, for reasons (which I shall hereafter relate) which Crœsus alleging against him, sent to consult the oracle, if he should make war against the Persians; and having received an illusory answer, which he interpreted to his own advantage, he led his army towards their territories. When he arrived at the river Halys, he caused his forces to pass over, as I believe, by bridges which were then built. But the common opinion of the Grecians is, that Thales the Milesian procured him a passage by other means. For, they say, whilst Crœsus was in doubt how his army should pass over the river, (for they say that there were no bridges at that time,) Thales, who was in his camp, caused the stream, which ran along the left[l] of the army, to pass likewise on the right, by this invention. They began a deep trench[m] by his direction at the head of the camp, in the shape of a half-moon, so that the water being turned into this from its old channel, it passed in the rear of the camp, and afterwards fell into its former course; so that as the river was thus divided it became fordable in both parts. Some say, that the ancient channel of the river became quite dry; but I cannot assent to their opinion; for how then could they repass, when they returned from that expedition?

LXXVI. However, Crœsus having passed the river with his army, entered into the country of Pteria. (Now Pteria is the strongest part of the whole of this country, and is over against Sinope, a city situated very near to the coast of the Euxine.) Encamping in that region, he ravaged the lands of the Syrians, took the chief city of the Pterians, and enslaved the inhabitants; he also took all the adjacent places, and expelled the inhabitants, who had given him no cause for blame.

Cyrus being informed of these things, assembled his army[n], and, having taken with him the forces of those countries

till the blood appears, which they reciprocally drink. In this manner the ancient Scythians and Babylonians ratified alliances, and almost all the nations of the east observe the same custom. *Civil and Natural History of Siam.*

[l] They would naturally go up the stream from the Euxine to find a convenient place to cross, and by that means they would have the river on the left. *Schweighæuser.*

[m] Anciently, when they wanted to construct a bridge, they began by digging another channel to turn off the water; when the ancient bed was dry, or nearly so, the bridge was erected, as we see chap. 186. It was consequently much less trouble for Crœsus to turn aside the river than to build a bridge. *Larcher.*

[n] Cyrus, intimidated by the threats of Crœsus, was inclined to retire into India. His wife Bardane inspired him with courage, and advised him to consult Daniel, who had more than once predicted future events to her and to Darius the Mede. Cyrus having consulted the prophet, received from him an assurance of victory. To me this seems one of those fables which the Jews and earlier Christians made no scruple of asserting as incontrovertible truths. Babylon not being yet taken, Cyrus could not know Daniel. *Larcher.*

through which he passed, marched towards the enemy. But before he began to advance, he sent heralds to the Ionians, to persuade them to revolt from Crœsus, and received a positive denial. When Cyrus had arrived and encamped opposite Crœsus, they tried their strength on the plains of Pteria in violent skirmishes; but when a general engagement took place, with great slaughter on both sides, they at last parted, on the approach of night, neither having been victorious. In this manner did the two armies engage.

LXXVII. But Crœsus being dissatisfied to see his forces much inferior in number to those of Cyrus, as indeed they were, and finding nothing attempted against him the day after the battle, retired to Sardis with his army, designing to send to the Egyptians for succour, pursuant to the confederacy he had made with Amasis king of Egypt, before he treated with the Lacedæmonians. In like manner, because the Babylonians with their king Labynetus[o], were also his allies, he resolved to require their assistance, and to fix a time for the coming of the Lacedæmonians, determining with these forces and his own to attack the Persians in the beginning of the next spring. With this design he returned home; and after he had dispatched ambassadors to his confederates, to require them to send their forces to Sardis before the end of five months, he disbanded the army that was with him, and that had fought against the Persians, which was composed of mercenary troops, not imagining that Cyrus, who had come off so equally, would venture to advance to Sardis.

LXXVIII. While these things were in agitation, a great number of serpents were seen in the lands about Sardis; which when the horses found, they left their pasture, and eat as many as they could take. Crœsus, thinking this to be a prodigy, as it really was, sent to consult the interpreters at Telmessus[p] by certain persons, who arriving in that place, received the answer of the Telmessians; but could not deliver it to Crœsus, because he was taken prisoner before they returned to Sardis. The

[o] This was the second of that name. He is called by Berosus Nabonid, which name does not differ from Labynetus so much as one would at first imagine. The ancient Latins said *vallum* for *vannum*; the Athenians λίτρον for νίτρον; πλεύμων for πνεύμων. He was the last king of Babylon, and united himself to Crœsus in order to repress the rising power of Cyrus. Amasis probably assisted for the same reason. *Larcher*.

[p] This Telmessus was on the border of Lycie, near the promontory Telmessus. Its inhabitants were famous as soothsayers. Telmessus was a son of Apollo, by a daughter of Antenor. The god had commerce with her under the form of a little dog; and to make her compensation, endowed her with the faculty of interpreting prodigies. Telmessus her son, who had the same gift, was interred under the altar of Apollo, in the city of Telmessus, of which he was probably the founder. *Larcher*.

interpretation of the Telmessians was, that a foreign army must soon be expected to invade his country, which on its arrival should conquer the natives; because, they said, the serpent is a son of the earth, and the horse is an enemy and a stranger. This answer they gave to Crœsus when he had been taken; yet without knowing what had happened to him and to Sardis.

LXXIX. When Crœsus had retired immediately after the battle of Pteria, Cyrus, having discovered that it was the intention of Crœsus to disband his army, found upon deliberation, that it would be to his advantage to march with all possible expedition to Sardis, before the forces of the Lydians could be a second time assembled; which resolution was executed with so great a diligence, that Cyrus himself at the head of his army brought this news of his own enterprize. Crœsus, though extremely alarmed at an attempt, which he neither foresaw nor expected, drew out the Lydians into the field, who in that time were as brave and warlike a people as any other of all Asia. They fought on horseback, armed with strong lances, and managed their horses with admirable address.

LXXX. The place where they assembled was a spacious plain[q], lying before the city, and watered by divers rivers, particularly by the Hyllus, which runs into the greatest of all, called the Hermus. This river descending from a mountain, sacred to Cybele mother of the Gods, falls into the sea near the city of Phocæa. Cyrus seeing the Lydians drawn up in order of battle, and apprehending the efforts of their horse, by the suggestion of Harpagus, a Mede, made use of this stratagem. He ordered all the camels that followed the army with provisions and baggage to be brought together; and having caused their loading to be taken away, commanded men clothed after the manner of the cavalry to mount those animals, and to march in the van of his forces against the Lydian horse. Behind the camels he placed his infantry, and all his cavalry in the rear. When all had been drawn up in order, he gave out strict orders through the whole army, not to spare any Lydian they should meet, but not to kill Crœsus, although when taken he should offer resistance. Cyrus placed the camels in the front of the cavalry, for this reason; a horse is afraid of a camel[r], and cannot endure either to see or smell him: this therefore was contrived, in order that the Lydian

[q] The word ψιλός shews that there were neither trees nor bushes.

[r] This natural antipathy of the horse for the camel is affirmed by the ancients; but it is disproved by daily experience, and decided by the best judges, the Orientals. *Gibbon.*

cavalry might be useless, on which Crœsus depended that he should signalize himself. Accordingly the battle no sooner began, than the horses, impatient of the scent and sight of the camels, turned their heads and ran away; which Crœsus observing, gave all his hope for lost. Nevertheless the Lydians, who perceived the cause of what had happened, were not presently discouraged, but dismounting from their horses, renewed the fight on foot; till at last after an obstinate dispute, in which great numbers fell on both sides, they fled to Sardis, and shutting themselves up within the walls of the city, were besieged by the Persians.

LXXXI. Crœsus, thinking the siege would be long, sent from the city other messengers to his allies; for those who were before sent to the different places requested that they would assemble at Sardis on the fifth month, but he sent out the last to request them to succour him with all speed, as he was already besieged.

LXXXII. Among the rest of his confederates he sent to the Lacedæmonians; who at the same time had a contest with the Argians about the country of Thyrea[a], which the Spartans had seized, though of right belonging to Argos. And indeed whatever lies westward of that city, even to Malea, on the continent, together with Cythera and the other islands, belongs to the Argians. The Argians having advanced to the defence of their country which had been seized upon, both parties upon a conference agreed, that three hundred men on each side should determine the dispute by combat, and the country be adjudged to the victorious. Yet in the first place, both armies were to depart, lest either side finding their countrymen in distress, might come in to their assistance. This agreement being made, and the armies retired; the fight began, and was maintained with such equal valour, that of the six hundred, three men only were left alive: neither had these all survived, if night coming on had not saved them. Two of the three were Argians, Alcinor and Chromius by name, who, thinking themselves victorious, ran to Argos with the news. But Othryades, the only survivor on the part of the Lacedæmonians, after he had collected the spoil of the Argians, and carried all their arms into the Spartan camp, continued at his post. The next day both armies, being informed of the event, met again in the same place, and both laid claim to the victory. The Argians alleged, that they had more than one left alive.

[a] Thyrea was part of Cynuria, and was, from its situation of great importance to the Argians, as they obtained by it a communication with all their other possessions on that side. *Larcher.* This tract of land was the cause of constant variance between the Argians and Lacedæmonians. See Thucyd. v. 41. where a singular proposal for the adjustment of those differences occurs.

But the Lacedæmonians urged, that the surviving Argians ran away; and that their countryman alone had kept the field, and pillaged the dead. From words they betook themselves to their arms; and after a bloody fight[t], in which many were killed on both sides, the Lacedæmonians obtained the victory. Upon this disaster, the Argians cutting off their hair, which to that time they had been obliged to wear of a considerable length, agreed to a law, and made a solemn vow, that they would not suffer their hair to grow long, nor permit their women to dress with ornaments of gold, till they should recover Thyrea. On the other hand, the Lacedæmonians made a contrary order, enjoining all their people to wear long hair, which they had never done before[u]. As for Othryades, who was the only surviving Spartan of the three hundred, they say he killed himself at Thyrea, ashamed to return home after the slaughter of all his companions.

LXXXIII. The affairs of the Lacedæmonians were in this condition, when the Sardian ambassador arriving in Sparta prayed their assistance on the part of Crœsus, who was besieged in Sardis; which they no sooner heard, than they resolved to succour him. But when they had made ready their ships, and prepared all things for the expedition, they were informed by another message, that the city of Sardis was taken, and Crœsus himself made prisoner; which they took for a great misfortune, and desisted from their enterprize.

LXXXIV. The city of Sardis was taken in this manner. On the fourteenth day of the siege, Cyrus ordered proclamation to be made by men on horseback throughout his camp, that he would liberally reward the man who should first mount the enemy's walls: upon which several attempts were made, and as often failed; till, after the rest had desisted, one Hyrœades[x] a Mardian endeavoured to climb on that part of the citadel where no guard was stationed, because there did not appear any danger that it would be taken on that part; for

[t] Plutarch affirms, that the Amphictyons coming to the spot and bearing testimony to the valour of Othryades, adjudged the victory to the Lacedæmonians. He makes no mention of a second battle. *Larcher.*

[u] All the Greeks formerly wore their hair long. Homer for this reason calls them *καρηκομῶντες*. Xenophon remarks, that the Lacedæmonian custom of wearing the hair long, was amongst the institutions of Lycurgus, who is reported to have said, "Long hair makes the handsome more beautiful, and the ugly more terrible." Plutarch affirms the same thing as Xenophon, &c. *Larcher.*

[x] Xenophon (Cyrop. vii. 2.) does not mention this person's name, but merely says, a Persian who had been the slave of a man on military duty in the citadel, served as a guide to the troops of Cyrus. In other respects his account of the capture of Sardis differs but little from that of our historian. *Larcher.*

By means of this very rock, and by a similar stratagem, Sardis was a long time after taken under Antiochus. The circumstances are described at length by Polybius, book vii. ch. 4, 5, 6, &c.

on that side the citadel was steep and impracticable. To this part alone of all the fortifications, Males, a former king of Sardis, never brought his son Leo, whom he had by a concubine; though the Telmessians had pronounced, that if he were carried quite round the works, Sardis should be for ever impregnable; but having caused him to be brought to every other part of the place, totally neglected this, which faces mount Tmolus, as altogether insuperable and inaccessible. Hyrœades the Mardian had seen a Lydian come down this precipice the day before, to take up a helmet that was dropped; and after he had attentively observed and considered the thing, he ascended the same way, followed by divers Persians; and being soon supported by greater numbers, the city of Sardis was thus taken and plundered.

LXXXV. Crœsus, as I have already said, had a son who was dumb, though in all other respects commendable; and as in the time of his prosperity, he omitted nothing that might contribute to deliver him from that infirmity, among other experiments, he sent to consult the oracle of Delphi concerning him, and received this answer from the Pythian:

O too imprudent Lydian! Wish no more
The charming sound of a son's voice to hear:
Better for thee, could things rest as they are;
For in an evil day he first shall speak.

Upon the taking of the city, a certain Persian, taking Crœsus to be another person, was advancing to kill him; Crœsus though he saw him approach from his present misfortune paid no attention to him, nor did he care about dying by his sword; but his speechless son, seeing the soldier ready to strike, and fearing for the life of his father, in that instant cried out, *Man, kill not Crœsus.* These were the first words he ever uttered; but from that time he continued to speak readily during all the rest of his life.

LXXXVI. In this manner the Persians became masters of Sardis, and made Crœsus their prisoner; who having reigned fourteen years, and been besieged fourteen days, put an end to his great empire, as the oracle had predicted. The Persians having taken Crœsus, and brought him to Cyrus, he commanded him to be fettered, and placed on a great pile of wood[y] already prepared, accompanied by fourteen young Lydians; designing either to offer this sacrifice to some God, as the first fruits of his victory; or to perform a vow; or perhaps to see, because he had heard of his devotion to the Gods,

[y] This conduct of Cyrus was the more cruel as Crœsus was his great uncle, Aryenis the sister of Crœsus having married Astyages. See chap. 73. Ctesias and Xenophon do not mention this circumstance. *Larcher.*

whether any Deity would save him from being burnt alive. When Crœsus had ascended the pile, notwithstanding the weight of his misfortunes, the words of Solon reviving in his memory, made him think he was inspired by some God, when he said, that no living man could be justly called happy. When this occured to him, it is said, that after a long silence he drew a deep sigh, and with a groan thrice pronounced the name of Solon; which when Cyrus heard, he commanded his interpreters to ask him, whose assistance he implored. They obeyed immediately; but Crœsus for a while kept silence; yet at last being constrained to speak, he said, "I named a "man, whose discourses I more desire all tyrants might hear, "than to be possessor of the greatest riches." When he gave them this obscure answer, they repeated their demand; and when they persisted in their importunity, Crœsus at length acquainted them that Solon an Athenian, having formerly visited him, and viewed his immense treasures, had despised all; and that the truth of what he then said was now verified, though his discourse was general, relating to all mankind as much as to himself, and especially to those who vainly imagine themselves happy. Crœsus gave this explanation, and the fire being now kindled, the flames began to ascend on every side. Cyrus, already informed by the interpreters of what he had said, relented on a sudden; and considering that being but a man, he was yet going to burn another man alive, who had been no way inferior to himself in prosperity; and fearing a retaliation, and considering that nothing human was constant, he commanded the fire to be instantly extinguished, and Crœsus with those who were about him to be taken down. Accordingly all endeavours were used to execute his orders; but they could not master the fire.

LXXXVII. In this distress, Crœsus, as the Lydians report, being informed that Cyrus had altered his resolution, and seeing every man toiling in vain to put out the fire, with a loud voice invoking Apollo, besought the God, if ever any of his offerings had been agreeable to him[a], to protect and deliver him from the present danger: they report, that he with tears invoked the God, and immediately clouds were seen gathering in the air, which before was serene, and a violent storm of rain ensuing, quite extinguished the flames; by which Cyrus understanding that Crœsus was a good and pious man, spoke to him as soon as he came down in these terms: "Tell "me, Crœsus, who persuaded you to invade my territories, "and to be my enemy rather than my friend?" "This war,"

[a] Herodotus surely had in view this verse of Homer: Εἴ ποτέ τοι χαρίεντ' ἐπὶ νηὸν ἔρεψα. Iliad, A. ver. 39.

said Crœsus, "as fortunate to you, O king, as unfortunate to "me, I undertook by the persuasion and encouragement of "the Grecian God. For no man is so void of understanding "to prefer war before peace; because in the time of war fa-"thers bury their children[a], and in time of peace children "perform that office to their parents. But, I suppose, it "pleased the Gods that these things should be so."

LXXXVIII. When he had thus spoken, Cyrus commanded his fetters to be taken off; and permitting him to sit down by his side, shewed him great respect; for both he and all those that stood about him were astonished at the things they had seen. Crœsus sat for some time pensive and silent: but afterwards having turned round and beheld the Persians sacking the city, he said to Cyrus, "Does it become me, O "king, to tell you what I think, or to keep silence on the pre-"sent occasion?" Cyrus bid him say with confidence whatever he wished; upon which Crœsus asked him, what those great numbers were now doing with so much diligence. "They "are," said Cyrus, "pillaging your city, and dispersing your "riches." "Not so," replied Crœsus; "they neither plunder "my city, nor my riches, for I have now no part in those "things, but they ravage and consume[b] what belongs to "you."

LXXXIX. The reply of Crœsus excited the attention of Cyrus; he therefore ordered all present to withdraw, and asked him, what he thought should be done in this conjuncture. "Since the Gods," said Crœsus, "have made me your ser-"vant, I am in duty obliged to acquaint you with all that may "conduce to your advantage. If you permit the Persians, "who are poor, and by nature insolent, to plunder and possess "great riches, you may expect that those who enrich them-"selves most, will be most ready to rebel. Therefore, if you "approve my sentiment, place some of your guards at every "gate, with orders to take the booty from all those who would "go out, and to acquaint them that the tenth must of neces-"sity be consecrated to Jupiter: thus, you will not incur their "hatred by taking away their plunder; and every one acknow-"ledging your intention to be just, will readily obey."

XC. Cyrus, when he heard this, was beyond measure delighted, as he conceived that Crœsus had advised him well; and having bestowed many commendations on him, he commanded the guards to do as he advised; and then turning to

[a] See Shakespeare's King Henry VI. part 3.

[b] *Ἄγειν καὶ φέρειν* properly signifies to plunder entirely; *ἄγειν* referring to cattle which you drive, or man whom you drag into slavery; *φέρειν* to the moveable and every inanimate thing which it is necessary to carry. See Xenoph. Anab. ii. 6. *Larcher.*

him again, said, "Crœsus, since your conduct and your words "evince a princely character[c], I permit you to ask immediately whatever thing you chiefly desire." "Sir," said Crœsus, "the most acceptable favour you can bestow upon "me is, to let me send my fetters to the God of the Grecians, "whom I have honoured more than any other deity; and to "ask him, if it be his custom to deceive those who deserve "best of him." Cyrus asked what cause he had to complain of the God, that might induce him to make this request: upon which Crœsus, recollecting all his thoughts on that subject, recounted all the answers he had received from the oracles, and particularly the donations he had presented; and how he was incited by an oracle to make war against the Persians; beseeching him again to grant him leave to reproach the God with these things. Cyrus, with a smile, assured him he would not only grant this, but whatever else he should desire: which Crœsus hearing, dispatched certain Lydians to Delphi, with orders to lay down his fetters at the entrance of the temple, and to demand of the God, if he were not ashamed to have encouraged Crœsus by his oracles to believe, that by undertaking a war against the Persians he should destroy the power of Cyrus, of which war such were the first fruits, (commanding them at these words to shew the fetters,) and to ask if the Grecian Gods were accustomed to be so ungrateful.

XCI. When the Lydians arrived at Delphi, and had said what was enjoined them, the Pythian is reported to have made this answer: "The God himself cannot avoid the predetermined decrees of fate; and Crœsus suffers for the crime of "his ancestor in the fifth generation[d], who being one of the "guard of the Heraclidæ, was induced by the artifice of a "woman to murder his master, and to usurp his dignity, to "which he had no right. Yet although Apollo used his best "endeavours, that the disaster of Sardis might be suspended "to the time of his sons, and not happen during the reign of "Crœsus, he could not set aside the fatal decree[e]; yet he "had done as much in his favour as that would permit, having delayed the subversion of his kingdom for three years. "And therefore let Crœsus know, that he was taken prisoner "three years later than the fates had ordained. In the next

[c] Literally; since you make it your study to act and speak as a prince, βασιλεὺς ἄνηρ does not mean a king, but was a common expression, to denote any person of distinction.

[d] Crœsus was the fifth descendant of Gyges, if we include the two extremes: for the house of the Mermnadæ was as follows; Gyges, Ardys, Sadyattes, Alyattes, Crœsus. This was the common way of counting among the Greeks, especially in speaking of the degrees of genealogy. *Bellanger.*

[e] The power of fate was commonly supposed immutable among the heathens. See Æsch. Prom. Vinct. 516. Ovid Met. IX. 429.

"place, when he was upon the point of being burnt alive, the "God came in to his relief. Then, as to the prediction of the "oracle, he has no right to complain; because Apollo only "foretold, that if he would make war against the Persians, he "should subvert a great empire; and had he desired to be "truly informed, he ought to have sent again to inquire, "whether his own or that of Cyrus was meant by the oracle. "But if he neither comprehended the meaning of the oracle, "nor would inquire again, the fault is his. And, he did not "understand the answer he received concerning the mule, "when he last consulted the God; for Cyrus was that mule: "inasmuch as he was born of parents, who were of different "nations, whose mother was also of a superior, and his father "of an inferior condition. For his mother was a Mede, and "daughter to Astyages king of Media; but his father was of "Persia, subject to the Medes; and being every way inferior "to her, had married his mistress." The Lydians having received this answer from the Pythian, returned, and made their report to Crœsus; who acknowledged the fault to be his, and that the oracle was wholly innocent. In this manner the kingdom of Crœsus was conquered, and Ionia the first time subdued.

XCII. Many other donations were consecrated by Crœsus in Greece, besides those already mentioned. For at Thebes of Bœotia he dedicated a tripod[f] of gold to the Ismenian Apollo; at Ephesus, he gave the golden heifers, with the greater part of the pillars; and sent a large shield of gold to Delphi, in the temple of Minerva Pronæa[g]. All these remain to this day; but others have been lost. The offerings he dedicated in Branchis, a city belonging to the Milesians, were, as I am informed, equal in weight and similar to those he presented at Delphi. These last, together with those he sent to Amphiaraus, were the first fruits of his domestic and patrimonial riches. But the rest arose out of the property of an enemy; who, endeavouring to put the kingdom of Lydia into the hands of Pantaleon[h], formed a party against Crœsus, to hinder his accession to the throne. Pantaleon was the son of

[f] We must not confound the tripods of the ancients with the utensil known to us by that name (Trepieds). The tripod was a vessel standing on three feet, of which there were two kinds, one appropriated to festivals, and wine and water were mixed in them; the other kind was placed on fire to warm water, &c. *Larcher.*

[g] There was at Delphi a temple of Minerva Pronæa; its situation opposite to that of Apollo gave it that name.

[h] When Crœsus mounted the Lydian throne he divided the kingdom with his brother. A Lydian remarked, that the sun obtains for mankind all the comforts which the earth produces, and that if deprived of its influence the earth would cease to be fruitful. But if there were two suns, it were to be feared that every thing would be scorched and perish. For this reason the Lydians have but one king; him they regard as their protector, but they will not allow two. *Stobeus, Serm.* 45.

Alyattes, and brother to Crœsus, though not born of the same mother; for Alyattes had Crœsus by a Carian, and Pantaleon by an Ionian woman. But when Crœsus obtained the kingdom pursuant to the designation of his father, he killed his opponent by tearing his flesh with a fuller's instrument[i], and having already vowed all his treasure to the Gods, he performed his promise by the donations he made to the places I mentioned before. And this I think sufficient to say touching these things.

XCIII. The territories of Lydia have nothing admirable and deserving mention, like other countries, unless some particles of gold, brought down from mount Tmolus. But the Lydians shew one monument of art, which in greatness much surpasses all others, except those of the Egyptians and Babylonians; I mean, the sepulchre of Alyattes[k], father to Crœsus, the basis of which is composed of stones of extraordinary dimensions, and all the rest is a mound of earth. This fabric was raised by merchants, artificers, and women who prostituted themselves for hire. On the summit of this monument there remained, even within my remembrance, five termini, upon which were inscriptions, certifying the measure of their labour, and shewing that the work of the females was the greatest. The daughters of the Lydians are accustomed to acquire their

[i] Κνάφος is properly a fuller's instrument set round with points, with which fullers scrape the cloth. It also signifies an instrument of torture made somewhat in the same way. *Wesseling*.

[k] The remains of this barrow are still conspicuous within five miles of Sardis, now called Sart. The mould, which has been washed down, conceals the basement; but that, and a considerable treasure, might perhaps be discovered if the barrow were opened. *Dr. Chandler's Travels in Asia Minor*, p. 263.

Clearchus relates, that a large mound was erected by Gyges in honour of one of his mistresses, (Athen. Deipnosoph, xiii. 4.) which must be the same with the one Herodotus here speaks of. *Larcher*.

The learned Mr. King considers this description as exactly corresponding with that of a large British or Irish barrow. The foundation is composed of large stones, which gives us some intimation of the probable existence of a passage and kitsvaen, or a small room under the foundation, designed for the reception of the bones and ashes; and formed of large rude stones, (as in some of our barrows,) over which there was then a vast tumulus or mount of earth, heaped very high. Mr. King objects to οὖροι being translated termini, or rude boundary stones; and says that it more properly means a ditch, or artificial trench, whilst at the same time ἐνεκεκολάπτο in reality rather implies, that letters or marks were impressed by being stampt or beaten in, than by being inscribed or cut. The expression therefore exactly agrees with that of rude characters or marks being stampt or beaten into the side of a dry ditch, (perhaps somewhat in the manner that those old memorials, the figures of the white horse, and of the white leaf cross, are formed on the sides of certain chalk-hills in our own country.) Herodotus then expressly says, it appeared by *measuring*, that the work of the girls was the greatest; and we may observe, it certainly would be, in every respect, if their ditch was, as it should seem to be, the outermost of five concentric ones, formed on the summit of the barrow.

It may be observed, with due deference to Mr. King, that if those trenches were concentric, there could be no occasion for measuring. The simplest explanation seems to be, that this tomb was raised not by the manual exertions, but by the contributions of these three classes of people, and that the contribution of the courtesans was the largest. *Beloe*.

dowries by prostitution; and are then permitted to marry as they please[l]. This sepulchre is six stades and two plethrons in circumference, and thirteen plethrons in breadth; contiguous to it is a large lake, which the Lydians say is fed by perpetual springs, and is called the Gygean lake.

XCIV. The customs of the Lydians differ little from those of the Grecians, except only that they prostitute their daughters. They were the first of all the nations we know, who introduced the art of coining gold and silver[m] to facilitate trade, and first practised the way of retailing merchandise. They pretend to be the inventors of divers games, which are now common to them with the Greeks; and, as they say, were found out about the time they sent a colony to Tyrrhenia, on this occasion. During the reign of Atys the son of Manes king of Lydia, a scarcity of provisions spread over the kingdom, which the people for a time supported with patience and industry. But when they saw the evil still continuing, they applied themselves to find out a remedy, and some devised one thing, some another; and at that time the games of dice, hucklebones[n] and balls, and all other kinds of games except chess[o], were invented; the Lydians do not challenge the invention of this last game; and to bear this calamity better, they used to play one whole day without intermission, that they might not be disquieted with the thoughts of food; eating and drinking[p] on the next day, without amusing themselves with any kind of game. After they had continued this alternate manner during eighteen years, and found their wants rather increasing than abating, the king divided the people into two parts, and ordered them to determine by

[l] They give themselves away in marriage. Ἐκδίδωμι is properly said of a father, who gives away his daughter in marriage. *Larcher.*

[m] It is impossible to decide who were the first people that coined gold and silver. According to some it was Pheidon, king of Argos, (see book vi. ch. 127.) According to others Demodice, wife of Midas. Xenophanes of Colophon, and Eustathius, agree with Herodotus. *Larch.*

[n] This game is played in several parts of England, and is called in some counties *cockals*, and in others *dibs.*

[o] Some suppose this game (πεσσοί) to be the same as the scrupus lusorious, mentioned by Quintil. ii. 2. and also by Ovid. Art. Am. iii. Others think that it is the same as the lusus latrunculus. Hesychius tells us it was played without dice, and therefore probably it did not depend on chance.

With regard to the origin of chess, we are much in the dark. It came to us from the Saracens, but it is by no means probable that they were the original inventors of it. According to some, it was invented by Diomedes, others say by Lydus and Tyrrhenus. Mr. Irwin (Irish Trans. vol. v.) supposes that it was invented by the Chinese. Sir William Jones concludes that it was of Hindoo invention. Asiatic Researches, vol. ii. mem. 9.

[p] That the Lydians may have been the inventors of games, is very probable; that under the pressure of famine they might detach half their nation to seek their fortune elsewhere is not unlikely; but that to soften their miserable situation, and to get rid of the sensations of hunger, they should eat only every other day, and that for eighteen years, appears perfectly absurd. *Larcher.*

H 2

lot which division should relinquish the country and which should remain in possession; he himself designing to reign over those who should have the fortune to stay, and appointing his son Tyrrhenus to command that part which should be obliged to remove. Those who by lot were constrained to depart, marched down to Smyrna; where having built a sufficient number of ships, and put all their moveables which were of use on board, they set sail in search of food and of a new habitation; till having passed by many nations, they arrived in Umbria, and built divers cities, which they inhabit to this day. There they changed their ancient name, and were no longer called Lydians, but Tyrrhenians[q], from their leader Tyrrhenus the son of their king. In this manner then the Lydians were conquered by the Persians.

XCV. My history naturally then proceeds to inquire who Cyrus was, that destroyed the kingdom of Crœsus, and how the Persians became masters of Asia. In which narration I shall follow those Persians only, who do not wish to magnify the actions of Cyrus, but to relate the plain truth; though I am not ignorant that there are three other ways[r] of relating his history. After the Assyrians had possessed the empire of upper Asia five hundred and twenty years, the Medes were the first that revolted from them, and in their struggle for liberty, proved themselves brave men; and having shaken off the yoke, they became free: afterwards other nations did the same.

XCVI. They made and enjoyed their own laws for some time all over that continent; but were again reduced under a tyranny, in the following manner; there lived among the Medes, a man famous for wisdom named Deioces, the son of Phraortes. This Deioces aiming at absolute power, practised the following conduct. The Medes were at that time distributed into several districts; and Deioces having already become distinguished in his own district, applied himself with more eagerness to the exercise of justice; and this he did, since great lawlessness prevailed throughout the whole of Media, and as he well knew that injustice and justice are

[q] Horace alludes to this in the following lines:

Non quia, Mæcenas, Lydorum quicquid Etruscos
Incoluit fines, nemo generosior est te.
1 Sat. vi. 1.

So Virgil,

Et terram Hesperiam venies; ubi Lydius, arva
Inter opima virûm, leni fluit agmine Thybris. Æneid. ii. 781.

This emigration of the Lydians is subject to considerable difficulties. They are considered by M. Freret, in the Memoires de l'Acad. des Belles Lettres, tom. xviii. Hist. p. 95. Some of his opinions are questioned by M. Larcher at considerable length.

[r] Ctesias, in the fragments of his Persian History, preserved by Photius, gives a different account; and every body knows the account given by Xenophon in his Cyropædia: Æschylus in his Persæ (ver. 767.) gives an account which differs from them all. *Larcher.*

ever at variance[s]. The Medes of the same district observing the equity of his conduct, chose him for their judge; and he, aspiring to compass the sovereign power, performed that office with all possible regard to justice. By this conduct he acquired so much honour in the district where he lived, that men of other districts hearing that Deioces was the only one who judged according to the rules of equity, having before met with unjust sentences, came from all parts to him, in order to obtain justice: till at last no man would commit the decision of a difference to any other person.

XCVII. In the end, the numbers of those who applied to him for redress augmenting in proportion to the great fame of his equity, Deioces, seeing the whole devolved upon his person, absented himself from the place where he used to sit to determine differences, and declared he would pronounce no more judgments; because it was not advantageous to him to neglect his own affairs, and spend the day in doing right to others. Upon this, rapine and all manner of injuries growing far more frequent in every part than before, the Medes called a general assembly, and as they were consulting about the present state of things, the partizans of Deioces, in my opinion, spoke nearly in the following manner: "Since it is "impossible for us to inhabit the country, if we continue in "our present condition, let us constitute a king, that the na-"tion may be governed by good laws; and that applying our "care to our own business, we may not be constrained to aban-"don our habitations by the disorders of anarchy." By some such words they persuaded them to be governed by a king.

XCVIII. When it was immediately proposed for their deliberation, "Whom they should appoint king," Deioces was universally named and commended, and at last they consented that he should be king. But he then commanded them to build him a palace suitable to the dignity of a king, and required guards for the security of his person. The Medes obeyed; and on the ground he chose, erected a strong and stately fabric for his use; permitting him at the same time to choose for his guard such persons as he should think fit out of the whole nation. Being thus possessed of the power, he compelled the Medes to build one city[t], that they might protect that, and pay less attention to the others. In this also he was obeyed; and those strong and magnificent

[s] Deioces, when he aspired to the throne, wished to gain popularity; and being fully convinced of the iniquity of the judges, and that those who were its victims abhorred injustice, he determined to administer justice with all possible impartiality, in order to render himself popular. This appears to be the meaning of the passage. *Larcher.*

[t] The conduct of Theseus, in collecting the inhabitants of Attica into one city, (Thucyd. book ii.) and of Gelon in fortifying and enlarging Syracuse, (Herod. book vii. ch. 156.) are exactly similar.

walls, which now go under the name of Ecbatana[w], were then built. They are of a circular form, one within the other, and each gradually raised just so much above the other as the battlements are high. The situation of the ground, rising by an easy ascent, was very favourable to the design. But that which was particularly attended to is, that the king's palace and treasury are built within the innermost circle of the seven which compose this city. The first and most spacious of these walls is equal in circumference to the city of Athens[x], and the battlements are white, those of the second are black, of the third purple, the fourth blue, and the fifth of a deep orange. The battlements of all these are coloured with different compositions; but of the two innermost walls, one is painted on the battlements with a silver colour, and the other is gilded with gold.

XCIX. Deioces, having thus provided for his residence and the safety of his person, commanded the rest of the people to fix their habitations around the citadel; which when they had done, he established these rules to be observed as standing orders; that no man should be admitted to the king's presence, but should transact all things with him by messengers; that none should be permitted to see him; and that either to laugh or spit in his sight, should be accounted indecent[y]. He established this solemn dignity for this purpose;

[w] The city of Ecbatana was unquestionably on or near the site of Hamadan, in Al Jebal. A great number of authorities concur in proving this, although many refer it to Tauris, or Tebriz, in Aderbigian; Mr. Gibbon and Sir W. Jones among the rest. The authorities are too numerous to be adduced here, we shall only mention that Isidore of Charax places it on the road from Seleucia to Parthia; that (says Pliny) that Susa is equidistant from Seleucia and Ecbatana; and that the capital of Atropatia (Adergian) is midway between Artaxata and Ecbatana. And finally, that it lay in the road from Nineveh to Rages, or Rey. *Rennell*, p. 272.

The following is the Scripture account of Ecbatana:

"In the twelfth year of the reign of "Nabuchodonosor, who reigned in Nineve, the great city; in the days of Arphaxad, which reigned over the Medes "in Ecbatane,

"And built in Ecbatane walls round "about of stones hewn three cubits "broad and six cubits long, and made "the height of the wall seventy cubits, "and the breadth thereof fifty cubits:

"And set the towers thereof upon the "gates of it, an hundred cubits *high*, and "the breadth thereof in the foundation "threescore cubits:

"And he made the gates thereof, even "gates that were raised to the height "of seventy cubits, and the breadth of "them was forty cubits, for the going "forth of his mighty armies, and for the "setting in array of his footmen." *Judith*, ch. i. ver. 1, 2, 3, 4.

Prideaux and Gray are of opinion that this Arphaxad is the same as Deioces.

[x] According to Diodorus Siculus, (lib. xvii. 110.) Ecbatana was 250 stadia in circumference, and Athens according to Thucydides (ii. 13.) 195.

[y] The Indians are not permitted to spit in the king's palace. (Le Blanc's Travels, p. 18.) The Arabians never spit before their superiors. Neibuhr (Description of Arabia, p. 53.) informs us, that he has frequently seen the master of a house sitting with a china spitting-pot near him. He however observes, that they do not often spit, although they continue smoking for many hours at a time. The Arabians are less punctilious with regard to this custom, since they have smoked tobacco. *Larcher.*

lest those who were once his equals and who were educated with him, and of no meaner family or inferior on the score of virtue, might grieve and conspire against him; but that if they did not see him they might conceive him to be a different kind of being.

C. When he had established these orders, and settled himself in the tyranny, he was very severe in the execution of justice. The parties contending were obliged to send him their case in writing; which when he had seen and considered, he used to send it back with his decision; and this was the method he took in judiciary matters. But if he received information that any man had injured another, he would presently send for him, and punish him in proportion to his offence, maintaining to that end many emissaries and spies in the provinces of his government.

CI. The power of Deioces extended not beyond the whole nation of the Medes; which consists of the Busæ, Parataceni, Struchates, Arizanti, Budii, and the Magi.

CII. He reigned fifty-three years, and his son Phraortes succeeded him in the kingdom; who, not contented to be king of Media only, made his first expedition against the Persians, and reduced them under the dominion of the Medes. And having united the forces of those two powerful nations, he subdued Asia; advancing his conquests gradually, and attacking one country after another; till at last he invaded the Assyrians, who inhabited the city of Nineveh[a], and had been the principal people of those nations, though at that time they were abandoned by their confederates, yet their affairs were otherwise in good condition, Phraortes having entered their territories, perished with the greatest part of his army in that enterprize, after he had reigned twenty-two years.

CIII. Cyaxares the son of Phraortes, and grandson to Deioces, succeeded him, and is generally esteemed to have been more brave and warlike than his ancestors. He first divided the people of Asia into cohorts[a], and divided into distinct bodies the spearmen, cavalry, and archers; whereas

[a] Both Diodorus, lib. ii. c. 1. and Strabo, p. 737. attribute the foundation of this city to Ninus, king of Assyria. Its situation is well known to be at the eastern side of the Tigris, opposite the city of Mosul, where, according to travellers of the highest authority, (Niebuhr among the rest,) traces of the remains of a city are found; such as mounds of earth, and heaps which indicate the rubbish of buildings, as at Babylon. It appears remarkable that Xenophon, whose fifth encampment from the Zabatus must have been near to it, or on its site, and Alexander, who passed so near it, in his way to the field of Gaugamela, (Arbela,) should neither of them have taken any notice of its ruins; the former especially, who notes the remains of two cities (Larissa and Mespyla) on his way towards the site of Nineveh, from the Zabatus. *Rennel*, p. 265.

[a] Military discipline appears to have been introduced among the Hebrews some time before. *Larcher*.

before they had been accustomed to mix in a confused manner. It was he that fought with the Lydians, when the day was on a sudden turned into night[b]: and united all Asia beyond the river Halys under him. Having assembled the forces of all his subjects, he marched against Nineveh to avenge the death of his father by the destruction of that place; but after he had obtained a victory over the Assyrians, and while he was besieging Nineveh, a great army of Scythians[c] came upon him, under the conduct of Madyes their king, and son of Protothyas. These Scythians had driven the Cimmerians out of Europe, and pursuing them into Asia, by that means entered the territories of the Medes.

CIV. The distance between the lake Mæotis and the river Phasis in the country of Colchis, is as much as an expeditious traveller can pass over in thirty days: but the way from Colchis to Media is not long, no other people than the Saspires lying between both. However, the Scythians did not pass through their territories but turned to the higher road by a much longer rout, having mount Caucasus on the right[d]; and there the Medes having engaged, were defeated and deprived of their dominion; but the Scythians became masters of all Asia.

CV. From thence they proceeded to Egypt, and when they were arrived in Palæstine of Syria, Psammetichus king of Egypt came thither to meet them, and by prayers and presents prevailed with them to advance no farther. In their return they came to Ascalon, a city of Syria, and most part of the army marched through the place without doing any injury. But some few, who were left behind, pillaged the temple of the celestial Venus[e]; which, as I am informed, is the most ancient of all those that are dedicated to this goddess. For her temple in Cyprus was built after that of Ascalon, as the Cyprians themselves confess; and that of Cythera was erected by Phœnicians who came from the same part of Syria. However, the goddess, to avenge this attempt, inflicted on those that robbed her temple, and all their posterity, the female disease[f]; so that the Scythians confess that they are afflicted

[b] See chap. 74.

[c] The Gog and Magog of Ezekiel must be understood to be meant for the Scythians, who made the above irruption into Media, and even carried their devastation into Palæstine and to the borders of Egypt. See Rennell, p. 111. who gives his reason for the supposition at length.

[d] Herodotus relates the same thing more clearly, lib. iv. chap. 12. and lib. vii. chap. 20.

[e] Pausanias says, that the Assyrians were the first who worshipped Venus Urania. He adds, that the inhabitants of Paphos in Cyprus, and the Phœnicians of Palæstine, received this worship from them, and afterwards communicated it to the people of Cythera. *Wesseling*.

[f] Few passages in Herodotus have caused more dispute than this. The president Bouhier (Dissert. sur l'Histoire d'Herodote) enumerates six different opinions, and decides in favour of the last.

with it on this account, and those who visit Scythia may see the condition of those that are called Enarees.

CVI. For twenty-eight years then the Scythians governed Asia, and every thing was overthrown by their licentiousness and neglect; for besides the usual tribute, they exacted from each whatever they chose to impose; and not satisfied with this, they rode round the country and plundered them of all their possessions. Cyaxares and the Medes invited the greatest part to a feast, and killed them when they were drunk: in consequence of which, the Medes recovered their former power, and all they had possessed before; and they took Nineveh, in a manner which I will relate in another work[g], and reduced the Assyrians into subjection, with the exception of the Babylonian district. Having accomplished these things, Cyaxares died, after he had reigned forty years, comprehending the time of the Scythian dominion.

CVII. Astyages the son of Cyaxares succeeding him in the kingdom, had a daughter named Mandane; he dreamt she made so great a quantity of water, as not only filled his capital city, but overflowed all Asia. He laid this before those of the Magi who interpret dreams, and was extremely alarmed when informed of each particular, and therefore he afterwards gave Mandane, when arrived at a suitable age, to no one who was worthy of her, through dread of the vision; but to a Persian, named Cambyses, descended of a good family, of a peaceful disposition, and one he thought inferior to a Mede, even of moderate condition.

CVIII. Within the space of a year after he had married Mandane to Cambyses, he had another dream; in which he seemed to see a vine shooting from the womb of his daughter, and extending its branches over all Asia. This he also communicated to the interpreters, and having heard their answer, sent to Persia for his daughter, who was then big with child;

Some suppose the female disease to be languor, weakness and impotence; others, a delicate way of living; others, the hemorrhoids; others, the disease now called venereal; others, the catamenia (τὰ γυναικεῖα;) and others, the vice against nature. Larcher refutes Bouhier, but establishes no opinion of his own. Herodotus says, that this malady was propagated to the posterity of those who plundered the temple, which will exclude some of the opinions. Hippocrates (De aëribus et locis, viii. ch. 50.) says that "continual exercise on horseback brought "upon the Scythians pains in their joints; "they immediately became lame, and "the hip shrank if the malady increas-"ed." He goes on to add, that they became impotent and acquired effeminate habits. The impotency, however, he attributes to the way in which the Scythians endeavoured to cure the disease. Professor Heyne supposes that it proceeded from a melancholic, hysteric, or other nervous affections; in consequence of which the intellect becomes disturbed.

g Several passages of our author seem to prove that Herodotus wrote other histories than those which have come down to us. In the 184th chapter of this book he speaks of his Assyrian history; in the 161st of the 2nd of the Lybian. Larcher has a note of considerable length on the subject.

and upon her arrival put her under a guard, resolving to destroy whatever should be born of her. For the Magi, considering his dream, had informed him that the issue of his daughter should reign in his place. And therefore, as soon as Cyrus was born, Astyages, mindful of the prediction, sent for Harpagus, who was his relation[h], the most faithful of all the Medes, and to whom he entrusted his affairs, and said to him, "Harpagus, fail not to perform the thing I now command. "Deceive me not; and do not by preferring another, draw "ruin upon thy own head[i]. Take Mandane's son; carry him "to thy house; kill him, and bury him as thou shalt think fit." Harpagus answered, "O king, you have never yet observed "in me any thing which has displeased you, and I shall take "care never to offend you hereafter. If therefore this thing "be agreeable to your intention, my part is to perform it with "diligence."

CIX. Harpagus having made this answer, when the child had been put into his hands, adorned as the dead usually are, returned home weeping; and upon his arrival acquainted his wife with all that had passed between Astyages and himself. "What then," said she, "are you resolved to do?" "Not "to obey Astyages," replied Harpagus, "in the manner he "has commanded; though he should be yet more outrageous "and mad than he is, I will not comply with his wishes, nor "will I serve him by performing this murder; and I will not "commit this murder for many reasons; but principally be"cause the child is related to me in blood, and Astyages is "old, and has no son to succeed him. So that after his "death, if the kingdom should devolve into the hands[k] of "his daughter, whose son he now murders by my means, "what else remains for me but the greatest danger? It is "indeed necessary for my preservation that the infant should "die, but as necessary that some person belonging to As"tyages should be the executioner, and not any person of "my family."

CX. In this resolution he immediately sent for one of the king's herdsmen, who he knew kept his cattle at the foot of certain hills, abounding with wild beasts, and on that account very commodious for his design. Mitradates was the name of the herdsman, and he had married a wife who was his

[h] Οἰκήϊον has been badly translated by familiarem. Harpagus in the following chapter, says that the child was related to him, and this could only be by Mandane the daughter of Astyages. *Larcher.*

[i] Περιπέσῃς in te ipsum cadus, a metaphor taken from a building which falls from its own weight.

[k] It is worth while to remark, that in Herodotus, and other authors, θέλει and ἐθέλει are frequently redundant. So in book ii. ch. 11. *Larcher.*

fellow-servant. Her name in the language of Greece was *Cyno*, and in that of the Medes *Spaco*[l], for the Medes call a bitch Spaco. The man kept his cattle in pastures that lie under the hills on the north of Ecbatana, towards the Euxine sea. For this part of Media, which borders upon the Saspires, is very mountainous, and covered with woods; whereas all the rest is plain and level. When the herdsman had received the message, he went with great diligence to Harpagus; who spoke to him in these terms: "Astyages com-"mands thee to take this infant[m], and to lay him down in the "most abandoned desert of the mountains, that he may pre-"sently perish; and has charged me to add, that if thou "shouldest venture to disobey him, and by any means save "the child, thou shalt die in the most exquisite tortures that "can be invented; and I am appointed to see the child ex-"posed."

CXI. Mitradates, having heard these words, took the infant, and returned by the same way to his cottage. It so happened that his wife, who had been all the day in hard labour, was brought to bed whilst he was absent in the city. During this time they had been both in a state of solicitude; the husband much concerned for the condition of his wife, and the woman no less disturbed about her husband; because Harpagus had not been accustomed to send for him before. So that when he returned and came up to her, she immediately asked him, as if she beheld him unexpectedly, why Harpagus had sent for him in such haste. "Wife," said he, "I have been in the city, where I have seen and "heard such things, as I wish had never been seen by me, "nor ever happened to our masters. The whole house of "Harpagus was filled with lamentations; and as I went in, "struck with horror, I saw an infant dressed in gold and the "richest colours, panting and crying on the floor. Harpagus "seeing me, ordered me to carry away the child with all "speed, and to leave him in that part of the mountain which "is most frequented by wild beasts; telling me at the same "time, that it was Astyages who imposed this task on me, "and threatening the severest punishment if I should fail.

l It is not known whether the dialect of the Medes and Persians was the same. In such remains as we have of the Persian language, Burton and Reland have not been able to discover any term like this. Nevertheless Lefevre affirms, that the Hyrcanians, a people in subjection to the Persians, call, even at the present time, a dog by the word Spac. *Larcher.*

m Shakespeare's Winter's Tale will necessarily occur to every reader. The speech of the king to Antigonus minutely resembles this:

———" Take it up straight,
" Within this hour bring me word 'tis
" done,
" And by good testimony, or I'll seize thy
" life."

"I took the infant, which I supposed to belong to some person of the family; having then no suspicion of his high birth, though I was astonished to see the gold and magnificence of the apparel, and also at the sorrow which evidently prevailed in the house of Harpagus. But soon after, on my way home, I understood all from the servant that accompanied me out of the city; who, delivering the boy into my hands, assured me he was born of Mandane our king's daughter, and of Cambyses the son of Cyrus, and that Astyages had commanded him to be killed."

CXII. As the herdsman uttered these last words, he uncovered the child, and shewed it to his wife; who, seeing him beautiful and large in size, embraced the knees of her husband, and with tears besought him by no means to expose it. He said that it was impossible to do otherwise; because the spies of Harpagus would certainly come to see the thing done, and because he himself had been threatened with the most cruel death, if he should fail. The woman, finding she could not prevail this way, had recourse to another. "Since then," said she, "I cannot persuade you not to expose the infant, do this at least, if the spies of Harpagus must see him exposed: take my child, which was born dead, leave him among the hills instead of the other, and let us bring up the son of Mandane as our own. For by that means we shall sufficiently consult our own safety, without doing any injury to our lords: the child that is dead shall have a royal sepulchre, and the surviving infant shall be preserved from an untimely death."

CXIII. The herdsman judged this expedient very proper in the present state of things, and resolving to do as his wife advised, delivered the infant, which he brought to destroy, into her hands; and having wrapped his own dead child in all the rich apparel, he put it into the same basket, in which he had brought the other, and carried it to the most desolate part of all the mountains. On the third day after this was done, having left one of the herdsmen in his place, he went to the house of Harpagus in the city, and told him he was ready to shew the carcase of the infant. Upon which Harpagus dispatched some of his guards, whom he most trusted, by whose means he saw what had been done, and buried the herdsman's child. The other, who afterwards had the name of Cyrus, was educated by the wife of the herdsman, who gave him some other name, and not Cyrus.

CXIV. But when he attained to the age of ten years, a circumstance of the following nature having happened to him, discovered him. Being one day playing in these pastures with boys of the same age, whilst he passed for the son of the herdsman, he was chosen king by his companions; and in virtue of that power distinguished them into several orders and offices, appointing some to be builders, and others to wait on him as guards; one to be his chief minister, who is called the eye of the king[n], and another to have the office of bringing messages to him. The son of Artembares, a man of eminent dignity among the Medes, being one of his companions in this play, and refusing to obey his orders, Cyrus commanded the others to seize him; and when they obeyed, he scourged him very severely. But as soon as the boy was dismissed, he hastened to the city, full of grief and indignation as having suffered great indignities, and with tears told his father what he had suffered from Cyrus, calling him the son of the king's herdsman; for at that time he had not the name of Cyrus. Artembares in a transport of anger went immediately to Astyages, and taking his son with him mentioned the indignities he had received; adding, "Are we, O king, to "receive this insolent treatment from the slave, the son of "the herdsman?" (At the same time he shewed the boy's shoulders.)

CXV. Astyages heard and saw what was done; and resolving, for the honour of Artembares, to avenge the indignity offered to the youth, commanded the herdsman and his son to be brought before him. When they came into his presence, the king looking upon Cyrus, asked him, how he, who was the son of so mean a man, had dared in so insolent a manner to abuse the son of one of the principal persons in his kingdom? "Sir," said Cyrus, "I have justly treated him in that manner. "For he with other boys of our neighbourhood, in our recrea- "tions, made me their king, because they thought me most "capable of that dignity. All the rest obeyed me, and per- "formed what I commanded; but he alone refusing to obey, "and slighting my orders, has suffered the punishment he de- "served: and if on this account I am deserving of punish- "ment, here I am in your power."

CXVI. As the boy was speaking, Astyages discovered who he was; the features of his face appeared to him like his own; his answer free[o]; and reflecting on the time when his grand-

[n] The ministers of the kings were thus called in the Asiatic courts. See Æschy.Pers.984 et seq. Aristoph.Acharn. 91 and 124. We are told in the embassy of Major Symes to the court of Ava, that the introduction to the sovereign was termed the introduction to the "golden feet." These same metaphorical expressions still prevailing. M. Le Comte Carli remarks in his American letters, that at Peru the commissary, whose office it is to examine into the public and private conduct of the Decurions, is called Cucuy Rioc, i. e. eye of all. He also remarks, on this subject, that in the laws of the Csar Peter 1st. the king's solicitor, is called the eye of the king. *Larcher.*

[o] Ἐλευθερωτέρε, more free than is usual in a boy of his age and condition. Several incidents in the plot of Douglas bear great resemblance to this story.

son was exposed, he found it agreeing with his age. Atonished at these things, he was long silent; and at last, having with difficulty recovered himself, (being desirous of sending Artembares away in order that he might examine the herdsman in private,) he said, "Artembares, I will take care that neither you nor "your son shall have any cause of complaint." In this manner he dismissed Artembares; and the servants at the command of Astyages conducted Cyrus into an inner room; and when the herdsman alone remained, he asked him where he had the boy, and from whose hands? Mitradates affirmed he was his own son, and that the mother of the boy was still living. Astyages told him, that he did not consult his own safety, since he wished to be compelled to speak the truth; and at the same time commanded his guards to seize him. The man, seeing himself reduced to this necessity, discovered the whole matter without reserve; and concluded with prayers and entreaties for pardon.

CXVII. Astyages, when the herdsman had confessed the truth, did not concern himself much about him afterwards; but being highly incensed against Harpagus, he sent his guards with orders to bring him to the palace; where, when he was come, Astyages asked him: "Harpagus, by what "kind of death did you destroy my daughter's child which I "delivered to you?" Harpagus, seeing the herdsman present, resolved to conceal nothing by a falsehood, lest he should be convicted by his testimony; and therefore said, "O king, after "I had received the infant, I carefully considered how your "command might be obeyed, and I, without offending you, "might not be guilty of the crime of murder against you and "your daughter. To that end I sent for this man, and gave "him the child; which I said you had commanded him to "destroy, and I told him the truth; for such indeed were your "orders. In this manner I put the infant into his hands; "charging him in the next place to lay him down in some "desert mountain, and to stay till he should see him perish, "threatening the severest punishment if he should not per-"form these things. When he had executed these orders, "and the child was dead, I sent some of the most trusty "among my eunuchs, and having by means of them beheld "*the dead child*, I buried him. This is the whole truth, O "king, and such was the fate of the infant."

CXVIII. Thus Harpagus explained the truth; and Astyages, dissembling the resentment which he felt towards him, related to him the whole matter as the herdsman had related

Lady Randolph is at first struck by the free answer and noble bearing of young Norval; and the examination of the old shepherd is very similar to the examination of the herdsman by Astyages.

it to him; and when he had repeated it, he ended by saying that the child was alive and all was well. "For," said he, "I was in great pain on account of this thing, and could not "easily bear the reproaches of my daughter: therefore since "fortune has taken a more favourable change, send your son "to accompany the boy I have recovered, and come yourself "to my supper; for I resolve to offer a sacrifice on account of "his preservation to those Gods, to whom that honour is due."

CXIX. As soon as Harpagus heard these words, he fell down and worshipped the king; and went home exceedingly pleased, that his fault had turned to so good account, and that he was invited to the feast which was to celebrate the fortunate event. At his return he sent his only son, of about thirteen years of age, to Astyages, with order to do as he should command; and acquainted his wife with what had happened, in expressions of the highest satisfaction. But the youth, when he arrived at the palace, was killed and cut in pieces by Astyages; who, after he had roasted some parts of his flesh and boiled others, kept them in readiness to be served. At the appointed hour, when Harpagus and all the company were come, the tables where the king sat, and the rest of those he had invited, were served with mutton; but before Harpagus all the body of his son[p] was placed, except the head, the hands, and the feet, which were laid together in a basket, and covered. When he seemed to have eaten sufficiently, Astyages asked him, if he was pleased with the entertainment. When Harpagus replied, that he was highly delighted, the officers appointed to that end brought the head, hands, and feet of the youth covered up. And when they had approached him, they requested him to uncover the basket, and take what pleased him best. He did as they desired, and saw the remains of his son's body, and was not astonished at the sight, but continued master of himself; and when Astyages asked him, if he knew what kind of flesh he had eaten, he said, he knew very well, and that whatever the king did, was agreeable to him[q]: after which answer, he collected the mangled parts, and went home, as I conjecture, to bury them together.

[p] The banquet of Thyestes will occur to every one. A similar example occurs in Titus Andronicus;

"Why there they are, both baked in that "pie,
"Whereof their mother daintily hath fed:
"Eating the flesh that she herself hath "bred."

[q] This reply of Harpagus, worthy of a servile courtier, brings to mind one of an English nobleman no less despicable, Edgar king of England, having killed Ethelwold in the forest of Harewood, the son of that nobleman arrived soon after on the spot; the king shewing him the body of his father, asked him how he found the game: the young man replied with perfect indifference: "That what"ever was agreeable to the prince, could "not possibly displease him." Quoted by Larcher from William of Malmesbury.

CXX. Astyages, after he had thus punished Harpagus, beginning to consider what he should do with Cyrus, sent again for the Magi, who had formerly interpreted his dream; and, when they came into his presence, asked them what judgment they had made of it. They gave the same answer as before; and said, that if the boy should continue to live, he must of necessity be a king. "He is living and safe," answered Astyages; "and while living in the country, was chosen "king by the boys of the village, and has already performed "all the offices which belong to a real king. For he exer-"cised that power, in appointing guards, door-keepers, mes-"sengers, and all other things requisite: and now I desire to "know to what these things appear to you to tend." "If the "boy be living," said the Magi, "and has already been a king "by such an accident, and not by contrivance, you may rest "satisfied in full assurance that he shall not reign a second "time. For our predictions often terminate in things of little "importance, and dreams especially are fulfilled by slight "events." To this Astyages replied, "I am most inclined "to the opinion, that my dream is accomplished, and that the "boy is no longer an object of alarm to me, since the title of "king has been given to him; yet consider well, and with all "possible circumspection advise what may be most conduc-"ing to the safety of my family and to yourselves." "Our "great interest," answered the Magi, "is that your kingdom "should be firmly established; because if the sovereignty be "alienated and transferred to this Persian, we, who are "Medes, shall become servants of the Persians, and be treat-"ed as foreigners with the utmost contempt; whereas now, "living under a king of our own country, we have a part in "the government, and enjoy the greatest honours. So that "it is altogether to our interest to look forward for you, and "your kingdom; and if in this case we perceived any thing "to be feared, we would have foretold the whole of it to you. "And therefore, since the dream has glanced off to a frivo-"lous event, we exhort you to lay aside your fears, as we "have already done, and to send away the boy to his parents "in Persia."

CXXI. Astyages heard this discourse with joy, and, calling for Cyrus, said to him, "Child, I have been unjust to "thee, by reason of a false dream; but thou hast survived "by thy own good destiny. Prepare now to go cheerfully to "Persia with those I shall appoint to attend thee; where "thou shalt find thy father and mother very different in con-"dition from the herdsman Mitradates and his wife."

CXXII. After these words, Cyrus was dismissed by Astyages; and, upon his arrival at the house of Cambyses, his parents received and embraced him with the greatest tenderness, as a child they had long given over for dead; and asked him by what means his life had been preserved. He said, that before that time, he knew not, but had wandered very far from the truth; for he believed he was the son of the king's herdsman; till those who accompanied him in this journey informed him of all that had passed. He related that he had been brought up by the herdsman's wife, whom he constantly praised, and Cyno formed the chief subject of his talk. His parents having laid hold of this name, (in order that the Persians might suppose, that the child was somewhat miraculously preserved for them,) spread abroad a report, that a bitch[r] had nourished him when exposed: hence this report was propagated.

CXXIII. When Cyrus had attained to the age of a man, and was become the most beloved and most brave of all his equals in years, Harpagus, vehemently desiring to be avenged upon Astyages, and despairing to accomplish his ends by his own power, because he was but a private man, courted him with presents; and, perceiving that Cyrus in his growth gave him hopes of vengeance[s], and thinking the injuries they had suffered to be of like nature, formed a friendship with him. He did yet more to bring about his purpose. For seeing the Medes oppressed by the cruelty of Astyages, he applied himself to the principal persons of the nation, one after another, and persuaded them that they ought to depose him, and advance Cyrus to the throne in his place. When he had done this, and prepared the Medes to second his design, he resolved to discover his intentions to Cyrus; and having no other way left, because guards were placed on all the roads that lead to Persia, he contrived the following artifice. He opened the belly of a hare, and, without tearing off any of the hair, put a letter, containing what he thought necessary to write, into the body; and having sewed it up, he delivered the hare with a net to the most trusty of his domestic officers, clothed in the habit of a hunter, and sent him to Persia; having by word of mouth commanded him to bid Cyrus, as he gave him the hare, to open it with his own hand, and not to suffer any one to be present when he did so.

CXXIV. The messenger executed his orders, and Cyrus, opening the hare with his own hands, found a letter, in which

[r] The story of Romulus and Remus involves many similar circumstances, and especially the origin of the report that they were suckled by a wolf, from the name of the woman, (Lupa,) who brought them up.

[s] The force of ἐπὶ, in ἐπιτρεφόμενον must be observed. Wyttenbach has well translated it, *Cirum videns crescere in spem vindictæ, (sibi crescere et ali vindicem.)* Ἐπιτρεφόμενον must be referred to τιμωρὸν, which is understood in the preceding word τιμωρίην. *Larcher.*

he read these words: "Son of Cambyses, the Gods watch "over you, or you could never have arrived at your present "fortune; resolve now to punish your murderer Astyages; "for as far as regards his wishes you are dead, but by the "care of the Gods and of me you survive. I need not repeat "what he has done against you, nor what I have suffered from "him for delivering you to the herdsman, instead of executing his bloody orders, because I suppose you have been long "informed of these things. At present, if you will follow my "counsel, all the dominions which Astyages possesses shall "belong to you. Persuade the Persians to revolt, and at the "head of their forces invade Media. The success is certain, "whether Astyages appoint me or any other illustrious Mede to "command his army. For all the principal persons among "the Medes will desert him; and, joining with you, will endeavour to dethrone him. Defer not the execution of this "enterprize, because all things are ready on our part."

CXXV. Cyrus, having read these words, began to consider what measures he should take to persuade the Persians to revolt; and after various thoughts, fixed upon this method as the most proper. He framed a letter in such terms as he thought fit, and called an assembly of Persians; in which, when he had opened and read the letter, he declared, that Astyages had constituted him captain-general of Persia: "And now," said he, "I command you to attend me, every "man with his hatchet." Now the Persians are divided into many tribes; some of which Cyrus summoned, and persuaded to revolt; those tribes are as follow, and upon them the rest of the Persians are dependent; the Pasargades, the Meraphians, and the Masians. But of all these, the Pasargades are esteemed the most brave, and comprehend the Achæmenian family, of which the kings of Persia are descended. The rest are, the Panthelians, the Derusians, and the Germanians[1], who are all husbandmen; but the Daians, the Mardians, the Dropicians, and the Sagartians, are keepers of cattle.

CXXVI. When they came to Cyrus with their hatchets, he ordered them to clear in one day a piece of land, containing eighteen or twenty stades, overgrown with briars; and after they had done that work, he bid them go home and wash, and attend him again the next day. In the mean time he ordered all his father's flocks and herds to be killed and dressed; providing wine, and the best of things in abundance, to treat the

[1] The Germanians are the same as the Caramanians. Some authors affirm, that the ancient Germans were descended from this people. Cluvier (German. Antiq.) has with much politeness explained their error: "But," adds M. Wesseling, "there are some persons so obstinate, that "since the discovery of corn, they still "prefer to feed on acorns. *Larcher.*

whole military power of Persia. The next day when they were all assembled, and seated on the turf, he feasted them plentifully; and, after they had dined, asked, whether what they had before, or their present circumstances, were more eligible. They answered, the difference was great; for on the preceding day they had every hardship, but on the present every thing that was good. Cyrus, perceiving the tendency of these words, discovered his intentions, and said, "Men of Persia, your affairs are thus circumstanced; if you "will hearken to my council, you shall enjoy these, and infinite other advantages, without any kind of servile labour; "but if you refuse, innumerable hardships like those of "yesterday are prepared for you. Believe me therefore, and "be a free people; for I am persuaded some divine power "brought me into the world, to be the author of your happiness: neither can I think you any way inferior to the "Medes; especially in military affairs: and since these "things are so, revolt with all speed from Astyages."

CXXVII. The Persians then having obtained a leader, gladly reassumed their liberty, having for a long time felt indignant at being governed by the Medes. Astyages, being informed of these transactions, sent a messenger for Cyrus; who by the same person returned this answer, "That he "would come sooner than Astyages desired." Which when the king heard, he armed all the Medes; and, as if the Gods had deprived him of understanding, made Harpagus general of his army, utterly forgetting the outrage he had done. So that when the two nations came to a battle, though some of the Medes, who knew nothing of the conspiracy, behaved themselves with courage, yet great numbers revolted to the Persians; and the far greater part, willingly losing the day, fled out of the field.

CXXVIII. The army of the Medes being thus shamefully dispersed, as soon as the news was brought to Astyages, he threatened Cyrus, that he should not long enjoy the pleasure of his victory. After which, having first commanded the Magi, who had interpreted his dream, to be crucified [u], for advising him to let Cyrus go, he armed all the Medes he found in the city, both old and young; and, marching out with these forces, engaged the enemy, and was defeated [x]

[u] Astyages broke all his officers, and put others in their place; he sought also for those who had been the cause of his defeat, and had them executed. His disposition was so inhuman and cruel, that his whole army detested him. The troops held assemblies, in which they resolved to revenge the death of their companions. See Diodor. Sicul. de Virt. et Vit.

[x] Xenophon relates that Cyrus quietly succeeded to the throne of Media; but see Larcher (Philosophie de l'Histoire,) and Plutarch (de Virtut Mulier.)

with the loss of his whole army, and was himself made prisoner by the Persians.

CXXIX. Harpagus, standing by Astyages after he was taken, reproached and insulted him openly; and among other discourse, tending to embitter his calamity, he recalled to his recollection the supper, in which he had feasted him with his son's flesh, and asked what he thought of slavery in exchange for a kingdom. Astyages, looking stedfastly on Harpagus, demanded, whether he thought himself the author of the late success obtained by Cyrus. He answered, Yes; because by his letter he had animated Cyrus to this war; and therefore might justly lay claim to the enterprize. Astyages said, he was then the weakest and most unjust of all men: the weakest, in giving the kingdom to another, which he might have assumed to himself, if indeed he had effected this change; and the most unjust, in enslaving the Medes on account of the supper. For if he was necessitated to confer the kingdom on another person, and not to take the power to himself, he might with more justice have advanced a Mede to that dignity than a Persian: whereas now the Medes, who before were masters of Persia, and had no part in the fault, were by his means reduced to the condition of servants; and the Persians, who had been servants to the Medes, were become their lords.

CXXX. In this manner Astyages was deprived of the kingdom, after he had reigned thirty-five years; and by his cruelty the Medes bent under the Persian yoke, after they had commanded in all those parts of Asia that lie beyond the river Halys, for the space of one hundred and twenty-eight years[y], the time of the Scythian dominion only excepted. Yet afterwards, repenting of what they had done, they revolted against Darius, but were again defeated[a] in a battle; and the Persians, who under the conduct of Cyrus had taken arms against Astyages and the Medes, have from that time been masters of Asia. As for Astyages, Cyrus kept him in his palace till he died, without exercising any farther severity

[y] According to Herodotus,

Deioces reigned	53 years
Phraortes	22
Cyaxares	40
Astyages	35
	150

If from this number we subtract 28, the time that the Scythians reigned, there remain but 122: so that in all probability a mistake has been made in the text by some copyist. The six years too many in the text cannot be applied to the time in which the Medes had no king, for I have proved in a memoir read before the academy, that there were 39 years of anarchy, (Mem. Acad. des Belles Lettres, tom xlv. p. 368, &c.) *Larcher.*

[a] They returned to their duty under the reign of Darius Nothus in the first year of the ninety-third Olympiad, and twenty-fourth year of the Peloponnesian war. (Xenop. Hellen. book i. ch. 2.) This passage is one of those which Herodotus added in his old age.

against him[a]. And this is the account of the birth, education, and advancement of Cyrus to the dignity of a king. How he afterwards conquered Crœsus, who had commenced an unjust attack, has been before related by me; by subduing whom, he became master of all Asia.

CXXXI. The Persians according to my own knowledge, observe the following customs. It is contrary to their practice to make images[b], or build altars[c] or temples; charging those with folly who do such things; because, as I conjecture, they hold the Gods to be altogether different in nature from men[d], contrary to the opinion of the Grecians. When they go to offer a sacrifice to Jupiter, they ascend the highest parts of the mountains; and call the whole circle of the heavens by the name of Jupiter[e]. They sacrifice to the sun and moon, to the earth, the fire[f], the water, and the winds. These are their original Gods; but they have since learnt from the Arabians and Assyrians to sacrifice to Venus Urania, who by the Arabians is called Alitta, by the Assyrians Mylitta, and by the Persians Mitra[g].

CXXXII. The following is the established mode of sacrifice to the abovementioned deities. When a man intends to sacrifice, he builds no altar, kindles no fire, makes no libation, nor uses either flutes, fillets, or consecrated cakes; but, wearing a tiara garnished chiefly with myrtle on his head, leads

[a] Isocrates, in his funeral oration on Evagoras, king of Salamis in Cyprus, says, that Cyrus put Astyages to death, but I do not find this asserted by any other author. *Larcher*.

[b] It is proper to remark here, that the more ancient nations were not worshippers of images. Lucian tells us, that the ancient Egyptians had no statues in their temples. According to Eusebius, the Greeks were not worshippers of images before the time of Cecrops, who first erected a statue to Minerva. And Plutarch tells us, that Numa forbade the Romans to represent the deity under the form of a man or an animal; and for seventy years this people had not in their temples any statue or painting of the deity. *Larcher*.

On the whole of this passage see Hyde on the ancient religion of the Persians, cap. iii. p. 93, &c.

[c] The theology of Zoroaster was darkly comprehended by foreigners, and even by the far greater number of his disciples; but the most careless observers were struck with the philosophic simplicity of the Persian worshippers; *Gibbon*: who gives a short and clear account of the fundamental doctrine of the system in ch. viii. of the decline and fall.

[d] This is translated by some, *born of men*. Bp. Warburton (Div. Legation of Moses, book ii. sect. 1.) is of that opinion; φυή however signifies shape, in Homer and Herodotus.

[e] The Greeks and Latins had a bad habit of applying the names of their own Gods, to the Gods of other nations. One or two similar attributes in each were sufficient to establish their identity. Thus they applied the name of Jupiter to the God who was considered supreme in any other country. *Larcher*.

[f] "I am of that impious race,
"Those slaves of fire, who, morn and even,
"Hail their Creator's dwelling place
"Among the living lights of heaven!" *Lalla Rookh*.

[g] Mihr or mihir, in the ancient Persian language, according to Hyde, cap. iv. p. 107. signified *love*. Hence Mitra and Mithra to designate the goddess who presided over love, *Venus Urania*.

the victim to a clean piece of ground, and invokes the God. He that offers is not permitted to pray for himself alone; but, as he is a member of the nation, is obliged to pray for the prosperity of all the Persians, and in particular for the king. When he has cut the victim[h] into small pieces, and boiled the flesh, he lays it on a bed of tender grass, especially trefoil; and after all things are thus disposed, one of the Magi standing up sings an ode concerning the original of the Gods, which they say has the force of a charm; and without one of the Magi they are not permitted to sacrifice. After this, he that offered having continued a short time in the place, carries away and disposes of the flesh as he thinks fit.

CXXXIII. They are persuaded that every man ought to celebrate his birth-day above all other days, and furnish his table in a more plentiful manner than at other times. Beeves, camels, horses, and asses, roasted entire, are seen in the houses of the rich on that day; and smaller cattle in those of the meaner sort. They are moderate in the use of common food, but eat of many after-dishes[i] which are brought in small quantities at a time; and they thence take occasion to say, that the Grecians rise hungry from table, and that if they had any thing good set before them after their repast, they would not leave off eating so soon. The Persians drink wine in abundance[k]; and are not allowed to vomit or make water before any man. These customs are observed to this day. They debate the most important affairs when warm with wine; but the master of the house where they meet to consult, proposes the same things the next day to the company; and if it pleases them when they are sober also, they put it in execution; if not, they reject it. And whatever they have first deliberated on when sober, they examine a second time after drinking.

CXXXIV. When they meet one another in the streets, a man may discover by the following custom, whether those who meet are equals. For if they are equals, they salute with a kiss on the mouth; if one be a little inferior to the other, they kiss on the cheek; but if he be of a much lower rank, he prostrates himself before the other. They give the greatest honour, next to themselves, to their nearest neighbour; the next, to the next; and observe this same gradation in honouring; and least of all they honour those who live at the greatest distance; esteeming themselves much more

[h] According to Strabo (lib. xv.) the Magi performs this.

[i] Ἐπιφορήματα means any thing which is brought on after the repast, which we call the desert.

[k] The Persians were originally sober. See note on chap. 71.

worthy in every thing than the rest of men, and others to participate of virtue only in proportion to the nearness of their situation; always accounting those the worst and most base, who inhabit farthest from them. During the empire of the Medes, each nation had a gradual superiority: for though the Medes had the supreme power, yet they exercised a more particular authority over those that were nearest to them; these again, over such as lived next beyond their borders; and the last in like manner over their neighbours of the adjoining country, (in the same manner the Persians honour,) for that nation extended its government and præfectures far and wide.

CXXXV. No nation has ever been more ready to admit foreign customs. They wear the habit of the Medes; which they think more becoming than their own; and in war they use the Egyptian cuirass. They learn of others by inquiry, and practice all kinds of enjoyments, and have learnt from the Greeks a passion for boys[l]. The virgins they take for their wives are many; but their concubines are far more numerous.

CXXXVI. To be a father of many children[m] is accounted the excellence of man, next to military courage; and such persons as can shew a numerous offspring, receive yearly presents from the king, because they think their strength consists in their numbers. From the age of five years to that of twenty[n], the Persians instruct their sons in three things only; to manage a horse[o], to shoot with the bow, and to speak truth. A son is not admitted to the presence of his father, but is brought up by women, till he attains the age of five years; lest if he should die before that time, his father might be afflicted by the loss.

CXXXVII. These customs relating to education I much approve; and likewise that, by which even the king is re-

[l] Plutarch (de Malig. Her.) affirms that this vice was derived from the Persians.

Harmer in his Observations on Passages of Scripture, has been at some pains to prove, that in all probability Sodom and Gomorrah were somewhere in Persia.

[m] A numerous posterity is, at the present day, the most fervent wish of the female inhabitants of Egypt. Public respect is annexed to fruitfulness. This is even the prayer of the poor, who earn their bread by the sweat of the brow.

Sterility is a reproach among the Orientals, and they still retain for fecundity all the esteem of ancient times. *Volney.*

[n] Xenophon gives a different account of the education of the Persians, which he says ended at sixteen or seventeen.

[o] This, in the time of Cyrus, did not constitute a part of Persian education. The Persians, at that period inhabited a country mountainous and without pasturage, (Xenop. Cyroped. I. cap. iii. 3.) and therefore could not feed horses; but as soon as they had conquered a country fit for this purpose, they learnt to ride, and Cyrus (Xenoph. Cyrop. IV. cap. iii. 5.) ordained that it should be considered disgraceful for any of those to whom he had given a horse to go any where on foot. *Larcher.*

strained from killing any man for a single crime; and every private Persian from exercising extreme severity against those of his family for one fault. He is first to consider the actions of the delinquent, and if his faults are found to overbalance his former services, he may punish him at pleasure. They say, no one has ever killed his father or mother; and if at any time such a crime has *apparently* happened, the person accused shall certainly upon due information be found to have been suppositious, or begotten in adultery; for they hold it utterly improbable, that a true father should be murdered by his own son.

CXXXVIII. They are not allowed even to mention the things which it is not lawful for them to do. To affirm a falsehood[p], is among them the utmost infamy; and to be in debt, is for many reasons accounted the next degree of disgrace, but especially because they think such a man always exposed to the necessity of lying. If any of the citizens have a leprosy[q], or scrofulous disease, he is not permitted to stay within the city, nor to converse with other Persians; having, as they believe, drawn this punishment upon himself, by committing some offence against the sun[r]. But if strangers are infected with those distempers, they expel them the country: and many expel white pigeons from motives of the same kind. They never spit, nor wash their hands in a river, nor defile the stream with urine or any other thing, nor will they allow any one else to do so, but they pay extreme veneration to all streams[s]

CXXXIX. Another circumstance also exists, of which the Persians themselves are not aware, but which is well known to us. All their names, which express personal or other distinction, terminate in that letter which the Dorians call

[p] The Persians were not always so scrupulous in speaking the truth. See book iii. ch. 72.

[q] Persons afflicted with leprosy are still kept secluded in many places of the East. *Niebuhr's Description of Arabia*, p. 120.

[r] When Æschines touched at Delos, on his way to Rhodes, the inhabitants of that island were greatly incommoded by a species of leprosy called *Leuce*. They attributed it to the anger of Apollo, because, contrary to custom, they had buried in the island the body of a man of rank. *Larcher*.

[s] Homer (Iliad xxi. 132.) gives us an example of the worship paid to rivers, when he speaks of throwing horses in the Scamander in honour of the God of the river. *Larcher*.

That the same superstitious veneration for rivers continues among unenlightened nations, appears from a passage in Horneman, the last traveller into the interior of Africa: "Not long "ago a custom was observed at Bornou, "as in ancient times at Cairo; a girl "very richly dressed was thrown into "the river Niger." *Beloe*.

"The ancient Cuthites, and the Persians after them, had a great veneration "for fountains and streams, which also "prevailed among other nations, so as to "have been at one time almost universal. "If these rivers were attended with any "nitrous or saline quality, or with any "fiery eruption, they were adjudged to "be still more sacred." *Bryant*.

"From those who kneel at Brahma's
"burning founts." *Lalla Rookh*.

San, and the Ionians *Sigma*. And every one upon inquiry will find, that all Persian names[t], without exception, end in the same letter.

CXL. These things I can with certainty affirm to be true, since I have myself observed them. But what relates to the dead are only secretly mentioned, and not openly; viz. that all the Persians are exposed for a prey to some dog or bird before they are buried; but I certainly know this to be the manner of the Magi, for it is done openly. The Persians cover the body with a sufficient quantity of wax[u], and afterwards lay it in the ground. Their Magi not only differ from all other men, but even from the Egyptian priests, who consider it essential to their purity not to kill any animal, except those they sacrifice to the Gods; whereas the Magi make no scruple to kill every thing with their own hands, except a man or a dog; and think they do a meritorious thing, when they destroy ants, serpents, birds, or reptiles[x]. And with regard to this custom, let it remain as it originally was. I will now return to my former narration.

CXLI. The Ionians and Æolians, as soon as the Lydians had been conquered by the Persians, sent ambassadors to Cyrus, before his departure from Sardis, to make an offer of their submission to him, on the same terms they obtained under the government of Crœsus. Which proposition Cyrus having heard, related this story to[y] them: "A piper seeing

[t] The language spoken anciently in Persia opens a wide field for unsatisfactory inquiry. Dr. Hyde derives it from that of Media; which is much the same as deducing one jargon of the Saxon heptarchy from another. The union of those people called by Europeans, the Medes and Persians, is of such high antiquity, that it is lost in darkness, and long precedes every glimmering we can discover of the origin of their speech. *Richardson on Eastern Nations.*

[u] Bodies thus enclosed continue perfect for ages. Some of the members of the Antiquarian Society being desirous of discovering the state of the body of Edward I. which had been covered with wax, obtained permission to inspect it. It was found entire, May 2, 1774. The wax had been renewed under Edward III. and Henry IV. by virtue of orders addressed to the Treasury, which are in the Fœdera of Rymer. It has not been renewed since. Edward I. died in 1307, at Burgh upon Sands, in Cumberland, when marching against the Scotch. *Annual Register for* 1774.

The Magi long preserved the exclusive privilege of exposing their bodies as a prey for carniverous animals. In succeeding times, the Persians threw all bodies to birds and beasts of prey. This custom still in part continues; the place of the burial of the Guebres, (Chardin's Travels, vol. ii. p. 186.) at the distance of half a league from Ispahan, is a round tower of free-stone; it is thirty-five feet in height, and ninety in diameter, without a gate, or any kind of entrance; they ascend it by a ladder. In the midst of the tower is a kind of trench, into which bones are thrown. The bodies are ranged along the wall in their proper clothes, &c. The ravens which fill the cemetery devour them. *Chardin.*

[x] Chardin (vol. ii. p. 185.) says, that the Guebres, or ancient fire-worshippers, think that it is not only lawful to kill insects, and all other useless animals, but that it is an action agreeable to God, and a meritorious work, as these creatures are the production of a bad principle, and wicked author, &c. *Larcher.*

[y] Λόγος is an apologue, a moral fable. *Larcher.*

"many fishes in the sea, and imagining he might entice them "to the shore by his music, began to play; but finding his "hopes disappointed, he threw a net into the water, and "having enclosed a great number, drew it to the land. "When the piper saw the fishes leaping on the ground, he "said, Since you would not come out when I played to you, "you may now forbear dancing at all." Cyrus told this story to the Ionians and Æolians, because the Ionians, when Cyrus pressed them by his ambassador to revolt from Crœsus, refused to consent, and now were ready to comply with his desires, because they saw the success of his arms. With this answer, which Cyrus gave in anger, the Ionians returned home; and having fortified their cities, met together at the Panionium, the Milesians only excepted, who were singly admitted into the alliance of Cyrus, on the same terms as their former agreement with the Lydian. All the rest of the Ionians met, and unanimously resolved to send ambassadors to Sparta, earnestly to desire succour from the Lacedæmonians.

CXLII. These Ionians, to whom the Panionium belongs, have built their cities in a country, which is the most excellent of all we know in temperature and *seasons*; for neither the regions that are above Ionia on one side, nor those that lie below on the other, nor any part situate either to the east or west, are at all the same as this country; because they are either chilled with cold and rain, or exposed to the excesses of heat and dryness. All the Ionians are not of the same language; but have four different dialects[a]. The city of Miletus[a] lies farthest south. The next are Myus and Priene. These three are situate in Caria, and use the same dialect. Ephesus, Colophon, Lebedus, Teos, Clazomene, and Phocæa, are part of Lydia; and though they vary not at all from one another in their manner of speaking, yet their language is different from the other. The rest of the Ionian communities are three, two of which inhabit the islands of Chios and Samos; but the Erythræans are placed on the continent. This people use the same dialect with those of Chios; whereas the Samians have one peculiar to themselves. And these are the four dialects which characterize the Ionians.

CXLIII. Among these Ionians, the Milesians were sheltered from apprehension, as they had made an alliance with Cyrus. The islanders also had nothing to fear; because the

[a] *Παραγωγὴ* is a deflexion, a kind of change or variety from the original; since *παράγειν* is to draw aside from the right way, to change, &c. *Schweighæuser.*
Although the Greeks had four principal dialects, each of these dialects were again subdivided: the Ionian dialect varied in the different Ionian cities. *Larcher.*

[a] For a particular account of the modern names and circumstances of these cities, consult Chandler and Pocock.

Phœnicians were not then under the obedience of the Persians, nor were the Persians at all acquainted with maritime affairs. This separation of the Milesians had no other foundation than the weakness of the Grecians in general, and of the Ionians in particular; who were the weakest of all, and in no manner of esteem. For, except Athens, there was no other city of note. But neither they nor others were willing to be called Ionians; as indeed in our time the greater part seem to me ashamed of the name. Yet the twelve cities not only gloried in their name, but built a temple, which from themselves they called Panionium[b], and resolved not to communicate the privilege of that place to any other Ionians; neither have others ever desired to participate in it, except the Smyrnæans alone.

CXLIV. In this they resembled those Dorians of the country called Pentapolis, which same was before Hexapolis; who not only constantly refused to admit any of the neighbouring Dorians into their temple at Triope[c], but excluded some of their own community for transgressing the established orders. For in those exercises that were performed there in honour of Apollo, a tripos of brass was the reward of the victorious; which yet no man might carry out of the temple[d], but was obliged to dedicate it in the temple to the God. Nevertheless, Agasicles of Halicarnassus[e] won the prize, and disregarded their custom, by carrying away the tripos, and hanging it up in his own house, the five cities of Lindus, Jalyssus, Camirus, Cos[f], and Cnidus[g], excluded that city,

[b] About sixteen miles to the south of Scala Nuova there is a Christian village, called Changlee. It is supposed to be the ancient Panionium, where the meeting of the twelve cities of Ionia was held, and a solemn sacrifice performed to Neptune Heliconius, in which the people of Priene presided. *Pocock.*

The Panionium assembly, being but a congress of ministers from independant states, wanted authority to enforce its resolutions, and the political connection produced by it remained very imperfect. *Mitford*, ch. vi. sect. 1.

[c] Triopium was a city of Caria, founded by Triopas, father of Erysicthon. Hence the Triopian promontory took its name, where was a temple known under the name of the Triopian temple, which was consecrated to Apollo. The Dorians here celebrated games in honour of that God. In this temple was held a general assembly of the Dorians of Asia, upon the model of that of Thermopylæ. *Larcher.*

[d] In the games to the honour of Apollo, or Bacchus, the victor was not permitted to carry the prize away with him. It remained in the temple, with an inscription signifying the name of the persons at whose cost the games were celebrated, with that of the victorious tribe. *Larcher.*

[e] The sincerity of Herodotus is eminently conspicuous, from the faithful manner in which he relates circumstances but little honourable, either for Halicarnassus, his country, or even for the Athenians, who had expressed themselves anxious to receive him into the number of their citizens, and before whom he had publicly recited his history. See also chap. cxlvi. of this book; as also different passages in the 3d, 5th, and 7th books. *Bouhier.*

[f] Cos was the birth-place of Hippocrates and Apelles.

[g] The historian Ctesias was born at Cnidus, and also the astronomer Eudoxus. Strabo informs us, that there

which was the sixth, from participating in the religious ceremonies; and punished the Halicarnassians in that manner.

CXLV. The Ionians seem to have formed themselves into twelve cities, and resolved to admit no more into their society, because they had been divided into just so many parts when they inhabited in Peloponnesus; as the Achaians, who drove out those Ionians, now consist of the same number. The city of Pellena is the first towards Sicyon; the next are Ægyra and Æge, which is watered by the perpetual streams of the river Crathis, from whence that of Italy takes its name; after these, Bura and Helice, to which place the Ionians fled when they were defeated by the Achaians; Ægion[h], Rhipes, Patras, Pharæ, and Olenus, through which runs the great river Pirus; the rest are Dyma and Tritæa, the only inland places among them.

CXLVI. These are the twelve parts of the Achaian territories, which formerly belonged to the Ionians; and on that account they constituted the same number of cities in their new establishment. For to say that these are more properly Ionians, or of more noble origin than other Ionians, is great folly; when we know that the Abantes[i] from Eubœa, who had neither name nor any other thing in common with the Ionians, are no inconsiderable part of this colony; and that the Minyan-Orchomenians, the Cadmæans, Dryopians, Phocians[k], (who separated themselves from the rest of their countrymen,) and Molossians, with the Pelasgians of Arcadia, the Dorian Epidaurians, and many other people, were intermixed with them, as well as the Athenians; who set out from the Prytaneum[l] of Athens, and thought themselves the most

was an observatory near this city, where observations were made on the movements of the celestial bodies. It also possessed the celebrated Venus of Praxiteles.

[h] The inhabitants of this place having vanquished the Ætolians in a naval fight, and taken from them a vessel of fifty oars, they made an offering of the tenth part to the temple of Delphi; at the same time they asked the God, who were the bravest of the Greeks? The Pythian answered thus: "The best cavalry are "those of Thessaly; the loveliest women "are those of Sparta; they who drink the "water of the fair fountain of Arethusa "are valiant; but the Argians, who live "betwixt Terinthus and Arcadia, abounding in flocks, are more so.—As for you, "O Ægians! you are neither the third, "nor the fourth, nor even the twelfth; "you inspire no respect, nor are of the "smallest importance." *Larcher.*

[i] This people cut off their hair before, and suffered it to grow behind; being a valiant race, they did this to prevent the enemy, whom they always boldly fronted, from seizing them by the hair. For the same reason Alexander ordered his generals to make his troops cut off their hair. *Larcher.*

[k] Pausanias informs us, that the Phocians formed part of these colonies, except those of Delphi, and this is the reason why Herodotus calls them φωκίες ἀποδάσμιοι, *Phocians separated from the others.* Thucyd. (book i. ch. 12.) has the word ἀποδασμὸς in the same sense. *Larcher.*

[l] When a colony was sent to any part, they used to take their arms, provisions, and fire from the Prytaneum. If the fire happened to be extinguished, it was necessary to send for fresh from the Pryta-

noble by birth of the Ionians. They had no wives with them when they came to settle in this country, but seized a sufficient number of Carian women, after they had killed their parents: and for that reason those women entered into a mutual compact, which they confirmed by an oath, and transmitted as sacred to their daughters, that they would never eat with their husbands, nor ever call them by their names; because they had killed their fathers, their husbands, and their children, and after such violences had forced them to submit to their will. This action was done in the country of Miletus.

CXLVII. The Ionians appointed kings to govern them; some choosing Lycians, of the posterity of Glaucus[m]; others electing out of the Pylian-Caucones, who are descended from Codrus the son of Melanthus; and some again from both those families. But, *perhaps some one may say that*, these are more attached to the name of Ionians than any others; I allow them to be genuine Ionians: all those, however, are Ionians, who derive their original from Athens, and celebrate the Apaturian festival[n], which is universally observed in Ionia, except by the Ephesians and Colophonians; but these alone are excluded, under the pretext of some murder.

CXLVIII. The Panionium is a sacred place in Mycale, situate to the northward, and dedicated by the Ionian confederacy to Neptune of Helicon[o]; and Mycale is a promontory on the continent, advancing in a western direction towards Samos. In this place the Ionians are accustomed to celebrate the Panionium solemnity; and we shall observe by the way, that not only the Ionian, but all the Grecian festivals terminate, like the Persian names, in the same letter. These then are the Ionian cities.

CXLIX. The following are the Æolian; Cyme, otherwise

neum of the metropolis. The Prytaneum was sacred to Vesta. It appears, that every other city of Greece had a Prytaneum, but that of Athens eclipsed the others. Thucydides informs us, (book ii. ch. 15.) that from the time of Cycrops to that of Theseus, the Athenians were dispersed in small boroughs, each of which had a Prytaneum and Archons. But Theseus established only one Senate, and one Prytaneum, having put an end to the others. *Larcher.*

[m] This Glaucus was general of the Lycians at the siege of Troy.

[n] For an account of the origin of this festival, and the manner of celebrating it, see Potter's Archæologia Græca, vol. i. book ii. ch. 20. p. 427.

[o] The Ionians had a great veneration for Neptune; they had erected to him a temple at Helice, a city of Achaia, when that country belonged to them. From this place the deity took his name of Heliconius. Homer calls him the Heliconian king. The Ionians giving place to the Achæans, carried with them to Athens (where they took refuge) the worship of Neptune: afterwards settling in Asia, they constructed, in honour of this divinity, a temple, on the model of that at Helice. This temple was in the territories of Priene, to which place the person that presided at the sacrifices was obliged to belong, its inhabitants giving out that they came from Helice. *Larcher.*

called Phriconis, Larissa, Neontichus, Tenus, Cilla, Notion, Ægiroessa, Pitane, Ægæa, Myrina, and Grynia. These are eleven of the twelve cities formerly belonging to the Æolians; but Smyrna, which was the other, was ruined by the Ionians. They all stand on the continent in a country of greater fertility, but inferior in climate to that of the Ionians.

CL. The Æolians were deprived of Smyrna in this manner. The inhabitants of Smyrna received into their city certain Colophonians, who were unsuccessful in a sedition and had been driven from their country. But some time after their arrival, while the people were celebrating the rites of Bacchus without the walls, they took that opportunity to shut the gates, and seize the city. Upon which, when the Æolians came with all their forces to succour the Smyrnæans, the dispute was determined by an agreement, conceived in these terms; That the Ionians should restore all moveable goods, and that the Æolians on their part should quit their claim to the city. The Smyrnæans, consenting to these conditions, were distributed into the other eleven cities, and permitted to enjoy the privilege of citizens.

CLI. These places belonging to the Æolians are on the continent; besides those about mount Ida, which lie at a great distance. In the islands they had the following cities: five in Lesbos[p]; for the Methymnians destroyed Arisba, which was the sixth, though they were of the same blood; one in Tenedos; and another in the Hundred Islands. The Lesbians, with those of Tenedos[q], and the Ionians of the islands, were under no fear of the Persian power; and all the other cities had taken a resolution to follow, wheresoever the Ionians should lead.

CLII. When the ambassadors of the Ionians and Æolians arrived at Sparta (for this was done with all possible speed;) they made choice of Pythermus, a Phocæan, to speak in the name of all; who, to bring a greater number of Lacedæmo-

[p] The Æolians of Lesbos affirmed, that they were present at the siege of Troy, under the command of Pylæus, whom Homer makes the general of the Pelasgi. A plain confession that they were then called Pelasgi as well as others. The names of Arion and Terpander, of Pittacus, of Alcæus, and of Sappho, and in after-times, of Theophanes the historian, concur in making the island of Lesbos a just object of classical curiosity. Arion and Terpander excelled all their contemporaries in the science and practice of music; Pittachus was eminent for his wisdom; and of Alcæus and Sappho little more need be said, than that they have ever been considered as the founders of lyric poetry. A proper opportunity seems here to present itself, of informing the English reader, that what has been said of the dissolute manners of Sappho is only to be found in the works of those who lived a long time after her. The wines of Lesbos was esteemed the finest in Greece: it is now called Mytilene, which was the name of the ancient capital of the island. *Beloe.*

[q] Nothing has rendered this island more famous in antiquity than the siege of Troy. The Grecian fleet lay there. It has not changed its name, and is at present inhabited by Greeks and Turks.

nians together, clothed himself in a purple habit[r], and in a long speech implored their assistance. But the Spartans rejecting his request, determined not to succour the Ionians in any manner: upon which the ambassadors returned home. Yet the Lacedæmonians, though they had dismissed the Ionian embassy with a plain denial, sent away certain persons by sea, to observe, as I conjecture, what should pass between Cyrus and the Ionians. These men arriving in Phocæa, sent Lacrines, who was the most eminent person among them, to Sardis, with instructions to acquaint Cyrus, that if he should commit any hostility against the Grecian cities, they would not pass by the indignity.

CLIII. Which when Cyrus heard, he inquired of the Grecians that were present, who the Lacedæmonians were, and what number of men they were, who thus imperiously addressed him. And being informed of the particulars, he said to the Spartan, "I was never yet afraid of those, who in "the midst of their cities have a place set apart, in which "they collect and cheat one another by mutual oaths; and if "I continue in life and health, not the calamities of the "Ionians shall be a subject for conversation, but their own." These words of Cyrus were levelled at all the Grecians in general, who in every city have some public place for the uses of buying and selling; but the Persians have none of these, nor any place of public meeting at all. After this, Cyrus having entrusted Tabalus a Persian with the government of Sardis, and appointed Pactyas a Lydian to bring away the gold found in the treasury of Crœsus and other parts of the city, took Crœsus with him, and departed for Ecbatana, thinking it of no consequence to march immediately against the Ionians[s]. For Babylon was an obstacle to this, and the Bactrians, the Saces and the Egyptians; against whom he resolved to lead his army in person and to send another general against the Ionians.

CLIV. But as soon as he was retired from Sardis, Pactyas prevailed with the Lydians to revolt, and going to the seacoast, with all the riches of Lydia in his possession, he hired mercenaries and persuaded the inhabitants of the coast to join him, and then having marched to Sardis, he besieged Tabalus, who had shut himself up in the castle.

CLV. Which news when Cyrus heard, as he was on his way, he spoke to Crœsus in these terms; "What will be the

[r] This dress was most likely to make him conspicuous, as being particularly affected by women. *Larcher.*

[s] Εἶναι is here redundant, as it frequently is in Herodotus. See lib. iv. 33. ii. 44, &c. also Hermann ad Viger. Adnotat. 177.

"end of these things; the Lydians, it seems, will never cease "to give disturbance to me, and to themselves. I am in "doubt whether it will not be better to reduce them to sla-"very, since I think that I have done as imprudently as "those, who, after having killed the father[t], should spare the "lives of his sons. For I compel you, who have been more "than a father to the Lydians, to follow me as a prisoner, "and at the same time have reinstated them in the possession "of their city: and now I wonder at their rebellion!" When Cyrus had thus plainly delivered his thoughts, Crœsus, fearing the utter ruin of Sardis, answered: "Sir, you have but too "much reason for what you say; yet you will do better to "moderate your indignation, and not to destroy an ancient "city, altogether innocent of this, as well as of the former "offence. I myself committed the first fault, and am now "bearing the punishment on my own head[u]. But as Pactyas, "who was entrusted by you, is guilty of this second, let him "be treated as his crime deserves, and let the Lydians be "pardoned. Yet to the end they may never more revolt, "nor be troublesome to you, command all their arms to be "taken away; and enjoin them to wear tunics under their "cloaks, and buskins on their feet, and to teach their sons to "sing, to play on the harp, and other arts likely to render "them effeminate[x]. For by these means you will soon see the "Lydians becoming women instead of men, so that they will "never any more give you any apprehensions about their re-"volting."

CLVI. Crœsus suggested this method to Cyrus, because

[t] This was a proverb in Greece; it is quoted by Aristot. Rhetor. i. 16. and ii. 17: Νήπιος, ὃς πατέρα κτείνων, παῖδας καταλείπει.

[u] Wesseling has very well explained this passage by the 92nd verse of the 19th book of Homer's Odyssey. The 445th of the Electra of Sophocles might be added with the explanation of the Scholiast. *Larcher.*

[x] The word καπηλεύειν signifies properly to retail, thence to keep a tavern. As every man who can brave the contempt of the public is not susceptible of sentiments of honour, the word κάπηλος came to signify those infamous men who keep houses for the resort of the dissolute. I conceive that it is here used in this sense, and I have preferred a general expression. This people became so effeminate, that the word Λυδίζειν signified to dance, and the Romans called dances and pantomimes, *Ludiones et Ludii*, from the Lydians, and not from *Ludus*; for the Latins used *Ludus, Surus et Suria*, for *Lydus, Syrus et Syria*. Xerxes compelled the Babylonians, who had revolted, to adopt a similar conduct. He forbade their carrying arms, obliged them to learn music, to have in their cities places of debauch, and to wear long tunics. The expressions in Herodotus and Plutarch are parallel. A nation, which debases itself by its vices, is no longer dang[erous]... the Lydians became effeminate, an[d the] most cowardly people of Asia, although they had before been the most valiant. (Polyæni Strategem. lib. vii. ch. 6.) One cannot help observing the process of tyrants. They begin with introducing luxury, and corrupting the morals of the people, whom they wish to oppress. "It "is, in fact, pleasure," as Æschines remarks in Timarch. "and insatiable desire, "which engage young men in the ser-"vice of tyrants to the overthrow of po-"pular governments." *Larcher.*

he judged the Lydians would be less unhappy under such circumstances, than if they should be sold for slaves; and was persuaded, that unless he could frame some plausible pretext, he should not prevail with him to alter his resolution: neither was he without apprehension, that if the Lydians should otherwise escape the present danger, they might hereafter revolt from the Persians, and bring utter ruin on themselves. Cyrus, pleased with the expedient, relaxed his anger, and said that he would follow his advice; and sending for Mazares, a Mede, commanded him to order the Lydians to conform themselves to the regulations proposed by Crœsus; and to treat all those as slaves, who had assisted in the attempt upon Sardis; but above all, to bring Pactyas alive to him: and having given these orders in his way, he returned to Persia.

CLVII. Pactyas, being informed that the army which was coming against him was close at hand, fled in great consternation to Cyme; and Mazares, with that part of the Persian forces he had, marched directly to Sardis. But not finding Pactyas and his followers there, he in the first place constrained the Lydians to conform themselves to the orders prescribed by Cyrus, and totally to alter their manner of life: after which he dispatched messengers to Cyme, to command them to deliver up Pactyas. The Cymæans called a council on this occasion, and resolved to refer the matter to the ancient oracle of Branchidæ, which was frequented by the Ionians and Æolians, and stands in the territory of Miletus, a little above the port of Panormus[y].

CLVIII. When the persons, who were sent to the oracle, arrived at Branchidæ, and prayed to be informed what they should do that might be most pleasing to the Gods, they were commanded to deliver Pactyas to the Persians: which answer being brought to the Cymæans, determined the majority to decree that he should be surrendered accordingly. But after they had taken that resolution, Aristodicus the son of Heraclides, one of the principal men of the city, either distrusting the faith of the oracle, or suspecting the sincerity of [illegible] consulters, prevented them from acting in that manner: [illegible] at last other messengers, among whom was Aristodicus, went to inquire concerning Pactyas.

CLIX. When they arrived at Branchidæ, Aristodicus consulted the oracle in the name of the rest, using these words: "O king, Pactyas the Lydian came to us as a suppliant, to "avoid a violent death from the hands of the Persians. They

[y] It will be proper to remark, that there were two places of that name; and that this must not be confounded with the port of Panormus, in the vicinity of Ephesus. *Beloe.*

"now demand him, and order the Cymæans to give him up. "We, who are under great apprehensions of the Persian power, "have not yet dared to surrender the suppliant, till we shall be "plainly informed by thee what we ought to do in this con- "jecture." Thus spoke Aristodicus; but the oracle gave the same answer as before, and again admonished them to surrender Pactyas to the Persians. Upon which Aristodicus, in pursuance of the design he had formed, walking round the temple, took away all the sparrows and other birds he found in the nests that were within the limits of the place; and when he had so done, it is reported, a voice was heard from the innermost part of the temple, directing these words to Aristodicus: "O thou most impious of all men, how darest thou thus "tear my suppliants from under my protection?" Aristodicus readily answered, "Art thou then so careful to succour thy "suppliants, and yet so forward to command the Cymæans to "abandon Pactyas to the Persians?" "Yes," said the voice, "I command it; that by having acted impiously, you may the "sooner perish, and never more disturb the oracle with ques- "tions of like nature."

CLX. When this last answer was brought to Cyme, the people, being unwilling either by surrendering Pactyas to be destroyed, or to draw a war upon themselves by protecting him, sent him away to Mitylene. Some say, the Mitylenæans, upon a message they received from Mazares, agreed to deliver Pactyas into his hands for a certain reward; but I cannot affirm this, because the thing was never effected. For the Cymæans, being informed of what was doing in Mitylene, dispatched a vessel to Lesbos, and transported Pactyas to Chios, where he was taken by violence from the temple of Minerva Poliuchus[a], and delivered up by the Chians; who in recompence were put into possession of Atarneus, a place situate in Mysia over against Lesbos. In this manner Pactyas fell into the hands of the Persians, and was kept under confinement, in order to be conducted to Cyrus. And for a long time after this action, none of the Chians would use the barley[a] of Artaneus in their offerings to the Gods, or make a confection of the fruits produced by that country; but the whole growth of those lands was kept away from the temples.

CLXI. When the Chians had delivered up Pactyas, Mazares marched with his forces against those who had assisted

[a] That is, Patroness or Protectoress of the citadel. At Athens the town was called ἄστυ and the citadel πόλις. Citadels were under the protection of this Goddess, and she also had usually a temple in them, as in that of Troy in Homer's Iliad vi. ver. 297. *Larcher.*

[a] They used to sprinkle on the head of the victim barley mixed with salt, which the Latins called *mola salsa*; hence the word immolate. *Larcher.*

in besieging Tabalus; and having first destroyed Priene, he over-ran all the plain that lies by the river Mæander, and abandoned the booty to his army. But after he had treated the Magnesians in the same manner, he fell sick and died.

CLXII. Upon which, Harpagus, who was also a Mede, and the same person that, having been entertained by Astyages at an impious feast and assisted Cyrus in ascending the throne, came down to command the army in his place. This man being appointed general by Cyrus, and arriving in Ionia, took several cities by throwing up earthworks to the walls, after he had forced the people to retire within their fortified places. Phocæa was the first of the Ionian cities that he attacked.

CLXIII. These Phocæans were the first of all the Grecians who undertook long voyages, and discovered the coasts of Adria, Tyrrhenia, Iberia, and Tartessus[b]. They made their expeditions in galleys of fifty oars, and used no ships of a rounder form. When they arrived at Tartessus they were kindly received by Arganthonius, the king of that country, who had then reigned fourscore years, and lived to the age of one hundred and twenty. They had so much of his favour, that he at first solicited them to leave Ionia, and to settle in any part of his kingdom they should choose; but afterwards, finding he could not prevail with the Phocæans to accept his offer, and hearing they were in great danger from the increasing power of the Mede[c], he presented them with treasure to defray the expence of building a wall round their city; which he did with so liberal a hand, that the whole structure, comprehending no small number of stades in circumference, was built with large and well-compacted stone.

CLXIV. Harpagus having arrived with his army before this city, first sent in a message to acquaint the Phocæans within, that if they would demolish one of the towers built upon their wall, and consecrate one edifice[d], he would rest contented. The Phocæans, detesting slavery, answered, that they would take one day to deliberate touching his proposal, in the mean time he would draw off his forces from about

[b] Tartessus was situated between the two branches of the Bœtis, (now Guadalquiver,) through which it discharges itself into the sea.

[c] Larcher confidently puts, *of Crœsus*, since the walls of Phocæa appear to have been built before Cyrus became formidable; he changes Μήδου into Λυδῶν.

[d] Commentators understand a temple. Reiske wishes to add τῷ Μήδῳ after ἓν. But the Persians did not confine their deity in walls. Perhaps, says Wesseling, Harpagus was satisfied with their consecrating one building, as a token of their subjection. For my own part, I think that the king, having a palace in every large town in his dominions, the building which Harpagus demanded, was probably intended for his residence, whenever he might happen to visit Phocæa; or it might perhaps be intended for the governor, his representative. *Larcher.*

the city. Harpagus said, that though he well knew their design, yet he would permit them to consult together, as they desired. But when he had withdrawn his army, the Phocæans made ready their ships; and having put their wives, children, and goods on board, together with the images and other things dedicated in their temples, except pictures, and works of brass or stone; they themselves embarked likewise, and set sail for Chios: so that the Persians at their return found the city desolate, and abandoned by all the inhabitants.

CLXV. The Phocæans arriving in Chios, desired to purchase the Œnussian islands of the Chians; but because the Chians would not consent to sell them, lest they should become the seat of trade, and their own island be excluded, they embarked again, directing their course to Cyrnus[e]; where, by the admonition of an oracle, they had built a city, which they named Alalia, twenty years before. Arganthonius was at that time dead. In their passage to Cyrnus, turning in at Phocæa, they cut in pieces the Persian garrison left by Harpagus in the city. Having destroyed these Persians, they pronounced terrible imprecations against those who should stay behind; and bound themselves by mutual oaths, never to return to Phocæa, till a burning ball of iron[f], which they threw into the sea on that occasion, should appear again unextinguished. Nevertheless, as they were making towards Cyrnus, more than one half of the fleet, moved by regret and affection for their native country, broke through all these engagements, and returned to Phocæa; while the rest, resolving to observe the oaths they had taken, pursued their voyage from the Œnussian islands to Cyrnus.

CLXVI. When they arrived there, they built divers temples, and lived five years in one community with the former colony. But because in that time they had ravaged the territories of all their neighbours, the Tyrrhenians and Carthaginians combined together to make war against them, each nation with sixty ships. The Phocæans on their part fitted out their fleet, consisting in all of sixty sail also; and coming up with the enemy in the sea of Sardinia, fought and conquered, but [illegible]tained a Cadmean victory[g]; for forty of their own ships were

[e] Herodotus occasionally mentions most of the larger islands in the Mediterranean; Cyrnus is Corsica. *Rennell*, p. 42.

[f] This is the proper signification of the word μύδρος, as we may see in Hesych. and Suidas. Hence it signified a mass of stone; in which sense it is taken by Horace, Epod. xvi. v. 25.

Sed juremus in hæc: simul imis saxa renarint
Vadis levata, ne redire sit nefas.
Larcher.

[g] This became a proverb to express a victory, which was mournful to the conqueror. Various reasons are given by Hesychius and Suidas for the proverb. Suidas, amongst others, says that it became a proverb, because Cadmus having destroyed the dragon, which guarded a fountain sacred to Mars, lived afterwards

sunk; and all the rest, having lost their prows, were utterly disabled. After this action returning to Alalia, they put their wives and children on board again, with as much of their goods as they could carry off, and leaving Cyrnus, sailed to Rhegium[h].

CLXVII. Of those Phocæans that lost their ships in the fight, many fell into the hands of the Carthaginians and Tyrrhenians, who divided them by lot, and having taken them on shore, stoned them to death in the territory of Agylla[i]. After which, all the men and cattle that passed by that spot, where the Phocæans who had been stoned lay, became distorted, lame, and seized with convulsions. In this extremity the Agyllians, being desirous to expiate the crime, had recourse to the oracle of Delphi; and the Pythian enjoined them to use those rites, which they still observe; for they commemorate the death of the Phocæans with great magnificence, and established gymnastic and equestrian contests. This was the fate of these Phocæans; and as for the rest, who fled to Rhegium, they left that place, and in Œnotria built a city, which is now called Hyela[k], by the advice of a certain Posidonian; who told them they had mistaken the oracle, and that the Pythian meant they should build a monument for Cyrnus the hero[l], and not a city in the island of that name.

CLXVIII. The conduct of the Teians in this conjuncture was not unlike that of the Phocæans. For when Harpagus by the advantage of his earthworks had made himself master of their walls, all the Teians went on board their ships, and, transporting themselves to Thrace, settled in the city of Abdera; which Timesius[m] of Clazomene had formerly founded; but was afterwards driven out by the Thracians, who would not suffer him to continue in possession of the place; where

for eight years, in servitude to that God. See further particulars in Erasmi Adagia.

h It is very surprising that Herodotus passes over in silence the foundation of Marseilles. The accounts of its foundation are collected by Larcher in a long note.

i This was Cære in Etruria; this name is still preserved in its modern name of Cervetère, abridged from Cere vetere, which means ancient Cere. *Larcher.*

k This the Latins called Velia; it was situated in the tract between Pæstum and Cape Palinurus. Œnotria was afterwards called Lucania.

l Cyrnus the son of Hercules gave his name to the island. The grammarian Servius is the only one who mentions him. *Larcher.*

m Larcher, on the authority of Plutarch and Ælian, reads *Timesias;* he was governor of Clazomene, and of great integrity. Envy, which always persecutes such characters, at last effected his disgrace. He was for a time regardless of its consequences; but it at length banished him from his country. He was passing by a school, before which the boys, dismissed by their master, were playing. Two of them were quarrelling about a piece of string. "I wish," says one, "I might so dash out the brains of Timesius." He concluded from this that he must be universally disliked, and therefore he voluntarily banished himself. Ælian. Var. Hist. xii. 9. Plutarch (Repub.) relates the same story.

yet he is honoured as a hero, at this time, by the Teians of Abdera.

CLXIX. These were the only people of all the Ionians, who chose rather to abandon their country than submit to servitude. The rest, except the Milesians, were conquered by Harpagus, after they had as strenuously defended their several cities, as those who left the country; and when they were forced to surrender to a superior power, they continued to inhabit the same places, and submitted to the will of the conqueror. But the Milesians having made a league with Cyrus, as I said before, kept themselves quiet during these commotions. And in this manner the Ionians of the continent were a second time enslaved[n]; which put the Islanders under such consternation, that they readily made their submission to Cyrus.

CLXX. Yet, as the Ionians, even in these circumstances, were permitted to meet in the Panionian council, I am informed that Bias of Priene offered them such salutary advice in one of those assemblies, that if they had hearkened to him, they might have been the most happy of all the Grecians. For he counselled the Ionians to transport themselves in their ships to Sardinia in one body, then to build one city for all the Ionians, by which means they would not only be delivered from servitude, but inhabiting the most considerable of the islands, and governing the rest, would become prosperous; whereas should they continue in Ionia, he saw no hope of recovering their liberty. This was the counsel of Bias the Prienean, after the Ionians were subdued; but Thales the Milesian, who was of Phœnician descent, gave them the most useful advice before that calamity happened, in admonishing the Ionians to constitute one general council of the whole league in the city of Teos, which stands in the centre of Ionia; and to esteem all the rest of the inhabited cities as so many different tribes. Such were the sentiments of those two persons.

CLXXI. Harpagus having subdued Ionia, led his army, which he reinforced with Ionians and Æolians, against the Carians, Caunians, and Lycians. The Carians came from the islands to inhabit on the continent. They were anciently called Leleges, and lived in the islands[o] under the protection of Minos, paying no kind of tribute, that I could ever find by inquiring into the remotest times. But when he had occasion for mariners, they assisted him with their ships in the great

[n] See chapters, 6 and 28.

[o] Thucydides (book i. ch. 4.) says, that Minos expelled the Carians from the Cyclades, and gave the government of them to his children. Probably he expelled them only from some, but left them in others on certain conditions. *Larcher.*

conquests he made, and raised themselves to a higher degree of reputation than any other nation. They were the inventors of three things now in use among the Grecians. For the Carians were the first who wore a crest upon their helmets; adorned their shields with various figures; and invented the handle[p], by which they are managed; whereas, before this invention, all who used shields, carried them without handles, directing them with leathern thongs, which hung round their necks and left shoulders. After a long time, the Dorians and Ionians expelled the Carians from the islands, who then settled on the continent: and this account the Cretans give of the Carians. But the Carians, not assenting to these things, affirm they were originally inhabitants of the continent, and always went under the same name. In testimony of which they shew an ancient temple at Mylasa[q], dedicated to the Carian Jupiter; where the Mysians and Lydians are admitted to participate with the Carians in their worship, as nations of the same blood. For, say they, Lydus and Mysus were brothers to Car, and on that account the use of this temple is communicated to their posterity; and not to any other people, though of the same language with the Carians.

CLXXII. The Caunians, as I conjecture, are originally of the country they inhabit, though they say their ancestors came from Crete[r]. But whether they have accommodated their language to that of the Carians, or the Carians have formed their speech by the Caunians, I cannot determine with certainty. In their customs and manners the Caunians resemble no other nation, not even the Carians; accounting it very becoming for men, women, and boys, to drink in great companies, with their friends, and with those of the same age. They anciently worshipped the Gods of other nations, but afterwards changing their opinion, and resolving to have no other than their own national deities, they all armed themselves, both young and old, and brandishing their spears in the air, marched up to the mountains of Calinda; crying as they went, that they were expelling the foreign Gods out of their country.

CLXXIII. The Lycians derive their original from Crete,

[p] It appears from Homer, (Iliad viii. v. 193.) that in the time of the Trojan war, the buckler had two handles of wood, one through which the arm was passed, the other was grasped by the hand to regulate its movement. Sophocles therefore (Ajax, 576.) has not observed the proper fashion, in giving the shield of Ajax a handle of leather. *Larcher.*

[q] This city was more decorated with temples, &c. than any in Caria. It is now called Melasso, or Marmora, from its quarries of beautiful white marble.

[r] Now called Candia: for an account of its present circumstances, see Savary's Letters on Greece. M. De Sainte Croix has given an excellent account of its ancient legislation, in his work entitled, Des Anciens Gouvernement Federatifs.

which in ancient time was entirely in the possession of barbarians[s]. But Sarpedon and Minos, the sons of Europa, contending for the kingdom, Sarpedon, being defeated by Minos, was driven out of the island with all his partizans, and landing in Asia, settled in Milyas; for that was the ancient name of the country which the Lycians now inhabit, though the Milyans were then called Solymi. During the reign of Sarpedon they went by the name they brought with them into Asia; and in our time are by their neighbours called Termilians. But when Lycus the son of Pandion was compelled by his brother Ægeus to quit Athens, he fled to Sarpedon and the Termilæ, and from him the people began to be named Lycians. Their customs are, for the most part, derived from the Cretans and Carians; but they have one peculiar to themselves, in which they differ from all other nations. For they take their names from their mothers[t], and not from their fathers[u]; so that if any one be asked who he is, and of what

[s] In the remotest times Crete was inhabited by barbarians, and its inhabitants were called Eteocretes, (i. e. true Cretans.) They were supposed to be Autochthones, and were governed by a king named Cres. After several generations the Pelasgians seized on part of the island. The third nation consisted of Dorians, who came chiefly from the country round mount Olympus, under the conduct of Tectamus, son of Dorus, and of Achæus from Laconia. This Tectamus afterwards became king of the island, and married the daughter of Cretheus, by whom he had Asterius. During the reign of Asterius, Jupiter carried off Europa from Phœnicia, who bore Minos, Rhadamanthus, and Sarpedon. Asterius afterwards married Europa, and as he had no sons of his own, he adopted the sons of Jupiter, and left them his kingdom. Minos was father of Lycastus, who was father to Minos the Second, who equipped a fleet, and became master of the sea. He espoused Pasiphæ, by whom he had Androgeus, Ariadne, &c. A mixed tribe of barbarians occupied Crete in the fourth place, who in time learnt the Greek language, which they found already established there. Lastly, after the return of the Heraclidæ, the Argians and Lacedæmonians sent colonies thither. *Larcher.*

[t] Bellerophon slew a wild boar, which destroyed all the cattle and fruits of the Xanthians, and received no recompense for his services. He therefore prayed to Neptune, and obtained from him, that all the fields of the Xanthians should exhale a salt dew, and be universally corrupted. This continued, till regarding the supplications of the women, he prayed a second time to Neptune, to remove this. Hence a law was instituted among the Xanthians, that they should derive their names from their mothers, and not from their fathers. *Plutarch on the virtues of Women.*

I am more inclined to believe that a promiscuous intercourse existed among this half civilized people, the women belonging to those who could first seize them; and as they afterwards became the property of those who could carry them off, or had the art to seduce them; and as the children of these irregular connections must therefore be ignorant of their fathers, they took the name of their mother. The country of the Xanthians was in Lycia. If this custom commenced with the Xanthians, the Lycians doubtless adopted it. Amongst these people the inheritance descended to the daughters, the sons were excluded. *Larcher.*

[u] They also call themselves sons of Thetis, as I have mentioned in another place; this probably they did in consequence of the strange custom here mentioned, and to confront the like ridiculous fictions of other nations.

Moreover, over the different companies (τα Συσσιτια, or Ανδρεια) into which the Cretans were divided, a woman presided, had the care and management of the whole family, provided for them, and at table distributed the choicest

family, he recounts his maternal genealogy, in the female line. Besides, if a free-born woman marry a servant, her children enjoy the full privilege of citizens; but should a man of ever so high dignity marry a foreigner or a concubine, his children would be incapable of any honour.

CLXXIV. The Carians were subdued by Harpagus, without doing any memorable action in their defence: and all the Grecians that inhabit those parts behaved themselves with as little courage. Among these were the Cnidians, a Lacedæmonian colony, whose territories descend to the Triopian sea. This region, beginning at the Bybassian peninsula, is entirely surrounded by water, except a small space, which is about five stades in breadth, having on the north side the Ceramic gulph, and on the south-west the sea which flows around Rhodes and Syme. The Cnidians there, while the arms of Harpagus were employed in the conquest of Ionia, formed a design to cut through the isthmus, and to make their country an island. For the whole of their dominions were within the isthmus. But as they were carrying on that work with great diligence, the shivers of the stones broken by their instruments, flew about so thick, and wounded so many men in the body, and particularly in the eyes; that falling into great consternation, and imagining some divine power had interposed, they sent to inquire of the Delphian oracle concerning this obstruction; and, as the Cnidians say, had the following answer from the Pythian:

> Build here no towers, nor through the isthmus cut:
> Had the God pleas'd that this should be an isle,
> The sea had wash'd your coast in every part [x].

Upon the reception of this oracle, the Cnidians desisted from their work, and when Harpagus appeared with his army, surrendered without resistance.

CLXXV. But the Pedasians inhabiting a midland coun-

pieces to those who had distinguished themselves, either at home or abroad. This female government arose from the foregoing plea, their pretended descent from Thetis: but the youth under seventeen were under the care of a master, who was called their father. See Meursius, c. 16, 17. *Creta.*

[x] This answer of the oracle brings to mind an historical anecdote, which may be here introduced. The Dutch offered Charles the Second of Spain to make the Tagus navigable as far as Lisbon at their own expence, provided he would suffer them to exact, for a certain number of years, a stipulated duty on merchandize, which should pass that way. It was their intention to make the Mansanazer navigable from Madrid to the place where it joins the Tagus. After a sage deliberation, the council of Castile returned this remarkable answer: "If it had pleased God to make these "rivers navigable, the intervention of hu-"man industry would not have been ne-"cessary; as they are not so already, it "does not appear that Providence intend-"ed them to be so. Such an undertaking "would be, seemingly, to violate the de-"crees of heaven, and to attempt the "amendment of those apparent imper-"fections visible in its works." *Clarke's Letters on the Spanish Nation. Letter* xv.

try, situate above Halicarnassus, were the only people of Caria that opposed Harpagus with vigour. For retiring to a mountain called Lyda, they fortified and defended themselves valiantly, and were not subdued without great difficulty. When any sinister event is about to fall upon the Pedasians and their neighbours, a long beard shoots suddenly from the chin of Minerva's priestess[y], and this prodigy has thrice happened.

CLXXVI. The Pedasians then were, after some time, subdued. The Lycians, when Harpagus marched towards the Xanthian plain, went out to meet him, and though inferior in number, displayed feats of valour. But being overpowered with numbers, and forced to retire into the city, they put their wives, children, and servants, with all their riches, into the citadel, and set fire to the place[z]. Which when they had done, and all was burnt, they engaged themselves by the strongest oaths to die together; and to that end returning to the field of battle, they renewed the fight, and were cut in pieces to the last man. All the Xanthian Lycians of our age are descended from strangers, except eighty families, which being absent at the time of this invasion, escaped with life. Thus Xanthus fell into the hands of Harpagus; and Caunia almost in the same manner; for the Caunians were accustomed to follow the example of the Lycians.

CLXXVII. While Harpagus subdued the lower, Cyrus conquered the upper Asia, by reducing every nation, and passing by no one. But I shall forbear to mention the greater part of his actions, and content myself to relate those which gave him most trouble, and are most worthy of being narrated.

CLXXVIII. When he had reduced all the continent of

[y] See Aristot. Hist. Animal. lib. iii. ch. 2. We express ourselves surprised at the blind credulity of the ancients: posterity, in its turn, will be astonished at ours, without being on this account perhaps at all more wise. *Larcher.*

The liquefying of the blood of St. Januarius at Naples, which by the majority of the people there, it would at this day be thought impiety to doubt, is recited in a very lively and entertaining manner by Dr. Moore, and is an instance of credulity no less striking than the one recorded by Herodotus of the Carian priestesses. *Beloe.*

[z] Similar despair actuated the Xanthians, when Brutus laid siege to their city, (Plutarch in Bruto.) When they were endeavouring to set fire to the engines of the Romans, a violent wind carried the flames to the walls, so that some houses took fire. The Romans, ordered by Brutus, ran to extinguish it, but were repelled by the Xanthians, who did all they could to assist the flames. Not only men and women, but even boys and children leaped into the flames, others threw themselves from the walls, others fell on their parents swords, opening their breasts and desiring to be slain. *Larcher.*

The burning of the city of Moscow, by the Russians when invaded by Bonaparte, bears some resemblance to the above deed.

Asia, he resolved to invade Assyria, which contains many famous cities; but the principal in strength and name is Babylon, where the seat of the kingdom was fixed, after the destruction of Nineveh. Babylon stands in a spacious plain, and being perfectly square, shews a front on every side, of one hundred and twenty stades[a], which make up the sum of four hundred and eighty stades in the whole circumference. So great was the size of the city of Babylon. It was adorned in a manner which surpasses any city we are acquainted with[b]. In the first place, a wide and deep ditch, always supplied with water, encompasses the wall; next there is a wall two hundred royal cubits in height, and fifty in breadth; every royal cubit containing three digits more than the common.

CLXXIX. And here I think myself obliged to give some account, how the Babylonians employed the earth that was taken out of so large a ditch, and in what manner the wall was built. As they dug the ditch, they made bricks of the earth that was taken out, and when they had shaped a convenient number, they baked them in furnaces prepared for that purpose. The cement they used was a bituminous substance heated on the fire; and every thirty orders of bricks were compacted together with an intermixture of reeds[c]. With these materials they first built up the sides of the ditch, and afterwards the wall in the same manner. Certain edifices, consisting only of one story, were placed on the edges of the

[a] The following are the statements of different authors, respecting the measures of Babylon.

	Circuit in stades.	Height of the walls.		Breadth of the walls.	
		cubits	feet	cubits	feet
Herodotus	480	200	300	50	75
Pliny, 60 M. P.	480				
Ctesias	360	*	300		
Clitarchus	365				
Curtius	368	100	150		32
Strabo	385	50	75		32

* 50 Orgyiæ are given, it should probably be 50 cubits. It appears highly probable that 360 or 365 stades was the true statement of the circumference. The 480 of Herodotus, taking a stade at 491 feet, would give about 126 square miles, or 8 times the area of London. It is evident however from Quintus Curtius that the whole was not built on. *Rennel.*

For an accurate account of the remains and situation of Babylon, the reader is referred to the elaborate publication of Rennel, sect. 14.

[b] The greatest cities of Europe give but a faint idea of that grandeur which all historians unanimiously ascribe to the famous city of Babylon. *Dutens.*

[c] It is not perhaps very easy to determine the use of the layers of reeds, where the cement was of so tenacious a quality. Layers were however introduced at different distances: each method had probably a reference to some particular object or use which we cannot understand. *Rennel.*

wall, fronting each other, and a space was left between those buildings sufficient for turning a chariot with four horses abreast. In the circumference of the wall one hundred gates of brass[c] are seen, with frames[d] of the same metal. Eight days' journey from Babylon stands another city, called Is[e], on a river of the same name, that falls into the Euphrates, and brings down great quantities of bitumen in lumps. From thence the bitumen was brought that was used in the wall of Babylon.

CLXXX. In this manner Babylon was encompassed with a wall; it consists of two parts, separated from each other by the river Euphrates; which descending from the mountains of Armenia, becomes broad, deep, and rapid, and falls into the Red sea. The arms of the wall are carried close down to the river, at those points angles are formed, and a rampart of burnt bricks extends along each bank of the river. The city, which abounds in houses three or four stories in height, is divided into straight streets, both the others and the transverse ones which lead to the river. At the end of each street a little gate is formed in the wall which extends along the river, so that there are as many gates as streets. These are all made of brass, and lead down to the edge of the river.

CLXXXI. The wall which I have mentioned is its chief defence; but within it another is built, not much inferior in strength, though not altogether so thick; and besides these, buildings are raised in the centre of each division, in one the royal palace[f], which is very spacious and strong; and in the other the temple of Jupiter Belus[g], being a square building,

[c] See Isaiah chap. xlv. 2.

[d] In the Greek σταθμοὶ καὶ ὑπέρθυρα: the posts and the part over the gate.

[e] We still find bitumen at Hit on the Euphrates, 128 miles above Hillah, which probably is the same as this *Is*, which should have been written *It*. *Rennel*.

[f] Herodotus has not said in which of the divisions of the city the temple and palace respectively stood; but it may be pretty clearly collected from Diodorus, that the temple stood on the east side, and the palace on the west; and the remains found at the present day accord with this idea. *Rennel*.

[g] The temples of the ancients consisted of a large space enclosed by walls, in which were courts and groves, pieces of water, and sometimes apartments for the priests; and lastly the temple, properly so called, and where most frequently the priests alone were allowed to enter. The whole enclosure was named τὸ ἱερὸν; the temple, properly so called, or the residence of the Deity, was named ναὸς, Ionicè, νηὸς, *the cell:* it is obvious that this last is the place particularly alluded to. *Larcher*.

This is in all probability the tower of Babel, repaired by Belus the 2nd king of Babylon, who is frequently confounded by ancient historians with Belus the First, or Nimrod. Berosus the Chaldee mentions that the tower of Babel was erected by giants, who waged war with the Gods, and were dispersed, and that the edifice was beaten down by the winds. That it was constructed with burnt bricks, (as related in Gen. xi. 3.) is attested by Justin, Quintus Curtius, Vitruvius, and other heathen writers, and also by the relations of modern travellers, who have described its ruins, which are about 5 miles distant from Hellah, and 950 yards from the bank of the Euphrates, and are called, by the natives Mukallibè, (or

extended to the length of two stades on every side, and having gates of brass, as may still be seen in our time. In the midst of this temple stands a solid tower, of one stade in height, and in breadth of the same measure. On this tower another is built, and a third upon that, till they make up the number of eight. The ascent to these is by a circular way, carried round the outside of the building to the highest part. About the middle of the ascent there is an apartment and resting seats, on which those who go up may sit down and rest; and within the uppermost tower a spacious chapel is built, in which a table of gold stands at the side of a large couch magnificently adorned. No image is seen in this place; nor is any mortal permitted to remain there by night, (as the Chaldæans[h], who are priests of this temple, say,) except only a woman chosen by the God out of the whole nation.

CLXXXII. They affirm for a truth, which nevertheless I think incredible, that the God comes by night, and lies in the bed: which resembles the account given by the Egyptians of their temple at Thebes. For there also a woman lies in the temple of Jupiter, and neither of these are suspected to have the company of men; in the same manner also the priestess, who utters the oracles at Pataræ in Lycia[i], when answers are given; where, though they have not a constant oracle, yet when an answer is to be delivered, she is shut up during the night in the temple with the God.

CXXXIII. In a chapel, which stands below, within the temple of Babylon, there is a large image of gold, representing Jupiter sitting; a large table of gold stands by him; the throne also and the footstool are of gold, which together weigh eight hundred talents, as the Chaldæans affirm. Without this chapel is an altar of gold; and another of a greater size, which is used when cattle of full age are sacrificed; for on the golden altar no other than sucking victims may be offered. On the great altar the Chaldæans consume yearly the weight of a thousand talents in incense, when they celebrate the festival of this God. There formerly stood within the precincts of the temple, a statue of solid gold, twelve cubits

Mujelibè,) which means overturned. See Faber's Horæ Mosaic. vol. i. p. 146—170. Dr. Hale's Analysis, vol. i. p. 350—355. Mr. Rick's Memoirs of the Ruins of Babylon, and Sir R. K. Porter's Travels, vol. ii. p. 308—332.

[h] Belus came originally from Egypt. He went, accompanied by other Egyptians, to Babylon; there he established priests: these are the people who are called Chaldeans by the Babylonians. The Chaldeans carried to Babylon the science of astrology, which they learned from the Egyptian priests. *Larcher.*

[i] According to Servius, Apollo communicated his oracles at Pataræ during the six winter months, and at Delos in the six summer. *Larcher.*

Horace probably alludes to this in the line,

Delius et Patareus Apollo.

Od. III. iv. 64.

high[k], which because I did not see, I shall only relate what I heard from the Chaldæans; who say, that Darius the son of Hystaspes, having formed a design to take away this statue, had not courage to effect his purpose: but that Xerxes the son of Darius not only took the statue, but killed the priest who had forbidden him to remove it. In this manner the temple of Jupiter Belus is built and adorned; not to mention divers other donations consecrated there by private persons.

CLXXXIV. There were many others who reigned over Babylon, and strengthened the walls and beautified the temples, (whose names I will mention in my account of the affairs of Assyria[l],) but two women particularly. The first of these, named Semiramis[m], lived five generations before the other, and raised mounds along the plain which are worthy of being visited; for before the river was wont to form a lake over the whole plain.

CLXXXV. But the other, whose name was Nitocris, having afterwards obtained the kingdom, and being much more provident, not only left monuments of herself, which I shall describe; but when she saw the power of the Medes grown formidable and restless, and that they had taken the city of Nineveh, with divers others, she made all imaginable provision for the defence of her territories. To that end in the first place, by causing channels to be dug above Babylon, she made the Euphrates, which before ran in a straight line, so very winding, that in its course it comes three times to Ardericca, an Assyrian village; and to this day, those who go from our sea to Babylon[n], when they go down the Euphrates towards it, are compelled to touch at Ardericca three times, on three several days. She raised on either side banks, which deserve admiration for their size and height. At a considerable distance above Babylon, turning aside a little from the river, she caused a spacious lake to be made, four hundred and twenty stades over on every side; and in depth till the workmen came to water. The earth that was dug out was heaped up on the sides of the river and formed the embankments; when it was completely dug, she brought stones and

[k] Beloe says, that it is by no means impossible but that this might be the identical image which Nebuchadnezzar set up. See Daniel iii. 1.

[l] See note, chap. 106.

[m] There were several princesses of this name; Herodotus distinctly marks which he alludes to. *Larcher.*

It may be worth while to observe the different opinions of authors, about the time when Semiramis is supposed to have lived. According to Syncellus she lived .... 2177 yrs. B. C.

Petavius 2060
Heloicus 2248
Eusebius 1984
Mr. Jackson 1964
Archbp. Usher .. 1215
Philo Biblius .. 1200
Herodotus...... 713 *Bryant.*

[n] Literally; *from this sea*, i. e. the Mediterranean: he uses the same expres-

built the sides of it with them. These two things she performed, and made the river winding, and this trench a lake, in order that the current, being broken by frequent turnings, might be more slow, and the navigation to Babylon tedious; or, if they should leave their ships[o] and endeavour to march by land, the great circumference of the lake might check them. All this was done in that part of the country which lies next to the Medes, and is their shortest way to Babylon; to the end they might have no opportunities of discovering her affairs by an easy communication with the Assyrians.

CLXXXVI. These defences she made around the city by digging[p], and after they were completed made this addition. For considering that Babylon was divided by the river into two parts, and that all persons, who passed from one side to the other during the reigns of former kings, had been necessitated to make use of boats, which in my opinion was very troublesome, she provided the following remedy; and after having sunk the receptacle for the lake I mentioned before, left this also for a monument of her fame. She ordered stones to be cut of large dimensions; and when they were ready and the place was completely dug, she turned the current of the Euphrates into that place. While this was filling, and the ancient channel had become dry, she lined the banks of the river on both sides with a facing of burnt bricks, where it flows past the city, and also the descents, which lead from the gates to the river, in the same manner as the walls were built. Which having done, she built a bridge about the midst of the city with the stones she had prepared; binding them together with plates of lead and iron. Upon these stones, planks of squared timber were laid by day, that the Babylonians might pass over from one side to the other, but were removed at night to prevent mutual robberies. When the trench that was dug had become a lake filled with the water of the Euphrates, and the bridge finished, she brought back the river to its ancient channel. And thus, this trench being made, a

sion in the first chapter. It is impossible for it here to signify the Erythrean, or the Persian gulf, because then it would be necessary to sail up; whereas Herodotus uses the word καταπλέοντες. It is also evident that the winding part of the river was to the north of Babylon, and therefore, if they sailed from the Erythrean, they would come to Babylon before they came to the winding part. It was probably the usual way for those who wished to go to Babylon, to sail to one of the Phœnician harbours, from thence to pass by land to the nearest point of the Euphrates, and embark there and sail down the river to Babylon.

[o] I have followed the explanation of Schweighæuser, which appears to me to be the best.

[p] Ἐκ βάθεος. This alludes to the lake and the canals which rendered the river winding. Ἐξ αὐτῶν has been badly rendered *ex eis*. There are an infinite number of instances in which ἐξ signifies *post*. See Viger. de Idiotismis, cap. ix. 3. *Larcher*.

lake appeared to have been done rightly, and a bridge[q] was built for the use of the inhabitants.

CLXXXVII. The same queen laid this snare for succeeding time: she prepared a sepulchre for herself over the most frequented gate of the city, exposed to open view, with the following inscription: IF ANY ONE OF MY SUCCESSORS, KINGS OF BABYLON, SHOULD FIND HIMSELF IN WANT OF MONEY, LET HIM OPEN THIS SEPULCHRE, AND TAKE AS MUCH AS HE SHALL THINK FIT; BUT IF HE BE NOT REDUCED TO REAL WANT, HE OUGHT TO FORBEAR; OTHERWISE HE SHALL HAVE CAUSE TO REPENT. This monument continued untouched to the reign of Darius; who judging it unreasonable that the gate should remain useless to the inhabitants, (for no man would pass under a dead body,) and an inviting treasure be rendered unserviceable, broke open the sepulchre, and instead of money, found only the body and these words; HADST THOU NOT BEEN INSATIABLY COVETOUS, AND GREEDY OF THE MOST SORDID GAIN, THOU WOULDEST NOT HAVE VIOLATED THE SEPULCHRE OF THE DEAD. And this is the account they give of Nitocris queen of Babylon.

CLXXXVIII. Cyrus made war against Labynetus the son of this queen, who had his name and the kingdom of Assyria from his father. When the great king[r] leads his army in person, he has with him cattle and other provisions in abundance. And more particularly the water of the river Choaspes[s], which flows past Susa, is taken with them, which water alone, and no other, the king drinks. A great number of four-wheeled carriages drawn by mules carry the water of this river, after it has been boiled in silver vessels, and follow him.

CLXXXIX. Cyrus, in his march against Babylon, ar-

[q] Diodorus Siculus represents this bridge as five stades long; but as Strabo assures us, that the Euphrates was only one stade wide, Rollin is of opinion, that the bridge could not be so long as Diodorus says. Although the Euphrates was, generally speaking, no more than one stade in breadth, at the time of a flood it was probably more; and doubtless, the length of the bridge was proportioned to the greatest possible width of the river: this circumstance Rollin does not seem to have considered. The Mansanares, which washes one of the extremities of Madrid, is but a small stream; but as, in the time of the flood, it spreads itself over the neighbouring fields, Philip the Second built a bridge 1100 feet long. This bridge of Nitocris must have been very inferior to ours, its length only excepted; as it consisted only of large masses of stone, piled one upon another, at regular distances, without arches: they were made to communicate by pieces of wood thrown over each pile. *Larcher.*

[r] This was the title by which the Greeks always distinguished the monarchs of Persia. The emperor of Constantinople is at the present day called the Grand Signior. *Larcher.*

[s] Milton, who seldom falls into errors in matters of history, confines the use of the waters of the Choaspes to kings alone, instead of confining kings to the use of those waters. *Paradise Regained,* book ii. Jortin controverts this opinion.

rived at the river Gyndes[t]. The Gyndes rises in the hills of Matiene, and descending through the Dardonians[u], falls into the Tigris; which, passing by the city of Opis, runs out into the Red sea. While Cyrus was endeavouring to pass this same river, which might be crossed in ships, one of the sacred white horses boldly plunged into the stream, and attempted to swim over, but the stream having violently whirled it round, carried it away and drowned it. Cyrus, much offended[x] with the river for this affront, threatened to render his stream so contemptible, that women should pass to either side without wetting their knees. After which menace, deferring his expedition against Babylon, he divided his army into two parts; and having marked out one hundred and eighty channels, by the line, on each side of the river, commanded his men to dig out the earth. His design was indeed executed by the great numbers he employed; but the whole summer was spent in the work.

CXC. Thus Cyrus punished the river Gyndes, by draining the stream into three hundred and sixty trenches; and in the beginning of the next spring advanced with his army towards Babylon. Upon his approach, the Babylonians, who in expectation of his coming had drawn out their forces, gave him battle, and being defeated, were shut up in their city. But having been long acquainted with the restless spirit of Cyrus, and his custom of attacking all nations, without distinction, they had laid up provisions for many years, and were under no apprehensions about a siege. On the other hand, Cyrus himself, finding much time consumed, and his affairs not at all advanced, fell into great doubt what he should do next.

CXCI. When at last, either by the suggestion of some other person, or of his own sagacious invention, he resolved upon the following stratagem. He posted one part of his army near the place where the river enters Babylon, and the rest in another station below, where the same river leaves the

[t] This Gyndes should be the river Mendeli, which descends from the quarter of mount Zagros, and passes by the country of Derne or Derna, probably the Darnea of Herodotus. From the description given by Aristagoras, (book v. ch. 52,) the Diala of modern geography must be the Gyndes. *Rennel.*

Larcher thinks the Mendeli is the modern Gyndes. *Table Geographique.*

[u] Chrytæus, Henry Stephens, and Cellarius, correct this to Darneans; Larcher and Rennel follow this alteration. Breiger conjectures δι' Ἀρμενίων.

[x] This portrait of Cyrus seems a little overcharged. The hatred which the Greeks bore to the Persians is well known. The motive of Cyrus for thus treating the Gyndes could not be such as here described. That which happened to the sacred horse, might make him apprehend a similar fate for the rest of his army, and compel him to divert the river into a great number of channels to make it fordable. A similar example occurs ch. 75. *Larcher.*

The anger of Xerxes towards the Hellespont will occur to every one.

city; with order to enter so soon as they should see the channel passable. Having given this direction, and encouraged his forces, he went with the less effective part of his men to the lake, and did as the queen of Babylon had done. For by opening a large trench, he turned the stream into the lake, which before was stagnant water[7], and by that means the river subsiding, the ancient channel became fordable: which the Persians observing, who were appointed to that purpose close to the channel of the river, when the river had retired so as to be so deep as nearly to reach to a man's thigh, entered the city through the bed of the river. Yet if the Babylonians had been well informed, or had foreseen the attempt of Cyrus, they would doubtless have destroyed his army, and not have supinely suffered the Persians to pass. For if they had shut all the little gates that lead down to the river, and mounted the brickworks that extend along the edge of the river, they might have taken them as if enclosed in a net; whereas, having no suspicion of such a design, they were unexpectedly surprised by the Persians. The extent of the city was such, that, if we may believe the Babylonians, when those who inhabited near the centre were taken, the people that dwelt about the extremities of Babylon heard nothing of their disaster; but were celebrating a festival[8] that day with dancing and all manner of rejoicing, till they received certain information[a] of the general fate. And thus Babylon was the first time taken[b].

CXCII. Among many things which I shall mention, to shew the power and wealth of the Babylonians, this is one. That, whereas all the dominions of the great king are charged with providing subsistence for his person and armies, over

[7] Observe the difference between λίμνη and ἕλος; the latter signifies a standing pool, enclosed on all sides by the land, without any passage to flow out; the former, that into which a river runs, or is joined by a trench, and again flows out. *Wesseling*.

[8] This brings to mind the feast of Belshazzar, described in Daniel, ch. v. ver. 1. "Belshazzar the king made a great "feast to a thousand lords, and drank "wine before the thousand," &c. They were profaning the sacred vessels, brought by Nebuchadnezzar from the temple at Jerusalem; and praising the Gods of silver, of brass, of iron, when the miraculous hand-writing appeared on the wall, from which Daniel foretold the destruction of the kingdom of Babylon, and the transferring of the empire to the Medes and Persians.—"In that night "was Belshazzar slain, and Darius the "Median took the kingdom." This Darius is supposed by the most judicious chronologers to be the same with Cyaxares, son of Astyages, whom Cyrus, as Xenophon (Cyrop. book vii. ch. 5.) relates, made king of the Chaldeans.

This account of the taking of Babylon exactly agrees with that given by Xenophon, and they both accord with the account in the sacred writings. See Rollin.

[a] They who were in the citadel did not know of the capture of the place till the break of day; which is not at all improbable: but that which Aristotle affirms exceeds belief, viz. that even on the third day it was not known in some quarters of the town that Babylon was taken. *Larcher*.

[b] It was again taken by Darius. See book iii. ch. 159.

and above the usual tribute; the territory of Babylon contributes as much as is sufficient for four of the twelve months that make up the year, all the rest of Asia furnishing no more than for eight months only; so that the country of Assyria[c] alone is accounted equivalent to one half of all the other parts of Asia. The government of this region, which the Persians call a satrapy, is much more considerable than any other, and yielded an artabe of silver every day to Tritæchmes the son of Artabazus, who was appointed governor by the king. The artabe is a Persian measure, containing three chœnices more than the attic medimnus. Besides this revenue, and his horses for war, a stud of eight hundred stallions, and sixteen thousand mares, one horse to twenty mares, was kept for him at the expence of the country; and his Indian dogs[d] were so many, that four considerable towns in the plain were exempted from all other taxes, on condition to provide food for those animals. Such advantages belonged to the governor of Babylon.

CXCIII. The land of Assyria is but little watered by rain, and the root of the corn is nourished by other means; it grows up by being watered from the river, and the corn becomes ripe; but not, as in Egypt, by the river overflowing[e] the fields, but by the hands of men and watering engines. For all the country about Babylon is, like Egypt, divided by frequent canals[f]; of which the largest is navigable, and beginning at the Euphrates, has a south-eastern direction, and falls into the river Tigris, on which the city of Nineveh formerly stood. No part of the known world produces so good wheat; but the vine, the olive, and the fig-tree, they do not even attempt to cultivate. Yet in recompence it abounds so much in corn, as to yield at all times two-hundred fold, and even three-hundred fold, when it is most fruitful. Wheat and barley carry a blade full four digits in breadth; and though I well know to what a surprising height millet and sesama grow in

[c] This province is excellently described by Gibbon, *Decline and Fall*, ch. 24.

[d] These were very celebrated. The ancients in general believed them to be produced from a bitch and a tyger. *Larcher*.

[e] The Euphrates does occasionally overflow its banks, but its inundations do not, like those of the Nile, communicate fertility. "The streams of the Euphrates and the Tigris do not," says Pliny, "leave behind them the mud, "which the Nile does in Egypt." *Larch.*

[f] The use of these artificial canals were various and important: they served to discharge the superfluous waters from one river into the other, at the seasons of their respective inundations; subdividing themselves into smaller and smaller branches, they refreshed the dry lands, and supplied the deficiency of rain. They facilitated the intercourse of peace and commerce; and as the dams could be speedily broken down, they armed the despair of the Assyrians with the means of opposing a sudden deluge to the progress of an invading army. *Gibbon.*

those parts, I shall be silent in that particular; because I am well assured, that what has already been related concerning other fruits is far from credible to those who have never been at Babylon. They use no other oil than such as is drawn from sesama. The palm-tree grows over all the plain; and the greater part bears fruit; with which they make bread, wine, and honey. This tree is cultivated[g] as the fig-tree; and they tie the fruit of that which the Grecians call the male palm, about those trees that bear dates, to the end that the worm may enter and ripen the fruit, lest otherwise the fruit fall before maturity; for the fruit of the male palm, like that of the wild fig-tree, produces a worm.

CXCIV. But the thing, which, next to the city, seems most wonderful to me, is this: the vessels that descend the river to Babylon are round, and composed of skins[h]. For when they have cut the ribs out of willows growing in the hills of Armenia above Babylon, they cover them with hides extended on the outside, to serve for a bottom; making no distinction of stem or stern. These vessels thus shaped in the form of a buckler, they stow with reeds, and venture upon the river, freighted with merchandize, and especially with casks of palm-wine. They are directed by two men standing upright with a pole in the hand of each, one pulling to, and the other putting off from himself: some of these boats are very large, and others of a less size; but the most capacious carry the weight of five thousand talents. Every vessel has an ass on board, and the greatest more. For after they arrive at Babylon, and have disposed of their goods, they sell the ribs of the boat with the reeds; and loading the hides on the asses, return by land to Armenia, the river not being naviga-

[g] On this subject Larcher has a note of considerable length. Pococke informs us, that "the male bears a large branch "something like millet, which is full of "a white flour, and unless the young "fruit of the female is impregnated with "it, the fruit is good for nought. And "to secure it, they tie a piece of the "fruit of the male to every bearing "branch of the female."

[h] The same kind of embarkation is now in use in the lower parts of the same river, under the name of *kufah*; (that is, a *round vessel*;) but they are most commonly daubed over with bitumen, skins being very seldom used; being perhaps much scarcer than formerly. These *kufah* are exactly in the form of a *sieve*, and require only a few inches depth of water to float in. The reader will immediately recollect the Welsh *corricles*, and the boats of reeds and willows made in other parts of the world. The *ark*, that is, the cradle of Moses, was formed of the *bulrush*, or reed of the Nile, and daubed over with *pitch*; we may suppose, *bitumen*, (Exod. ii. 3.) *Rennel.*

Lucan alludes to the same;

Primum cana salix, madefacto vimine, parvam
Texitur in puppim; cæsoque inducta juvenco,
Vectoris patiens, tumidum supernatat amnem.
Sic Venetus stagnante Pado, fusoque Britannus
Navigat oceano; sic cum tenet omnia Nilus,
Conseritur bibula Memphitis cymba papyro. Pharsal. lib. iv. 131.

These boats however do not appear to have been lined with reeds.

ble upwards, by reason of the rapidity of the stream. For this cause they use skins rather than timber in fitting up these vessels; and at their return to Armenia with their asses, they build more after the same manner. The boats then are of this kind.

CXCV. For their dress, they wear a linen tunic[i] which reaches down to the foot, upon which they have a vest of woollen cloth, and a white mantle over all. Their shoes are made in a fashion peculiar to the country, not unlike those of the Bœotians[k]. They wear long hair, covering the head with a mitre, and anoint the whole body with perfumed oils. Every man has a ring with a signet, and a staff curiously wrought; on the top of which is placed either an apple, a rose, a lily, an eagle, or some other thing; for to wear a stick without such an ornament, is accounted improper[l].

CXCVI. They have the following institutions; and this one is, in my opinion, the wisest; which I hear the Venetians, a nation of Illyricum, likewise use. In every district this custom used to be observed every year. When they had assembled all the virgins of a marriageable age, they used to lead them in a body to one place. A crowd of men used to collect around. The crier used to make them to stand up, and sell them one after another[m], beginning with the most beautiful; and when she had been sold for a great sum of money, he used to put up the one who was next in beauty. They were sold on condition that they should be married. On this occasion the richest of the Babylonians who were desirous of marrying, used to outbid one another, and purchase

[i] Herodotus not only calls linen those which are made of flax, (*ex lino*,) but those which are made of cotton. A very similar dress among the Egyptians is mentioned, book ii. ch. 81. *Schweigh.*

[k] The Bœotian shoe was made of wood, and was a kind of Cothurnus which came up part of the leg. They were called κρουπίζια.

[l] The kings of Greece wore on their sceptres the figure of a bird, and often that of an eagle. The monarchs of Asia had the same custom. The eagle is always represented as crowning the summit of Jupiter's sceptre. See Pindar, Pyth. Od. i. ver. 10. *Larcher.*

[m] Herodotus here omits one circumstance, of consequence in my opinion, to prove that this ceremony passed with decency. It was conducted under the eyes of the magistrates; and the tribunal, whose office it was (Strabo, lib. xvi.) to take cognizance of the crime of adultery, superintended the marriage of the young women. Three men, respectable for their virtue, and who were at the head of their several tribes, conducted the young women that were marriageable to the place of the assembly, and there sold them by the voice of the public crier. *Larcher.*

If the custom of disposing of young women to the best bidder was peculiar to the Babylonians, that of purchasing the person intended for a wife was much more common. It was practised amongst the Greeks, the Trojans, and their allies, and even amongst the Deities. See Homer's Iliad, ix. 145. xii. 366. xvi. 178. 190. xxii. 472. Odyssey, vii. 318. Vulcan gave a great price to Jupiter in order to obtain his daughter Venus: when he surprised her with Mars, he refused to release them until Jupiter had restored all he had received for her. *Bellanger.*

the handsomest. But the lower people had no need of a beautiful form, but used to take the more ugly with a sum of money. For when the herald had sold all the handsome ones, he used to make the most deformed stand up, and demand, who would marry her with the least sum; until she was assigned to the man who engaged to take the least. This money was obtained from the *sale of* the beautiful virgins, and thus the handsome portioned out the ugly and deformed. A father was not allowed to give his daughter in marriage to whom he pleased, neither might the purchaser carry off the woman, without having brought forward some people to be security, that he would certainly live with her as his wife; if they did not agree, a law was enacted that the money should be restored. It was lawful for any one who pleased, to come from another district to purchase. Such was their best institution; it has not continued to exist. They have lately adopted another regulation to prevent them from treating the women unjustly, and carrying them away to another city. Since the taking of the city, in which they suffered great misfortunes, and were ruined in their private fortunes, all the meaner sort, from want of a livelihood, prostitute their daughters.

CXCVII. They have also this other custom, which is second on the score of prudence. All sick persons[n] are brought out into the most frequented places, (for they use no physicians,) and as those, who come thither, always inquire concerning the disease of the patient, when they find that they have been afflicted with the same, or have seen others in a like condition, they advise him to do as they did to cure themselves, or as others they knew had done in the same case. For, to pass silently before the sick, without inquiring into the nature of their distemper, is among them accounted a crime.

CXCVIII. They embalm the dead in honey, and their funeral lamentations are like those of the Egyptians. When a Babylonian has had communication[o] with his wife, he burns

[n] We may from hence observe the first rude commencement of the science of medicine. Syrianus is of opinion, that this science originated in Egypt, from those persons who had been disordered in any part of their bodies, writing down the remedies from which they received benefit. *Larcher.*

Herodotus (book ii. ch. 84.) tells us, that they had a separate physician for each disease, which may support the opinion of Syrianus.

[o] It seems most probable that the legislator, who appointed these purifications, wished to infuse an exalted idea of chastity, so difficult to practise in such a climate. I much approve of the reply of Theano, wife of Pythagoras. A person inquired of her, what time was required for a woman to become pure, after having had communication with a man. "She is pure immediately" replied Theano, "if the man be her husband, but if not, no time will make her "so." *Larcher.*

incense, sitting on one side, while she does the same on the other; and about break of day they go both into a bath, as the Arabians likewise do, refusing to touch any vessel till they have washed.

CXCIX. Nevertheless they have one established custom, which is infamous in the highest degree. For every woman is obliged, once in her life, to sit down openly in the temple of Venus, in order to prostitute herself to some stranger[p]. Yet because the most wealthy disdain to expose themselves in public among the rest, many come in covered chariots to the gates of the temple, and make that their station, with a numerous train of servants attending at a distance. But the far greater part enter into the temple, and sit down crowned with a circle of cords, some continually going out, and others coming in. The galleries where they sit are built in a straight line, and open on every side, that all strangers may have a free passage to choose such women as they like best. When a woman has seated herself, she must not return home till some stranger throw a piece of silver into her lap, and lie with her at a distance from the temple; using this form as he gives her the money; *I beseech the Goddess Mylitta*[q] *to favour thee:* for the Assyrians call Venus by that name. The law forbids any woman to refuse this present, how small soever, because such money is accounted sacred; and commands her to follow the first that offers it, without rejecting any man. Having satisfied this obligation, and performed her duty to the Goddess, she returns home; and after that time is never more to be obtained by any presents, how great soever. Those women who excel in beauty and shape are soon dismissed; but the deformed are sometimes necessitated to wait

[p] This, as an historical fact, is questioned by some, and by Voltaire in particular; but it is mentioned by Jeremiah who lived two centuries before Herodotus, and by Strabo who lived long after him; so also Barrich, vi. 42. "The women also with cords about them sitting "in the ways, burn bran for perfume. "But if any of them, drawn by some that "passeth by, lie with him, she reproach"eth her fellow, that she was not thought "as worthy as herself, nor her cord "broken." Married women and their daughters prostituted themselves at Heliopolis in Phœnicia, in honour of Venus, and at several other places. Voltaire's objection is stated and answered by Larcher in a note of considerable length.

Mr. Bryant remarks, that instead of women, it should probably be read virgins; and that this custom was universally kept up wherever the Persian religion prevailed.

Strabo is more particular: "not only," says he, "the men and maidservants "prostitute themselves, people of the "first fashion devote in the same man"ner their own daughters. Nor is any "body at all scrupulous about cohabit"ing with a woman who has been thus "abused."

"Truly," says Voltaire, "it must "have been a fine solemnity and very "devotional, to see merchants of camels, "horses, &c. running into the churches "to lay before the altar with the prin"cipal ladies of the city."

[q] Mylitta, or Mylidath, is a Chaldaic word, which according to Scaliger signifies *genetrix*, which is an epithet of Venus. *Larcher*.

three or four years, before they can satisfy the law. The Cyprians have a custom not unlike to this in some parts of the island.

CC. The Babylonians have three tribes among them, who eat nothing but fish; which they order in this manner: when they have taken and dried the fish in the sun, they throw them in a mortar: and after having reduced the whole substance to a kind of meal, with a pestle, they sift it through a piece of fine cloth; and then those who wish, make it up as cakes or bake it as bread.

CCI. Cyrus, having subdued this nation, grew very desirous of conquering the Massagetæ, who are accounted a great and a valiant people. They inhabit towards the east and the rising-sun beyond the river Araxes, over against the Issedonians; and some say they are Scythians[r].

CCII. Many think the Araxes to be greater than the Ister, and others less; containing, as they say, divers islands, equal to Lesbos in circumference, and inhabited by men, who during the summer feed upon all manner of roots, which they dig out of the ground; and for their winter provision lay up the ripe fruits they find upon the trees. They add, that a certain tree growing in this country produces fruit of such a nature, that when the inhabitants meet together in company, and throw a quantity of it upon the fire, they become intoxicated as they sit round the steam, no less than the Grecians by drinking wine; that the more they fling on, the drunker they grow, until they rise up to dance and sing. In this manner these islanders are reported to live. The Araxes[s]

[r] It would appear that Herodotus was not decided in his opinion whether or no the Massagetæ were to be regarded as a Scythian nation; but subsequent writers have almost universally reckoned them so. So that the *proper* Scythians of Herodotus were those of the Euxine; and those of succeeding writers, at the Caspian (or rather the Aral) and Jaxartes. For our author, who calls the Massagetæ a great and powerful nation, says, "they are by *some* esteemed a Scythian "nation;" and that, "in their clothes "and food they *resemble* the Scythians;" implying that they were not confessedly a Scythian nation. He says moreover, what the Greeks assert *in general* of the *Scythians*, is true only of the Massagetæ. Clio, 201, 215, 216. *Rennel*, 47.

See also pag. 132 and 217 of his learned work.

[s] Herodotus falls into a great mistake respecting the source of the Jaxartes, which he calls Araxes. In his description the Jaxartes and Oxus (Sirr and Jihon) are confounded together; (he had perhaps heard certain particulars of both rivers, but might refer them to one only;) for there are circumstances that may be applied to each, respectively, although most of them are applicable only to the former. It may be observed that our author mentions only one large river in this part of the empire of Cyrus; that is, the river which separates it from the Massagetæ, which is unquestionably the Sirr or Jaxartes; for there is no question that Sogdia was included in the empire of Cyrus; and it lay *between* the Oxus and Jaxartes. The Oxus therefore has no *distinct* place in the geography of our author, although of much greater bulk and importance than the Jaxartes. But that the Oxus was intended, when he says that the larger stream continued its even course to the Caspian, appears *probable*; although the numerous branches that formed the large islands, and were

descends from the hills of Matiene, (as I observed before of the river Gyndes, which Cyrus turned into three hundred and sixty trenches,) and, except one stream which runs into the Caspian sea, without any impediment, discharges all its waters by forty several passages into certain fens and lakes; where it is said the inhabitants feed only upon raw fish, and clothe themselves in the skins of sea-calves. The Caspian is a sea by itself, having no communication with any other sea; whereas, that which the Grecians navigate, together with the Red sea, and the Atlantic, lying beyond the columns of Hercules, are but one sea.

CCIII. The length of the Caspian[t] is as much as a vessel with oars can make in fifteen days; and to cross the breadth in the widest part, requires eight. This sea is bounded on the west by mount Caucasus, the greatest and highest of all mountains; containing many different nations, who for the most part live upon such things as the earth produces without cultivation. In this country, it is said, they have a certain tree, the leaf of which, when bruised and diluted with water, serves to paint the figures of various things on their garments with a colour that never fades; that these figures are not washed out by water, but continue to wear, as if they had been woven in the cloth; and that these people never conceal themselves when they use the company of women, any more than do cattle.

CCIV. Mount Caucasus, as I said before, is extended on the west of the Caspian sea; and on the east, towards the

afterwards lost in bogs and marshes, agrees rather to the description of the *Aral* lake and lower part of the *Sirr*. It is indeed possible, that the *Jaxartes* may, at some period, have sent a branch into the *Oxus*; or vice versa, the *Oxus* into the *Jaxartes*; but no such idea is warranted by the ancients.

The remarkable mistake of our author's deriving this Araxes from the mountains of Matiene, and giving it an *easterly* course (Melp. 40.) must have arisen from his having heard of the Armenian Araxes, and confounded it with the other. There is no possibility of getting rid of his error in this matter; for he refers the source of the Massagetan Araxes to the same quarter with that of the Gyndes. It can only be said that it is a prodigious mistake. *Rennel*, p. 204. seq.

[t] This Herodotus rightly describes as a sea, distinct from all others; that is, a lake. The dimensions given are not very different from the truth; only that the width is too great if meant for the Caspian alone; but as Alexander, and all geographers from his time, to that of Delisle, included the *Aral* as a part of the Caspian, it is probable that Herodotus did the same, since he conducts the Jaxartes into the *Caspian*, and not into a *separate lake*. The real length of this sea is about 640 Gr. miles in N. by W. and S. by E. direction: and it contracts to less than 130 miles at the northern neck, and to about 100 at the southern. This knowledge concerning the unconnected state of the Caspian was lost in the time of Eratosthenes, Strabo and Pliny, but regained in that of Ptolemy. *Rennel*, p. 193. seq.

[u] Τὰ πολλὰ πάντα is properly taken adverbially. Τὰ πολλὰ has the same meaning as ὡς ἐπὶ πολὺ, *generally, for the most part;* and with the addition of *πάντα, by far the most part:* they scarcely live upon any thing else than what the earth spontaneously produces. *Schweigh.*

rising of the sun, a plain which presents no limit to the eye, succeeds. The greater part of this country is inhabited by the Massagetæ, against whom Cyrus was so vehemently inclined to make war. The motives that pushed him on to this enterprize were many and powerful; principally, because his birth had inspired him with an opinion that he was something above a man; and secondly, the good fortune which had so constantly attended him in all his military expeditions, that wherever Cyrus turned his arms, it was impossible for that nation to escape.

CCV. The Massagetæ were at this time under the government of Tomyris, who had been wife to their last king; and this gave Cyrus a pretext to send ambassadors to her, with proposals of marriage in his name. But Tomyris, believing he only courted the kingdom, and not her person, sent to forbid them to proceed in their journey. Upon this Cyrus, perceiving his artifice ineffectual, pulled off the mask; and openly advancing with his army against the Massagetæ, arrived at the river Araxes; over which he laid bridges of boats for the passage of his forces, and fortified with towers the boats which carried over part of his army.

CCVI. Whilst he was employed in this work, Tomyris sent him a message by a herald in these terms: "King of "the Medes, desist from the enterprize thou hast begun with "so great diligence; for thou art not sure the end will prove "fortunate. Be contented to govern thy own dominions, and "suffer us to rule the country we possess. But if thou wilt "not hearken to my counsel, and art resolved to prefer every "thing before peace; in a word, if thou hast so great a desire "to make trial of thy forces against the Massagetæ, toil no "longer to build bridges over the Araxes; but pass boldly to "this side, whilst I retire with my army full three days' "march from the river: or, if this condition please thee not, "receive us into thy territories on the same terms." When Cyrus heard this message, he called a council of all the principal Persians; and after he had laid the proposal before them, and demanded their opinion, they unanimously advised him to let Tomyris pass with her army into his dominions.

CCVII. But Crœsus the Lydian, who was present in the assembly, disapproving their counsel, delivered a contrary opinion in these words: "O king, in pursuance of the pro"mise I made you, when Jupiter delivered me into your "hands, I will always to the uttermost of my power endea"vour to prevent the misfortunes I see impending over your "head; and my own calamities[x], however severe, have con-

[x] This appears to have been a proverb παθήματα μαθήματα.

"tributed something to my instruction. If you think yourself immortal, and your army to have the like prerogative, it is needless for me to tell you my opinion. But if you know you are no more than a man, and that the forces you command are men likewise, consider, in the first place, that the continual rotation of human affairs never suffers the same person to be always prosperous. For this, and other reasons, I am obliged to dissent from the advice of all this assembly touching the question now before us. For if we shall receive the enemy into this country, there is in that plan this danger; that you, if you are defeated, will also lose all your dominions; because no man can imagine that after such a victory the Massagetæ would presently retire with their forces; but rather immediately fall upon your territories: and if you should conquer, the victory will not be so important, as if, having crossed the river, you should have conquered the Massagetæ, and pursued them in their flight; for to that, I oppose this, that if you are victorious, you will immediately march into the heart of the dominions of Tomyris. Besides, the disgrace is too great and intolerable, for Cyrus the son of Cambyses to retreat before a woman. My opinion therefore is, that you would resolve to pass the river; and when you are advanced near the enemy, then to use the following stratagem, in order to surprise their forces. I have heard the Massagetæ live hardly, and are unacquainted with the luxuries of the Persians. And therefore I advise, that great numbers of cattle, killed and dressed, with plenty of unmixed wine, and all other provisions in abundance, should be prepared in our camp for these men; and that, leaving the weakest of our forces behind, all the rest should return towards the river; for the Massagetæ, if I mistake not, when they see so much exquisite fare, will turn to immediately, and by that means afford us an occasion of striking a blow of importance."

CCVIII. Of these two opinions, Cyrus rejected the first; and approving that of Crœsus, sent a message to Tomyris, requiring her to retire, whilst he should pass the Araxes with his army. The queen, mindful of her promise, did as he desired; and after Cyrus had committed the care of the kingdom, and of Crœsus, to his son Cambyses[y], commanded him, if the expedition against the Massagetæ should prove unfortunate, to honour Crœsus, and treat him with favour, he dismissed both, with orders to return to Persia, and passed the river with all his forces.

[y] When the Persian kings went on any expedition, it was customary with them to name their successor, in order to prevent the confusion unavoidably arising from their dying without having done so. See book vii. Init. *Larcher.*

CCIX. Cyrus having passed the Araxes, entered the country of the Massagetæ, and in the night dreamt he saw the eldest son of Hystaspes with wings on his shoulders; which he spread, and shaded Asia with one, and Europe with the other. Hystaspes the son of Arsames was of the Achæmenian blood, and the name of his eldest son was Darius; who having then scarce attained to the age of twenty years, had been left in Persia, as too young to sustain the hardships of war. Cyrus, when he awoke, considered his dream with attention; and judging it to be of the last consequence, sent for Hystaspes, and taking him aside, said, "Hystaspes, thy son "has formed a design against me and my government, and I "will tell thee how I know this with certainty. The Gods, "solicitous for my preservation, ever give me timely notice "of all impending dangers: and therefore last night, as I "slept, I saw in a dream the eldest of thy sons, having wings "on his shoulders; with one of which he covered Europe, "and Asia with the other. Since then I have seen this vi-"sion, it is impossible that your son has not formed designs "against me; I therefore order thee to return immediately "to Persia, and to take care, that when I come home with "victory, you bring your son before me to be examined."

CCX. These words Cyrus said, in a full persuasion that Darius had formed a design against him: but the Deity by this previous admonition signified, that he should die in the enterprise he had undertaken, and that his kingdom should devolve upon Darius. Hystaspes answered, "God forbid, O "king, that one who is born a Persian should conspire "against thee! But if any such be found, may sudden destruc-"tion overtake him. For thou hast not only enfranchised the "Persians, who before were servants, but advanced them "from the condition of slaves, to the power of commanding "other nations; and therefore if any vision has represented "my son as contriving any thing against thee, I freely sur-"render him to be treated in the manner thou shalt com-"mand." Having made this answer, Hystaspes repassed the river Araxes, and went to Persia, in order to watch over his son Darius for Cyrus.

CCXI. In the mean time Cyrus advanced one day's march beyond the river; and afterwards, pursuant to the counsel of Crœsus, retired again with all his best troops; leaving only the worst of his men behind him. These the Massagetæ attacked with a third part of their army, and, after some resistance, cut in pieces. Which having done, and having perceived a plentiful feast prepared, they eat and drank to such excess, that they fell asleep upon the spot. In this condition they were surprised by the Persians, who killed many, and took a greater number prisoners; among them Spargapises, son to Tomyris, and general of the Massagetæ.

CCXII. The queen, having learnt the misfortune of her son and one part of her army, sent a herald to Cyrus with a message in these words: "O Cyrus, insatiable of blood, " be not elate with the late event, if, by the fruit of the vine, " which none of you can bear without raving, and which never " enters into your bodies without bringing up all manner of " unbecoming language; if, I say, by this treacherous poison, " thou hast circumvented my son, instead of conquering him " by valour in the field. However, for the present, take the " best council I can give. Restore my son; depart out of " this country, and rest satisfied with having insolently dis-" graced[z] a third part of the army of the Massagetæ. But if " thou wilt not do these things, I swear by the sun, who is " the Lord of the Massagetæ, to give thee blood enough, in-" satiable as thou art."

CCXIII. After this message, which had no effect upon Cyrus, Spargapises, the son of Tomyris, being recovered from his wine, and perceiving the disaster that was fallen upon him, begged of Cyrus to be unbound; and having obtained his request, no sooner found his hands at liberty, than he immediately killed himself.

CCXIV. But Tomyris, finding her advice slighted by Cyrus, assembled all her forces, and engaged the Persians in a battle; which I think to have been the most obstinate that ever was fought by barbarians. At first, as I am informed, whilst the two armies were at a distance, they sent showers of arrows upon each other; and after they had quite emptied their quivers, and thrown all their javelins, they joined in close fight with their swords and spears. In this manner they continued for a long time fighting with equal fury: but at length the Massagetæ had the victory, most of the Persian army being cut in pieces, and Cyrus himself killed in the place, after he had reigned twenty-nine years. Tomyris found the body of Cyrus among the slain; and having cut off the head, threw it into a vessel filled with human blood, which she had purposely prepared; saying in an insulting manner, "Thou hast indeed ruined me, though I am alive and have " conquered thee in battle, since thou hast destroyed my son " by stratagem; but I will now, as I threatened, glut thee " with blood[a]." Such was the end of Cyrus; and though

[z] Καθυβρίσας; Ὑβρίζω frequently governs a dative case; καθυβρίζω rarely. There is, however, another example in Soph. Ajax. 153. *Larcher*.

[a] With this story of Cyrus that of the Roman Crassus nearly corresponds. The wealth of Crassus was only to be equalled by his avarice. He was taken prisoner in an expedition against the Parthians, who poured melted gold down his

many other things are said of him[b], I have restrained my relation to these, which to me seem best attested.

CCXV. The Massagetæ resemble the Scythians in their habit and way of living: they have both horse and foot in their armies; their weapons of war are arrows, javelins, and battle-axes; they make use of brass and gold for all things; for the blade of their scymetar is brass, and their javelins and arrows are pointed with the same metal; but the coverings of their heads and the belts, which they wear round their waists and over their shoulders[c], are adorned with gold. They arm their horses with a breastplate of brass, and the bridle, with all the rest of the furniture, is enriched with gold. They use no silver nor iron, for neither of those metals are found in their country, but brass and gold are found in abundance.

CCXVI. As for their manners, every one marries a wife; but they lie with those women in common; and the Grecians mistake, when they attribute this custom to the Scythians, which is peculiar to the Massagetæ; among whom, whenever a man desires to have the company of a woman, he hangs up his quiver[d] at the head of his chariot, and uses her without shame. The years of life are not limited by any law. But after a man has attained to old age, all his relations meet, and sacrifice him[e], with cattle of several kinds; and when they

throat, in order, as they said, that he, whose thirst of gold could never be satisfied when he was alive, might be filled with it when dead. *Beloe.*

[b] Xenophon (Cyrop. 8.) makes Cyrus die peaceably in his bed; Strabo inclines to this opinion. Lucian says, that he died when more than a hundred years old, from grief that his son Cambyses had caused most of his friends to be put to death. On his tomb there was this inscription: "Man, I am Cyrus, the son of "Cambyses; I acquired the empire of "Persia, and I reigned over Asia; be "not then jealous of my monument." *Larcher.*

[c] Μασχαλιστὴρ: this word is derived from *μασχάλα, axilla;* for the proper meaning of the word see Bloomfield's Glossary to the Prometheus Vinctus of Æschylus, 71.

[d] Amongst the Nasamones, in Africa, whose habits were nearly the same, a *staff* was fixed in the ground before the *tent* as a signal of privacy; Melp. 172. Dowe says, in his dissertation prefixed to his Indian History, p.37, that the Facquirs of some part of India leave one of their *slippers* at the door, when engaged in certain visits, in which they are supposed to be privileged by the *sanctity* of their order. Some of our ancestors are accused of the same want of delicacy as the Messagetæ and the Nasamones; but we have no particular record of their domestic customs. Herodotus acquits the Western Scythians of this custom so contrary to decency and sentiment. *Rennel*, p. 78.

[e] Hellanicus, speaking of the Hyperboreans, who lived beyond the Rhipean mountains, observes, that they learn justice, that they eat no meat, but live entirely on fruit. Those of sixty years of age they carry out of the town, and put to death. Timæus says, that in Sardinia, when a man has passed seventy years, his sons, in honour of Saturn, and with seeming satisfaction, beat out his brains with clubs, and throw him down a precipice. The inhabitants of Julis, in the isle of Ceos, oblige those who are past sixty to drink hemlock, &c. However improbable this custom may appear, it is practised at the present day in the kingdom of Aracan; "The inhabitants of this "country" (Natural and Civil History of "Siam) accelerate the death of their "friends and relations, when they see "him afflicted by a painful old age or "incurable disease; it is with them an "act of piety." *Larcher.*

have boiled all the flesh together, they sit down as to a feast. This death they account the most happy; for they never eat the bodies of those who die by sickness; but bury them in the earth, and think it a great misfortune that they did not attain to be sacrificed. Their drink is milk; and they sow nothing; contenting themselves with the flesh of animals, and fish, which the river Araxes yields in abundance. They adore the sun only of all the Gods, and sacrifice horses[f] to this deity; judging it most proper to offer the swiftest of all animals to the swiftest of all the Gods.

[f] This was a very ancient custom; it was practised in Persia in the time of Cyrus, (Xenoph. Cyrop. viii. 3.) and was probably anterior to his time. Horses were thrown into the sea and rivers in honour of Neptune, (Iliad xxi. 132.) *Larcher.*

Placat equo Persis radiis Hyperiona cinctum,
Ne detur celeri victima tarda Deo.
Ovid.

It is unquestionable that there is a great similarity between many of the customs of the Messagetæ and those of the Scythians; which can only be referred to imitation. We shall only enumerate a few of them. Not to mention the Nomadu life common to both, which might also have been followed by others in North Asia, we shall only observe,

1. That the *clothes* and *food* of the *Massagetæ* resemble those of the *Scythians*, chap. 215.

2. That both nations lived in *waggons*, or carriages; Clio, 216. Melp. 46, 121.

3. That they fought chiefly or horseback; Clio, 215. Melp. 46, 136.

4. That they sacrificed *horses* to their deities. The Messagetæ in particular to the sun. Clio, 216. Melp. 61.

It however happens, unfortunately, that Herodotus is much too brief in his account of the Massagetæ, to allow any great scope for comparison; otherwise it is probable that more points of resemblance might be found. *Rennel*, p. 78.

The following account of an important point of history may serve to illustrate chapter 145. Hellen, son of Deucalion, reigned in Phthia, between the Peneus and the Asopus. (Strabo viii. p. 587.) He left his estates to his eldest son, and sent the others to seek settlements elsewhere. Dorus estabalised himself in the neighbourhood to Parnassus, and gave his own name to the people who assembled there. Xuthus passed into Attica, where he espoused a daughter of Erectheus. Pausanias, (Achaic. sive lib. vii. 1.) relates that Xuthus was expelled from Thessaly by his brothers, because he endeavoured to obtain his father's wealth. Both historians however agree, that he went to Attica, where he married the daughter of Erectheus, king of the country, by whom he had two sons, Achæus and Ion. Achæus, having committed an involuntary homicide, passed into Laconia, and the Lacedæmonians and Argians were called from him *Achæi*, till the return of the Heraclidæ. Attica became at this time very populous and hardly able to support its inhabitants.

The Athenians (Strabo viii. p. 588.) sent a colony into the Peloponnese, under the conduct of Ion. This colony settled at Ægialeia, which is situated along the coast, between Elis and Sicyonia.

Ion was afterwards recalled by the Athenians to take the command of their armies, against the Thracians, who under Eumolpus had possessed themselves of Eleusis. The oracle had promised victory to Erectheus, if he would sacrifice his daughter. He did not hesitate, and the Thracians were defeated. Euripides has made the sacrifice of this female the subject of a Tragedy, called Erectheus. The Athenians, to acknowledge the services of Ion, gave him the chief part of the government, and called themselves Ionians from him.

He divided the Athenians into four tribes, Geleontes, Argades, Ægicores and Hopletes; from the names of his four sons.

After the death of Erectheus a contest arose between his children concerning the succession to the throne. (Pausan. Achaic. sive vii. 1.) Xuthus, being chosen umpire, adjudged the crown to Cecrops the elder. Achæus did not remain long in Laconia. He passed into Thessaly with some troops from Ægialeia and Athens, and recovered the estates of his fathers. Two of his children, Archander and Achiteles, left Phthiotis, and went to Argos, where they married two daughters of Danaus, a prince of Argos. The Achæans remained in this country, till the return of the Heraclidæ who expelled them. They retired into Ægialeia, where the Ionians kindly received them, on account of their common origin. Jealousy soon arose between them, and the Ionians were compelled to abandon the country to the Achæans, who preserved the Ionian divisions, but called it, from themselves, Achæa.

The Ionians (Pausan. Achaic. cap. 1.) returned into Attica, where they were received by Melanthus, who had deposed Thymœtes, and obtained the kingdom. They continued in that country under his reign, and under that of Codrus his successor. The sovereign power having been abolished in Athens after the death of Codrus, Neleus, his youngest son, passed into Asia Minor, and led with him the Ionians. *Larcher.*

THE HISTORY OF HERODOTUS.

BOOK II.

EUTERPE.

AFTER the death of Cyrus, Cambyses succeeded him in the kingdom. He was the son of Cyrus, and of Cassandane the daughter of Pharnaspes; who having died some time before, Cyrus deeply lamented her, and commanded all his subjects to exhibit signs of mourning[a]. Born of these parents, Cambyses having considered the Ionians and Æolians as his servants by inheritance, made an expedition against Egypt, having taken with him his other subjects; and particularly the Greeks, whom he also ruled over.

II. The Egyptians, before the reign of Psammetichus, thought themselves the most ancient[b] people of all the world. But since the experiment he made, to find out the truth of that matter, they have yielded the priority to the Phrygians, still esteeming themselves the second in antiquity. For after Psammetichus had long endeavoured in vain to discover who were the first men, he at last contrived this expedient. He took two children newly born of poor parents, and putting them into the hands of a shepherd to be brought up among his flocks, commanded him not to permit any one to speak in their hearing; but to lay them in a solitary cottage by themselves; to bring them goats to suck at certain times, and when he should perceive they were satiated with milk, to

[a] Admetus paid this tribute of respect to the memory of his deceased wife Alcestis. See Eurip. Alcest. 425.

[b] There is no doubt but that Egypt is one of the most anciently peopled countries in the world. The subject of their claims to antiquity is impartially discussed by Larcher in his Essay on Chronology.

attend to his other employments. These orders Psammetichus gave, that he might be informed what word would first break from the children, when the inarticulate sounds of infancy should have ceased; and the success was answerable to his expectation. For at the end of two years, as the shepherd, to whose care they were committed, was one day entering the cottage, and had already opened the door, both the children ran to him, and, holding out their hands, cried Becos[c]. The shepherd, when he first heard it, said nothing; but when this same word was always repeated to him when he went and attended to the children, he acquainted the king with what had happened, and by his command brought the children into his presence. Psammetichus having heard the same, inquired in the next place if any nation made use of the word Becos: and when he found by inquiry that the Phrygians call bread[d] by that name, the Egyptians consented to take this for a proof, that the Phrygians[e] were the more ancient people.

III. This relation I had at Memphis from the priests of Vulcan. But the Greeks, among many other ridiculous things, report, that Psammetichus delivered these children to be brought up by certain women, whose tongues he caused to be cut out. Divers other things I heard at Memphis, in several conferences I had with the priests of Vulcan. And on this very account I went in particular to Thebes[f], and to Heliopolis[g], in

[c] These infants in all probability pronounced the word *Bec*, the cry of the goats, which they endeavoured to imitate, *os* being a termination appropriate to the Greek language. In the fifteenth century James IV. of Scotland confined two infants in the isle of Inckeith, one of the Hebrides, under the care of a dumb attendant. When they grew up, they spoke the language of Paradise, i. e. pure Hebrew. Henry, who relates this in the sixth volume of his History of England, laughs at it with reason, as Herodotus might have done also. *Larcher.*

[d] Hipponax, speaking of the people of Cyprus, uses this word as signifying bread. *Larcher.*

[e] Psammetichus must have been very little acquainted with the origin of the Phrygians, who were of European descent and lately transported into Asia. (Herod. b. vii. 73.) We may remark that the faculty of speech is not the gift of nature, but an acquired art. Infants would not speak if so much pains were not taken with them. The wild boy found in the woods of Hanover, under the reign of George the First, could never be taught to speak. This art may also be forgotten, as well as others. Selkirk, the Scotchman, who was cast on a desert island, not only forgot how to speak, but found great difficulty in learning again. There are also in all languages letters which can never be properly pronounced, unless they are practised in early years. Such was the Greek *theta*, which the English at the present day so easily pronounce; and the *ch* of the Germans and Scotch. If God, in creating man, had not giving him a language, the human race might have passed through many generations without being able to discourse otherwise than by signs.

[f] The ruins of Thebes occupy a space at least half a league in circumference; for a description of which, see Savary, Letter XXXIV.

[g] There were two places of this name which have caused great confusion and perplexity among geographers. See Larcher's Table Geographique.

This city is universally allowed by travellers to have been at Materea. It is supposed to have been the On of the Scriptures, and was celebrated as a

order to see whether their accounts might agree with what I had heard at Memphis; for the Heliopolitans are esteemed the most skilled in antiquity of all the Egyptians. What I heard concerning their deities, I am not very willing to publish, except only their names; supposing that all men think alike concerning them: and therefore I shall say no more of those matters than the thread of my narration absolutely requires.

IV. But as for human affairs, they all agree, that the Egyptians were the first inventors of the year, which they divided into twelve parts, by means of the knowledge they had of the stars: in this, as I think, more able than the Grecians, who on account of the seasons, throw in an intercalatory month every third year[h]: whereas the Egyptians, allowing thirty days to each of the twelve months, add five supernumerary days to each year, and by that means the seasons[i] in their revolution, return at the same point. They said also, that the Egyptians were the first who gave names to the twelve Gods; and that the Greeks had those names from them[k]; that they erected the first altars, images, and temples to the Gods, and carved the figures of animals on stone; most of which they demonstrated to be so in fact. They added, that Menes was the first king who reigned in the world; and that in his time all Egypt, except the country of Thebes, was one morass; no part of the present land appearing then below the lake Myris, which is seven days' passage from the sea by the way of the river.

V. Indeed to me they seemed to speak rationally touching this region. For any man of understanding will easily perceive at sight, though he had never heard these things, that those parts of Egypt which the Greeks frequent with their shipping, are an accession[l] of land bestowed upon the Egyp-

school of science from very early times. We learn from Strabo that it was the school of Plato and Eudoxus. *Rennel*, p. 495, 535.

Eusebius, Cyril, Augustine, and others affirm, that Plato got his information in Egypt; and Bryant says there can be no doubt of it. Plato resided three years at Heliopolis, where he was very intimate with the priests of the sun. Egypt was also the school of Musæus, Melampos, Dædalus, Homer, Lycurges, Solon, Democrites, &c.

[h] At the end of two years or the beginning of the third; this mode of speech was customary among the Greeks. See Aristoph. Plut. 583; compare Herod. i. 32.

[i] If the Egyptian year had consisted of 365 entire days, the seasons would be far from returning regularly at the same period. After some ages the winter months would be found to return at the spring, and so of other seasons. *Larcher*.

[k] At the same time that Plato confesses that the Grecian mythology was of foreign original, he derives Artemis from a Greek word signifying integrity. Diodorus says, that the Greeks not only borrowed the names of their Gods from Egypt, but also their knowledge of the arts and sciences. *Beloe*.

[l] This opinion was adopted by all the ancients and a great part of the moderns. If it be true, all the country from Memphis to the sea must have been formerly

tians by the river: and so is all that country, which men see beyond the lake during a passage of three days; of which yet these Egyptians said nothing. For the nature of the soil of Egypt is of this kind, when a ship bound to Egypt rides at a distance of a whole day's sail from the port, if a man try the sounding, he shall draw up his plummet covered with mud, even where the sea is eleven fathoms deep; which plainly shews that all that earth was brought down thither by the river[m].

VI. The extent of Egypt along the sea-coast, according to our division, from the bay of Plinthene to the lake Selbonis, under mount Casius, is sixty schœni. And here we must observe, that those who have only small[n] portions of land, measure their land by the orgya; such as have more, by the stade; and those who have very much, by parasangs; each consisting of thirty stades. But those who have very extensive domains measure by the schœnus; which is an Egyptian measure, equal to sixty stades. So that the whole coast of Egypt is three thousand and six hundred stades in length[o].

VII. From the sea upwards, to the city of Heliopolis, the country is a spacious level, without rivers, and a slimy soil. The distance from the sea to Heliopolis, is about the same as from the altar of the twelve Gods[p] in Attica, to Pisa and

a gulf of the Mediterranean parallel to the Arabian gulf. The earth must have been raised up by little and little, from a deposit of the mud which the waters of the Nile carry with them. Larcher has a note of twelve pages on the subject. See also Rennel, sect. xviii. on the Floods and Allusions of Rivers, &c, more particularly on those of the Nile.

m Shaw says, that the black mud appears by soundings at the distance of twenty leagues. Surely the soil of Ethiopia must be of an extraordinary depth, in having not only bestowed upon Egypt so many thousand annual strata, but in having laid the foundation likewise of future additions to it in the sea. *Beloe.*

For seven or eight leagues from the land they know by the sounding plummet if they are near Egypt, as within that distance it brings up the black slimy mud of the Nile, that settles at the bottom of the sea, which is often of great use in navigation, the low land of this country not being seen far off. *Pococke.*

n It appears to me most probable, that he is here speaking of measures in use among different nations, according to the extent of their country. The Greeks, whose territories are not considerable, measured by stades; the Persians, whose country was greater, by parasangs; the Egyptians, whose country was still more spacious, by schœni. Herodotus, when he observes that this last is an Egyptian measure, indirectly informs us, that the stade and parasang were not there used. *Larcher.*

o In the report of Herodotus respecting the extent of Egypt, he has made use of a stade, which is totally different from that which he uses when he refers to Greece or Persia. This appears in a remarkable instance, where he assigns the same number of stades within fifteen to the space between Athens and Pisa, as between Heliopolis and the sea-coast of Egypt, although the former be about one hundred and five, the latter eighty-six miles only; the one giving a proportion of seven hundred and fifty-five, the other of one thousand and twelve to a degree. So that he appears to have used stades of different scales without a consciousness of it. It appears that the error arises from his having taken the schœni one third above the real standard; that is, sixty stades instead of forty, as it really appears to be. *Rennel*, p. 19 and 427.

p This was in the forum at Athens. Pisistratus, (Thucyd. vi. 54.) son of Hip-

the temple of Olympian Jupiter. For whoever will compare these ways, shall find by computation, that they differ not one from the other above fifteen stades; the road leading to Pisa wanting no more of one thousand five hundred stades, which is just the number that lie between the sea and Heliopolis.

VIII. From this city upwards[q] Egypt is narrow; for on the one side the mountains of Arabia extend, which form a continued line, extending from the north to the south and south-west, till they reach the Red sea. In these hills are found quarries of stone, which were used in building the pyramids of Memphis; in that part the mountain[r] ends, and turns into the country I mentioned. But I have heard, that to travel this country over in the widest part, from east to west, is a journey of two months; and that the most eastwardly limits produce frankincense in abundance. On that side of Egypt which borders upon Lybia are other mountains, very rocky, and covered with sand. They contain divers pyramids, and extend in the same manner as those of Arabia, which stretch to the southward. So that from Heliopolis, the country which belongs to Egypt, is not very extensive, but for four days sail[s] up the river it is very narrow. Between the mountains before mentioned the land is level, and in the narrowest part seems to me not above two hundred stades in breadth, from the Arabian to the Lybian hills; but beyond these straits the country grows wider again.

IX. Such is the form and situation of this region. From Heliopolis to Thebes[t] men pass by water in nine days, the distance between those two cities being four thousand eight hundred and sixty stades, which amount to eighty-one schœni. To put these measures together, the coast of Egypt, as I said before, contains in length three thousand and six hundred stades; Thebes is distant from the sea six thousand one hun-

pias the tyrant, dedicated it to the twelve Gods when he was Archon. *Larcher.*

[q] Egypt, in proportion as it recedes from the Mediterranean, is regularly elevated.

[r] The mountain ending in that part where the quarries are, (i. e. not going on any longer in a direction from north to south,) takes a turn towards that part which I have mentioned, viz. to the Red sea, (as he said in line 4.) and then continues upwards with that sea, (and thus takes an eastern or south-eastern direction,) extending to the country of frankincense. *Schweighæuser.*

[s] Aristides affirms that Egypt, far from becoming wider at this distance from Heliopolis upwards, became so contracted, that the two chains of mountains united, and that the Nile at their junction formed cataracts. Herodotus was not ignorant of this, but he conceived that Egypt became wider during the four first days sail. This affirmation of Herodotus is confirmed by Norden, &c. *Larcher.*

[t] Herodotus says, from Heliopolis to Thebes there are 4860 stades, and from the sea to Heliopolis (ch. 7.) 1500. Therefore, according to these measures, from the coast to Thebes there are 6360. In the text he has 6130; so that there is an error of 240 stades. The mistake must fall on the copyists.

dred and twenty; and the city of Elephantis, eight hundred and twenty from Thebes.

X. The greater part of all this country, as the priests informed me, and as I judge by what I saw, is an acquisition of land to the Egyptians. For the plains that lie between the mountains beyond Memphis, seem to me to have been formerly a bay of the sea; and I have the same opinion of those about Ilium[u], Teuthrania, Ephesus, and the plain of the Mæander; if I may be permitted to compare small things with great, for none of all the rivers that have thrown out earth in this manner on those regions can justly be brought in competition with any one of the five mouths[x] of the Nile. I might mention other rivers which have wrought the like effect, and, though not so considerable as the Nile, have yet done great things[y] of this nature. Of these, one of the most remarkable is the Achelous; which passing through Acarnania, and falling into the sea by the Echinades[z], has already joined one half of those islands to the continent.

XI. Besides, there is a bay, not far from Egypt, branching out from the Red sea, though belonging to Arabia, which is long and narrow, in the manner I shall here describe; from the innermost part of this bay to the broad sea, the passage is of as great a length as a vessel with oars can perform in forty days; and yet the breadth in the widest place is no more than half a day over. The tides[a] of this gulf are strong; the waters ebb and flow daily; and I am of opinion, that Egypt was anciently penetrated in like manner by an arm of the sea, entering on the north side, and ascending towards Ethiopia; as that of Arabia, which I mentioned before,

[u] Grelot, an author worthy of credit, assures us, in his description of his voyage from Constantinople, that the Scamander is a very small stream, which loses itself in the sea soon after its source. Yet in the time of Homer it was very considerable. *Bellanger.*

[x] This he fully explains at the end of ch. 17.

[y] What prodigious changes great rivers occasion on the surface of the globe! how incessantly they repel the sea, by accumulating sand on sand! how they elevate at their mouths islands, which at length become large portions of the continent! It is thus that the Nile has formed almost all the Lower Egypt, and created out of the waters the Delta, which is ninety leagues in circumference. It is thus that the Mæander, constantly repelling the waves of the Mediterranean, and gradually filling up the gulf into which it falls, has placed in the middle of the land the town of Miletus, formerly a celebrated harbour. It is thus that the Tigris and the Euphrates let loose from the Armenian hills, and sweeping with them in their course the sands of Mesopotamia, are imperceptibly filling up the Persian gulf. *Savery,* Letter I.

[z] These islands are described by Thucydides, book ii. ch. 102.

[a] Diodorus Siculus relates, (book iii. 40.) that the Ichthyophagi had records of a very considerable reflux of the tide in this gulf, which left it totally dry, but soon after the sea returned. This bears great similarity to the miraculous parting of the waters which saved the Israelites. *Larcher.*

stretches from the south towards Syria; and that the extremities of these two had only a narrow tract of land lying between, and separating the one from the other. Now, if the Nile would turn its stream into the Arabian gulf, what could hinder it from being filled with earth by the river? I, for my part, expect that it would be filled in ten thousand years. How then is it not possible, that during the time which has been before my birth, that this, or even a much greater channel, might have been filled up by such a vigorous and abounding river.

XII. The things, therefore, which I heard concerning Egypt, together with the testimony of my own eyes, induce me to this opinion; especially having observed that this country projects farther into the sea than the next adjoining region; that shells[b] are found on the hills; that a saline humour issuing from the earth corrodes the stones of the pyramids[c]; and that among all the mountains of Egypt, this alone, which is situate above Memphis, abounds in sand. Besides, Egypt is utterly unlike all the adjacent countries, whether of Arabia, Lybia, or Syria, (for the maritime parts of Arabia are inhabited by Syrians,) the soil being black and crumbling, as if it were mud and loose earth, brought down by the river from Ethiopia; whereas we know that the earth of Lybia is reddish, and somewhat more sandy; as that of Arabia and Syria is either stony, or mixed with clay.

XIII. Another particular, of great moment to confirm what is said touching this country, I had from the priests; who affirm, that, under the reign of Mœris, if the Nile rose to the height of eight cubits, all the lands of Egypt below Memphis were sufficiently watered; and yet Mœris had not been nine hundred years dead when I received this information. But in our time, unless the river swells to sixteen cubits[d], or

[b] It is very certain that shells are even to this day found upon the mountains of Egypt, but this by no means proves the Egyptian gulf. Shells are also found upon mountains much higher than those of Egypt; in Europe, Asia, and America. This only proves, that all those regions have in part been covered by the waters of the sea. I say in part, because it is certain, from the observations of the most skilful naturalists, that the tops of the highest mountains have not been covered with water. These, in times of such general deluges, were like so many islands. *Larcher.*

[c] Norden informs us, that the stones of the great pyramid on the north side are rotten, but assigns no cause.

[d] The majority of travellers inform us, that upon an average, the water usually rises every year to twenty-two cubits. In 1702 it rose to twenty-three cubits four inches; in the year preceding, to twenty-two cubits eighteen inches. According to travellers, the favourable height is from twenty-two to twenty-three; according to Herodotus, from fifteen to sixteen. *Larcher.*

There seems to have been no addition during the space of 500 years, to the number of cubits taken notice of by Herodotus. This we learn, not only from the sixteen children that attend the statue of the Nile, but also from a medal of Trajan, where we see the figure of the Nile with a boy standing upon it, who

fifteen at least, the country is not covered with water. So that if the soil continues[e] to increase in the same proportion as in ages past, I am persuaded, that those who inhabit below the lake Mœris, and in all that part which is called Delta, must for ever suffer by a deficiency of water; the same calamity, they used to say, must at some time fall upon the Grecians. For having heard that all the lands of Greece were watered by rain, and not, as Egypt, by rivers; they said the Grecians at some time or other would be disappointed in their great expectations, and miserably starve; meaning, if the deity should not afford rain, but send dry seasons in the place of wet, they must perish by famine, since they had no other resource for water, except from Jupiter only.

XIV. I acknowledge this discourse is not altogether groundless; but I will now state how the Egyptians are situated: if, as I said before, all the land below Memphis, which visibly rises every year, should continue to increase in the same proportion as it has in time past, what else will happen, but that the Egyptians who inhabit this part will starve? especially if their land shall neither be watered by rain[f] from heaven, nor the river be sufficient to inundate the fields. At this day, indeed, no people in the world, nor in the rest of Egypt, enjoy the productions of the earth with so little labour; for there is neither labour in breaking up the furrows, nor in digging, nor in performing any other of those things which other men labour at with regard to corn. For as soon as the river has voluntarily overflowed the corn fields, and having watered them has retired, each man sows his land and turns in his swine[g]; and when the seed has been trodden

points to the number sixteen. Fifteen cubits are recorded by the emperor Julian, as the height of the Nile's inundation. Three hundred years afterwards, the amount was no more than sixteen or seventeen cubits; and at present, notwithstanding the great accumulation of soil, when the river rises to sixteen cubits the Egyptians make great rejoicings, and call out Wafaa Allah! God has given all we wanted. *Pococke's Description of the East*, &c.

e All rivers and streams must at times overflow, because there is no provision made in their beds for a sudden increase of water; for this sudden increase being immediately diffused over the country, can have no effect in deepening and enlarging the beds; so that, notwithstanding the continued increase of soil, the river must still continue to overflow. *Rennel*, p. 514.

f In upper Egypt they have sometimes a little rain; and I was told, that in eight years it had been known to rain but twice hard for about half an hour. *Pococke*, vol. i. p. 195.

According to the meteorological observations of Dr. Shaw, (vol. ii. Appendix, p. 142.) in 1689, it rained sixteen times in January, and snowed once, and rained eight times in February.

g Plutarch, Eudoxus, and Pliny, relate the same fact. I am of opinion, that Herodotus is only mistaken with regard to the time when they were admitted into the fields. It was probably before the corn was sown, that they might eat the roots of the aquatic plants, which might prove injurious to the grain. *Larcher*.

Norden says, that there is scarcely a country where the land has greater need of culture than in Egypt.

in by the swine, he expects the harvest without farther care; and when that season comes, lets in his swine again[h], to shake the grain out of the ear, and has no other trouble than to lay up his corn.

XV. But if we should follow the opinion of the Ionians, who say that the country of Delta alone is properly called Egypt; extending along the shore, from the tower of Perseus to the Taricheea[i] of Pelusium, forty schæni in length, and from the sea upwards, to the city of Cercasorum, where the Nile divides, and descends towards Pelusium and Canopus[k]; attributing the rest of Egypt, partly to Lybia, and partly to Arabia, we should evidently infer that the Egyptians had not formerly any country. For they themselves acknowledge, and I concur in opinion with them, that Delta is formed of the soil which the river has brought down, and has lately (if I may so express myself) appeared above the water. If then they formerly had no country, to what end were they so solicitous to be thought the most ancient of all people? Surely they might have forborne to try by an experiment, what language children would first speak. For my own part, I am not of opinion that the Egyptians commenced their existence with the country which the Ionians call Delta; but that they always[l] were, since men have been; and that as the soil increased gradually, many came slowly down from the higher parts to inhabit the new formed earth, and many continued in their former possessions. For the province of Thebes went anciently by the name of Egypt, and is six thousand one hundred and twenty stades in circumference.

XVI. If, therefore, we judge rightly of these things, the opinion of the Ionians is erroneous; but if their sentiment be well grounded, we shall shew that neither the Greeks nor the Ionians reason well, when they say the world is divided into three parts[m]; Europe, Asia, and Lybia; for they ought to

[h] Larcher reads in this place, and in the one immediately before, *τῦσι ζοῦσι*.

They spread out the corn, when reaped, and an ox draws a machine about on it, which, together with the treading of the ox, separates the grain from the straw, and cuts the straw. *Pococke*, vol. i. p. 208.

[i] This name is probably derived from their preserving in this place the embalmed bodies; and therefore common to several other places in Egypt. *Larcher*.

[k] This is the same as the modern *Aboukir*. According to Strabo, (lib. 17.) Diodorus Siculus and St. Epiphanes, it received its name from Canopus the pilot of Menelaus, who died there. This confirms the opinion of Homer, that Menelaus landed in Egypt.

[l] Diodorus Siculus informs us, that the Ethiopians consider the Egyptians as one of their colonies, at the head of which was Osiris. He observes also in another place, that the inhabitants of the Thebaid consider themselves as the most ancient of mankind. This historian, doubtless, had a view to the traditions of the two people, without giving us any opinion of his own. *Larcher*.

[m] Many of the ancients divided the world into two parts only, Europe and Asia. Africa was made to belong to Europe.

add a fourth, viz. the Delta of Egypt, if it be not a part either of Lybia or of Asia. For, by their reasoning, the Nile does not separate[n] Asia from Lybia; that river dividing at the point of Delta, and rolling down on each side of it: so that it must be between Lybia and Asia.

XVII. But not to insist longer on the opinion of the Ionians, I presume, that all the countries which the Egyptians inhabit ought to be accounted Egypt, as those of the Cilicians and Assyrians are known by the names of Cilicia and Assyria. Neither can I imagine what parts may be properly called the bounds of Asia and Lybia, except the limits of Egypt. Yet if we follow the opinion which the Greeks embrace, we shall suppose that all Egypt, beginning from the Catadupians and the city of Elephantis, is divided into two parts, and partakes of both names; one belonging to Lybia, and the other to Asia. For the Nile descending from the Catadupians, passes through the midst of Egypt, in one channel towards the sea, to the city of Cercasorum; and there separates into three[o]. That

Tertia pars rerum Libye, si credere famæ
Cuncta velis: at si ventos cœlumque sequaris,
Pars erit Europæ.
Lucan. Pharsal. ix. 411.

Isocrates (Paneg. vol. i.) says, the whole earth is divided into two parts, Europe and Asia; yet some authors add Africa to Asia.

Æoliis candens austris, et lampade Phœbi
Æstifero Libye torretur subdita cancro
Aut ingens Asiæ latus, aut pars tertia terris.
Silius Italic. lib. i. 193.

[n] Herodotus excludes Egypt from Africa, as well as from Asia; which appears very extraordinary, and can only be accounted for on the ground that he does not, like others, distribute the habitable world into *continents*, but *regions*; and that Egypt might be considered as a region of itself. He seemed to think Egypt, if we may so say, *extra-continental*; in effect, he thought the *land of Egypt* alone constituted the natural and proper limits or boundary of Asia and Africa. He says, (Melp. 39.) that Asia *terminates* at Egypt, and Lybia *begins* where Egypt ends, 41. And again, (Eut. 65.) Egypt is said to be *near to Africa*. These notices seem to be clearly in favour of the arrangement, which makes Egypt distinct from Africa or Lybia. But on the other hand, he says, in Melp. 41 and 42. except in that *part* which is *contiguous* to Asia, the *whole* of Africa is surrounded by sea, &c. The reader will determine for himself; but it appears, on the whole, as if Herodotus had either no decided opinion of his own on the subject, or that in one of the places he has merely expressed the opinion of others, without explaining his own. *Rennel*, p. 3 and 411.

[o] This river, whose source has not yet been explored, comes by one single channel from Ethiopia to the point of the Delta; arrived here, it separates itself into three principal branches: of these, one takes an eastern direction, and is called the Pelusian channel; a second proceeds northward, and is called the Sebennitic branch; the third flows towards the west, and takes the name of Canopic. The Sebennitic arm is subdivided into two others, the Saitic and Mendesian; the Saitic is between the Bolbitine, which is an artificial branch, and the Sebennitic. The Bucolic also is the production of the inhabitants, and flows betwixt the Sebennitic, from which it proceeds, and the Mendesian. Thus the seven branches of the Nile, from east to west, are the Pelusian, the Mendesian, the Bucolic, the Sebennitic, the Saitic, the Bolbitine, and the Canopic. Such is the account of Herodotus. *Larcher*.

Rennel, p. 411. seems to have mistaken Herodotus; for he makes him only assign six mouths to the Nile. By means of this chapter, the five mouths of chap.

which runs out to the eastward is called the Pelusian mouth; the second, inclining westward, goes by the name of Canopic; and the third channel descending from above by a straight line, passes through the midst of Delta, and being no way inferior to the other two in fame or quantity of water, is called the mouth of Sebennytus; whence two more are derived, which take their names from the cities of Sais and Mendis, and flow into the sea. For those of Bolbitis and Bucolis were not formed by nature; but are owing to the industry of men.

XVIII. To this opinion concerning the extent of Egypt, I have the concurring testimony of the oracle of Ammon; which yet I had not heard before I was fully persuaded of these things. For the people who inhabit the cities of Apis and Marea, situate on the frontier of Egypt next to the borders of Lybia, impatient of the religious ceremonies of the Egyptians, and unwilling to abstain from the flesh of heifers, were very desirous to be accounted Lybians rather than Egyptians; and to that end consulting the oracle of Ammon, professed they had no relation to the Egyptians, because they lived out of Delta, and could by no means agree with them, but desired to eat all manner of food without distinction. Nevertheless the God did not permit them to do so, but pronounced, that Egypt comprehends all the territories which are overflowed by the Nile; and that all those who drink of that river below the city of Elephantis, are Egyptians[p].

XIX. The inundations of the Nile not only cover Delta, but the frontier of Lybia also, and sometimes that of Arabia, to the extent of about two days' journey, more or less, on each side. And though I was very desirous to be informed touching the nature of this river, I could not learn, either from the priests or any other persons, what should cause the Nile to come down in such abundance during a hundred days[q], beginning at the summer solstice, and when it has completed this number, it retires; the quantity of water diminishing, so that it

x. are understood; Herodotus did not count the artificial mouths.

For an exact account of the several mouths of the Nile, collected from ancient and modern authorities, the reader is referred to Rennel's 19th section.

The Arabian account of the Nile, and its different divisions, may be found in *Herbelot Bibliotheque Orientale*, which the curious reader will do well to compare with the description given by Herodotus, and that of modern travellers, particularly Pococke, Norden, Volney, and Savary. *Beloe.*

[p] The ancients, says Strabo, confined the appellation of Egypt to the inhabited country watered by the Nile, from the environs of Syene to the sea. *Beloe.*

[q] The inundation regularly commences about the month of July, or three weeks after the rains have begun to fall in Ethiopia. In 1714 it began the 30th of June; in 1715, the 1st of July; in 1738, the 20th of June. The Nile is not the only river which increases in the summer, it has this property in common with many others of Africa and India. *Larcher.*

continues low all the winter, and even to the return of the next summer solstice. Of these particulars I could get no account from the Egyptians, though I inquired whether this river have any peculiar quality, so as to be different in nature from other rivers; and my great desire to be informed not only led me to ask these questions, but also how it comes to pass that the Nile alone, of all the rivers in the world, never emits the least breeze[r] on the adjacent parts.

XX. Nevertheless some of the Greeks, pretending to distinguish themselves by their knowledge, have named three several causes of these inundations, which are scarcely worth mentioning, except merely as I wish to shew what they are. One of them affirms, that the Etesian winds[s] are the cause of the swelling of this river, by repelling the stream, and preventing it from discharging into the sea. But the Nile has sometimes performed its work before the Etesian winds begin to blow; and besides, if those winds were the cause of these inundations, all other rivers that are exposed to the same winds must of necessity be liable to the same effect; and the rather, as they are less and have weaker currents: yet the rivers of Syria and Lybia, which are many, were never subject to the like influence.

XXI. The second opinion is more ignorant than the former, though more marvellous; affirming, that the Nile, flowing from the ocean[t], performs these things; and that the ocean surrounds the whole earth.

XXII. The third way of resolving this difficulty is the most probable, and yet most untrue. For by saying that the waters of the Nile are produced by melted snow[u], they say nothing, for this river descends from Lybia through the midst of Ethiopia into Egypt; how therefore, since it runs from a very hot to a colder region, can it flow from the snow? Many reasons will readily occur to men of good understanding, to shew the improbability of this opinion. First and principally, because the winds which blow from Ethiopia are always hot. In the second place, neither rain nor ice[x] is seen

[r] Αὖρα differs from ἄνεμος. Αὖρα is a wind that rises from exhalations from watery places, as a river, &c. and is therefore cold; Ἄνεμος is an agitation of the air. Over all rivers there is a current of fresh air; over the Nile there is a current, but it is warm. *Larcher*.

[s] This was the opinion of Thales according to Seneca, Nat. Quæst. iv. 2. These winds however contribute something to the overflowing of the river, as Maillet has remarked in his description of Egypt, p. 55.

[t] This was the opinion of Euthymenes of Marseilles. If we believe Diodorus Siculus, (book i. 37.) it was also the opinion of the Egyptian priests. *Larcher*.

[u] This was the opinion of Anaxandrides, Diodorus Siculus, and also of Euripides, Fragm. ex Archelai Tragœd. and Helen. v. 3.

[x] Nonnus relates, in the history of his embassy, that during the period when the Nile inundates Egypt, there are very violent storms in different parts of Ethiopia; the atmosphere becomes exceed-

in those countries; and yet rain always follows within the space of five days[y] after snow: so that if snow falls in those regions, rain must. Besides, the inhabitants are rendered black by the excessive heat; swallows and kites continue there all the year; and the cranes, to avoid the cold of Scythia, come to pass the winter in that country: all which could not be, if in even the smallest quantity snow fell in the parts adjacent to the source and passage of the Nile.

XXIII. The person who attributed this to the ocean, since he has referred it to an obscure fable, does not deserve refutation: neither do I know any river so called; but conjecture that Homer or some other ancient poet having invented that name, inserted it in their writings.

XXIV. Yet if, after I have expressed my dissatisfaction with the opinions before mentioned[z], I must give my own concerning so intricate a question, that which causes the Nile to overflow in summer is, in my judgment, this. During the winter the sun, being driven by the cold from his former course, retires to the upper regions of Lybia; which in few words comprehends the whole matter; for it is natural that that country nearest to, and over which this God is, should be most in want of water, and that the streams of the neighbouring rivers should be dried up.

XXV. But to explain[a] my meaning more amply, I say, that the sun passing over the remoter parts of Lybia, acts in the following manner; as the air of that country is constantly serene, and the country is always hot, since there are no cooling winds; the sun when passing through that region does the same as it used in the summer, when passing through

ingly cloudy, and the rains fall in such torrents as to inundate the country.

The Portuguese missionaries inform us, that from June to September there does not pass a day in Abyssinia without rain, and that the Nile receives all the rivers, streams and torrents which fall from the mountains. *Larcher.*

[y] Herodotus had probably remarked, that at Halicarnassus or Thurium, where he lived, snow was, in the space of a few days succeeded by rain. *Wesseling.*

[z] It must be supposed that the north winds are the cause of its overflow, which begin to flow about the latter end of May, and drive the clouds formed by the vapours of the Mediterranean southward, as far as the mountains of Ethiopia, which stopping their course, they condense and fall down in violent rains. It is said that at this time not only men from their reason, but that wild beasts by a sort of instinct, leave the mountains. The wind, which is the cause of the rise of the Nile, driving the clouds against those hills, is also the cause of it in another respect, as it drives in the water from the sea, and keeps back the waters of the river in such a manner as to raise the waters above. *Pococke.*

[a] This reasoning of Herodotus is refuted by Diodorus Siculus and by Aristides. "If the sun attracted moisture "from the Nile during the winter season "it would be the same with respect to "the other rivers of Lybia, and in like "manner diminish the force of their "currents. As this is not the fact, the "reasoning of this author falls to the "ground. The rivers of Greece are increased during the winter, not on account of their distance from the sun, "but from the frequency of the rains." Diodorus Sic. b. i. c. 38.

the centre of the heavens, for it attracts the moisture and throws it back again upon the higher regions; where it is received and liquified by the winds, which in this climate blow generally from the south and south-west, and consequently most attended with wet of any other. Yet I am of opinion that the sun may retain some part about itself, and not discharge every year all the water of the Nile. But when the rigours of winter are past, and the sun returns again to the midst of the heavens, all rivers are attracted by the heat in equal proportion. To which time all other streams, being mixed with abundance of rain, as the country has been watered by showers and torn up by torrents, run high, and overflow the adjacent parts; whereas in summer being destitute of rain, and at the same time exhaled by the sun, they become reduced; but the Nile, being destitute of rain, and attracted by the sun, is the only river that flows much weaker in winter than in summer; for in summer it is attracted equally with the others, but in winter it is alone oppressed. From all which, as I conceive, the sun is the cause of the inundations of the Nile[b].

XXVI. And in my opinion the dryness of the air in those parts proceeds from the scorching heat of the same being, which affects in an extraordinary manner all that lies near its passage: and for this occasion the upper regions of Lybia are always hot. Now if such a change of seasons and the situation of the heaven could be made, that the south winds might take the place of the north, and the north winds be transferred to the southward, the sun retiring from the north in winter to the upper regions of Europe, and passing through those parts, as now he does through Lybia, would, I suppose, cause the same effects in the Ister, which we now see in the Nile.

XXVII. And whereas I said before that no wind blows from this river; my opinion is, that it is very improbable that winds should blow from hot countries, but that they are wont to blow from cold.

XXVIII. But I leave these things as they are, and as they always were.

Touching the source of the Nile[c], no man of all the Egyp-

[b] The more ancient Egyptians superstitiously believed that the overflowing of the Nile was occasioned by the sacrifice which they annually paid to the supposed divinity of the river. Every year, on the twelfth of their month Baoni, corresponding with our June, they threw a young woman superbly ornamented into the river. *Beloe.*

[c] In spite of all the researches posterior to the time of Herodotus, these sources were not better known, when rather more than a century ago, the Portuguese Jesuits imagined that they had discovered them. But it appeared that they had taken one of the rivers which fall into the Nile, for the Nile itself. The source therefore remains as little known as before. *Larcher.*

The point fixed upon by Bruce agrees

tians, Lybians, or Grecians I have conversed with, ever pretended to know any thing certain; except a scribe[d], who had the charge of Minerva's treasury at Sais, a city of Egypt. And though I thought he trifled with me, when he said he was perfectly informed of this secret, I shall yet give a place here to his relation. Crophi, said he, and Mophi, are two mountains, with heads of a pyramidical form, situate in the way from Elephantine to Syene[e], a city of Thebais; and between these hills is a profound abyss, which contains the springs of the Nile. One half of the water issuing from this place runs into Egypt northward; the other half passes southward to Ethiopia: and that the fountains of the Nile are bottomless, Psammetichus king of Egypt found by an experiment. For having caused a line twisted to be many thousand fathoms in length, he sounded the depth, but could not find a bottom. Which, if admitted for true[f], would induce me to believe, that there are violent whirlpools and reverberations of the water; and, as the water dashes against the rocks, a sounding line, when let down, cannot reach the bottom.

XXIX. I was unable to learn any thing more of any one. But thus much have I learnt concerning the farthest extent *of higher Egypt*; since, I went and made my own observations as far as Elephantine; the rest I heard upon inquiry. Those who ascend the river above the city of Elephantine, find a country in their passage so steep, that every vessel, like a cow, is drawn by ropes fastened to each side, and must be hurried down the stream by the impetuosity of the torrent if the ropes should happen to break. This region is four days' voyage from Elephantine, and the Nile is there as full

very nearly with that fixed on by Father Lobo; and Larcher severely reproves Bruce for claiming the merit of having first discovered the source of the river.

Rennel supposes that the remote sources of the Nile are rather to the south than the west, or nearer to the meridian of Abyssinia, though by no means within that country. Ptolemy, Edrisi, and Abulfeda place them in the same position, though greatly too far to the southward, p. 433. See the whole of that section for an accurate examination of this subject.

[d] Michaelis (Dissert. on the Memoires of the Acad. Gotting. vol. i. p. 271.) shews, that χραμματεὺς implies a person skilled in the knowledge of hieroglyphics, and who possesses the art of divination. Χρήματα are not only money, but every thing precious of whatever kind, as vessels, &c.

[e] Is a town of Egypt, on the confines of Ethiopia. It has the island of Elephantine before it, and is situated immediately under the Tropic. A well is dug there, which marks the summer solstice. When that day arrives the vertical sun darts his rays to the bottom of the well, and his whole image is painted on the water that covers the bottom. *Strabo*, lib. 17.

We still see the ruins of this place on an eminence to the south of a village in Assuan. *Savary*, Letter XXXVII. *Pococke*, vol. i. p. 116. This (Assuan) is the same as the ancient name with the Coptic vowel. See note on ch. 91.

[f] Herodotus could not have told us more explicitly that he disbelieved the whole of this narrative.

of windings as the Mæander. There are twelve schœni, which it is necessary to sail through in this manner; and from thence you will come[g] to a spacious plain, and an island called Tachompso appears in the midst of the Nile. The Ethiopians inhabit the country beyond Elephantine, and one half of the island Tachompso; the other half being in the possession of the Egyptians. Near to this island lies a vast lake, the borders of which are inhabited by Ethiopian herdsmen; and after sailing through that lake, you will enter again into the channel of the Nile. A little beyond this place you will be obliged to go ashore, and to travel forty days by the side of the river, because the frequency of rocks and shelves renders the navigation of those parts utterly impracticable. At the end of these forty days you must go on board another vessel, and you will arrive in about twelve more at the great city of Meroe[h], which is accounted the capital of all Ethiopia. The inhabitants of that place worship no other Gods than Jupiter and Bacchus[i]; but these they adore with extraordinary pomp. They have an oracle of Jupiter; and make war, when that God commands by an oracle, and wherever it orders.

XXX. Sailing from this city, you will arrive at the country of the Automoli, in the same time as you were travelling from Elephantine to the capital of the Ethiopians. This people is called by the name of Asmak, which in the language of Greece signifies, *those that stand at the left hand of the king.* Their ancestors were Egyptians; and being in number two hundred and forty thousand military men, revolted to the Ethiopians on the following occasion. Some of them were placed in garrison at Elephantine against the Ethiopians, others at the Pelusian Daphnæ, against the Arabians and Syrians, others at Marea against Lybia: which method of Psammetichus we have seen imitated by the Persians of our time, who maintain guards both in Elephantine and Daphnæ. These Egyptians, after they had continued three years in their respective posts, without hearing any thing of being relieved, consulted together; and unanimously resolving to abandon Psammetichus[k], marched away to Ethiopia. When

[g] Longinus admires the elegance of this narrative. "The change of person," says he, (sect. xxvi.) "makes the thing "present, and the hearer frequently "fancies himself in the midst of the dan-"ger."

[h] The city of Meroe is in an island of the same name formed by three rivers; viz. the Nile, Astapus and Astaboras, or by the Bahr El-Biad, Abawi, and Tacazze. *Larcher.*

[i] Strabo, in describing the manners of the Ethiopians, makes no mention of either Jupiter or Bacchus. Every thing, therefore, must have been changed between the age of Herodotus and that of Strabo, or these two authors received very different impressions with respect to the two countries. *Larcher.*

[k] Diodorus Sic. (book i. 67.) assigns a very different reason for the revolt of these Egyptians. Psammetichus having meditated an expedition against Syria, gave the places of honour to strangers,

the king heard what was doing, he followed, overtook, and adjured them not to forsake the Gods of their fathers, with their own wives and children. But in answer to his exhortation, one of the Egyptians is reported to have uncovered his private parts, and to have said, that wheresoever these were, there could not be wanting either wives or children. So continuing their march, they presented themselves to the king of Ethiopia[l]; who in recompence sent them into a country which was disaffected to him, with orders to expel the inhabitants, and to possess their lands: by the settlement of which colony the Ethiopians became more civilized, and learned the manners of the Egyptians.

XXXI. Thus to the extent of four months journey, partly by land and partly by water, the Nile is known, without including its passing through Egypt. For upon computation, so much time will be found necessary to those who travel from Elephantine to the Automoli[m]. This river descends from the west and the setting of the sun; but no one is able to speak with certainty of what is beyond, because the excessive heat renders the rest of the country desert and uninhabited.

XXXII. I was also informed by some Cyrenæans, that in a journey they took to the oracle of Ammon, they had conferred with Etearchus king of the Ammonians; and that, among other things, discoursing with him concerning the head of the Nile, as of a thing altogether unknown, Etearchus acquainted them, that certain Nasamones[n], a nation of Lybia inhabiting the Syrtis, and a tract of land of no great extent eastward of the Syrtis, came into his country, and being asked by him if they had learned any thing new touching the Lybian deserts, answered, that some petulant young men, sons to divers persons of great power among them, had, after many extravagant actions, resolved to send five of their number by lot to the deserts of Lybia, to see if they could make any farther discovery than others had done. For the northern coast of Lybia, from Egypt to the promontory of Solois[o], where Lybia ter-

&c. These strangers must have been the Ionians and Carians, who assisted Psammetichus against his eleven colleagues. See ch. 152, 154. Aristotle alludes to this narrative in his third book, ch. 2. *Larcher.*

During the late distressing mutiny and revolt of a part of the fleet, it is said that a *like answer* was made by some of the mutineers, though not accompanied by the act of indecency recorded by Herodotus.

l It is certain that Herodotus (like the rest of the ancients) gives a wide range to Ethiopia; since he designs by it the whole of the southern part of Africa, extensive, as from his own descriptions, he must have conceived it to be. For it was with him "the extremity of the habitable world," and included all those countries, which, for want of the means of discrimination, he was compelled to comprise in one mass, as we may do, by the remote inland parts of *North America*, or *New Holland*. *Rennel*, p. 430.

m This word means deserters.

n See book iv. ch. 172.

o See note on ch. 43. book iv.

minates, is inhabited by Lybians of various nations; except those parts alone, which are possessed by the Grecians and Phœnicians. Above this coast, and those nations which reach down to the sea, the next country abounds in beasts of prey; and all beyond that is destitute of water, covered with sands, and utterly desolate. The young men chosen by their companions to make this expedition, having furnished themselves with water and other necessary provisions, first passed through the inhabited country; and when they had likewise traversed that region which abounds in wild beasts, they entered the deserts, making their way towards the south-west. After they had travelled many days through the sands, they at length saw some trees growing in a plain, and they approached and began to gather the fruit which was on them; and while they were gathering, several little men, less than men of middle size, came up, and having seized them carried them away; and the Nasamones did not at all understand what they said, neither did they understand the speech of the Nasamones. However, they conducted them over vast morasses to a city built on a great river running from the west to the east, and abounding in crocodiles; where the Nasamones found all the inhabitants black, and of no larger size than their guides.

XXXIII. To this relation Etearchus added, as the Cyrenæans assured me, that the Nasamones returned safe to their own country, and that the little men were all enchanters; but for the river, which passes by their city, he conjectured that it was[p] the Nile, which reason confirms; because the Nile descends from Lybia, dividing the country in the midst; and, as I form my conjectures of things unknown on things known, may probably take its rise from the same parts as the Ister[q]. For the Ister beginning to appear at the city of Pyrene[r] among the Celtæ, who inhabit beyond the columns of Hercules[s], and

[p] It may however with great probability be supposed, that the river seen by the Nasamones, was that which, according to the present state of our geography, is known to pass by Tombuctoo, and thence eastward, through the centre of Africa, (in effect, the river commonly known by the name of Niger,) but which we cannot agree with Herodotus, in supposing to be the upper part of the Nile.

Herodotus calls the Indus the second river which produced *crocodiles*, meaning the Nile as the first. But here we have a *third*; and Hanno, who doubtless preceded him, mentions the Senegal river, (though not by name,) which makes of course the fourth. *Rennel*, p. 431.

[q] Our author conjectures that these two rivers took their rise towards the same part of the world; the Nile in the western part of Africa, the Ister in the western part of Europe. *Larcher*.

[r] Many critics, and among others Bellanger, have supposed that Herodotus here alludes to the Pyrenean mountains, but that he was wrong for want of knowing the situation of those mountains. He however alludes to a small village near which the Ister took its rise, in the country of the Celtæ. *Larcher*.

[s] Africa is divided from Spain by a narrow strait of about twelve miles, through which the Atlantic flows into the Mediterranean. The columns of Hercules, so famous among the ancients, were two mountains which seemed to

border on the territories of the Cynesians[t], which lie in the extremity of Europe to the westward; divides in its course Europe in the middle[u], and ends at the Euxine sea, at that point where a Milesian colony inhabits the country of Istri.

XXXIV. Now the Ister is generally known, because the adjacent parts are every where well peopled; but the springs of the Nile are undiscovered, because this river passes through the uninhabited deserts of Lybia. I shall therefore say no more concerning the course of the Nile, having already mentioned as much as I could learn by the most diligent inquiry; only that it flows into the sea by the way of Egypt, which lies, as near as may be, opposite to the mountains of Cilicia; from whence an expeditious man may travel in five days to Sinope, a place situate on the Euxine, and directly facing the mouth of the Ister. So that in my opinion the Nile, which traverses all Lybia, may be properly compared with the Ister. And thus I have finished my account of the Nile.

XXXV. I shall now proceed[x] in my discourse concerning Egypt; which will be very ample and particular, because that country far surpasses all others in things admirable, and beyond expression remarkable. For as their climate is different from all others, and their river exhibits a different nature from other rivers; so the Egyptians have framed their laws and manners very different from the rest of mankind. The women of Egypt are employed in trade and business[y], while

have been torn asunder by some convulsion of the elements; and at the foot of the European mountain Gibraltar is now situated. *Gibbon's Decline and Fall.* ch. i.

[t] Who these are intended for, we know not. They are again mentioned, Melp. 49. *Rennel*, p. 42.

[u] This description is just; for its general course does really divide the central parts of Europe in the midst; and having arrived in the neighbourhood of the Euxine, it takes a sudden turn to the north-east, towards Scythia. *Rennel*, p. 43.

[x] Μηκυνέων is the Ionic participle of the future.

[y] This custom was contradictory to the manners of Greece. There the women never went to the market.

The employments of the two sexes prove, that in Egypt the women had more authority than their husbands, although Herodotus says nothing of the matter. But Diodorus Siculus (Book i. 27.) is of this opinion; and he thinks that by this custom they wished to perpetuate the gratitude which they felt from the mild government of Isis. "Thus," says he, "in Egypt the queens are more honoured than the kings, and the influence of the women is greater in private life. In the contracts of marriage it is stipulated, that the woman shall be mistress of her husband, and that he shall obey her in every particular."

Nymphodorus (Scholia Æd. Col. of Soph.) remarks, that Sesostris, seeing Egypt become exceedingly populous, and fearing lest the inhabitants should conspire against him, obliged them to employ themselves in feminine occupations, in order to enervate them. *Larcher*.

The present aspect of Egypt presents a very different scene; "Each family," says Savary, (Letter XV.) "forms a small state, of which the father is king; the members of it, attached to him by the ties of blood, acknowledge and submit to his power. When the master of the family dines, the women stand, and frequently hold the bason for him to wash, and serve him at table; and on all occasions behave to him with the extremest humility and reverence. The

the men stay at home to spin and weave. Other nations in weaving, shoot the woof above; the Egyptians, beneath. The men carry burdens on their heads; the women on their shoulders. The men squat down[z] when they make water, but the women perform that action standing. The Egyptians discharge their excrements at home[a], and eat in public; alleging, that whatever is indecent, though necessary, ought to be done in private; but things no way unbecoming should be done openly. No woman may be a priestess of any God or Goddess; men only are employed in those offices. Sons are not constrained[b] to make provision for their parents, if they are not willing; but daughters, however unwilling, are compelled to this duty.

XXXVI. In other countries the priests of the Gods wear hair; in Egypt they are all shaved. Among other people[c], the general custom in the time of mourning is, that those who are most nearly concerned shave their heads; but when any one dies in Egypt, his relations cease to shave, and let the hair grow on their heads and faces. In other regions, men live separate from beasts; whereas in Egypt man and beast live together. Other nations use barley and wheat for food, which would be a very great reproach among the Egyptians; who make bread of spell, which some call zea[d]. They knead the dough with their feet; but mix clay and take up dung with their hands. The Egyptians are circumcised[w] in their secret

"women spend their time principally "among their slaves in works of embroi- "dery," &c.

[z] The Indians of Hudson's bay differ from almost all other nations in their manner of making water, for here the men always squat down, and the women stand upright. *Ellis*, p, 198.

[a] The Greeks on the contrary went out of doors. *Larcher.*

[b] This law appears to me so barbarous, that I cannot in it discern any of that boasted wisdom of the Egyptians. The law of Solon seems much more commendable; this permitted a young man to neglect the maintenance of his father and to refuse him admission into his house, if he had been prostituted by his means. He was nevertheless obliged, after his death, to give him sepulture, with the usual funeral solemnities. *Larcher.*

The best reason for this law may be found in a former note of Larcher's, where we are informed that the women had more authority than their husbands. *Beloe.*

[c] Amongst the Greeks, when any sad calamity befalls them, the women cut their hair close, the men wear it long; in general the women wear their hair long, the men short. *Plut. Quæst.*

[d] See Martyn's Virgil's Georgics, i. 73. note on the word *farra.*

[w] "I am aware," says Mr. Gibbon, "how tender is the question of circum- "cision." He affirms, however, that the Ethiopians have a physical reason for the circumcision of males and even of females; and that it was practised in Ethiopia long before the introduction of Judaism or Christianity.

The above is one of Gibbon's sneers; of his two assertions on this subject, the one is very doubtful, and the other a positive falsehood.

The commencement of circumcision with the Jews was unquestionably with Abraham, and by the command of God. Marsham is of opinion, that the Hebrews borrowed it from the Egyptians, and that God was not the first author of this custom. This latter is contrary to the testimony of Moses; the former position will admit of more debate. This practice, as it prevails amongst the Jews and Egyptians, had a very different object; with the first it was a ceremony of religion,

parts, which all other men leave as they are formed by nature; those only excepted, who have learnt this custom from them. The men wear two garments, the women but one. They fasten the ropes and hooks of their sails to the inside, and all other nations to the outside. When the Grecians write or calculate with counters, they carry the hand from the left to the right; but the Egyptians on the contrary from the right to the left: and yet pretend in doing so, that their line tends to the right and ours to the left. They have two sorts of letters[e]; one of which they call sacred, the other vulgar.

XXXVII. They are of all mankind the most excessive worshippers of the Gods, and use these ceremonies. They drink in cups of brass, which they scour every day; and this custom is not only practised by some particular men, but by all the Egyptians in general. They wear garments of linen fresh washed, taking particular care to have them always clean, and are circumcised principally for the sake of cleanliness[f], which they esteem more than ornament. The priests shave all parts of the body once in three days, lest lice or any other impurity[g] should be found about those who officiate in the service of the Gods. They are clothed in linen[h], wear shoes of the byblus, and are not permitted to dress in any other

with the latter a point of decency or cleanliness, or as some say, of physical necessity. With the former it was performed on the eighth day from the birth of the child; with the latter not till the thirteenth year, and then on the girls as well as boys.

From the pain attending the operation, when performed at an advanced age, Mr. Harmer takes occasion to explain a passage in the Old Testament, concerning which commentators have materially differed. See Observations on Passages of Scripture, vol. ii. p. 500. The above observations are compiled from the different writers on this curious topic. It may not be improper to add, that circumcision is sometimes used medicinally.

Upon this subject see also Spencer de Legibus Hebræorum, and Marsham's Canon Ægyptiacus. *Beloe.*

[e] Diodorus Siculus agrees in this respect with Herodotus. Clemens of Alexandria and Porphyry remark, that the Egyptians used three different sorts of letters; the first is called epistolary, the second the sacerdotel, the third, the hieroglyphic. Warburton in his Divine Legation, (Book iv. sect. 4.) attributes to the Egyptians four sorts of letters. Although I am ignorant of the time when the Egyptians first began to have an alphabet, I am satisfied it must have been long before the invasion of Cambyses. *Larcher.*

[f] Philo relates that circumcision was established to prevent a disease, which is dangerous and difficult to cure, called the *charbon*, and which principally afflicts those who have not been circumcised. De Circum. tom. ii. This is also mentioned by Niebuhr in his description of Arabia, pag. 68.

The inhabitants of Otaheite practise circumcision for the same reason: Journal of a voyage round the world in the Endeavour in the year 1768, 1769, 1770, and 1771. See the London Chronicle, vol. xxx. p. 321.

[g] The Jews also were scrupulous in this respect. If a priest found any dirt or dead vermin betwixt his garments and skin, he might not perform the duties of his office.

[h] The fine linen of Egypt is mentioned in the Scriptures. "Fine linen, with "embroidered work from Egypt, was "that, which thou spreadest forth to be "thy sail." Ezek. xxvii. 7.

"I have decked my bed with cover- "ings of tapestry, with carved works, "with fine linen from Egypt." Prov. vii. 16.

manner. They constantly bathe themselves twice in cold water by day, and twice by night[i]; using so many other religious ceremonies, that we may say their number is infinite. On the other hand they enjoy great advantages[k], for they do not consume[l] or expend any of their private property; but sacred food is prepared for them and a considerable quantity of beef and geese is allowed each of them every day. They have an allowance of wine[m]; but may not taste of fish[n]. Beans[o] are never sowed in any part of Egypt, and if some happen to grow there, the Egyptians will not eat them either crude or dressed. As for the priests, they abhor the sight of that pulse, accounting it impure and abominable. The service of every God is performed, not by one, but by many priests, the principal being called the arch-priest; and, when he dies, his son is substituted in his place[p].

XXXVIII. They consider bulls as belonging to Epaphus, and for that reason make the following trial. If they find one black[q] hair upon him, they adjudge him to be unclean; which that they may know with certainty, the priest, appointed to this purpose, views every part of the animal both standing, and laid down on the ground. After this he draws out his tongue, to see if he be clean by certain signs, which I shall

[i] Porphyry (de Abstinent. iv. 7.) says, that they bathed three times a day in cold water; when they arose in the morning, before dinner, and immediately before they went to bed. If by chance they had any nocturnal pollution, they bathed themselves on the spot. Those who were the most strict bathed themselves in the water the ibis had drank of; for that bird particularly avoids all impure water.

[k] They enjoyed one great advantage which is not noticed by Herodotus. They were judges of the nation, as Ælian (book xiv. 34.) positively affirms, and as may be inferred from Diodorus Siculus, (book i. 73, 74.) We are struck with these points of resemblance between the customs of the Egyptian and Jewish high priests. 1. The high priest administered justice before the establishment of kings, unless there was any judge specially appointed. 2. The Urim and the Thummim of the high priest resemble the image which was worn by the chief judge of the Egyptians; both hung upon the breast by golden chains, and were composed of gold and precious stones. (Diod. Sic. i. 48.) *Larcher.*

[l] "Only the land of the priests bought "he not; for the priests had a portion "assigned them of Pharaoh, and did eat "their portion which Pharaoh gave them: "wherefore they sold not their lands." Gen. xlvii. 20.

[m] The Greek adds, *made of the grape*, to distinguish it from the *οἶνος ἐκ κριθέων*, *barley-wine*, or *beer*.

[n] The true reason of this is the hatred they bear to the sea, which they consider as an element foreign to us, or rather an enemy to human nature. Plut. Symp. viii. q. 8.

[o] This was imitated by the Pythagoreans. Piny says, (Hist. Nat. xviii. 12.) that it was forbidden because it was supposed to deaden the senses and cause dreams. So also Cicero, de Divinat. i. 30.

[p] The priests composed a distinct class among the Egyptians, as the Levites among the Jews, and the Brachmans among the Indians. There were also at Athens certain families to which the functions of priesthood belonged, as the Eumolpidæ, the Ceryces, the Eteobutades, &c. *Larcher.*

[q] "Speak unto the children of Israel, "that they bring thee a red heifer with-"out spot, wherein is no blemish, and "upon which never came yoke." Num. xix. 2. If they have only two white or black hairs together......they were deemed unfit for sacrifice. Maimonides, Leb. de Vaccâ ruffâ, &c. cap. i.

mention in another discourse. In the last place, he looks upon the hairs of his tail, that he may be sure they are as by nature they ought to be. If after this search the beast is found unblemished, he marks it by rolling a piece of the byblus round his horns, and then having put on it some clay fit to receive an impression, he applies his ring[r] to it, and the animal is then led away and secured; it is death to sacrifice one of these animals, unless he has been marked with such a seal: in this manner the animal is examined.

XXXIX. The established mode of sacrifice is this; when they have brought the victim, which has been stamped, to the altar, where they intend to sacrifice him, they kindle a fire. They then pour wine upon the altar, opposite to the victim, and having invoked the God, they kill him. This done, they flay the body, and cut off the head, which they carry with many imprecations to the market, if they have any, and sell it to some Grecian merchant; but if no such is to be found, they throw it into the river, using this form of execration; "May "all the evils impending over those that now sacrifice, or over "the Egyptians in general, be averted on this head[s]." These ceremonies of the libation of wine, and the manner of devoting the head of the sacrifice, are practised in all the temples of Egypt; and for this reason no Egyptian will eat of the head of any animal.

XL. But the inspection of the entrails and the manner of burning them is different in different rites. The Goddess they principally worship is called Isis, and they celebrate her festival with all imaginable solemnity. On the preceding day they fast, and, after they have prayed, they sacrifice a bullock; after having stript off the skin, they take out the intestines, leaving the fat with the vitals in the carcase. This done, they cut off the legs and end of the loin, together with the shoulders and neck; and, having filled the body with fine bread, honey, raisins, figs, incense, myrrh, and other perfumes; they burn it, and pour in a great quantity of oil. They sacrifice, after they have fasted, beating themselves[t] during all the

[r] The impression of this, according to Castor, represented a man on his knees, with his hands behind his back and the point of a sword at his throat. *Plutarch. de Iside et Osir*, p. 363.

[s] "And Aaron shall lay both his hands "upon the head of the live goat, and "confess over him all the iniquities of "the children of Israel, and all their "transgressions, putting them upon the "head of the goat, and shall send him "away by the hand of a fit man into the "wilderness." *Leviticus*, ch. xvi. 21.

[t] Xenophanes the Physician seeing the Egyptians scourging themselves and weeping in their sacrifices said, "If your "Gods are really Gods, do not lament "for them, if they are men do not sacri- "fice to them." *Plutarch. de Superst.* p. 171.

Larcher says this saying is well enough in the mouth of Xenophanes, but considers that Athenagoras, who also ridicules the custom, has shewn but little judgment in so doing.

time the flesh lies on the fire; and when they have so done, they feast upon the rest of the offering.

XLI. All the cattle of this kind, whether full grown or calves, used by the Egyptians in their sacrifices, are unblemished males; but the females, being sacred to Isis, are forbidden to be offered[u]: for the image of Isis is always made in the form of a woman with the horns of a cow on her head, as the Grecians represent Io; and for this reason all the Egyptians pay a greater reverence to that animal than to any other. So that no man or woman among them will ever be persuaded to kiss a Grecian on the mouth; or to use the same knife, pot, or spit; nor to eat the flesh even of unblemished cattle, which has been cut up with the knife of a Greek[x]. When any beast of this sort happens to die, they dispose of the body in the following manner; they throw the females into the river, and inter the males in the parts adjoining to the city, with one horn, and sometimes both, appearing above the ground, for a mark of the grave. When the flesh is putrified and the appointed time arrives, a vessel comes to each city from Prosopitis, an island of Delta, which comprehends nine schoeni of land in circumference, and several cities. The vessel is sent to take up the bones of the oxen, by one of these called Atarbechis[y], where a temple stands dedicated to Venus, and from whence many others are dispatched to different parts. After they have thus collected all the bones, they bury them together in one place; and the same rites are observed with relation to other cattle. For the Egyptians are forbidden by their laws to kill any.

XLII. Those who worship[z] in the temple of Jupiter at Thebes, or belong to that district, abstain from sheep, and sacrifice goats only. For the Egyptians are not unanimous in their manner of honouring the Gods, if we except Isis and

[u] Porphyry and St. Jerome say, that this was done on account of the scarcity of oxen. This rule, wise in its principle, degenerated into superstition. The Brachmans probably abstained from them originally for the same reason. In our colonies, it is not lawful to kill a cow without the permission of the governor. *Larcher.*

[x] From similar customs, the Egyptians necessarily became adverse to strangers. "And they set on for him "by himself and for them by themselves, "and for the Egyptians which did eat "with him by themselves, because the "Egyptians might not eat bread with "the Hebrews, for that is an abomination to the Egyptians." *Genesis,* ch. xliii. 32.

[y] The temple gave this name to the city. Atar or Athar (Etymologic. magn. voc. Ἄθυρ.) signifies Venus, and Bek a city: as Balbeck, the city of the sun, called by the Greeks Heliopolis. Baki is still found in the same sense among the Copts, and in their language *a* is pronounced as *e*. It is merely a Greek termination; Strabo and Pliny call it Aphroditespolis. *Larcher.*

[z] Ἵδρυνται is equivalent to ἱδρυμένον ἔχουσι, or ἱδρύκασι ἑαυτοῖς; so ch. 44. ἱδρυσάμενοι ἔκτηνται. Larcher ridiculously translates this, "Tous ceux, "qui ont fondé le temple de Jupiter "Thébéen." *Schweigh.*

Osiris, who, they say, is no other than Bacchus: but in the worship of these deities they all agree. On the other hand, those who frequent the temple of Mendes, with all the inhabitants of that territory, abstain from sacrificing goats, and offer sheep only. Now the Thebans, and all those who abstain from sheep after their example, pretend that this custom was established among them by the means of Hercules, who was very desirous of seeing Jupiter, whereas the God was unwilling to be seen; until at last Jupiter, yielding to his importunity, contrived this artifice. Having separated the head from the body of a ram, and flayed the whole carcase, he put on the skin with the wool, and in that form shewed himself to Hercules. For this cause the Egyptians represent Jupiter by an image wearing the head of a ram: in which they have been imitated by the Ammonians, who are a colony of Egyptians and Ethiopians, speaking a language composed of words taken from both those nations; and, as I conjecture, have given themselves the name of Ammonians, because Jupiter is by the Egyptians called Ammon[a]. For the same reason the ram is accounted a sacred animal, and never killed by the Thebans, except once in every year on the festival of Jupiter; when, after they have flayed the body, and put the skin upon the image of the God, they bring a statue of Hercules, into his presence: which done, all the assistants by beating themselves[b] weep for the ram, and afterwards bury him in a consecrated coffin.

XLIII. I have been informed that this Egyptian Hercules[c] is one of the twelve Gods; but of the other, who is known to the Grecians, I could never hear the least mention in any part of Egypt. And I have many good reasons to believe, that the Egyptians did not borrow this name from the Grecians, but rather the Grecians (and especially those who gave it to the son of Amphitryon) from the Egyptians; principally, because

[a] Ammon, says Plutarch, (de Iside et Osir. p. 354.) is the Egyptian name for Jupiter. This God was particularly worshipped at Thebes, called by the sacred books *Hamon-no*, the possession of Hammon; and by the Septuagint, (Ezek. ch. xxx.) the city of Ammon. The Greeks and Romans called it *Diospolis*, the city of Jupiter. Amongst the astronomers of Egypt Ammon represented the sun.. Jablonski (vol. i.) derives the word from Am-oein, *shining*. *Savary*, Letter LI.

[b] The word *τύπτεσθαι* is used in the same sense in ch. 61, and 132. The Latins also said *plangere aliquem*: *κόπτεσθαί τινα* is very common.

[c] Cicero also calls this Hercules *nilo genitus*, (de Natur. Deor. iii. 16.) M. de Pauw asserts, that there was only one Hercules. Hercules among the Greeks was originally only a hero. But the Greeks having remarked that there was a slight similarity between the Chon of the Egyptians, the Melcarth of the Tyrians and their Hercules, foolishly concluded that they were the same God.

The same remark may be applied to Bacchus, he was only a hero, till Orpheus, in order to flatter the Thebans, transferred the birth of Osiris to a more modern time. See Diodor. Sic. book i. ch. 22. from whom the latter part of this note is taken. *Larcher*.

Amphitryon and Alcmena[d], father and mother to the Grecian Hercules, were both of Egyptian descent. Besides, the Egyptians affirm they know not the names of Neptune, Castor, and Pollux[e], and that they have never been admitted into the number of their Gods; yet if they had borrowed the name of any deity from the Grecians, they would certainly have mentioned these in the first rank, had any of the Grecians then frequented the sea, and been acquainted with the use of shipping, as I believe they were. And therefore the Egyptians must have known the names of these Gods, rather than that of Hercules. But however this be, Hercules is one of the ancient Gods of the Egyptians; who say, that seventeen thousand years before the reign of Amasis, the number of their Gods, which had been eight, was increased to twelve[f], and that Hercules was accounted one of these.

XLIV. And being desirous of learning something certain concerning this matter, from whatever source I might be able, I sailed to Tyre in Phœnicia, because I had heard there was a temple dedicated to Hercules. That temple I saw, enriched with many magnificent donations, and among others with two pillars, one of fine gold, the other made of emerald[g], which shines by night in a surprising manner. Conversing with the priests of this God, and inquiring how long this temple had been built, I found these also to differ from the Greeks. For they assured me that the temple was built at the same time with the city, and that two thousand three hundred years were already past since the foundation of Tyre. In this city I saw another temple dedicated to Hercules by the name of Thasian; and when I arrived in Thasus, I found there also a temple of the same God, built by those Phœnicians, who founded that city during the expedition they made in search of Europa; which was five generations[h] before Hercules the

[d] The inscription on a tablet of brass found at Haliartus in Bœotia, on the tomb of Alcmena, shews this. Plutarch (de Socr. Genio.) relates, that Agesilaus carried it to Sparta, and that the inscription could not be understood, but the characters were very similar to the Egyptian. *Larcher.*

[e] Wilford remarks, that as it is positively asserted in the Paranas, that the Dioscuri were venerated on the banks of the Nile, they must have been revered under other names. Indeed Harpocrates and Halitomerion, the twin sons of Isis and Osiris, very much resemble them. *Beloe.*

[f] Larcher, contrary to the meaning of the author, has translated this, "Il est du "nombre de ces douze Dieux, qui sont "nés des huit Dieux." *Schweigh.*

[g] This pillar could not have been a true emerald, and according to Theophrastus, it was a pseudosmaragdus. But as this kind of stone does not emit any light during the night, if Herodotus was rightly informed, I readily believe, with the authors of the English Universal History, that it was composed of painted glass, the interior of which was illuminated by lamps. *Larcher.*

[h] From Cadmus to Œdipus, who was cotemporary with Hercules, there are exactly five generations. For the difficulties which this passage has caused, see Larcher's note, and his Essay on Chronology, ch. xi.

son of Amphitryon appeared in Greece. The researches then that I have made evidently prove, that the Egyptian Hercules is a God of great antiquity; and therefore, in my opinion, those Grecians act most rationally, who build temples to both; sacrificing to the first, as to an immortal being, under the name of Olympian, and honouring the other as a hero.

XLV. But the Grecians say many other things on this subject without due examination, and in particular have invented the following silly story. When Hercules, say they, arrived in Egypt, the Egyptians crowned him with a garland, and designing to sacrifice him to Jupiter, conducted him to the altar in great ceremony: during the way he was silent; but when they had placed him before the altar, and were beginning the preparatory ceremonies[i], he collected all his strength, and killed every man that was there present. Now those who tell this story seem to me utterly ignorant of the character and laws of the Egyptians. For how can we imagine that a people forbidden to sacrifice any kind of animal, except geese, swine, and such bulls and calves, as they find without blemish, would sacrifice men? and how could Hercules kill so many thousands, being then alone, and at that time by their own confession no more than a man? Nevertheless, I desire the Gods and the heroes would take in good part what I have said concerning these things.

XLVI. The reason that prevails with the Mendesians[k] I mentioned before, not to sacrifice the goat, either male or female, is, because they account Pan one of the eight Gods, who, they say, are more ancient than the twelve. And indeed their painters and sculptors represent Pan with the face and legs of a goat[l], as the Grecians do. Not that they imagine this to be his real form, for they think him like other Gods; but I have no inclination[m] to mention the reason they give for representing him in that manner. However, the Mendesians pay a religious worship to all goats, but to the males much more than to the females[n]; and the goatherds have also great honours; and particularly one he-goat[o], who is honoured at his death by public lamentations in all parts of

[i] This was the sprinkling of barley, and pouring libations on the head of the victim.

[k] The traveller who may be desirous of finding the ruins of Mendes, if he consults Herodotus and Strabo, must look for it at some distance from the canal of Achmoum, on the side of Menzale. *Savary*, Letter XXIV.

[l] All the images of Pan, that have come down to us, describe Pan with a man's face, and with the horns, ears, and feet of a goat.

[m] The comparative is often put for the positive, and particularly by the Attics. In the next chapter we have *εὐπρεπέστερος* for *εὐπρεπής*. *Larcher.*

[n] The Egyptians venerated the he-goat for the same reason as the Greeks did Priapus.

[o] I have followed the interpretation of Wesseling, Larcher, and Schweighæuser. See Schweighæuser's note.

the district. In the language of Egypt, Pan and a goat are equally called by the name of Mendes: and in my time a goat lay with a woman of that country in so public a manner, that all men knew the prodigy to have really happened.

XLVII. Swine are accounted such impure beasts[p] by the Egyptians, that if a man touches one, even in passing by, he presently hastens to the river, and in all his clothes plunges himself into the water. For this reason swineherds, although natives of Egypt, are not suffered to enter any of their temples; neither will any man give his daughter in marriage to one of that profession, nor take a wife born of such parents; so that they are necessitated to intermarry among themselves. The Egyptians deem it unlawful to sacrifice swine to any other deities than to Bacchus, and to the moon, when completely full; at which time they may eat of the flesh. There is a sacred tradition related by the Egyptians, to account for their abhorring swine on all other festivals, and sacrificing them on that; but it is more becoming for me, though I know it, not to mention it: and therefore shall only say, that when they offer this sacrifice to the moon, and have killed the victim, they put the end of the tail, with the spleen and fat, into a caul found in the belly of the animal; all which they burn on the sacred fire, and eat the rest of the flesh on the day of the full moon, though at any other time they would not taste it. Those, who on account of their poverty cannot bear the expence of this sacrifice, mould a paste into the form of a hog, and make their offering.

XLVIII. On the day before the[q] festival of Bacchus, though every one be obliged to kill a swine before the door of his house, yet he immediately restores the carcase to the swineherd that sold him. The rest of this festival is celebrated in Egypt to the honour of Bacchus with the same ceremonies as in Greece[r]; only, instead of the Phallus, they

[p] The reason of the aversion of the Egyptians to swine is, that the milk of the sow occasioned leprosies, and the animal itself from its fat has within it the seeds of leprosy. The Jews would never eat swines flesh, the Egyptians did once a year. *Larcher.*

[q] This custom was borrowed from hence by the Ionians in their festival of Apaturia. See Potter's Grecian Antiquities, and also Hesych. and Suidas in voc.

[r] Bacchus and Osiris were the same, or in other words the Bacchus of the Greeks was the Osiris of the Egyptians. What Clemens of Alexandria and Arnobius relate of the origin of this custom, are too indecent to relate. Plutarch gives another reason. Isis collected all the limbs of Osiris, with the exception of the virile member, which she could not find. It had been thrown into the Nile, and the Lepidotus, the Phagrus and Oxyrinthus had immediately devoured it; and it is for this reason that the Egyptians hold these fish in great abomination. In its place she consecrated the phallus, which is an imitation of it, in memory of which to this day the Egyptians hold a festival. De Iside and Osiride, p. 358.

These phalli were made in a variety of shapes, sometimes in the shape of a cross surmounted by a handle. *Larcher.*

have invented certain images of one cubit in height, so artificially contrived with strings, that the virile member, almost equal in bigness to the rest of the body, moves: while the women, who make the procession, carry the images, singing the praises of Bacchus, and preceded by a flute. But why this part is so disproportioned to the body, and why it alone moves, is accounted for by a sacred story.

XLIX. For my own part, I think Melampus[s] the son of Amytheon was not ignorant of any thing relating to this ceremony, but perfectly well instructed in all these rites. For he first introduced the name and sacrifices of Bacchus among the Grecians, together with the procession of the Phallus; though he did not so fully explain every particular, as other learned persons have done, who lived after him. But Melampus was certainly the first that taught the Grecians to carry the Phallus in procession to the honour of Bacchus, and introduced all the ceremonies they use on that occasion. I for my part pronounce him to have been a wise man, skilful in the art of divination; and that he instructed the Grecians in many things, which were derived from Egypt[t]; but especially in the worship of Bacchus, changing only some few particulars. For I shall not say that the worship paid this God by the Egyptians and Greeks, had their origin at the same period[u]; because in that case they would be conformable to the rest of the customs of the Greeks, and not lately introduced: neither shall I pretend that the Egyptians have borrowed these, or any other rites from the Grecians. But I am of opinion that Melampus was instructed in the ceremonies of Bacchus, chiefly by Cadmus the Tyrian, and those Phoenicians who accom-

[s] Melampus was exposed by his mother Rhodope when a child. All his body was covered except his feet, these the rays of the sun scorched and made black. Hence he was called Melampus. He was a celebrated soothsayer and physician, and after death received divine honours. See also book ix. ch. 33.

[t] As Egypt was then distinguished for sciences and arts, the Greeks who were beginning to emerge from barbarism, travelled thither to obtain knowledge, which they might afterwards impart to their countrymen. With this view the following illustrious men visited it: Orpheus, Musæus, Melampus, Dædalus, Homer, Lycurgus the Spartan, Solon the Athenian, Plato the philosopher, Pythagoras of Samos, &c. But superstition, which was the prevailing trait in the Grecian character, prevented their reaping the fruits they might have expected. They went from their country superstitious from ignorance, they returned superstitious from system. *Larcher.*

[u] The verb *συμπίπτειν* is sometimes used with a dative case in the sense of, *to agree, to coincide*, (vi. 18. 6. vii. 151. 1.) but never with the addition of any idea of chance; which many learned men think we must adopt in the present passage. This verb is frequently used by our author in another sense, so that those things are said *συμπίπτειν*, which *happen or exist at the same time*; sometimes with the addition of ὁμοῦ, τοῦ αὐτοῦ χρόνου, &c. (i. 82. 3. v. 36. 2. viii. 141. 7. ix. 100. 7.) and now and then without, (v. 36. 6. viii. 132. 16.) in which sense it appears to be used in the passage before us. *Schweigh.*

panied him to that country, which now goes under the name of Bœotia[x].

L. And indeed the names of almost all the Gods came into Greece from Egypt; for I discovered by inquiry that they came from a barbarian country, and in my opinion chiefly from Egypt. Only we must except Neptune[y], Castor and Pollux, as I mentioned before; Juno[z], Vesta, Themis, the Graces, and the Nereides; the names of all the others have always been familiar to the Egyptians, in this I repeat, what the Egyptians affirm; but those names which they say they are not acquainted with, I think are derived from the Pelasgians, except that of Neptune, which they learned from the Lybians, for no other people possess the name of this God, except the Lybians, who have always worshipped him. The Egyptians pay no religious honour to heroes[a].

LI. These and other rites, which I shall afterwards mention, the Grecians received from the Egyptians; but they learned of the Pelasgians to make the images of Mercury with an erected penis, the Athenians having been the first who practised this manner, and others by their example. For in that time the Pelasgians inhabited part[b] of the Athenian territories; and, because the Athenians were accounted among the nations of Greece, came likewise to be esteemed Grecians. Whoever is initiated in the Cabirian mysteries[c] of the Samothracians, which they received from the Pelasgians, knows what I say. For these Pelasgians were inhabitants of Samothracia, before they came into the country of Attica, and had instructed the Samothracians in the mysteries; as they after-

[x] Bœotia took its name from Bœotus, son of Itonus and the nymph Menalippe, and grandson of Amphictyon. Diodor. Sic. (book iv. ch. i.) says, that Bœotus was the father of Itonus, that he reigned in Thessaly, then called Æolis, and his subjects were called Bœotians. This author however does not inform us how the Bœotians passed into the country, which was known afterwards by the name of Bœotia. But this information is supplied by Thucydides, (book i. ch. 12.) who relates that they were driven from Arne by the Thessalians, sixty years after the fall of Troy, and that they established themselves in Bœotia, then called Cadmeis. *Larcher*.

[y] This God came originally from Lybia. See book iv. ch. 188.

[z] Manetho speaks of the Juno of the Egyptians, and informs us that three men were daily sacrificed to her, who were examined like calves. Amasis abolished this barbarous sacrifice, and substituted three figures of wax. (Porphyry de Abstin. ii. 55.) Whenever the Greeks discovered any slight resemblance in any foreign deity to their own, they did not fail to call them by the same name.

Hence the Egyptian divinity, which other nations call Venus, is by them called Juno. *Larcher*.

[a] "Ne leur rendent aucun honneur "funèbre," is Larcher's translation of *νομίζουσι οὐδὲν*, who shews that such is the meaning of the word.

[b] See book i. ch. 57. and particularly book vi. ch. 137.

[c] The Cabiri, according to Mnaseas, (see the Scholiast. Apoll. Rhod. book i. ver. 917.) were Axieres or Ceres, Axiokersa or Proserpine, Axiokersos or Pluto; to which is added a fourth, Casmilus or Mercury. Those who were initiated, (Scholiast. Aristoph. Pac. ver. 277.) were esteemed happy men, they had no-

wards did the Athenians, who by that means were the first of all the Grecians that formed the images of Mercury in the manner above mentioned: for which the Pelasgians pretend certain sacred reasons, explained in the mysteries of Samothracia.

LII. In all their sacrifices before that time, they used to pray to the Gods in general, as I was informed at Dodona, without attributing either name or surname[d] to any deity, which in those times they had never heard: but they called them by the name of Gods, because they disposed[e] and governed all actions and countries. After a long time, the names of the other Gods were brought among them from Egypt, and last of all that of Bacchus: upon which they consulted the oracle of Dodona, still accounted the most ancient, and then the only oracle in Greece; and having inquired, whether they should receive these names from barbarians, the oracle answered, they should. So from that time they invoked the Gods in their sacrifices under distinct names, and the same were afterwards received by the Grecians from these Pelasgians.

LIII. But what original is to be assigned to each of those Gods; whether they always were, and of what form, was utterly unknown till of late, and, to use a common expression, of yesterday. For I am of opinion that Hesiod and Homer, who lived not above four hundred years[f] before my time, were the persons that described in verse[g] the genealogy of the Gods

thing to fear in dangers or tempests. They who had learnt their names, says Plutarch, (de profect. in Virt. sent. p. 85.) used them as an amulet to avert dangers, by pronouncing them slowly. See book viii. ch. 65. *Larcher.*

[d] It is hence evident that the Pelasgians can have acknowledged but one God; for where many gods are believed, distinguishing appellations will and must be given; but the unity of the Deity precludes the necessity of names. *Mitford*, ch. ii. sect. 1.

[e] This is founded on the Etymology of *θεός*. Θεὸς is he who arranges every thing, ὁ παντὰ τεθεὶς καὶ ποιῶν. Eustat. ad Iliad, lib. xviii. Plato (in Cratylo) derives it from θέω, *to run*, on account of the perpetual movement of the stars, the sun, &c. which were the first objects of the adoration of the Greeks. *Larcher.*

It seems probable that the word θεὸς had a more ancient origin than any derivation within the Greek language. *Mitford*, ch. ii. sect. 1.

[f] According to Aulus Gellius, Herodotus was born fifty-three years before the Peloponnesian war, i. e. 484 B. C. Consequently Homer and Hesiod were born about 884 before our era. According to the life of Homer attributed to Herodotus, that poet was born 622 years before the invasion of Xerxes; this will give 1102 for the birth of Homer, which is very different from the former.

It appears to me very certain, that the life of Homer is not the production of our author, which might be easily proved, &c. See Larcher's long note, and Essay on Chronology, for an account of the opinions on this passage. Herodotus does not inform us how this period was calculated, but many things remaining from other early authors, and among them the dates reported by Thucydides, tend to make the assertion probable, and it has been generally admitted. *Mitford*, c. iii.

[g] The word in Greek is ποιεῖν, which signifies to compose or write in verse. They did not invent the stories of the deities, &c. as is evident from their writings, for they do not mention them as

among the Grecians; imposed names upon each; assigned their functions and honours; and clothed them in their several forms. As to the other poets, supposed to be more ancient, I think they lived after these. As to what relates to Homer and Hesiod I speak on my own opinion; but the rest, which I related before, I had from the priestesses of Dodona[h].

LIV. Concerning the oracles of Greece and Lybia, the Egyptians give the following account. The priests of the Theban Jupiter told me, that two women, employed in the temple, were carried away out of that country by certain Phœnicians; who afterwards, as they were informed, sold one of them in Lybia, and the other in Greece; and that these two women established the first oracles among those people. When I inquired how they knew this to be true, they answered, that indeed the women were never found, though all possible diligence was used to that end; but they had since learned, that things had passed as they related.

LV. This account I received from the priests of Thebes. On the other hand the principal priestesses of Dodona say, that two black pigeons flew away at a certain time from Thebes in Egypt: that one of these arrived in Lybia, and the other in Dodona; that this last, as she sat pearched on a beech-tree, admonished the inhabitants, with an articulate voice, to erect an oracle in that place to Jupiter; and that the people, believing this to be a divine revelation, readily obeyed. They add, that the other pigeon, which flew into Lybia, commanded the Lybians to found the oracle of Ammon dedicated to the same God. These things are said by the priestesses of Dodona, and affirmed by all that belong to the temple. The eldest of these women is named Promenia, the second Timarete, and the third Nicandra.

LVI. But my opinion is, that if the Phœnicians did really carry off the two priestesses before mentioned, and sold the one in Lybia and the other in Greece, this last was bought by

new. They introduced legends and fables handed down by tradition, &c. In this passage Herodotus expresses an opinion that the Grecian theogony was the invention of Homer and Hesiod; but whoever reflects on its nature, its complication and contrivance; its countless, but coherent relations and dependencies, must be sensible that this was impossible. Butler's Reminiscences, Sect. ii.

[h] According to another tradition, (Strabo, lib. vii. 7.) men originally delivered the oracles at Dodona. They were called Selli or Helli, from the Thessalian Hellus, from whom the neighbouring country was called Hellopia. These priests practised great austerities. They were also called Tomures from τέμνω and from οὐρὰ, *caudam demeto, castro*; probably, because they underwent that operation, in order to keep themselves chaste. The office consequently was not much sought for; and we find that women of an advanced age were appointed in their stead, who retained the name of Tomores. Strabo pretends that they were so called, because they were guardians of mount Tmaros or Tomaros, on which the temple of Dodona was situated. *Larcher.*

the Thesprotians, who inhabited those parts which are now called Hellas, and in that time were known by the name of Pelasgia[i]: that under her servitude she consecrated an altar to Jupiter under a beech; nothing being more natural, than to suppose that she who had been an attendant in the temple of that God in Thebes, would not be unmindful of his worship in another place; and, when she had learned the Greek language, she instituted an oracle, and related that her sister had met with the like fortune, and had been sold in Lybia by the same Phœnicians.

LVII. The Dodonæans, as I conjecture, gave them the name of pigeons, because they were barbarians, and their speech resembled the chattering of birds: but as soon as this woman became able to speak their language, they presently reported that the pigeon had spoken with a human voice; for while she continued to use a barbarous tongue, she appeared to speak like a bird. If these things are not so, I desire to be informed how a pigeon should come to speak the language of men. In a word, by saying that the dove was black, they shew that the woman was an Egyptian. The manner in which oracles are delivered at Thebes and Dodona are similar; and also the manner of divination from victims came from Egypt.

LVIII. The Egyptians were also the first inventors of meetings at festivals[k], ceremonies, and supplications[l]; all which I persuade myself the Grecians received from that people; because they plainly appear to have been very ancient among the Egyptians, and but lately introduced in Greece.

LIX. The Egyptians have not one, but several meetings on festivals in a year[m], particularly, and with the greatest zeal, in the city of Bubastis, where they assemble to worship Diana; and in Busiris, a place situate in the midst of Delta, where there is a very large temple of Isis[n], by the Grecians called Demeter, is built. The festivals of Minerva are solemnized in the city of Sais, and those of the sun in Heliopolis. Latona

[i] The whole of Greece was formerly called Pelasgia, of which Thesprotia was part. *Schweighæuser.*

[k] The people receiving without labour the produce of the earth, were able to celebrate so many festivals without any prejudice to themselves. In a country less favoured by nature, too many festivals would waste valuable time and accustom the inhabitants to idleness and excess. *Larcher.*

[l] Προσαγωγὴ is a term borrowed from the court of kings; Herodotus applies the word to these ceremonies of religion, which bring us into the presence of the Deity. *Larcher.*

[m] From the great number of festivals observed in ancient Egypt, it seems that the inhabitants must have been a gay and cheerful people. Yet Winkleman observes that they were of a grave, dull character. Modern narratives justify the picture drawn by Herodotus. *Larcher.*

[n] Sicard has described the ruins of this temple, and gives us a grand idea of what it once was. *Memoires des Missions du Levant.*

is particularly worshipped in Butus, and Mars in the city of Papremis.

LX. The manner observed in the festivals of Bubastis is this: men and women embark promiscuously in great numbers, and during the voyage, some of the women beat upon a tabor, while part of the men play on the pipe, the rest of both sexes singing and striking their hands together at the same time. At every city they find in their passage they bring the boat to land, and some of the women continue their music; but others either provoke the women of the place with opprobrious language; or dance, and draw up their garments; and this they do at every town that stands by the shore. When the arrive at Bubastis, they celebrate the festival with numerous sacrifices, and consume more wine than in all the rest of the year. For the inhabitants say this assembly usually consists of about seven hundred thousand men and women, besides children.

LXI. I have already related how the worship of Isis is performed in the city of Busiris[o]; and shall only add, that, after the sacrifices, all the men and women then present, who always amount to many thousands, lament some one by beating themselves; but whom they lament it is impious for me to discover. In this devotion the Carians that live in Egypt surpass all; for they cut their foreheads with swords, and by this action distinguish themselves to be strangers, and not Egyptians.

LXII. When they meet to sacrifice in the city of Sais[p], they hang up by night a great number of lamps filled with oil and a mixture of salt[q], round every house, the wick swimming on the surface. These burn during the whole night, and the festival is thence named *the lighting of lamps*[r]. The Egyptians who are not present at this solemnity, observe the same ceremonies wherever they be; and lamps are lighted that night, not only in Sais, but throughout all Egypt. Nevertheless, the reasons for using these illuminations, and paying so great respect to this night, are kept secret.

LXIII. Those who assemble on such solemn occasions at Heliopolis and Butus, offer sacrifices only, without any farther ceremonies. But in Papremis, when they have per-

[o] The situation assigned to this place in ch. 59. agrees with the position of the modern village of Bousir. *Savary*, Letter XXII.

Bou, among the Egyptians, signifies a tomb, a sepulchre. Thus Busiris will be the tomb of Osiris. *Larcher*.

The manner of sacrificing to Isis was related in the 40th chapter.

[p] This is now called *Sah*.

[q] Salt was used in every religious ceremony.

[r] This feast, which much resembles the feast of lamps, observed from time immemorial in China, seems to confirm the opinion of M. de Guignes, who was one of the first who suspected that China was a colony of Egypt. *Larcher*.

formed their worship, and finished their offerings as in other places, a small number of priests, at the setting of the sun, attend about the image of Mars; but the far greater part place themselves before the gates of the temple, with clubs in their hands; while other men who have devoted themselves to this service, and frequently amount to above a thousand, armed in like manner, assemble together in a place opposite to them. The image of the God, which is kept in a little tabernacle of wood gilded with gold, is brought on the eve of the festival, and placed within another; and those few, who are appointed to attend, draw both the tabernacle and the image to the temple on a chariot of four wheels. But the priests, who stand at the entrance, refusing to give them admittance, the votaries, bringing succour to the God, begin to strike with their clubs, and an obstinate combat ensues, in which many heads are broken; so that, as I conjecture, many die of the wounds they receive, though the Egyptians affirm the contrary.

LXIV. These rites, if we may believe the inhabitants, were instituted for the following cause. They say, that Mars was educated abroad till he attained to the age of a man; when coming home to visit his mother, who dwelt in this sacred place, he was denied entrance by her servants, and driven away by violence; because they had never seen him before; that Mars, having brought a good number of men from another city, handled the servants rather roughly, and entered by force; in commemoration of which action, this combat is represented on his festival. The Egyptians were likewise the first who made it a point of religion, that men should abstain from women in the temples; and not enter any sacred place without washing, after the use of a woman. For almost all other nations, except the Egyptians and Grecians, neither scruple to perform that action in temples, nor to go thither unwashed after they have had the company of women; thinking mankind to be like other animals. And because they frequently see beasts and birds coupling together in sacred inclosures[a] and temples, they imagine that if this action were disagreeable to God, these creatures would abstain in those places. But I cannot approve the conclusion they draw from this observation.

LXV. The Egyptians are beyond measure scrupulous in all things concerning religion; especially in the ensuing particulars. Egypt, though adjoining to Lybia, abounds not in variety of beasts; yet all those they have, both wild and tame, are accounted sacred. But if I should take upon me

[a] See Book i. ch. 199.

to give the reasons why they are consecrated, I must enter into a long discourse of divine things, which I avoid with all possible care[t]; and whatever I have touched upon in the course of my narrative, I have mentioned from necessity. They have a custom, however, relating to beasts of the following kind. In the first place, men and women are appointed to feed and bring up all domestic animals by themselves; and the son succeeds the father in this office. All the inhabitants of the cities perform their vows[u] to these, and to the deities to which they are sacred, with the following ceremonies. They shave the heads of their children, either entirely, or one half, or at least a third part, and weigh it in a balance against a piece of silver, and when the silver preponderates, they give it to the woman who keeps[x] the animals; who for that reward provides them with fish cut in pieces, which is their usual food. If any person kills one of these beasts voluntarily[y], he is punished with death; if involuntarily, his punishment is referred to the discretion of the priests. But if a man kill either a hawk or an ibis, whether with design or not, he must die without mercy.

LXVI. The beasts that are brought up among men are many, and would be much more numerous, if accidents of the following kind did not frequently happen to the cats. For when the females have been delivered of their young, they care no longer for the male; the male being desirous of obtaining a second commerce, and not being able, contrives this artifice. He waits an opportunity to rob the female of her young, and having done so, kills them all, but abstains from eating their flesh. The female, seeing herself deprived of

[t] The ancients were remarkably scrupulous in every thing which regarded religion; but, in the time of Diodorus Siculus, strangers did not pay the same regard to the religious rites of the Egyptians. Thus this historian was not afraid to acquaint us with the motives, which induced the Egyptians to pay divine honours to animals. See Diod. Sic. i. 21. *Larcher.*

[u] These vows regarded the health of their children. See Diod. Sic. i. 83.

[x] These were not the only funds to procure food for these animals. Diodorus Siculus (i. 83.) says, that there was a piece of ground consecrated to each kind of animal, from the revenue of which food was purchased.

[y] *Ne fando quidem auditum est crocodilum, aut ibim, aut felem violatum ab Ægyptio.* Cicero de Nat. Deor. i. 29.

Ægyptiorum morem quis ignorat? Quorum imbutæ mentes pravis erroribus quamvis carnificinam prius subierint quam ibim, aut aspidem, aut felem, aut canem, aut crocodilum violent, quorum etiamsi imprudentes quidpiam fecerint, pœnam nullum recusent. Cicero, Tusculan. Quæst. v. 27.

When Ptolemy had not yet been declared the friend of the Roman people, and the Egyptians were paying all possible attention to any one who came from Italy, and were carefully avoiding every thing which might give a pretext for war, a Roman happened to kill a cat; and notwithstanding all this the people surrounded his house, and neither the entreaties of the nobles, who were sent by the king, nor the terror of the Roman name, were able to rescue the suppliant from their fury, although he had done it involuntarily. *Diodorus Siculus*, i. 83.

her young, and being very desirous of more, begins again to follow the male; for this creature is exceedingly fond of its young. When a conflagration takes place, a supernatural[a] impulse seizes on the cats. For though the Egyptians standing at a distance neglect the progress of the flames, and take much greater care to preserve the cats than the house; yet, either by creeping slily along the ground, or leaping over the heads of the men, the cats throw themselves into the fire; and on these occasions great lamentations are heard among the Egyptians. In whatever house a cat dies of a natural death, all the family shave their eyebrows; and if a dog die[a], they shave the whole body.

LXVII. All dead cats are carried to certain sacred houses, where being embalmed, they are afterwards buried in the city of Bubastis. Bitches are laid in consecrated coffins, and interred in the cities where they die, and so are ichneumons[b]; but hawks and field-mice are carried to the city of Butus. The ibis is carried to Hermopolis[c]. The bears, which are few in number, and wolves[d] no bigger than foxes, are buried in the places where they are found dead.

[a] It is astonishing that Herodotus should consider this as a prodigy. The cat is a timid animal, and fire makes it more so; the precautions taken to prevent its perishing render it more alarmed, and deprive it of its senses. It is then not surprising that they should throw themselves in the fire. *Larcher.*

[a] This was because the dog was consecrated to Anubis, who was represented with the head of a dog. Virgil (Æneid viii. 698.) and Ovid (Met. ix. 692.) call him *Latrator Anubis*; Propertius (III. Eleg. xi. 41.) and Prudentius, (Apotheos, 196.) *Latrans Anubis.* The Egyptians paid greater honours to dogs than any other animals; but when Cambyses killed Apis, the dog alone of all the animals touched it: this deprived it of its honours. See Plutarch de Isid. et Osir. *Larcher.*

[b] Diod. Sicul. (i. 87.) relates that this was a kind of rat, a mortal enemy to the crocodile, whose eggs it destroys, and while it is asleep creeps down its throat and devours its entrails. Pococke (vol. i. p. 203.) says he was unable to learn in Upper Egypt whether the ichneumon destroyed the eggs of the crocodile, and creeped down its throat. The former he thought probable, the latter improbable. He relates, that there was an animal in Egypt called the rat of Pharaoh, which passed in Europe for the ichneumon; its make is somewhat like that of the ferret, but much larger. M. Camus, in his notes on Aristotle's Hist. of Animals, pretends that the Egyptians kept them in their houses, as we do cats. In this he is certainly deceived. For else how could Maillet say, that he had only seen the representations of this animal in stone; and Pococke, who travelled long after, not have remarked it during his long stay in the country. Maillet informs us (Description de l'Egypte, vol. ii. p. 130.) that, according to the representations in stone, it is a kind of wild pig, very handsome. *Larcher.*

[c] There were three places of this name in Egypt. Larcher thinks, with Wesseling, that the one in Upper Egypt is here meant; because the building called Ibeum (apparently from these birds) was not far from it.

[d] Sonnini (vol. i. p. 155.) affirms that there are neither wolves nor foxes in Africa. Larcher thinks his testimony outweighed by the united authorities of Herodotus, Aristotle, Pliny and Prosper Alpinus. Wolves were honoured in Egypt, from their resemblance to the dog; and because formerly, when Isis and her son Osiris were on the point of fighting with Typhon, Osiris came to their assistance in the shape of a wolf. Others relate that the Ethiopians having made an expedition against Egypt were put to flight

LXVIII. As for the crocodiles, they are of a strange nature. They eat nothing during the four coldest months[e]; and though they have four feet, yet they equally frequent the water and the land. They lay their eggs and hatch them on dry ground; staying ashore the greater part of the day. But they pass all the night in the water, because the water is then warmer[f] than the air and dews. No living thing that we know grows to so vast a size from so small a beginning. For their eggs are little bigger than those of a goose, and their young at the first appearance proportionable: but they afterwards grow to the length of seventeen cubits and more[g]. They have the eyes of a hog, and large and projecting teeth in proportion to the rest of the body. Of all animals, these alone have no tongue[h], and move the upper jaw only when they eat; the lower never. They have claws exceedingly strong, and a scaly impenetrable hide[i]. The crocodile is blind in the water, but very quick-sighted by land: and because he lives for the most part in the river, his mouth is

by a great number of wolves, whence the place where this happened was called Lycopolis. *Larcher from Eusebius.*

[e] Pococke (vol. i. p. 203.) relates that he saw great numbers of crocodiles during the whole month of January.

[f] Water exposed to violent heat during the day, preserves its warmth in the night, and is not then so cold as the external air. *Larcher.*

[g] "In my wanderings on the Nile, I "have seen crocodiles of all sizes, from "three to twenty-six or twenty-eight "feet in length: many officers worthy "of credit, assured me that they met "with one no less than forty feet long. "They are by no means so ferocious as "is pretended; their favourite resorts "are the low islands of the river, where "they are seen basking in the sun, (the "most intense heat of which appears "highly gratifying to them,) by numbers "at a time, asleep and motionless like so "many logs of wood; surrounded by birds "who appear quite unmindful of them. "What is the food of these large "animals? Many stories are related of "them, but we have not yet had an "opportunity of verifying a single one. "We were not once attacked by them, "though constantly bathing in the Nile, "nor did we ever meet with one at a "distance from the water. It appears "probable, that they find in the Nile "itself a sufficient quantity of easily "procurable food, which they digest "slowly, being, like the lizard and serpent, cold-blooded, and of an inac"tive stomach. General Beliad had a "young one in his possession, which "lived four months without eating, "without appearing to suffer, or to grow "larger, or to become leaner, and to "the last was as untractable as ever." *Denon's Travels in Egypt*, vol. ii. p. 308.

Mr. Harmer is of opinion that the dragon of the Old Testament is the crocodile; in confirmation of whom see Hurdis.

[h] "On the 27th we found a dead cro"codile on the shore of the river; it "was still fresh; the length was eight "feet; the upper jaw, which is the only "one that has any motion, seems to "close but indifferently with the under, "but the throat supplies the deficiency, "for it hangs as loose as a purse, and "its elasticity performs the office of a "tongue, of which this animal is en"tirely destitute; the nostrils and ears "shut like the ear-holes of a fish; and "its small close-set eyes add much to "the frightfulness of its general ap"pearance." *Denon.* vol. ii. p. 82.

[i] "We here saw three, one much "larger than the rest, was nearly "twenty-five feet long; they were all "asleep, so that we could approach "within twenty paces: I fired at one "with a heavy musquet, the ball struck "him and rebounded off from his scales, "he made a leap of ten feet, and dived "into the river." *Denon.* vol. ii. p. 186.

generally infested with leeches; so that though all other beasts and birds equally avoid him, yet he lives in peace with the trochilus[k], because he receives a benefical service from that bird. For when the crocodile goes out of the water, and opens his mouth, which he does most commonly towards the west, the trochilus enters and devours the leeches; with which good office the crocodile is so well pleased, that he never hurts it[l].

LXIX. One part of the Egyptians esteem the crocodile sacred; but others pursue him to death[m] as a common enemy. Those who inhabit the country of Thebes, and that adjoining to the lake of Mœris, pay a peculiar veneration to him. For each of these people train up a crocodile to be so tame as to endure the hand[n], putting strings of jewels or gold through its ears[o], and a chain on its fore-feet. They feed it with sacred food, prescribed by law, and treat it while alive as well as possible; and when it is dead it is embalmed, and buried in a sacred coffin. But the inhabitants of Elephantine are so far from accounting the crocodile sacred, that they eat its flesh. The Egyptian name of this animal is Champsæ[p]; for the Ionians were the first who called them crocodiles; because they thought them to be like certain creatures they find in hedges[q], and call by that name.

[k] Marmol (in his Africa, tom. iii.) assures us that this is a white bird, about the size of a thrush. The greater part of translators interpret this word wren, but the wren haunts ruins, old walls, &c. whereas the trochilus delights in the borders of morasses, lakes, rivers, &c. Mr. Camus (Arist. Hist. Anim. tom. ii.) says, that it is a species of wren, and inclines to the opinion of Salerne, who thinks it is the swift, (*Courier.*) Father Sicard, the learned and pious missionary informs, us that it is the saq-saq; a bird I do not know. *Larcher.*

[l] Blanchard pretends, "that retreat "would not be certain to the trochilus, "if nature had not given to its feathers, "both on the back and the extremity of "its wings, a stiffness which would "sorely prick the fleshy parts of the "mouth of the crocodile." He cites Pliny, book viii. and Arist. Hist. Anim. ix. 6. Aristotle and Pliny mention the trochilus, but say nothing of the properties stated by Mr. Blanchard. *Larcher.*

[m] These were the people of Tentyra, now called Dandera. They used to seek them on purpose to kill them, and were famous for their intrepidity in destroying them. See Strabo Geograph. xvii. Seneca Nat. Quæst. iv. 2. and Pliny, Hist. Nat. viii. 25. See also Savary, Letter XXXII.

[n] It appears that this was a particular kind of crocodile. Great honours were paid them in the district of Arsinoe. They are tamed by the priests, and called *Sonchis.* Champsæ appears to be the generic term. *Larcher.*

[o] This seems to suppose, that the crocodile has ears externally; nevertheless those the Sultan sent to Louis XIV. and which the Academy of Sciences dissected, had none. They found in them indeed apertures for the ears placed below the eyes, (but concealed and covered with skin,) which had the appearance of two eyelids entirely closed. When the animal was alive, and out of the water, these lids probably opened. However this may be, it was, as may be presumed, to these membranes that the earrings were fixed. *Larcher.*

For an account of the whole crocodile, see the Memoires de l'Academie des Sciences, tom. iii. p. 3.

[p] The modern Egyptians call them Timsah, according to Pococke. This is very much like Champsæ, and may have been altered by copyists. *Larcher.*

[q] This is in fact the guana, an animal very well known in the hot climates.

LXX. The ways of taking the crocodile[r] are various, but I shall only describe that which to me seems most worthy of being mentioned. They fasten the chine of a hog to an iron hook, which they let down into the river, beating a living pig on the shore at the same time. The crocodile hearing the noise, and making that way, meets with the chine, which he devours, and is drawn to land; where, when he arrives, they presently throw dirt in his eyes, and by that means do what they will with him, which otherwise would be difficult.

LXXI. The hippopotamus[s] is esteemed sacred by the inhabitants of Papremis, though in no other part of Egypt. It has the following nature and shape. It is a quadruped, with cloven feet, and hoofs like a bull; his nose is short and turned up; but his mane, tail and voice, resemble those of a horse, and his teeth grow out in the manner of tusks. He is equal in bigness to the largest bull; and his skin is so thick, that spear-handles are made of it when dry.

LXXII. Otters are likewise seen in the river; which, with the eel and lepidotus[t], are the fish called sacred to the Nile, as the vulpanser[u] is among the birds.

LXXIII. The phœnix[x] is another sacred bird, which I have never seen except in effigy. He rarely appears in Egypt; once only in five hundred years, immediately after the death of his father, as the Heliopolitans affirm. If the painters describe him truly, his feathers represent a mixture

[r] The most common way of killing the crocodile is by shooting it. The ball must be directed towards the belly, where the skin is soft and not armed with scales like the back. Yet they give an account of a method of catching them, something like that which Herodotus relates. They make some animal cry at a distance from the river, and when the crocodile comes out, they thrust a spear into his body, to which a rope is tied; they then let him go into water to spend himself; and afterwards drawing him out, run a pole into his mouth, and jumping on his back tie his jaws together. *Pococke*, vol. i. p. 203.

[s] Bochart contends that the Behemoth of Job, ch. xl. 15. is the same as the hippopotamus, and he has supported his opinion with so much plausibility and learning, that it has been generally received since his time.

[t] This word signifies scaly and a particular species of fish, but what species I know not. Linnæus calls it the red carp of the Nile, *cyprinus rubescens Niloticus*. Syst. Nat. vol. i. p. 528.

This probably is the same fish as that described under the name of *bichir* by Geoffrey de St. Hiliaire, with remarkable accuracy. "The bichir is covered "with strong and impenetrable scales, "which defend it from any fatal contact, "and from the tooth of any animal that "might attempt to attack it. This solidity arises from a bony substance which "lines each scale underneath, and which "is so thick and compact, that very few "of our cutting instruments will penetrate it." There is also a description of the same fish, with a drawing of it, in the Annales du Musée d'Hist. Nat. tom. i. p. 57, et seqq. *Schweigh.*

[u] This bird in figure greatly resembles the goose, but it has all the wit and cunning of a fox. *Larcher.*

[x] It was not believed in the time of Herodotus that the phœnix rose again from its ashes. The Fathers of the Greek and Latin church added credit to this fable, and did not fail to cite it as a solid proof of the resurrection, which it was impossible to refute. This was first alleged by St. Clement of Rome. *Larcher.*

of crimson and gold; and he resembles the eagle in outline[7] and size. They affirm that he contrives the following thing, which to me is not creditable. They say that he comes from Arabia; and bringing the body of his father inclosed in myrrh, buries him in the temple of the sun; and that he brings him in this manner. First he moulds as great a quantity of myrrh into the shape of an egg, as he is well able to carry; and after having tried the weight, he hollows out the egg, and puts its parent into it, and stops up with some more myrrh the hole through which he had introduced the body, so that the weight is the same as before: he then carries the whole mass to the temple of the sun in Egypt. Such is the account they give of the phoenix.

LXXIV. In the country of Thebes a small kind of serpent is found, esteemed sacred by the Egyptians; having two horns growing on the top of the head, and no way hurtful to men[8]. When any of these serpents die they are buried in the temple of Jupiter, because they are thought to belong to that God.

LXXV. There is a place in Arabia, nearly opposite the city of Butus, to which I went, when I heard what is related of the flying serpents[9]; when I arrived there, I saw an incredible quantity of their bones and spines amassed in many heaps of different bigness, some greater and others less. The place where these spines are scattered about, is at the narrow passage between mountains opening into a spacious plain, which is contiguous to Egypt; and to this place, the inhabitants say, the flying serpents advance in the beginning of every spring; but are prevented by the ibis from proceeding farther, and destroyed in the pass; for which service the ibis is highly reverenced by the Egyptians, as both they and the Arabian sacknowledge.

LXXVI. This bird is in colour of the deepest black, and

[7] The Greek word seems to express the same as the French word *contour*. *Schweigh.*

[8] Phylarchus relates, that great honours were paid in Egypt to asps; that they were tame, and lived with their children without doing any harm. They came from their holes when called, and at a certain noise made with the fingers. The Egyptians, after dinner, put on the table meal mixed with wine and honey, and the asps at their call came and fed. (Ælian, Nat. Hist. Anim. xvii. 5. and x. 31.) These asps were called *thermonthis*. The statues of Isis were crowned with them. *Larcher.*

It is supposed that by means of these the Egyptian magicians turned their rods into serpents. See Sykes on Miracles, pp. 166—168; Shaw's Travels, Pref. p. 5, also p. 429; Supp. p. 62.

[9] We ought not to be too prompt, either to believe or disbelieve things which are uncommon. Although I have never seen winged serpents, I believe that they exist; for a Phrygian brought into Ionia a scorpion with wings like those of the grasshopper. *Pausanias*, book ix. ch. 21.

"The burden of the beasts of the "South; into the land of trouble and "anguish, from whence come the young "and old lion, the viper, and fiery flying "serpent," &c. *Isaiah*, ch. xxx. ver. 6.

in bigness equal to a crex[b]; his beak is crooked, and his legs like those of a stork. This is the form of the black ibis which kills the serpents. Another sort of ibis[c], which comes more in the way of men, has white feathers on every part of his body, except the head, neck, and extremities of the wings and tail; which are of as deep a black as those of the other kind: but part of his head, and all his neck, have no feathers. The serpent is in shape like the water-snake; but his wings are destitute of feathers, and smooth, like those of a bat. And here I leave this discourse concerning sacred animals.

LXXVII. The Egyptians who inhabit those parts of Egypt which are sown with corn, of all nations I ever saw, are the greatest cultivators of memory[d], and most skilled in antiquities. Their manner of life is this. They purge themselves every month, three days successively, by vomiting and glysters, in order to preserve health; supposing that all diseases among men proceed from the food they use. For otherwise, the Egyptians are by nature the most healthy[e] people of the world, the Lybians only excepted; which, as I conjecture, is to be attributed to the regularity of the seasons and constancy of the weather, most distempers beginning upon some alteration, and particularly the change of the seasons. They make their bread of olyra, and call it by the name of cyllestis; but their wine is made of barley[f], because

[b] The crex is a species of bird (Arist. Hist. Anim.) with a very pointed beak and long legs. Gesner pretends that this bird is found in England, with long legs, resembling the quail, only somewhat larger, and at the commencement of the summer incessantly repeats these words, *Crex, crex.* There are several other opinions on the subject. It must have been common in Greece, as Herodotus uses it to explain the other. *Larcher.*

[c] This bird was consecrated to the moon, and, according to Ælian, it would starve itself if carried out of Egypt. There has been, however, one for several years at the menagerie at Versailles; an exact description of which is given in the Memoires de l'Academie des Sciences, vol. iii. *Larcher.*

[d] Thamus, king of Egypt, is reported to have said to Theuth, who was praising, in his presence, his invention of letters, as an assistance to the memory: "You, since you are the father of letters, "have, from prejudice in their favour, "spoken the contrary to what they "effect; for this invention will produce "forgetfulness, as the cultivation of the "memory will be neglected." *Plato in Phædro.*

[e] This assertion was true previous to the time of Herodotus, and a long time afterwards; but when they began to neglect the canals the water putrified, and the vapours which exhaled rendering the air of Egypt very unhealthy, malignant fevers soon began to appear; these became epidemical, and these vapours concentrating and becoming every day more pestilential, finally caused that dreadful malady, the plague. It was not so before canals were sunk at all, or as long as they were kept in good order; but probably that part of Lower Egypt which inclines to Elearchis has never been healthy. *Larcher.*

[f] The most vulgar sort of people make a sort of beer of barley without being malted; they put something in to make it intoxicate, and call it *bonny:* they make it ferment; it is thick and sour, and will not keep longer than three or four days. *Pococke.*

Hops were unknown in that country; they put in chervil and lupines to give it a bitter taste. *Larcher.*

The invention of this liquor of bar-

they have no vines[g] in that country. They eat some fish raw, when they have dried them in the sun, others salted[h]; together with quails, ducks, and smaller birds, preserved in salt, without any other preparation. Whatever other birds or fishes they have, except such as they account sacred, are eaten without scruple, either boiled or roasted.

LXXVIII. At the feasts of the wealthy, when they begin to taste the wine after supper, a person appointed to that end carries about in a coffin the image of a dead man carved in wood, and representing the original in colour and shape. These images, which are always of one, and sometimes of two cubits in length, are carried round all the company, and these words pronounced to every one distinctly: "Look upon "this[i], then drink and rejoice; for thou shalt be as this is." This they do at their banquets.

LXXIX. They observe the institutions that have been handed down from their forefathers, but will not increase their number by new additions. Among other memorable customs, they sing a song like that which is sung by the Phoenicians, Cyprians, and other nations, who vary the name according to the different languages they speak. It is evident that it is the same which the Greeks sing, and which they call Linus[k]. And as I confess my surprise at many things I found among the Egyptians, so I more particularly wonder whence they had this knowledge of Linus; because they seem to have celebrated him from time immemorial. The Egyptians call it Maneros; and say, that Maneros was the only son of the first of their kings, but happening to die by an untimely death in the flower of his age, he is lamented by the Egyptians in this mourning song; which is the most ancient and only composition of the kind used in Egypt.

ley is universally attributed to Osiris. *Beloe.*

[g] Dupuy has rightly perceived that Herodotus only speaks of that part of Egypt which was marked out for the cultivation of corn. To other proofs may be added the following, from Numbers, ch. xx. ver. 5: "And wherefore have "ye made us to come up out of Egypt "to bring us unto this evil place? it is "no place of seed, or of figs, or of *vines*, "or of pomegranates; neither is there "any water to drink." *Larcher.*

[h] The Egyptians abhorred sea salt, and therefore used fossil salt. See Arrian, Exped. Alexand. iii. cap. 4.

[i] The idea of enjoying oneself while life lasted was common among the ancients. See Anacreon. Od. iv. The example of Sardanapalus will occur to every reader, and also the line:

Ede, bibe, lude, nulla est in morte voluptas.

See also Cicero Tuscul. Quæst. v. 35.

[k] Linus was the first inventor of rythm and melody among the Greeks. Having become admired for his poetry and music, he had several scholars, of whom the most illustrious were Hercules, Orpheus, and Thamyris. Hercules was learning to play on the harp, when Linus, impatient at his dulness, struck him; upon which Hercules in his anger gave him so violent a blow with his harp, that he killed him. *Diodorus Siculus*, iii. 66.

Eustathius says that there was a Linus more ancient than the master of Hercules. *Larcher.*

LXXX. In one particular the Egyptian manner is like that of the Lacedæmonians[l] only, among all the Grecians; for the young men turn aside to make way when they meet their elders, and rise up from their seats[m] when they approach; in this they do not agree with any other nation of Greece. Instead of addressing one another when they meet in the streets, they bow the body and let their hands hang down to the knee.

LXXXI. They wear linen tunics with fringes round the legs, which they call calasiris[n], over these they throw shawls[o] made of white wool; but to enter into any temple with this garment, or to be buried in any thing made of wool, is accounted profane. This custom is observed by those who are initiated in the rites of Orpheus and Bacchus[p]; which are the same as the Egyptian and Pythagorean[q]. For among them also, to inter the dead in woollen garments is accounted irreligious, and certain mysterious reasons are alleged to justify their opinion.

LXXXII. The Egyptians were also the inventors of divers other things. They assigned each month and day to some particular God; observing the time of men's nativity;

[l] Another point of resemblance between these two people, is mentioned in book vi. ch. 60.

[m] The following story is related by Valerius Maximus: (lib. iv. 5:) an old Athenian going to the theatre, was not able to get a place among his countrymen; coming by accident where the ambassadors from Sparta were sitting, they all respectfully rose and gave him the place of honour. The people were loud in their applause, which occasioned a Spartan to remark, that "the Athenians knew what was virtuous, but "the Spartans practised it." The same story is related nearly in the same manner by Plutarch.

When the *Cheik* (this word signifies old man, and was the title of the eldest of the family) speaks, the young hold their tongue, and listen attentively. Every one rises up when he appears in company. The precedence is given him in all public places, and he is every where treated with consideration and respect. This custom existed in Egypt in the time of Herodotus; and the despotism which crushes the country contributes still to preserve it. *Savary,* Letter XIII.

[n] Pococke, with other modern travellers, informs us, that the dress of the Egyptians has undergone very little change; the most simple dress being only a long shirt with wide sleeves, tied about the middle. When they performed any religious ceremony, we find from Herodotus, they were clothed only in linen; and at this day, when the Egyptians enter a mosque, they put on a white garment, which circumstance, Pococke remarks, might probably give rise to the use of the surplice. To this simplicity of dress in the men, it appears that the dress of the females, in costliness and magnificence, exhibits a striking contrast.

[o] Shawls are in universal use at this day in all these countries; and it is not unworthy of remark, that one of Buonaparte's objects in robbing the caravan from Syria to Mecca, was the rich shawls destined for Cairo. See Denon's Travels.

[p] According to Diodor. Sic. (iii. 64.) Orpheus new modelled the mysteries of Bacchus, and after that time they were called Orphica. Cicero (de Nat. Deor. i.) says, that Aristotle questioned the existence of Orpheus.

[q] Pythagoras adopted the mode of living which the Egyptian priests practised, and which was founded on the nature of their climate, without considering that the same was not suitable to the climate of Greece. *Larcher.*

predicting what fortune they shall have, how they shall die, and what kind of persons they shall be. All which the Grecian poets have made use of in their poems. More prodigies have been discovered in Egypt, than in all the rest of the world; for when any prodigy occurs, they carefully preserve the consequences in writing; out of an opinion, that if the like happen at another time, the event will be the same.

LXXXIII. The art of divination is attached to no human being, but only to some of the Gods. For Hercules, Apollo, Minerva, Diana, Mars, and Jupiter have their several oracles. Yet that which they reverence above all others, is the oracle of Latona in the city of Butus. They are not all administered in the same manner, but differently.

LXXXIV. In these countries the art of physic is distributed into several distinct parts, and every physician applies himself wholly to the cure of one disease only, no man ever pretending to more. By which means all places abound with physicians; some professing to cure the eyes[r], others the head, teeth, or parts about the belly, whilst others take upon them the care of internal distempers.

LXXXV. Their manner of mourning for the dead, and their customs relating to funerals, are these. When a man of any consideration dies, all the female sex of that family besmear their heads and faces with dirt; and, leaving the body at home, run, attended by all their relations of that sex, through the streets of the city, with naked breasts, and girdles tied about the waist, beating themselves as they go: while the men on their part, forming another company, gird and beat themselves in like manner. When they have done this, they carry the body to be embalmed.

LXXXVI. For this purpose there are certain men who practise the art of embalming the dead; and as soon as the dead body is brought, the embalmers, shewing several models made of wood and painted, ask them which sort they would have. One of these models is finished with the greatest care, and called by a name which I am not permitted to discover[s]; the second is of an inferior sort and less expensive; and the third is the cheapest of all. When those who are concerned have concluded an agreement, they return home, and the artists remaining in their houses, thus proceed in the most expensive manner. First they draw out the brains through the nostrils with a crooked instrument of iron; some they take

[r] This, and one other passage, ch. 11. of this book, are the only allusions to that cruel disease, the ophthalmia, with which Egypt is now so much tormented.

[s] This was without doubt the figure of some divinity, probably of Osiris. *Larch.*

out in this manner; the rest by the infusion of drugs[t]. Then with a sharp Ethiopian stone they make an incision in the side, and take out the bowels[u]; to which, after they are cleansed and washed in palm wine, they again cleanse with pounded aromatics. When this is done, and the belly filled with pounded pure myrrh, cassia, and other odours, frankincense excepted, they sew all up again, and lay the body in nitre[x] for seventy[y] days, which is the longest time allowed. At the expiration of this term, they wash the whole body, and, enveloping it entirely in bandages of cotton[z], cover it with gums[a], which the Egyptians commonly use instead of glue. All being thus finished, the relations of the dead receive the body, and place it in a frame of wood, shaped in the figure of a man, which they set upright against the wall of the edifice reserved to that end. And this is the most costly way of preserving the dead.

LXXXVII. Those who, to avoid so great expence, will be contented with the middle way, they serve in the following manner. They fill syringes with oil of cedar, which they inject, without cutting the belly, or taking out the bowels; but they inject it at the fundament, and after they have prevented the liquid from escaping, they lay the body in nitre, during the appointed number of days; on the last, the oil of cedar is let out by the fundament, and by a peculiar virtue

[t] M. Rouelle has discovered aromatic drugs in the heads of several mummies. *Larcher.*

For accurate information on the subject of embalming, see M. Rouelle's Memoir in the Academy of Sciences, for 1750, and Dr. Hadley's Dissertation in the Philosophical Transactions, vol. liv. p. 3.

[u] Herodotus does not inform us what becomes of these intestines. Porphyry (de Abstin. iv. 10.) informs us, that they are put in a chest, and one of the embalmers makes a prayer for the deceased, addressed to the sun, as follows: "O "sun, sovereign master, and all ye Gods, "who have given life to men, receive "me and permit me to dwell with the "eternal Gods; I have persevered all "my life in the worship of the Gods, as "I was taught by my forefathers; I have "always honoured my parents; I have "killed no man; I have not set up a de-"spot; I have done no other ill. If I "have committed any fault during my "life, whether by eating or drinking, it "was not for myself, but for these." The embalmer then points to the chest, which is afterwards thrown into the river. Plutarch also agrees with Porphyry. *Larch.*

[x] Larcher says, this was not of the nature of our nitre, but a fixed alkaline salt.

[y] If the nitre had been suffered to remain longer, it would have attacked the solids, and dissolved them; if it had been a neutral salt, like our nitre, this precaution would not have been necessary. *Larcher.*

[z] Mr. Greaves (Work, vol. i. p. 68.) asserts, that these bandages were made of linen. Rouelle, who examined them with particular care, says that all that he has examined are of cotton. I remarked the same thing in the mummies in the British Museum, which I examined in 1752, with the late Dr. Maty. *Larcher.*

[a] This was gum arabic. Pococke (vol. i. p. 69.) says, it was produced from the acacia, which is very common in Upper Egypt, where it is known under the name of sount, the same as the cyale in Arabia Petræa.

[b] Rouelle remarks, that it was impossible to make an injection of this kind at the fundament, without some incision.

brings away all the guts and vitals shrunk and putrified, the nitre having in all this time consumed the flesh, and left nothing remaining except the skin and the bones. When this is done, they deliver the body without any further operation.

LXXXVIII. The third and last manner of preserving the dead, used only for the poorer sort, is performed by the injection of a liquor called surmaia[c] to cleanse the bowels, and laying the body in nitre for seventy days; after which they deliver it to be carried away by the persons concerned.

LXXXIX. The wives of considerable persons, and all women who have been beautiful and of importance, are not delivered to the embalmers presently after death, but kept at home three or four days before they are carried out, in order to prevent those artificers from abusing the bodies of such persons; one of them having been formerly accused of this crime by his companion.

XC. If any Egyptian, or even a stranger, be found killed by a crocodile, or drowned in the river; wherever the body comes ashore, the inhabitants are by law compelled to pay all the charges of embalming and placing it among the consecrated monuments, adjusted in the most costly manner. For none of his friends, or relations, or any other, may touch his body, except the priests of the Nile[d], who bury him with their own hands as something more than human.

XCI. They avoid using the Grecian customs; and to say all at once, will not receive the usages of any other people. All the other Egyptians are particular in this. But the city of Chemmis[e], standing in the province of Thebes not far from Nea, has a temple of a quadrangular form dedicated to Perseus the son of Danae. This fabric is surrounded with palm-trees, and adorned with a spacious portico of stone, on which two vast statues, of stone likewise, are erected. In a chapel built within the circumference of the walls, an image of Perseus is placed. The Chemmitæ affirm, that the hero fre-

[c] Some think that this was composed of salt and water, others of the juice of a plant. The word occurs in chap. 125. where it signifies a radish.

[d] The Egyptians worshipped the Nile, and built temples to it. There was a magnificent one at Nilopolis, in Arcadia, a province of Egypt. It would appear from this passage that there were priests of the Nile, in every place on its banks. *Larcher.*

[e] The Egyptians called the place Chemmo. Chemmis seems to have a Greek termination; it is the same with Panopolis. Plutarch informs us that Pans and Satyrs once dwelt near Chemmis, which tradition probably arose from the circumstance of the worship of Pan commencing at this place. It was very ancient, but I will not venture to affirm with Leo the African, Vansleb and other Arabians, that it was founded by Ichmin son of Misrain. However that may be, its modern name is Akmin, Achmin or Ekmin, or Ichmin. Jablonski remarks, that the Copts prefix a vowel to words beginning with a consonant. If we take away the vowel, the modern becomes very much like the ancient name. Pococke describes its remains, (vol. i. p. 77, 78.) *Larcher.*

quently appears to them in their country, and often in the temple; that they have one of the sandals he wore, which is two cubits in length; and that after his appearance, a plentiful year always ensues in Egypt. These things they say; and have instituted all manner of gymnastic exercises[f] in honour of Perseus, entirely agreeing with those used in Greece, rewarding the victorious with cattle, apparel and skins. When I inquired what might be the reason that Perseus appeared only to them, and why they differed from the rest of Egypt in appointing these gymnastic exercises; they answered, that Perseus was a native of their city. For, said they, Danaus and Lynceus were both Chemmitæ, and sailed together into Greece; enumerating the several generations down to Perseus; who passing through Egypt, in order to fetch the gorgon's head from Lybia, (as the Grecians likewise acknowledge,) arrived in this country, and having formerly heard the name of Chemmis from his mother, recognised his relations, and by his command these games were first instituted.

XCII. Those of the Egyptians who live above the morasses, observe the customs I have before mentioned; but those who live in the fenny parts, are conformable in manners to the rest of Egypt, and as in other things, so particularly in this, that each man has no more[g] than one wife, like the Greeks. They have the following other inventions, to procure food more easily. For when the river has become full and made the plains like a sea, great numbers of lilies, which the Egyptians call lotus[h], shoot up through the water. These they cut

f Larcher translates this, " Jeux gymniques, qui, de tous les jeux, sont les " plus excellens;" in which he follows Wesseling. I have followed Schweighæuser.

The games were five in number, and are expressed in this one line

Ἅλμα, ποδώκειαν, δίσκον, ἀκόντα, πάλην.

g Diodorus Siculus remarks, that in Egypt the people of rank might marry as many wives as they pleased. But though this is the case, yet they might have been satisfied with one; so that Herodotus does not differ from him. The Turks, we are informed by Lady Wortley Montague, are allowed by the Mahometan law to have as many as four wives, but scarce an example occurs of a married man having used this privilege. This is also remarked by Niebuhr. *Larcher.*

h The lotus is an aquatic plant peculiar to Egypt, which grows in rivulets and on the sides of lakes; there are two species of it, the one with a white, the other with a blueish flower. The calix of the lotus blows like a large tulip, and diffuses a sweet smell, resembling that of the lily; the first species produces a round root like that of the potatoe; the inhabitants of the banks of the lake Menzala (Tennis) feed upon it. The rivulets in the environs of Damietta are covered with this majestic flower, which rises upwards of two feet above the water. M. Pauw asserts, that it has disappeared in Egypt, and gives a description which bears no resemblance to it; (Recherches sur les Egyptiens et les Chinois, tom. i.) but it is not wonderful that this learned author should be mistaken, since the greatest part of the travellers, who have passed through Egypt, have never seen the lotus, which is not to be found in the great canals of the Nile, but in the rivulets that pass through the interior of the country. *Savary*, Letter I. note.

The lotus is of the lily species. We find this singular remark in the Memoire sur Venus, " Le lys etoit odieux à Venus

down, and after they are dried in the sun, take out the heart of the plant; which resembling the poppy they grind and make into bread, and afterwards bake it. The root also of the lotus is eatable, and is sweet and round, and equal to an apple in bigness. Another lily grows in the same places, much like to a rose, with a certain fruit found in a calyx which grows on a separate stem, springing from the side of the root in form not unlike a wasp's nest, and containing divers kernels of the size of an olive stone, which are eaten either tender or dried. The byblus[i] which is an annual plant, they gather in the fens, and divide into two parts; the head is reserved for other uses, but the lower part, being of a cubit in length, is eaten and sold. When any one is desirous to eat these stems dressed in the best manner, he cooks it in a red-hot oven. Some among these people live together upon fish, which they disbowel and dry in the sun, and then eat them without any farther dressing.

XCIII. Fishes that are gregarious seldom breed in the river; but when the desire of engendering seizes them, leave the waters they frequent, and drive out in shoals to the sea, the males leading the way, and scattering their spawn. This the females swallow as they come up, and are thus impregnated. When they find themselves full, they return to their accustomed haunts; though not under the conduct of the males, but of the females; which in their way home, do as the males did in their passage outwards. For they eject their little eggs[k] in small numbers, which the males that follow devour; yet such as remain undevoured are sometimes nou-

"parce qu'il lui disputoit la beauté. "Aussi pour s'en venger fitelle croitre "au milieu de ses petales le membre de "l'âne." The above is translated from the Alexipharmaca of Nicander. *Beloe.*

[i] I have seen whole forests of papyrus, of which the ancient Egyptians made their paper. Strabo, who calls it *byblus*, gives an accurate description of it:

"The byblus grows in lakes and marshes, and rises to about ten feet in height. Its stalk is bare and has on the top a woolly tuft. The byblus does not grow in great quantities about Alexandria, because it is not cultivated. But it is found in great abundance in the Delta. There are two kinds of it of an inferior, and another of a better quality, called sacred, (appropriated for sacred purposes,) and those who wish to increase the public revenue, employ with regard to this plant the contrivance which the Jews adopted with regard to the date-tree, for they will not suffer it to grow in many places, and its scarcity increasing the price, augments the revenue of the state, at the expence of the public utility." *Strabo*, lib. xvii. p. 1151.

It is the avidity of these *publicans*, and their care in destroying it, that occasions the scarcity of papyrus in Egypt. I only met with it in the neighbourhood of Damietta and of lake Menzala. Travellers in general, who have not visited this interesting part of Egypt, have not made mention of it. Others less circumspect have denied its existence, and have circulated fables on the subject. *Savary*, Letter XXIII. and notes.

[k] The eggs of the fish are not compared with the grains of the millet, but *κέγχροι* mean *grains in general;* and *τῶν ὠῶν οἱ κέγχροι, the grains of the eggs,* mean the eggs themselves. The construction is *ἀποῤῥαίνουσι (μέρος τι,* or *τινὰς) τῶν κέγχρων τῶν ὠῶν κατ' ὀλίγους. Schweig.*

rished and become fish. If any of these fish happen to be taken in their passage towards the sea, they are found bruised on the left side of the head; if in their return, on the right: because they swim outwards leaning towards the land on the left side, and when they return keep close to the shore, and touch it as much as possible, for fear of being carried down by the stream. When the Nile begins to overflow, the hollow vales and morasses that lie near the river first begin to be filled by the water which filters through from the river, and immediately swarm with infinite numbers of small fishes; the reason of which, as I conjecture, is this: whilst the annual inundation of the Nile is reteating back, the fishes lay their eggs on the slime, and go off with the last of the waters; and when the river returns to overflow the same places again after the revolution of a year, these fishes are immediately produced from those eggs.

XCIV. The Egyptians who inhabit about the fens use an oil called Kiki[k], drawn from the fruit of the sillicyprian shrub, which they sow upon the borders of rivers and lakes. This plant grows wild in Greece; but is sowed in Egypt, and bears great abundance of fruit, though of an ill scent. Some bruise it in a press, and squeeze out the oil; others prepare it by fire[l], and collect the liquid which flows from it, which is unctuous, and no less useful in lamps than other oil; but it emits an oppressive smell.

XCV. These parts are much infested with gnats, and therefore the inhabitants have contrived to defend themselves from that insect by the following means. Those who live above the marshes go up to take their rest in towers built to that end; because the gnats are prevented by the winds from mounting so high: and those who inhabit the lower parts, use this artifice instead of such towers. Every man has a net[m], which serves him by day to take fish, and at night to defend the place where he sleeps; for if he should wrap himself up either in his clothes or any kind of linen, the

[k] The plant which supplies this oil is called *ricin*, from the Latin ricinus, which name was given it on account of its resemblance to a tick. Some suppose it to be the same as the *palma Christi*. When commerce flourished in the country, oil of olives was carried thither from Judæa and Greece. Plato defrayed the expences of his voyage to Egypt, by the sale of oil. M. Savary relates from Elmacin's life of Omar, that Amron, the general of Omar, found in Alexandria 12,000 dealers in fresh oil. In the Latin translation of Elmacin, by Erpenius, it is 12,000 *olitores vendentes olus viride*. It is very surprising that Savary should have taken olitores for oil-dealers, and olus for oil. *Larcher.*

[l] Literally; after having roasted it, they boil it.

[m] This is called by Juvenal *conopeum*, from *κώνωψ, a gnat*, (Sat. vi. ver. 80.) which the Scholiast thus explains; linum tenuissimum maculis variatum. Quia latine conopeum *culicare* dicunt.

gnats would not fail to bite, but never attempt to pass the net.

XCVI. Their ships of burden are made of the acanthus[n], which in shape resembles the Cyrenæan lotus, and distils a sort of gum. From this tree they cut timber of about two cubits square, and putting them together like bricks, they build their ships in the following manner. They connect these pieces of wood with many long nails[o], and afterwards put benches upon them. They use no kind of ribs, and strengthen the joints on the inside with the byblus; having only one rudder, which passes quite through the keel of the ship, with a mast of acanthus, and sails of byblus. These vessels are altogether unable to sail up the stream, and therefore are always drawn up, unless the wind prove very fresh and favourable. But when they go with the current, they fasten a hurdle of tamarisk with a rope to the prow of the vessel. This hurdle is strengthened with bands of reeds, and so let down into the water. They have likewise a stone, pierced through the middle, of about two talents in weight, which they also let down into the river by another rope made fast to the poop; and by this means the stream bearing hard upon the hurdle carries down the ship (which is called baris) with great expedition, whilst the weight of the stone balances and keeps it steady. These vessels are very numerous in those parts, and some of them carry a burden of many thousand talents.

XCVII. When the Nile has overflowed, nothing is seen in Egypt except the cities, which appear very nearly like the islands of the Ægean sea. All the rest of the country becomes a sea, and vessels hold not the same course as at other times by the channel of the river, but through the midst of the plains. Those who would pass from Naucratis to Memphis, sail by the pyramids[p]; but this is not the usual course, which passes by the point of Delta and by the city of Cercasorum[q],

[n] This acanthus very much resembles the lotus of the island Cercina. It must not however be confounded with that tree. It is the same as the *acacia*. *Larcher*.

[o] Τόμφος signifies *a peg* or *a nail*, as we see in Homer (Odys. v. 6, 58.) Ζυγὰ are the pieces of wood which are laid across. *Transtra* is used in the same sense in Latin. Ἐν ὧν ἐπάκτωσαν cannot signify *inferciunt*. He is not here speaking of filling up the intervals with byblus as with tow, but of strengthening this assemblage, and this is the meaning of the verb ἐμπάκτοω. Eustatius (ad Odyss. v. 58.) very rightly explains it by καταοφαλίζονται. *Larcher*.

[p] The pyramids, denominated from Gizu, are always intended by *the* pyramids, and Herodotus mentions no others. *Rennel*, p. 496.

[q] It appears not improbable that Letus or Latone may have succeeded to Cercasorum, on the same, or nearly the same site, before the date of the Itinerary. *Rennel*, p. 506.

Savary, Letter XXII. places Cercasorum at the modern village of *Charakhania*. D'Anville places it on the western bank of the Nile, at the village of *El-Arksas*.

and the passage from Canopus and the sea to Naucratis is through the plains, by the cities of Anthylla[r] and Archandropolis.

XCVIII. Since Egypt has been under the dominion of the Persians, the revenues of Anthylla, which is a considerable city, have been always appropriated to the wife of the reigning king of Egypt, for her expence in shoes[s]. And the other, as I conjecture, was named Archandropolis, from Archander of Phthia, son of Achæus, who married the daughter of Danaus[t]. It is possible there may have been another Archander; but it is most certain that this name is not Egyptian.

XCIX. Hitherto I have only related what I actually beheld, or what was my opinion on the subject, or what I learnt by inquiry: but I shall now proceed to give some account of the Egyptian history according to what I heard related, which yet will be interwoven with divers things that I saw. The priests informed me, that Menes, who was the first king of Egypt, among many other things which he performed, by raising mounds[u], rendered Memphis secure from inundation; for the river formerly ran close to the sandy mountain on the side of Lybia; but Menes having filled up the arm of the river which turned towards the south, about a hundred stadia above Memphis[x] dried up the old channel, and con-

[r] It appears to me to be the same as Gynæcopolis, which is situated to the west of the Canopic branch. The excellence of its wine made it in after-times celebrated. *Larcher.*

[s] Athenæus says, (Deipn. i. 25.) that it was given *εἰς ζώνας, for her girdles.*

[t] This was not the Danaus who went from Egypt, and afterwards became king of Argos. See Larcher's Essay on the Chronology of Herod. x. 4. and xv. 3.

[u] *Γέφυρα*, as Schneider has remarked in his Lexicon, not only signifies a bridge properly so called, but also an embankment, a mound, as in the fifth book of the Iliad, ver. 89. and *γεφυροῦν* not only to join by a bridge, but also to fill up with a mound, to block up with an embarkment. Iliad, xxi. 245. So an isthmus is called *πόντου γέφυραν*, Pindar, Nem. vi. 67. and *γέφυραν ποντιάδα*, Isthm. iv. 84. So that *ἀπογεφυρῶσαι, τὴν Μέμφιν* may be easily understood to signify by raising mounds to seperate Memphis from the Nile, and make it safe from inundation. *Schweigh.*

[x] It is very extraordinary, that the situation of Memphis should not be well known, which was so great and famous a city, and for so long a time the capital of Egypt. See Pococke, vol. i.

It appears that Memf, Menf, or Menouf, which is rather a *position* than a *village*, as perhaps referring to the site of the *latest* remains of Memphis, lies within half a mile (and that to the N. E.) of the position pointed out by the meeting of the two lines of distance from Fostat and the Pyramids. And that this Menf is on the site of Memphis there is little doubt; since Abulfeda describes the situation of Memphis, as a considerable city, so late as the seventh century, when Egypt was conquered by the Mahomedans. This author says, that it stood at a short day's journey from Cairo; and as the site of Menf may be taken at fourteen road miles from Cairo, it agrees very well. To this may be added, that Maillet, Pococke, Bruce and Browne, agree that there are remains which prove the existence of a former city. Thus the site of the centre of Memphis falls in the parallel of 29°, 53′, and its northern skirt in about 29°, 55′, being 8 minutes of latitude south of Cairo, and 18 south of the point of the Delta; which latter is fixed by the celestial observations of M. Nie-

ducted the Nile[y] into another, which was equally distant from each mountain: this passage is diligently preserved in our time, and annually repaired by the Persians; because if the river should at any time break through the bank, the whole city would probably be drowned. They added, that the same Menes, after he had diverted the course of the water, built the city which to this day is called Memphis, within the ancient bed of the river; and indeed this place is situate in one of the narrowest straits of Egypt; that on the north and west side he caused a lake to be made without the walls from the river, which passes on the eastwardly part, and founded the magnificent and memorable temple of Vulcan in the same city.

C. After this the same priests read to me from a book the names of three hundred and thirty kings who had reigned after Menes. During all which time eighteen were Ethiopians[z], one woman, and the rest Egyptians. The woman, like the queen of Babylon, was called by the name of Nitocris[a]; and they informed me, that after she had received the power from the hands of the Egyptians, who had slain her brother and immediate predecessor, in order to revenge the death of her brother, destroyed many of them by stratagem. She caused an extensive apartment to be made under ground, pretending that she was going to consecrate it[b], but in reality intending something else. For having invited all those she knew to have been principally concerned in the death of her brother to a great feast, she let in the river by a private channel, and drowned them altogether; they added, that after this she threw herself into an apartment filled with

buhr, in 30°, 13'. *Rennel*, p. 497, &c. See also the whole of Savary's twenty-first Letter.

y From this description, (a part of which however is obscure) together with the description of the ground, in Dr. Pococke, and the aid of our own observations on other capital rivers, it appears very clearly that the Nile in ancient times ran through the plain of the Mummies, near Sakkara; and thence along the foot of the rising ground, on which the pyramids of Gizu stand, and finally in the line of the canal of *Beheira*, into the bay of Abukeir or Canopus. This appears more particularly from the remarks of Dr. Pococke, (vol. i. p. 40, 41.) *Rennel*, p. 500.

At the moment I am writing this channel is not unknown; it may be traced across the desert, and passes to the westward of the lakes of Natrum. Petrified wood, masts, lateen yards, and the wreck of vessels which have formerly navigated there, mark its ancient traces. The Arabs still bestow the name of *Bahr Belama* (sea without water) on this channel, which is almost choaked up. *Savary*, Letter I.

z These eighteen Ethiopian princes seem to prove, that the throne was not always hereditary in Egypt: and we are also informed by authors worthy of credit that the king was elected. *Larcher*.

a We find in this name traces of that of Minerva, whom the Egyptians called Neith, according to Plato Timæus, vol. iii. p. 21. Eusebius interprets Nitocris, Minerva the victorious, (Chronic. p. 21.) *Larcher*.

b It appears that καινοῦν has the same signification as καινίζειν, and that καινίζειν has the same force as the compound ἐγκαινίζειν, (i. e. καθοσιοῦν, καθιεροῦν,) is evident from the testimonies of Callim. and Hesych. cited by Valck. *Schweigh.*

ashes, in order that she might avoid the vengeance of the nation. This account they gave of Nitocris.

CI. But of the other kings not one obtained distinction, as the priests did not mention any memorable action; except Mœris, who being the last of them, built the portico of Vulcan's temple, fronting to the northward, and caused a lake to be made, (the dimensions of which I shall describe hereafter[c],) with pyramids, which I shall also mention when I come to speak of the lake. In a word, they assured me that he had done these great things, and all the rest nothing.

CII. And therefore I shall pass them by, and will make mention of the king that succeeded them, whose name was Sesostris[d]. The priests affirmed, that this king was the first who, passing through the Arabian gulf with a fleet of long ships[e], subdued those nations that inhabit about the Red sea; and continued his expedition till he arrived at a sea which was not navigable on account of the shoals; that returning to Egypt, he assembled a numerous army, with which he landed on the continent, and conquered all the countries where he passed; that wherever he met with any valiant people who were very ardent in defence of their liberty, he erected a column in that place, with an inscription declaring his own name and country, and that he had conquered them by his power: but when he subdued a nation, either without fighting, or by an easy victory, he caused a pillar and inscriptions to be erected, as among the nations who had proved themselves brave men, with the addition of figures representing the secret parts of a woman[f], wishing to make it known that they were unwarlike.

CIII. In this manner extending his conquests through the

[c] See chap. 149.

[d] This prince lived not quite an age before the Trojan war, and was nearly cotemporary with Hercules, son of Alcmena. He ascended the throne after these 330 kings whom he has mentioned, of whom Mœris was the last. About 900 years had elapsed since the death of Mœris when Herodotus went to Egypt; (see ch. 13;) about 800 from the Trojan war to his time, and 900 from Hercules. *Wesseling.*

Tacitus calls Sesostris Rhamsès. Scaliger remarks, that he had two other names, Ramesès and Egyptus; he is called Ramestis on an obelisk described by Ammianus Marcellus, Ramessès and Rampsès in Josephus, Sésoosis and Sésouchis in Diodorus Siculus, and Sésosis in some manuscripts of Pliny, xxxvi. 9. *Larcher.*

This prince is supposed by some to be the same as Shishak, mentioned in 1 Kings, ch. xiv. ver. 25; and again, 2 Chron. ch. xii. ver. 2; where his infantry is said to consist of the Lubims, (Lybians,) the Sukkiims; (Trogladytes,) and the Ethiopians.

[e] To the number of 400, according to Diodorus Siculus, (i. 55.) who adds, that Sesostris was the first king of Egypt who built long vessels.

[f] Diodorus Siculus (i. 55.) adds, that among the people that had bravely resisted, he caused the private parts of a man to be engraved.

It is related, that Margaret, the valiant queen of Denmark, in order to upbraid the Sueones with their cowardice, stamped coins with the private parts of a woman.

continent, he at length crossed over from Asia into Europe; and subdued the Scythians and Thracians[g]. For so far, and no farther, the Egyptian army appears to have penetrated, because their pillars are to be seen in those countries, and no where beyond them. From thence he turned back towards Egypt; and when he arrived at the river Phasis, I cannot affirm whether he appointed[h] part of his army to inhabit that country, or whether some of his forces, grown uneasy with the fatigues of their expedition, did voluntarily remain in that region.

CIV. For the inhabitants of Colchis seem to me of Egyptian extraction; which struck me before I heard any thing from others; and when it had become a matter of curiosity to me, I inquired of both nations, and discovered that the Colchians had more recollection of the Egyptians, than the Egyptians had of the Colchians; yet the Egyptians say they believe them to be descended from a part of the army of Sesostris; which I conjectured, because their complexion is black, and their hair curly, which however comes to nothing; because others are so likewise. But I ground my opinion more upon this circumstance, that the Colchians, Egyptians, and Ethiopians, are the only nations of the world, who from time immemorial have been circumcised. For the Phoenicians, and those Syrians[i] that inhabit Palestine, acknowledge they received the circumcision from the Egyptians; as the other Syrians, who possess the countries adjacent to the river Thermodon and Parthenion, with their neighbours the Macrones, confess they very lately learned the same custom from the Colchians. And these are the only nations that are circumcised[k], and appear to perform it in the same manner as the Egyptians But whether the Ethiopians had this usage from the Egyptians, or these, on the contrary, from the Ethiopians, is a thing too ancient and obscure for me to determine. But there is this great evidence, that other nations learnt it in their intercourse with the Egyptians; that we see that none of those Phoenicians who have any commerce with the Grecians, continue to imitate the Egyptians in this usage, of circumcising their children.

CV. One thing more I shall mention, in which the Colchians resemble the Egyptians. They alone of all people

[g] According to another tradition, preserved in Valerius Flaccus, (Argon. v. 418.) the Getæ, the most brave and the most just of the Thracians, (Herod. iv. 93.) vanquished Sesostris; and it was, doubtless, to secure his retreat that he left a detachment of his troops at Colchis.

[h] Pliny (Hist. Nat. xxxiii. 3.) assures us, I know not on what authority, that Sesostris was vanquished by the Colchians. *Larcher.*

[i] The Greek word is Σύροι. Σύριοι, when they are distinguished from the Syri, mean the Cappadocians. Σύροι, the inhabitants of Syria, from the Mediterranean to the Euphrates. *Gronovius.*

[k] See note on chap. 36.

manufacture[l] their linen after the manner of Egypt; and the way of living, as well as the language, is similar in both nations; though the Grecians call the linen they import from Colchis by the name of Sardonian[m], and that which comes from Egypt by the proper name of the country.

CVI. The pillars erected by Sesostris king of Egypt in the countries he subdued, are for the most part demolished; yet I saw some of them standing in the Syrian Palestine[n], with the inscriptions I mentioned before, and the genital parts of a woman. Two figures likewise of this king, carved on a rock, are seen in Ionia, upon the ways that lead from Ephesus to Phocæa, and from Sardis to Smyrna. In both places a man is carved, four cubits[o] and a half in height, holding a spear in his right hand, and in his left a bow, and the rest of his armour is in unison, for it is partly Egyptian and partly Ethiopian[p]. An inscription, in the sacred characters of Egypt, extends across his breast from one shoulder to the other, which says, "*I acquired this region by the strength of these arms*[q]." The stone does not discover who the person represented was, nor from whence he came; and though this is well known by other means, yet some who have seen the monument, have supposed that it is the statue of Memnon, but they are very far from the truth.

CVII. The priests farther informed me, that Sesostris, followed by great numbers of captives drawn out of the countries he had conquered, landed in his return at the Pelusian Daphnæ; where his brother[r], to whom he had committed the government of Egypt during his absence, desired him to accept the entertainment of his house for himself and sons;

[l] See chap. 35.

[m] Larcher proposes to read Σαρδιανικόν, *linen of Sardis*; and observes, that Sardis was a more convenient market for this kind of linen than Sardinia; and that its dyes were very famous. The prince of Mingrelia, whose dominions formed part of the ancient Colchis, pays at this time an annual tribute of 120,000 yards of linen to the Turks.

[n] If the country in which Herodotus saw these pillars had belonged to David or Solomon, we cannot doubt but that these princes would have overthrown them, and consequently our historian could never have seen them. There is, however, great probability that Herodotus, under the name of Palestine, comprehended a country much more extended than what was contained under that name in the time of David and Solomon; and that our historian speaks of a country which had never been subject to these princes. *Larcher.*

[o] The σπιθαμή is *half a cubit*; and as τρίτον ἡμιτάλαντον signifies *two talents and a half*, and ἕβδομον ἡμιτάλαντον *six talents and a half*, so πέμπτη σπιθαμή signifies *four cubits and a half*. *Schweigh.*

[p] The bow is very particularly used among the Ethiopians. See book iii. ch. 21.

[q] The following line from Claudian, says Larcher, seems to be a translation from Herodotus:

> *Ast ego, quæ terras* humeris *pontumque subegi.* Bell. Gildon, v. 114.

[r] According to Manethon, his name was Armais, and he was the same person the Greeks called Danaus. Larcher discusses the matter in his Chronology, ch. x. on the kings of Argos, sect. 4.

and having prevailed with the king to stay, he caused a great quantity of combustible matter to be piled around the house, and set on fire: that Sesostris being informed of the danger, immediately deliberated with his wife, who had accompanied him in his expedition; she advised him to take two of his six sons, and by extending their bodies on the fire, form a kind of bridge over which they might escape; that her counsel was put in execution, and two of his sons thus perished in the flames: he himself, with all the rest, was preserved.

CVIII. Sesostris, when he had returned to Egypt, and punished his brother, employed the multitude of prisoners he brought with him from the countries he had subdued, partly in drawing those immense stones, which are seen in the temple of Vulcan, and partly in digging the canals of Egypt; by their involuntary[s] labours they made Egypt, which before was in every part practicable for horses and carriages to pass over, deprived of these things; for from that time Egypt, though it was one level plain, became unfit for horses or carriages, and this is caused by these canals which are numerous, and in every direction. Yet this was designed by Sesostris, to the end that those who inhabit the cities and other places that lie remote from the river, might be plentifully supplied with water to drink, who when the river retired, being in want of water, used to drink water that was rather salt[t], which they drew from wells; and for this reason, these canals were cut throughout Egypt.

CIX. They told me also that this king made an equal division of all the lands in Egypt, and assigned a square piece of ground to every Egyptian, reserving to himself a certain rent, which he commanded them to pay annually; yet if the river happened to diminish any man's portion, he presently went with his complaint to the king, who always deputed certain inspectors to measure the remainder of the land, and adjust the payment in proportion to the loss. Hence geometry, as I conjecture, had its beginning, and was afterwards intro-

[s] According to Volney, Sesostris was anterior to Moses. This prince, according to Herodotus, by causing a great number of canals to be cut, made it impossible to travel in chariots. Therefore, says Volney, the Bible must relate a fable, when it tells us that Pharoah pursued the Israelites in six hundred chariots. Exod. xiv. 7.

Unfortunately for Volney the first assertion is not true. The passage of the Red sea took place one hundred and seventy-five years before the time of Sesostris. This miracle took place 1531 B. C. Sesostris began to reign B. C. 1356. *Larcher.*

[t] Pococke (vol. i. p. 198.) says, that all through Egypt the water of the wells was salt. Diodor. Sic. (i. 57.) says, that Sesostris cut these canals in order that merchandize, &c. might be more easily carried from one place to another, and principally to protect his country from the incursions of the enemy. These two reasons appear to me very probable. *Larcher.*

duced among the Greeks[w]; but the pole, the gnomon[x], and the division of the day into twelve parts[y], they received from the Babylonians.

CX. Sesostris alone of all the Egyptian kings was master of Ethiopia; and left as monuments[z], divers statues of stone erected at the entrance of Vulcan's temple. Two of these, representing himself and his wife, are thirty cubits in height; and four other statues, representing his four sons, are of twenty cubits each. Many ages after, when the statue of Darius the Persian was brought thither, the priest of Vulcan would not suffer[a] it to be placed before those of Sesostris, saying openly that the actions of the Persian were not so illustrious as those of the Egyptian king. For Sesostris had subdued other nations, not inferior to those which Darius had, and besides these the Scythians, whom Darius could not subdue; and therefore to place before the offerings of Sesostris the statue of a man who had not surpassed him in glorious actions, would be unjust. All which was forgiven by Darius[b].

CXI. After the death of Sesostris, his son Pheron[c] succeeded him in the kingdom. But he undertook no military expedition, and became blind by this accident. At a time when the Nile had overflowed in an extraordinary manner, to the height of eighteen cubits above the surface of the earth,

[w] Thales the Milesian learnt geometry of the Egyptians, and carried it into Greece.

Dr. Halley (in Wotton's Observations on Learning, ch. xxiii.) observes, that the Greeks appear to have been the first practical astronomers, who endeavoured to make themselves masters of the science; and that Thales was the first who predicted an eclipse in Greece, not 600 years B. C. and that Hipparchus made the first catalogue of fixed stars, not above 150 years B. C.

[x] Wesseling understands by πόλον, *a sun-dial*. Larcher, *the pole of the heavens*, and by γνώμονα, *a sun-dial*. Others more properly consider them to be astronomical instruments, one used to shew the changes of the seasons, the other to shew the parts of the day. See Menag. ad Laert. ii. 1. and Bailly Hist. de l'Astronomie ancienne, p. 384. *Schw.*

[y] From this passage it appears that in the time of Herodotus the day was divided into twelve parts. But we must not conclude with Leo Allatius and Wesseling, that they were called hours. It is not certain when the twenty-four parts of the day were called hours; but it was doubtless very late, and the passages cited from Anacreon and Xenophon to prove the contrary, ought not to be interpreted by what we call hours. *Larch.*

[z] Larcher adds to this, *of the danger which he had escaped.* This he does on the authority of Diodor. Sic. (i. 57.) who relates, that these statues were erected by Sesostris in gratitude to Vulcan; by whose assistance he escaped from the treachery of his brother.

[a] Diodor. Sic. (i. 58.) relates the same fact, and adds, that Darius said, that if he should live as long as Sesostris, he would endeavour to equal him, and invited the priest to compare what both had done at the same age, which would be the most just proof of their virtue.

[b] It does not appear from hence that Darius himself was in Egypt at this time.

[c] Eusebius calls him Pharaoh, and Diodorus Siculus, Sesostris. If it be true, as we learn elsewhere, that Pharoah, Pheron, or Phouroh, was a name common to the kings of Egypt, he might have been called Pharaoh-Sesostris; as Pharaoh-Neco, Pharaoh-Hophra, who are the same as Neco and Apries, c. 158, 161. *Wesseling.*

a great storm of wind arose, and put the waters into a violent agitation. Upon this the king in an insolent humour took a javelin in his hand, and having thrown it into the midst of the vortex, was presently seized with a pain in his eyes, which made him blind for ten years. In the eleventh year an oracle was brought from the city of Butus, importing, that the time of his punishment was expired, and he should recover his sight, if he would wash his eyes with the urine of a woman, who had never known any other man than her own husband. In obedience to the oracle he first tried the urine of his own wife; but finding no relief, made use of that of others indifferently, till at last his sight was restored. Upon which he collected all those women whose urine he had tried, except the one by whose urine he had recovered his sight, in a city which is now called Erythrebolus; where he caused them to be burnt[d] together with the city, and married the woman by whose[e] means he had been cured of his blindness. After this he dedicated many considerable offerings in all the temples, to perpetuate the memory of his recovery; but the most memorable were two magnificent obelisks which he erected in the temple of the sun, each of one stone only, a hundred cubits in height, and eight cubits in breadth.

CXII. The priests farther informed me, that a native of Memphis, who in the Grecian language would be named Proteus[f], succeeded him in the kingdom; there is to this day an inclosure, sacred to him, at Memphis, which is very magnificent, and richly adorned, standing on the south side of that dedicated to Vulcan. The parts adjacent to it are inhabited by Phœnicians of Tyre, and all that region is called the Tyrian camp[g]. In this spot is a chapel dedicated to Venus the Stranger, which I conjecture to be the temple of Helen the daughter of Tyndarus, both because I have heard that she resided for some time in the court of Proteus, and because it has the title[h] of Venus the Stranger. For of all the temples that are dedicated to Venus, not one is known by this name.

CXIII. And, indeed, when I inquired of the priests con-

[d] We may hence easily see the necessity of Abraham's precaution (Gen. ch. xii. ver. 4.) when entering Egypt; and cannot be surprised at the conduct of Potiphar's wife (Gen. ch. xxxix. ver. 7.) to Joseph. *Larcher.*

[e] Diodor. Sic. (i. 59.) says, that this woman was the wife of a gardener.

[f] Diodor. Sic. (i. 60.) relates, that a great many kings ascended the throne between Pheron, whom he calls Sesostris and Proteus, &c. Diodorus says, he was called by the Egyptians Cetes. This name gave occasion to the fable of his feeding the flocks of Neptune; *κῆτος* in Greek signifying *a sea animal—Cetus, bellua marina. Larcher.*

[g] In chap. 154. we have the camp of the Ionians and Carians.

[h] Ἐπωνύμιον, i. q. *ἐπώνυμον*, scil. *τὸ ἱερόν*. Pindar, Ol. x. 95, and Pyth. i. 58. has also used *ἐπωνύμιος* for *ἐπώνυμος*. *Schweigh.*

cerning Helen, they told me, that when Alexander[i], after having carried her off[k] from Sparta, was sailing away to his own country, and when he was in the Ægean, he was driven by adverse winds into the Egyptian sea[l], and from thence (as the winds did not abate) to Egypt, up the Canopic mouth of the Nile to Tarichex. On that shore stood a temple of Hercules, which remains to this day; whither, if the servant of any person flies, and devoting himself to the God, takes upon him certain sacred marks, he may not be forced from thence under any pretext; and this privilege has been preserved to our time the same as it was at its first institution. When, therefore, the slaves of Alexander had heard of this immunity, they fled to the temple, and as suppliants putting themselves under the protection of Hercules, accused their master with a view to injure him, relating how things stood with regard to Helen, and his injustice towards Menelaus. These complaints were made in the presence of the priests, and before the governor of that province, whose name was Thonis[m].

CXIV. Upon which the governor immediately dispatched a messenger to Proteus, at Memphis, with orders to inform him, "that a certain stranger, born at Troy, was arrived, "who had been guilty of a most nefarious action in Greece; "having seduced the wife of his host, and carried her away, "with immense riches; that a violent tempest had forced "him to land in Egypt, and that therefore the king would "determine whether he should be permitted to depart with "impunity, or whether he and all he had brought with him "should be seized." Proteus sent back the messenger with the following answer: "Whoever the man is that has acted "so impiously toward his host, seize him and bring him to "me, that I may know what he will say for himself."

CXV. Which answer being brought to Thonis, he seized the person of Alexander, detained his ships, and sent him to Memphis, with Helen[n], his riches, and also the suppliant

[i] Paris. Homer most frequently calls him Alexander.

[k] Larcher, in his Essay on Chronology, ch. 14. argues that the taking of Troy was 1263 years B.C.

[l] Herodotus not only calls that sea which washes the coast of Egypt the Egyptian sea, but that also which washes the adjacent coasts. *Wesseling*.

[m] Some writers pretend (Eustath. ad Hom. Odyss. iv. 228.) that Thonis was king of the Canopic mouth of the Nile, and that he was the inventor of medicine in Egypt. Before he saw Helen, he treated Menelaus with great respect; but when he had seen her, he paid attention to her, and endeavoured to violate her person. Menelaus having heard of it, put him to death. The city of Thonis, and Thoth the first Egyptian month, take their names from him. This narrative seems less probable than that of Herodotus. Thoth, or the Mercury of the Egyptians, is quite different from Thonis, and it is from him that the month has its name. *Larcher*.

[n] Euripides (in his Helen) supposes that Helen was never at Troy, and that Paris carried thither a cloud which resembled her; Theaclymenus, son of

slaves. When they arrived there, and Proteus had asked Alexander who he was, and whence he came, he gave him an account of his family, country, name, and from whence he had set sail. But the king proceeding to demand in what place he had met with Helen, he became embarrassed in his answer, and did not speak the truth; till the fugitive suppliants openly accused him, and discovered all the circumstances of his crime. At last Proteus pronounced this judgment: "If I did not think it of great consequence, not "to put any stranger to death who may be forced by the "winds to take refuge in my territories, I would avenge the "injuries you have done to that Grecian; since, O basest of "men, you have committed the most impious action when "you met with hospitable treatment; you have seduced the "wife of your host, and not content with this, by your per-"suasive words[o] have taken her away by stealth[p]. And "since this was not sufficient, you have plundered the house "of your host, and come hither with the spoils: therefore, "though I cannot persuade myself to kill a stranger, yet I "will not suffer you to carry away the woman, or the riches "you have plundered; but shall preserve both, in order to "restore them to your injured host upon his demand, com-"manding you and all your companions to depart out of my "kingdom within three days, under pain of being treated as "enemies."

CXVI. In this manner the priests reported the arrival of Helen at the court of Proteus. And I am of opinion that Homer had heard the same relation; but not thinking it so fit for epic poetry as the other which he has adopted, he altered the relation, though he has plainly shewn he was not ignorant of what I have mentioned; as is sufficiently manifest in his Iliad, and never retracted[q] in any part of that work. For describing the wanderings of Alexander, while he was carrying Helen with him, he says, that when driven in uncertainty to various places, he arrived at Sidon in Phœnicia; which he has mentioned in the description of Diomede's valour[r]:

Proteus, is on the point of marrying Helen, when Menelaus arrives and succeeds in carrying her off.

[o] In the Greek it is *ἀναπτερώσας*; having filled her with good hopes; having raised her expectations; and in a manner furnished her with wings to fly away.

[p] Οἴχεαι ἔχων ἐκκλέψας. The word *ἔχων* must be joined with *οἴχεαι*, i. e. *οἴχεαι ἔχων αὐτὴν*; as we meet also with *ἔρχομαι ἔχων*, *I bring*; and *ἄπειμι ἔχων*, *I carry away*; properly, *I depart, taking with me*, &c. *Schweigh.*

[q] Ἀναποδίζω literally means, *I retrace my footsteps, I say, a second time.*

[r] The different parts of Homer's poems were anciently known by names taken from the subjects. Thus the fifth book of the Iliad was the Bravery of Diomede; the eleventh, the Bravery of Agamemnon; the first, the Anger of Achilles. The verses quoted, however, are from the sixth Iliad, ver. 289, &c.

> These garments lay, in various colours wrought,
> The work of Sidon's dames, from Sidon brought
> By godlike Paris, when he plowed the seas,
> And high-born Helen wafted o'er from Greece.

And also in the Odyssey[a], in the following lines:

> Jove's daughter had an antidote in store,
> Which she receiv'd from Polydamne's hand,
> Wife to th' Egyptian Thonis: for that soil
> Abounds no less with good than noxious plants.

To which may be added these words of Menelaus to Telemachus:

> The Gods detained me on th' Egyptian shore,
> Because I fail'd whole hecatombs to pay,
> Which they expected.

He shews in these verses, that he was acquainted with Alexander's arrival in Egypt. For the coast of Syria lies next adjoining to that of Egypt, and the Phœnicians of Sidon are inhabitants of Syria.

CXVII. So that these lines, together with the mention of this region, plainly prove that Homer was not the author of the Cyprian verses[b], but some other person. For they affirm, that when Alexander brought away Helen from Sparta, he had a favourable wind and a smooth sea, so that he arrived at Troy in three days; whereas Homer in his Iliad says he was driven about to various places, while taking Helen with him. And so I take my leave of him and the Cyprian verses.

CXVIII. When I asked the priests whether the account of the Trojan war, as related by the Grecians, was an unfounded story, they assured me they were informed by Menelaus himself, that after the rape of Helen, the Grecians, resolving to assist him, formed a numerous army, and landed in Teucris: that upon their landing they pitched a camp, and sent ambassadors to Ilium, of which embassy Menelaus was one: that these embassadors went to the city, and demanded Helen, with all the treasures Alexander had stolen, and satisfaction for the injuries done: that the Trojans protested both

[a] The first lines are from the 4th book, v. 227. the next from the same book, v. 351.

[b] The subject of these verses was the Trojan war from the time of the birth of Helen. Venus caused this princess to be born, that she might be able to promise Paris, an accomplished beauty; and Jupiter, by the advice of Momus, consented, in order to destroy again the human race by the war of Troy, which was to take place on her account. As the author of this poem refers all the events to Venus, Goddess of Cyprus, the work derived its name from her. Ælian (Var. Hist. lib. ix. 15.) says, that Homer gave these verses as a marriage portion to his daughter. I conceive that Herodotus did not know the author, or else he would have mentioned his name. Heyne, in his first Excursus to the second Æneid, has discussed this matter with great skill. *Larcher.*

with and without oaths, both at that time and since, that neither Helen, nor the riches they accused them of having in their possession, were in their power, but in Egypt; and therefore to demand restitution from them, of things that were in the possession of Proteus king of Egypt, was unjust: that the Greeks, taking this answer for a mere mockery, began the siege, which they continued till the city was taken; that when they were masters of Troy, finding the Trojans still persisting in their asseverations, and Helen no where appearing, they gave credit to their former protestations, and sent Menelaus to Proteus.

CXIX. When Menelaus arrived at Egypt, he sailed up to Memphis, and having truly related what had passed, was very hospitably entertained by the king; had his wife with all his treasures restored to him without any injury done to her person; and that notwithstanding this kindness, Menelaus proved unjust to the Egyptians: for when he was desirous of sailing away, contrary winds detained him; and when things continued the same for a long time, he devised an impious deed; for having taken two children of the people of the country, he sacrificed them[u]; when the deed became known, he was detested and pursued by the Egyptians, but he escaped with his ships to Lybia; where he went to from thence, they could not tell: some of these circumstances they said they knew by inquiring of others, and were fully assured of the rest, because they were done among them.

CXX. These things the Egyptian priests related to me; to this story of Helen, I also assent from the following consideration. If Helen had been within the territories of Ilium, doubtless the Trojans would have surrendered her to the Grecians, either with or without the consent of Alexander. For certainly Priam and all those about him could never be so infatuated to bring themselves, with their children and the whole kingdom, into the utmost hazard, only that Alexander might enjoy Helen. But let us suppose they might take such a resolution at first; yet after the slaughter of such vast numbers of Trojans, and two or three of the king's sons, or even more if we may believe the poets, that were killed fighting against the Greeks, I cannot forbear to think that if Priam himself had married Helen, he would have restored her to the Greeks, to be delivered from so great a calamity. Besides, the kingdom would not next devolve upon Alexander, so that

[u] This was doubtless to appease the winds. This kind of sacrifice was frequent in Greece, the sacrifice of Iphigenia at Aulis is well known.

Sanguine placastis ventos et virgine cæsa.
Sanguine quærendi reditus.
Virg. Æneid. ii. 116.

as Priam was old, the administration of affairs would be in his power, but Hector, who was older and more brave than he[x], would receive the kingdom after the death of Priam, who could not with any decency abet and support the injustice of his brother; by whose means so many evils had already happened, and were daily impending over his own head, and over all the Trojans in general. But indeed they had it not in their power to restore Helen, though the Greeks would not believe them when they spoke the truth; heaven ordaining, as I conjecture, that they should be utterly destroyed, in order to convince men that the Gods have great punishments in reserve for atrocious crimes. And thus I have delivered my opinion concerning these things.

CXXI. The priests likewise informed me, that upon the death of Proteus, Rhampsinitus succeeded him, and for a monument of his magnificence added to the temple of Vulcan a portico fronting to the west, and erected two statues before this building of twenty-five cubits each. One of these looks to the northward, and is adored by the Egyptians under the name of Summer: the other facing the south, is altogether neglected[y], and goes by the name of Winter.

Rhampsinitus, they informed me, possessed great riches, which no one of the succeeding kings[z] could surpass or even nearly come up to; and being desirous to treasure up his wealth in safety, built an apartment of stone, which had one wall on the outside of the palace. This situation the architect[a] made use of to deceive the king, and placed one of the stones in so loose a manner, that it might be easily taken out by two or even one man. When the building was finished the king laid up his treasures in it. In the course of time the architect finding his end approaching, called his two sons to him and explained to them, how, with a view that they might live in abundance, he had contrived, when building the king's treasury; and having clearly explained all the particulars they were to observe in taking out the stone, he gave them the dimensions[b] of it, and told them, if they would observe his instructions, they might be the managers of all the king's riches. The sons waited not long after the death of their father to put his counsel in execution, and went by night to the palace; where hav-

[x] Literally; more a man than he was.

[y] This they scourged on certain occasions, because it represented Typhon. It is in the month of February that the southerly wind begins to be felt, which causes hurricanes, and makes the air unhealthy. *Savary*, Letter, LXV.

[z] Ἐπιτραφέντων, (i. q. ἐπιγενομένων,) from ἐπιτρέφω, which is used in a similar sense, i. 123. and iv. 3. But in i. 7, 10. it is rightly written ἐπιτραφθέντες from ἐπιτρέπω. *Schweigh.*

[a] Pausanias relates a similar story of Trophimus, whose cave became so famous. *Larcher.*

[b] Not only the size of the stone, but its distance from the bottom and the sides, &c. *Schweigh.*

ing found the place, they removed the stone without difficulty, and carried off a great quantity of money.

Rhampsinitus entering one day into the treasury, and seeing his vessels which contained his treasures much diminished, fell into a great surprise; and knew not whom to blame since the seals were unbroken, and the apartment in appearance well secured. But after the king had two or three times successively visited his treasures, and they constantly appeared diminished, (as the thieves did not cease plundering,) he ordered traps to be made, and spread about the vessels that contained his money. The thieves coming as before, one of them entered, and going to a vessel filled with silver, was presently taken in the snare. Finding himself in this extremity, he immediately called his brother, and acquainting him with his misfortune, desired him to come in, and cut off his head without delay, lest, if he was seen and recognised, he should ruin him also. The brother, comprehending the reason of his request, did as he desired, and having put the stone in its proper place, returned home with the head.

Early in the morning the king coming to the treasury, was not a little astonished to find the body of the thief taken in the trap without a head, and the whole edifice entire, without any place for a person to go out or come in. In this perplexity he went away, and commanded the body to be hanged on the wall; appointing a guard, with strict orders, if they should see any one weeping at the spectacle, or pitying the person, to bring him immediately before the king. But no sooner was the body thus exposed, than the mother fell into a great passion, and commanded her surviving son, by any means he could contrive, to take down and bring away the corpse of his brother: threatening, if he refused, to go to the king, and let him know that he was the person who had the treasures.

When the mother treated her surviving son harshly, and when with many entreaties he was unable to persuade her, he contrived the following plan; he made ready some asses, and having loaded them with skins filled with wine, and driven them near the guards that were appointed to watch the dead body that was hanging up, he unfastened two or three of the openings of the skins which hung down: and when he saw the wine running out, struck himself upon the head, and cried out lamentably; as if his confusion had been so great, that he knew not to which of his asses he should run first. The guards seeing so much wine lost, ran presently to the asses with pots in their hands to receive the liquor, and make use of the present opportunity; which the man perceiving, feigned himself highly incensed, and railed bitterly against the soldiers. But they on the contrary giving him good words, he grew calm again, and pretending to be pacified, led his asses out of the way, as if he designed to secure the rest of his wine; until at last falling into a dialogue of mirth and raillery with the guards, he gave one of the skins among them. The soldiers determined to sit down at once and drink it, and, having taken him by the hand, desired him to stay and drink with them; he, as he intended, was persuaded, and as they kindly treated him during the drinking, he gave them another skin; and the guards taking very copious draughts, became exceedingly drunk, and being overpowered by the wine fell asleep in the place. By this means he took down his brother in the dead of night; and having, in derision, shaved all the guard on the right cheek[c], he laid the body upon one of his asses, and drove it home, having performed his mother's injunctions.

They added, that the king hearing the body of the thief had been stolen, was very indignant; and, resolving by any means to find out the contriver of this artifice, formed a design, which to me seems incredible; he commanded his daughter to sit in a brothel[d], and to admit to her embraces all comers indifferently, after having first obliged every one in particular to let her know the most subtle, and most wicked actions of his whole life; and, when any one should discover himself guilty of the fact relating to the thief, that she should lay hands on him, and not suffer him to escape. His daughter obeyed; and the thief, not ignorant to what end this contrivance tended, and desirous to out do the king in versatile craft, cut off an arm from the body of a man newly expired, and putting it under his cloak, went to the daughter of Rhampsinitus. At his coming, when she asked him the same questions she had proposed to others, he answered, that he had perpetrated the most impious action, when he cut off his brother's head who was caught in a snare in the king's treasury;

c This was, throughout all the east, the greatest insult to any one. Thus Hanun king of the Ammonites, shaved the messengers of David by way of contempt, and sent them away, 2 Sam. x. 4, 5.

Beloe says, that Larcher here makes a false reference; viz, to the second Book of Kings, instead of the second Book of Samuel. But Beloe does not appear to have been aware that the two Books of Samuel are styled in the Vulgate the first and second Books of Kings, and the two Books of Kings, the third and fourth, since those four contain the history of the Kings of Israel and Judah.

It was one of the most disgraceful punishments inflicted on cowardice in Sparta, that those who fled in battle were obliged to appear abroad with one half of their beard shaved, the other unshaved. Many of the Arabs would rather die than lose their beards.

d Οἴκημα among the Athenians particularly signified *a brothel, a place of prostitution; lussanar* is also used in this sense in ch. cxxvi.

and the most subtle, when he contrived to make the guard drunk, and by that means to carry off the body. When she heard this, she endeavoured to seize him, but he in the dark held out to her the hand of the dead man, which she seized, and imagined that she held the hand of the thief, and he having let it go, fled away through the door.

When the king was informed of this event, he was astonished at the invention and audaciousness of the man; and at last, caused proclamation to be made in all places, that he would not only pardon him, but reward him amply, if he would discover himself. The thief, in confidence of this promise, went directly to the palace; and Rhamsinitus, in admiration of his subtlety, gave him his daughter in marriage; accounting him the most knowing of all men, because he knew more than the Egyptians, who are wiser than the rest of mankind.

CXXII. After this, they said, Rhampsinitus descended alive into those places which the Grecians call Hades; where playing at dice with Ceres[e], he sometimes won, and other times lost[f]: that at his return he brought with him as a present a napkin of gold. On account of his descent, after his return, they informed me that a festival was celebrated by the Egyptians, which I have seen them observe in my time: but whether that adventure, or some other thing, gave birth to this solemnity, I cannot determine. However, the priests every year at that time, clothing one of their order in a cloak woven the same day, and covering his eyes with a mitre, guide him into the way that leads towards the temple of Ceres, and then return: upon which, they say, two wolves come and conduct him to the temple, twenty stades distant from the city, and afterwards lead him back to the place from whence he came.

CXXIII. Any person, to whom these things may appear probable, is at liberty to adopt as true, the things that are related by the Egyptians; as for me, it is my object throughout the whole of the history, to write what I heard from each people. The Egyptians hold, that the sovereign power of the infernal regions is exercised by Ceres and Bacchus; and were the first of all mankind, who affirmed the immortality of man's soul[g]; which, they say, upon the death of the body

[e] In the Greek, *Demeter*. The Egyptians, says Diodor. Sic. (i. 12.) regarded the earth as the receptacle of every thing which is born, and called it mother. The Greeks call it Demeter, which bears relation to the same word, and has been changed a little by time.

[f] Szathmari applies this to the years of plenty and scarcity, which happened under Pharoah. See his Dissert. on the Pharaohs, printed by Franiher. *Valck.*

[g] Herodotus does not say that the Egyptians were the first who believed the immortality of the soul, but the first who affirmed that it passed into some other animal. I have no doubt that the Egyptians always believed in the immortality of the soul. It was derived from Mis-

always enters into some other animal; and passing, by a continued rotation, through the different kinds of aerial, terrestrial, and marine beings, returns again into a human body; and that this revolution is performed in three thousand years. Yet this opinion divers Greeks have published for their own[h], in these and former times; but I shall forbear to mention them, though I am not ignorant of their names.

CXXIV. They told me likewise, that to the reign of Rhampsinitus, justice and good order were preserved in Egypt, and that the kingdom flourished in plenty; but that Cheop[i], who succeeded him, plunged into every vice. For after he had shut up all the temples, and forbidden the public sacrifices, he oppressed the Egyptians with hard labour; appointing some to receive the stones that were dug out of the quarries in the Arabian mountains, and to draw them down to the Nile, and when they had been transported in vessels to the other side of that river, he appointed others to receive them, and to drag them to the mountain called the Lybian. About a hundred thousand men were employed in this labour, ten thousand every three months: as to the time during which the people were thus harrassed by toil, first of all, ten years were spent in constructing the causeway[k], along which they

raim, the grandson of Noah, who peopled Egypt. The doctrine of immortality gradually degenerated into that of transmigration. The Indians however claim this last opinion. Osiris and Sesostris, who subdued them, probably brought it into Egypt. A great deal has been written on the subject without throwing any light upon it. *Larcher.*

h The poetry of Homer shews, that the immortality of the soul was long known in Greece. Pherecydes and Pythagoras are probably alluded to by Herodotus. The Gauls also supposed that the soul passed from the body of one man into that of another. (Cæsar de Bello Gallico, vi. 15.) *Larcher.*

i Diodorous Siculus, (i. 63.) after Rhampsinitus, whom he calls Rhemphis, puts in seven other kings. The eighth he calls Chembes or Chemmes, or Chemmis, who is the Cheops of Herodotus.

M. de Voltaire was justified in regarding the construction of the pyramids, as a proof of the slavery of the Egyptians, and with justice remarks, that it would not be possible to compel the English to erect similar masses, who are far more powerful than the Egyptians at that time were. *Larcher.*

k The stones might be conveyed by the canal, that runs about two miles north of the pyramids, and from thence part of the way, by this extraordinary causeway. For at this time there is a causeway from that part extending about a thousand yards in length, and twenty feet in breadth, built of hewn stone. The length of it agreeing so well with Herodotus, is a strong confirmation that this causeway has been kept up ever since, though some of the materials of it may have been changed, all being now built with free-stone. It is strengthened on each side with semicircular buttresses, about fourteen feet in diameter, and thirty feet apart; there are sixty-one buttresses beginning from the north. Sixty feet farther it turns to the west for a little way, then there is a bridge of about twelve arches, twenty feet wide, built on piers that are ten feet wide. Above one hundred yards farther there is such another bridge, beyond which the causeway continues about one hundred yards to the south, ending about a mile from the pyramids, where the ground is higher. The country over which the causeway is built, being low, and the water lying on it a great while, seems to be the reason for building this causeway at first, and continuing to keep it in repair. *Pococke,* vol. i. p. 42.

drew the stones, which I think to be a work, little less considerable than the pyramid. For it is five stades in length, sixty feet broad, and in the highest part forty-eight feet in altitude; all of polished stone, and carved with the figures of various animals. Ten years were occupied in constructing this, and also in forming subterraneous apartments[l] in the hill[m], on which the pyramids are, which he intended as a sepulchre for himself, in an island, which he formed, by digging a canal from the Nile. Twenty years were spent on the pyramid, which is quadrilateral, every face containing eight plethra[n] in length, and the same measure in height. All the stones are thirty feet long, well polished, and jointed with the greatest exactness.

CXXV. This pyramid was built in the form of steps, which some call stairs, and others little altars. When they had commenced in that manner, they raised the other stones by

These two bridges are also described by Norden, the dimensions given by these two travellers differ essentially. Larcher suspects that Norden describes the second bridge, which Pococke only mentions without giving the measures.

[l] The second pyramid has a fosse cut in the rock to the north, and to the west, which is about ninety feet wide and thirty deep. There are also small apartments cut in the rock: *Pococke*, vol. i. p. 45.

[m] The pyramids are not situated in a plain, but upon the rock, which is at the foot of the high mountains, which accompany the Nile in its course, and make the separation between Egypt and Lybia. It may have fourscore feet of perpendicular elevation above the horizon of the ground that is always overflowed by the Nile. *Norden's Travels in Egygt and Nubia*, vol. i. p. 67, 71.

[n] To determine the dimensions of the great pyramid is still a problem. From the time of Herodotus, it has been measured by a great number of travellers, and learned men, and their different calculations, far from clearing up doubts, have only increased the uncertainty. I will give a table of them, which will serve at least to prove how difficult it is to come at the truth.

	Height of the great pyramid.	*Width of one of its sides.*
ANCIENTS.	FEET.	FEET.
Herodotus	800	800
Strabo	625	600
Diodorus Sicul.	600 & a fraction.	700
Pliny		708
MODERNS.	FEET.	FEET.
Le Brun	616	704
Prosper Alpinus	625	750
Thevenot	520	612
Neibuhr	440	710
Greaves	444	648

Number of the layers of stone or steps.

Greaves	207
Maillet	208
Albert Lewenstein	260
Pococke	212
Belon	250
Thevenot	208

To me it seems evident that Greaves and Neibuhr are prodigiously deceived in the perpendicular height of the great pyramid. All travellers agree that it has at least two hundred layers, which are each from two to four feet high. The highest are at the base, and they decrease insensibly to the top. I measured several which were more than three feet high, and I found none less than two; therefore the least mean height is two feet and a half, which, even according to Greaves's calculation, who reckons 207 layers, would make 517 feet six inches perpendicular height. *Savary*, Letter XVII.

Savary next proceeds to shew, that it is at present 600 feet high, but that in the time of Herodotus, when the sand was not accumulated round its base, it would have been much more. It is to the astonishing accumulation of sand that the difference between the accounts of historians is to be attributed. See also

machines[o] made of small pieces of wood, raising them first from the ground to the first range; when the stone arrived there, it was put on another engine, which stood on the first step, from which step it was raised to the second, and so on: for these engines thus employed were equal in number to the several orders of stone; or perhaps the engine was but one, and being easily managed, might be removed as often as they placed a stone; for I may be allowed to relate it in both ways, as it was related to me. The highest were first finished[p], and the rest in their proper order; but last of all those that are lowest and nearest the ground. On this pyramid an inscription is seen, declaring, in Egyptian characters[q], how much was expended in radishes, onions, and garlic, for the workmen; which the interpreter, as I well remember, after reading the letters, informed me, amounted to no less than the sum of sixteen hundred talents of silver. And if this be true, how much more may we think was expended in iron tools, in bread, and in clothes for the labourers, since they occupied in building this edifice the time which I mentioned, and no short time besides, in my opinion, in heaving and drawing the stones, and in constructing the subterraneous apartments.

CXXVI. In the end, Cheops, having exhausted his treasures, arrived to such a degree of infamy, that he prostituted his own daughter[r] in a brothel, commanding her to get a certain sum of money, but the sum they mentioned not. She collected as much as her father ordered her; and at the same time contriving to leave a monument of herself, asked every one that came, to give her a stone towards the edifice she designed. By which means she built that pyramid which stands in the midst of the three, before the great pyramid, and extends to the length of a plethron and half on every side of the base.

CXXVII. Fifty years, as the Egyptians say, Cheops reigned, and when he was dead, his brother Chephren[s] suc-

Letter XVIII. for remarks on the interior structure of the great pyramid, &c. which are extracted from Maillet.

[o] Larcher thinks these machines were inclined planes.

[p] Ἐκποιέειν signifies *to complete, to perfect, to ornament, to put the finishing stroke to.* Herodotus alludes to the coating of the pyramid. He uses the word in this sense, lib. v. 62.

Shaw, Thevenot, and others, who pretend that this pyramid was never finished, are in error. It is only necessary to observe the remains of the mortar, with the splinters of white marble, which are to be found in many parts of the steps, to see that it has been coated. *Savary,* Letter XVII. This coating was marble.

[q] Probably in common letters; not in the sacred, or hieroglyphics. *Larcher.*

[r] This story has been thought so horrible, that many have doubted the truth of it: but we have had in England an instance of a crime as detestable. Mervin, Lord Audley, prostituted his wife. See State Trials.

[s] Diodorus Sic. (i. 64.) says, that some affirm that his son Chabryin, or Chabryen, succeeded him; this probably was the same word, differently written, according to a different pronunciation. *Larcher.*

ceeded to the kingdom; imitating him in other things, and particularly in building a pyramid; which does not come up to the dimensions of that of Cheops, (for we ourselves measured them,) and neither has it subterraneous chambers, nor a channel, like the other, derived from the Nile, and forming a kind of island within, on which they say the body of Cheops lies deposited[t]. The lower range of this fabric is built with Ethiopian marble[u] of various colours; the pyramid is forty feet[x] less in height than the other, near which it stands. They both stand on the same hill; which rises to the height of about a hundred feet. Chephren, they said, reigned fifty-six years.

CXXVIII. The Egyptians having been thus oppressed with all manner of calamities, during one hundred and sixty years, in all which time the temples were never opened, have conceived so great an aversion to the memory of the two kings, that no Egyptian will mention their names[y]; but always attribute their pyramids to one Philitis a shepherd, who kept his cattle in those parts.

CXXIX. They said also, that after him, Mycerinus the son of Cheops became king; and, disapproving the conduct of his father, opened the temples, and permitted the people, who were reduced to the last extremities, to have leizure to apply themselves to their own affairs, and to sacrifices, and that he made the most just decisions of all their kings. On this account they praise him above all the kings that ever reigned in Egypt; for he judged well in other respects, and also, when any man complained of a hard sentence, he used

[t] Although the kings destined these for their sepulchres, yet it came to pass that no one of them was buried there. The people indignant at the labours they had undergone, and the cruelty and violence of the treatment they had met with, threatened to take their bodies from the tombs and tear them in pieces. Thus these two kings ordered their friends to bury them secretly in some unknown place. *Diod. Sic.* i. 64.

[u] I am of opinion that this is the stone which Pliny calls pyropœcilos, and that it is granite. This, Pliny says, is brought from Syene, which being on the borders of Ethiopia, might in less accurate language be said to be Ethiopic. *Larcher.*

The quarries of this beautiful marble are situated at the extremity of Egypt, in the mountain, at the foot of which stands Syene. There are three kinds of it; the first is a perfect black; the second is only spotted with black; and the last is speckled with red. The granite of the two former kinds was employed in the construction of the tombs. The other in columns and obelisks. *Savary*, Letter XIX.

[x] I have followed Schweighæuser's reading ὑποβάς, *the King having built it lower than*, &c.

[y] This is probably the reason that historians agree so little about the names of the princes, who built these pyramids. Qui de iis (Pliny, Hist. Nat. xxxvi. 12.) scripserint, sunt Herodotus, Euhemerus, Duris Samius, Aristagoras, Dionysius, Artemidorus, Alexander Polyhistor, Butorides, Antisthenes, Demetrius, Demoteles, Apion. Inter eos omnes non constat a quibus factæ sint, justissimo casu obliteratis tantæ vanitatis auctoribus. *Larcher.*

to make him some present out of his own treasury and satisfy his anger: that while he was thus beneficient to his people, and careful of their welfare, the first misfortune that befel him was the death of his only daughter; with which calamity being extremely afflicted, he resolved to bury her in an extraordinary manner; and having caused the image of a cow to be made of wood richly gilded with gold, he put the body of his daughter into it.

CXXX. This cow was not interred in the ground; but continued to my time exposed to open view, in a magnificent chamber of the royal palace in the city of Sais, where they burn all kinds of aromatics every day, and illuminate the place by night with a lamp. In another room contiguous to this are seen the images of Mycerinus's concubines, as the priests of Sais affirm: and indeed about twenty statues of wood stand naked in that place; but, touching the women they represent, I know no more than they were pleased to tell me.

CXXXI. Yet some giving a different account of this monument, and of these statues, say, that Mycerinus, falling in love with his daughter, used violent means to obtain her; they add, that she from grief hanged herself, and was buried in this manner by her father; that her mother cut off the hands of her maids, for assisting Mycerinus in the rape of his daughter; and for that reason, say they, the statues are made, as the originals were mutilated for their offence. But these things, as I conjecture, are trifling fables; especially in that particular relating to the hands of the images, for I plainly saw that they had lost their hands from age, as they were lying at their feet even in my time.

CXXXII. The body of the cow is covered with a purple cloth, except the head and neck, which are covered with very thick gold; and a circle of gold in imitation of the sun is placed between the horns. This animal is represented kneeling, and equal to a large living cow. The Egyptians annually carry her out of the apartment where she is placed; and after having beat themselves and lamented a certain God, not to be named by me on this occasion, they bring her into the light; which they say is done because the daughter of Mycerinus desired her father before she died, that he would permit her to see the sun once every year.

CXXXIII. Another calamity fell upon this king, after the death of his daughter. For a prophecy was brought to him from the city of Butus, importing, that he had no more than six years to live, and should die in the seventh: which denunciation having heard with impatience, he sent a reproach to the God[z], complaining, that his father and uncle, who had shut up the temples, despised the Gods, and destroyed vast numbers of men, had lived long, and he, notwithstanding his piety and religion, must die so soon. But the oracle in an answer sent him another message, to acquaint him, that his life was shortened, because he had not acted in conformity to the decrees of fate; which had determined that Egypt should be afflicted during one hundred and fifty years; and that this was well known to the two kings his predecessors, though not understood by him. Mycerinus, finding himself thus condemned by the Gods, commanded a great number of lamps to be made and lighted every night, that he might without ceasing, either day or night, drink and enjoy himself: roving frequently by night and by day about the plains and groves, wherever he could hear of places most suited for pleasure[a]: imagining by this artifice to convict the oracle of falsehood, and by turning the nights into so many days, to live twelve years instead of six.

CXXXIV. This king likewise left a pyramid of a quadrangular form, but lower by twenty feet than that of his father, every side extending to the length of three plethrons, and built to the middle[b] with Ethiopian stone[c]. Some of the Grecians, without reason, attribute this monument to the courtesan Rhodopis[d]; but to me they seem ignorant who she

[z] Valckenaer proposes *τῇ θεῷ*, as it was Latona that had an oracle at Butos. We are however informed that Apollo had a temple there also, c. 155, 156.

[a] Ἐνηβητήρια, pleasant places in which youth gives itself up to enjoyment: agreeable places adapted to inspire pleasure.

[b] To the east is a third pyramid, said to be built by Mycerinus. Herodotus speaks of it as three hundred feet square. I measured it at the top, fourteen feet on the north side, and twelve on the east; and counting seventy-eight steps at one foot nine inches broad, it amounts to about the number of feet. Our author affirms that it was built half way up with Ethiopian marble, that is, cased with it. Diodorus mentions fifteen tier, so that computing each tier on the outside to be five feet deep, as I found them, that will amount to seventy-five feet, which answers within six feet of the height, computed at one hundred and fifty-six feet, supposing the steps to be two feet high. On this account, Strabo says, it was as expensive a work as the others. All round it are remains of the granite it was adorned with, which has been pulled down, and great part of it carried away. *Pococke*, vol. i. p. 47.

[c] If Herodotus wished to speak of the same stone, as in ch. cxxvii. he would have expressed himself in the same manner. It is most probable that it is the stone which we call Basalte. *Larcher*.

[d] Some say that this is the tomb of Rhodopis. Some of the governors of the districts caused this pyramid to be built in order to win her good graces. *Diodorus Siculus*, i. 64.

It is said that this pyramid was erected by the lovers of Rhodopis, who is by Sappho called Doricha; she was the mistress of her brother Charaxus, who traded to Naucratis with Lesbian wine. It is reported of her, that one day when she was in the bath, an eagle snatched one of her slippers from an attendant, and carried it to Memphis. The king was then sitting in his tribunal; the eagle, settling above his head, let fall the slipper into his bosom: the prince, astonished at this singular event, and at the smallness of the slipper, ordered a search to be made through the country for the female to whom it belonged. Being found at Naucratis, she was presented

was; for they would not else have attributed to her the building a pyramid, on which, to speak in few words, numberless thousands of talents are expended, and besides she did not live in the same time, but under the reign of Amasis, very many years after the death of those kings who founded the pyramids. She was a native of Thrace, servant to Iadmon the Samian, son of Hephæstiopolis, and fellow-servant with Æsop, the inventor of the fables[e], who likewise belonged to Iadmon, as appears by this testimony chiefly. For when the Delphians had several times demanded, in obedience to the oracle, if any one wished to require atonement for the death of Æsop[f], no man appeared except Iadmon, the grandson of this Iadmon who was the master of Æsop.

CXXXV. Xanthus the Samian transported Rhodopis to Egypt; she was brought in order to gain money by her person, but Charaxus of Mitylene, son to Scamandronymus, and brother to Sappho the poetess, purchased her liberty with a great sum. By this means, being delivered from servitude, Rhodopis continued in Egypt; and as she was extremely beautiful, acquired great treasures for a person of her condition, though no way sufficient to defray the expence of such a pyramid. For it is possible, for every one who wishes, to see the tenth of her wealth, so that it is not necessary to attribute any great wealth to her. For out of a desire to leave some memory of herself in Greece, she contrived such a monument as no person ever yet devised and dedicated in a temple; appropriating the tenth of all her wealth to purchase a great number of iron spits, strong enough to carry an ox, which she sent as an offering to the temple of Delphi; where they are still piled up behind the altar, which the Chians dedicated opposite the inner chapel. The courtesans of Naucratis are generally beautiful; for not only the person we mention became so famous that no Grecian was ignorant of the name of Rhodopis; but also another named Archidice[g],

to the king, who made her his wife; when she died she was buried in the manner we have described. *Strabo, Geograph.* xvii. p. 1161.

[e] Λογοποιὸς signifies *both an historian and a writer of fables*; it is used in chap. 163, in the former sense. Λόγος, however, when opposed to μῦθος, signifies *the truth*, or *moral*, of the fable. *Larcher.*

[f] Plutarch (de his qui a sero numine puniuntur, p. 556.) informs us, that Æsop was sent by Crœsus, with a large sum of money, to Delphi to sacrifice to Apollo, and to distribute four mina to each citizen. But having had some quarrel with the Delphians, he offered the sacrifice, but sent the money back. The enraged Delphians accused him of sacrilege, and put him to death by throwing him from the rock Hyampea. Apollo, to punish them, afflicted them with all sorts of diseases and made their land barren. And it was to remove this, that they made the proclamation alluded to by Herodotus.

[g] A young man was enamoured of Archidice a courtesan of Naucratis. Proud of her charms, and difficult of access, she made people pay dear for her favours. When he made her a present, she at first yielded, but soon rejected him. Being then unable to obtain her favours, on account of his poverty, he dreamed in the

who lived after her, was highly celebrated in Greece, though not talked about so much as the former. As for Charaxus, who purchased the liberty of Rhodopis, he returned to Mitylene, and was not a little ridiculed by Sappho in an ode she composed against him. But I shall say no more concerning Rhodopis.

CXXXVI. After the time of Mycerinus, the priests said, that Asychis[h] was king of Egypt, and that he built the most beautiful and largest portico of Vulcan's temple, which fronts to the rising sun: for though the other porticos are adorned with various figures of excellent sculpture, and many curious pieces of architecture, yet this is preferable to all: they relate that under his reign, when commerce was checked for want of money, a law was made, that any man, by giving as a pledge the body of his father, might borrow money; and it was also added, that the lender should have power over the whole sepulchre; and that, if he afterwards refused to repay the debt, he should neither be buried[i] in the same place with his father, or in any other, nor have the liberty of burying the dead[k] body of any of his friends; that this king desiring to out do all his predecessors, erected a pyramid of brick for his monument, with this inscription: "Do not despise me in comparison with the pyramids of stone, which I excel as much as Jupiter surpasses the other Gods. For dipping down to the bottom of the lake with long poles, and then collecting the mire that stuck to them, men made bricks, and formed me in that manner." These were the principal actions of Asychis.

CXXXVII. After him, the priests informed me, that Anysis, a blind man, born in a city of the same name, succeeded in the kingdom; that during his reign Sabacon[l], king of Ethiopia, at the head of a powerful army, invaded Egypt, and that the blind man fled to the fens: that the Ethiopian king reigned fifty years in Egypt, and in all that time put no Egyptian to death[m] for any crime; contenting himself to com-

night that he enjoyed her, and his love immediately ceased. Upon this Archidice pretended that the young man ought to pay her, and summoned him before the judges; the judge ordered the man to put the required sum in a purse, and to put it so that its shadow might fall on Archidice; meaning by that, that the young man's pleasure was but the shadow of the real one. *Ælian. Var. Hist.* xii. 63.

[h] Diodorus Siculus does not here agree with Herodotus. He does not mention Asychis or Anysis, (i. 65.) but puts in their place Bocchoris, and adds, that long after him Sabacon reigned in Egypt. I am of opinion that Diodorus is mistaken. *Larcher.*

[i] The laws of England allow the arrest of a person's dead body till his debts are paid.

[k] Ἀπογενόμενον does not signify born of, but *dead*, so lib. ii. 85. iv. 4. and Thucyd. *Wesseling, Valckenaer and Larcher.*

[l] Usher and Marsham suppose him to to be the same as So, king of Egypt, mentioned in 2 Kings, xvii. 4.

[m] In ch. 152. however we are told that he put to death Necos the father of

mand every delinquent, in proportion to his offence, to carry a certain quantity of earth to the city of which he was an inhabitant; and by this means the situation of the Egyptian cities was much elevated; for those who cut the canals in the time of Sesostris, had already brought thither all the earth they took out of them; but under this Ethiopian king they were raised much higher; and none more, in my opinion, than the city of Bubastis[n], which has a temple dedicated to Bubastis, who is no other than the Diana of the Grecians. This temple very well deserves mention. For though others may be more spacious and magnificent, yet none can afford more pleasure to the eye.

CXXXVIII. The temple is built in a peninsula, no part except the entrance joining to the land, and almost surrounded by two canals cut from the Nile, each of which flow as far as the entrance of the temple, without mixing together. Each canal is a hundred feet broad, shaded with trees on both sides. The portico is ten fathoms in height, adorned with excellent statues of six cubits each. This fabric stands in the midst of the city, open on all sides to the public view; as the city has been raised up, and the temple not being moved, but being as it originally was, it may be looked down upon. A wall runs round it beautified with various figures wrought in the stone, and inclose a grove of lofty trees, that encompass a chapel, in which an image is placed. This temple contains a full stade in length, and as much in breadth. From the avenue eastward lies a way through the public place, leading to the temple of Mercury[o], about three stades in length, and four plethrons in breadth, all paved with stone, and planted with trees on each side, that seem to reach the heavens. And such is the description of this temple.

CXXXIX. They informed me that the Ethiopian departed[p] on this occasion; they said, he fled from Egypt upon

Psammetichus; but perhaps Necos was of the royal family, and Sabacon might fear that he would aim at the throne. *Larcher.*

[n] Bubastis was a virgin who presided at child-births, and was the symbol of the moon. This resemblance caused the Greeks to name her the Diana of the Egyptians. The resemblance, however, was not perfect, for she was not the Goddess of the mountains. *Larcher.*

[o] The Egyptian mercury was Thoth or Theuth. Thoth with the Egyptians was the inventor of the sciences; and as Mercury with the Greeks presided over the sciences, this last people called Thoth, in their tongue, by the name of Hermes or Mercury: they had also given the name of Mercury to Anubis, on account of some fancied resemblance. "It "is not," says Plutarch, (de Iside et Osir. p. 355.) "a dog properly so called, "that they revere under the name of "Mercury, it is his vigilance and fidelity, "the instinct which teaches him to distinguish a friend from an enemy, which "(to use the expression of Plato) makes "this animal a suitable emblem for this "God, the immediate patron of reason." Servius (on Virgil, Æn. viii. 698.) has a similar remark. *Larcher.*

[p] Τέλος δε τῆς ἀπαλλαγῆς. I understand by this, the same as by τέλος θάνατοιο, τέλος γάμοιο in Homer, which

a vision he had in a dream, representing a man standing by him, and advising him to assemble all the Egyptian priests, and to cut them in two by the middle of the body; that after he had reflected on his dream, he concluded that the Gods had a design to lay before him an occasion of committing an impious action, to the end he might be punished, either by themselves, or by men; but rather than be guilty of such a crime, he would return to his own country; because the time was then expired, which the oracles had assigned for the duration of his reign in Egypt: for whilst he was yet in Ethiopia, he had been admonished by the oracles of that country[q], that he should govern the Egyptians fifty years. In conclusion, Sabacon, seeing the term of those years elapsed, and being exceedingly disturbed by the vision, voluntarily abandoned Egypt.

CXL. After his departure, the blind king returned to the exercise of the government from the fens, where he had continued fifty years, and had formed an island for his habitation, composed of ashes and earth. For when any Egyptian went to him by order with provisions, he always desired him to bring some ashes thither, without discovering the secret to the Ethiopian. This island, which goes by the name of Elba, and comprehends ten stades in length, and the same measure in breadth, lay undiscovered more than seven hundred years[r], till the reign of Amyrtæus; and was never found out by any of that king's predecessors.

CXLI. After him succeeded Sethon, a priest of Vulcan[s], who slighting the military men of Egypt as persons altogether useless to him, among other indignities took away the lands they possessed, and which had been assigned to them by former kings as a distinction, twelve aruræ[t] to each man. For this reason, when Sennacherib king of Arabia and Assyria invaded Egypt with a numerous army, the military men refused to assist him; so that the priest in great perplexity, betook himself to the temple; and, prostrate before the image of the God, deplored the calamities which he was in danger of un-

are for *θάνατος, γάμος*. Or perhaps we ought to put a comma after *τέλος δὲ*, and to read *τὴν ἀπαλλαγήν*. *Larcher.*

[q] These were the oracles of Jupiter. See Chapter 29.

[r] Larcher alters this into five hundred. His reasons are stated at length in his Essay on Chronology, ch. i. 12.

[s] A prince, says Plato, (in Politic. vol. ii. p. 290.) cannot reign in Egypt if he be ignorant of sacred affairs. If an individual of any other class comes by accident to the crown, he is immediately admitted into the sacerdotal order. The priests have the privilege of censuring the prince, says Diodorus Siculus, (i. 70.) of giving him advice, and regulating his actions. By them is fixed the time when he may walk, bathe, or visit his wife. See also Plutarch, (de Isid. et Osirid. p. 354. *Larcher.*

[t] The arura was an Egyptian measure, containing a square of 100 Egyptian cubits.

dergoing. In the midst of these lamentations he fell asleep, and dreamed he saw the God standing by his side, exhorting him to take courage, and assuring him, if he would march out against the Arabians, he should receive no hurt, for he would send him assistants. In confidence of this vision, the priest took with him the artificers, traders[u], and all the populace, who were willing to follow him, and encamped on the frontier near Pelusium, without any of the military order in his army. But the night after his arrival, an infinite number of field-mice[x] being spread over the enemy's camp, gnawed their quivers, bows, and the handles of their shields in pieces. So that on the next day they fled without arms, and many of them fell. For which cause a statue of stone, representing this king, stands, even at the present day, in the temple of Vulcan, with a mouse in one hand, and these words issuing from his mouth; *Whoever beholds me, let him learn to revere the Gods*.

CXLII. Thus far the Egyptians and the priests are the authors of this relation, and gave an account of three hundred forty and one generations, from their first king to the reign of Sethon, priest of Vulcan, and last of these monarchs; in which time the number of high priests was found equal to that

[u] The Egyptians were divided into three classes; (Diod. Sic. i. 28.) those of rank, who, with the priests, occupied the most distinguished honours of the state; the military, who were also husbandmen; and artizans, who exercised the meaner employments. Diodorus probably speaks of the three principal divisions; as Herodotus mentions seven, (ch. 163.) *Larcher*.

[x] This is founded on the fact related in 2 Kings, ch. xix. 35. 2 Chron. xxxii. 21. and Isaiah, xxxvii. 36. The Babylonish Talmud hath it, that this destruction upon the army of the Assyrians was executed by lightning, and some of the Targums are quoted for saying the same thing; but it seemeth most likely, that it was effected by bringing on them the hot wind, which is frequent in those parts; and often, when it lights among a multitude, destroys great numbers of them in a moment, as it frequently happens in those vast caravans of the Mahometans, who go their annual pilgrimages to Mecca; and the words of Isaiah, which threatened Sennacherib with a blast that God would send upon him, seem to denote the same thing. Herodotus gives us some kind of a disguised account of this deliverance from the Assyrians, in a fabulous application of it to the city of Pelusium, instead of Jerusalem; and to Sethos the Egyptian, instead of Hezekiah. It is particularly to be remarked, that Herodotus calls the king of Assyria Sennacherib, as the Scriptures do, and the time in both doth also agree very well; which plainly shews, that it is the same fact that is referred to by Herodotus, although much disguised in the relation; which may be easily accounted for, when we consider that it comes to us through the hands of such as had the greatest aversion both to the nation and to the religion of the Jews, and therefore would relate nothing in such a manner as would give reputation to either. *Prideaux's Connection*, book 1. sub anno 710. pt i. pag. 25. edit. 1720.

The blast, or hot pestilential south wind, called the Simoom, is well described by Mr. Bruce in his Travels, vol. v. pp. 80. 295. 322. 350.

It is remarkable, that the blast which destroyed the Assyrians happened in the night; whereas the *Simoom* usually blows in the day time, and mostly about noon, being raised by the intense heat of the sun. *Dr. Hales, Analysis of Chronology*, vol. ii. p. 407.

of the kings[y]. Now three hundred generations are ten thousand years, every three generations being accounted equivalent to a hundred years: and the forty-one that remain above the three hundred, make one thousand three hundred and forty years. Thus, they said, in eleven thousand three hundred and forty years, no God had put on the form of a man; neither had they ever heard of such a thing in Egypt, under their more ancient or later kings. They said, indeed, that in those days the sun had four times altered his regular course[z], having been twice observed to rise where he now sets, and to go down twice where he now rises; yet without producing any change, in the things in Egypt, either with regard to the productions of the earth or the river, or with regard to diseases and deaths.

CXLIII. Some time before, the priests of Jupiter did to Hecatæus[a] the historian, when he traced his genealogy and referred to a God as his sixteenth progenitor, the same as they did to me, though I did not trace my genealogy. For they conducted me to a spacious edifice, and shewed me large images of wood, representing all their preceding high priests; and pointing to each in order as they stood, the son after the father, they went through the whole number I mentioned before, repeating their genealogy in a gradual descent; for every high priest places his image there during his life. But when Hecatæus, in the account of his family, came to mention the sixteenth God, they would by no means admit of

[y] This becomes impossible in a great number of ages, though it might have happened in one or two. The priests undoubtedly abused the good nature of Herodotus. How could the Egyptians, who had at first no knowledge of hieroglyphics, much less of writing, have any annals? How, in a time when they had no idea of sculpture, could they have any statues? *Larcher*.

[z] We cannot read this without referring to the narrative in Joshua, ch. x. 12. and the fact related of Hezekiah, Isaiah, ch. xxxviii. The priests of Egypt professed to explain the revolutions of the Nile, the fertility of their country, and the state of public health, by the influence of the sun; and therefore in mentioning these unexampled traditional phœnomena, they adverted to a circumstance, which to them appeared as remarkable as the facts themselves, that those singular deviations of the sun from its course, had produced no sensible effects on the state of the river, on the productions of the soil, on the progress of diseases, or on deaths. The circumstances are *not* mentioned in the same form in the Scriptures, and by Herodotus; but they are in substance the same in both. And supposing the traditions to be founded in facts, it can scarcely be doubted, that they relate to the same events; especially when we recollect, that where so much is ascribed to the influence of the sun, such remarkable deviations from the course of ordinary experience would not fail to be handed down through many ages. *Horne's Introduction to the Crit. Study of the Scriptures.*

Marsham, in his Chronic. Canon. Egyptiac. p 252. attributes this to the defect of the solar year.

Larcher thinks this one of the extravagant inventions of the priests, in order to shew the antiquity of their nation.

[a] Antiquity mentions several authors by the name of Hecatæus. The one of whom Herodotus speaks was an historian, a native of Miletus, and son of Hegesander. (Herod. v. 36 and 125; vi. 137.) He is distinguished from Heatæus of Abdera, &c. by the name of Milesian.

his supposition, that a man could be begotten by a God; but opposed to him this genealogy, that each of the images he saw represented a piromis[b], begotten by another piromis; and that of the whole number, amounting to three hundred and forty-five[c], no one had referred his origin to a God or a hero; the word *piromis* signifying in their language an honest and virtuous man.

CXLIV. They declared that all the kings, whose images those were, bore that character, and yet were far inferior to the Gods; that, indeed, before the time of these men, the Gods had been the sovereigns of Egypt, but were not conversant with mortals; that one of them always exercised the supreme power, and that the last of those kings was Orus[d], the son of Osiris, who dethroned Typhon, and by the Greeks is called Apollo, as Osiris[e] by the same people is named Bacchus.

CXLV. The Greeks also think that Hercules, Bacchus, and Pan, are the youngest of all the Gods; but in Egypt Pan is esteemed the most ancient, and one of the eight pri-

[b] Mr. Bryant distinguishes between Pharaon, as it is written by Josephus, and the Pirôm of Herodotus. The former, he thinks, is compounded of *Phi* and *ourah*, implying the voice of Orus; because it was no unusual thing among the ancients to call the words of their prince, the voice of God. The observations of Herodotus and Josephus, however, so far coincide, as to make it evident they meant the same title, though they may have both, perhaps, altered the original word, by expressing it in the characters of their respective languages. In a treatise "On Providence," by Synesius, the celebrated bishop of Cyrene, is a passage which coincides with, and is illustrative of, Herodotus. He says, "the father of Osiris and Typhon was at the same time a king, a priest, and a philosopher. The Egyptian histories also rank him among the Gods; for the Egyptians are disposed to believe, that many divinities reigned in succession, before their country was governed by men, and before their kings were reckoned in a genealogical series, by Peirôm after Peirôm." It seems to be admitted that Pharaoh is a title signifying dignity, honour, exaltation. May it not be analogous to our title of highness? "I conceive," says a late celebrated writer, "that the expression in Herodotus, pyromis after pyromis, signifies, a great man after a great man." Assuming this to be the radical import of the Egyptian title, we may, perhaps, discover the meaning of Exod. ix. 16. *Robinson's Theolog. Dict. Art.* Pharaoh.

M. Lacroze observes, that Brama, which the Indians of Malabar pronounce *Biroumas*, in the Sanscreet, or sacred language of India, signifies the same as *Piromis;* and that *Piramia*, in the language of Ceylon, means a man. Is this coincidence the effect of chance, or of the conquests of Sesostris, who left colonies in various parts of Asia? *Larcher.*

[c] In the former chap. he has 341. This must be owing to the carelessness of copyists. *Larcher.*

[d] According to Plutarch, (de Iside et Osirid. pag. 380.) the Egyptians held two principles, one good, the other evil. The good principle was composed of three persons, father, mother, and son; Osiris was the father, Isis the mother, and Orus the son. The bad principle was Typhon, who dethroned his brother Osiris, and killed him. Orus fought with him, and after a combat which lasted several days, he made him prisoner.

[e] Some suppose (Plutarch. de Is. et Osir. p. 363.) that he was the Nile which made the earth, or Isis, fruitful. According to Macrobius, (Saturn. i. 21.) he was the sun. *Larcher.*

Jablonski (vol. i.) derives Osiris from Osch-Iri; he who makes time. Diodorus Sic. (lib. i.) says Osiris signifies one who has many eyes.

many deities: Hercules is among those that are second in antiquity, and go under the name of the twelve; and Bacchus is of the third order of Gods, who derive their being from the former.

I have already declared[f] how many years the Egyptians account from Hercules to the reign of Amasis; but their computation from Pan contains a greater number, and from Bacchus fewer years than from either, though from this God to the reign of Amasis they reckon no less than fifteen thousand years. The Egyptians say they know these things with certainty, because they have always computed the years, and kept an exact register of them. Now from Bacchus, who is said to have been the son of Semele the daughter of Cadmus, to our time, about sixteen hundred years[g] have passed; and from Hercules the son of Alcmena, about nine hundred; but from Pan, who, as the Grecians say, was the son of Mercury by Penelope, not more than eight hundred; which is a less number of years than they account from the siege of Troy.

CXLVI. Let every man embrace the opinion he judges most probable; as I have declared my own touching these things. For if these deities had been well known, and had grown old in Greece, like Hercules the son of Amphitryon, and particularly Bacchus the son of Semele, and Pan the son of Penelope, some one might have said that these others, though men, obtained the names of those ancient Gods. But because the Grecians report that Jupiter received Bacchus as soon as he was born, and having sewed him into his thigh, carried him to Nyssa in Ethiopia, beyond Egypt; and because they have nothing at all to say touching the place of Pan's education, I am fully convinced, that the Grecians had not heard of these till they were made acquainted with the names of the other Gods, and therefore they ascribe their generation to that time, and not higher.

CXLVII. These things[h] then the Egyptians themselves relate. I shall now relate such things as other nations, no less than they, acknowledge to have been done in Egypt, and shall add some particulars of which I was an eye-witness. The Egyptians being free, upon the death of their king, (the priest of Vulcan, for they were never capable of living without a kingly government,) divided Egypt into twelve parts, and constituted a king over each division. These twelve

[f] See chapter 43.

[g] We learn from Apollodorus, (ii. 1, 2, and 3.) and Diodorus Sic. (iv. 2.) that there were only five generations between Bacchus and Hercules, which cannot make 700 years, the time according to the present numbers in Herodotus. Larcher has, with Reizius and Borheck, introduced 1060.

[h] That is, all that has been related of the three ranks of Gods, who formerly governed Egypt, and also of the ancient kings, who were men. *Schweigh.*

kings contracted alliances by mutual marriages, and made these engagements: that they would not attempt the subversion of one another, nor one seek to acquire more than another; but should be united in the strictest friendship. Which engagements they made and carefully strengthened, because they had been admonished by an oracle when they assumed the government, that whoever among them should offer a libation in the temple of Vulcan out of a bowl of brass, should be sole king of Egypt; for they used to assemble in all the temples indifferently.

CXLVIII. But being desirous to leave a public monument of their reign at the common charge, they built a labyrinth near the city of Crocodiles, a little above the lake of Mœris, which I saw, and found far surpassing the report of fame. For if any man will impartially consider the buildings and monuments of the Grecians, he will plainly see upon comparison, that this labyrinth is a work of more labour and greater expence; though I confess the temples of Ephesus and Samos particularly deserve mention. The pyramids are beyond expression magnificent, and, singly, comparable to many of the greatest structures in Greece considered together. And yet the labyrinth is more admirable than the pyramids. For this building contains twelve courts enclosed with walls, with as many opposite doors; six opening to the north, and six to the south, contiguous to one another; and the same exterior wall extends around them. Fifteen hundred chambers are comprehended within the upper part of this edifice, and an equal number under ground. I went through and viewed every room of the upper part, and only report what I saw. But of the subterraneous apartments I know nothing but from inquiry; for the Egyptians who kept the place would by no means permit me to go in; because, said they, the sepulchres of the holy crocodiles, and of those kings that built the labyrinth, are there. I am therefore confined only to report the things I heard concerning the subterraneous buildings. But the upper part, which I carefully viewed, seems to surpass the art of men; for the passages through the buildings, and the variety of windings, afforded me a thousand occasions of wonder, as I passed from a hall to a chamber, and from the chamber to other buildings, and from chambers into halls. All the roofs and walls within are of stone; but the walls are farther adorned with figures of sculpture. The halls are surrounded with pillars of white stone, very closely fitted. And at the angle where the labyrinth ends[1] a pyramid is erected, forty

[1] In the midst of the ruins of *Casr Caroun* a large edifice rises up, of which there are several halls remaining, filled with trunks of columns. A portico half

fathoms in height, with large figures carved on it, and a subterraneous way leading into it.

CXLIX. Nevertheless, though this labyrinth be such as I have described, yet the lake of Mœris[k], by which that monu-

demolished encompasses it. One may distinguish staircases, by which they mounted to different apartments; and others, by which they descended into subterraneous passages. But what particularly attracts attention, is the view of several low, narrow, and very long cells, which seem to have had no other destination, than to contain the bodies of the sacred crocodiles, brought hither from Crocodilopolis, where they were fed by the priest, and honoured by a particular worship. These ruins, placed towards Lybia, at a league's distance from *Birket Caroun*, formerly lake Mœris, can only correspond with the labyrinth, for ancient authors assigned it this position, and point out no town on that side. See Strabo, book xvii. p. 1165. Ptolemy iv. and Herod. ii. All these authors agree in placing the labyrinth beyond the city of *Arsinoe*, on the Lybian side, and on the banks of the lake Mœris. This is exactly the situation where we meet with the ruins I have been describing. Although the account of Strabo, who visited the same monument several ages after, does not agree with that of Herodotus in every respect, it however confirms it. Diodorus Siculus, Pliny, and Pomponius Mela have described it without having seen it. The founder of the edifice is unknown. Each writer names one or more, and almost all different. This variety of opinions affords a presumption, that it was not the work of one, but of several kings. Strabo attributes it to Pharaoh *Imandes*, and pretends that his body is deposited in the pyramid at the termination of it. Pliny to Petesue or Tithoé. Diodorus Siculus thinks that the labyrinth is the work and tomb of Pharaoh Mendes. Pomponius Mela attributes it to Psammetichus. *Savary*, Letter XXVIII.

Pococke has given a minute description of it in vol. i. p. 61.

[k] Herodotus, Strabo, &c. mark out the situation of this lake; and we see in our days a lake known by the name of Birket Caroun, more than fifty leagues in circumference; but this, though less than the dimensions given by Herodotus and Pliny, by no means shews that they were deceived in their calculations. Considering the revolutions which have molested Egypt for a series of two thousand years, it might have undergone still greater changes. One of the Pharaohs, called Mœris, knowing perfectly the situation of the country, conceived one of the noblest designs ever projected, and had the glory of carrying it into execution. He determined to change a hollow covered with barren sand into an useful lake. After some thousands of men had cleared out and dug the soil in several places, he drew a canal of 40 leagues in length, and 300 feet wide, for the purpose of conducting thither the waters of the Nile. This great canal, which still subsists entire at this day, is known by the name of *Bahr Jouseph*, Joseph's river. There were two other canals, with sluices at their mouths, which were kept shut during the increase of the Nile, and then the waters conveyed by the canal of Joseph were collected in the lake Mœris. During the six months that the Nile was on the decline, these sluices were opened, and a surface of water of about eighty leagues in circumference, and thirty feet higher than the ordinary level of the river, formed a second inundation to be directed at pleasure. This work united every advantage. It supplied the deficiency of water in years of moderate inundation, by retaining those waters which would have been expended in the sea. It was still more beneficial in times of too great inundation, by receiving that superfluity which would have prevented seed time. At present this lake has lost almost all its advantages. The canal of Joseph is choked up with mud. The depth of 300 feet must be exaggerated, but much less so than might be imagined. The bottom which it occupies is formed by the mountains, and it is very low. The pyramids, described by Herodotus, no longer exist. It appears even that they existed not in the time of Augustus, since Strabo does not speak of them. In our days, we may remark to the north of Birket Caroun, a promontory, which doubtless was formerly an island. It is terminated by a rock covered with ruins. This was perhaps the foundation of these Mausolea. *Savary*, Letter XXVIII.

ment stands, is more wonderful; containing the full measure of three thousand and six hundred stades, or sixty schœnes in circumference; which is equal to the length of all the sea coast of Egypt. The figure of this lake is oblong, stretching to the north and south; and in the deepest parts has fifty fathoms of water. But the two pyramids built about the middle of the lake, which raise their heads fifty fathoms above the surface of the water, and conceal as many underneath, shew undeniably that this work was performed by the hands of men: on each of these a statue of marble is placed, seated in a throne. By which account, the pyramids are one hundred fathoms in height; and one hundred fathoms make up just a stade of six plethrons. The fathom is a measure containing six feet, or four cubits: the foot comprehends four palms, and the cubit six. This lake is not fed by springs; for all those parts are excessively dry; but by waters derived through channels cut from the Nile, which flow into the lake six months of the year, and return to the river the other six. During all the six months of the river's retreat, the fishery yields a talent of silver every day to the king's treasury[l]; and the rest of the time, twenty mines only.

CL. The inhabitants assured me that this lake runs under the earth and discharges itself into the Syrtis of Lybia, leaning always to the westward, towards the inland country, and passing by the mountain, which is above Memphis. But when I did not see any where the heap of the earth that was dug out[m], for this I was also anxious to learn, I inquired of the people, who lived nearest the lake, where it was; they told me where it had been carried, and easily persuaded me, because I had heard that the like had been done at the city of Ninus in Assyria. For when certain thieves had formed a design to steal the vast treasures of Sardanapalus, king of Ninus, which were preserved in subterraneous vaults, they carried on a mine from their own habitations, towards the palace according to the measures they had taken; and every night throwing the earth they had taken out into the river Tigris, which passes by the city, they at last effected their design. The same method was taken in Egypt, with

See also Norden, plate 79. vol. ii.; Pococke, vol. i. pp. 64, 65. Browne, p. 169. says, "Nothing can present an "appearance so unlike the works of "men. On the N. E. and S. is a rocky "ridge, in every appearance primeval." See also Denon's Egypt.

l Βασιλήϊον properly signifies *the king's palace*. The treasury probably was in the palace. Τὸ βασιλικὸν signifies *the treasury*; where we understand ταμιεῖον.

m Pococke justly finds fault with the credulity of Herodotus in this matter, especially as the river was ten miles from the nearest point of the lake, and fifty or sixty from the further, even though they might contrive water carriage for a great part of the way. Schweighæuser wonders that it was not employed in making embankments, or raising the soil.

this exception only, that they wrought here by day and not in the night. For they informed me, that all the earth they dug was carried by the Egyptians to the Nile, which swept it away, and began to disperse it; and in this manner the lake of Mœris is reported to have been made.

CLI. The twelve kings continued to observe justice; when meeting altogether at a stated time to sacrifice in the temple of Vulcan, and being about to offer a libation on the last day of the solemnity, the high priest by mistake brought no more than eleven of the twelve golden bowls, which were reserved for these occasions. So that to supply the deficiency, Psammetichus, who stood last in order, took off his helmet of brass, and holding it in his hand, performed the ceremony of libation with the rest. All the other kings were in the habit of wearing[n] the same kind of helmet, and wore them at that time: Psammetichus therefore did this without any bad design; but they having taken into consideration the action of Psammetichus, and the prediction of the oracle, "that he who should "offer a libation out of a bowl of brass, should be sole king "of Egypt;" though they thought it unjust to put him to death, because upon examination they found him free from any evil design, nevertheless unanimously agreed to divest him of the greatest part of his power, and to banish him into the fens, with a strict prohibition not to remove, or communicate with the rest of Egypt.

CLII. Long before this event, Psammetichus had been forced to fly into Syria, to escape the fury of Sabacon king of Ethiopia, who had killed his father Necos, and to continue in exile till he was recalled by the inhabitants of Sais, after the Ethiopian had been induced by the terror of a dream to abandon Egypt. Then reigning in conjunction with the eleven kings, he was again constrained to withdraw into the fens, for using his helmet at the libation. Sensible of the unjust treatment he had met with, he began to form plans for revenging himself against his persecutors; he sent to the oracle of Latona, in the city of Butus[o], which is accounted the most infallible in Egypt, and received for answer, "that he

[n] Ἐφόρεον. The aorists, the future, and sometimes the imperfect, ought to be rendered, *in that manner they used, were accustomed*, &c. For want of observing this, authors have often been made to say what they have not. *Larcher.*

[o] This goddess, one of the eight most ancient divinities of the country, was called Buto, and particularly honoured in a city of that name. She had been the nurse of Apollo and Diana, that is to say, of Orus and Bubastis, whom she had preserved from the fury of Typhon; the mole was sacred to her. Antoninus Liberalis informs us, that she assumed the form of this little animal to elude the pursuit of Typhon. Plutarch says, that the Egyptians rendered divine honours to the mole, on account of its blindness; darkness, according to them, being more ancient than light.

"should be revenged by men of brass suddenly rising out of "the sea." This oracle plunged him into the deepest incredulity; not comprehending the possibility of receiving succour from men of brass. But not long after, some Ionians and Carians, who had sailed out in order to plunder, were carried by storms to Egypt, where they landed in armour of brass. Upon which an Egyptian, who had never before seen men armed in that manner, went to the fens, and acquainted Psammetichus, that certain men of brass had risen out of the sea, and were ravaging all the lands adjacent to the shore. He, understanding the accomplishment of the prediction, made an alliance with these Ionians and Carians; and having, by promises of ample gratifications, persuaded them to stay, did, with their assistance, and the help of such Egyptians as were well affected to him, subdue and dethrone all the other kings[p].

CLIII. Thus being in possession of all Egypt, he added a portico to Vulcan's temple at Memphis, facing the south; and in front of this portico built another spacious edifice, adorned with various figures of sculpture, and surrounded with colosses twelve cubits high, in the place of pillars, designed for the habitation of Apis, by the Grecians named Epaphus, whenever he might appear.

CLIV. He rewarded the Ionians and Carians who had assisted him, with lands situate on each side of the Nile, and separated by that river; calling those habitations, the camp. And besides these lands, he gave them whatever he had promised before the expedition; and put divers Egyptian children under their care, to be instructed in the knowledge of the Greek language. So that those who now perform the office of interpreters in Egypt, are descended from this colony. The Ionians and Carians continued for a long time to inhabit those parts, which lie near the sea, below the city of Bubastis, in the pelusian mouth of the river Nile; till in succeeding time, Amasis king of Egypt caused them to abandon their habitations, and settle at Memphis, that they might be his body-guard against the Egyptians. But from the time of their first establishment, the Greeks had so constant a communication with them, that we know with certainty, all that has happened in Egypt since the reign of Psammetichus to our age. They were the first people of a different language who settled in Egypt; and the ruins of their buildings, together

p The oracle of Ammon had cautioned Tementhes king of Egypt to beware of cocks. Psammetichus being informed by Pigres, that the Carians were the first who wore crests on their helmets, comprehended the meaning of the oracle. He engaged a large body of Carians to assist him, &c. Polyænus, vii. 3. This Tementhes was undoubtedly one of the eleven kings. *Larcher.*

with the remains of the stations and arsenals they had for shipping, are seen to this day, in the place from which they were removed. And in this manner Psammetichus became master of all Egypt.

CLV. Of the Egyptian oracle, I have frequently before made mention; and shall now farther enlarge on the same subject, as a thing that deserves a singular regard. The temple is dedicated to Latona, and built in the great city of Butus, as I mentioned before, near the Sebennytic mouth of the Nile, as men navigate from the sea up that river. Apollo and Diana have also temples in the same city; and that of Latona, which contains the oracle, is a magnificent structure adorned with a portico sixty feet high. But of all the things I saw there, nothing seemed so astonishing to me, as a quadrangular chapel in the sacred inclosure[q], cut out of one single stone, and containing a square of forty cubits on every side, entirely covered with a roof of one stone likewise, having eaves[r] of four cubits.

CLVI. This chapel, I confess, appeared to me the most prodigious thing I saw in that place; and next to this, the island of Chemmis, situate in a broad and deep lake near the temple of Butus. The Egyptians say this is a floating island[s]; but I could not see it either float or move, and wondered when I heard it, whether any island really floats. The island of Chemmis contains a spacious temple dedicated to Apollo, and three altars; with great numbers of palms, and other trees, as well of such as produce fruit, as of those that do not bear fruit. The Egyptians, when they affirm that it floats, add the following story; they say that Latona, one of the eight primary deities, residing in Butus, where her oracle now is, received Apollo from the hands of Isis, and preserved his life by concealing him in this, which is now called the floating island, when Typhon, arriving in those parts, used all

[q] This enormous rock, two hundred and forty feet in circumference, was brought from a quarry in the isle of Philæ, (or Philoe,) near the cataracts, on rafts, for the space of two hundred leagues, to its destined place, and without contradiction was the heaviest weight ever moved by human power. Many thousand workmen, according to history, were three years employed in taking it to its place of destination. *Savary*, Letter XXXVII.

[r] If I am not mistaken, *παρωροφὶς* signifies *the projecting part of the roof which extends, παρὰ τὸν ὄροφον*. *Wess.*

[s] I am ignorant whether Chemmis has ever been a floating island. The Greeks pretend that Delos floated. I am persuaded they only invented that fable from the recital of the Egyptians who settled amongst them; and that they attributed to Delos, the birth place of Apollo; what the Egyptians related of Chemmis, the place of retreat to their Apollo. A rock two thousand toises long, could not float upon the waves; but the Greeks, who dearly loved the marvellous, did not examine things so closely. Theophrastus, (Hist. Plant. iv. 59.) Pliny, (Hist. Nat. ii. 15. p. 116.) and Seneca, (Nat. Quæst. iii. 25.) speak of floating islands, but they are formed of united trunks of trees. *Larcher.*

possible diligence to find out the son of Osiris. For they say that Apollo and Diana are the offspring of Dionysius and Isis; and that Latona was their nurse and preserver; calling Apollo and Ceres by the names of Orus and Isis; and Diana by that of Bubastis. Now from this account, and no other, Æschylus[t], the son of Euphorion, took his information, when he alone of all the former poets introduced Diana as the daughter of Ceres, and said that the island was made to float on this occasion. These things are thus reported.

CLVII. Psammetichus reigned in Egypt fifty-four years; nine and twenty of which he was sitting down before and besieging the large city until he took it by assault. This Azotus[u] held out against the siege, the longest time of all the cities we know.

CLVIII. His son Necos succeeded him, and began a canal of communication between the Nile and the Red sea, which Darius the Persian afterwards carried through. Two triremes may row abreast, and perform the whole voyage in four days. This canal[x] begins at the Nile, a little above Bubastis, and passing by Patumon, a city of Arabia, flows into the Red sea. It is cut through the plains of Egypt, that lie towards Arabia, the mountain which stretches towards Memphis, and which contains the quarries, hangs over this plain and is contiguous to it. And therefore this canal is carried along the foot of those hills from the west to the eastward, and then turned through the chops of the mountains towards the south into the Arabian gulf. But the shortest and most compendious passage from the northern sea to the southern, or Red sea, is by mount Casius, which separates Egypt from Syria. For this mountain is not above a thousand stades distant from the gulf of Arabia. So that this is the shorter way, the other being rendered more tedious by the frequent turnings of the canal. One hundred and twenty thousand Egyptians employed in this labour perished under the reign of Necos; and when the work was half done, he stopped, because an oracle impeded him, which declared that he was working for a barbarian; for that name is given by the Egyptians to all those who do not speak the same language as they do.

CLIX. Thus Necos abandoning his design, turned his thoughts to military affairs, and built a fleet of gallies on the

[t] This was doubtless in some piece not come down to us.

[u] The modern name of this place is Esdoud, and it is the same as the Ashdod of Scripture, 1 Sam. v. 1. It is also mentioned in the Acts, viii. 40.

[x] Diodorus Siculus (i. 33.) informs us, that it was not finished by Darius, because he was informed by some that he would cause Egypt to be deluged, as the Red sea was higher than the land of Egypt. Ptolemy the Second finished it, and made sluices in the proper places.

northern sea[y], and another in the Arabian gulf, at the mouth of the Red sea, as appears by the ruins of his arsenals and havens remaining to this day. These fleets he used upon occasion; and was no less formidable by land. For he fought a battle against the Syrians in the plains of Magdolus[z]; and after he had obtained the victory, took the great city of Cadytis. The garments he wore on these actions he consecrated to Apollo, and sent them to the Milesian Branchidæ. He reigned sixteen years; and at his death left the kingdom to his son Psammis.

CLX. During the reign of this king, ambassadors from Elis arrived in Egypt, boasting that they had outdone all mankind, in establishing the Olympian exercises under the most just and excellent regulations, and did not think that the Egyptians, though they were the wisest people of the world, could make any addition to their institution. Being arrived, and having acquainted the king with the cause of their embassy, he summoned an assembly of such persons as were esteemed the wisest among the Egyptians: they assembled and heard the Eleans relate what their office was with regard to the games: when they had explained every thing, they said, that they came to learn whether the Egyptians could invent any thing more equitable. After some deliberation they inquired of the ambassadors, if the citizens of Elis were permitted to enter the lists: and the Eleans answering that they and all other Grecians, who wished, were allowed to contend; the Egyptians replied, that in so doing they had totally deviated from the rules of justice; no consideration being sufficient to restrain men from favouring those of their own country to the prejudice of strangers. But if they were sincerely desirous to act justly, and had undertaken this voyage into Egypt with that intention, they advised them to establish games for strangers, and to make it unlawful for

y Herodotus here means the Mediterranean.

z This Necos is the Pharaoh-Necho of Scripture, (2 Kings, ch. xxiii. ver. 29, &c. 2 Chron. ch. xxxvi. ver. 1. &c.) He carried arms to the Euphrates, and took Carchemish, supposed to be the same as Circesium. He fought with Josias king of Judæa near Megiddo, or Magdiel, and not at Magdolus, a place in Lower Egypt. Larcher thinks the resemblance of names deceived Herodotus. The learned are not agreed about the city of Cadytis; some will have it to be Cades in Arabia Petræa; some Cedes in Galilæ in Naphthali; others Jerusalem, which is the opinion of D'Anville, Rennel, and Prideaux.

This is also confirmed by the researches of M. Belzoni, in the tomb of Psammethis or Psammis, the son of Pharaoh-Necho. See his Narrative of the operations and recent discoveries within the pyramids, &c. &c. in Egypt and Nubia, pp. 242, 243. (4to. edit. 1820.) and also Nos. 4, 5, and 6, of his Atlas.

The Arabian name is Al Kads, the *Holy*; it is sometimes also called Kadesh. Herodotus again mentions it (Thalia, c. 5.) as a city of Palæstine, not much less than Sardis.

any but strangers to contend. This admonition the Eleans received from the Egyptians[a].

CLXI. Psammis reigned only six years; and having undertaken an expedition against the Ethiopians, died soon after, and left the kingdom to his son Apries[b]. This king lived twenty-five years, in greater prosperity[c] than any of his predecessors, except his grandfather Psammetichus. In which time he invaded Sidon with an army, and engaged the Tyrians in a sea-fight. But when it was destined for him to meet with adversity, his misfortunes began upon an occasion, which I shall briefly mention in this place, and more largely explain[d] when I speak of the Lybian affairs. Apries having sent an army against the Cyrenæans, received a very great defeat; the Egyptians, blaming him on this account, revolted, suspecting he had designedly sent them into certain ruin, that after their destruction he might govern the rest with greater security; both those that returned and the friends of those who perished, being very indignant at this, openly revolted against him.

CLXII. When Apries heard of this defection, he dispatched Amasis to pacify them with kind expressions. As soon as he found them, and was endeavouring to dissuade them from their enterprize, an Egyptian came behind Amasis and put a helmet upon his head[e], and said that he put it on him to make him king. Which was not done against the wishes of Amasis, as the event shewed. For when those who had revolted appointed him king, he prepared to lead an army against Apries; who being informed of all that had passed, sent Patarbemis, a considerable person among the Egyptians that adhered to him, with orders to bring Amasis alive into his presence. Patarbemis arriving in the camp, summoned Amasis; but he, as he sat on horseback, lifting up his thigh, and breaking wind, bid him carry that to Apries. Patarbemis, *they add*, nevertheless ordered him to go to the

[a] The Eleans did not profit by the advice of the king of Egypt; nevertheless we cannot reproach them of having ever judged with partiality. When they were subject to the Romans, some of the great men of Rome occasionally wrote to them in behalf of some of the combatants; but the judges of the games made a point of not opening these letters till after the prizes had been decided. *Larch.*

[b] This is the same as the Pharaoh-Hophra, who made an alliance with Zedekiah king of Judah, and attempted to assist him against Nebuchadnezzar. Against him Ezekiel denounced several prophecies. See Ezekiel, ch. xxx. and Habbakuk, ch. ii. verses 15 and 16; Isaiah, ch. xix. xx; and Jeremiah, ch. xlvi. ver. 17.

[c] Herodotus, doubtless, speaks of the time preceding the revolt. *Larcher.*

[d] Herodotus certainly refers to book iv. ch. 159. as Wesseling and Bouhier have observed. But he probably forgot the promise here made. *Larcher.*

[e] The helmet in Egypt was the sign of royalty. See ch. 151. ἐπὶ βασιληΐῃ, *to put him in possession of the crown.* Examples of this preposition in this sense are very common. Ἐπὶ βλάβῃ, *nocendi causâ, to injure him.* *Larcher.*

king, who had sent for him; to which he answered, that he had been long preparing to visit him, and that he might give him no cause of complaint, he would not only appear himself, but would bring some company with him. Patarbemis perceiving the design of Amasis by the words he had heard, and the preparations he saw, departed in haste, as he wished to inform the king of these things as soon as possible; and coming into his presence without Amasis, Apries said not one word to him, but in a sudden transport of passion commanded his ears and nose to be cut off. The rest of the Egyptians, who to that time had continued faithful to Apries, seeing one of the most distinguished among them treated in so unworthy a manner, went immediately over to those who had revolted and offered themselves to Amasis.

CLXIII. Which when Apries heard, he drew out his auxiliary forces, consisting of Carians and Ionians, to the number of thirty thousand; and marching from Sais, where he had a beautiful and magnificent palace, led his troops against the Egyptians; whilst Amasis led the army he commanded against the foreigners. They met in the neighbourhood of Momemphis, and prepared to try each other's strength.

CLXIV. The Egyptians are distinguished into seven classes[f]; priests, soldiers, herdsmen, swineherds, tradesmen, interpreters, and pilots; they all take their names from the professions they exercise. The military men are called either Calasirians or Hermotybians, according to the districts they inhabit. For all Egypt is divided into districts or jurisdictions.

CLXV. The Hermotybians are of the district of Busiris, Sais, Chemmis, Papremis, the island called Prosopitis, and one half of Natho. From these districts a hundred and sixty thousand Hermotybians may be drawn, when they are most numerous. None of these ever learn any mechanic art, but apply themselves wholly to military affairs[g].

[f] The Indians are divided into four principal casts, each of which is again subdivided; the Bramins, the military, labourers, and artizans. The Indians and Egyptians bear so much relation to one another in their religious and civil customs, that I am troubled to persuade myself that one of these was not colonized by the other. I am most inclined to suppose that Egypt colonized India. We know that before the expedition of Sesostris, Bacchus conquered the Indians. The details are fabulous, but the event is not the less true. We know of no tradition of the Indians having conquered Egypt. *Larcher*. See also Robertson's India.

[g] Every country which encourages a standing army of foreigners, and where the profession of arms is the road to the highest honours, is enslaved, or on the point of being so. Foreign soldiers in arms are never so much the defenders of the citizens, as the attendants of the despot. Patriotism, that passion of elevated souls, which prompts them to noble actions, weakens and expires. *Larcher*.

CLXVI. The Calasirians are of the jurisdictions of Thebes, Bubastis, Aphthis, Tanis, Mendes, Sebennitus, Athribis, Pharbæthis, Thmuis, Onuphis, Anysis, and of Myecphoris, which is situated in an island over against Bubastis. These districts of the Calasirians may furnish two hundred and fifty thousand men at most; who being likewise restrained from exercising any mechanic profession, are obliged to apply themselves, from father to son[h], to the art of war only.

CLXVII. I am unable to decide whether the Greeks received this custom from the Egyptians, especially considering that the Thracians, Scythians, Persians, Lydians, and almost all barbarous nations, hold in less honour those who learn any art, and their descendants judging such as abstain from those employments, and particularly those who devote themselves to war, to be of a more generous spirit. Yet all the Greeks have entertained the same maxim, and principally the Lacedæmonians; though the mechanic arts are accounted least dishonourable among the Corinthians.

CLXVIII. These alone of all the Egyptians have the following distinguished privileges. Twelve select aruræ are assigned to each free from tribute; each arura contains a square of one hundred Egyptian cubits, which are equal to so many cubits of Samos. They all enjoy these advantages, but are admitted to other profits by turns. For a thousand Calasirians, and as many Hermotybians, serve the king annually for a guard; and, besides the revenue of their lands, receive a daily allowance, consisting of five minæ of bread, and two of beef, with four arysteres[i] of wine to each man.

CLXIX. The two armies having met at Momemphis, Apries at the head of his auxiliaries[k], and Amasis with all the Egyptians, they fought a battle, in which the foreigners behaved themselves with great courage; but being oppressed with numbers, were defeated. It is reported, that Apries fondly thought he had so well established his authority, that the power of a God would not prove sufficient to dispossess him of the kingdom; and yet he was beaten, taken prisoner, and confined to the palace of Sais, formerly his own, and now belonging to Amasis; where he was kept for some time, and

[h] Children, by always following the profession of their fathers, apply themselves to it without talents or genius. Thus industry has never made any progress among these people; if they invented different arts, we may be assured that they could never carry them to any degree of perfection. *Larcher.*

[i] Hesychius makes the aryster the same as the cotyle.

[k] Jeremiah alludes to the mercenaries of Apries. "Also her hired men are in "the midst of her, like fatted bullocks; "for they also are turned back, and are "fled away together; they did not "stand, because the day of their calamity was come upon them, and the "time of their visitation." Ch. xlvi. ver. 21.

treated with great humanity. But the people complaining that he did not act right in preserving a man who was the greatest enemy of both parties, he was constrained to deliver Apries into the hands of the Egyptians, who strangled him[l], and laid his body in the sepulchre of his ancestors, erected in the temple of Minerva adjoining to the palace, on the left hand as you enter. For the inhabitants of Sais have always buried the kings that were of their province in this temple. The monument of Amasis is placed at a greater distance from the palace than that of Apries and his progenitors. In the court of this temple there is a large chamber, adorned with columns of stone cut to extraordinary dimensions, and resembling palm-trees in figure, together with many other ornaments; in that chamber are two doors[m], within which is a sepulchre.

CLXX. In the same temple of Minerva at Sais, certain sepulchres are built behind the chapel and joining the whole of the wall, being the tomb of a person whose name it is not right for me to mention[n] on such an occasion. Vast obelisks stand erected on the consecrated ground, near a lake of orbicular form, the edges of which are covered with stone, and in my opinion equal to that of Delos, which is called Trochoeides[o].

CLXXI. In this lake the Egyptians exhibit a representation of the accidents which befel him, and which they call mysteries. But for the sake of decency, I shall not explain these things[p], though the far greater part are well known to

[l] "Thus saith the Lord, I will give "Pharaoh-Hophra, king of Egypt, into "the hand of his enemies, and into the "hand of them that seek his life." Jeremiah xliv. 30.

Herodotus, nor any other Greek who has written an Egyptian history, has made mention of the conquest of Egypt by Nabuchodonosor, king of Babylon. See Larcher's long note, and also his Essay on Chronology, chap. 5.

[m] This passage is one of the most difficult in Herodotus, and has given me much trouble.

Παστὰς signifies *a chamber*, and also *a chamber to sleep in*. Παστὰς μεγάλη must be *a large chamber*. Διξὰ θυρώματα appears to me to be *a closet with two doors*, formed in the thickness of the walls. *Larcher*.

This accords very well with the description of the catacombs of Alexandria, described by Pococke, vol. i. pag. 9.

The most extraordinary catacombs are towards the farther end, and may be reckoned among the finest that have been discovered, *being beautiful rooms cut out of a rock, and niches in many of them, so as to deposit the bodies in, adorned with a sort of Doric pilasters on each side.*

Θύρωμα is the same as θύρα, as is evident from many authors. Therefore διξὰ θυρώματα are *two doors*, or *folding doors*, and ἐν τοῖς θυρώμασι is the same as ἐντὸς τῶν θυρωμάτων. *Schweigh.*

[n] This is Osiris.

[o] Apollo, when he was not yet four years old, erected an altar near a round lake, (Callim: Hymn. Apoll. v. 59.) which was in after-times so much reverenced that they built a temple over it. The temple of Delos then was close by the lake Trochoeides, as is also evident from Plutarch (de Solert. Anim. p. 983.) and Theognis (Sentent. v. 8.) This then is the same lake which Spon has described in his Travels in Italy, Dalmatia and Greece, vol. i. p. 106. *Larcher*.

[p] Εὔστομα κείσθω became from this

me. Neither shall I utter one word more than is permitted, touching the sacred rites of Ceres, which in Greece are called Thesmophoria[q]. The daughters of Danaus brought these ceremonies from Egypt[r], and instructed the Pelasgian women in the use of them. But upon the expulsion of the Peloponnesians, these rites were almost abolished; but the Arcadians, who were not ejected by the Dorians, alone preserved them.

CLXXII. Apries being thus dethroned, Amasis, who was born in a city called Siuph in the district of Sais, mounted the throne. At the beginning of his reign, the people rather despised him, and held him in no great estimation, as having been formerly a plebian[s] and of no illustrious family; but he conciliated them by his address, without any haughtiness. For among other infinite treasures, he had a bason of gold, in which he and all those who were admitted to eat at his table were accustomed to wash their feet. This bason he caused to be broken in pieces, and formed into the statue of a God; which having placed in the most frequented part of the city, the Egyptians with great reverence paid their devotions to the image. In the mean time Amasis, informed of their behaviour, calls a general assembly, and acquaints the Egyptians, that the image they now worshipped so devoutly, was made out of the bowl, in which they had so often pissed, vomited, and washed their feet; and that his condition was not unlike that of the image: for though he had been formerly an ordinary person, yet being now their king, he required them to honour and obey him: and by this means he persuaded the

expression of Herodotus a phrase. So Soph. Philoct. *εὔστομ' ἔχε, be silent.*

[q] Ceres is the same as Isis, who was called Thesmophoria or Lawgiver by the Greeks, because she first gave laws to men. For a full account of these festivals see the learned work of M. de Sainte-Croix on the Mysteries of the Ancients. *Larcher*. See also Potter's Antiquities of Greece, book II. ch. xix.

[r] In an ingenious Dissertation on Grecian Mythology by Dr. S. Musgrave, it has been endeavoured to prove that Cecrops was a native Greek, and that the religion of Athens was not derived from Egypt. Other works however of deeper inquiry, abundantly support the contrary position; particularly Blackwell's Life of Homer, Monboddo on Languages, Bryant's Analysis, &c. We learn from Herodotus and Thucydides that the Athenians were a mixed people. The early communication between Greece and Egypt is also established, and that this intercourse operated powerfully on Grecian religion is not reasonably to be doubted. We may easily conceive Attic vanity, in later times, hurt by the idea that the founder of Athens was an Egyptian, and that even their tutelary deity, whom they were fond of esteeming their peculiar protectress was borrowed. Both facts militated with their title of Autochthones, but Thucydides seems to have had no faith in this title, and Herodotus, Plato, &c. agree that the Athenian Minerva is the same goddess that is worshipped at Sais in Egypt. *Mitford*, ch. i. sect. 3. note.

[s] We are told by Athenæus (Deip. xv. p. 680.) that he insinuated himself into the good graces of Apries by a chaplet of flowers which he presented to him on his birth-day. The king enchanted with the beauty of the chaplet, invited him to a feast which he gave on that occasion, and received him amongst the number of his friends.

Egyptians to think themselves obliged in duty to pay him all that respect and submission, which is due to a king.

CLXXIII. He regulated his affairs in the following manner; in the morning[t] until the time that the public square begins to be filled, he used assiduously to perform whatever was brought before him; from that time he used to drink and jest with his companions, and indulge in witty and indecent jokes[u]. But his friends, offended at his conduct, admonished him in these words; "You do not, O king, well direct your con- "duct, since you make yourself to become contemptible. "For he who sits on a throne ought to pass the whole day in "the administration of public business; that the Egyptians "may know they are governed by a great king, and speak "honourably of his person. Whereas your conduct is alto- "gether unbecoming the royal dignity." Amasis in answer said, "Those who have bows, bend them, when they want to "use them; when they have finished using them, they loosen "the string, because a bow that should always continue bent, "would either break, or be rendered useless in time of "need. The condition of man is precisely the same: for if "a man should incessantly attend to serious studies, and not "give himself up any part of his time to ludicrous recrea- "tions, either madness or stupidity would steal upon him: of "which truth being perfectly convinced, I have contrived to "divide the time between business and diversion."

CLXXIV. And indeed the Egyptians say that Amasis, whilst he was a private person, loved to drink, and divert himself with jesting and raillery; and was so far from being a man of diligence and industry, that he betook himself to stealing, when his resources failed him while indulging in drinking and pleasures: for which being frequently accused by those he had robbed, and always denying the fact, he was often carried to the oracle of the place; where he was many times convicted, and as often acquitted. But after his accession to the throne, he neglected the temples of all those Gods who had acquitted him; and abstaining from their sacrifices, would never bestow any thing upon them, whether for repairs or ornament; well knowing they deserved no regard, by the experience he had of the falsehood of their oracles. Whereas, on the contrary, he paid particular attention to those who had

[t] No one, in my opinion, has better explained the different parts of the day than Dion Chrysostom. (De Gloria Orat, lxvi. p. 614.) Πρωὶ *is the sun rise, the early part of the morning;* περὶ πλήθουσαν ἀγορὰν, *the middle of the morning,* i. e. *the third hour;* τὰς μεσημβριὰς *mid-day, or noon;* περὶ δείλην, *the middle of the afternoon, the ninth hour;* ἑσπέρα, *the evening, the sun-setting. Larcher.*

[u] Παιγνιήμων is used to signify *a person who uses polished and witty sayings, witticisms, which are suitable for a man of rank.* Μάταιος, *one who utters those which offend against decency and good manners. Larcher.*

convicted him[x] of being a thief, considering them as really Gods, who delivered true oracles.

CLXXV. He both built that admirable portico which stands before the temple of Minerva in Sais, far surpassing all others in circumference and elevation, as well as in the dimensions and quality of the stones; and also adorned the building with Colossian statues, and the immense figures of Androsphynx[y]; he also brought other large stones to repair the temple, some of which were cut in the quarries of Memphis; but those of the greatest magnitude were conveyed by water from the city of Elephantis, distant from Sais as far as a vessel can make in twenty days. But that which I beheld with greatest admiration, was a house he brought from Elephantis, made of one stone. Two thousand men, all pilots, who were appointed to conduct it, were occupied during three whole years in the transportation of this house. The exterior length of this structure is twenty-one cubits; in breadth fourteen, and eight in height. And this is the measure of the outside. The inside is eighteen cubits and twenty digits in length, twelve in breadth, and five cubits in height. This wonderful edifice is placed by the entrance of the temple; for they relate that it was not drawn into the temple, because the architect, regreting the time he had spent in so tedious a labour, fetched a deep sigh, as the edifice was being dragged along; which Amasis having revolved in his mind[z], would not suffer it to be drawn any farther. But others affirm, that one of the men who was attempting to move it by levers was crushed to pieces in the way to the temple, and on that account it was not dragged into the temple.

[x] Observe the opposition of the words *καταδῆσαι* and *ἀπολῦσαι*, which occurs again in book iv. ch. 68.

[y] The Androsphynx is a monstrous figure with the body of a lion and face of a man. The artists of Egypt, however, commonly represented the sphynx with the body of a lion and the face of a young woman. They were generally placed at the entrance of temples, to serve as a type of the ænigmatic nature of the Egyptian theology. *Larcher.*

Facing the second pyramid on the eastern side, is the enormous sphynx, the whole body of which is buried in the sand. The top of its back only is visible, which is more than 100 feet long. It is of one single stone, making part of the rock on which the pyramids are placed. Its head rises about twenty-seven feet above the sand. The Arabs, inspired by Mahomet with a horror for all representations of men or animals have disfigured its face with arrows and lances.

M. Pauw says (Recherches Philosoph. sur les Egypt. et Chinois) that the sphynxes found in Egypt, composed of the body of a virgin grafted on that of a lion, are images of the divinity, who was represented as an hermaphrodite. This explanation does not seem to me fortunate. It is under the sign of the Lion and the Virgin that the Nile swells, overflows its banks, and gives fertility to Egypt. The sphynx was an hieroglyphic, which taught the people the period of the most important event of the whole year. *Savary*, Letter XIX.

[z] Larcher translates *ἐνθύμιον*, or *ἐνθυμιστὸν ποιεῖσθαι*, *in religionem, in omen vertere*. So Duker on Thucyd. vii. 18. and Portus Ion. Lex. voc. *ἐνθύμιον*. Schweighæuser sees no reason for altering the original meaning of the word, since the verb *ἐνθυμίζεσθαι* is known to signify the same as *λογίζεσθαι*.

CLXXVI. Among the many magnificent donations which Amasis presented in the most famous temples, he caused a Colossus, lying with the face upwards, seventy-five feet in length, to be placed before the temple of Vulcan at Memphis: and on the same basis erected two statues of twenty feet each, made of Ethiopian stone, and standing on each side of the great statue. Like this, another is seen in Sais, lying in the same posture, cut in stone, and of equal dimensions. He likewise built the great temple of Isis in the city of Memphis, which well deserves to be visited.

CLXXVII. Under the reign of Amasis, Egypt particularly flourished in all the conveniences derived from the river to the country, or from the country to men, and contained twenty thousand inhabited cities[a]. He established a law, commanding that every Egyptian should annually declare before the governor of the province, by what means he maintained himself; and if he omitted to do this, or did not shew that he lived by honest means, he should be punished with death. This law Solon[b] the Athenian brought from Egypt, and established it at Athens; where it is inviolably observed, since it cannot be found fault with.

CLXXVIII. Amasis, being partial to the Greeks, bestowed many other favours on individuals; and in particular to as many as came to Egypt, he gave the city of Naucratis to dwell in; and granted that those who would not settle there, but chose rather to attend their commerce by sea, might erect altars and temples to the Gods in certain places assigned to that end. The greatest, noblest, and most frequented of these temples is that which is generally known by the name of Hellenium, or the Grecian temple, built at the common expence of the Ionian cities of Chios, Teos, Phocæa,

[a] "This country," says Diodorus Siculus, (i. 31.) "was once the most "populous of the known world, and is "not now inferior to any. In ancient "times it had 18,000 *considerable* "*towns and cities*, as may be seen in "the sacred registers. In the time "of Ptolemy Lagus there were three "thousand which still remain. It once "had seven millions of inhabitants, and "now there are not less than three." Ancient Egypt supplied food to eight millions of inhabitants, and to Italy and the neighbouring provinces likewise. At present the estimate is not one half. I do not think with Herodotus and Pliny that this kingdom contained twenty thousand cities in the time of Amasis: but the astonishing ruins every where seen, and in uninhabited places, prove that they must have been thrice as numerous as they are. *Savary.*

[b] "Ejusdem urbis sanctissimum consilium Areopagus, quid quisque Atheniensium ageret, aut quonam quæstu sustentaretur, diligentissime in quirere solebat, ut homines honestatem, vitæ rationem memores reddendum esse sequerentur." Valer. Maxim. ii. 6. sect. 3, 4.

It appears that Draco established the law, and that Solon softened it, by commuting the punishment of death to that of infamy, against all those who had thrice offended. Those who had offended five times were fined 100 drachms. *Larcher.*

and Clazomenæ; in conjunction with the Dorian communities of Rhodes, Cnidus, Halicarnassus, Phaselis; and the city of Mitylene only of the Æolians. So that this temple belongs to these cities, and they appoint officers to preside over the emporium[c]: and all other communities that lay claim to it, claim a thing which does not belong to them. Besides this, the people of Ægina built a temple to Jupiter at their own charge; the Samians one to Juno, and the Milesians another to Apollo.

CLXXIX. The city of Naucratis was anciently the only place of resort for merchants in all Egypt[d]: and if a man put into any other mouth of the Nile, he was obliged to swear he arrived unwillingly, and after he had made that oath, to depart in the same ship by the first opportunity; and that if contrary winds should prevent him from reaching the port of Canopus, he was forced to unload his goods, and carry them in boats round the Delta to Naucratis. So great were the privileges of that city.

CLXXX. When the Amphyctions agreed to pay three hundred talents for rebuilding the temple of Delphi, which had been burnt by an unknown accident[e], it fell upon the Delphians to supply a fourth part of the sum, who went about desiring assistance of divers cities, and brought home no small contributions from Egypt. For they received a thousand talents of alum[f] from Amasis, and twenty mines from the Grecians who were settled in his kingdom.

CLXXXI. Amasis made also an alliance of mutual amity and defence with the Cyrenæans; and resolving to take a wife of that country, either out of a desire of having a Grecian woman, or from a peculiar affection to that people, he married Ladice, the daughter, as some say, of Battus, others,

[c] Their proper name was Timuchi, as we are informed by Athenæus, (Deipn. vi. 3.) Ἐμπόριον signifies *a place of commerce*, προστάτης τοῦ ἐμπορίου does not signify a judge to preside over commerce in particular, but, *judge of the place*. *Larcher*.

[d] The position of Naucratis falls precisely at Salhadjar, about 289 miles above Rosetta, at the east side of the river, or within the Delta. M. Niebuhr says, vol. i. p. 78. that there are indications of an ancient and extensive city at that place; and that he, in consequence, visited them. But he found little to repay his curiosity; he does not, however, appear to have referred them once to Naucratis.

Perhaps the restriction originated in the same jealousy, which in the empire of China limits the trade of Europeans to the port of Canton: and one cannot help remarking how parallel the two cases are in this respect. The Greeks were permitted to have a commercial settlement at Naucratis, and they were allowed places for the construction of temples for their religious rites. *Rennel*, p. 530.

[e] We are ignorant of the real cause of this conflagration. The Scholiast on Pindar (Pyth. viii. ver. 10.) attributes it to the Pisistratidæ, i. e. to Hipparchus and Hippias. See also book v. ch. 62. *Larcher*.

[f] The best alum came from Egypt according to Pliny, Hist. Nat. xxxv. 15.

of Arcesilaus[g]; though a third sort pretend she was the daughter of Critobulus, a person of distinction among the Cyrenæans. Whenever he lay with her he found himself afflicted with an imbecility, which was not the case with respect to other women; upon the continuance of this, he said to her, "O woman, you have used charms against me, and "no contrivance will prevent your perishing by the most "cruel death that any woman has undergone." Ladice denied the fact, and endeavoured to pacify him: but when nothing would prevail, she sighed out a mental prayer to Venus; and vowed, if Amasis should be enabled to do the part of a husband that night, (which was the only remedy left,) she would send a statue of the Goddess to be erected in Cyrene. No sooner had she made this vow, than Amasis found himself like other men, and continued to use Ladice as his wife with all possible tenderness and affection. On the other hand, Ladice performed her vow to the Goddess, for she caused a statue to be made, and sent it to Cyrene, which stands entire to this day looking out of the city of Cyrene[h]. And when Cambyses had conquered Egypt, and learnt who she was, he sent her back to Cyrene, without injury.

CLXXXII. Amasis sent several consecrated donations to Greece. He presented a gilded statue of Minerva to Cyrene, with his own picture[i]; to Lindus he gave two statues of stone representing the same Goddess, together with a linen corselet[k] well worth seeing; and sent two images of himself carved in wood to the city of Samos; where to this

[g] Larcher, with Wesseling, reads Battus, the son of Arcesilaus, who (b. iv. ch. 159.) was the cotemporary of Apries, and therefore of Amasis.

[h] It seems very probable that this statue was placed in the city and looked out towards the country, which is the sense I have followed; but the text may signify that it was out of the city and turned on its side. *Larcher.*

[i] The art of painting was probably known in Egypt in the first ages, but they do not seem to have succeeded better in this art, than in sculpture. Antiquity does not mention any painter or sculptor of Egypt who had acquired celebrity. *Larcher.*

They possessed the art of staining marble; and to this day may be seen, amongst the ruins of superb edifices, marbles artificially stained, so exquisitely fresh in point of colour, that they seem recently dismissed from the hand of the artist. *Norden.*

[k] The Egyptians were celebrated for weaving and embroidery:

Hæc tibi Memphitis tellus dat munera; victa est
Pectine Niliaco jam Babylonis acus.
Martial. Epigr. lib. xiv. 150.

Candida Sidonio perlucent pectora filo,
Quod Nilotis acus percussum pectine Serum
Solvit——
Lucan. Pharsal. x. ver. 141.

Mirentur hoc ignorantes in Egyptii quondam regis, quem Amasim vocant, thorace, in Rhodiorum insula ostendi in templo Minervæ, CCCLXV filis singula fila constare: quod se expertum nuper prodidit Mucianus ter Consul, parvasque jam reliquias ejus nunc superesse hoc experientium injuria. Plin. Hist. Nat. xix. 1.

See also book iii. ch. 47. where Herodotus describes a similar corselet. *Larcher.*

day they are seen standing in the great temple of Juno behind the gates. Amasis made this donation to Samos, on account of the mutual obligations of hospitality, contracted between him and Polycrates the son of Æaces; and the other to Lindus, without any engagement of that nature, but because the daughters of Danaus[1] are reported to have founded the temple of Minerva in that city, when they touched there in their flight from the sons of Egyptus: and these were the donations of Amasis. He was the first who conquered Cyprus, and constrained the Cyprians to pay him tribute.

[1] Strabo (lib. xiv. p. 967.) says also that it was built by the daughters. But Diodorus Siculus (v. 58.) attributes the temple and statue to Danaus himself.

THE HISTORY OF HERODOTUS.

BOOK III.

THALIA.

AGAINST this Amasis, Cambyses the son of Cyrus made an expedition with an army, consisting of his own subjects, and the Grecian forces of the Ionians and Æolians. The cause of the war was this. Cambyses sent a herald into Egypt to demand the daughter of Amasis; to which he was persuaded by an Egyptian physician, who was dissatisfied with Amasis because he had separated him from his wife and children, and had sent him, in preference to all the others, as a present to Persia, when Cyrus by a message desired Amasis to send him the best physician for the eyes[a] that could be found in Egypt. The angry Egyptian incessantly endeavoured[b] to induce Cambyses to make this demand, to the end that Amasis, if he should comply, might be mortified with the loss of his daughter, or irritate the king of Persia by his refusal. Under these difficulties Amasis could not easily determine what resolution to take; for he dreaded the Persian power; and knew Cambyses demanded his daughter, not to make her his wife, but his concubine. At last he resolved upon this expedient. His predecessor Apries had left an only daughter, tall and beautiful, whose name was Nitetis[c]. This virgin Ama-

[a] As diseases in the eyes were very frequent in Egypt, it is probable that the best physicians would be found there. We may conclude from ch. cxxix. that Egyptian physicians were considered superior to others.

[b] The construction of the sentence is, ἐνῆγε τῇ συμβουλίῃ τον Καμβύσεα, κελεύων αὐτὸν αἰτέειν.

[c] There is in this passage a little difficulty. M. Wesseling is reasonably astonished that Nitetis was still beautiful. She must have been more than forty years old, since Amasis put her father to death forty-four years before the Persian expedition into Egypt. Herodotus, it is

sis adorned with magnificent apparel, and sent her to Persia for his own daughter: not long after, when Cambyses saluted her as the daughter of Amasis, she said, "O king, you are "ignorant that you have been deceived by Amasis, who sent "me hither with all these ornaments as if he was giving you his "daughter; whereas indeed I am the daughter of Apries his "master, whom he put to death, after he had revolted with "the rest of the Egyptians." These words and this incident induced Cambyses, in great anger, to march against Egypt. Thus the Persians report the matter.

II. But the Egyptians claim a relation to Cambyses by blood, and pretend that he was the son of this Nitetis[d]; and that Cyrus, not Cambyses, was the person who sent for the daughter of Amasis. Nevertheless this account is not correct. For if any people of the world are well informed of the Persian customs, the Egyptians certainly are; and therefore could neither be ignorant that a natural son is never admitted to be king of Persia, when a legitimate heir is alive; nor that Cambyses was the son of Cassandane daughter to Pharnaspes of the race of Achæmenes, and not of an Egyptian woman. But they pervert the truth, that they may pretend a relation to the family of Cyrus.

III. Another story is also asserted which to me seems improbable. They say, that a Persian lady being admitted to the presence of the king's women, and seeing the children of Cassandane beautiful and tall, very much admired and praised them; to whom Cassandane the wife of Cyrus replied, "Though "I am the mother of such children, Cyrus holds me in dis-"honour, and prefers the Egyptian slave:" this she said from anger towards Nitetis, upon which Cambyses, the eldest of her sons, said, "Mother, when I am a man, I will on your "account turn all Egypt upside down:" that this discourse of Cambyses, who had not then attained to more than ten years of age, struck all the women present with admiration; and that he kept his revenge in memory till he grew up; and when he was possessed of the kingdom, made an expedition into Egypt.

IV. Another circumstance of the following nature occurred, which contributed to induce him to undertake this expedition. Among the auxiliaries of Amasis was a person named Phanes,

true, passes almost immediately from the defeat to the death of Apries, but it appears very probable that several years passed between those two events. We may suppose that Apries lived twenty years after he was dethroned, in that case Nitetis might not have been more than twenty-two. *Larcher.*

Jablonski (Pantheon Ægypt. part i. p. 55, &c.) has rightly observed, that the names of Nitetis, Nitocris, and the like, are derived from Neith, the Egyptian Minerva.

[d] This is the opinion of Dinon, Lynceas, and Polyenus in his Stragmat. viii. 29. *Larcher.*

a native of Halicarnassus, a man of considerable prudence, and a brave warrior. This man, dissatisfied with Amasis, on I know not what occasion, departed by sea from Egypt, with a design to confer with Cambyses. But Amasis, who knew him to be a man of no small consequence among the auxiliaries, and very accurately acquainted with the Egyptian affairs, resolved to pursue him with all diligence: and to that end sent one of the most trusty among his eunuchs with a trireme, who surprised him in Lycia, but did not bring him back to Egypt, because Phanes overreached him by artifice. For he intoxicated his guard, and by that means escaping into Persia arrived at the time when Cambyses was preparing all things for his expedition to Egypt, and much perplexed how he should pass the deserts that were destitute of water. He discovered many important affairs of Amasis to the king of Persia, and advised him to desire the king of Arabia by a message to grant him a safe passage through his territories.

V. By this way alone is a passage opened into Egypt. For whatever is situate between Phœnicia and the borders of Cadytis[e], belongs to the Syrians of Palestine, but from the city Cadytis, which in my opinion is little inferior to Sardis, all the trading places on the coast to the city of Jenysus belong to the Arabian king. And the whole tract of land that lies extended from Jenysus, as far as the lake Serbonis, near which mount Casius stretches to the sea, is again a Syrian territory. But from the lake of Serbonis[f], in which Typhon is reported to have concealed himself[g], the country belongs to Egypt. And all that space which lies between the city of Jenysus[h], mount Casius, and the lake, being no less than three days' march, is utterly destitute of water.

VI. But in this place I shall mention a thing which has not been observed by many who have passed by sea into Egypt. Twice every year earthern vessels, filled with wine, are carried to Egypt from every part of Greece, and also from Phœnicia, and yet you cannot see afterwards a single one, if I may so say, of these wine jars. But some one may ask, "where then I pray are these used?" This I will also relate. The governor of every province is obliged to collect all those vessels that he can find within his jurisdiction, and

[e] See note on ch. 159. book ii.

[f] Jenysus was an Arabian town, on this side the lake Serbonis with regard to Syria, and on the farther side with regard to Egypt. This Rennel (p. 259.) identifies with the Khan, or *caravanserai*, of Iönes.

[g] This appears to have been a kind of inland Syrtis. Diodorus describes its borders as being formed of a very dangerous kind of quicksand, (lib. i. 3.) and says (lib. xvi. 9.) that Artaxerxes Memnon lost part of his army there, in his march into Egypt, about B. C. 350. M. Maillet p. 103, supposes it to be quite filled up. *Rennel*, p. 647.

[h] See Apollonius Rhodius, ii. 1215, and the ancient commentaries.

send them to Memphis; where they are filled with water[i], and then conveyed to those arid parts of Syria. So that all the earthern vessels which are brought and landed in Egypt, are continually added to those already in Syria.

VII. In this manner the Persians, as soon as they became masters of Egypt, facilitated the passage into that country, by supplying it with water in the above mentioned manner. But, as before this expedition, water was not thus prepared in those parts, Cambyses by the advice of Phanes the Halicarnassian, sent ambassadors to solicit the king of Arabia to permit him to pass in safety; and upon mutual assurances of amity obtained his request.

VIII. The Arabians are most religious in observing[k] the engagements they make; which are attended with these ceremonies. When they enter into mutual obligations, a third person, standing between the parties, makes an incision with a sharp stone, in the palm of the hand, under the longest fingers, of both the contractors; and taking some of the nap from the garment of each, dips it in the blood, and anoints seven stones brought thither to that end, invoking at the same time Bacchus and Urania. After this invocation, the person who has made the engagement pledges his friends to the stranger, or the citizen if the contract be made with a citizen, the friends also profess themselves bound in justice to observe the treaty. They acknowledge no other Gods than Bacchus and Urania, whom they call by the names of Urotal[l] and Alilat. They shave their temples, and cut their hair to a circular form; in the same manner, they say, as Bacchus shaved himself.

IX. The Arabian, after the conclusion of this treaty with the ambassadors of Cambyses, caused a great number of camels' skins to be filled with water, and loaded on all his living camels: which being done, he drove them to the arid deserts, and there expected the arrival of Cambyses with his army. This account seems to me the most credible[m]: yet I must not

[i] The water of the Nile never becomes impure, whether reserved at home, or carried abroad. On board the vessels which pass from Egypt to Italy, the water, which remains at the end of the voyage, is good; whilst that which they happen to take in by the way, corrupts. The Egyptians are the only people we know who preserve this water in jars, as others do wine. They keep it three or four years, and sometimes longer, and the age of this water is with them an increase of its value, as the age of wine elsewhere. Aristidis Orat. Ægyptiac, fol. 96.

Savary, Letter XLIV. bears testimony to the excellence of the waters of the Nile. Our mariners say much the same thing of the water of the Thames.

[k] For the force of the phrase ὅμοια τοῖσι μάλιστα, see Matth. Greek Gram. sect. 289.

[l] Urotal, according to Scaliger and Selden, signifies the sun and the light. Alilat, the new-moon, she was also called Alitta. Herod. i. 131. *Larcher.*

[m] Perhaps the truth might have been, that water was conducted through pipes into reservoirs, either from small running springs, whose waters were ordinarily absorbed by the sands of the desert; (which is the case in many places;) or

omit to mention another expedient, (though less probable,) because it is affirmed likewise. There is a large river in Arabia called Corys, which discharges itself into the Red sea. And they say that the king of Arabia, by sewing together the hides of oxen and other animals, made a canal from this river to the deserts, and conveyed the water thither by that means into large reservoirs, which he had caused to be made, where they might preserve the water. But that, because the way between the river and this dry country was no less than twelve days' journey, he contrived to convey the water by three several canals into three different places.

X. Psammenitus the son of Amasis lay encamped with his army at the Pelusian mouth of the Nile, in expectation of Cambyses; for Cambyses did not find Amasis alive when he marched to Egypt; but Amasis died after a reign of forty-four years, during which no great calamity had happened. His body was embalmed, and buried in the sepulchre which he had built for himself in the temple. During the reign of Psammenitus a most remarkable prodigy was seen in Egypt. Showers of rain fell at Thebes; which the Thebans say, had never happened before, nor since, even to this day. For no rain ever falls in the upper regions of Egypt[n]; but at that time they had rain, in distinct drops.

XI. The Persian army having marched through the unwatered country, and encamped near the Egyptians, as if with a design of engaging; the Greeks and Carians, who were auxiliaries to the Egyptians, in order to shew their detestation of Phanes, for introducing a foreign enemy into Egypt, adopted this expedient; they brought his sons, who had been left behind in Egypt, into the camp, and having placed a bowl between the two armies, killed them one by one over the bowl, in sight of their father. Then they poured water and wine into the blood; and, after all the auxiliaries had tasted[o] of this mixture, they began the attack. The battle was obstinately fought, and great numbers fell on both sides, but at last the Egyptians were put to flight.

XII. On this spot of ground I saw a very surprising thing, which the people of the country informed me of. For as the bones of those who were killed in that fight are scattered

from *draw-wells*. It appears morally impossible to have supplied a *Persian* army, and its *followers*, and beasts of burthen, with water, by means of *skins*, during the whole march. Arabia could scarcely have supplied skins. The caravans at the present day carry their water on camels, in skins of camels. *Rennel*, p. 257.

[n] See note on ch. 13. book ii. Violent rains frequently fall in Lower Egypt, and in Upper Egypt it sometimes rains a little. Aristid. Orat. Ægypt. p. 92.

[o] The blood of an human victim, mixed with wine, was often used in the solemn forms of execration among the ancients. Catiline made use of this form to bind his adherents. See Sallust.

about separately; those of the Persians lying in one place, and those of the Egyptians in another; I found the skulls of the Persians so weak, that one might break them if he wished with a single pebble; whereas those of the Egyptians were so hard, that you could scarcely penetrate them with a large stone. They told me, and I assented to their experience, that this difference is owing to the Egyptian custom of shaving the heads[p] of their children early; by which means the bone is rendered thicker and stronger, through the heat of the sun, and the head preserved from baldness: and indeed we see fewer persons bald in Egypt than in any other country. This, therefore, is the cause that the Egyptian skulls are so hard; but the heads of the Persians are softened by a contrary custom. For from their infancy they are accustomed to the shade, and wear tiaras. And I observed the same thing at Papremis, in those who were defeated with Achæmenes[q] the son of Darius, by Inarus[r] the Lybian.

XIII. The Egyptians, after they had lost the battle, fled away in complete disorder. When they had shut themselves up in Memphis, Cambyses sent a Persian herald thither in a ship of Mitylene to exhort them to surrender. But when they saw the vessel entering the port of Memphis, they rushed in great numbers out of the walls, destroyed the ship, tore the men in pieces[s], and carried their mangled limbs into the city. Upon this the Epyptians were besieged, and after some time forced to submit[t]. The neighbouring Lybians, fearing what had befallen Egypt, gave themselves up without a blow, and they both imposed a tribute on themselves, and sent divers presents to Cambyses. The Cyrenæans and Barcæans being

p The same custom still subsists. I have seen every where the children of the common people, whether running in the fields, assembled round the villages, or swimming, with their heads shaved and bare. Let us but imagine the hardness a skull must acquire thus exposed to the scorching sun, and we shall not be astonished at the remark of Herodotus. *Savary*, Letter XXIV.

q Herodotus and Diodorus Siculus say that it was Achæmenes, the brother of Xerxes and uncle of Artaxerxes, the same who before had the government of Egypt in the beginning of the reign of Xerxes, that had the conduct of this war; but herein they were deceived by the similitude of names; for it appears from Ctesias, that he was the son of Hamestris, whom Artaxerxes sent with his army into Egypt. *Prideaux's Connections.*

r This Inarus was the son of Psammetichus, (Herodot. vii. 7.) and might probably be of the royal family of Egypt, but certainly could not be the son of that Psammetichus who was king; for he died B.C. 617. Inarus killed Achæmenes B.C. 458. Thucydides mentions the same Inarus, i. 104. Herodotus merely calls him Inarus the Lybian, but he usually designates kings in that manner; and also Thucydides (*loc. citat.*) so styles him. *Larcher.*

s They were two hundred in number, as appears from the next chapter, where we find ten Egyptians put to death for every one that thus perished, and that two thousand Egyptians were deprived of life. *Larcher.*

t The second aorist of the verb ἵστημι and of its compounds, as also the perfect and future middle, are used passively. *Larcher* and *Schweigh.*

under the same apprehensions, surrendered likewise as the Lybians had done. Cambyses very favourably received the presents of the Lybians; but was highly displeased at those of the Cyrenæans, as I conjecture, because they were inconsiderable. For they sent no more than five hundred mines of silver, which he took, and dispersed them with his own hand among the soldiers.

XIV. On the tenth day after the taking of Memphis, Cambyses, to try the magnanimity of Psammenitus, who had reigned only six months, ordered him to be ignominiously made to sit down in the suburbs of the city, accompanied by other Egyptians; and at the same time ordering his daughter to be dressed in the habit of a slave, and furnished with a pitcher, commanded her, with other virgins of the principal families in Egypt clothed in the same manner, to bring water from the river. As the virgins, with loud lamentation and weeping, came up to their parents, all the other parents answered them with wailing and weeping, when they beheld their children in so wretched a condition. But Psammenitus alone, who saw and heard no less than they, only turned his eyes towards the ground. These virgins having passed by with water, Cambyses in the next place sent the son of Psammenitus thither also, attended by two thousand Egyptians of like age, all with halters about their necks, and a curb in the mouth, to suffer death in satisfaction for the lives of those Mitylenæans who perished with their ship. For the king's judges had determined that ten of the principal Egyptians should be sacrificed for every one of those men. Yet when Psammenitus perceived them passing, and knew that his son was going to die, he did no more than he had done at the sight of his daughter; though all the rest of the Egyptians about him made loud lamentations. When they had passed by, it happened that one of those who formerly had shared his table, a man somewhat advanced in years, plundered of all, and possessing no more than a mendicant, while begging alms of the army, passed by Psammenitus and the other Egyptians that were seated in the suburbs; Psammenitus, when he saw him, wept bitterly, and calling him by his name, struck himself upon the head. All these things being reported to Cambyses, by persons who were placed about Psammenitus to observe his actions, he was struck with wonder, and sent a message to him in these words: "Psammenitus, "thy master Cambyses is desirous to know why, after thou "hadst seen thy daughter so ignominiously treated, and thy "son led to execution, without any exclamation or weeping, "thou shouldest be so highly concerned for a poor man no "way related to thee, as he is informed." To this question

Psammenitus returned the following answer: "Son of Cyrus, "the calamities of my family are too great to leave me the "power of weeping; but the misfortunes of a companion, "who, at the commencement of his old age[u], has fallen from "abundance and prosperity into poverty, may be fitly lamented with tears." His answer being brought to Cambyses[x], it is reported that he approved of it; and the Egyptians say, that not only Crœsus, who accompanied him in this expedition, and all the Persians that were present, could not refrain from tears, but that Cambyses himself touched with remorse, sent immediate orders to preserve his son out of those who were to perish, and to bring the father from the suburbs into his presence.

XV. Those who were sent for the purpose found the son already dead, having been the first that suffered, but conducted Psammenitus to Cambyses, with whom he afterwards lived, without experiencing any manner of violence. And if he had not been suspected[y] of attempting some innovation, he might probably have been entrusted with the administration of Egypt. For the Persians are accustomed to pay so great respect to the sons of kings, that even if they have revolted, they nevertheless bestow the government upon their children; and it may be proved, that they usually do this, from many other examples, and also by those of Thannyras the son of Inarus the Lybian, who was invested with his father's government; and of Pausiris the son of Amyrtæus, who met with the same fortune; though greater disasters never fell upon the Persians, than by the means of those two kings. But Psammenitus designing to raise new disturbances, received his reward, for he was detected in soliciting the Egyptians to rebel, and when this became known to Cambyses he was compelled to drink the blood of a bull, and died immediately[z].

[u] The expression *ἐπὶ γήραος οὐδῷ* may equally signify at the commencement or at the extremity of old age, because both those who go out and those come in, arrive at the *threshold* of the house. In the Iliad, xxiv. ver. 486, it is used in the latter sense. In Odyssey xv. ver. 346, in the former. I am inclined to the former, in the present passage, because *ἀπηλιξ*, which is used a little before, signifies a man who has ended the virile age, and entered upon old age. *Larcher.*

[x] Herodotus seems to have used a participle with *ὡς*, instead of a finite verb, or an infinitive mood; so that *ταῦτα ὡς ἀπενειχθέντα* has the same force as *ταῦτα ὡς ἀπενείχθη*. So also vi. 31, 79. *Schweigh.*

[y] Schweighæuser derives the word *ἠπιστήθη* from *ἀπίστεω*, so that the phrase becomes the same as *εἰ μὴ ἐπιστεύθη πολυπρηγμ.* So also Thucyd. i. 10. and xxi. 101.

[z] Egypt, after the conquest of Cambyses, passed under the dominion of the Persians. The Greeks afterwards subdued it, and then the Romans. The Arabians took it from the Romans, and after having passed successively into the hands of the Saracens, and the Mamelukes, it acknowledges the power of the Grand Signior, and is governed by Beys. Ezekiel predicted this in these terms: "Thus saith the Lord God; I will also "destroy the idols, and I will cause "*their* images to cease out of Noph; "and there shall be no more a prince "of the land of Egypt; and I will

XVI. From Memphis Cambyses went to the city of Sais, with a design to do what he did effect; and to that end going into the palace of Amasis, he presently commanded his body to be taken out of the sepulchre; which being done, he gave farther orders to whip him, to pull off his hair, to prick him with pointed instruments, and to abuse the corpse with all manner of indignity. But after they had tired themselves with this employment, (for the dead body, since it was embalmed, resisted their efforts and did not at all fall in pieces,) Cambyses commanded the body to be burnt: which was an action of impiety, because the Persians venerate fire as a divinity[a]; and to burn a dead body is not permitted in either nation. For the Persians say it is a violation of religion to offer to a God the dead body of a man; and the Egyptians hold that fire is a savage animal, which devours all that comes within his reach, and after he has glutted himself with food, expires with the things he has consumed; for it is their law, by no means to give the bodies of dead men to wild beasts, and for that reason they embalm them, lest they should be eaten by worms. So that Cambyses commanded a thing altogether repugnant to the manners of both nations. But the Egyptians pretend this was not the body of Amasis, but of another Egyptian, of the same stature, whom the Persians, mistaking him for Amasis, treated so opprobriously. For they say, that Amasis being admonished by the oracle of what should happen to him after death, in order to prevent that which threatened him, buried the body of the man who was scourged near the door of his sepulchre[b], and commanding his son to deposit his own in the remotest part of the same monument; though I am of opinion that these pretended commands of Amasis, touching his own funeral, and this Egyptian, were never given, but that the Egyptians vainly boast of them.

"put a fear in the land of Egypt," c. xxx. 13. This prophecy has been literally fulfilled.

The twelfth verse, "and I will sell "the land into the hand of the wicked," appears to me to allude to the Beys, under whose government Egypt groans.

The fifteenth verse, "and I will cut "off the multitude of No," appears to me to allude to the great diminution of the people by the conquests of the Babylonians and Persians, and it has never recovered its population. *Larcher.*

See also note on ch. 177. b. ii.

[a] This expression must not be understood in too rigorous a sense. Fire was certainly regarded by the Persians as something sacred, and perhaps they might pay it some kind of worship, which in its origin referred only to the deity, of which it was an emblem. But this nation did not believe fire to be a deity, otherwise how would they have dared to extinguish it, all over Persia, on the death of th· sovereign. When the king of Persia joined in any procession, fire was carried before them, (Xenoph. Cyrop. viii. 3, 12.) This custom was borrowed from the Persians by the Roman Emperors, when they became masters of Asia; and was also practised by the magistrates in the provinces: this is what Horace alludes to Sat. l. i. v. 36.

Prætextam et latum clavum, prunæque batillum. Larcher.

[b] See book ii. ch. 169.

XVII. After this, Cambyses resolved to undertake three several expeditions; one against the Carthaginians, another against the Ammonians, and a third against the Macrobian Ethiopians[c], who inhabit that part of Lybia which lies upon the South sea. He designed to send against the Carthaginians a naval armament, and against the Ammonians a detachment of his land forces. But before he would make war against the Ethiopians, he determined to send some persons into the country, who under pretence of carrying presents to their king, might see whether the table of the sun[d], which was said to be among the Ethiopians, did really exist, and might also explore other things.

XVIII. They say this table of the sun is a certain meadow in the suburbs, furnished with the cooked flesh of all sorts of four-footed animals, which being regularly carried there by the magistrates of the city in the night, serve to feast all comers in the morning. The inhabitants say that the earth of itself daily produces these things; and this is their account of the table of the sun.

XIX. Cambyses, in pursuance of his resolution touching the spies, sent to Elephantine for such persons among the Ichthyophagi[e], as understood the Ethiopian language; and in the mean time commanded all his naval forces to sail towards Carthage. But the Phœnicians alleging they were bound by the most sacred obligations to the Carthaginians, and that they should act impiously if they made war against their own children[f], refused to execute the orders of Cambyses. And the rest not being fit for such an enterprize, the Carthaginians thus escaped the slavery which threatened them from the Persians. For Cambyses did not think it convenient to compel the Phœnicians to obey, because they had voluntarily submitted to him, and the whole of his navy depended upon them; the Cyprians had done the same, and were likewise employed against the Egyptians.

XX. When the Ichthyophagi arrived from Elephantine, Cambyses sent them away to Ethiopia, (having instructed

[c] The epithet Macrobian is given them by Herodotus on account of their longevity. In this Mr. Bruce is deceived, and also in supposing that they are the same as the Shangallas. Rennel concludes with reason that they are the Abyssinians. See his Geographical System, &c. p. 229. *Larcher*.

[d] This table was called the table of the sun, because it was common to all the Ethiopians, as the sun gives its light for all mankind.

[e] Strabo (xvi. p. 1113.) says, that the Ichthyophagi are on the right as you sail from Heroopolis to Ptolemais Epitheras. They were neither Ethiopians nor Egyptians, but spoke both languages. There were some of them in the island of Elephantine, and of these Herodotus here speaks. We are ignorant of their real name; Herodotus calls them Ichthyophagi from their feeding on fish. *Larcher*.

[f] See also the appeal of Themistocles to the Ionians, b. viii. ch. 22.

them what to say,) with presents, consisting of a purple vest, a necklace, bracelets of gold, an alabaster[g] box of rich ointment, and a cask of palm wine. These Ethiopians are reported to surpass all other men in beauty and large proportion of body; and to have customs also, which are different from those of other nations, (and one of the following kind, with regard to the supreme authority,) for they confer the royal dignity upon the man who is of the largest size, and of strength proportionable[h] to his person.

XXI. After the arrival of the Ichthyophagi among this people, when they made their presents to the king, they addressed themselves to him in these words: "Cambyses king "of the Persians, being desirous to enter into mutual en-"gagements of friendship and hospitality with thee, has given "us commission to treat of this affair, and sent these pre-"sents, which are such as he himself is most delighted with." To which the Ethiopian, not being ignorant that they were spies, returned this answer: "It was not from any considera-"tion of my friendship that the king of Persia sent you to me "with these presents; neither have you spoken the truth; "but are come as spies to my kingdom. If Cambyses were "a just man, he would desire no more than his own; and not "endeavour to reduce a people under servitude who have "never done him any injury. However, give him this bow "from me, and let him know that the king of Ethiopia advises "the king of Persia to make war against the Macrobian Ethio-"pians, with more numerous forces, when the Persians shall "be able thus easily to draw so strong a bow; and in the "mean time to thank the Gods, that they never inspired the "Ethiopians with a desire of extending their dominion be-"yond their own country."

XXII. When he had said this, he loosened the string, and delivered the bow to the ambassadors. Then taking up the purple garment[i], he asked what it was, and how made; and

[g] Naturalists make a distinction between alabaster and alabastrites, it was of this last that boxes for ointment, &c. were made, which was hard and capable of being polished; the alabaster was soft. *Larcher.*

We find mention of these boxes in Matthew, ch. xxvi. ver. 7. and Mark, ch. xiv. ver. 3.

[h] *Condere cœperunt urbeis, arcemque locare*
Præsidium Regis ipsi sibi, perfugiumque:
Et pecudes, et agros divisere, atque dedere
Pro Facie cujusque, et Viribus, Ingenioque;
Nam Facies multum valuit, viresque vigebant. Lucretius, v. 1107.

[i] Naturalists are not decided on the kind of shellfish that yielded this celebrated dye. There are found at Peru certain snails which produce it; and it is very probable that it is the same animal; see on this subject the History of the European Establishments and Com-

after they had informed him touching the colour, and manner of the tincture, "The men," said he, "are deceitful, and so "is the clothing they wear." In the next place he questioned them concerning the necklace and bracelets; and when they had explained to him the nature of those ornaments, the king, supposing them to be fetters, laughed, and told them that chains of a far greater strength were to be found in Ethiopia. Of the ointment he gave the same judgment as of the purple garments. But when he came to the wine, and inquired concerning the way it was made, he was very much delighted with the draught, and desired to know what provisions were used at the king of Persia's table, and to what age the longest life of a Persian might reach. The ambassadors answered, that the food of the king of Persia was bread, taking occasion from that demand to describe the nature of wheat; and that the longest period of the life of a Persian was about fourscore years. The Ethiopian king replied, that he was not at all surprised, if men who eat nothing but dung, did not attain to a longer life; and was persuaded they could not arrive even to that age, unless they mixed it with this drink, (meaning the wine,) acknowledging the Persians to have the advantage of the Ethiopians in that particular.

XXIII. Then the Ichthyophagi inquiring in their turn concerning the life and diet of the Ethiopians, the king said, that they usually attained to a hundred and twenty years, and some to a greater age; that they fed upon cooked flesh[k], and used milk for their drink. But seeing the spies astonished at the mention of so great a number of years, he brought them to a fountain, which rendered the bodies of men smooth, if they washed with the water of it, as if it had been a fountain of oil, and that an odour arose from it like that of violets. The water of this fountain, as the spies said, is too light to bear either wood[l], or other substance lighter than wood; but every thing presently sinks to the bottom. This water, if indeed they have any such, from being on every occasion used by the inhabitants, might be the cause of their longevity. From this fountain the king conducted them to see the prisons, where the prisoners are fettered with chains of gold; for among these Ethiopians the most rare and valuable of all metals is brass. The next thing they viewed was the place which is called the table of the sun.

merce in the two Indies, tom. iii. p. 243.

[k] Mr. Bruce (Vol. i. book ii. p. 452.) says that they eat raw flesh dried in the sun, (and again 453.) He seems to have been very inaccurate in what regards the ancient history of this country.

[l] Boerhave (Element. Chemica, tom. i. p. 550.) supposes that the wood was heavier than our wood, and the water lighter than ours.

XXIV. After this, they saw last of all the sepulchres, which are said to be made of crystal in the manner following. When they have dried the body after the Egyptian fashion, or some other way, they lay on a covering of white plaister, which they paint with colours as near as possible to the likeness of the person deceased, then they enclose the body within a hollow column of crystal[m], which they dig up in great abundance, and is easy to work. The dead are plainly seen through these transparent glasses; emitting no ill scent, nor any thing else that is disagreeable, and both the column[n] and the body may be seen in every part. They are kept a whole year in the houses of their nearest relations; and during that time are honoured with sacrifices, and the first fruits of all things; after which they are carried out, and placed upright round the parts adjoining to the city.

XXV. The spies having seen every thing, returned to Cambyses; and after they had acquainted him with all that had passed, he fell into a violent passion, and ordered his army to march immediately against the Ethiopians, without making any provision for their subsistence, or once considering that he was going to make an expedition to the remotest parts of the world; but as soon as he had heard the report of his messengers, like one, who was mad and deprived of his senses, he began to move with the whole body of his land forces; commanding only the Greeks to stay behind with their ships. When he arrived at Thebes, he selected about fifty thousand men, ordering them to enslave the Ammonians, and to burn the oracle of Jupiter Ammon, whilst he with the rest of his army should march against the Ethiopians. But before the army had passed over a fifth part of the way[o], all the provisions[p] that they had failed them, and afterwards the beasts of burden were eaten and failed: and if upon the first information of this want, Cambyses had conquered his determination, and after the fault which he had committed at the beginning, had led back his army, he had given some proof of his wisdom. But without reasoning with himself, he obsti-

[m] According to Ludolf (Hist, Ethiop. i. 7.) in some places in Ethiopia a great quantity of fossil salt is found, which is transparent and becomes hard, when exposed to the air; this is probably what was taken for glass. *Wesseling.*

[n] Herodotus says, the column has every part conspicuous, as the body itself. The Egyptian mummies could only be seen in front, the back was covered by a box or coffin; the Ethiopian body could be seen all round, for the column of glass was transparent and there was no wall behind it. *Schweighæuser.*

[o] We must suppose that it never got through the desert of *Selima*; that is, on a supposition that Thebes was the place of outset, and *Sennar* the entrance into the country of the Macrobians. *Rennel*, p. 252.

[p] The Greek is *σιτίων ἐχόμενα*. This expression is very common in Herodotus. So book i. 120. *τὰ τῶν ὀνειράτων ἐχόμενα, dreams.* So also v. 44, and viii. 142.

nately continued his march. The soldiers fed upon herbs, so long as they found any in their way; but when they arrived in the sandy deserts, some of them were guilty of a horrid action; for they cast lots among themselves, and eat every tenth man; which Cambyses hearing, and fearing they would continue to devour one another[q], he desisted from his enterprize against the Ethiopians, and retreated to Thebes, after he had lost a great part from his army. From Thebes he went down to Memphis; where, at his arrival, he dismissed the Greeks, with leave to retire in their ships to their own country; and thus ended this expedition of Cambyses against the Ethiopians.

XXVI. As for that part of the army which he sent against the Ammonians, they marched from Thebes, and by the help of their guides it is certain they arrived at the city Oasis[r], inhabited by Samians, who are reported to be descended from the Eschrionian tribe, and situate seven days' march from Thebes, through the sands. This country in the Greek language is called the Fortunate Island, and it is said, that the army arrived in this place. But what was their fate afterwards, is related by none, except the Ammonians, or those who have conversed with them, for they never reached the Ammonians, nor returned back. The Ammonians say, they marched from Oasis, and after they had passed one-half of the sands which lie in the way from that city, a strong and impetuous wind began to blow from the south at the time of their dinner, and raised the sands to such a degree, that the whole army was buried alive[s], and that in this manner they disappeared.

[q] Seneca (de Irâ iii. 20.) informs us, that the table of Cambyses was notwithstanding supplied with the same delicacy and profusion as before.

[r] The Oasis are *insulated*, fertile *spots* like islands, in the midst of an expanse of desert. They are aptly compared to islands in a *sea* of *sand*, but they surpass those of the ocean, in that they are almost universally fruitful, whilst the others are commonly naked and barren; the former, probably, owing their very growth and existence to that principle, which fertilizes them, *vis.* fountains of water springing up in the desert; while the latter are either the *ruins* of ancient lands, the production of volcanoes, or an accumulation of marine substances. Thomson thus poetically styles them,

————————" the tufted isles
" That verdant rise amid the Lybian world." *Summer*, 912.

It may be satisfactorily made out (we trust) that the most consistent descriptions, ancient and modern, agree in fixing *three* Oasis, *two* of which properly belong to Egypt, and the *third* to Lybia. Herodotus appears to have known but one. He describes the *greater* Oasis under the name of *Oasis* as *appropriate* to it: not having, we may suppose, heard of its application generally, to the islands of the desert. But he nevertheless describes those of Ammon, Angela, the Garamentes, &c. though not under the *name* of Oasis. The greater Oasis is the same as the *Al Wah* of the moderns. *Rennel*, p. 545, &c.

For an accurate account of the Oasis, see his work, sections 20, 21.

[s] It is unquestionable that the route from Thebes to Ammon must have lain through the greater Oasis; but the proper and safe route would have been from Memphis; from whence also it was about one-third nearer than from Thebes.

M. Savary and M. Poncet have both

XXVII. When Cambyses was returned to Memphis, Apis, or, as the Grecians call him, Epaphus[t], appearing among the Egyptians, they put on the richest of their apparel, and feasted splendidly. Cambyses, seeing them thus occupied, and feeling fully convinced that they made these rejoicings on account of his ill success, sent for the magistrates of Memphis, and asked them why the Egyptians had done no such thing when he was in Memphis before, but did so now, when he had returned with the loss of a great part of his army. They answered, that when their God manifested[u] himself, which he was accustomed to do after considerable intervals, the Egyptians had been always accustomed to celebrate his appearance with the greatest demonstrations of joy. Which when Cambyses heard, he told them, they lied; and put them to death, as liars.

XXVIII. Then he sent for the priests, and having received the like answer from them, he said, that he would not be ignorant whether any God, who might be led by the hand, had appeared among the Egyptians, and without more words commanded the priests to bring their God. So they departed to put his orders in execution. This Apis, or Epaphus, is the calf of a cow incapable of bearing another, and the Egyptians affirm, that lightning descends upon it from heaven by which it conceives and bears Apis. The marks that distinguish him from all others are these: his body is black, except one square of white on the forehead; he has the figure of an

given a frightful idea of the journeys across the Lybian sands. Nothing however appears more likely than that the armies perished through fatigue and want of water. Mr. Browne does not so readily give into the belief of the possibility of a living person being overwhelmed with sand. See his book, p. 248, &c. *Rennel*, p. 578.

[t] This he mentioned in book ii. ch. 153.; compare also book ii. ch. 38.

Epaphus was the son of Io, daughter of Inachus. The Greeks pretended that he was the same as Apis, which the Egyptians rejected as a fable, and said that Epaphus was posterior to Apis by many hundreds of ages.

Æschylus (Prom. Vinct. v. 853.) says, that his name was derived from the touch of Jupiter; ἐπαφῶν χειρὶ, *touching you with his hand*. *Larcher*.

[u] Apis probably was not a God from the beginning; perhaps he was regarded as a symbol of Isiris; and it was most likely in this quality that he was adored by the Egyptians; others assert that he was the same as Osiris. Apis was sacred to the moon, as the bull Mnevis to to the sun. (Ammianus Marc. xxii. 14.) Others think that they were both sacred to Osiris, who is the same as the sun. (Diodor. Sic. i. 31.) When he died there was a general mourning throughout all Egypt. They then sought for another, and when they had found one the mourning ended. The priests conducted him to Nilopolis, where they fed him forty days. He was then transported in a magnificent vessel to Memphis, where he had an apartment ornamented with gold. During the forty days abovementioned, women only were allowed to see him. They stood round him, and lifting up their garments, discovered to him what modesty forbids us to name. Afterwards, the sight of the God was forbidden them. Every year they brought him a heifer, (Ammianus Marc. xxii. 14.) which was known by certain marks. According to the sacred books, he was only to live a certain time, at the end of which he was drowned in a sacred fountain. *Larcher*.

eagle on his back; double hair on his tail[x]; and the figure of a beetle on his tongue[y].

XXIX. When the priests had brought their God into the presence of Cambyses, like a man not very much in his senses, he drew his dagger, and designing to thrust it into the belly of Apis, wounded him in the thigh; then falling into a fit of laughter, "Ye wretches," said he, "are there any Gods "such as these, composed of flesh and blood, and so able to "feel the blow of a weapon. This God truly is worthy of the "Egyptians. But I will let you know that you shall not ridi-"cule me with impunity." When he had said these words, he commanded the proper officers to whip the priests, and to kill all the Egyptians they should find making public demonstrations of joy. Thus the festival was interrupted; the priests punished; and Apis languished some time, from his wound, in the temple, and after his death the priests buried him[z] without the knowledge of Cambyses.

XXX. The Egyptians say Cambyses grew mad immediately after this sacrilegious action, though before that he was not quite in possession of reason. The first crime he committed was against his brother Smerdis, who was born of the same father and mother with himself, whom he sent back from Egypt to Persia from envy, because he alone of all the Persians had been able to draw the bow, which the Ichthyophagi brought from the Ethiopian king, as much as two digits. After his departure, Cambyses saw in his sleep the following vision; he imagined that a messenger arrived from Persia to inform him that Smerdis was seated on the royal throne, and touched the heavens with his head. Upon which, fearing his brother would kill him, and assume the kingdom, he sent Prexaspes, one of his principal confidents, to Persia, with orders to kill Smerdis. Prexaspes, having gone up to Susa, put an end to the life of Smerdis; some say, when he had led him out to hunt, others that he got him to the Red sea and drowned him.

XXXI. This is related to be the commencement of the crimes of Cambyses. His second was the murder of his own sister, who had accompanied him into Egypt, and was also his wife. He married her in the following way: for before his time, the Persians were not accustomed to marry their

[x] The Scholiast of Ptolemy says, but I know not on what authority, that the tail of the bull increased or diminished according to the age of the moon. *Larcher.*

[y] Nodus sub lingua quem *cantharum* appellant. (Pliny, Hist. Nat. viii. 46.) From this Larcher and Jablonski propose ὑπὸ, instead of ἐπί. Porphyry also has ὑπὸ τῇ γλώσσῃ, and Euseb. Præpar. Evang. iii. 13.

[z] Plutarch (de Isid. et Osir. p. 368.) says, that Apis having been killed by Cambyses was by his order exposed and devoured by the dogs.

sisters. Cambyses became enamoured with one of his sisters, and being desirous of making her his wife, and, being aware that he intended to do what was not customary, he summoned all the royal judges together. These judges are certain chosen Persians, who continue in their offices during life, unless they are convicted of a crime. They decide all controversies, interpret the laws, and all things are referred to their determination. Of these persons Cambyses demanded whether they had any law that permitted a man to marry his sister[a]; to which they gave this cautious and proper answer; that indeed they could find no law to permit a man to marry his sister, but had discovered another, which gives a liberty to the kings of Persia to do whatever they wish. And by this means they did not abrogate a law for fear of Cambyses; but that they might not lose their lives by protecting the law, they found out another in favour of the king, who was so desirous of marrying his sister. Upon their answer, Cambyses married the sister he loved[b], and a little time after, another[c]. The youngest of these, who followed him into Egypt, he put to death.

XXXII. With regard to her death, as well as that of Smerdis, there are two reports. For the Greeks say, that Cambyses one day made a young dog fight with the whelp of a lion, and that this sister was also looking on; and that this dog being over-matched, another of the same litter broke loose, and ran to his assistance, by which means the two dogs worsted the lion: that whilst Cambyses was pleasing himself with this entertainment, the young woman, who sat by him, began to weep; of which, when the king had asked her the reason, she answered, that seeing the little dog come to the succour of his brother, she could not refrain from tears, as she remembered Smerdis, and felt certain that there was no one to revenge him; and the Greeks affirm that for these words Cambyses killed her. But the Egyptians say, that as they were both at table, she took a lettuce, and having stripped off its leaves, asked her husband, "Whether the lettuce, "when whole, was most beautiful, or when deprived of its "leaves." He answered, "when whole." "Then," said she, "you have truly represented this broken lettuce, by dis"membering the house of Cyrus:" that upon these words

[a] At Athens a man was permitted to marry his sister by the father, but forbidden to marry his sister by the mother. At Lacedæmon a man was allowed to marry his sister by the mother, but not his sister by the father.

[b] According to the Scholiast on Lucian, her name was Atossa; she afterwards married Smerdis the Magus, (Herod. iii. 88.) and then Darius son of Hystaspes. *Larcher*.

[c] Her name was Meroe; if Libanius (Antioch. p. 343) may be credited. *Wesseling*.

Cambyses in a rage struck her with his foot, and caused an abortion, of which she died.

XXXIII. Thus Cambyses exercised his fury against those of his own family; whether from the death of Apis, or from any of those other evils, which are wont to befal mankind. And indeed we are informed that Cambyses was afflicted from his infancy with the great malady, by some called the *sacred disease*[d]: and then, it is nothing improbable that his mind should not be sound in so distempered a body.

XXXIV. Besides these, he was guilty of other outrageous extravagances against the Persians, and among them against Prexaspes, who had always been honoured by him in an extraordinary manner, and used to bring him all messages, and had a son that served him as cup-bearer, which is no small honour. For when he asked Prexaspes what the Persians said of him, and what character they usually gave him, Prexaspes answered, " Sir, you are highly applauded in all other things, " but they say you are too much addicted to wine." " What." replied Cambyses with indignation, " the Persians say then " that by my fondness for wine, I become beside myself and not " in my senses; if so, their former words were not true." For Cambyses being formerly present in a great assembly of Persians, where Crœsus likewise assisted, and asking what opinion they had of him in comparison with his father[e] Cyrus, they told him, he far surpassed his father; because he was not only master of all that Cyrus possessed, but had added Egypt and the sea to his dominions. Crœsus not being pleased with their decision, spoke thus to Cambyses; " Son of Cyrus, I " cannot persuade myself that thou art equal to thy father, " for thou hast not yet such a son as he left behind him:" which words were so grateful to Cambyses, that he highly commended the judgment of Crœsus.

XXXV. Therefore, on this occasion remembering what had passed at that time, he said with indignation to Prexaspes, " See now, whether the Persians have spoken the truth, " or are distracted themselves, when they say these things of " me; for if I shoot this arrow and hit the heart of thy son, " who stands there under the portico, the Persians have said " nothing to the purpose; but if I miss, they have spoken " the truth, and I am mad." He had no sooner pronounced

[d] This was the epilepsy, which was always called, as Hesychius informs us, *μεγάλη νόσος*, &c. Hippocrates tells us, (de Morbo Sacro ii. p. 325.) that it was called *sacred*, by jugglers and ignorant people, who did not know how to cure it; and in order to hide their ignorance, referred it to the Gods. *Larcher.*

[e] *Πρὸς τὸν πατέρα τελέσαι* Κῦρον. Πρὸς is used to signify *comparison.* Reiske and Abresch, rightly take the phrase, *ὥστε τελέσαι, that he might come up to his father, or equal him.* Wesseling.

these words, than drawing his bow, he hit the boy; when he had fallen to the ground, he commanded them to open him and examine the wound; when it was found that the arrow was in the heart, he laughed, and with great joy said to the father, "Prexaspes, it has been clearly shewn to you that "the Persians are mad, and not Cambyses. Tell me, didst "thou ever see a man shoot more surely than I have done?" But Prexaspes perceiving him to be delirious, and being under great apprehensions for his own life, "Truly sir," said he, "I believe a God could not shoot more dexterously." At another time, he commanded twelve Persians of the first rank[f] to be seized, and without any just cause to be buried alive up to the head.

XXXVI. But whilst he was proceeding in this furious manner, Crœsus the Lydian thought fit to admonish him in these words: "O king, do not give yourself up entirely to "youth and anger, but restrain and moderate your passions. "To look forward is advantageous, and forethought is the "part of wisdom. You have destroyed divers of your own "countrymen upon slight occasions, and have not spared "their children; consider, if you persist in such a course, "whether the Persians may not rebel. For my own part, "I cannot refrain from giving you this advice, because your "father Cyrus expressly commanded me to admonish you, "and suggest to you whatever I might discover to be ex-"pedient for your affairs." Crœsus in this advice shewed his kind wishes; but Cambyses answered, "Do you presume "to advise me, you, who have so wisely governed your own "kingdom. It was admirable counsel you gave my father, "when you persuaded him to pass the river Araxes, and "march against the Massagetæ, instead of permitting them "to enter our territories, as they were willing to do. You "first ruined yourself by badly governing your own country, "and then destroyed Cyrus, since he followed your advice. "But you shall not long enjoy the pleasure of that action; "for I have for a long time been desirous of a pretext for "your destruction." No sooner had he pronounced these words, than he took up his bow to shoot Crœsus; but the Lydian saved himself by running immediately out of his presence. Cambyses, when he could not hit him, commanded his officers to seize him, and put him to death. But they, who knew his manner, resolved to conceal Crœsus; that if Cambyses should repent of his rashness, and inquire for him, they might, by producing, receive rewards for preserving his

[f] Xenophon, in his Cyropædia, calls this rank, Ὁμοτιμοι.

life; or dispatch him afterwards, if they should find that Cambyses had neither altered his opinion, nor desired to see him. In a little time the king, as they expected, regretted Crœsus, which the officers understanding, acquainted him that Crœsus was still living. "I am very glad," said Cambyses, "that he is alive, but will never forgive those who "saved him." And indeed he made good his word, for he put them all to death.

XXXVII. Many more actions of this nature he did whilst he staid at Memphis, not only against the Persians, but also against his confederates. He opened many ancient sepulchres to view the bodies of the dead; and entering into the temple of Vulcan, derided the image of the God; which indeed resembles those Phœnician figures that are placed on the prow of their ships, and called Pataïci[g], which I will describe to those who have not seen them; it is a representation of a pigmy. He likewise went into the temple of the Cabiri[h], (which no man except the priest may presume to enter,) and after he had ridiculed the form of their images, ordered them to be thrown into the fire; these also are like that of Vulcan, whose sons they are said to be.

XXXVIII. All these things convinced me that Cambyses was outrageously mad; else he would never have attempted to make a mockery of national religions and customs. For if any one should propose to all men, to select the best customs and institutions from all that there are, after they had deliberated, they would each choose their own; so true it is, that each thinks his own by far the best. It is not, therefore, probable that any one else but a madman would make such things the subject of his ridicule. That this is the common sentiment of all mankind, I could prove by many instances, but shall content myself with one. Darius, having assembled the Grecians who lived under his empire, asked them for how great a sum they would eat the dead bodies of their parents; and they answered, that they would not do it for any sum. He afterwards sent for certain Indians called Calatians, who are accustomed to eat their parents, and demanded in the presence of the Greeks, who learnt what was said by an interpreter, how much money they would take to burn their parents after death, they made loud exclamations, and begged he would speak words of better omen. This is

[g] Herodotus is the only one who mentions these Pataïci, and does not call them Gods. Hesychius, however, does call them Gods; but I am inclined to think that they are not, because the images of the tutelary deities were always placed at the stern, and not at the prow. *Larcher.*

[h] See Book ii. ch. 51.

the effect of custom: and therefore Pindar, in my opinion[i], says judiciously, *That custom is the king of all men.*

XXXIX. Whilst the arms of Cambyses were employed in this expedition, the Lacedæmonians made war against Samos and Polycrates, and against the son of Æaces, who had made an insurrection and seized on Samos[k]. He at first divided his acquisition with his two brothers, Pantagnotus and Syloson; but afterwards having put the elder to death, and expelled Syloson, who was the younger, he became sole master of all, and made a treaty of friendship with Amasis king of Egypt; which was confirmed and cultivated on both sides by mutual presents. In a short time his power increased, and was noised abroad through Ionia and the rest of Greece; for wherever he turned his arms, every thing went on prosperously. He had a hundred gallies of fifty oars each, and a thousand archers. He plundered all without distinction; pretending to do a greater favour[l] to his friends by restoring what he had taken away, than by not taking them at all. He subdued many of the islands; took divers cities on the continent; and defeated the Lesbians in a sea fight, as they were going to assist the Milesians with their whole fleet: the prisoners were put in chains and compelled to dig the whole of the ditch that surrounds the walls of Samos.

XL. It so happened that the prosperity of Polycrates did not escape the notice of Amasis, but it was the object of his anxiety. And when he heard that it increased daily, he sent a letter to Samos in these terms: "Amasis to Polycrates: "It is pleasant to hear of the good fortune of a friend and ally. "But the excess of thy prosperity does not please me, because I know how envious the Gods are. As for me, I would 'rather choose that my affairs, and those of my friends, 'should alternately participate of good and bad fortune 'through the whole course of life, than be always accompanied with uninterrupted felicity. For I cannot remember "that I ever heard of a man, who having been always happy, "did not at last utterly perish. Be advised therefore by

[i] The passage alluded to is preserved in the Scholia on Nem. ix. ver. 35. See Heyne's Pindar, vol. iii. pt. 1. p. 76, &c.

[k] Polyænus (Stratag. i. 23, 2.) says, that a solemn procession of the Samians in arms, was made in honour of Juno to her temple. When they arrived at the temple and laid down their arms in order to sacrifice, Polycrates and his party seized their arms, put to death those who opposed, and having got possession of the most advantageous posts, sent for Lygdamis king of Naxos, by whose assistance they got possession of the citadel. *Larcher.*

[l] This sentiment is false, and Libanius (Anec. Græc. tom. ii. p. 16.) rightly remarks, that gain naturally does not give so much pleasure to a man, as the loss of it does sorrow.

It is not less certain, that he who takes away the property of another inflicts a deep wound, by restoring which he does not heal. The mind of the man who has received the injury remains always ulcered. *Larcher.*

"me; and act against good fortune in this manner: consider "what you value at a high rate, and would be much con- "cerned to lose; deprive yourself of this precious thing so "effectually, that it may be utterly lost; and if your pros- "perities still continue without other vicissitude, repeat the "remedy which you have now from me."

XLI. When Polycrates had read this letter, and conceived that Amasis had given him good advice, he considered, by the loss of which of his valuables he should be most afflicted, and at last found this; he had a seal-ring[m], which he occasionally wore, made of an emerald, set in gold by the hand of Theodorus the son of Telecles the Samian; and when he determined to lose it, he did thus. He went on board a galley of fifty oars completely manned, and commanded the mariners to put out into the open sea; and when they had advanced to a considerable distance from the island, he took the jewel in his hand, and in the presence of all the company threw it into the sea. This done, he commanded them to carry him back, and at his return he mourned for its loss.

XLII. But on the fifth or sixth day after, a certain fisherman having taken a large and beautiful fish, and thinking it a present worthy Polycrates, went to the gates of his palace, and desired admission, which being granted, he presented the fish to the king, and said, "Though I get my living by "hard labour, yet I could not persuade myself to carry this "fish, which I have taken, to the market, because I thought "it a fit present for a king." Polycrates, pleased with these words, replied, "You have done well, and I give you double "thanks for your speech and your present, and I invite you "to supper." The fisherman thinking a great deal of this, went away to his own habitation. In the mean time the servants opening the fish, find the seal-ring of Polycrates in the belly; and when they had taken it out, hastened with much satisfaction to Polycrates, and as they gave him the ring, acquainted him in what manner they had found it. Polycrates, persuaded that the event was divine, wrote down what he had done, as well as what had happened to him afterwards, and entrusted it to a man to carry to Egypt.

XLIII. By which Amasis being convinced that no man can deliver another from the destiny that was impending, and that the life of Polycrates would not terminate happily, since he had been successful in every thing, and even found what he had thrown away, sent a herald to Samos with

[m] Pliny, Hist. Nat. xxxvii. 1. says, that the stone was a Sardonyx; Clemens of Alexandria says, that it represented a lyre; and Larcher thinks that they both describe another ring, and not the one which Polycrates threw into the sea.

orders to renounce his friendship[n], and dissolve all obligations of hospitality that had been contracted between them; lest if any dreadful and great calamity should befal Polycrates, he might himself be grieved for him, as for a friend.

XLIV. Against this Polycrates, so universally happy in all his affairs, the Lacedæmonians prepared to make war, at the solicitation of those Samians who afterwards founded the city of Cydonia in Crete. Polycrates, having sent a messenger to Cambyses the son of Cyrus, as he was collecting an army to invade Egypt, had entreated[o] him to send to him at Samos and demand some troops. Which, when Cambyses heard, he readily dispatched a message to Polycrates, desiring he would furnish a fleet to assist him in his Egyptian expedition. Upon this demand, Polycrates drew out all those he suspected of seditious designs, and sent them with forty galleys to Cambyses, requesting at the same time that he would not send them back[p] to Samos.

XLV. Some affirm that these Samians never arrived in Egypt, but that in their passage through the Carpathian sea they deliberated upon the matter, and came to a resolution not to proceed farther in their voyage; others say, that they arrived in Egypt, but finding themselves observed and under guard, they took an opportunity to make their escape, and in their return to Samos met the fleet of Polycrates, which they defeated, and landed in their own country; where they fought an unsuccessful battle by land, and afterwards set sail for Lacedæmon. Yet some pretend they had the victory in this action also; but I think their opinion is not correct. For they could not have been under a necessity of imploring the aid of the Lacedæmonians, if they had found themselves able to reduce[q] Polycrates. Besides, it is repugnant to reason to imagine, that one who had a numerous army of foreign mercenaries in his pay, and such a body of Samian bowmen, should be beaten by so unequal a number as those were who returned from Egypt; especially, if we consider that Polycrates had brought together the wives and children of all

[n] This does not do much honour to Amasis. Diodorus Sic. (i. 95.) makes him act from a very different motive. Polycrates, he says, treated both his subjects and all strangers who came to Samos with great injustice and caprice. Amasis sent an ambassador to exhort him to use his power more moderately; which advice Polycrates did not listen to, and therefore Amasis foreseeing that his fate was unavoidable, took care not to be involved in his ruin.

[o] The verb δεῖσθαι is here used in two different senses. It first signifies *to beg, to entreat;* in the second, *to send for, to demand. Larcher.*

[p] It might be inferred from a passage in Apuleius, (Florid. xv. p. 790.) that Pythagoras was among the number that were thus sent to Cambyses; but he adds, that the general opinion was, that he went to Egypt of his own accord. *Larcher.*

[q] For the force of παραστήσασθαι, see note of ch. xiii. of this book.

those who were subject to him into the docks, resolving to burn them, together with the docks, if he should find himself betrayed to the returning exiles.

XLVI. These Samians, thus expelled by Polycrates, arrived in Sparta; and having been brought before the magistrates, made a long harangue, as people who very earnestly entreated. But at this first audience, the Lacedæmonians gave them no other answer than that they had forgotten the first part of their speech, and therefore could not comprehend the last. At their second appearance, the Samians brought a sack, and said nothing else than that the sack[r] wanted flour; to which the Lacedæmonians replied, that the word *sack* was superfluous: it was, however, decreed that they should assist them.

XLVII. When all things were ready for the expedition, the Lacedæmonians transported their army to Samos, in requital for a benefit, as the Samians say, because they had formerly assisted them with some ships, when they were engaged in a war against the Messenians; though the Lacedæmonians say, they did not so much undertake this enterprize out of good will to the Samians, as to revenge themselves of that people, for intercepting the bowl they sent to Crœsus, and robbing them the year before of a curious corselet, which Amasis king of Egypt had sent to them. This corselet was made of linen, adorned with many figures woven into the work, and enriched with gold and cotton; each thread of it deserves particular admiration; for each thread, though itself fine, is composed of three hundred and sixty threads, all distinctly visible. Such another is seen at Lindus[s], presented to Minerva by the same Amasis.

XLVIII. The Corinthians readily assisted in exciting this war; because they also had been injured by the Samians in the age preceding this expedition, about the same time as the bowl was intercepted[t]. For when Periander[u], the son of Cypselus, had sent three hundred youths, born of the noblest families of Corcyra, to Alyattes king of Sardis, that they might be made eunuchs, and the Corinthian ships which transported them touched at Samos, the Samians, who were not ignorant of the design of this voyage, in the first place instructed the boys to take sanctuary in the temple of Diana, forbidding the Corinthians to use any violent means to remove them, because they were under the protection of the Goddess;

[r] Schweighæuser is here followed for the opinion of others. See his note. Θύλακος is properly a *leathern sack*.

[s] See book ii. ch. 182.

[t] See book i. ch. 70. Larcher has a long note to ascertain the exact chronology of these circumstances.

[u] Periander is by some considered as one of the seven sages; his maxim was, *restrain your anger*.

and when the Corinthians refused to give them subsistence, the Samians on their account instituted a festival, which they observe to this day. For at the approach of night, as long as the suppliants were in the temple, they assembled the young men and virgins to dance, and ordered them to carry about certain cakes made of sesamum[v] and honey, that the Corcyræan youths might snatch them out of their hands, and by this means sustain themselves; which practice they continued till the Corinthians, who had charge of the boys, went away and left them, and then the Samians sent home the boys to Corcyra.

XLIX. Now if the Corinthians had lived in amity with the Corcyræans after the death of Periander, they would not have taken part with the Lacedæmonians against Samos on this occasion: but, indeed, from the first peopling of that island, their dissensions have been perpetual, though they have the same origin[x]. The Corinthians, therefore, not forgetting the usage they received at Samos, joined their forces to the Lacedæmonians. Periander had selected the sons of the principal Corcyræans to send to Sardis to be castrated, in order to avenge himself, because the Corcyræans had first committed an outrageous injury against him.

L. When he had killed his wife Melissa[y], he found that calamity attended by another. She left him two sons, one of seventeen, and another of eighteen years of age. These young men Procles, tyrant of Epidaurus[z], their grandfather by the mother, sent for to his court, and caressed with that tenderness which is usually shewn to the children of a daughter. And when they were returning home, he said to them

[v] The cakes of Samos were celebrated. See Athen. Deipnosoph. xiv. 13.

[x] Corcyra was founded by a colony from Corinth. See Thucydides, book i. ch. 24.

[y] Pythænetus, in the third book of his History of Ægina, says that Periander having seen Melissa, the daughter of Procles of Epidaurus, dressed, after the custom of the Peloponnesians, without any robe, with one simple vest, pouring out drink for the labourers, became enamoured of her, and married her. He had two sons by her, Cypselus and Lycophron. Some time after, being exasperated by the calumnies of his concubines, he killed her, by kicking her when she was pregnant, and afterwards caused them to be burnt. Diogenes Laert. i. 94.

According to Pausanias (ii. 28.) her monument was near Epidaurus. Whether Periander sent her body to Procles, or this was merely a cenotaph, I cannot pretend to decide. *Larcher.*

[z] The Poets frequently confound Τύραννος with Βασιλεὺς; but prose writers, in my opinion, make a great difference; for instance, they never call the kings of Persia, Lacedæmon and Athens, *Tyrants*; but they give that name to the kings of Syracuse, to Pisistratus, &c. Tyrant, among the Greeks, signifies *an usurper* who governs a people *contrary* to their wishes and assent, even though he may govern according to the rules of justice. This is evident from many instances and several authorities. Herodotus also (v. 92.) puts into the mouth of Sosicles the Corinthian deputy, words which necessarily imply a distinction between the two terms. *Larcher.*

See also Mitford's Greece, chap. v. 5. note 20.

as he was accompanying them part of the way, "Do you "know who killed your mother?" The elder made no reflection on these words; but the younger, whose name was Lycophron, when he heard it, was so grieved, that at his return to Corinth he neither addressed his father, regarding him as the murderer of his mother, nor did he converse with him, or answer a word to the questions he asked; till at last Periander in great anger turned him out of his house.

LI. After this, he inquired of the elder brother what discourses they had heard from their grandfather. He acquainted him that they had been received by Procles in the kindest manner; but he did not mention the words he said at their departure, because they had made no impression on his mind. But Periander affirmed that it was impossible that their grandfather had not suggested something to them; and plied him so long with questions, that in the end the young man recovered his memory, and repeated the words to his father, which he having attentively considered, and resolving not to shew the least indulgence, sent to the persons that had given him reception, forbidding them to harbour him for the future. Lycophron being removed from this house retired to another; from whence, upon the menaces and positive commands of Periander, he was expelled[a] in like manner. But betaking himself to another, he was received as the son of Periander, though they were not without fear of his displeasure.

LII. At last Periander made a proclamation that whoever should receive him in his house, or converse with him, should pay a sacred fine to Apollo; the amount of which was mentioned. After which, when every one declined conversing with him, or receiving him, and he did not choose to attempt it, as it was forbidden, he wandered about in the porticos. Periander finding him without food and covered with filth[b], began to relent, and relaxing his anger approached him, and said, "Son, are you better pleased with this miserable way "of living, than by accommodating yourself to my wishes, "to enjoy all the power and riches I possess? You who are "my son, and a king in the rich city of Corinth, have "chosen a vagabond life, by opposing and shewing anger "towards him, whom you by no means ought. For if any "incident has occurred, from which you have conceived "any suspicion towards me, it has fallen more heavily on "me, inasmuch as I murdered her. Therefore, do you, since "you have thus learnt how much better it is to be envied

[a] For the force of ἂν with ἀπελαύνετ', see Matthiæ's Gr. Gr. sect. 598.

[b] The Greek expression ἀλουσίῃσι shews that he had not been in a bath. Before the use of linen, baths were necessary both for health and cleanliness, especially in hot climates. *Larcher.*

" than pitied[c], and how prejudicial to provoke a parent and a " powerful man, return home." With such words did Periander endeavour to check his son. But Lycophron returned no other answer to his father, than that he had incurred the penalty of his own edict by speaking to him. So that Periander perceiving the obstinacy of his son to be insuperable and without remedy, removed him out of his sight, and sent him by sea to Corcyra, which was a part of his dominions. After the departure of Lycophron, Periander made war against his father-in-law Procles, as the principal author of these troubles; took the city of Epidaurus, and Procles prisoner at the same time.

LIII. At length growing old, and being conscious that he was no longer able to inspect and manage public affairs, he sent for Lycophron from Corcyra to take the government upon him, because he did not consider his eldest son[d] capable, as he seemed somewhat dull; but Lycophron would not vouchsafe to give an answer to the messenger. Nevertheless Periander, still fond of the young man, sent another message to him by his own daughter, who was sister to Lycophron, thinking she might persuade him to return. At her arrival she spoke to him in these terms: " Brother," said she, " hadst thou rather see thy father's dominions fall into the " hands of others, and our family utterly destroyed, than re- " turn to Corinth and take possession of all[e]? Come away from " this place, and cease to punish thyself. Obstinacy is an in- " auspicious quality: think not to cure one evil by another. " Many have preferred equity before the rigour of justice; " and many have lost their paternal inheritance by pursuing " a maternal claim. A tyranny is an uncertain possession[f], " and courted by numerous pretenders. Thy father is old, " and past the vigour of life. Let nothing therefore prevail " with thee to abandon to others the advantages which belong " to thyself." Thus she pressed him with these arguments which were most likely to influence him, as she had been instructed by her father. But Lycophron, refusing to comply, assured her he would never return to Corinth so long as he should hear his father was living. With this answer she departed, and, having informed Periander of what had passed, he sent a third message by a herald, to acquaint his son, that

[c] Pindar Pyth. i. v. 164. says the same.

[d] This was Cypselus, see note on chap. 50. After ἐνεώρα τὸ εἶναι δυνατὸν τὰ πράγματα διέπειν, or something similar, is understood.

[e] Οἶκος signifies the wealth and possessions of the father, the patrimony. Σφὲ like μιν has the same force as αὐτὸν, αὐτὴν, αὐτὸ, and therefore may be referred to οἶκον. In Homer Il. xii. 111. and xx, 265. σφε is used to signify a plural number. *Schweigh.*

[f] Compare Euripides Iphig. in Aulid. 21. and a fragment quoted by Stobæus Sentent. Tit. xlvii. p. 343. *Larcher.*

he himself designed to retire to Corcyra; and urged him to return to Corinth and become his successor in the kingdom. To this proposition Lycophron consented; and as Periander was preparing to remove to Corcyra, and his son to Corinth, the Corcyræans informed of the design, and unwilling to receive Periander into their country, killed the young man: and this was the cause that moved Periander to revenge himself against the Corcyræans.

LIV. The Lacedæmonians, arriving with a great fleet, besieged Samos; and having assaulted the walls, they penetrated beyond a tower, which was built upon the shore near the suburbs; but Polycrates at the head of a considerable force falling upon their army, compelled them to retire. Soon after, a good body of Samians, in conjunction with their auxiliary forces, sallied out from another tower, which stands on the ridge of a hill, and attacked the Lacedæmonians; but fled away after a short dispute, and were pursued with great slaughter.

LV. And if all the Lacedæmonians who were in that action had behaved themselves as well as Archias and Lycopas, Samos had been taken that day. For these two men alone of all those who pursued the Samians, entered the city at their heels, and finding all hopes of retreating cut off, died valiantly fighting within the walls. I remember to have met with one Archias, the son of another of that name, and grandson to this Archias, in Pitane[g]; for he was of that tribe. This person esteemed the Samians above all other strangers, and said, that the surname of Samian was given to his father, because he was son to that Archias who fell so gloriously at Samos; and that he himself should always pay a peculiar respect to the Samians, because they had honoured the memory of his grandfather with a magnificent funeral at the public charge.

LVI. The Lacedæmonians, after they had been forty days before Samos, and the siege was not at all advanced, retired to Peloponnesus; though a groundless report has been raised, that Polycrates, having caused a great number of pieces made of gilded lead to be coined, purchased their departure with that money. This was the first expedition[h] the Dorians of Lacedæmon undertook against Asia.

LVII. After their departure, those Samians who had brought this war upon Polycrates, finding themselves abandoned, and their treasures exhausted, set sail for Siphnos[i]. The affairs

[g] This was a small town of Laconia, situated on the Eurotas, and subject to Sparta. See Cellar. Geograph. Antiq. tom. i. p. 1207. See also note on chap. 52. of book ix.

[h] In book i. chap. 152. we find that they had before interfered in the affairs of Asia, but this was the *first expedition*.

[i] This is one of the Cyclades. It is situated to the west of Paros, N.N.E. of

of the Siphnians were then in a flourishing condition[k], and they were the richest of all the islanders; since the island abounded in mines of gold and silver[l], so that the tenth of their revenues, transported to Delphi, made up a treasure equal to the greatest; and they used once every year to divide the riches they drew from their mines. When the Siphnians established this treasure, they consulted the oracle, to know if their prosperity should long continue, and received this answer from the Pythian:

When public structures shall be cloth'd in white,
A wise man's care should fence against the rage
Of wooden troops, and red ambassadors.

The Prytaneum and Forum of Siphnos, were in that time adorned with white Parian marble.

LVIII. Yet the Siphnians could not comprehend the intention of the oracle, either before, or upon the landing of the Samians; though immediately after their arrival they sent an embassy to the city in one of their ships. In former times, all ships were coloured over with red. And this was the thing meant by the Pythian, when she forewarned the Siphnians to beware of a wooden force and red ambassadors. These Samians being admitted to an audience, desired a loan of ten talents; but receiving a denial, they began to ravage the territories of Siphnos. Upon which the Siphnians, drawing all their forces together, fought a battle and were defeated by the Samians; who took many prisoners in the pursuit, by cutting off their retreat to the city; and they afterwards exacted one hundred talents.

LIX. The Samians then sailed to Hermione, and instead of money, received the island of Thyrea, situate near Peloponnesus, which they committed to the care of the Trœzenians; and afterwards landing in Crete, founded the city of Cydonia; though they came not thither with that intention, but only to expel the Zacynthians out of the island. Five years they continued in this settlement, attended with such prosperity, that they built the temple of Dictynna[m], and all the other tem-

Melos, and S.S.E. of Seriphos. Tournefort (Voyages to the Levant, vol. i. p. 172.) gives a description of its present state. It is now called Siphanto, or Siphano.

[k] It appears that afterwards they were not so prosperous. Compare Demosth. περὶ Συντάξεως, p. 102. 52. *Larcher.*

[l] Tournefort (vol. i. p. 174.) says, that the situations of these are not easily found in the present day.

[m] Britomartis was the daughter of Jupiter and Carma, and was born at Cænos in Crete. She invented hunters' nets, and hence received the name of Dictynna. Some confound her with Diana, as she was often in company with that Goddess. Diodor. Sic. (v. 86.) rejects the story, that in her flight from Minos she jumped into the sea, and was caught in some fishers' nets. Βριτὸ, is a Cretan word, which signifies *sweet*, μαρτις, *a virgin*. *Larcher.*

ples which remain to this time in Cydonia. But in the sixth year, they, together with the Cretans, were entirely defeated in a sea-battle, and enslaved by the Æginetæ; who took off the prows of their ships, which represented boars, and dedicated them in the temple of Minerva. The people of Ægina did this on account of a grudge they bore the Samians, because they had before, when Amphicrates[n] was their king, made war against them, which had reduced both sides to great extremities.

LX. I have been more prolix in relating the affairs of the Samians, because they have three things more considerable than are seen in any other parts among the Grecians. They have opened a way through a mountain, one hundred and fifty fathoms high. The length of this passage, which pierces the hill from one side to the other, is full seven stades; and the height and breadth eight feet each. A canal twenty cubits deep, and three feet broad, runs quite through[o] the aperture, and serves to convey the water of a plentiful spring into the city, through various pipes. Eupalinus of Megara, the son of Naustrophus, was the contriver and director of this work. The second thing worthy to be observed, is a mole of one hundred and twenty feet in height, embracing the harbour, and advancing above two stades into the sea. The third is a temple, greater than all those I ever saw, and of which the first architect was Rhœcus[p] the son of Phileus, a native of Samos. These things have induced me to enlarge my discourse concerning the Samians.

LXI. Whilst Cambyses the son of Cyrus tarried in Egypt, and was acting extravagantly, two magi, who were brothers, made an insurrection against him. One of these, whose name was Patizithes, had been by Cambyses made governor of his household during his absence. This person being well informed of the death of Smerdis, which was kept private, and known to few of the Persians, (who, for the most part, thought him still alive,) undertook to invade the throne in the following manner. He had a brother, as I have said, for his accomplice; in person very much resembling[q] Smerdis the son of Cyrus, who had been murdered by Cambyses, and

[n] Who Amphicrates was, and when he reigned is not known. Herodotus, I believe, is the only author that mentions him. *Larcher.*

[o] This appears to have been within the other, and as it was only three feet broad, and the other was eight, there was probably a dry path of two feet and a half on each side, in order that the channel might be repaired if necessary.

[p] This Rhœcus also invented, with the assistance of Theodorus, the art of making moulds of clay. (Plin. Hist. Nat. xxxv. 12.) He had two sons, Telecles and Theodorus, both ingenious statuaries. *Larcher.*

[q] Many instances might be quoted from the history of almost every state, where a resemblance of person has produced great commotions.

moreover bearing the same name. Patizithes, after he had persuaded him that he would carry every thing through for him, placed this man on the throne, and sent heralds to all places, and particularly to the army in Egypt, commanding them for the future to obey Smerdis the son of Cyrus, and not Cambyses.

LXII. The other heralds made this proclamation: and he who was dispatched to Egypt, finding Cambyses with his forces at Ecbatana in Syria, placed himself in the midst of the army, and openly proclaimed the orders of Patizithes. Cambyses, who was present at the proclamation, believing the words of the herald to be true, and imagining that he had been betrayed by Prexaspes, (as if he, though sent to kill Smerdis, had not done so,) looked towards him and said, "Prexaspes, hast thou thus performed that which I enjoined "thee?" To which Prexaspes answered, "Sir, the words "you have heard are false: your brother Smerdis cannot "rebel against you, neither can you have any dispute, great "or small, with him. I myself put your order in execution, "and buried him with my own hands. If indeed dead men "can rise again, expect another rebellion from Astyages the "Mede; but if the course of things be not altered, no harm "to you will spring from him. However, I am of opinion "we ought to go after the herald, and examine who sent "him to proclaim to us that we should obey king Smerdis."

LXIII. Cambyses approving his advice, commanded the herald to be pursued; and when he was brought back, Prexaspes said to him, "Friend, since thou sayest thou art the "messenger of Smerdis the son of Cyrus, speak the truth, "and thou shalt be dismissed with impunity. Didst thou "see Smerdis, and receive these orders from his mouth, or "from any one of his ministers?" "Truly," answered the herald, "I have not seen Smerdis the son of Cyrus since "Cambyses departed from Egypt; but the magus, whom he "appointed governor of his domestic affairs, gave me these "orders, and told me that Smerdis the son of Cyrus com-"manded me to publish them here." Thus the man spoke without feigning any thing: whereupon Cambyses said, "Prexaspes, you, like a faithful man, have executed my "orders, and escaped all blame: but what Persian can this "be, who has revolted against me, and assumed the name of "Smerdis?" "O king," replied Prexaspes, "I think I un-"stand the intrigue: the conspirators are the two magi, Pa-"tizithes, governor of the household, and his brother Smer-"dis."

LXIV. When Cambyses heard that, he was struck with the truth of his words, and the dream, in which he had seen a messenger, who came to acquaint him that Smerdis was placed in the royal throne, and touched the heavens with his head. Reflecting how he had destroyed his brother without a cause, he wept; and after he had lamented him, and bitterly complained of the calamity, he leaped upon his horse, with a resolution to return in all diligence to Susa, and make war against the magus. But as he mounted his horse, the sheath fell from the sword[r], which being thus naked wounded him on the thigh, in that part where he had formerly struck the Egyptian god Apis. Cambyses, when he thought that the blow was mortal, asked the name of the city, and was informed that the place was called Ecbatana[s]. He had formerly received an oracle from Butus, that he should end his life in Ecbatana; and therefore imagined he should die an old man in the place of that name in Media, where all his treasures were; but the oracle meant, as appeared in the event, the Syrian Ecbatana. Thus having heard the name of the city, though vexed with the injury of the magus, and afflicted with his wound, he recovered his understanding; and rightly interpreting the sense of the oracle, said, "Fate "has decreed that Cambyses the son of Cyrus shall die in "this place."

LXV. These words he said at that time; and about twenty days after, having assembled all the principal men of the Persians who were with him, he spoke to them in these terms: "I am necessitated to acquaint you with a thing, "which above all others I desired to conceal. When I was "in Egypt I saw a vision in a dream, which I wish I had "never seen, representing a messenger arrived from Persia, "with tidings that Smerdis was seated on the royal throne, "and touched the heavens with his head. Induced by this "dream, I feared my brother would deprive me of the king- "dom, and acted with more precipitation than prudence: "for no human power is able to turn aside the decrees of "fate. I foolishly sent Prexaspes to Susa with orders to "kill Smerdis; and have lived in the profoundest security "since the execution of that crime; not at all suspecting "that any other mortal would rebel against me, after I had "removed him out of the world. But having been mistaken "as to what was about to happen, I became a fratricide, in "violation of my duty, and nevertheless am deprived of the

[r] Until we are better informed of the shape, &c. of the Grecian and Persian swords, we cannot explain this passage with certainty. It appears from the Scholiast on Nicander, (Alexipharm. v. 103.) that the μύκης held the sheath fast; but we have no idea of what this might be. *Larcher*.

[s] This was a village of Syria, situated at the foot of Mount Carmel, towards Ptolemais. A similar fulfilment of feigned prophecy occurs in Shakespeare, Henry IV. part ii. and in Livy, book viii. ch. 24.

" kingdom. For the God who sent me that vision meant no " other person than Smerdis the magus, when he admonished " me that Smerdis would invade my throne. The crime has " been perpetrated by me, and remember that Smerdis the " son of Cyrus is no more; but that two magi (I mean Pati-" zithes and Smerdis) have taken possession of the kingdom: " the first of these I appointed governor of my household " during my absence, and the other is brother to him. Now " because he, who of right should have revenged the in-" dignity I suffer from the magi, has perished impiously by " the hand of his nearest relation, I think myself obliged in " this exigency to let you know what I would have you do " for me after my death. In the first place I command, and " by the Gods of the royal family adjure you all, especially " those among you who are of the Achæmenian blood, never " to permit the government to return into the hands of the " Medes: and if at any time they should usurp the supreme " power by artifice, to use the like means to recover it; or if " they should acquire the dominion by arms, then likewise to " recover it by arms. On this condition, may the earth " bring forth fruits; may your wives bring you many chil-" dren; your herds and flocks increase; and your liberty re-" main inviolable for ever. But if you do not recover, nor " attempt to recover, the dominion from the Medes, may the " contrary imprecations overtake you; and besides, may the " same end befal every Persian which has befallen me." When Cambyses had finished these words, he again passionately lamented his condition.

LXVI. And all the Persians seeing their king so deeply afflicted, wept abundantly, and tore their garments in pieces. But in a little time, when the bone became infected and the thigh mortified, it carried[t] off Cambyses the son of Cyrus, after he had reigned seven years and five months[u], having never had any children of either sex. He was no sooner dead, than the Persians, who had accompanied him, began to enter into a violent suspicion, that whatever he had said concerning the usurpation of the magi, and the death of his brother, was fictitious, and contrived by Cambyses with design to render all the Persians enemies to Smerdis. This incredulity easily wrought them into a persuasion, that Smerdis the son of Cyrus was really the person who had taken possession of the kingdom: and Prexaspes contributed not a little to this delusion, by denying utterly that he had killed Smerdis. For indeed, after the death of Cambyses, he could

[t] You may either put in ἡ γοῦσος, or τὸ κακὸν, or τὸ ὀστέον σφακελίσαν καὶ ὁ μηρὸς σαπείς. Compare vi. 27. *Schw.*

[u] Clemens Alexandrinus (Stromat. i.) makes him reign ten years, and Ctesias (Hist. Per. 12.) eighteen. *Larcher.*

not safely own that he had murdered the son of Cyrus with his own hand.

LXVII. The magus[x] Smerdis, by assuming the name of Smerdis the son of Cyrus, reigned in security during the seven months that remained to complete the eighth year of Cambyses; in which time he treated the people with such beneficence, that all the nations of Asia, the Persians only excepted, felt regret at his death. For upon his accession to the throne, he dispatched orders through all parts of his dominions, to proclaim a general exemption from tribute and military services for the space of three years.

LXVIII. But in the eighth month he was discovered in this manner. Otanes the son of Pharnaspes, a man equal to the greatest of the Persians, both in fortune and blood, was the first who suspected him to be an impostor, and not the son of Cyrus, because he never went out of the castle, nor summoned any of the principal men of Persia to his presence. In this suspicion he contrived the following artifice, in order to discover the truth. His daughter Phædyma had been one of the wives of Cambyses, and was kept, as all the rest were, for the use of Smerdis. To her therefore he sent a message, to inquire of her whether the person she lay with was Smerdis the son of Cyrus, or some other man: she sent back word, that she did not know, for she had never seen Smerdis the son of Cyrus, and that she did not know with whom she lay: he sent to her a second time, saying, "If you "do not yourself know Smerdis the son of Cyrus, then in-"quire of Atossa who this man is, with whom you and she "cohabit, for she must of necessity know her own brother." But his daughter replied, "I can neither obtain a conference "with Atossa, nor see any of the other women; because the "king, whoever he was, had from the beginning of his reign "dispersed all his wives into distinct and separate apart-"ments."

LXIX. The matter appeared much more plain to Otanes when he heard this, and he sent a third message to Phædyma in these words: "Daughter, being descended of an illustrious "family, you ought to undertake the most hazardous enter-"prize, in obedience to the commands of your father. If this "Smerdis is not the son of Cyrus, but the person I suspect

[x] That Cambyses was the Ahasuerus, and Smerdis the Artaxerxes, that obstructed the work of the temple, is plain from hence, that they are said in Scripture to be the kings of Persia that reigned between the time of Cyrus and the time of that Darius by whose decree the temple was finished; but, that Darius being Darius Hystaspes, and none reigning between Cyrus and that Darius in Persia, but Cambyses and Smerdis; it must follow from hence, that none but Cambyses and Smerdis could be the Ahasuerus and Artaxerxes, who are said in Ezra to have put a stop to this work. *Prideaux's Connections.*

'him to be, he ought by no means, since he possesses your 'person, and the Persian power, to escape with impunity, but 'to suffer the punishment due to his offences. Follow there- 'fore my advice; and when you lie by him, and perceive him 'to sleep, carry your hand to his head; and if you find he has "ears, be assured that you cohabit with the son of Cyrus; "but if he has none, with Smerdis the magus." To this message Phædyma answered, that the danger was exceedingly great; because if the king had no ears, and she should be discovered in touching him, she well knew that he would put her to death; nevertheless she would make the attempt. Thus she took upon herself to satisfy the doubt of her father touching this Smerdis, (whose ears had been formerly cut off, for a reason of importance, by Cyrus the son of Cambyses.) In pursuance therefore of her promise, Phædyma the daughter of Otanes carefully executed the orders of her father; and going in her turn to the king's bed, as the manner of the Persian women is, she no sooner perceived him to sleep profoundly, than she easily discovered by her hand that the man had no ears; and early the next morning sent an account to her father of what she had done.

LXX. Otanes took with him Aspithines and Gobryas, who were the noblest of the Persians and most fit to be trusted, and related to them the whole affair; these also had of themselves suspected that the case was so. When Otanes had related his story, they readily assented; and came to an agreement with him, that each of three should nominate one of his most trusty friends among the Persians, to be admitted to a participation of their counsels. Pursuant to this resolution, Otanes introduced Intaphernes, Gobryas Megabyzus, and Aspathines Hydarnes. At the same time Darius the son of Hystaspes arriving in Susa[y] from Persia, where his father was governor, the six Persians resolved to admit him into their society.

LXXI. These seven having met, after mutual assurances of fidelity, entered into a debate touching the thing in question. But when Darius came to speak in his turn, he said, "I thought no man, except myself, had known that the "kingdom is usurped by a magus, and that Smerdis son of "Cyrus is dead; and therefore I came to this place in haste, "in order to contrive his death. But since I find that you "also are informed of this indignity, my opinion is to dispatch "the enterprize with all expedition, because delays in such a "conjuncture are not safe." "Son of Hystaspes," said Ota-

[y] Susa, although in some degree the capital of the Persian kingdom, and particularly made the residence of the king, was not situated in Persia, properly so called, but in Cissia or Susiana. See ch. xci. *Schweighæuser.*

nes, "thou art born of a noble father, and you appear to shew "that you are not inferior to him, but do not so inconsiderately hasten this attack, but undertake it with more moderation; for we ought not to undertake this enterprize "without augmenting our number." Darius replied, "Believe me, friends, if you follow the advice of Otanes, you "will all inevitably perish: for some one will not fail to discover the conspiracy to the magus for private advantage: "and indeed you alone, who first formed the design, ought to "have put it in execution immediately; but since you have "thought fit to communicate your intentions to a greater "number, and to me among others, let us make the attempt "this day; or be assured, that if this day pass away, no one "shall be before me in accusing, but I myself will disclose it "to the magus."

LXXII. Otanes perceiving Darius so eager; "Since "then," said he, "we are necessitated to precipitate our enterprize, and not permitted to defer the execution, pray tell "us in what manner we shall enter the palace; which, as "you know, or at least have heard, is defended by guards "placed in all the passages; and I desire to be informed how "we shall pass them." Darius answered, "Some things, "Otanes, may be explained by action, that cannot be demonstrated in words; while other things, which seem easy in "discourse, produce no considerable effect in the execution. "No man here can imagine that we shall find any great difficulty in passing the guards, because our quality is such that "every one, either from a motive of reverence or dread, will "presently give us way. Besides, I am furnished with a "most specious pretext; for I will say I come directly from "Persia, and bring a message to the king from my father. If "it is necessary for a falsehood to be spoken[a], let it be spoken, "for men aim at the same thing by both. Some make use of "an untruth, when by persuading with falsehoods, they are "likely to gain something; whilst others on the contrary "speak the truth, in order that, by the truth, they may acquire some advantage, and something farther may accrue to "them; and thus by different practices we aim at the same "end. But if they were not likely to gain, there will be "little difference between truth and falsehood. As for the "guards, they who willingly permit us to pass, shall be rewarded in due time; but whoever offers to resist must be "treated as an enemy, and when we have forced our passage, "we must execute our purpose."

[a] This appears remarkable, when we remember that the Persians were particularly taught to speak the truth. See book i. ch. 138.

LXXIII. To this Gobryas added, "Friends, it will be 'more glorious for us Persians to recover the sovereign 'power, or die in the attempt; since, though Persians, we 'are governed by a magus of Media, and one without ears. 'Those among you who attended Cambyses during his sick- 'ness, well remember the imprecations he uttered at the 'point of death against the Persians, if they should neglect "to use their utmost endeavours to repossess themselves of "the kingdom; though his discourse made little impression "upon us at that time, because we imagined he spoke out "of hatred to his brother. Therefore I concur with the opi- "nion of Darius, and think we ought not to go any where "else than directly to the magus upon the breaking up of "this meeting." Which proposal was unanimously approved.

LXXIV. Whilst they were concerting this attempt, it happened by chance that the magi, after a consultation, determined to engage Prexaspes in their interests; as well because he had been ill used by Cambyses, who shot his son dead with an arrow, as because he alone of all the Persians knew certainly that Smerdis the son of Cyrus was not living, having dispatched him with his own hand; and besides this, he had acquired a general esteem among the Persians. For these reasons they sent to Prexaspes, and having obtained a promise of his friendship, they obliged him to give his word, confirmed by an oath, that he would keep to himself, and never discover to any man the fraud they had put upon the Persians, assuring him, in consideration of this service, they would give him every thing in abundance. When Prexaspes had promised that he would do what they persuaded, they next proposed that they should assemble all the Persians under the walls[a] of the palace, and desired that he would ascend a certain tower, and from thence publicly proclaim, that Smerdis the son of Cyrus, and no other person, was the king then reigning. This command they laid upon him, because they not only knew he was a man of principal authority among the Persians, but also that he had frequently affirmed with great asseveration, that Smerdis the son of Cyrus was still living, and utterly denied that he had killed him.

LXXV. When Prexaspes said that he was ready to do that also, the magi having summoned the Persians together, commanded him to mount the tower, and from thence to harangue the assembly. But he willingly forgot the words they had desired him to speak, and, beginning with Achæmenes,

[a] This was the citadel. The kings anciently lodged there for safety. Herodotus observed in ch. lxviii. that the magus would not quit the citadel; and in ch. lxxix. says, that the conspirators left behind, in the citadel, such of the party as were wounded. *Larcher.*

he related the genealogy of the family of Cyrus; and afterwards put them in mind of the great benefits the Persian nation had received from that king. When he had finished this part, he confessed the whole truth, and told them, that the apprehensions he had of the hazards he must inevitably run by publishing the fraud, had constrained him to conceal it so long; but now seeing the necessity of discovering the secret, he acknowledged, that being compelled by Cambyses, he had with his own hand destroyed Smerdis the son of Cyrus, and that the magi at present reigned over them. Then after he had uttered many imprecations against the Persians, if they should neglect to recover the sovereignty, and punish the magi, he precipitated himself headlong from the tower[b]. Thus died Prexaspes, a man highly esteemed during the course of his whole life.

LXXVI. In the mean time the seven Persians having determined to execute their design against the magi without delay, set out after they had implored the assistance of the Gods; and in the midst of their way were informed of all that Prexaspes had said and done, which obliging them to retire and confer together, Otanes earnestly exhorted them to defer the enterprize, and not to attempt any thing in the present disorder of affairs; but Darius still insisting upon immediate execution, and rejecting all propositions of delay, the dispute grew warm; and as they were contending, seven pair of hawks appeared pursuing two pair of vultures in the air, pulling and tearing them to pieces, which, when the seven Persians observed, they accepted the omen, fell in with the opinion of Darius, and proceeded with confidence to the palace.

LXXVII. When they arrived at the gates, it happened as Darius had supposed. For the guards respecting their dignity, and no way doubting such a design from persons of their rank, as if they were guided by Providence, permitted them to pass, and no one asked them any question. But when they passed on to the hall, they fell in with the eunuchs who attended to receive messages, who inquired what business they had there; and threatened the guards for permitting them to pass, and also endeavoured to prevent the seven who were desirous of proceeding farther. Then the seven Persians animating each other, drew their swords, killed all that opposed their passage, and in an instant penetrated to the apartment of the men.

[b] Larcher is unable to reconcile this last noble action of Prexaspes with the mean answer which he gave to Cambyses when he murdered his son, ch xxxv.

LXXVIII. The two magi happened at that time to be both waiting, and were consulting about the late action of Prexaspes; who, when they heard the exclamations and tumult of the eunuchs, went together to the door, and perceiving what was doing, had recourse to courage. To that end one of them quickly taking up a bow, and the other a javelin, they began to engage in the combat. He who had the bow soon found that weapon of no use, since their enemies were at hand and pressing upon them, but the other with his javelin wounded Aspathines in the thigh, and struck out the eye of Intaphernes, though the wound was not mortal. Thus one of the magi wounded two of the Persians; whilst he who found his bow useless, ran to a chamber adjoining to the apartment of the men, with design to shut the door upon himself, but Darius and Gobryas broke into the chamber with him; and as Gobryas was struggling with the magi, Darius stood still, doubting how to direct his blow in the dark, which Gobryas perceiving, and asking him why he held his hand, Darius answered, because he feared he might hurt him; "Strike," said Gobryas, "though you strike through the bodies of both." Upon this Darius in obedience thrust forward his sword and by good fortune killed the magi.

LXXIX. When the seven had dispatched the magi, they cut off their heads; and leaving the two Persians who were wounded to secure the palace, because they could not be serviceable elsewhere, the other five, carrying the heads of the magi, marched out with great tumult and exclamation; and, calling to the Persians, related what they had done, shewed them the heads, and killed all the magi they found in their way. The Persians were no sooner informed of what had passed, and of the deceit of the magi, than they likewise thought it right to act in conformity to the seven, killed every magi they met; and if night coming on had not prevented, no one of that order had been left alive. All the Persians celebrated this day with the greatest solemnity, and call the festival by the name of Magophonia, or, *The slaughter of the magi*. On that day no magi may be seen abroad, but every one of them is constrained to shut himself up in his own house.

LXXX. When the tumult was appeased, and five days had elapsed, those who had been concerned in the attempt against the magi, met to consult about the government, and made the following speeches; notwithstanding some among the Grecians fondly imagine they are fictitious. Otanes urged that they should resign the administration of affairs to the people, saying, "My opinion is, that we ought not to entrust the supreme power with any single person among us;

"because a monarchical government is neither good nor popular. You know to what excesses Cambyses was transported, and have sufficiently experienced the insolence of the magus. And indeed how can that government be well arranged, where one man may do whatever he wishes, without being accountable? for even the best of all men, when placed in such power, would go beyond his accustomed prudence. Insolence is produced in a man by the presence of power, and envy is implanted in man at his birth; when a man has these two, he has every vice. Puffed out with insolence, he commits many nefarious crimes, and many when bloated with envy. One would think a tyrant should not be envious, because he possesses such eminent advantages above other men; but experience demonstrates the contrary. He envies the best, and favours the worst men of the nation; he hearkens to calumny with pleasure; and his conduct is so irregular, that if any one commend him modestly, he grows angry, and thinks he is not treated with sufficient reverence; on the other hand, if he be highly admired, he is no less offended, because he suspects he is flattered.

"The things of the greatest importance I am now about to relate. He overthrows the orders and customs of the country; violates the chastity of women; and murders the innocent unheard. But a popular government deservedly bears the charming name of equality[c], and is never guilty of those excesses that are the constant attendants of monarchy. The magistrates are appointed by election, every officer is obliged to give an account of his administration, and refers all matters of deliberation to the common assembly of the citizens. My opinion therefore is, that we ought to reject monarchy, and establish a popular government; for no valuable quality can be wanting in a numerous assembly." Otanes delivered this opinion.

LXXXI. Megabyzus spoke next; and recommending an oligarchy to their choice, said, "I readily concur with Otanes in the advice he has given to abolish the tyranny; but in counselling us to confer the whole power upon the multitude, he hath widely deviated from the best opinion, for nothing can be imagined more foolish and arrogant than an useless crowd; and therefore nothing can be more extravagant, than that we, who are endeavouring to avoid the insolence of a tyrant, should fall under the caprice of an un-

[c] The word in the original means *equality of laws;* we have no one word to express it. Euripides has expressed the same sentiment in his Medea, verses 119—126.

"restrained multitude[d]. A tyrant knows what he does, but "the populace are unable to know; for how should they "know any thing, who are bred under no discipline, and have "no idea of virtue, or even of common order; and they "hurry on matters without reason like an impetuous torrent[e]. "Let those then who desire the ruin of the Persians, promote "the establishment of a popular state; as for me, I am of "opinion that we ought to place the sovereign authority in a "select council of the best men; both because we ourselves "shall be of their number, and because, in all appearance, "the best men will give the best advice." Megabyzus laid this opinion before them.

LXXXII. Darius next declared his opinion in these terms: "The things which have been said by Megabyzus against a "popular government, seem to me very just and right; but "what he said with regard to an oligarchy, not so. For if "three forms are proposed, and each of these which I allude "to, the best in its kind, a most perfect democracy, oligarchy "and monarchy, I affirm that the last is far superior. Cer-"tainly nothing can be imagined more excellent than the go-"vernment of a single person, if he be completely virtuous: "following the best counsel, he would govern the people "without blame, and would most of all keep his designs "against the enemy secret. Whereas in an oligarchy, whilst "many are practising virtue in advancing the public service, "private enmities will frequently and unavoidably arise; and "every man being willing to be the principal manager, and "desirous to see his own opinions prevail, animosities of the "most dangerous consequence must necessarily ensue. From "this source seditions arise; from sedition murder; and from "mutual murders, things naturally tend to monarchy; which "is sufficient to prove this kind of government highly prefer-"able to any other. On the other hand, in a popular state, "it is impossible for wickedness not to exist; and when that "happens, they will not produce enmity, but the strongest "friendship, for those who injure the commonwealth, act in "concert and support one another; until at last some person "puts himself at their head, and stops the proceedings of the "conspirators; on account of this he is admired by the peo-"ple, and afterwards he commonly becomes a real monarch, "and shews by this that a monarchy is the most excellent of "all governments. To finish all in a word; from what cause,

[d] Fenelon says, Directions pour la Conscience d'un Roi, "The despotism "of the multitude is a foolish and blind "power, which rages against itself; a "people spoiled by an excessive li-"berty, is the most insupportable of all "tyrants."

[e] "Illæ undæ comitiorum, ut mare pro-"fundum et immensum, sic effervescunt "quodam quasi æstu, ut ad alios acce-"dant, ab aliis autem recedant." *Cicero pro Plancio*, sect. 6.

"and by whose means were we made a free nation? Did we "receive our liberties from the people; from a few select "persons; or from a monarch? My opinion therefore is, that "since we were delivered from servitude by a single person, "we would resolve to confirm that kind of government, and not "to alter the custom of our country, which has been so ad-"vantageous to us: for we should not find our account in the "change."

LXXXIII. After these three opinions had been proposed, four of the seven embraced that of Darius; and Otanes, who had endeavoured to introduce an equal republic, finding his sentiment overruled by number, thus spoke before the assembly: "Since it appears evident, that it is necessary for some "one of us to be made king, either by the chance of the lot, "the election of the Persian multitude, or by some other "way, I will not be your competitor, because I resolve nei-"ther to govern nor be governed, but quit all my right, on con-"dition that neither I nor any of my posterity may be account-"ed subjects." When he had said this, and the six had consented to his demand, he accordingly did not join in the contest, but withdrew from the assembly; and his descendants alone of all the Persians retain their liberty to this day; being no farther subject to the king than they think convenient, but without transgressing the customs and manners of the country.

LXXXIV. After his departure, the other six entered into a deliberation touching the most equitable manner of constituting a king; and in the first place resolved, that if any one of their number obtained the kingdom, Otanes, and his posterity after him, should every year receive a Median vest, accompanied with all other presents which are accounted most honourable among the Persians. They decreed that these things should be bestowed upon him, because he had been the author of the enterprise, and brought them together into this association. These honours were conferred on Otanes in particular; and they made the following resolutions with regard to the whole body; that any one of the seven should have full liberty to enter into all the apartments of the palace without being introduced; unless the king should happen to be in bed with one of his women; and that he should not be permitted to marry a wife out of any other family than of the conspirators. With regard to the kingdom they decreed that he should possess it, whose horse should first neigh in the suburb at sun-rise[f], while they themselves were mounted on them.

LXXXV. In this resolution the assembly parted, and Da-

[f] The Persians were accustomed to worship the rising sun.

rius was no sooner returned home, than calling for Œbares, who had the charge of his horses, and was a man of ingenuity, he said to him, "Œbares, we have determined to dispose of "the kingdom in this manner; he, whose horse shall neigh "first after the rising of the sun, is to have the sovereign "power. Now therefore, if thou hast any invention, exer-"cise thy talent, that I may obtain this glory, with the exclu-"sion of all other persons." "Sir," answered Œbares, "if "it depends on this, whether you shall be made king or not, "be confident on that account, and be in good spirits; since "no one else shall be king in preference to you; I have such "a charm." "If thou hast such an artifice," said Darius, "it "is time to use it without delay; for the trial is to be made "to morrow." Œbares having heard this, departed; and when night came, he led a mare, which the horse of Darius loved, to the suburbs, and tied her up; then he brought his master's horse thither also; and after he had led him several times round the mare, gradually bringing it nearer, he at last let him cover her.

LXXXVI. The next morning, at day-break, the six Persians appearing on horseback pursuant to their resolution, rode about the suburbs; and as they passed by that part where the mare had been tied the preceding night, the horse of Darius ran to the place and neighed, which he had no sooner done, than flashes of lightning were seen issuing from a clear sky, and followed by a clap of thunder. These additional circumstances, as if they arose from some concerted scheme, consummated the auspices. All his competitors dismounted from their horses and adored him as king[g].

LXXXVII. This account is most commonly given of the artifice used by Œbares; but others say, (and the Persians relate the story both ways,) that having rubbed his hand upon the genital part of the mare, he kept it warm under his garment[h], and that after the rising of the sun, when the horses were ready to set forward, Œbares drew out his hand and stroked the nostrils of his masters horse, who taking the scent, began to snort and neigh immediately after.

LXXXVIII. However this be, Darius the son of Hystaspes was declared king, and all the people of Asia submitted to his government, whom Cyrus had first subdued, and afterwards Cambyses. The Arabians alone[i] were never

[g] Darius was twenty years old (i. 219.) when Cyrus perished. Cambyses reigned seven years and five months, and the magus seven months; hence Darius was twenty-nine years old, when he came to the crown. *Larcher.*

[h] The anaxyrides were large breeches, which reached down to the ancle. *Larcher.*

[i] It was foretold of Ishmael, Gen. xvi. 12. "And he will be a wild man; "his hand will be against every man, "and every man's hand against him." Sesostris, Cyrus, Pompey, Trajan, and

reduced to the condition of subjects by the Persians, but were accounted their friends, and gave them a free passage into Egypt, which they could not have compassed without their permission and assistance. Darius contracted the most noble alliances with the Persians, for he married two daughters of Cyrus, Atossa and Artystona. The former had been wife to her brother Cambyses, and also to the magus, but Artystona was a virgin. To these he added Parmys, the daughter of Smerdis the son of Cyrus, together with that daughter of Otanes[k] who detected the magus. His power was fully established on all sides. He first erected a statue of stone, representing a man sitting on horseback, and bearing this inscription, DARIUS THE SON OF HYSTASPES OBTAINED THE KINGDOM OF PERSIA BY THE SAGACITY OF HIS HORSE, (here the name of the horse was read,) AND BY THE ADDRESS OF OEBARES, MASTER OF HIS STABLES.

LXXXIX. Having done this, he divided his dominions into twenty provinces or satrapies, and constituted a governor in each division. Then he appointed the tribute which every nation should be obliged to pay into his treasury; and for this purpose he joined to certain nations the neighbouring people, and then passed by these neighbouring people, and assigned to them other people which were more remote. In this manner did he distribute the satrapies and the annual payment of tribute. He also ordained, that all those who brought their portion in silver should make their payments by the Babylonian talent, which is equal to seventy Eubœan mines; and those who paid in gold, should bring in their part by the standard of the Eubœan talent. During the reign of Cyrus there was no fixed regulation[l] with regard to tribute, nor even afterwards under Cambyses, but the people made voluntary presents to the king; and, therefore, from the establishment of these taxes, and other things of like

other potentates, vainly attempted to subjugate the wandering Arabs; and though they had temporary triumphs over some tribes, they were never ultimately successful. From the commencement of the Ishmaelites to the present day, they have maintained their independence. For a full account of the prophecies concerning Ishmael, see Bp. Newton's Second Dissertation.

[k] Darius had no children by Phædyme, but by the daughter of Gobryas he had three; Artobazanes, (vii. 2.) Ariabignes, (ibid. 97.) Arsamenes; (ibid. 68;) by Atossa he had Xerxes, Masistes, Achæmenes, and Hystaspes; (ibid. 64, 82, and 97;) by Artystona he had Arsames and Gobryas; (ibid. 69 and 72;) by Parmys, Ariomardus; (ibid. 78;) by Phratagune, Abrocomas and Hyperanthes; (ibid. 224;) in all twelve sons. *Larcher.*

[l] This appears to contradict what was said in ch. 67, that the magus exempted the Persians for three years from every kind of impost. It must be observed, that these imposts were not continual; they only subsisted in time of war, and they were rather a gratuity than an impost. Those which Darius established were perpetual; therefore Herodotus does not contradict himself. *Larcher.*

nature, the Persians say Darius was a trader[m], Cambyses a master, and Cyrus a father. For Darius made profit of every thing; Cambyses was severe and negligent from haughtiness; but Cyrus was mild, and always contriving advantages for his people.

XC. The Ionians and Asiatic Magnesians[n], with the Æolians, Carians, Lycians, Milyens, and Pamphylians, were appointed to pay a tribute of four hundred talents in silver, and composed the first satrapy. The Mysians, Lydians, Alysonians, Cabalians, and Hygenians[o], were the second, and paid five hundred talents of silver[p]. The people who dwell on the right hand of those who sail through the Hellespont, together with the Phrygians, Asiatic Thracians, Paphlagonians, Mariandynians[q], and Syrians[r], paid three hundred and sixty talents, and made up the third government. The Cilicians were the fourth, and furnished Darius with three hundred and sixty white horses; that is, one for every day of the year, besides five hundred talents in silver; a hundred and forty of which were consumed in the payment of the cavalry which guarded Cilicia[s], and the remaining three hundred and sixty were paid into the treasury.

XCI. The fifth comprehended all the countries that lie extended from the city of Posideum, built in the mountains of Cilicia and Syria, by Amphilochus the son of Amphiaraus[t], down to Egypt, excepting only the Arabian territories, which are free from any tribute; this portion, containing all Phœnicia, the Syria which is called Palæstine[u], and Cyprus, was taxed at three hundred and fifty talents. Egypt, and those

[m] Æschylus throughout his tragedy of the Persians bears honourable testimony to the character and administration of Darius. Mitford translates κάπηλος *a broker*, ch. vi. 2.

[n] There were also Magnesians in Thessaly. The Milyens are probably the same with those in book i. ch. 173.

[o] Of this people we know nothing. Wesseling proposes to read Obigenians. Obigene was a division of Lycaonia. See Plin. v. 32.

[p] This division, which is by far the smallest of the twenty, does not appear to have touched the sea on any part. The greatness of the tribute paid by this satrapy, in proportion to its very confined limits, requires explanation; and none appears more satisfactory, than that the sources from whence the vast riches of Crœsus were derived, were contained in it. *Rennel*, sect. xi.

[q] This people occupied a part of the coast of the Euxine, between Bithynia and Paphlagonia. *Rennel*, sect. xi.

[r] By Syrians are meant Cappadocians. See note on book ii. ch. 104.

[s] Cilicia was a post of great importance. According to the hands into which it fell, it either connected or separated the two countries of Asia Minor and Persia on the one hand, and Asia Minor, Syria, and Egypt, on the other. *Rennel*, ch. xi.

[t] For an account of Amphiaraus, see note on book i. ch. 46. Amphialochus became king of Argos, but was forced to fly from the throne; he thence went to the Ambracian gulf and founded Argos Amphilochium. He shared divine honours with his father at Oropus. His oracle at Mallus, in Cilicia, acquired celebrity. The answers were given in dreams.

[u] The country, which is named by the Greeks *Palæstine*, is called by the Arabs *Falastin*, and is the Philistine of the Scriptures.

parts of Lybia which border upon Egypt, together with Cyrene and Barce, made up the sixth government, and contributed seven hundred talents, besides the revenue arising from the fishery of the lake Mœris, and a sufficient quantity of corn for one hundred and twenty thousand Persians and their auxiliaries, who had their station within the white fortress[x] of Memphis. The seventh satrapy, consisting of the Sattagydæ[y], Gandarii, Dadicisæ, and Aparytæ, paid one hundred and seventy talents. Susa[z], and the rest of the country of the Cissians, were the eighth, and contributed three hundred.

XCII. A thousand talents of silver, and five hundred young eunuchs, were furnished yearly by the city of Babylon and other parts of Assyria; this was the ninth division. Ecbatana, and the rest of Media, with the Parycanians and Orthocorybantes, were the tenth[a], and paid a tribute of four hundred and fifty talents. The Caspians, Pausicæ, Pantimatians, and Daritæ, contributed two hundred talents, and composed the eleventh satrapy[b]. The twelfth,[c] which extended

[x] Memphis consisted of three parts; the third part was the castle or fortress, which was built of white stones, whence it derived the appellation of the *white*; it is also mentioned by Thucydides, i. 104. *Larcher*.

[y] No name like this can be found. From what scanty notices we have, it can only be supposed that the seventh satrapy of Herodotus was made up of the province of Margiana, and some tracts adjoining to it on the west, and that it had for its boundaries on the south, the ridge of mountains that separate Aria; on the west, the countries of Baverd, Toos, &c. the original seats of the Parthians; on the north, the desert towards the Oxus; and on the east, Bactria. In effect, that it was surrounded on three sides by the sixteenth, and on the fourth, by the twelfth satrapy. *Rennel*.

[z] This division answers to the modern *Khusistan*. As it contained the *then* capital of the empire, and had a rich soil, it was enabled to pay so large a tribute. The wealth of Susa is mentioned by Aristagoras, in the fifth book, ch. 49. *Rennel*.

[a] It is well known that there were two countries of the name of Media at the time of the Macedonian conquest; the *greater* and *less*. The greater answers to the modern division of *Al Jebal*, or *Irak Ajami*; the less, to *Aderbigian*, called by the Greeks *Atropatia*. We conclude that Herodotus intended the greater Media only, because he classes *Matiene*, which lay between the two, as distinct from Media, and because also, Aderbigian appears to form a part of the Saspires and Caspians. The *Oathocorybantes* may be taken for the people of *Corfiana*, now *Currinabad*, the southern part of Media; and by the *Paricanii* we conclude are meant the *Paretaceni*, the people of the eastern province of Media, which extends from *Persis* to the Caspian straits. *Rennel*.

[b] There are found in Strabo and Ptolemy some notices respecting the Pasicæ and Aspasicæ, who appear to be the Pausicæ of our author. (Strabo, p. 513; Ptolemy, Asia, Tab. 7.) They are placed near the Chorasmians. The *Caspians* inhabited the shore of the sea of that name, from the mouth of the river Cyrus southward. Hence this satrapy constitutes one vast natural division of country, and that of the most fertile and productive kind, being the modern provinces of *Ghilan*, *Mazanderan*, (or *Taberistan*,) *Korkan*, *Dahestan*, &c. known in ancient geography by the names of Gela, Maxere, Tapuri, Hyrcani, and the country of the Dahæ. Hyrcania should have been included in this division, although omitted in the statement of Herodotus. *Rennel*.

[c] No rule is given by which we can form any idea of the extent of this satrapy, unless the modern province of

from the Bactrians to the Ægles, brought in three hundred and sixty talents.

XCIII. Pactyice, with the Armenians and other neighbouring parts, down to the Euxine sea, made the thirteenth[d] government, and was ordered to pay four hundred talents. The fourteenth[e] consisted of the Sagartians, Sarangæans, Thamanæans, Utians, Mycians, and those who inhabit the islands of the Red sea, where banished persons were confined by the king, all these together were obliged to bring in six hundred talents. The fifteenth[f] comprehending the Sacæ and Caspians, paid two hundred and fifty. The Parthians, Chorasmians, Sogdians, and Arians, were the sixteenth[g] government, and furnished three hundred talents.

XCIV. Four hundred were required from the Paricanians, and Asiatic Ethiopians, who made the seventeenth[h] division. The eighteenth[i], consisting of the Matieni, Saspires, and

Balk and its dependencies are taken for the country of the *Bactrians* at large. There is little question but that the present *city* of Balk is the Bactra or Bactria of the ancients; but whether the modern *province* answers to the ancient one cannot be known: but Æglos is an unknown position. According to the context, we might suppose Bactrians to form the western quarter, and look for Æglos in the eastern. Now the most remote eastern province of Balk is *Kil*, *Gil*, or *Kilan*; may not this be the Kilos, Ekilos, or Æglos of our author? *Rennel.*

[d] The Pactyans in Polymina, 67, should be taken for the Bactearis, seated in the mountains on the west of Ispahan; and the Pactyans of Armenia quite a different people, and quite unknown to us. When our author extends this satrapy to the Euxine, he appears to contradict what he says of the nineteenth. *Rennel.*

[e] This must be regarded as comprising *Sigistan*, together with such parts of the country between it and the Persian gulf as were not exempted from tribute by Darius. We conceive *Carmania* in general, as well as the country of *Lar*, bordering on the Persian gulf, and the islands of it, to belong to this satrapy. *Rennel.*

[f] The Sacæ possessed the countries of *Kotlan* and *Saganian*, which were adjacent to Baetriana, Sogdia, and mount Imaus. The *Caspians* may probably be the *Casians* of Ptolemy; that is, *Kashgur*, which borders on the country of the Sacæ. *Rennel.*

[g] The provinces of this satrapy are all contiguous, and form one of the largest of those divisions. The original Parthia of Herodotus appears to be nothing more than the mountainous tract between Hyrcania, Margiana, Aria, and the desert of Chorasmia. *Soghd* or Samarcand between the Oxus and Jaxartes is doubtless *Sogdia*, excluding *Kotlan*, *Saganian*, and *Kilan*, as parts of the Sacan or Bactrian satrapies. *Chorasmia* must be taken for *Khowarezm*, at large; and *Aria* for Herah, which is sometimes written without the aspirate, at this time. *Rennel.*

[h] These Paricanii we refer to the country of *Gedrosia*, i. e. *Kedge* or *Makran:* considering the town of *Fahraj* or *Pooraj*, as the *Poorah* of the historians of Alexander; and this *Poorah* we regard as the capital of the Paricanii. We must regard the Ethiopians of Asia as the people of *Makran*, *Haur*, and other provinces in the south-east angle of Persia towards India. *Rennel.*

[i] The position of Matiene is well known. It was, properly speaking, the north-west part of Media major, lying above the ascent of mount Zagros; and between Ecbatana and the lake of Maraga. The *Saspires* (or whatsoever may be their proper name) must occupy the space in the line between the Matiene and Colchis, in modern geography the eastern part of Armenia. The *Alarodians* we cannot find any authority for placing; but may suppose their country to be parts of Iberia and Albania, bordering on the Colchians and Saspires. *Rennel.*

Alarodians, brought in two hundred talents. The Moschians, Tibarenians, Macronians, Mosynæcians, and Mardians, were enjoined to pay three hundred talents, and composed the nineteenth[k] satrapy. The Indians were the twentieth[l]; and as they are more numerous than any other people we know, the tribute charged upon them was proportionably great; for they were obliged to bring in yearly three hundred and sixty talents of gold.

XCV. Now, if the Babylonian talent be compared with the Eubœan, we shall find in this account nine thousand five hundred and forty talents[m]; and if we estimate the gold at the value of thirteen times[n] silver, the sum will amount to four thousand six hundred and eighty Eubœan talents. All this computed together, shews that Darius received the yearly tribute[o] of fourteen thousand five hundred and sixty talents of the Eubœan value, besides other sums of less consequence, which I forbear to mention.

XCVI. The revenues were paid to Darius by the inhabitants of Asia, and a small part of Lybia; but in succeeding times another tribute was laid upon the islands, and divers parts of Europe as far as Thessaly. The king preserves his treasures in this manner; he causes the metals to be melted down and poured into earthern pots; which done, the vessels are broken, and when occasion requires, so much is cut off as seems necessary.

[k] This satrapy must have extended along the south-east coast of the Euxine, and was confined on the inland, or southern side by the lofty chain of Armenian mountains. On the east it was bounded by the heads of the Phasis and Cyrus; and on the west by the Thermodon. *Rennel.*

[l] How much of India was possessed by Darius is not known. For a perspicuous account of this and all the other satrapies, the reader is referred to the learned work of Major Rennel, sect. xi, xii. where the reasons for the situation of them are clearly stated.

[m] These numbers as they now stand involve some difficulty. Larcher without hesitation reads nine thousand eight hundred and eighty. See also Schweighæuser's note.

[n] In the time of Plato the proportion of gold to silver was twelve to one, in the time of Menander ten to one. *Larcher.*

[o] Herodotus has undertaken to give an account, in some detail, of the produce of the Persian taxes; on what authority we are not informed. But we know that it is even now, with all the freedom of communication through modern Europe, extremely difficult to acquire information, at all approaching to exactness, of the revenue, and still more of the resources of the neighbouring states. Mr. Richardson, in his Dissertation on the Languages of the East, has observed, that the revenue of Persia, according to Herodotus's account, was very unequal to the expences of such an expedition as that attributed to Xerxes; and therefore, he says, Herodotus must stand convicted of falsehood in one case or the other. Unprejudiced persons will have little difficulty to chuse their belief. The principal circumstances of the expedition fell necessarily under the eyes of thousands. The revenue could be known to very few, and the resources probably to none. Yet a very acute inquirer into ancient politics has observed, that valuable information is derived from Herodotus's account of the Persian revenue. See Gibbon's History of the Roman Empire, vol. i. ch. 8. note 1. and vol. ii. ch. 24. *Mitford's Greece*, ch. vi. 2. note 14.

XCVII. These then are the satrapies and the imposts on each. Persia is the only country which I have not mentioned as tributary; for the lands of the Persians are free from all taxes. But the Ethiopians, who border upon Egypt, and were conquered by Cambyses in his expedition against the Macrobians, together with those who inhabit the sacred city of Nissa, and celebrate the festival of Bacchus, are not enjoined to pay tribute, but send a yearly present to the king. These Ethiopians, and the adjoining people, who live in subterraneous dwellings, and use the same grain[p] with the Calantian Indians, make a present every third year of two chœnices of unrefined gold, two hundred blocks of ebony, five Ethiopian children, and twenty elephants' teeth of the largest size: which custom they continue to this day. The Colchians numbered themselves among those who gave presents, with the nations that lie between their country and mount Caucasus; for so far the dominions of Persia extend. But the people who inhabit the north side of that mountain, pay no regard to the Persian power. The present sent by the Colchians, consisting of one hundred boys, and the same number of virgins, was delivered every fifth year. The Arabians also brought every year a thousand talents of frankincense. These gifts were brought to the king besides the tribute.

XCVIII. I shall now explain in what manner the Indians collect that great quantity of gold dust, which serves to pay the tribute imposed upon them by the king. That part of India which faces the rising sun is covered with sand; and of all the people who inhabit Asia, and are known to us by certain information, the Indians are placed in the most eastwardly situation. The country which most advances towards the east, is rendered desert by the sands. The Indians consist of many nations, which speak different languages: some apply themselves to the keeping of cattle, and others not. Some inhabit the morasses of the river, and feed upon raw fish, which they take by sailing out in boats composed of reeds; each boat is formed of one single joint of the reed[q]. These Indians wear garments made of rushes, which they cut

[p] This is rice or a kind of millet, which is also mentioned in chap. 100. See Denon's Travels in Egypt, vol. i. p. 75. and other travellers. *Schweigh.*

[q] Arundini quidem Indicæ arborea multitudo, quales vulgo in templis videmus. Spissius mari corpus, fœminæ capacius. Navigiorum etiam vicem præstant (*si credimus*) *singula internodia*. Pliny Hist. Nat. xvi. 36. See also vii. 2; compare also Theophrast. Hist. Plant. iv. 12. Ctesias, ch. 6. &c.

It must be supposed that Herodotus meant the people who inhabit the banks of the Ganges, the *proper* and *Sanscrit* name of which is Padda; Ganga being the appellative only; so that the *Padæi* may answer to the Gangaridæ of later Greek writers. *Rennel.*

in the river, and weaving them together like a mat, wear them, like a cuirass.

XCIX. Eastward of this people lie the Padæi, who keep cattle, eat raw flesh, and are reported to use the following customs. When any one of the community is sick, his nearest connections put him to death, alleging that if he wasted by disease, he would spoil his flesh; he denies that he is sick, but they, not agreeing with him, kill him, and feast upon his flesh. And if a woman be in the same condition, she is treated in the same manner by the women most acquainted with her. They kill those who happen to live until they are old, and eat their flesh with rejoicing; but few among them attain to long life, for before that, they put to death every one that falls into any distemper.

C. On the other hand, some Indians observe a quite contrary custom; for they neither kill any animal[r], nor sow any seed, nor are they accustomed to have houses; but live upon herbs. They have a kind of grain about the size of millet, and enclosed in a calyx, which springs spontaneously from the earth: this they collect, and having boiled it, together with the calyx, they eat it. When any one among them is sick, he retires into the desert, where no care is taken of him, whether he live or die.

CI. All these Indians I have mentioned resemble the Ethiopians in complexion, and perform the act of generation in public[s] like other animals. The seed they emit is not white, as that of other men, but of equal blackness with their skin; and such also is the seed of the Ethiopians. This part of India is situate to the southward, very remote from the Persians, and was never subject to Darius.

CII. Other Indians, inhabiting towards the north, and bordering upon the territories of Caspatyrus[t] and Pactyica, resemble the Bactrians in their manner of living, and are the most valiant people of all India. These are they who go to collect gold upon the uninhabited sands of their country. In this desert, and among the sands, there are found a kind of ants[u], less indeed than dogs, yet of a larger size than foxes. Some of them are kept in the palace of the Persian king, which were taken in this place. These ants are in shape exactly like those of Greece; and making themselves habitations under ground, they throw up the sand in the same man-

[r] Nicholas Damascenus says these people were called Aritonii. *Larcher.*

[s] See book i. ch. 216.

[t] See book iv. ch. 44. and note.

[u] These are also described by Pliny, Hist. Nat. xi. 31. Nearchus informs us, (Arrian. Hist. Indic. xv. 4.) that he had never seen the animal itself, but a great many of their skins, which were brought into the Macedonian camp. M. De Thou, an author of great credit, informs us, that Schah Thomas, Sophi of Persia, sent in the year 1559, to Soliman, an ant like these here described. *Larcher.*

ier. The sand thus thrown up is mixed with gold dust. For his sand therefore the Indians make journeys into the desert; every man employed in that work tying three camels together, a male on each side, and a female in the middle, which he mounts himself, and always takes care that he may have torn her from her young as recently born as possible. These camels are not less swift than horses, and much more able to carry burdens.

CIII. What the form of the camel is, I shall not describe to the Greeks, as they are acquainted with it; I will only mention those particulars which are not known; a camel has four thighs[x] and four knees on his hinder parts, and the genital member turning towards his tail.

CIV. When the Indians have prepared and harnessed their camels in the manner above mentioned, they set forward towards the desert; having before calculated the time, so as to be employed in their plunder during the most scorching heat of the day, because the ants are then all under ground. In this climate the sun is not, as in other regions, hottest at noon, but in the morning[y], from the time that it has risen to any height in the heavens, to the hour when men usually retire from the forum[z]; during which time it scorches there much more than at noon in Greece; so that, it is reported, these Indians are accustomed at that time to bathe in cold water[a]. At noon the heat is little different from that which is felt in other countries, but soon after becomes as moderate as the morning elsewhere; gradually diminishing as the sun declines, and upon the setting changes into excessive cold.

CV. The Indians arriving in this place, fill their sacks with the sand, and return with all possible expedition. For the ants, as the Persians say, immediately having discovered it by the scent, pursue them; they affirm, that they are superior to every other animal in swiftness, so that if the Indians did not make some progress while the ants were collecting, no one would get away safe. The male camels, as they are inferior in speed to the females, fail in their strength[b], and at different times keep up with great difficulty; whilst the

[x] This, as Aristotle has remarked, (Hist. Anim. ii. 1.) is not true. *Larcher.*

[y] Some traveller had told Herodotus, that when it was the third hour, or nine o'clock in Greece, the sun was vertical in India; and from his want of knowledge on that subject the difficulty appears to have arisen. *Larcher.*

[z] The time of full forum appears to have been about nine.

[a] This is the general way of translating the passage. Schweighæuser thinks that it alludes to intense perspiration, as in French, the phrase, "nager dans "l'eau." The Latin word *sudor* is the exact Greek word ὕδωρ.

[b] I have followed Schweighæuser, who considers *παραλύεσθαι* as signifying, *to fail in strength*, &c. Coray translates it, "Les chameaux mâles se sépareroient des femelles (resteroient en arrière,) s'ils n' étoient point tirés ensemble et à coté d'elles.

females, which are more swift than the males, and animated by the remembrance of their young, spare no efforts to return with all possible speed. In this manner the Indians collect the greatest part of their gold, as the Persians say; for that which they dig out of the mines is not so considerable.

CVI. Thus the remotest part of the inhabited world possesses some of the most excellent things; as Greece is more happily blessed with an agreeable temperament of air and seasons. For in these regions, which, as I said before, lie farthest to the eastward, and are called India, all animals, both quadrupeds and birds, are bigger than in other places; except only horses, which are not so large as the Nysæan horses of Media. There is likewise abundance of gold, either dug out of the mines, or brought down by the rivers, or robbed from the ants in the manner I have related; besides a certain tree, growing wild, and instead of fruit, bearing a wool[c] which excels that of sheep, both in beauty and quality, and is used by the Indians for clothing.

CVII. Arabia is the last inhabited country lying to the southward; and the only region which produces frankincense, myrrh, cassia, cinnamon, and ledanum. All these things the Arabians gather with some difficulty, myrrh only excepted. They collect the frankincense by burning styrax, which the Phœnicians export into Greece; for flying serpents, small of body and with variegated skins, guard the trees which bear the frankincense, a great number round each tree. These are the same serpents as attack Egypt. They are driven from the trees with nothing else but the smoke of the styrax.

CVIII. These serpents, the Arabians say, would fill all the country, if they were not subject to the same effect which is experienced in vipers: and we may rationally conjecture that the wisdom of Divine Providence has made all those creatures, which are naturally fearful, and serve for food, to be very prolific, lest the species should be destroyed by constant consumption; and on the contrary, such as are rapacious and cruel, to be almost barren. Hence the hare[d], which is hunted by beasts, birds, and men, is so very prolific that it alone of all beasts conceives to superfetation, having in its womb some of its young covered with down, others bare, others just formed, and at the same time conceives another. Whereas a lioness, which is the strongest and fiercest of

[c] This was doubtlesss the cotton plant, called by the ancients Byssus, and was by them regarded both as a species of linen, and as a sort of wool which grew on trees in India. See Pollux Onomast. viii. 75. *Larcher*. See also Palmerius Exerc. in Gr. Script.

[d] The astonishing fecundity of this animal has made some authors imagine that they are hermaphrodites. Xenophon, (Cyneg. p. 572.)

Aristotle and several other ancient authors make the same remark with regard to the superfetation of the hare.

beasts, bears one once[e] in her life, because she ejects her matrix with her whelp; for he is no sooner capable of motion, but with his claws, sharper than those of any other beast, he begins to tear the part where he lies; until, increasing in strength, he at last rends it in pieces, and leaves nothing sound behind him at his birth.

CIX. So that if vipers and the winged serpents of Arabia should generate as their nature admits, men could not possibly live. But when they couple together, and the male emits his seed, the female seizes him by the neck, and presses so hard with her teeth, that she never lets him go until she has torn it through. In this manner the male dies[f], and the female escapes not long with impunity; for when her young ones are entirely formed, they open a way for themselves with their teeth through her bowels, and thus revenge the death of their father; whilst other serpents, which are not hurtful to men, lay their eggs, and produce great abundance of their own kind. As for vipers, they are found in all parts of the world; but flying serpents are found in thick swarms in Arabia, and no where else, and therefore they appear to be very numerous.

CX. Having related the manner of gathering frankincense, I shall now give some account of the way they take to furnish themselves with cassia, which is this; they cover all the body and face, except the eyes, with hides and skins, and go down to the lake where the cassia grows: this lake is not deep, but infested with great numbers of winged beasts, in form resembling a bat, making hideous cries, and assaulting boldly. From these the Arabians take care to defend their eyes, and thus gather the cassia.

CXI. They collect the cinnamon[g] in a still more wonderful manner. In what place and country it is produced they cannot tell; some however, reasoning not improbably, affirm that it grows in those countries where Bacchus received his education; and from thence, say they, certain great birds bring those sticks (which we, from the Phœnicians, call cinnamon) to build their nests, which are fastened by means of clay, to mountainous cliffs, inaccessible to men. The Arabians, to surmount this difficulty, have invented the following artifice: they cut oxen, asses, and other large cattle into great pieces, and when they have carried and laid them down as near as is possible to the nests, they retire to some distance from the

[e] This is perfectly false. The lioness generally has two at once, never more than six, and sometimes only one. Lionesses in Syria litter as many as five times. *Larcher.*

[f] This is entirely fabulous. *Larcher.*

[g] By cinnamon the ancients understood the small branches of the tree with the bark on; by cassia, the bark only. *Larcher.*

place. In the mean time the birds descend to the flesh, and carry up the pieces to their nests, which not being strong enough to support such a weight, fall down immediately to the ground. The Arabians approaching gather up the sticks, and by this means they and other nations are furnished with cinnamon[h].

CXII. But the gathering of ledanum[i], which the Arabians call ladanum, is far more wonderful. For though it is found in a most stinking place, it is itself most fragrant. For it is found, like gum, sticking to the beards of he-goats, which collect it from the woods. It is useful for many ointments, and is more generally burnt by the Arabians than any other perfume.

CXIII. But I have said enough of these odours. For the rest, the air of Arabia is divinely sweet, and the country produces two sorts of sheep, which are very strange, and no where else seen. The first kind has a tail at least three cubits[j] long, which would certainly ulcerate, if they were suffered to draw it after them upon the ground. But every shepherd knows so much of the carpenter's art as to make little carts, upon which he places the tails of the sheep, and fastens them. The other sort has a tail of a full cubit in breadth.

CXIV. South-west of this country lie the regions of Ethiopia, which are the utmost limits of the inhabited world, abounding in gold, ebony, and elephants of a prodigious size. The trees grow wild and uncultivated, and the inhabitants are very tall, beautiful, and of very long life.

CXV. These are the extremities of Asia and Lybia; but I have nothing certain to relate concerning the western bounds of Europe; neither can I assent to those who tell us of a river, by the Barbarians called Eridanus[k], which, they

[h] The mode here described of getting the cinnamon resembles in many particulars one of the adventures of Sinbad the sailor, in the Arabian Nights Entertainments.

[i] The Ledum is a flowering shrub which grows to the height of two or three feet. A complete description of it is given by Tournefort. The goats browse upon the leaves, on which there is a gummy substance, which clings to their beard. (Dioscorid. Mater. Medica, i. 128. The peasants collect it with wooden combs made for the purpose, then they form it into a mass, and give it the name of *Ledanum* or *Ladanum*. *Larcher*.

[j] Between Senegal and Gambra there are sheep with tails so long and heavy, that the shepherds support them on a kind of carriage; the sheep of the Cape of Good Hope have also very long and broad tails. See Penant's Zoology.

[k] Bellanger was of opinion, that Herodotus here intended to speak of a river in Italy; Pliny thought so too, and is surprised that Herodotus, who passed so long a time at Thurium, in Magna Græcia, should have been unable to meet any one who had seen this river. This Eridanus could be no other than the *Rho-daune*, which empties itself into the Vistula, near Dantzic, on the banks of which we now find amber in large quantities. *Larcher*. This is also the opinion of Major Rennel.

say, furnishes amber, and runs northward into the sea. I know as little of the islands called Cassiterides[l], from whence our tin comes. Indeed the very name of Eridanus, which is Greek, and not Barbarous, discovers it to be the fiction of some poet; and though I have diligently inquired, yet I have never seen any man who by his own experience could inform me concerning the nature of that sea, which bounds the extremities of Europe. However, it is certain that amber and tin come from the remotest parts.

CXVI. And it appears certain, that by far the greatest abundance of gold is found in the north of Europe[m], but in what manner I am not able to relate with certainty, though it is said that the Arimaspians[n], a people who have only one eye, steal it from the griffins; but I cannot believe that men are born with one eye, and yet resemble the rest of mankind in all other things. In a word, these extreme parts, which enclose and contain within themselves the rest of the earth, seem to possess whatever we account most excellent and rare.

CXVII. There is a plain in Asia encompassed on every side with a ridge of hills, opening into five several passages. This country was formerly in the possession of the Chorasmians, and is on the confines of these same Chorasmians, of the Hyrcanians, Parthians, Sarangæans, and Thomanians, but since the establishment of the Persian power, belongs to the king. A great river, known by the name of Aces[o], flows from these hills, and formerly being divided several ways, used to water the lands of the nations before mentioned, being conducted to each nation through a separate opening. But these people have suffered the following thing since they were reduced under the dominion of the Persian; for the king caused the apertures to be blocked up, and gates placed

[l] It has been very much the custom to refer the Cassiterides to the Scilly islands alone; but the idea ought to be extended to Cornwall at least, and it is possible that very great changes have taken place in the state of Scilly and Cornwall since the date of that traffic. There are some curious particulars in Diodorus Siculus respecting an island near the British coast, to which carriages laden with tin came at low water, in order to its being embarked in vessels for the continent. See book v. 2. The want of information of Herodotus on these matters can only be referred to the jealousy of the Phœnicians. *Rennel.*

[m] The north-west part of Asia is here meant. The Europe of Herodotus extended far into north Asia. See Rennel, sect. 3.

[n] See book iv. ch. 13 and 27. Milton uses this fable in his second book of Paradise Lost.

[o] This story, so improbably told, seems to relate to the *Oxus*, or to the *Ochus*, both of which have undergone considerable changes in their courses, partly by the management of dams, partly by their own depositions, for they certainly flow near the countries of the Chorasmians, the Hyrcanians, and Parthians; but the *Sarangæans*, if taken for the people of Zarang, that is, Segistan, as no doubt they ought to be, are out of the question as to any connection with these rivers. *Rennel.*

at each, so that the water being prevented from escaping, the whole plain between the mountains became a sea; and the people who before had been supplied with those waters, being deprived of a thing so necessary, were reduced to great extremities; for though, as other countries, they have rain in winter, yet in summer, when they sow panicum and sesamus, they stood in need of water; and therefore, finding themselves totally excluded from the benefit of the river, they went with their wives to the king's palace, howling and making loud exclamations before the gates: upon which the king gave order that the passages should be opened towards those lands that were in the most pressing want, and shut up again when they were sufficiently watered, and afterwards to do the like to the rest, in such order as should be found necessary. But, as I am informed, he opens it when he has exacted great sums of money, besides the usual tribute.

CXVIII. It happened that Intaphernes, one of the seven who had conspired against the magus, lost his life from the following act of insolence: soon after that enterprize, he went to the palace in order to confer with Darius, pursuant to the agreement before mentioned, by which provision was made, that all the accomplices might, without a messenger to announce him, go in to the king at any time, except when he should happen to be in bed with one of his wives. Intaphernes, therefore, in confidence of this privilege, attempting to enter the royal apartment without an introducer, was stopped by the door-keeper and messenger, under colour that the king was then accompanied by one of his women; but Intaphernes, suspecting they lied, drew his scimitar, and after he had cut off the ears and noses of both these officers, and had fastened them to the bridle of a horse, he hung them round their necks, and so let them go.

CXIX. In this condition they went in, and shewing themselves to the king, acquainted him with the cause of the ill usage they had received. Upon which Darius, fearing the six might have concerted this attempt together, sent for them, one after the other, and examined their opinions, whether they approved the action. But finding by their answers that Intaphernes was singly guilty, he caused him to be seized, with his children and family, having many reasons to suspect that he and his relations might raise a rebellion. Whilst they were under confinement, and bound, in order to execution, the wife of Intaphernes went to the gates of the palace weeping and lamenting loudly, which she continued so assiduously, that at last Darius, moved with compassion, sent a messenger to speak to her in these terms: "Woman, "the king gives you the life of any one among your captive "relations whom you wish to deliver." "Since the king," said she, after some deliberation, "will grant me no more "than one, I choose my brother." Darius, when he heard her answer, wondering at her choice, dispatched another messenger to ask her in his name, "Why she had shewn so little "regard to her husband and children, and rather chosen to "save the life of her brother, who was not so near related to "her as her children, nor could be so dear to her as her husband?" She answered, "That by the permission of heaven "she might have another husband[p] and other children, if she "should be deprived of those she had, but could never have "another brother, because her father and mother were "already dead." The king was so well pleased with this answer, that he not only pardoned her brother, but gave her likewise the life of her eldest son, and put all the rest to death. Thus Darius caused one of the seven to be executed in the beginning of his reign.

CXX. As near as may be about the time of the illness of Cambyses, the following circumstances happened. Orœtes, a Persian, had been appointed governor of Sardis by Cyrus; this man conceived the impious project of seizing and putting to death Polycrates the Samian, though he had never seen him, nor ever received any injury from him by word or deed. But the most current report is, that the cause was this. As he was one day sitting at the gates of the palace[q] with another Persian, whose name was Mitrobates, at that time governor of Dascylium, they fell from ordinary discourse into a dispute concerning valour; in which Mitrobates upbraided Orœtes in these terms: "Art thou then," said he, "to be accounted a man of any esteem, who hast not yet reduced "the island of Samos to the king's obedience; which lies "near thy government, and is so easy a conquest, that one of "its own inhabitants having made an insurrection with fifteen "armed men, obtained possession of it, and now reigns "over it?" This reproach, they say, left a deep impression on the mind of Orœtes, and made him take a resolution to

[p] An exactly similar sentiment occurs in Sophocles, Antig. v. 924. Abaucha, a Scythian, in Lucian, (Toxar. s. Amicit. tom. ii. c. 61.) is described as neglecting his wife and children, and saving his friend from the flames. When asked the reason, he replied, "Other children "I may easily have, and they are at "best a precarious blessing; but I "should not find such another friend as "this in a long time."

Edward the First, when he heard at the same time of the death of his father and son, said, "that the death of a son "was a loss which he might hope to "repair; the death of a father was a "loss irreparable. *Hume.*

See also the lines quoted in the Antiquary, vol. iii. ch. 11.

[q] The grandees used to wait at the gates of the palaces of the kings of Persia. This custom, established by Cyrus, continued as long as the monarchy, and at this day, in Turkey, we say the Ottoman port, for the Ottoman court. *Larcher.*

revenge himself; not upon Mitrobates, who had said this, but against Polycrates, as the cause of the affront he had received.

CXXI. Others, but not so many, affirm that a messenger, dispatched by Orœtes to Polycrates, to demand something, which is not mentioned, found him reposing in the men's apartment, with Anacreon[r] of Teos near him, and (whether from previous determination he despised the affairs of Orœtes, or by chance it so happened) when the herald delivered his message, Polycrates, as his face chanced to be towards the wall, never turned about, nor condescended to make him any answer.

CXXII. Both these reasons are alleged to have been the cause of the death of Polycrates; and I leave every man to believe whichever he pleases. However, Orœtes, who resided in the city of Magnesia[s], upon the river Mæander, being acquainted with the intentions of Polycrates, sent a message by Myrsus a Lydian, the son of Gyges, to Samos; for Polycrates[t] was not only the first of all the Grecians we know, who formed a design to render himself master of the sea, except Minos[u] of Crete, or perhaps some other before his reign, but the first of all men[x], who to that time had entertained great expectations of subduing Ionia and the islands. Orœtes therefore, well informed of his design, sent him a message in these words: "Orœtes to Polycrates. I understand that you are devising vast enterprizes, but have not "money answerable to your projects. Now, if you will "hearken to my advice, you will succeed in your enterprizes, "and preserve me; for I have certain information that Cambyses has resolved to take away my life. Receive me there"fore with my treasures, part of which take yourself and per"mit me to enjoy the other: by these means you cannot fail "to acquire the dominion of Greece. If you doubt what I "say concerning my riches, send to me one of the most faith"ful persons about you, to whom I will shew them."

[r] It is by no means surprizing to find in the court of a tyrant a man who is perpetually celebrating wine and love. These verses are full of the praises of Polycrates. After the death of that prince, Hipparchus, tyrant of Athens, sent a fifty-oared vessel to conduct him to him. *Larcher.*

[s] This is added to distinguish it from the Magnesia *ad Sipylum*, a town of Lydia at the foot of mount Sipylus, to the north-west of Sardis and east of Phocæa. It is called by the Turks Guzel-Hisar. There was also a country called Magnesia in Thessaly, &c.

[t] Mitford (Hist. Greece, vi. 3.) says, that Polycrates appears to have been the Macihavel of his time, with the advantage of possessing the means to prove the merit of his theory by practice.

[u] This is confirmed by Thucydides, book i. ch. 4 and 13. and also by Diodorus, iv. 60.

[x] Τῆς ἀνθρωπηΐης λεγομένης γενεῆς. This Larcher translates, *Mais quant a ce que l'on appelle les temps historiques;* and says that ἀνθρωπηΐη γενεὴ, *true historical times*, are opposed to μυθικὴ, *fabulous times.*

CXXIII. Polycrates having heard this was delighted and willing to comply, and as he was very desirous of wealth, he first sent his secretary, Mæandrius, the son of Mæandrius, to take a view of his wealth. This man was a citizen of Samos; and not long after presented all the magnificent furniture, found in the apartment of Polycrates, to the temple of Juno. When Orœtes learnt that a person was expected to examine his wealth, he caused eight chests to[y] be filled with stones, except a very small space round the edge, and having spread a thin covering of gold upon the surface, he made them fast with cords[z], and kept them ready till the arrival of Mæandrius, who, when he had inspected the pretended treasure, departed, and at his return acquainted his master with what he had seen.

CXXIV. Upon this information, Polycrates resolved to go in person to Orœtes, though he was earnestly dissuaded by his friends, and by the oracles, and moreover, though his daughter had seen in a dream this vision; she imagined she saw her father elevated in the air, washed by Jupiter, and anointed by the sun. Deeply affected with her dream, she endeavoured by all means possible to divert him from going from home; and, as he was going to embark on a galley of fifty oars, persisted in uttering words of bad omen. On the other hand, he threatened her, if he returned safe, that she should long continue unmarried; which she willingly imprecated upon herself, choosing rather to remain a virgin than to lose her father.

CXXV. Thus Polycrates, rejecting all counsel, went away to Orœtes, accompanied by divers of his friends, and, among others, by Democedes the Crotonian, the son of Calliphon, a physician by profession, and the most skilful practitioner of his time. When he arrived in Magnesia, he was put to death in an infamous manner, unworthy of his person and magnanimity: for none of all the Grecian tyrants, with the exception of those of Syracuse[a], are to be compared with Polycrates in magnificence. But Orœtes put him to death in a manner not to be mentioned[b] without horror, having caused him to be

[y] Annibal made use of a similar stratagem to free himself from the dangers which threatened him from the avarice of the Cortynians. See Corn. Nepos, ch. xxiii. 9. Justin, xxxii. 15. See also the way in which the Egestæans deceived the Athenians. Thucyd. vi. 46.

[z] Before the invention of locks, it was the custom in ancient times to fasten doors, boxes, &c. with knots. Every one has heard of the famous Gordian knot. This custom is alluded to by Homer, (Odyss. viii. ver. 447.) upon which passage Eustathius informs us that keys were invented by the Lacedæmonians. It is very singular that the Lacedæmonians, who held every thing common, should be the inventors of keys.

[a] Herodotus alludes to Gelon and his brother Hiero.

[b] Orœtes doubtless flayed him alive, which was a common punishment in Persia. According to Diodorus Sic. (Excerpt de Virt. &c. tom. ii. p. 557.)

crucified: of those that attended Polycrates, he dismissed all that were Samians, bidding them to feel thankful to him for their liberty: the strangers and servants he detained and treated as slaves. Thus Polycrates accomplished the dream of his daughter: for, as he hung upon the cross, he was washed with the reign of Jupiter, and anointed by the sun, as the moisture of his body was exhaled. And such was the end of all his prosperities, as Amasis, king of Egypt, had foretold.

CXXVI. Not long after the avenging furies of Polycrates pursued Orœtes: for after the death of Cambyses, and during the usurpation of the mages, Orœtes continuing at Sardis, gave no manner of assistance to the Persians, who had been fraudulently dispossessed of their power by the Medes; and not only took that opportunity to murder Mitrobates, governor of Dascylium, because he had upbraided him on the subject of Polycrates, together with his son Cranaspes, both highly respected by the Persians, but, among an infinite number of other insolent actions, caused a messenger, who brought an unwelcome message to him from Darius, to be assassinated in his return, by certain persons appointed to way-lay him, and bury him privately with his horse, after they had put their orders in execution.

CXXVII. Darius, therefore, upon his accession to the throne, resolved to punish Orœtes for all his crimes; and especially for the death of Mitrobates and his son. But because his own affairs were not yet tranquillized, and he had but just gained the kingdom, and he understood that Orœtes, besides a guard of one thousand Persians, could draw together great forces out of his governments of Phrygia, Lydia, and Ionia, he declined to send an army against him; he therefore contrived the following project openly. He summoned the principal of the Persians together, and spoke to them in these terms: "Which of you, O Persians, will undertake to accomplish for me this by address, and not by violence or numbers of men? for where prudence is required, force is unnecessary. Which then of you will bring me the body of Orœtes, either alive or dead? Of Orœtes, I say, who has never yet done any service to the Persians, but brought infinite mischiefs upon them: who has already murdered two of us, I mean Mitrobates and his son; and, with intolerable insolence, assassinated the messengers I sent to recall him. He must therefore be stopped by death, before he has perpetrated any greater evils against the Persians."

Orœtes inflicted this cruel death to punish the perfidy of Polycrates, in having put to death some Lydians, who had implored his protection, in order to possess himself of their treasures. *Larcher.*

CXXVIII. When Darius had thus spoken, thirty of those who were present undertook it, being each separately desirous of performing this; and every one contending for the employment, Darius ordered them to determine the dispute by lot; which being done, Bagæus, the son of Artontes, was charged with the enterprize, and performed it in this manner. He wrote divers letters about several affairs, and, after he had sealed them with the signet of Darius, he departed for Sardis; and, coming into the presence of Orœtes, delivered the letters one after the other, to be read by the king's secretary; for every governor has one of these secretaries attending him. This he did in order to see if the guards would shew any signs of defection: and perceiving they paid great respect to the letters, and much greater to the contents, he put another into the hands of the secretary, containing these words: "Persians, "king Darius forbids you to serve any longer for guards to "Orœtes:" which they no sooner heard, than they laid down their lances. When Bagæus saw them so readily obey, he took greater confidence, and delivered his last letter to the secretary, written in these terms: "King Darius commands "the Persians who are in Sardis to kill Orœtes." Upon the reading of which, the guards drew their scimitars, and killed him immediately. Thus vengeance overtook Orœtes the Persian for the death of Polycrates.

CXXIX. When the possessions had been removed, and had arrived at Sardis, it happened not long after that Darius, in leaping from his horse while hunting, twisted his foot with such violence that the ancle-bone was dislocated; and thinking he had the best of the Egyptian physicians about him, he made use of their assistance. But they, by violent pulling and twisting the part, made the evil worse, and from the pain which he felt, he lay seven days and seven nights without sleep. On the eighth day Darius, still continuing in a bad condition, was informed of the ability of Democedes the Crotonian, by one who had heard of him at Sardis, and presently commanded him to be brought into his presence. He was found among the slaves of Orœtes, altogether neglected; and introduced to the king loaded with fetters, and clothed in rags.

CXXX. When he was brought before him, Darius asked him whether he understood the art of physic. But he, fearing such a confession might for ever prevent his return to Greece, would not acknowledge his skill. But he appeared to Darius to dissemble, although he was skilled in the art, and he therefore commanded those who had brought him thither to bring out the instruments of whipping and torture, and upon this Democedes presently declared, that indeed he could not pretend to understand the art in perfection, but had learned something by the conversation of one who was a physician. Upon which, when Darius put himself under his care, by using Grecian medicines, and applying lenitives after violent remedies, he caused him to enjoy sleep, and in a little time restored him to his health, though the king had before despaired of ever recovering the strength of his foot. When he had performed this cure, Darius presented him with two pair of golden fetters; but Democedes asked him, if he meant to reward him with a double evil for restoring his health. With which answer Darius was pleased, and sent him to the women's apartment, attended by some of his eunuchs; who having informed them that this man had saved the king's life, every one of his wives taking gold[c] out of a chest in a vase, gave it to him with the vase, and in such an abundant gift, that a servant Sciton, who followed him, collected a considerable treasure of the staters he took up as they fell to the ground.

CXXXI. This Democedes became acquainted with Polycrates after having left Crotona on the following account. He suffered restraint from his father, who was austere in his temper, and being unable to endure this, he removed to Ægina; having settled there, in the first year, though he was altogether unprovided with the instruments requisite to his profession, he surpassed the most skilful of their physicians; and the second year obtained a talent for his salary out of the public treasury. The third year he was engaged by the Athenians, at the rate of a hundred minæ; and the fourth by Polycrates, with a reward of two talents; and on that occasion went to Samos. The Crotonian physicians became very famous by the reputation of this man; for at this period the physicians of Crotona were said to be the first throughout Greece. The Cyrenæans possessed the second place; and the Argives were at the same time accounted the most skilful in the art of music.

CXXXII. Democedes, having thus cured Darius, lived at Susa in a magnificent house; was admitted to the king's table, and enjoyed every thing in abundance, except the liberty of returning to Greece. He obtained a pardon for the Egyptians, who, having been the king's physicians, were condemned to be empaled for suffering themselves to be outdone by a Greek; and procured the liberty of a certain prophet of Elis, who had attended Polycrates, and lay neglected

[c] This is one of the most perplexed passages in Herodotus, Ὑποτύπτειν is used in the same sense as in book ii. ch. 136. viz. *to dip a vessel down into any thing to fill it*, as into water. Θήκη has also caused great doubts. I have followed Valckenaer; see his note.

among the prisoners. In a word, Democedes was the principal favourite of Darius.

CXXXIII. Not long after these things had passed, Atossa, the daughter of Cyrus, and wife to Darius, had a tumour in her breast; which afterwards broke and spread considerably. As long as it was not very large, she concealed it, and from delicacy informed no one of it; when it became dangerous, she sent for Democedes and shewed it to him. He promised to cure her, but bound her by an oath, that she would confer upon him in return whatever favour he might ask, and that he would ask nothing which might bring disgrace on her.

CXXXIV. When he had by the application of remedies restored her to health, Atossa, as she was instructed by Democedes, addressed herself to Darius, as she lay in his bed, with these words: "It is strange that a king of so great "power should be inactive, and not rather conquer nations, "and enlarge the empire of the Persians. A young prince, "possessed of such vast treasures, ought to render himself considerable by his actions, and to convince his subjects that "they are governed by a man. Two reasons oblige you to "this conduct; first, that the Persians may know they are "commanded by a valiant king; and then that they may be "employed in war, and not tempted by too much ease to "rebel. You should therefore perform some illustrious "action, while you are in the flower of your years: for as "the faculties of the mind keep equal pace with the body "in advancing to their utmost vigour, so both decline[d] together gradually, and become blunted to every thing." Thus Atossa expressed herself according to the instructions she received from Democedes; and Darius in answer said, "Thou hast advised me to do as I had already determined: "for I have determined to make a bridge and march from "this continent to the other, against the Scythians, which I "will do in a short time." Atossa replied, "Lay aside, I "beg of you, your intentions of first marching against the "Scythians, who will be in your power whenever you please; "but take my advice, and lead an army into Greece: for "the account I have heard of the Lacedæmonian, Argian, "Athenian, and Corinthian women, has inspired me with a "vehement desire to have some of them for servants. Besides, you have the fittest man in the world to inform you "of every thing concerning Greece; I mean the person who "cured your foot." "Since then," replied Darius, "you are "of opinion that I ought to make my first attempt against

[d] The same sentiment occurs in Homer's Odyss. book ii. v. 315. and in Lucretius iii. v. 446. Compare also Livy, vi. ch. 23.

"Greece, I think it better to send some Persians thither "with the man you mention, in order to discover what they "can relating to the country; and when I have learnt every "particular, I will turn my arms against them."

CXXXV. Having said this, he soon began to make good his word[e]; for as soon as day dawned he sent for fifteen eminent Persians, and commanded them to accompany Democedes in taking a view of all the maritime places of Greece, and to bring him back again, without affording him any opportunity of making his escape. After he had given these instructions to the Persians, he sent also for Democedes, and enjoined him to return so soon as he had pointed out and shewn to them all the parts of Greece; he also commanded him to take and carry all his goods and furniture for a present to his father and brothers, promising to furnish him with many times as much at his return. He assured him farther, that he would provide a ship for the transportation of his presents, and would cause all things necessary and convenient for his voyage to be embarked in her. My opinion is, that Darius promised him all these things without any deceitful intention; but Democedes, fearing the king might have a design to try him, did not eagerly receive[f] all that was given, but said, that he would leave his own goods in his house till he should return, and only to accept the ship, which Darius had promised as a present to his brothers. Darius having given him these instructions, sent them down to the coast.

CXXXVI. When they reached Phœnicia and Sidon, a city of Phœnicia, they caused two galleys to be made ready with all diligence for the transportation of their persons, and another ship of great burden to attend them with all things necessary and commodious, they set sail for Greece; where they touched at, and viewed the maritime places, and wrote down a description of them; at length when they had observed whatever is accounted most remarkable in that country, they passed on to Italy, and landed at Tarentum. But Aristophilides, king of the Tarentines, out of favour[g] to Democedes, took off the rudders of the Median ships, and seized all the Persians as spies, and confined them. During which Democedes went to Crotona, and when he had reached his own

[e] Compare Homer's Iliad, xix. v. 242.

[f] Ἐπιτρέχειν signifies *to seize with eagerness.* It is used in the same sense by Appian. Punic. c. 94. Εὗ is an Ionicism for *οὗ, sui ipsius*: it is here written *εὑ* as being an enclitic. *Schweigh.*

[g] Ἐκ ῥηστώνης τῆς Δημοκήδεος. This passage has caused great doubts; *ῥηστώνη* is the same as *ῥαστώνη, indulgentia, facilitas*, and Δημοκήδεος is the genitive used objectively, a relation, which in English is sometimes expressed by prepositions. See Matthiæ's Gr. Gr. 313. The genitive is used in the same way in book v. ch. 43.

country, Aristophilides set the Persians at liberty, and restored all that he had taken out of their ships.

CXXXVII. The Persians set sail from Tarentum in pursuit of Democedes; and arriving in Crotona, found him in the forum, and laid hands on him. Some of the inhabitants, dreading the Persian power, were for delivering him up; but others took hold on the Persians, and beat them with clubs, though they admonished the Crotonians to desist, in these terms: "Men of Crotona, consider what you do, in protect-"ing one who is a fugitive from the king: how will king Da-"rius bear with patience this great insult? And what will be "the event, if you force this man from us? Shall we not cer-"tainly make war against your city before all others, and use "our utmost endeavours to reduce you into servitude?" Yet these words were not sufficient to persuade the Crotonians; for they not only detained Democedes, but seized the merchant-ship that attended the Persians; who, being thus deprived of their guide, reembarked in order to return to Asia, without endeavouring to inform themselves farther concerning Greece. At their departure Democedes required them to tell Darius, that he was engaged to marry the daughter of Milo[h], for he was not ignorant that the name of Milo, the famous Athlete, was well known to the king. And I am inclined to believe, that Democedes spared no expence to hasten the conclusion of this match, that he might appear to Darius to be no inconsiderable person in his own country.

CXXXVIII. After the Persians departed from Crotona, they were driven to Iapygia, and being taken, and made slaves there, were ransomed by Gillus, a banished Tarentine, and conducted by him to Darius: for which service the king professed himself ready to reward Gillus in the manner he should desire. But he, relating the cause of his banishment, asked nothing more than to be restored to his country by the authority of Darius. Yet lest he should throw all Greece into confusion, if on his account a great fleet should be sent through their seas, that he should be satisfied if the Cnidians alone were to restore him; since he thought that a return would be most easily effected by them, as they were in amity with the Tarentines. Darius having undertaken this, performed it; and having dispatched a messenger to require the Cnidians to conduct Gillus to Tarentum, they readily obeyed his orders, but could not persuade the Tarentines, and were not strong enough to constrain them by force. In this man-

[h] Milo carried off the prize of wrestling six times in the Olympic games, and seven times in the Pythian. For a full account of him, see Aulus Gellius Noct. Att. xv. 16.

ner these things passed; and the Persians I have mentioned were the first who went from Asia to discover the affairs of Greece.

CXXXIX. After these transactions, Darius conquered Samos; which was the first of all the cities he took either from the Grecians or Barbarians. The cause was this. During the expedition of Cambyses the son of Cyrus against Egypt, many Grecians resorted thither; some, as one may conjecture, on account of trade, some to serve as soldiers, others to view the country. Among the last was Syloson the son of Æaces, brother to Polycrates, and an exile of Samos. His good fortune led him to make use of a scarlet cloak, with which he covered himself, and walked publicly in the streets of Memphis. Darius, who was one of Cambyses's guards, and made no great figure at that time, saw him and became desirous of the cloak, and went up to him, and asked him if he would sell it[i]. Syloson, perceiving Darius to be passionately fond of the garment, made this answer, as if he had been extraordinarily inspired, "I would not sell my cloak for any riches; "yet, if you desire it so much, I will give it you for a present." Darius, accepting his offer with thanks, took the cloak.

CXL. Syloson thought afterwards that he had lost this cloak by his simple generosity. But when, after the death of Cambyses, and the destruction of the magus by the seven Persians, Darius, who had been one of that number, was advanced to the throne; Syloson, hearing that the kingdom had devolved upon the man he had presented with his cloak in Egypt, went to Susa, and, sitting at the gates of the palace, said he had been a benefactor to Darius: which being reported to the king by one of the door-keepers, he answered with surprize, "What Grecian is this, to whom I, who have "but lately obtained the kingdom, owe gratitude[k] for any "thing? Few or none of that country have come up hither: "nor can I mention any thing which I owe a Greek. How- "ever bring in the man, that I may know the meaning of "his words." The door-keeper presently introduced Syloson, and as he stood in the midst of the company, the interpreters asked him who he was, and what he had done, that he said he had been a benefactor to the king. Then Syloson related what had passed between Darius and himself concerning the cloak; and having said that he was the person who had made him that present, the king answered, "O thou most generous "of men! art thou then the man who made me a present, "when as yet I had no power? and although it was small,

[i] For the force of the imperfect *ὠνέετο*, see note on book i. ch. 68.

[k] The word *προαιδεῖσθαι* is used in the same sense, book i. ch. 61.

ng from the citadel to the sea. In the mean time Charilaus, having armed the auxiliaries, set open the gates, and sallying out upon the Persians, who expected not any hostility, and thought every thing had been agreed, surprised and killed the principal men among them as they were sitting in their seats. But the rest of the army taking the alarm, came into their succour, and repulsed the auxiliaries into the citadel.

CXLVII. When Otanes, the general, saw the great loss he had sustained by the slaughter of these Persians, he neglected to obey the orders given him by Darius at his departure, importing that he should neither kill nor take prisoner any Samian, but deliver the island to Syloson without damage; and on the contrary commanded his army to put all the Samians they should find to the sword, without sparing the children. So that while one part of his forces was employed in besieging the citadel, the rest killed all they met, as well within the temples as in other places.

CXLVIII. Mæandrius made his escape by sea, and fled from Samos to Lacedæmon; and after his arrival, when he had placed in safety the riches he had carried off, he did as follows. When he had set out his cups of gold and silver, his servants began to clean them, and at the same time holding a conversation with Cleomenes the son of Anaxandrides, and then king of Sparta, he conducted him to his house. The king, viewing the cups, was filled with surprise and astonishment, which Mæandrius perceiving, solicited him to take whatever he desired, and repeated his offer several times. But Cleomenes shewed himself a most upright man, by refusing stedfastly to accept any thing; and afterwards considering that by giving to other citizens he would get assistance[l], he went to the Ephori, and told them it would be more expedient to expel this Samian out of Peloponnesus, lest he should corrupt him or others of the Spartans. Upon which they took his advice, and banished him by public proclamation.

CXLIX. In the mean time, the Persians having taken Samos as in a net[m], put it into the hands of Syloson[n] entirely destitute of inhabitants. But Otanes, the Persian general, repeopled the city afterwards, upon a vision he saw in a dream, and a distemper which seized him in his private parts.

[l] *Τιμωρίῃ* is used in this sense in Thucyd. i. 58. and a few lines after, *εὕροντο* in the same sense as *εὑρήσεται* in the present passage. See Valckenaer's note.

[m] The manner of taking an island in this way is described in book vi. ch. 31.

[n] Syloson had a son named Æaces, as his father was, who succeeded him in the kingdom of Samos, and was dethroned by Aristagoras of Miletus. See book vi. ch. 13.

CL. Whilst these forces were employed in this naval expedition against Samos, the Babylonians revolted, being very well prepared in every thing. For during the usurpation of the magus, and the insurrection of the seven, they had made use of those times of confusion to prepare themselves to sustain a siege, and had not been discovered. But when they appeared in open rebellion, they took the following method to prevent the consumption of their provisions. They preserved their mothers in general; and after they had permitted every man to select besides one female from his family whom he liked best, to make his bread, they assembled all the rest together and strangled them[o].

CLI. Darius, being informed of these affairs, drew all his forces out, marched to Babylon and besieged the city. But the Babylonians, not at all solicitous about the event, mounting the ramparts of the wall, fell to dancing, and derided Darius with his army, and some one among them spoke in this manner to the Persians: "What business have you here "to detain you? decamp rather and march off, for you will "not be masters of this place until mules bring forth;" which words were spoken by the Babylonian in full assurance that a mule could never breed.

CLII. When Darius had spent a year and seven months before Babylon, and as well as his army became annoyed at not being able to take the city, he endeavoured by various stratagems and artifices to take the place, and, among others, he tried that in particular by which Cyrus took it; but all his efforts were rendered ineffectual by the unwearied vigilance of the Babylonians.

CLIII. In the twentieth month of this siege a prodigy happened in the quarters of Zopyrus the son of Megabyzus, one of the seven Persians who dethroned the magus; for a mule that carried his provisions brought forth, which Zopyrus hearing, and doubting the truth of so strange an event, he went to the place, and, after he had fully satisfied himself, strictly commanded all that were present to conceal the thing: and because he well remembered the words of the Babylonian, who at the beginning of the siege said, "The city "might be taken when mules, barren as they were[p], should

[o] By this action the prophecy of Isaiah was fulfilled, ch. xlvii. ver. 9. "But "these two things shall come to thee "in a moment in one day, the loss of "children, and widowhood: they shall "come upon thee in their perfection, "for the multitude of thy sorceries, and "for the great abundance of thine en-"chantments."

[p] Mules rarely engender. When it did sometimes happen, it was regarded as a prodigy which required expiations. Pliny, Nat. Hist. viii. 44. says, "*Theo-"phrastus vulgo parere in Cappadocia "tradit: sed esse id animal ibi sui ge-"neris.*" *Larcher*.

The particle περ gives great force to the expression; so in Homer, Iliad xx.

"breed;" he concluded that the man had spoken, and the mule brought a colt, by the influence of a divine power; on account, therefore, of the presage[q] of this saying, he thought that Babylon might be taken.

CLIV. In this persuasion Zopyrus went to Darius, and asked him whether he very much valued the taking of Babylon, and having learnt that he valued it at a high price, he began to consider by what means he alone might accomplish the work; for among the Persians great achievements are honoured in a very great degree. And after mature deliberation, finding no other possible way to compass his design than by mutilating his body, and in that condition deserting to the enemy, he considered that as a light matter, and inflicted on himself an irremediable mutilation; for having cut off his nose and ears, he whipped himself, and cut his hair in a shocking manner, and went thus into the presence of Darius.

CLV. Darius was very much grieved when he beheld a man of his rank so ignominiously treated, and having leaped hastily from his throne, with loud exclamation asked who had been the author of that outrage, and on what occasion; "There is no one," answered Zopyrus, "but yourself who "could have sufficient power to treat me in this manner; no "stranger has done this, but I have done it to myself, as I "considered it a particular indignity that the Assyrians "should deride the Persians." "Wretched man," said Darius, "thou hast endeavoured to put the fairest name on the "foulest action; pretending to have inflicted this indignity "on thyself by reason of the siege. Art thou so foolish to "believe the Babylonians will surrender the sooner because "you are mutilated? Have you not lost your senses[r], since "you have thus ruined yourself?" "Had I," replied Zopyrus, "informed you of my intentions, you would not have "permitted me to proceed; but because I consulted only "with myself, I have executed my design, and if you do not "fail we shall take Babylon. For I will desert to the Babylonians in this condition, and tell them I have suffered "these indignities from you; and when I shall have persuaded them of my sincerity, I doubt not to obtain the "command of their forces. My opinion therefore is, that on "the tenth day after my departure you would command a "thousand men of those whose loss you do not regard to

ver. 65. Τά τε στύγεουσι θεοί περ, *which the Gods, as many as there are*, &c. See Hoogeveen, Doctrina Partic. Græc. xliv. 3. *Larcher.*

[q] Φημη is what the Latins called *omen.* "*Omen,*" says Festus, *quasi* "*ormen, quia fit ab ore.*"

[r] Ἐκπλώειν, literally, *to sail out of harbour.* The word is used in the same way in book vi. ch. 12.

"march up to the gate of Semiramis, two thousand on the "seventh day after to the gate of Ninus, and after an interval of twenty days, four thousand more to that of the "Chaldæans; but let neither the first nor these carry any "other arms than swords only for their defence. After the "twentieth day is passed, command all the rest of the army "to march up directly to the walls, with particular orders to "the Persians to post themselves at the gates of Belus and "Cissia; for unless I deceive myself, the Babylonians will "not fail among other things to entrust me with the keys of "the gates, in consideration of my great actions; and then "I and the Persians will take care to perform the rest."

CLVI. When he had given this advice, he took his way towards the city, and frequently turned round to look behind him, as if forsooth he was really a deserter. The guards who were placed on the towers seeing him approaching, went down, and drawing back one door of the gate a little, asked him who he was, and what business brought him thither. He answered, he was Zopyrus, and desired to be received into the city, which the guards hearing, they conducted him to the assembly of the nation[a]; when he was brought before it, he began to deplore his condition, and assured them he had suffered from Darius what indeed he had done to himself, for advising him to break up the siege, because he saw no means of taking the city. "Now therefore," said he to the Babylonians, "I put myself into your hands, with a resolution to "do you the greatest service, and all possible mischief to "Darius, his army, and to the Persians; for he certainly "shall not escape with impunity, since he has thus disgracefully mutilated me, as I am perfectly informed of all his "counsels and designs."

CLVII. The Babylonians, seeing a man of that distinction among the Persians deprived of his ears and nose, and covered with stripes and blood, never doubted the truth of his words; and assuring themselves of his assistance, shewed a readiness to grant him whatever he would ask. Accordingly he desired the command of some forces; and having obtained his request, acted as he had preconcerted with Darius: for on the tenth day he sallied out of the city at the head of the Babylonians, and surrounding the thousand men that he had instructed Darius first to place there, he cut them all in pieces on the spot. When the Babylonians saw that his actions were suitable to his promises, they expressed their joy in an ex-

[a] Τὰ κοινὰ signifies either *the assembly of the people*, or that of *the senate and people*, or that of *the senate* only; according to the form of government established in Babylon. I am inclined to the second. *Larcher.*

traordinary manner, and declared themselves ready to supply him with all things he should demand. Zopyrus therefore, at the time prefixed by Darius and himself, drew out another party, and killed two thousand more of his men; which second action so pleased the Babylonians, that the name of Zopyrus became the general subject of their praises. In conclusion, he marched out a third time, and leading his troops to the place appointed, surprised and cut in pieces the other four thousand. Upon which success Zopyrus acquired so great credit in Babylon, that he was constituted general, and guardian of their walls.

CLVIII. But when Darius made an assault all round the city, pursuant to the agreement they had made, then Zopyrus discovered his treachery; for whilst the Babylonians were defending themselves from the walls against the army of Darius, Zopyrus opened the gates of Belus and Cissia, and introduced the Persians into the city. Those who saw this traitorous action, fled into the temple of Jupiter Belus; and those who perceived nothing of what passed, continued in their several posts, till they also discovered that they had been betrayed.

CLIX. Thus Babylon was taken a second time; and Darius, becoming master of the place, not only demolished the walls and gates[1] which had been left entire by Cyrus, but commanded about three thousand of the principal leaders to be impaled, and then gave leave to the rest to continue in their habitations. And because the Babylonians had strangled their women, as I said before, in order to prevent the consumption of their provisions, he took care to furnish them wives, that they might not be destitute of children; and to that end enjoined the neighbouring provinces to send a certain number of women to Babylon, taxing each at a certain number, so that altogether fifty thousand came together; and from these the Babylonians of our time are descended.

CLX. No Persian, in the opinion of Darius, either of those who came after, or lived before, surpassed Zopyrus in great achievements, Cyrus only excepted; with whom no Persian ever thought himself worthy to be compared. It is also reported that he frequently used to say, he would rather wish Zopyrus had suffered no hurt, than to acquire twenty more

[1] It must be remarked, that Darius lived about a century and a half before Alexander, in whose time the walls appear to have been in their original state; or at least, nothing is said that implies the contrary. And it cannot be believed, that if Darius had even taken the trouble to level thirty-four miles, of so prodigious a rampart as that of Babylon, that ever it would have been rebuilt in the manner described by Ctesias, Clitarchus, and others, who describe it at a much later period. Besides, it would have been quite unnecessary to level more than *a part* of the wall to lay the place open: and in this way probably the historian ought to be understood. *Larcher.*

Babylon. However, he rewarded him magnificently; for besides annual presents, consisting of all those things which are accounted most honourable among the Persians, he gave him the revenues of Babylon for life, free from any manner of charge. Megabyzus, afterwards general in Egypt against the Athenians[u] and their allies, was son of this Zopyrus[x], and father to another of that name, who abandoned the Persians, and voluntarily deserted to Athens.

[u] This is related in Thucydides, book i. chapters 104, 109, &c.

[x] Zobyrus, son of Megabyzus, and grandson of the famous Zopyrus, revolted from Artaxerxes (Ctesias apud Phot. Cod. 72. p. 124) after the death of his father and mother, and advanced towards Athens, on account of the friendship which subsisted between his mother and the Athenians. He went by sea to Caunus, and commanded the inhabitants to give up the place to the Athenians, who were with him. The Caunians replied, that they were willing to surrender it to him, but they refused to admit any Athenians. Upon this he mounted the wall; but a Caunian, named Alcides, knocked him on the head with a stone. His grandmother Amestris afterwards crucified this Caunian. *Larcher.*

THE

HISTORY

OF

HERODOTUS.

BOOK IV.

MELPOMENE.

AFTER the reduction of Babylon, Darius next undertook an expedition against Scythia; and seeing Asia flourishing in men and riches, grew very desirous to revenge himself upon the Scythians, who without provocation had formerly invaded the territories of Media, and defeated all those who appeared in arms against them. The Scythians, as I have said already[a], continued twenty-eight years in the possession of Upper Asia, having entered those provinces in pursuit of the Cimmerians, and suppressed the power of the Medes, who before that time were masters of all Asia. But after they had spent so many years abroad, they met with as great difficulties in returning to their own country, after such an interval, as they had encountered before in Media, and found an army of no inconsiderable force ready to oppose their entrance; for during so long a time of absence, the wives of those Scythians had used the company of their slaves.

II. The Scythians deprive all their slaves of sight for the sake of the milk[b] which they drink, and which they milk in this manner; they have bones shaped like flutes, which being applied to the genital part of a mare, one of these slaves

[a] See book i. ch. 103 and 105.

[b] Homer calls them Galactophagi and Hippomolgi. "J'entendis et vis moi-"même, à Basra," dit M. Niebuhr, (Descript. de l'Arab. p. 146.) "que "lorsqu'un Arabe trait la femelle du "buffle, un autre lui fourre la main et "le bras jusqu'au coude dans la *vulva*, "parce qu'on prétend savoir par expé-"rience, qu'étant chatouillée de la "sorte, elle donne plus de lait. Cette "méthode ressemble beaucoup à celle "des Scythes." *Larcher*.

blows with his mouth whilst another milks the beast. They say this is practised, because the veins of the mare, being thus inflated, are filled, and the dugs are depressed. When they have finished milking, they pour it into hollow vessels of wood, the blind men, placed in order[c] round the tubs, agitate it for some time; then they skim off the substance which lies uppermost[d], which they esteem the most precious, leaving the rest, as of less value. And on this account the Scythians put out the eyes of all the prisoners they take; for they do not apply themselves to husbandry, but only to the keeping of cattle.

III. Born of these slaves and the wives of the Scythians a new generation had grown up, who knowing their own extraction, marched out to oppose the return of those who came from Media. To this end they cut off the country by a broad ditch[e], carried on from mount Taurus to the very large lake Mæotis; and afterwards they encamped opposite, and came to an engagement with the Scythians, who were endeavouring to force a passage. The Scythians repeated the attempt several times, and were unable to obtain any advantage; upon which one among them said, "Men of Scythia, what are we doing by making war with our slaves? If we are killed our own power diminishes, and, if we kill, we lessen the number of those we ought to command. My opinion therefore is, that we should lay aside our bows and spears, and every one taking his horsewhip in his hand, go directly to them in that way; for so long as they saw us armed, so long they considered themselves equal to us, and born of as good blood as we; but when they shall perceive

[c] Literally, Having placed the blind men in a continued series round, &c. Περιστίζειν is used in the same sense in ch. 202.

[d] It is somewhat surprising that neither the Greeks nor the Latins had any word to express *cream*. *Larcher*.

[e] The Chersonesus Taurica is surrounded on all sides by the Euxine, the Cimmerian Bosphorus, and the Palus Mæotis, except in one narrow neck, which separates the gulf of Carcinitis from the Palus Mæotis. It is in this spot, I suppose, that the trench mentioned by Herodotus was sunk. It commences at the spot called Taphræ, where we now find the city Précops; which, according to P. Briet, in Tartary, signifies *a trench*. The Emperor, Constantine Porphyrogenitus (de Administ. Imp. 42.) tells us, that in his time the trench was filled up. The mountains of which Herodotus speaks were within Tauris, there are none *without*. *Larcher*.

Herodotus speaks again of the same trench in ch. 20. as the eastern boundary of the Royal Scythians. No mountains, however, are marked in any position corresponding to the above idea; and we have never heard of any mountains of *Tauris*, save those within the *Krimea*. It is probable, therefore, that the trench intended was that which shut up the peninsula; and more especially as such trenches or walls, or both, are clearly pointed out by other historians. In this case, therefore, some other word than *mountains* should be read; and the trench (which in fortification always implies a rampart also) would have been drawn from the Palus Mæotis to the opposite shore of Tauris. *Rennel*, p. 95.

"us approaching with our whips instead of arms, they will "soon be convinced they are our servants, and under that "apprehension will resist no more."

IV. The Scythians did as he advised, and the slaves, struck with astonishment, forgot they were to fight, and fled away. Thus the Scythians, who had the dominion of Asia, and were afterwards expelled by the Medes, returned to their own country; and Darius, desiring to take revenge, assembled an army in order to invade their territories.

V. The Scythians say their nation is of a later original[f] than any other, and began in this manner. The first man that appeared in Scythia, then an uninhabited desert, was Targitaus[g], concerning whom they relate things incredible to me; for they affirm that he was born of Jupiter and a daughter of the river Borysthenes; that he had three sons, who went by the names of Lipoxais, Apoxais, and Colaxais; that during their reign a plough, with a yoke, an axe, and a bowl, all of gold, fell down from heaven into Scythia; that the eldest, who saw those things first, approached with design to take them up, and as he approached, the gold burst out into a blaze; when he had retired the second went up, and the gold became as before; the blazing gold accordingly repulsed these, but when the youngest went up, it became extinguished and he carried them home with him; and that the elder brothers having learnt this event, surrendered the kingdom to the youngest.

VI. They farther say, that those Scythians, who are called Auchatæ, are descended from Lipoxais; those, who are called Catiari, and Traspies, from the second Apoxais; and the race of their kings, which they call Paralatæ, from Colaxais, the third son of Targitaus. They give themselves the general name of Scoloti, which is also the surname of their king; but the Grecians call them Scythians.

VII. This account they give of their original, and reckon about a thousand years at most from the reign of Targitaus, the first king of Scythia, to the time that Darius crossed over against them. The kings take all imaginable care to preserve the sacred gold, and annually approach it with magnificent sacrifices in order to render it propitious. If he who has the guard of these things on the festival day happen to fall asleep in the open air, the Scythians say he cannot live

[f] Justin (Hist. ii. 1.) says, that the Scythians contended with the Egyptians concerning their antiquity. See Rennel, p. 80.

[g] The Targitaus of Herodotus has in its root some affinity to the name Turk; as that of Paralatæ, the tribe descended from the youngest son of Targitaus, has to Perlas, or Berlas, which designed the tribe last in rank of those descended from Turk. Targitaus was the son of Jupiter; Turk of Japhet. See D'Herbelot, Art. Turk. *Rennel*, p. 73.

through the year, and therefore make him a present of as much land as he can ride over on horseback in one day[h]. Colaxais, perceiving the country to be of vast extent, divided the kingdom between his three sons, and made that share most considerable where the gold which fell from heaven is kept. The Scythians say that those parts which are situate to the northward of their territories, can neither be seen nor passed through, by reason of the feathers[i] that fall continually on all sides: for the earth is entirely covered, and the air so full of these feathers, which shut out the view.

VIII. These things are related by the Scythians concerning themselves, and the regions that lie above them; but the Greeks who inhabit Pontus give a different account, and say, that as Hercules was driving away the cows of Geryon, he arrived in the country now possessed by the Scythians, which was then an uninhabited desert; and that Geryon lived in an island, by the Greeks called Erythia, beyond the Pontus, and situate not far from Gades, beyond the columns of Hercules in the ocean. They likewise affirm that the ocean, beginning in the east, flows round the whole earth, but do not demonstrate it by fact: that Hercules, in his return, passed through the country which is now called Scythia, and as a storm and frost overtook him, he drew his lion's skin over him and went to sleep; and in the meanwhile his mares, which were feeding apart from his chariot, vanished by some divine interference.

IX. They add, that Hercules, when he awoke, sought them all over the country, and coming to a place called Hylæa[k], found a monster[l] of an ambiguous nature, resembling a virgin from the thighs upwards, and a serpent in the lower parts. Astonished at the sight, he asked her if she had seen his mares. She told him they were in her power, but that she would not restore them unless he would lie with her; to which he consented on these terms. Nevertheless she delayed to perform her promise, out of a desire to enjoy the company of Hercules as long as she could; he however was

[h] This was not given, says Larcher, because he would not live through the year; but, on account of the danger, this reward was given to him who had properly watched it.

[i] See chap. 31.

[k] Hylæa was the name of the peninsula adjacent to Taurica on the N. W. formed by the lower part of the Borysthenes, the Euxine, the gulf of Carcinitis, and the river Hypacyris, which flowed into it. It is now named *Jambeylouk*. This tract, unlike the rest of *maritime* Scythia had trees in it. This circumstance is not only confirmed by Pliny, but by the testimony of Baron Tott in modern times, which is very satisfactory. This province was also remarkable for containing a flat tract of a very singular form, (that of a sword,) which projected into the sea, called the course of Achilles. *Rennel*, p. 63.

[l] M. Pelloutier calls this monster a Siren. But Homer represents the Sirens as very beautiful women. Diodor. Sic. (ii. 43.) describes this monster in the same way as Herodotus. He makes her the mistress of Jupiter, by whom she had Scythes. *Larcher*.

desirous of recovering them and departing; at last she restored the mares, and spoke to him in these terms: "I preserved your mares when they strayed hither, and you "have given me the recompence of my care, for I have three "sons by you; tell me, therefore, how I shall dispose of them "when they are grown up: whether they shall continue to "live in this country, where I am mistress, or whether I shall "send them to you." To this question Hercules answered: "When you see the children arrived to the age of men, you "cannot err if you do this: give this country to that son "whom you shall find capable of drawing this bow, and putting on this belt as I do, and send away those who shall fall "short of these injunctions. If you do this, you will consult "your own happiness, and perform my orders."

X. Then having drawn one of his bows, (for he carried two at that time,) and having shewn her the belt, he put into her hands both the bow and the belt, which had a golden cup hanging at the clasp, and afterwards departed. When her sons had attained to the age of men, she named the eldest Agathyrsis, the second Gelonus, and the youngest Scythes; and remembering the orders of Hercules, put them in execution as he had enjoined; but finding two of her sons, Agathyrsis and Gelonus, unable to come up to the proposed standard, she sent them out of the country, retaining Scythes, her youngest son, with her, because he had accomplished the will of his father. All those who have in succession ruled over Scythia have been the descendants of this Scythes the son of Hercules; and from his time the Scythians have always carried a cup fastened to their belts. These things are reported by the Grecians who inhabit Pontus.

XI. But another relation, which seems more probable to me, runs in this manner. The Scythian Nomades were once inhabitants of Asia, and being harrassed by the Massagetæ with frequent wars, they passed the river Araxes, and entered the country of the Cimmerians; who, they say, were the ancient possessors of those regions which are now inhabited by the Scythians. The Cimmerians, finding themselves invaded by the Scythians with a numerous army, assembled in council, but could not come to any agreement, because the kings and the people were of different sentiments; both violently supported, though that of the kings was the more brave: for the people were of opinion that it would be best to retreat[m], and that there was no necessity to run into any hazard against

[m] Since *πρῆγμά ἐστι*, with an infinitive after it, signifies *it is worth while and useful to do this*, it can scarcely obtain that meaning without understanding *πρῆγμά ἐστι δεόμενον, the thing requires, the case demands, that this should be done.* So that there is no necessity to alter the reading. *Schweigh.*

so great a multitude; but the kings on the contrary advised that they should fight it out with the invaders of their country. Thus when neither the people would assent to the persuasions of the kings, nor the kings to those of the people; and one party resolved to depart without fighting, and leave their possessions to the invaders, whilst the other, reflecting on the great advantages they had enjoyed at home, and the apparent evils they must suffer if they should forsake their country, determined to die, and be buried in their own country, and not to betake themselves to flight with the multitude. In this contrariety of opinions they divided, and being equal in numbers, the two parties engaged in battle; and all those who fell in the dispute were buried by the rest of the people near the river Tyras, where their sepulchre remains to this day. When the Cimmerians had performed that office, they abandoned the country, and the Scythians, when they arrived, took possession of the deserted country.

XII. There are even to this day in Scythia fortifications and Porthmia[n], which retain the name of Cimmerian, together with a whole province, and a bosphorus or narrow sea. It appears certain that the Cimmerians fled from the Scythians into Asia, and settled in that peninsula where the city of Sinope, a colony of the Grecians, was afterwards built; and it is no less evident that the Scythians, pursuing them, mistook their way and entered Media: for the Cimmerians, in all their flight, never abandoned the coast of the sea; whereas the Scythians in their pursuit leaving mount Caucasus on the right hand, deflected towards the midland countries, and so entered Media. This report is generally current, as well among the Grecians as Barbarians.

XIII. But Aristeas[o], a poet of Proconnesus, and son to Caustrobius, says in his verses, that he was transported by Apollo into the territories of the Issedones, beyond which the Arimaspians inhabit, who are a people that have only one

[n] This, according to Stephan. Byz. was the name of a village at the mouth of the Palus Mæotis. *Wesseling.*

Respecting the *walls*, &c. still found in the time of Herodotus under the name of Cimmerian, he does not say that they were in the peninsula, but the context implies it, and it is not improbable that he had seen them. Baron Tott saw in the mountainous part of the Krimea, ancient castles and other buildings, a part of which were *excavated* from the *live* rock, together with subterraneous passages from one to the other. These were, he says, always on mountains difficult of access. He refers them to the *Genoese;* with what justice we know not; it is possible they might have *made use* of them, but it is more probable that these are the works alluded to by our author, for it may be remarked that works of this kind are commonly of very ancient date. *Rennel*, p. 74.

[o] He wrote an epic poem in three books, upon the wars of the Griffins and Arimaspians. Longinus (X.) has recorded six of his verses, which he considers rather florid than sublime. Tzetzes (Chiliad. vii. 688.) has preserved six more. *Larcher.*

ye; that the next region abounds in griffins[p], which guard he gold of the country; and that the Hyperboreans are ituate yet farther, and extend themselves to the sea; that ll these, except the Hyperboreans, following the example f the Arimaspians, were continually employed in making war against their neighbours; that the Issedones were exelled by the Arimaspians, the Scythians by the Issedones, nd that the Cimmerians, who inhabited on the south sea, were forced by the Scythians to abandon their country. So hat this Aristeas also does not agree with the Scythians n the account he gives of these regions.

XIV. I have already mentioned the place of his birth, and hall now add what I heard concerning him in Proconnesus nd Cyzicus. Aristeas, say they, who was inferior to no nan of the city in family, entering one day into a fuller's hop, died suddenly: upon which the fuller, after he had hut up his door, went and acquainted the relations of the leceased with what had happened. When the news of his leath had spread over the city, a certain Cyzicenian arriving from Artace, disputed the truth of the report, affirming that he had seen and conversed with him in his way to Cyzicus[q]; and while he persisted obstinately to maintain his assertion, the relations of Aristeas had been at the fuller's shop with ll things necessary for carrying out the body to be buried, out could not find him either alive or dead. In the seventh year he appeared again in Proconnesus, composed those verses, which by the Greeks are called Arimaspian, and then lisappeared a second time. These things are commonly reported in the cities I have mentioned.

XV. But to my own knowledge the following circumstance happened among the Metapontines of Italy, three hundred and forty years after the second disappearing of Aristeas the Proconnesian, as I found by computation in Proconnesus and Metapontum; at which time, the Metapontines say, Aristeas appeared in their city, and exhorted them to erect an altar to Apollo, and a statue by that altar, which should bear the name of Aristeas the Proconnesian, telling them, "they were "the only nation of the Italian coast, which had ever been "favoured with the presence of Apollo; that he himself

[p] These are not people, but fabulous animals. Pausanias (Attic. i. p. 57.) says, that Aristeas describes them as animals resembling lions, with the beaks and wings of an eagle. *Larcher*. These griffins are mentioned by Æsch. Prom. Vinc. 830.

[q] Plutarch (in Romulo, p. 35.) relates a story of a certain Cleomedes of Astypalæa, who seeing himself pursued, jumped into a great chest, which closed upon him; after many ineffectual attempts to open it, they broke it in pieces, but no Cleomedes was to be found, alive or dead. I should never end, were I to wish to relate all the similar stories that there are, ancient and modern. *Larcher*.

"attended the God, and was then a crow[r], though now he "went under the name of Aristeas." Having pronounced these words, he vanished; and the Metapontines say they sent to Delphi to inquire of the God concerning the apparition, and that the Pythian in answer admonished them to obey the phantom, and their affairs should be prosperous. In pursuance therefore of this oracle, they did as Aristeas had desired; and his statue is seen to this day in the public place, erected near the image of Apollo, and surrounded with laurels. Thus much concerning Aristeas.

XVI. No man knows with certainty the countries that lie beyond those, about which I design to speak; neither could I ever hear of a person who had viewed them with his own eyes. Aristeas himself, who is just now mentioned, says in his verses, that he went no farther than the Issedones, and that he learnt from them whatever he relates touching those parts. Nevertheless I shall relate with accuracy[s] as much I have been able to learn by the reports of others.

XVII. From the port of the Borysthenitæ[t], which is situate exactly in the midst of the maritime places of Scythia, the first people are the Callipidæ[u], who derive their original from Greece; and next to these is another nation, called Alazones[x]. Both these observe the customs of the Scythians, except only that they sow wheat, onions, garlic, lentils, and millet, for food; whereas the Scythians, who lie beyond the Alazones, and are husbandmen, sow wheat, not for food, but sale. The Neuri[y] dwell above these, and as far as I am able to learn, the parts to the north of their country are utterly uninhabited. These nations are situate along the river Hypanis, on the west side of the Borysthenes.

XVIII. But if we pass over to the other side of the Borysthenes from the sea, we shall first enter into Hylæa[z], and then into another region, possessed by Scythians, who apply

[r] "Aristeæ enim visam (animam) "evolantem ex ore in Proconneso, corvi "effigie, magna, quæ sequitur, fabulosi-"tate." Pliny, Hist. Nat. vii. 52.

[s] Notwithstanding some ambiguities, and apparent contradictions, in the geography of Scythia, Herodotus had certainly paid uncommon attention to the subject; and by the solemnity of his declaration at setting out, we may suppose that he meant to be very impressive. And perhaps it has seldom happened, that a traveller who collected his information concerning the geography of so extensive a tract, in so casual a way, has produced a description in which so many circumstances have been found to agree. *Rennel*, p. 81.

[t] The port of Cherson, (near the embouchure of this grand river,) rendered famous by the marine arsenals and docks, established by the immortal Catharine of Russia, must be nearly in the same situation with the port of the Borysthenitæ. *Rennel*, p. 57.

[u] These are the Callipodes of Solinus, and appear to have occupied the lower course of the Hypanis. *Rennel*, p. 72.

[x] These must be placed in part of Padolia and Braclaw. *Rennel*, ibid.

[y] See ch. 51, 105.

[z] See note on ch. 9.

ıemselves to agriculture, and are called Borysthenitæ[a] by ıose Greeks who inhabit on the Hypanis, though they give ıemselves the name of Olbiopolitans. These Scythian husandmen possess, to the eastward, a country of three days' ›urney, extending to the river called Panticapes; and of leven days' sail[b] up the Borysthenes to the northward. Beond this region the country is desert for a great distance, nd beyond that desert lies a country inhabited by the Androhagi[c], or men-eaters, who are a distinct people, and not of ›cythian extraction. All beyond this is entirely desert, no ıen being found there, that we know.

XIX. To the eastward of those Scythians who apply hemselves to the culture of land, and on the other side of the iver Panticapes the country is inhabited by Scythians, who either plough nor sow, but are employed in keeping cattle; one of those parts produce trees, except Hylæa only. These erdsmen possess a tract of land of fourteen days' journey owards the east, as far as the river Gerrhus.

XX. On the other side of this river is situated that which s called the *royal country*[d], and the most numerous and nost valiant of the Scythians, who think all the rest to be ›nly their slaves. Their country extends towards the south s far as mount Taurus, and towards the east to the intrenchnents that were made by the sons of the blind men, and to he port of Cremni, on the lake Mæotis; besides that part vhich borders upon the river Tanais. Above these Royal Scythians, the Melanchlæni[e] inhabit to the northward; a disinct nation, and not of Scythian race. But beyond them all s full of fens, and uninhabited, as we are informed.

XXI. The regions that lie beyond the river Tanais are no ›art of Scythia. The first portion belongs to the Sauromatæ[f], vho inhabit a country of fifteen days' journey from the farhest part of the lake Mæotis to the northward, destitute of ıll kind of trees, either wild or cultivated. Above these the Budini[g] occupy the second division, and they inhabit a counry covered with all sorts of trees.

XXII. Towards the north, above the Budini, there is at irst a desert of seven days' journey. Next to which, and a

[a] It would appear from ch. 53, that hese people dwell also on the west side ›f the Borysthenes, near its mouth, as ar as the influx of the Hypanis, (Bog.) *Rennel*, p. 65.

[b] In ch. 53. he says ten.

[c] See ch. 106.

[d] According to these notices, the Royal Scythians, who may be consilered as the great body of *freemen* of the nation, occupied the tract, generally, between the Mæotis on the south, the Tanais on the east, the river Gherrus and the Nomades on the west, and the river Desna and its eastern branch on the north. *Rennel*, p. 72.

[e] See ch. 107.

[f] See ch. 116.

[g] See ch. 108.

little deflecting to the eastward, the Thyssagetæ inhabit, who are a separate people, very numerous, and support themselves by hunting. The Iyrcæ[h] are contiguous to these, and possess the same region; these subsist also by hunting in this manner: they climb the trees (which abound in all places) and wait for the game, attended by a dog and a horse, taught to lie down upon his belly, that he may not be much above the ground. When the hunter sees the beast from the tree, he lets fly an arrow, mounts his horse, and pursues with his dog. The next region to the eastward is inhabited by Scythians, who, separating from the Royal Scythians, settled themselves there.

XXIII. Thus far Scythia is a plain country, and of a deep soil; but the rest is rocky and uneven. After passing through a considerable space of the rough country, a people are found living at the foot of some lofty mountains, who are said to be, both men and women, bald from their infancy. They have flat noses[i], and great chins, speak a peculiar language, wear the Scythian habit, and feed upon the fruit of a tree which they call ponticon, equal to the fig-tree, as near as may be, in size, and bearing fruit like a bean, with a kernel. When this fruit is ripe, they press and strain it through cloth, and squeeze out a thick and black liquor, called aschy, which they suck, and drink mingled with milk, making cakes of the sediment, to serve instead of other food; for they have few cattle in these parts, as they have no good pastures. They sleep in the winter under trees, which are covered with a thick white wool; in the summer without any other covering than the tree. No man offers violence to this people, for they are accounted sacred, and have no warlike weapon among them. They determine the differences that arise among their neighbours; and whoever flies thither for refuge, is permitted to live unmolested. They go by the name of Argippæi[k].

[h] It is in vain that M. M. Falconet and Mallet are desirous of reading here Τύρκοι, *the Turks*, the same as it occurs in Pomponius Mela; (i. 19;) it would be better, with Pintianus, to correct the text of the geographer by that of Herodotus. Pliny also (vi. 7.) joins this people with the Thyssagetæ. *Larcher.*

[i] The Tartars at present have flat noses. *Larcher.*

[k] We regard the Argippæi as the people who inhabited the eastern part of the *great Steppe*, bordering *northward* on the great chain of mountains that divides the *Steppe* from S.E. to N.W. and which separates the northern from the southern waters in that quarter. It is a marked feature in the geography; and is described by the Arabian geographers to be remarkably lofty, steep, and difficult of access.

The Argippæi would also border eastward, on the mountains that separate the Oigur country from the Steppe, or which, perhaps with more propriety, may be regarded as the western declivity of the elevated region, inhabited by the Kalmuc Eluths. A part of these mountains are named *Arga* and *Argia*, in the Strahlenberg, and the map of Russia. According to these suppositions, the Argippæi must have occupied the northern part of the tract now in possession of the *greater* or *eastern* horde of the *Kirgees*,

XXIV. As far as these bald people, the country and the nations which are before them are very clearly known[l]; for some Scythians frequently go there, of whom it is easy to learn by inquiry, as also some of the Greeks, who inhabit the ports of the Borysthenes, and of Pontus. The Scythians who go to this country transact business by means of seven interpreters and seven languages.

XXV. Thus far, therefore, things are known; but no man can speak with certainty of those regions that are situate beyond these bald men, for high and inaccessible mountains separate the country, and no one crosses them; but these bald men pretend that those mountains are inhabited by men who have feet like goats[m], which is to me incredible; and that beyond those hills another people is found, who sleep continually the space of six months, which I do not at all admit. We certainly know that the Issedones[n] inhabit to the eastward of this bald nation; but whatever lies to the northward, either of the Argippæi or Issedones, is utterly unknown, except only from what they are pleased to tell us[o].

XXVI. The Issedones are said to observe these customs. When a man's father dies, all his relations bring sheep, which when they have sacrificed, and divided into pieces, they likewise cut up the body of the dead parent of their host, and having mingled all this flesh together, sit down to feast. Then taking off the hair, and cleansing the head, they gild the skull[p], and annually celebrate magnificent sacrifices to it, and use it as a sacred vessel. Every son performs these funeral rites to his father, as a Greek solemnizes the day of his father's death[q]. This nation is likewise accounted just,

who are dependant on China, as the middle and western hordes are on Russia. *Rennel*, p. 134.

[l] Πολλὴ *περιφάνεια* does not signify an extensive view, but a clear knowledge of, &c. *Wesseling*.

[m] Larcher supposes that those men are called figuratively goat-footed who climb the precipices of mountains like goats.

[n] These may be regarded as the ancestors of the people now denominated *Oigurs* or *Yugures* by the Tartars, *Eluts* or *Eluths* by the Chinese. *Rennel*, p. 134.

[o] For a more full account of the several nations mentioned in Herodotus, the reader is referred to Rennel, sect. 4, 5, &c.

[p] We learn from Livy, (xxiii. 24.) that the Boii, a people of Gaul, did exactly the same with respect to the skulls of their enemies.

It appears that the Issedones do the same by the skulls of their *friends*, as the Scythians and others with those of their *inveterate enemies*. The author has seen brought from *Bootan*, nearly in the same region with *Oigur*, (the country of the *Issedones*,) skulls that were taken out of temples, or places of worship; but it is not known whether the motive to their preservation was friendship or enmity; it might very probably be the former. They were formed into drinking-bowls, in the manner described by Herodotus, Melp. 65. by "cutting them off "*below the eyebrows*;" and they were neatly varnished all over. *Rennel*, p. 144.

[q] Τενέθλια signifies *the anniversary of a man's birth*; *γενέσια*, that of *one's*

and the women have equal authority with the men. These countries are not unknown.

XXVII. But the Issedones affirm, that the regions beyond them are possessed by men who have only one eye, and by griffins, that guard the gold. The Scythians repeat these things from the Issedones, and we have them from the Scythians, who give the name of Arimaspians to the people above mentioned, because *Arima*, in the Scythian language, signifies one, and *Spou*, an eye.

XXVIII. All this country is so infested with cold during the winter, and frosts so intolerable[r] for eight months of the year, that if a man pour water on the earth he shall not make clay without kindling a fire. Even the sea freezes, together with the whole Cimmerian bosphorus, in such a manner, that the Scythians who live within the intrenchment[s], lead their armies, and drive their chariots over the ice to the opposite coast, to the Sindi[t]. Eight months their winter continues, and during the other four it is cold. The winter is different from the winter in all other climates, for no rain worth mentioning[u] falls in the proper season, and during the summer it never leaves off raining. Thunder is heavy in summer, but seldom heard at those times when it is most common in other parts. If any happen in winter, it is taken for a prodigy; and an earthquake, either in summer or winter, is no less astonishing. Their horses endure and hold out against the cold, but their mules and asses cannot at all endure it: whereas, in other places, horses, if they stand in the cold, waste away, but mules and asses easily bear it.

XXIX. These winters seem to me to be the cause why their cows and oxen have no horns; and the following verse of Homer, in his Odyssey, confirms my opinion:

And Libya, where the lambs have early horns[x].

Rightly intimating, that the horns of cattle shoot speedily in hot countries; for in those which are violently cold, they either cannot shoot at all, or never grow to any bigness.

death. Ammonius de Voc. Different. p. 34.

[r] For the force of the phrase ἀφόρητος οἷος, &c. see Matthiæ's Gr. Gr. sect. 445.

[s] Herodotus means that which was dug by the slaves in ch. 3. *Larcher*.

[t] Sindica is, by his own statement, somewhere near the Mæotis; for in Melp. 86. he says, that the broadest part of the Euxine is between the river *Thermodon* and *Sindica*; which latter must therefore, of course, be looked for opposite to the river Thermodon. *Rennel*, p. 198.

[u] Ἐν τῷ (i. q. ἐν ᾧ, sc. χειμῶνι *during the winter in Scythia*) τὴν μὲν ὡραίην οὐκ ὕει, in the time that it usually does in other countries, no rain falls. Ὡραίη may be supposed to agree with ὥρῃ, but it will be best to consider it as a substantive formed from ὥρη, in the same manner as ἀναγκαίη from ἀνάγκη, &c. See Schæfer ad Bos. Ellips. p. 577. *Schweighæuser*.

[x] This is the 85th verse of the 4th book

XXX. These are the effects of cold in Scythia: I am surprised (for my narration has from its commencement sought for digressions,) that no mules are engendered in all the territories of Elis, though the climate be no way distempered with cold, nor any visible cause of this defect appear. The Eleans pretend they are under the force of a curse[y] in this particular; and therefore at the times of breeding, they lead their mares to some of the parts adjacent, where they cause them to be covered by he-asses, and after they have conceived, bring them home again.

XXXI. Touching the feathers[z], with which the Scythians say the air is so filled that men can neither see nor pass farther upon the continent, my opinion is, that perpetual snows fall in those parts, though probably in less quantity during the summer than in winter: and whoever has observed great abundance of snow falling, will easily comprehend what I say, for snow is not unlike to feathers. On this account therefore, as I conjecture, the northern regions of this continent are uninhabited, and the Scythians, with other adjoining people, call it feathers, from the resemblance. But I have insisted long enough on those regions, which are said to be the most remote.

XXXII. Concerning the Hyperboreans[a], nothing is said either by the Scythians or any other nation that inhabits those parts, except the Issedones; and, as I think, they say nothing, for if they did the Scythians would mention it, as they have done of the people with one eye: Hesiod indeed mentions the Hyperboreans, and Homer speaks of them in his Epigoni[b], if Homer was in reality the author of those verses.

XXXIII. But the Delians say very much more than any others about the Hyperboreans; affirming that their sacred things were transmitted to Scythia, wrapped in a bundle of wheat-straw, and from the Scythians each contiguous nation in order received them, and carried them as far westward as

[y] This is mentioned by Pausanias, Eliac. Prior. c. 5.

[z] The Psalmist compares snow to fleeces of wool: "Who sendeth his snow "like wool." Psalm cxlvii. ver. 5.

[a] It appears from the Scholiast on Pindar, (Pyth. iv. ver. 324.) that the Greeks called the Thracians, Boreans; there is, therefore, great probability that they called the people beyond these Hyperboreans. *Larcher.*

It may be concluded, that in the idea of Herodotus, the country of the Hyperboreans began about the meridian of Tanais, and extended indefinitely eastward: and that the Russians and Siberians, and particularly such of the latter as are situated on the upper parts of the rivers *Oby* and *Irtish*, represent the Hyperboreans of our author. *Rennel*, p. 148, 157.

[b] This poem is very ancient, although in all probability Homer was not the author. The Scholiast of Aristophanes (Pax, ver. 1270.) attributes it to Antimachus; but according to Sindos, Antimachus of Colophon was posterior to Herodotus, or at least his cotemporary. The subject of this poem was the second Theban war. *Larcher.*

the Adriatic[c]: that from hence they were conducted towards the south, and that the Dodonæans were the first of all the Greeks who received them: that from these they descended to the Maliac gulf, passed into Eubœa, and from thence through various cities to Carystus: that from this they passed by Andros[d]; but that the Carystians transported them to Tenus, and the Tenians to Delos: in this manner the Delians say they received these offerings. They add, that the Hyperboreans had first sent two virgins to carry these sacred things abroad, and call them by the names of Hyperoche and Laodice: that for their security they appointed five citizens to accompany them, whose memory is to this day in great veneration among the Delians, and who are known by the title of Perpherees: but the Hyperboreans, finding that none of those they had sent came back, and considering it a serious thing that it should always happen that they should send people and not receive them back, they carried their offerings bound in wheat-straw to their borders, and enjoined their neighbours to conduct them to the next nation. And thus the Delians say these sacred rites were introduced, through many other parts, into their island. Something like these mysteries I have observed among the Thracian and Pæonian women, when they sacrifice to Diana the queen; for they never carry sacred things in procession[e] without using the straw of wheat, as I myself have seen.

XXXIV. These Hyperborean virgins died in Delos, and their memory is honoured by the Delian maids and young men in this manner. The maids cut off a lock of their hair[f] before marriage, which they wind about a distaff, and dedicate upon the sepulchre of those virgins, built within a spot consecrated to Diana, on the left hand of the entrance, and covered by an olive-tree. The young men twist their hair about a tuft of grass, and consecrate it on the same monument. Such veneration is paid to these virgins by the inhabitants of Delos.

XXXV. They likewise say, that Arge and Opis, two other Hyperborean virgins, passed through the same nations, and came to Delos, before Hyperoche and Laodice: that these last came only to bring the acknowledgment they had vowed

[c] The regions to the north of the Adriatic were generally attributed to the Hyperboreans, before the northern parts of Europe were much known. D'Anville in Mem. de l'Acad. Inscrip. xxxv. p. 589.

[d] They were carried straight from Carystus to Tenos without touching at Andros. *Reiske.*

[e] Schweighæuser translates ἰχοῦσας τὰ ἱρὰ, *sacra manu tenentes et in pompa gestantes,*

[f] The custom of offering the hair is of very great antiquity. Sometimes it was deposited in temples, as in the case of Berenice, who consecrated her's in the temple of Venus; sometimes it was suspended upon trees. It was a sign of grief. *Larcher.*

o Lucina for a speedy delivery; but that Arge and Opis rrived with the Gods, and are therefore honoured by the Deians with other solemnities; for the women collect alms for hem[g], calling on their names in a hymn, composed by Olen he Lycian[h], which the Ionians and Islanders afterwards earnt from them, and celebrate Arge and Opis, mentioning heir names and assembling together; (now this Olen came rom Lycia, and was the author of other ancient compositions which are sung in Delos;) the ashes of the sacrifices burnt on he altar are thrown upon their sepulchre, which stands beiind the temple of Diana, facing to the east, and adjoining to he room[i] of the Ceians.

XXXVI. And this I think sufficient to say concerning the Hyperboreans; for I shall not mention the fable of Abaris[k], who, they say, was of that country, and, without eating, was arried by an arrow[l] round the whole earth. Yet if there be ny Hyperboreans lying so far to the northward, we may as vell presume there are other Hypernotians inhabiting to the outhward. And here I cannot forbear laughter, when I see hat many men have described the circumference of the earth, nd have no prudence to guide them, who pretend that the cean surrounds the whole, that the earth is round as if made y a machine, and that Asia is equal in extent to Europe. I hall therefore briefly discover the dimensions of each part, nd give a just description of their form.

XXXVII. The countries inhabited by the Persians, xtend southward to the Red sea; to the northward they ave the Medes; beyond the Medes are the Saspires, and be-

g 'Αγείρειν is applied to those, who lemand a contribution for the Gods, as hey pretend, but in reality for themelves, as is also done now in many laces. *Wesseling*.

h Olen, a priest and very ancient oet, was before Homer; he was the irst Greek poet, and the first who delared the oracles of Apollo. The inhabitants of Delphi chanted the hymns, which he composed for them. In one of his hymns on Ilithya, he calls her the Mother of Love; in another on Juno, he affirms that she was educated by the Hours, and was the mother of Mars and Hebe. He composed another hymn on Achæa, who came to Delos, from the country of the Hyperboreans. *Larcher*.

Mitford (Hist. Greece, i. 4.) infers from this passage, and Pausanias, that the language both of Thrace and Lycia was Greek.

i The Athenians and the inhabitants of the Cyclades, celebrated at Delos, with great magnificence, festivals in honour of Apollo, which they called Delia. They were held at the beginning of every fifth year. The inhabitants of each island sent bands of youths, &c. and there was a building appropriated to the deputies of each island, where they lodged, as we may conjecture from this passage of Herodotus. *Larcher*.

k Some say he was the son of Seuthes, and lived in the age of Crœsus. Others place him in the third Olympiad, and others in the twenty-third.

l Larcher gives the following from the Anecdota Græca, (tom. i. p. 20.) A famine having appeared among the Hyperboreans, Abaris went to Greece, and engaged in the service of Apollo. The God taught him to give oracles. In consequence of this, he travelled through Greece, declaring oracles, having in his hand an arrow, the symbol of Apollo.

yond these the Colchians, whose country reaches to the North sea, into which the river Phasis runs. These four nations possess whatever lies between those seas.

XXXVIII. To the westward, two tracts[m] opposite to one another, reach from hence to the sea, which I shall describe. One of these, on the north, begins at the Phasis, and extends toward the sea along the Euxine, and the Hellespont, down to the Trojan Sigæum; and on the south, this same tract beginning at the Myriandric[n] gulf, which is adjacent to Phœnicia, extends as far as the promontory of Tropium. This region is inhabited by thirty several nations.

XXXIX. The other begins at Persia, and reaches to the Red sea; it comprises Persia, Assyria which is next, and Arabia; it terminates, but only from custom, at the Arabian gulf, into which Darius carried a canal[o] from the Nile. The countries that lie between the Persians and Phœnicians are spacious and of great extent. From Phœnicia the same tract stretches along this sea by the Palestine Syria and Egypt; terminates there, and contains only three nations[p]. These regions are situate in Asia, from Persia to the westward.

XL. Those that lie beyond the Persians, Medes, Saspires, and Colchians, are bounded on the east by the Red sea, and on the north by the Caspian, and the river Araxes, which flows towards the rising sun. All Asia is inhabited as far as India; but beyond India, whatever lies to the eastward is desert, and no one is able to describe what it is. Such and so great is Asia.

XL. Lybia is in another region, and begins where Egypt terminates. In this part the tract is narrow, and no more than a hundred thousand orgyiæ, or one thousand stades, are computed from this sea to the Red sea[q]. Beyond this narrow part there is a very wide country, which is called Lybia.

XLII. I wonder therefore at those who have made the division and separation of Europe, Lybia, and Asia, because the disproportion is great; for though Europe extends in length along both of them, yet in breadth it is not comparable to either. Lybia is clearly surrounded by the sea, except in that part which borders upon Asia: and this discovery was

[m] Larcher translates *ἀκτὴ peninsula:* for an exact account of these divisions of Herodotus, see the elaborate treatise of Rennel, sect. ix.

[n] So called from the city Myriandus. It was also called the bay of Issus.

[o] See book ii. ch. 158.

[p] Assyria, Arabia, and Syria.

[q] We must necessarily understand the isthmus between the Mediterranean, and the Arabian gulf, or Red sea. Herodotus says, book ii. ch. 158. that the shortest way from one sea to the other, is one thousand stadia. Agrippa says, on the authority of Pliny, (Hist. Nat. vii.) that from Pelusium to Arsinoe on the Red sea, was one hundred and twenty-five miles, which comes to the same thing, as that author always reckons eight stadia to a mile. *Larcher.*

first made by Necus king of Egypt; who, after he had desisted from opening the channel that conveys the waters of the Nile into the Arabian gulf, sent certain Phœnicians in ships, with orders to come back through the columns of Hercules into the sea which is to the north of Lybia, and then to return to Egypt. These men set sail from the Red sea, and entering into the southern sea[r], went ashore in Lybia, about the time of the autumn, and having sowed the land in what part soever they arrived, waited the time of harvest, and when they had cut the corn, put to sea again. After they had spent two years in their voyage, they passed by the columns of Hercules in the third, and returning to Egypt, related a thing which I cannot believe, though perhaps others may; affirming, that as they sailed round the coast of Lybia they had the sun on their right hand[s]: and in this manner Lybia was first discovered[t].

XLIII. Since that time, the Carthaginians say that Sataspes the son of Teaspes, one of the Achæmenian blood, was sent with orders to sail round Lybia, and did not finish his enterprize; but tired with the length of the voyage, and the inhospitable deserts, returned home without accomplishing this labour, which was imposed upon him by his mother, for forcing a virgin, who was daughter to Zopyrus the son of Megabyzus. Xerxes had condemned him to be impaled for this crime; but his mother, who was sister to Darius, saved him from that death, by assuring the king she would inflict a greater punishment upon her son than he had appointed, for she would constrain him to sail round the coast of Lybia, till he should arrive in the gulf of Arabia. Xerxes having agreed on these terms, Sataspes departed into Egypt, where, having furnished himself with ships and men, he set sail; and passing by the pillars of Hercules, doubled the Lybian cape of Solois[u], and steered to the southward. But after he had been

[r] This is the ocean which washes the eastern and southern coasts of Africa. Herodotus, therefore, was not ignorant that the Atlantic and Erythrean communicated. Eratosthenes, as Strabo says, (i. p. 97.) was also aware of it. This was unknown to Hipparchus and Ptolemy, and was also forgotten, until Barthelemy Dius and Vasco de Gama doubled the Cape of Good Hope in 1486 and 1487. *Larcher.*

[s] Brief as this narration is, it contains, as M. Larcher remarks, a circumstance which is in evidence to the truth of the voyage, viz. that of the sun being on their *right hand* in sailing round Africa; and which, says he, could never have been imagined in an age when astronomy was yet in its infancy. *Rennel*, p. 718.

[t] We must here put in after εγνωσθη, περιῤῥυτος εουσα, &c. from the commencement of the chapter, in order to complete the sense, as it was not the interior of Africa that was discovered. *Valckenaer* and *Larcher*.

[u] It appears that the *Soleis* of Hanno and of Scylax, and the *Solis* of Pliny and Ptolemy, must have been situated between the Capes *Blanco* and *Geer*, on the coast of Morocco; in which quarter also the Solois of Herodotus, as being part of the *inhabited* tract, must of necessity be situated, and probably is the

many months at sea, and found many more would be necessary to finish his voyage, he discontinued his course, and returned to Egypt. From thence he went to Xerxes, and told him that in the most distant part he sailed past a nation of little men, clothed in garments made of the leaves of the palm-tree, who upon the approach of his ships left their cities and fled to the mountains; that he had indeed taken some provisions in their country, but he had not done them any other injury. Then, to excuse himself for not completely sailing round Lybia, he alleged that his ship became immoveable, and could not proceed farther[x]. But Xerxes, being persuaded that he did not speak the truth, put the former sentence in execution, and commanded him to be impaled, because he had not accomplished the enterprize imposed on him; upon which the eunuch of Sataspes, hearing of his master's death, ran away with great riches to Samos, which a certain Samian, whose name I forbear to mention, detained.

XLIV. Much of Asia was discovered by Darius. For that king, being desirous to know in what part the Indus, which is the second river that produces crocodiles, runs into the sea, sent Scylax of Caryanda[y], with others of approved fidelity, to make the discovery. Accordingly they departed from Caspatyrus[z] and the country of Pactyice, and sailed down the river eastward to the sea[a], and then altering their course towards the west, arrived in the thirtieth month at that place where the king of Egypt had caused the Phoenicians I mentioned before to embark, in order to sail round the coast of Lybia. After this voyage, Darius subdued the Indians, and became master of that sea. By which means, without accounting those regions that are situate in the eastern parts, the rest of Asia is known to exhibit things similar to Lybia.

same with *Cape Cautin*, as D'Anville appears to have supposed. *Rennel*, p. 421.

[x] It is very probable that Sataspes was discouraged from prosecuting his voyage by the adverse winds and currents that prevail on the coast of Serra Leona, &c. from April to October, and which would be felt by those who left Egypt or Carthage in the *spring*; a more likely season to undertake an expedition of this sort than in *winter*, when the order of things is different. *Rennel*, p. 716.

[y] Vossius and Dodwell think that this is a different Scylax from the one whose Periplus we have. See Dodwell's Dissert. vol. i. p. 42. But M. de Sainte Croix thinks they are the same in a Dissert. in xcii. vol. de l'Acad. des Inscript. p. 350, &c. *Larcher*.

[z] A city of Pactyice on the western shore of the Indus. Dodwell places it on the Ganges. Rennel supposes it to be Puckoli, but that place is beyond the Indus. It appears to me that Pactyice was a part of Gandaria, and that it reached the western bank of the Indus at the south-east of Bactriana, and the north-west of Mount Paropamisus. *Larcher*.

[a] Larcher thinks that Herodotus must have been mistaken or misinformed, and that Scylax must have known that he was sailing southward.

XLV. But Europe has not been fully discovered by any man, and we have no account whether it be bounded on the north and east sides by the sea, or not; only we know, that it extends in length as far as[b] the other parts. And I cannot comprehend with what reason men have imposed three distinct names upon the earth, which is but one, and those properly names of women, and the boundaries have been laid down[c] to be the Egyptian Nile, and the Colchian Phasis, (some say, the river Tanais, the Mæotian river[d], and the Cimmerian Porthmeia.) Nor could I ever learn the names of those who made this division, nor from whence they gave them those names. The most prevailing opinion among the Greeks is, that Lybia was so called from a woman of that name and country; and Asia from the wife of Prometheus. But the Lydians put in a claim to the last, and say, that Asia had its name from Asius the son of Cotys and grandson of Manes, and not from Asia the wife of Prometheus; from whom also a tribe in Sardis is called the Asian tribe. In conclusion, no man knows whether Europe be surrounded by the sea, nor from whence that name was derived. Neither are we more certain who was the first imposer, unless we will say that the Tyrian Europa[e] gave her name to that region, which, therefore, like the rest, before her time had none. But yet she appears to have been of Asia, and never to have come into these parts which are now called Europe by the Grecians; but only passed as far as Crete from Phœnicia, and from thence sailed to Lycia. Thus having reported the common opinions, I shall say no more concerning these things.

XLVI. Except the Scythian, the nations of the Euxine to which Darius was preparing to lead an army, are most ignorant, for we are unable to mention any one on account of his wisdom; nor ever heard of any learned man among them, Anacharsis and other Scythians only excepted. But in Scythia one thing is observed, more prudently contrived than in

[b] It is not surprising that Herodotus should have formed this opinion of Europe and Asia, since with the exception of the Massagetæ, Arabia, and part of India, he only knew those parts of Asia which were subject to Darius. He assigned to Europe that immense country which is to the north of Caucasus, the Caspian and Massagetæ. *Larcher.*

[c] It is proper to remark that Herodotus considered, and perhaps rightly, the whole of the earth then known, as one single continent; regarding Europe, Asia, and Africa, as nothing more than divisions of that continent. *Rennel,* p. 3.

[d] Since τὸν Μαιήτην is the only reading, I see no reason why the Tanais should not be here called the Mæotian, (i. e. that which runs through the Mæotian borders,) as the Nile is called the Egyptian, and the Phasis the Colchian. *Schweighæuser.*

[e] Bochart (Geogr. Sacra iv. 33.) thinks that this part of the world was called by the Phœnicians Ur-Appa, because of the whiteness of their complexions. *Larcher.*

any other nation we know; but their other customs I do not admire. This most important thing is, that no one who has come against them can ever make his escape; and that it is impossible to catch them, if they do not wish to be found, because they have no cities nor inclosed places; but every man has a moveable house[f]; and fights on horseback, armed with a bow and arrows. They have not their subsistence from the plough, but from the cattle, and have their houses on waggons. Why must not such people be invincible[g], and difficult to come to an engagement with?

XLVII. The situation of their country, which is level, and the frequency of their rivers, have greatly contributed to these advantages: for the soil is rich and well watered, and the rivers are almost as numerous as the canals of Egypt. Of these, the most celebrated and navigable from the sea are, the Ister, the Tyres[h], the Hypanis, the Borysthenes, the Panticapes, the Hypacyris, the Gerrhus, and the Tanais.

XLVIII. The Ister is the greatest of all the rivers we know, flowing with an equal stream both in summer and winter; we meet with it first in Scythia at the west of the others, and it becomes the greatest, because many other rivers discharge themselves into it. In the first place, five several rivers, passing through Scythia, contribute to swell its stream. The first of these is by the Scythians called Porata[i], and by the Grecians Pyretos. The other four go under the names of Tiarantus, Aratus, Naparis, and Ordissus. The Porata is a considerable river, and running towards the east, communicates with the Ister. The Tiarantus is less, and deflects rather to the westward; the Ararus, Naparis, and Ordissus, pass between both, and fall likewise into the same river. These rivers take their rise in Scythia and swell the waters of the Ister.

[f] Æschylus, who lived forty-one years before Herodotus, mentions the same thing in the Prom. Vinct. 715, &c. and Horace iii. Od. xxiv. 9:

[g] Thucyd. (ii. 97.) supposes, that no nation either of Europe or Asia would be able to oppose the Scythians if they were unanimous. Herodotus does not consider them invincible on account of their bodily strength or numbers, but rather on account of their customs, &c. *Valckenaer.*

[h] Of these the Ister or Danube is the most western: the Tanais the most eastern. *Rennel*, p. 65.

[i] M. D'Anville recognizes the Porata in the Pruth; the Ararus in the Siret; the Naparis in the Proava, which is also called Jalomnitzas; and the Ordessus in the Argis; but the Tiarantus he has not made out. It cannot be for the Tibiscus or Teisse, for in the succeeding chapter it is enumerated amongst other adjuncts of the Danube, under the name of Tibisis; although by mistake it is made to descend from Mount Hæmus instead of the Bastarnian Alps in the opposite quarter. However as our author says that it has an *inclination* to the *west*, and is smaller than the Porata; as also that the three others take their courses between these two, it appears that the *Olt* or *Alut* should be meant for the Tiarantus. The Olt however has its source in *Transylvania*, which the context evidently allots to the Agathyrsi; but it is

XLIX. From the Agathyrsi the river Maris[k] flows and mixes with the same stream. The Atlas, the Auras, and the Tibisis[l], three great rivers rising in mount Hæmus, and descending northward; besides the Athres, Noes[m], and Atarnes, which pass through Thrace and the Thracian Crobyzi[n]; and the river Cius, beginning in the Pæonian and Rhodopean hills, and flowing through the midst of Hæmus; all these likewise discharge their waters into the Ister. In like manner the Angrus, a river of Illyria, flowing towards the north, and crossing the plains of Triballis, enters into the Brongus; and both these, considerable in themselves, are received together by the river Ister. And lastly, from the regions that are situate above the Umbri, two other rivers, which go by the names of Carpis[o] and Alpis, descending to the northward, fall into the same stream. The Ister rises in the country of the Celtæ, who with the Cynetæ[p] inhabit the remotest parts of Europe to the westward, and traversing all the European regions, enters one of the extreme parts of Scythia.

L. And thus by the addition of the waters I have mentioned, with the contributions of divers other streams, the Ister becomes the greatest of all rivers. For if we compare the waters of the Nile with those that properly belong to the Ister, we shall find the former much superior in quantity; because no river or fountain[q] enters into the Nile, nor contributes any thing to increase it. The Ister is of equal height in summer and in winter, for this reason, as I conjecture.

certain, notwithstanding, that its source is on the borders of Scythia; and as it is probable that our author had not a critical knowledge of the geography, the expression ought not to be taken too literally, when he says that *all* these rivers have their rise *in* Scythia. *Rennel*, p. 59.

[k] Some of the most learned historians suppose that this is the *Marosch* or *Merisch*, which rises in Transylvania. I am more inclined to believe it to be the Temesh, which joins the Danube some leagues from Belgrade. *Larcher*.

[l] Herodotus in mentioning the rivers of Scythia goes from the east to the west. The Atlas and the Auras are not known. The Tibisis is probably the same as the Caralom. The Athrys ought to be written Iathrys and is the Iautra, the Noes is the Novæ of Ptolemy, the Artanes the Utus of Pliny. The Cios ought to be read the Oscus, and is the modern Ischa. The Brongus is the Margus of Strabo, and the Morave of Bulgaria, the Angrus is the Morave of Servia. *Larcher*.

[m] Mr. Bryant in his Analysis of Heathen Mythology, pretends that this is the proper name of the Danube without the prefix. Thus we should say Da-Nau, Da-Nauos, Da-Nauvas, Da-Naubus.

[n] These dwelt between the Ister and Mount Hæmus, to the west of the Getæ and east of the Triballi, from whom they were separated by the Œscus. *Larcher*.

[o] D'Anville calls this river the Vicegrad.

[p] See book ii. ch. 33.

[q] The Astapus, or Abarvi, the Astaboras or Atbara, which are very considerable rivers, and a great number of others which come from Abyssinia and the adjacent countries, and are swollen by the trophical rains, discharge their waters into the Nile in Ethiopia. But perhaps our author meant that it did not receive any contribution after having entered Egypt. *Larcher*.

During the winter it is about as large as it usually is, and perhaps a little larger; for this country is very little moistened by rain during the winter, but it is entirely covered with snow. But the immense quantity of snow which fell in the winter, being melted in the summer, runs from all sides to the Ister, and together with violent and frequent rains, keeps the river full. By how much the more therefore the sun draws up in summer than in winter, so much the more copious are those waters which mix with it; these things therefore being opposed, an equilibrium results, so that it always appears equal.

LI. The first river then of Scythia is the Ister; the second is the Tyres, which comes from the north, issuing out of a vast lake, and separates Scythia from Neuris. At the mouth of this river certain Grecians inhabit, who are called Tyritæ.

LII. The third is the Hypanis[r], which flows from Scythia and runs from a great lake, which is deservedly named the mother of the Hypanis. Great numbers of wild white horses graze about the borders of this lake. The Hypanis, which takes its rise from this lake, is small and its waters are sweet for five days sail; but from thence to the sea, a voyage of four days, it is very bitter. For a fountain discharges itself into it, which though small, is so very bitter as to infect the Hypanis; which, nevertheless, is of moderate size. This spring rises in the borders of the Scythian husbandmen and the Alazones, and from that part of the country is called by the name of Exampæus, which in the Grecian language signifies, *The sacred ways*. The Tyres and Hypanis run near together along the territories of the Alazones, and then separating, leave a wide space between each channel.

LIII. The Borysthenes[s], which is the fourth and greatest river of Scythia after the Ister, surpasses, in my opinion, not only the rest of the Scythian rivers, but all others, except the Egyptian Nile; to which it is impossible to compare any other. This river affords highly excellent and rich pasture for

[r] There were other rivers of the name of Hypanis. The river *Kuban* in Asiatic Scythia bore that name.

As the Hypanis is the third in order of these rivers, and placed next to the Borysthenês, both here and in Melp. 17. (where it is said to lie to the west of the Borysthenes, and to form a junction with it near the sea,) it can answer to no other river than the Bog; as the Tyres, which immediately preceded it, can be no other than the Dniester. The circumstance of the near approach of the two, shews how well our author was informed; for those rivers do really approach very near to each other at Braclaw and Mohilow, in the early part of their courses; and afterwards diverge very considerably in their way to the Euxine. *Rennel*, p. 56.

[s] This is now called the Nieper or Dnieper.

There is some reason to suspect, that our author was not apprized of the famous cataracts of this river, which occur at about the height of 200 miles above its embouchure, and are said to be 13 in number. *Rennell*, p. 56.

cattle; and fish, which are by far the most excellent and numerous; and its water is of a very pleasant taste. The streams are pure and limpid, though in the neighbourhood of turbid rivers; and the bordering plains produce excellent corn, with plenty of grass in the places which are not sown. At the mouth of this river abundance of salt is incessantly formed of itself; and a sort of whale is taken, of great bigness, and without any spinous bones, which the Scythians salt, and call by the name of Antacæus: and also many other things which deserve admiration. So much of the Borysthenes is known as may be navigated in a voyage of forty days, from the north of the country of Gerrhus; but no man can affirm any thing certain concerning the remoter parts, through which this river passes. Probably they are uninhabited deserts, down to the regions of the Scythian husbandmen, that lie extended along the river during a sail of ten days. The head of the Borysthenes, as well as that of the Nile, is unknown to me, and I think to all other Grecians. This river and the Hypanis join at a little distance from the sea, and discharge their waters into the same morass. The space that lies between the two rivers, which is a projecting piece of land[t], is called the promontory of Hippoleon, in which a temple, dedicated to Ceres, is built; and beyond that temple the Borysthenitæ inhabit the country to the river Hypanis. Thus much concerning these rivers[u].

LIV. The fifth river is the Panticapes[x], which also descends from the north, and out of a lake; and between this river and the Borysthenes, the country is inhabited by Scythian husbandmen. The Panticapes enters into Hylæa, and after having passed through that region, mixes with the Borysthenes.

LV. The Hypacyris is the sixth river; which, beginning in a lake, traverses the country of the Scythian herdsmen; and then closing in the borders of Hylæa on the right, together with that place, which is called the Course of Achilles, rolls into the sea at the city of Carcinitis[y].

LVI. The seventh is the Gerrhus; which is separated from

[t] Ἔμβολον signifies *the beak of a ship*, i. e. this place takes the form of a beak of a vessel, as we are also informed by Dion Chrysostom, (Orat. xxxvi. p. 437.) *Larcher*.

[u] Ἀπὸ has nearly the same force in this passage as if he had said τὰ περὶ τούτους, &c. so iv. 195, and vii. 195. *Schweigh*.

[x] The descriptions of the courses and confluences of the Panticapes, Hypacyris and Gherrus, cannot be reconciled to modern geography, and, as far as we can understand, cannot have been of any great bulk. The Gherrus is expressly said to be a *branch* of the Borysthenes, and it is obvious, that as the other two are described to be situated between the Borysthenes and the Gherrus, they must either have been very unimportant in point of bulk, or branches of the Borysthenes or Gerrhus. *Rennel*, p. 57.

[y] This according to D'Anville was afterwards called Necro-Pyla.

the Borysthenes, near the place, as far as which that river is first known. Being from that place distinct from the Borysthenes, it has the same name as the country, viz. Gerrhus; and as it flows towards the sea it divides the territories of the herdsmen from those of the Royal Scythians, and then falls into the Hypacyris.

LVII. The eighth river is the Tanais[z], originally descending from a great lake, and entering into another yet greater, called Mæotis, which separates the Royal Scythians and the Sauromatæ. The river Hyrgis[a] runs into the Tanais.

LVIII. Thus with all these celebrared rivers are the Scythians furnished. The grass that grows in this country is the most productive of bile of any we have seen, as experience shews at the opening of the cattle.

LIX. These very great advantages are in such great abundance. Their customs and ceremonies are established in this manner. They worship no other Gods than these: in the first place Vesta, who is their principal deity; then Jupiter, and the Earth, which is accounted his wife; after them Apollo, Venus Urania, Hercules, and Mars. All these are generally acknowledged: but those who go under the name of Royal Scythians, sacrifice likewise to Neptune. Vesta, in the Scythian language, is called Tabiti; Jupiter is, in my opinion, very rightly named Papæus[b]; the Earth, Apia; Apollo, Œtosyrus; the celestial Venus, Artimpasa; and Neptune, Thamimasades. They erect no images, altars, or temples, to any other God except Mars alone.

LX. The same mode of sacrifice is established in all sacred places[c] alike, and is in this manner: the animal is placed before them with its fore-feet tied together; he who sacrifices standing behind it, by pulling the end of the rope throws it down; as it falls he invokes the God to whom it is sacrificing. This done, he throws a halter about its neck, and by putting in a stick and twisting it round strangles it, without kindling any fire, or any preparatory ceremony[d] or libation.

[z] This river is in modern geography the Don, and cannot be misunderstood. The modern name Don, seems to be a corruption of Tana, the proper name of the river, as well as of a city, which stood on, or near the site of Azoph; and not far from its embouchure in the Palus Mæotis. The Tanais does indeed spring from a lake, but it appears to be a very small one; and is not even marked in the Russian maps. *Rennel*, p. 57.

[a] Bayer and Wesseling think with reason that this is the Seviersky, which is also called the Donetz, or little Don. *Larcher*.

[b] It is well known that in every language ap, pa, papa, are the first sounds which children pronounce, and that they in this manner designate their fathers. *Larcher*. See also Des Brosses, Mechanisme des Langues, tom. i. p. 231—247.

[c] It appears to me more natural to understand by τὰ ἱρὰ sacred places than rites. Although the Scythians had no temples, it is, however, very probable that they met in the open air in certain places which they regarded as sacred. *Larcher*.

[d] This is remarked, because the Greeks

When he has performed this office, and taken off the skin from the body, he immediately applies himself to dress the flesh.

LXI. But because the country is very ill furnished with wood, the Scythians have found out this contrivance in order to cook their flesh. When they have flayed the victim, they strip the bones, and put the flesh into cauldrons, which are peculiar to the country, if they happen to have any. These cauldrons very much resemble the bowls of Lesbos in form, except that they are much larger; then making a fire under them of the bones, they boil the flesh of the animal. If they have no cauldron at hand, they throw all the flesh into the paunch[e], with a competent quantity of water, and burn the bones underneath. These bones burn very well, and the paunch easily contains all the meat separated from the bones; so that the ox, and all other victims each boils itself. When the flesh is sufficiently prepared, he that sacrifices, in the first place makes an offering[f] of part of the meat and intestines, which he throws out before him. They make use of divers sorts of cattle in these sacrifices, but chiefly of horses.

LXII. In this manner, and these victims, they sacrifice to the other Gods, but to Mars they sacrifice in this way. In each district, in the place where the magistrates assemble[g], a temple is erected of the following kind. Bundles of faggots are heaped together to the length and breadth of three stadia, but to a less height. On the top of this there is a level square, three of the sides are perpendicular, and the fourth a gradual declivity, of easy access. One hundred and fifty loads of faggots are annually piled up in this place, because it always sinks from severe weather. On each of these heaps an old scymetar[h] of iron is erected, which they call the image of Mars, and honour with yearly sacrifices of horses and other cattle, in greater abundance than they offer to the rest of their Gods. They likewise sacrifice to this deity every hundredth man of the prisoners they take from their enemies; but in a different

always sprinkled the victim with lustral water, scattered on its head some barley meal mixed with salt, and cut off some of the hair from the head and threw it into the fire.

[e] The Bedouin Arabs, the Greenlanders and several of the people of Tartary, have at present this custom. *Wesseling*.

There is a remarkable instance of the using bones for fuel in Ezekiel, ch. xxiv. 5. "Take also the choice of the flock, "and burn the bones under it, and make "it boil well."

[f] Ἀπάρχεσθαι is after the victim is killed and dressed; κατάρχεσθαι before it is killed. *Schweigh.*

[g] Ἀρχήιον signifies *the Senate*, the place where the senators, &c. assemble. This in Scythia where there are no houses, would be an open plain. *Larch.*

[h] Other barbarians used to worship the God of war under the emblem of a scymetar. Ammianus Marcell. (xxxi. 2.) informs us, that the Huns did. At Rome, according to Varro, a pike sometimes represented Mars. *Larcher*.

manner from the offerings they make of other animals: for after they have poured a libation of wine on the head of the prisoner, they cut his throat over a bowl, and then ascending the heap of faggots, pour the blood over the sword. While they are carrying this to the top, those below, after they have killed the man, cut off his right arm by the shoulder, which they throw into the air, and leave on the ground where it falls. Thus the body lies in one part, and the arm in another. When they have performed these and other ceremonies, they depart.

XLIII. And such are the sacrifices instituted by the Scythians. They make no use of swine, nor will suffer any to be kept in their country.

XLIV. The military affairs of Scythia are ordered in this manner. Every Scythian drinks the blood of the first prisoner he overthrows, and presents the king with the heads of the enemies he has killed in fight: for if he brings a head, he is entitled to a share of the booty, otherwise not. They strip the skin off these heads[i] in the following manner. Having made a circular incision round the ears, they take hold of it and shake it out; after they have cleared off the flesh with the rib of an ox, they soften the skin with their hands; and these skins thus prepared serve instead of napkins; each man hangs them on the bridle of the horse which he rides, and considers them an honour; for he who has the greater number of these napkins, is accounted the most valiant man. Many Scythians clothe themselves with the skins of their enemies, sewing them together like shepherd's garments[k]; and frequently stripping the right hands of the enemies they have killed, together with their nails, use them for coverings to their quivers: the skin of a man is thick, and of a brighter white than that of any other animal. Many take off the skins of men entire, and carry them about on horseback, stretched out upon a board. These usages are received among the Scythians.

LXV. They do this to the heads of their greatest enemies only. They saw off all below the eye-brow, and having cleansed the rest, if they are poor, they content themselves to cover the skull with leather; but the rich, besides this covering of leather, gild the inside with gold; and these serve instead of cups for their drink. They do the same to their familiar friends; if upon any dispute they conquer them in the presence of the king. When they entertain any stranger of consideration, they set these heads before him, and relate how, though they were formerly friends, they made war against

[i] This manner of scalping is nearly the same as that practised by the American Indians. A finished picture of this people is drawn by the masterly hand of the historian of the Decline and Fall of the Roman Empire, ch. 26, 34.

[k] The βαίτη was made of skins of beasts sewed together. *Larcher.*

them, and how they overcame them, considering these as feats of valour.

LXVI. Every governor of a district provides a vessel of wine once a year in his own province, from which all those Scythians, who have killed enemies, drink: whilst those who have not performed any such exploit, sit at a distance in dishonour, and are not permitted to taste the liquor, which is accounted the greatest disgrace[l]: but they who have killed very many men, drink at the same time from two cups joined together[m].

LXVII. The Scythians abound in prophets, who divine by rods of willow[n], in the following manner. They collect great bundles of these twigs, which they lay down, and open on the ground: then separating the whole parcel one from the other, they begin to utter their predictions; and whilst they are yet speaking, gather up the rods again, and tie them together as before. This way of divination was learnt from their ancestors; but the Enarees[o], or Androgyni, pretend that Venus gave them the power of predicting by the bark of a linden-tree, which they split in three places, and twist about their fingers, and as they untwist it, they prophecy.

LXVIII. When the king of Scythia is sick, he sends for three of the most famous of these prophets, who prophecy in the manner above mentioned; and they generally tell him that such and such a citizen, whom they name, has perjured himself, in swearing falsely by the royal lares; for it is a custom of the Scythians to swear by the king's lares[p], when they would use the most solemn oath. The person accused is presently seized, and brought into the king's presence; where the prophets charge him with perjury, and pretend to have discovered by their art, that he has sworn falsely by the lares of the palace, and so brought this distemper upon the king. He then denies the fact, and, affirming that he has not sworn falsely, becomes indignant; thereupon the king sends for a double number of prophets, and in case they confirm the former judgment, after they have performed the usual ceremonies, the man immediately loses his head, and the first three divide his riches among themselves; but if they

[l] "Ut quisque plures interemerit; ita "apud eos habetur eximius. Cæterum "expertem esse cædis, inter opprobria "vel maximum." Pompon. Mel. ii. 1.

[m] Schweighæuser thinks that *σύνδυο* only means *two cups.*

[n] Ammianus Marcellinus, speaking of the Huns, says, "Futura miro præsagiunt modo; nam rectiores virgas vimineas colligentes, easque cum incantamentis quibusdam secretis præstituto "tempore discernentes, apertè quiddam "portendatur, norunt," xxxi. 2. I have seen some traces of this superstition among the shepherds in the province of Berry. *Larcher.*

[o] See note on book i. ch. 105.

[p] The Turks at this day swear by the Ottoman Porte. *Larcher.*

judge him innocent, more and more of these diviners are called; and if he is at last acquitted by a plurality of voices, those who first accused him are condemned to die.

LXIX. They put them to death in this manner: when they have filled a waggon with wood, and yoked oxen to it, they tie the feet of the prophets and fasten their hands behind their back, and having gagged them, they secure them in the midst of the faggots; then after having set fire to them, and having terrified the oxen, they let them go. Many of these beasts are consumed with the diviners, and many escape very much scorched, when the shafts have been burnt asunder. In this manner, and sometimes for other reasons, they burn these men, and call them false prophets. The king never spares the sons of those he puts to death, but destroying all the males, does not hurt the female children.

LXX. The Scythians in their alliances and contracts use the following ceremonies with all men. They pour wine into a large earthen vessel, and mingle it with blood taken from those who are to swear, by making a slight wound[q] in their flesh with a knife or sword. When they have done this, they dip a scimitar, some arrows, a hatchet, and a javelin, in the vessel; after which they make many solemn prayers, and then both those who make the contract, and the most considerable of those who are with them, drink off the liquor.

LXXI. The sepulchres of the kings are in the country of the Gerrhi, as far as which the Borysthenes is navigable. When their king dies they dig a great hole in the ground of a quadrangular form, and when this is prepared, they take the body, which is covered with wax, after it has been opened and cleaned, having been filled with bruised cypress, aromatics, seeds of parsley and anise, and sown up again, and then carry it in a chariot to another province, where those who receive it imitate the Royal Scythians in the following custom. They cut off part of one ear, shave their heads, wound themselves on the arms, forehead, and nose, and pierce the left hand with an arrow. From hence they carry the body of the king to another province of the kingdom, and the people of the former province accompany them. When they

[q] See book i. ch. 74. Larcher relates the following from Le Pére Daniel, Histoire de France, tom. x. p. 532. 4to. "When Henry the Third entered Poland to take possession of the crown, "he found on his arrival thirty thousand cavalry ranged in order of battle. "The general of these advancing towards him, drew his sword, pierced "his arm with it, and receiving in his "hand the blood which flowed from the "wound, drank it, saying, 'Evil be to "him among us who would not shed "in your service every drop of his "blood; and it is from this principle "that I deem it nothing to shed my "own.'"

have carried the body round all the provinces they arrive among the Gerrhi, who are the most remote of the kingdom, and at the sepulchres. Here they lay him in the sepulchre, upon a bed of leaves, and having fixed spears on each side, they lay pieces of wood over it, and cover it with twigs of willow. In the spaces that remain vacant they place one of the king's concubines, strangled, with a cup-bearer, a cook, a groom, a servant, a message-bearer, certain horses, first-fruits of all other things, and cups of gold; for silver and brass are not used among them. This done, they throw up the earth with great emulation, and endeavour to raise the mound[r] as high as possibly they can.

LXXII. After the revolution of a year, they perform these things farther; they choose such servants as they judge most fit out of the rest of the king's household, which consists wholly of native Scythians; for those wait on the king whomsoever he may order, and they have no servants bought with money. When they have strangled fifty of these servants[s], and with them fifty of the most beautiful horses[t]; and after they have emptied and cleansed their bellies, they fill them with chaff, and sow them up again. Then they place upon two pieces of wood the half of a wheel, with its concave side uppermost, and the other half on other pieces of wood in the same manner; and when they have erected a sufficient number of these, they set the horses upon them, having thrust stout pieces of wood through them, lengthwise, up to the neck; and thus one semi-circle supports the shoul-

[r] Modern discoveries abundantly prove the general truth of our author's report concerning the sepulchres of the ancient Scythians; if it be allowed that a part of the *tumuli* found in the plains towards the upper branches of the *Irtish*, *Oby*, &c. are of so ancient a date; or, on the other hand, if the sepulchres in question are not so ancient, it at least proves that the same custom prevailed amongst their descendants. It appears that tumuli are scattered over the whole tract, from the borders of the Wolga to the lake Baikal. Those amongst them which have attracted the greatest notice on the score of the gold and silver (but principally the former) contained in them, lie between the *Wolga* and the *Oby*; for those which are farther to the east, and more particularly at the upper part of the *Jenesei*, have the utensils contained in them of copper.

It has not come to our knowledge, that any of these monuments have been found in the *Ukraine*, where the sepulchres described by Herodotus should have been; however, it may be conceived that it is a sufficient testimony of the general truth of his description, that they are found so far to the west as the *southern* parts of *Russia*, and on the banks of the Okka, Wolga, and Tanais; since much the same sort of customs may be supposed to have existed amongst the Scythians and Sarmatians generally: and it is certain that the *Sarmatians* and *seceding Scythians* occupied the tracts just mentioned. *Rennel*, p. 108.

[s] In the mild and polished country of China, the Emperor, Chun-Tehi, (Hist. Gen. de la Chine, tom. i. p. 43.) having lost one of his wives in 1660, caused more than thirty slaves to be sacrificed upon her tomb. He was a Tartar, that is, a Scythian. This instance makes the narration of Herodotus more credible. *Larcher*.

[t] The Kalmucs are still in the habit of burying horses, arms, &c. with their chiefs. *Rennel*, p. 109.

ders of the horse, the other his belly near the thighs, and his legs are suspended in the air. After this they put a bit and a bridle on the horses, and stretching the bridle in front, fasten it to a stake; they then mount one of the fifty young men they have strangled upon each horse, and fix him in the seat by driving a straight stick upwards along the spine as far as his neck, and fix the extremity of the stick which comes out below, into an aperture in the piece of wood that passes through the horse; then placing these horsemen round the monument, they all depart.

LXXIII. And this is the manner in which they bury their kings. But when any other Scythian dies, his nearest relations carry him about in a chariot among his friends, who receive and entertain the whole company in their turn, setting the same things before the dead man as before the rest. In this manner all private men are carried about forty days before they are buried[u]; and those who have assisted at these funerals purify themselves thus. When they have cleansed their heads with a kind of soap, and washed it off, they do thus with regard to the body; they set up three pieces of timber leaning against each other, and extend around woollen coverings[x], and when they have joined them together as closely as possible, they throw red-hot stones into a vessel placed in the middle of the stakes and coverings.

LXXIV. In this country a sort of hemp grows, very like to flax, only larger and thicker, and in this it very far surpasses flax: it grows both spontaneously and from cultivation. The Thracians clothe themselves with garments made of this hemp; so well resembling flax that a man must have great experience in those materials to distinguish one from the other; and he who had never seen this hemp would think their clothes were wrought out of flax.

LXXV. The Scythians, when they have taken the seed of this hemp, go under the woollen coverings and put it upon the burning stones, this begins to burn and emits so powerful a vapour that no Grecian stove[y] would surpass it. The company

[u] The Scythians did not all of them observe the same customs with respect to their funerals: some suspended the dead bodies from a tree and left them to putrify. See Silius Italic. xiii. v. 486. Capt. Cooke also relates, that in Otaheite they leave dead bodies to putrify on the surface of the ground till the flesh is entirely wasted, they then bury the bones. See Hawkesworth's Voyages, London Chronicle, June 29, 1773, p. 5. *Larcher.*

[x] Πῖλος εἰρίνεος *is a woollen cloth.* The term ὑποδύνουσι shews that the opening by which they entered was very small. In fact it ought to be, and there is every probability that they closed it as soon as they had gone in, in order that the vapor might not escape. These must have reached down to the ground, and therefore might be called *tents.* Compare ch. 23. Dr. Cooke (Voyages and Travels through the Russian Empire, vol. i. p. 307.) relates, that the Kalmucs at present live in tents. *Larch.*

[y] The Indians of Hudson's Bay have

extremely transported with the vapor, howl aloud; and this manner of purification serves instead of washing, for they never bathe their bodies in water. But their wives, grinding the wood of cypress, cedar, and incense, upon a rough stone, and infusing the powder in water, compound a thick substance, which they spread over all the parts of the body and face. This composition gives them an agreeable odour, and when they take it off on the following day, they become clean and bright.

LXXVI. They studiously avoid the use of any other customs than their own, not admitting even those of their Scythian neighbours, and are particularly averse to those of the Grecians, as the examples of Anacharsis[a], and afterwards of Scyles, sufficiently demonstrate: for Anacharsis, after he had viewed many countries, and given proofs of great wisdom, sailing through the Hellespont in his return to Scythia, and landing at Cyzicus, found the inhabitants of that place celebrating a festival to the mother of the Gods with great solemnity; and made a vow to the Goddess, that if he returned in health and safety to his own country, he would sacrifice in the same manner as he saw the inhabitants of Cyzicus, and would also celebrate the vigils[a]. Accordingly, when he arrived in Scythia, he went privately into the country of Hylæa, situate near the Course of Achilles, and which is covered with trees of all kinds. There he fully performed all the rites of the Goddess, holding a timbrel in his hand, and having some little images hung about him[b]. But a certain Scythian, observing what he was doing, discovered the whole matter to the king Saulius, who, coming to the place and seeing Anacharsis thus employed, shot at him with an arrow, and killed him on the spot: and at the present time if any man question the Scythians concerning Anacharsis, they presently say they know nothing of him, because he travelled into Greece and affected foreign customs. Nevertheless I have been informed by

a very similiar custom. When they wish to throw themselves into a perspiration they make a large stone red hot. This they take into a small cabin which they carefully close in; they go into this cabin naked with a vessel of water, with which they sprinkle the stone. The water changes into a hot vapor, which causes almost immediate perspiration. (Histoire des Voyages, XIV. p. 666.) *Larcher.*

[a] The life of Anacharsis is given at length by Diogenes Laërtius. His character for learning produced the excellent work of the Abbé Barthelemy. Galen (Suasoriâ ad Art. tom. i. p. 2.) says, that he was called the *wise*, although a barbarian by birth.

[a] These festivals properly commenced on the evening before the day on which they were celebrated; and it seems most probable that they passed the night in singing hymns in honor of the God or Goddess, in whose honor the feast was instituted. See the Peroigilium Veneris. *Larcher.*

[b] The priests of this Goddess carried a timbrel and little statues or images, which hung round their necks. See Apollon. Rhod. i. ver. 1139.

Timnes, the guardian of Ariapithes, that Anacharsis was uncle to Idanthyrsus, king of Scythia, son to Gnurus, and grandson of Lycus the son of Spargapithes; and if he was of that family, he was killed by his own cousin german; for Idanthyrsus was the son of Saulius, and Saulius killed Anacharsis.

LXXVII. But I had a different account from the Peloponnesians, who said, that Anacharsis was sent abroad by the king of Scythia; that he became a disciple of the Grecians; and at his return told the king that all the Greeks were employed in acquiring knowledge[c], except the Lacedæmonians, who only studied how to speak and answer with prudence: but this is a fiction contrived in Greece. Anacharsis therefore was killed in the manner I have mentioned, because he affected foreign customs, and had intercourse with the Grecians.

LXXVIII. Many years after this event, Scyles the son of Ariapithes, king of Scythia, met with the like fate. Ariapithes was the father of many other children; but he had Scyles by an Istrian[d], not a Scythian woman. His mother instructed him in the Grecian language and letters; and when, after some time, Ariapithes was killed by the fraud of Spargapithes, king of the Agathyrsi, Scyles took possession of the kingdom, and married Opæa, his father's wife, a native of Scythia, and mother of Oricus, another son of Ariapithes. But though Scyles was king of the Scythians, he was by no means pleased with the Scythian mode of life, but was much rather inclined to the Grecian manners on account of the education he had received, and therefore he acted thus. Leading the Scythian army to the city of the Borysthenitæ[e], which they say is a colony of the Milesians, and arriving before the place, he used to leave his Scythians without the walls, and entering alone, cause the gates to be immediately shut; then having laid aside his Scythian garment, he used to take the Grecian habit, and in this dress used to walk in public, without guards or other attendants. And that no Scythian might see him dressed in this manner, he placed sentinels at every gate; conforming himself to the Grecian customs in the worship of the Gods, no less than in all other things: and after he had stayed a month or more in this place, he used to resume the Scythian habit, and depart. This practice he frequently repeated; he also built a palace in the city, and married a native of the place to inhabit it[f].

[c] This character of the Greeks corresponds with that given by St. Paul, 1 Cor. i. 22, "The Greeks seek after wisdom."

[d] Istros or Istria, or according to Pliny (iv. 2. and 12.) Istropolis, was situated on the Euxine to the south of the southern mouth of the Nile.

[e] Olbiopolis or Olbia. See ch. 18.

[f] Γυναῖκα ἔγημε ἐς αὐτά. Αὐτά refers to *οἰκία*, *uxorem duxit in istas ædes*. See Valckenaer's note.

LXXIX. Since however it was destined that misfortune should befal him, it happened on this occasion. He was very desirous to be initiated in the rites of Bacchus; and when he was just upon the point of being initiated, a very great prodigy happened. The outward court of the magnificent palace, which, I have said, he built in the capital of the Borysthenitæ, was adorned quite round with images of white marble, representing sphinxes and griffins. Upon this place the thunder of heaven descended, and the whole was burnt to the ground; yet Scyles still persisted in his resolution, and accomplished his initiation. Now because the Scythians reproach the Grecians with these bacchanals, and say, that to imagine a God driving men into the most violent transports of madness, is not agreeable to right reason, one of the Borysthenitæ, after Scyles had been initiated, carried the information[g] to the Scythian army in these words: "You Scythians," said he, "laugh at us, because we celebrate bacchanals, and are possessed by the God; but now the same deity "has taken possession of your king; for he also celebrates "the rites of Bacchus, full of a divine fury; and if you will "not believe me, follow, and I will shew you the fact." The principal of the Scythians accompanied him accordingly; and he conducted them in, and secretly placed them in one of the towers: when Scyles went past with a thyasus, and they saw him acting the bacchanal, they regarded it as a great calamity, and having gone back to the camp, acquainted all the army with what they had seen.

LXXX. After this, when Scyles returned home, the Scythians revolted from him, and elected his brother Octamasades, born of the daughter of Tereus; which Scyles hearing, and understanding the reason of their proceeding, he fled to Thrace. Octamasades, being informed of his flight, marched with an army against Thrace, and arriving on the banks of the Ister, found the forces of the Thracians advancing to meet him: but as both sides were preparing for a battle[h], Sitalces the Thracian sent a herald to Octamasades, with this message; "Why should we try the fortune of war? "Thou art the son of my sister, and hast my brother with "thee. Surrender my brother to me, and I will deliver "Scyles into thy hands, and so neither of us shall run the "hazard of a defeat." For the brother of Sitalces, having formerly fled from him, was now with Octamasades, who, ac-

[g] *Δεπρήστευσε.* Stephens in his Thesaurus give to the word *διαπρήστευω* the signification of *Indicium defero, indico*; it does not occur in any other author. Schweighæuser purposes to read *διεδρήστευσε.*

[h] *Συνάπτω* is taken absolutely, as *committo* among the Latins: *μάχην* is understood; so also Eurip. Phœniss. 1390. *Larcher.*

cepting the condition, surrendered his uncle by the mother's side to Sitalces, and received his brother Scyles in exchange. Sitalces, upon the delivery of his brother, decamped with his army, and Octamasades took off the head of Scyles the same day. Thus the Scythians guard their own customs, and thus they punish those who introduce foreign manners.

LXXXI. The discourses I heard concerning the numbers of the Scythians were so various, that I could not obtain any certain information on that subject; some pretending they were exceedingly numerous, and others saying that there were very few real Scythians; thus much however they shewed me. There is a spot of land between the Borysthenes and the Hypanis, called Exampæus[i], which I mentioned a little before, and said that there was in it a bitter fountain, the water of which rendered the Hypanis unfit to be drank. In this place lies a bowl of brass, six times bigger than that which was placed by Pausanias[k] the son of Cleombrotus, at the mouth of the Euxine sea. They who have not been eye-witnessess may be here informed, the Scythian vessel is six digits thick, and large enough to contain full six hundred amphoras. The inhabitants say it was wrought up out of the points of arrows, by the order of their king Ariantes; who being desirous to know the number of the Scythians, commanded every one to bring him the point of an arrow, on pain of death; by which means so great a number was brought together, that resolving to leave a monument of the thing, he cause this bowl of brass to be made, and dedicated in Exampæus. This I heard concerning the numbers of the Scythians.

LXXXII. Their country has nothing wonderful, except the rivers, which are very many and very great; but whatever may seem worthy of observation, besides the rivers and extent of the plains, shall not be omitted. They shew the print of the foot of Hercules, upon a stone lying by the river Tyres, shaped like the step of a man, and two cubits in length[l]: but I will now return to the subject I at first set out to relate.

[i] See ch. 52.

[k] Nymphis of Heraclea relates (Athen. xii. 9.) in the sixteenth book of the history of his country, that Pausanias, who vanquished Mardonius at Platæa, in violation of the laws of Sparta, and from his pride consecrated, near Byzantium, a brazen bowl to those Gods whose statues may be seen at the mouth of the Euxine; which bowl still exists. Vanity and insolence had made him so far forget himself that he presumed to state in the inscription, that he himself consecrated it, "Pausanias the Lacedæmonian, son of "Cleombrotus, and of the ancient race "of Hercules, general of Greece, has "consecrated this bowl to Neptune as a "monument of his valour." *Larcher.*

Another very similar instance of the vanity of Pausanias, is mentioned by Pausanias the historian, book i. ch. 132.

[l] The length of the foot of Perseus was the same. See book ii. ch. 91.

LXXXIII. Whilst Darius was making preparations[m] against the Scythians, and sending messengers to command some to raise land forces, others to provide a fleet, and others to lay a bridge over the Thracian Bosphorus; Artabanus the son of Hystaspes, and brother of Darius, was desiring him by no means to make an expedition against the Scythians, representing the poverty of Scythia; and when he found that although he gave him good counsel he could not persuade him, he desisted. But Darius, when every thing was prepared, led his army from Susa.

LXXXIV. At that time Œobazus[n], a Persian, who had three sons in his army, came and desired him that one of the three might be left at home. The king replied to him as to a friend, and to one who made a moderate request, that he would leave him all his sons: which answer Œobazus received with great joy, because he hoped his sons would have their dismission from the army. But Darius commanded the officers appointed for such purposes to put all the sons of Œobazus to death, and in that condition left them to their father.

LXXXV. Then marching with his army from Susa, he advanced to Chalcedon upon the Bosphorus, where a bridge was laid ready[o] for his passage; and going on board a ship; he sailed to the Cyanean islands[p], which the Grecians say for-

[m] Herodotus's account of this expedition affords remarkable proof of his propensity to relate wonderful stories which he had heard, and of his honest scruple to invent what he had not heard; and at the same time adds powerfully to the instances before occurring, of his having information of distant countries and transactions beyond what, for his age and circumstances, might be expected. Nothing can be more improbable and inconsistent, not to say impossible, than his story of the Persian monarch's cruelty to Œobazus and his sons. All the most authenticated circumstances in the life of Darius mark him as a politic prince, yet of singular humanity. But that execution, as it stands reported by Herodotus, appears scarcely less absurd in its impolicy than abominable for its cruelty. Yet, that about the time of Darius's march for Scythia, there may have been executions in Persia, in a family of rank, is by no means impossible: and while the policy of a despotic government would conceal the real circumstances of the crime; perhaps also forbidding conversation upon it, the absurd tale which Herodotus has transmitted to posterity, might pass in whispers as far as Asia Minor. Mitford's Greece, ch. vi. 3. note 15. See also the remainder of his note.

[n] The same story is told by Seneca de Irâ, iii. 16.

[o] This bridge was thrown across the Bosphorus, now called the canal of Constantinople. Although he seems to speak as if the bridge had been at Chalcedon, yet it must only be taken for a loose and general way of speaking; Chalcedon being the nearest town of note to the bridge. In chap. 87. he speaks more accurately and critically. Besides, Chalcedon is situated *beyond* the opening of the Bosphorus, into the Propontis; and has an expanse of water of more than double the breadth of the Bosphorus, between it and Constantinople. *Rennel*, p. 117, &c.

[p] The Cyanean rocks were so near to one another, that, when viewed at a distance, they appeared to touch. This optical illusion probably gave rise to the fable, and the fable gained credit from the dangers encountered on this sea. See Apollon. Rhod. ii. ver. 320, &c. and 559, &c. *Larcher*.

merly floated about. There, sitting in the temple[q], he took a view of the Euxine sea, which truly merits admiration. This sea, of all others the most admirable, is eleven thousand one hundred stades in length, and, in the widest part, three thousand three hundred in breadth. The mouth is four stades over; and the length of the strait, which is called the Bosphorus, where the bridge of communication was laid, contains about a hundred and twenty stades, and extends to the Propontis. The Propontis[r] is five hundred stades in breadth, one thousand four hundred in length, and flows into the Hellespont[s]; which being seven stades over in the narrowest place, and extending to four hundred stades in length, falls into a more open sea, which is called the Ægean.

LXXXVI. These seas were measured in the following manner. A ship commonly advances about seventy thousand orgyæ in a long day, and about sixty thousand in the night. Now a voyage from the mouth of the Euxine sea to the river Phasis, which is the utmost point, may be performed in nine days and eight nights; comprehending the measure of one million, one hundred and ten thousand orgyæ, or eleven thousand and one hundred stades. From Sindica[t] to Themiscyra, situate on the river Thermodon, which is the broadest part of the Euxine sea, the passage is made in three days and two nights, being three hundred and thirty thousand orgyæ, or three thousand and three hundred stades over. These are the dimensions of the Euxine, the Bosphorus, and the Hellespont, which are situate as I have related. The Euxine receives the waters of a lake called Mæotis, not much inferior[u] in circumference to that sea, and usually named the mother of the Euxine.

LXXXVII. When Darius had looked over this sea, he

[q] Jupiter was invoked in this temple under the name of Urius, because this deity was supposed to be favourable to navigation; οὖρος signifying *a favourable wind*. There could never be more need of his succour than in an extremely stormy sea. Spon and Wheler have given us the inscription that is on the base of the statue of that God, which is also given more correctly by Chishull in his Appendix to the Asiatic Antiquities. *Larcher*.

[r] Between the Bosphorus and the Hellespont, the shores of Europe and Asia, receding on either side, enclose the sea of Marmara, which was known to the ancients by the name of Propontis. The navigation from the issue of the Bosphorus to the entrance of the Hellespont, is about 120 miles. Gibbon's Decline and Fall, ch. 17.

[s] For a description of this sea, and of the whole of the adjacent coast, see Gibbon's Decline and Fall, ch. 17. which is collected from the best accounts of ancient and modern writers. See also Major Rennel's work, pp. 53, 120. and seq.

[t] This country is now called Kuban; and is said to be inhabited by the Nekrassonian Cossacks. Herodotus mentioned the people in ch. 28. *Rennel*, ib.

[u] In order to get room for this, he must have extended it a vast way to the *north*, and *east*, beyond the truth. The ideas of Polybius, lib. iv. c. 5. on this subject, are worth attention, as well from the matter of them, as that they serve to explain the idea of Herodotus in this place. *Rennel*, p. 54.

returned to the bridge, which was contrived by Mandrocles, a Samian architect. He likewise viewed the Bosphorus, and erected two columns of white stone on the shore, with an inscription in the Assyrian tongue on the one, and in the Grecian language on the other, mentioning the several nations he had in his army, which was composed of men drawn out of every country of his empire, and amounted to the number of seven hundred thousand horse and foot, besides six hundred sail of ships. In succeeding times these pillars were removed by the Byzantians into their city, and used in building an altar to the Orthosian Diana[x]; except one stone, full of Assyrian letters, which they left near a temple, dedicated to Bacchus, in Byzantium. The place where Darius caused the bridge to be laid over the Bosphorus was, as I conjecture, in the middle of the way between Byzantium and the temple which stands at the mouth of the Euxine.

LXXXVIII. The king was so pleased with the performance, that he rewarded the Samian architect, Mandrocles, with ten of every thing[y]. And Mandrocles, having painted[z] the bridge across the Bosphorus, with Darius sitting on a throne, and his army passing over the bridge, dedicated the picture in the temple of Juno, as the first-fruits of the presents, with this inscription:

> To Juno sacred, by Mandrocles plac'd,
> This piece describes the artful bridge he laid
> Over the fishy Bosphorus. He join'd
> The fertile Asia to Europa's shore,
> Pleas'd the great king Darius, and acquir'd
> Fame to his country, to himself a crown.

This memorial was left by the person who contrived the bridge.

LXXXIX. And Darius, after he had rewarded Mandrocles, ordered his army to pass into Europe; having commanded the Ionians to sail by the Euxine sea to the Ister; there to wait his arrival, and lay a bridge over that river: for his naval forces consisted of Ionians, Æolians, and Hellespontines. They passed accordingly by the Cyanean islands, shaping their course directly to the Ister; and after they had sailed up the river during two days, arriving at that neck where the stream divides into several mouths, they formed a

[x] There was in Arcadia a mountain called Orthius. Diana was worshipped there, and from thence took the name of Orthian or Orthosian. She was worshipped under that name in Tauris, and at Sparta. In Tauris men were sacrificed to her; at Lacedæmon, boys were flagellated before her altars with the greatest severity, without uttering the least complaint. *Larcher.*

[y] See the note on book i. ch. 50.

[z] *Ζῶα γραψάμενος* is the same as *ζωγραφήσας*; see also the note on book i. ch. 70.

bridge. In the mean time Darius had passed over the Bosphorus, and marched through Thrace, and when he arrived at the sources of the river Tearus, he encamped there with his army three days.

XC. The inhabitants of the country say, this river is more excellent than any other for the cure of various distempers, and especially of ulcers, either in men or horses. The springs of the Tearus are thirty-eight; and though some of these are hot, and others cold, yet all descend from the same rock. They are at an equal distance from Heræopolis, near Perinthus, and Apollonia on the Euxine sea, two days' journey from each. The Tearus runs into the Contadesdus, the Contadesdus into the Agrianes, the Agrianes into the Hebrus, and the Hebrus into the sea by the city Ænus.

XCI. Darius, having encamped, was so delighted with this river, that he erected a pillar with the following inscription: THE SPRINGS OF THE TEARUS YIELD THE BEST AND MOST BEAUTIFUL WATER OF ALL RIVERS: DARIUS THE SON OF HYSTASPES, KING OF THE PERSIANS, AND OF ALL THE CONTINENT, THE BEST AND MOST EXCELLENT OF MEN, LEADING AN ARMY AGAINST THE SCYTHIANS, ARRIVED HERE.

XCII. Darius having departed from this, arrived at another river, called Artiscus, which passes through the country of the Odrysians, where, at his arrival, he marked out a certain spot of ground, and commanded every man of the army to bring a stone thither as he should pass by the place; and when they had executed his order he moved again, having thus left vast heaps of stones.

XCIII. But before he reached the Ister, he subdued the Getæ, who think themselves immortal; for the Thracians of Salmydessus, together with the Scyrmiadæ and the Nypsæi, who inhabit above the cities of Apollonia and Mesambria, submitted to Darius without resistance; but the Getæ by a foolish infatuation opposed him, and though they are the most valiant and honest of all the Thracians, were easily conquered and reduced to servitude.

CXIV. They think themselves immortal in this manner. They imagine that the man who ceases to live is not dead, but goes to Zalmoxis[a], accounted by some among them to be the same with Gebeleïzis[b]. Every fifth year they elect a

[a] I prefer this reading to that of Zamolxis, because it is that of the best and greatest number of manuscripts, and because Zalmos, in the Thracian language, means the *skin of a bear*; and Porphyry, in the Life of Pythagoras, (xiv. p. 16.) observes, that he was called Zalmoxis, because he was covered with the skin of that animal as soon as he was born. *Larcher.*

[b] Bayer interprets this word, *he who gives repose*. He rests his interpretation on the Lithuanian language. *Larcher.*

person by lot, and send him to Zalmoxis, with orders to let him know what they want. This messenger they dispatch thus. Certain persons are appointed to hold three javelins erected, whilst others taking the man they are to send by the hands and feet, throw him up into the air, that he may fall down upon the points. If he is pierced and dies, they think the God propitious; if not, they load him with reproaches, and, affirming he is a bad man, send another, whom they furnish with instructions while he is yet alive. These Thracians, in time of thunder and lightning, let fly their arrows towards the heavens, and threaten their God, whom they think the only deity.

XCV. But, as I am informed by the Greeks who inhabit about the Hellespont and the Euxine sea, this Zalmoxis was a man, and lived at Samos, in the service of Pythagoras[c] the son of Mnesarchus; and having procured his liberty, and acquired great riches, he returned to his own country; and finding the Thracians ignorant and miserable, he, who had learnt the Ionian way of living and manners, (more polite than those of Thrace,) by conversing with Grecians, and with Pythagoras, who was not the meanest philosopher in Greece, built a hall, in which he received and feasted the principal persons of the country, and taught them, that neither he nor any of those present, or their posterity, should ever die, but go into a place where they should live eternally, and have every kind of blessing. In the mean time he contrived a subterraneous habitation for himself, and having finished the building, went down, and continued there during three years. The Thracians, seeing him no more, regretted their loss, and lamented him as dead; but in the fourth year he appeared again, and by that means persuaded them to believe the things he had said. Thus the story is told.

XCVI. And for my own part I neither absolutely reject, nor entirely believe, the account of this person and his subterraneous habitation; but I am of opinion that Zalmoxis lived many years before Pythagoras. Yet whether this Zalmoxis were a man or a native deity among the Getæ, I bid him farewell. However, that people, observing such customs as I mentioned before, followed the army of Darius after they were subdued.

XCVII. The king arriving with all his land forces[d] at the

[c] This philosopher had framed the doctrine of the Metempsychosis, or transmigration of souls in Egypt. He pretended that he was present at the Trojan war, and was the Euphorbus who wounded Patroclus. See Horace i. Od. xxviii. 10, &c.

[d] Ὁ πεζὸς στρατός always signifies in Herodotus, Thucydides, Xenophon, Demosthenes, and others, *a land army*, and is frequently used in opposition to *ναυτικὸς στρατός*.

Ister, passed over the river, and commanded the Ionians to break the bridge, and join the army with the men they had on board. But as they were preparing to execute his orders, Coes the son of Erxandrus, and general of the Mitylenians, after he had asked Darius if it would be agreeable to him to hear an opinion from any one who wished to speak, addressed him in these terms: "O king," said he, "since we are "going to make war in a country in which we shall see no "ploughed land, nor any inhabited cities, let the bridge remain "entire, under the guard of those who put it together, that "whether we find the Scythians and succeed in our enter-"prize, or whether we be unable to find them, we may at "least secure our retreat. I am not at all afraid that the "Scythians will defeat us in battle; but rather, if we are "unable to find them, that we may suffer somewhat by wan-"dering about the country. Perhaps some may think I say "this for my own sake, in order to continue here; but, O "king, I sincerely propose what I judge most conducing to "the good of your affairs, for I will follow you, and would "by no means be left behind." Darius, pleased with his advice, answered him thus: "Lesbian friend, if I return "home in safety, fail not to come into my presence, that I "may reward the best of counsels with the greatest acknow-"ledgment."

XCVIII. Then tying sixty knots* upon a string, and calling for the Ionian commanders, he said, "Men of Ionia, I "have altered the resolution I had made concerning the "bridge, and therefore take this string and do as I direct. "Every day, after you see me beginning to march against "the Scythians, untie one of these knots; and if I return "not within that time, and the days of my absence exceed "the number of the knots, you may depart with your ships "to your own country. Till that time, since I have changed "my determination, do you guard the bridge, and apply the "utmost of your care to preserve and secure it; and if you "do this, you will exceedingly oblige me." And after Darius had spoken these words, he hastened onward.

XCIX. The territories of Thrace lie extended in front of Scythia, and descend to the sea. A bay is formed by this country, and at that place Scythia begins, and the Ister flows through it, and falls into the sea towards the east. I will proceed to give the measurement of those regions of Scythia that begin at the Ister, and stretch down by the sea coast.

* About a century and a half after this time, they used to drive a nail once a year into the wall of the temple of Minerva, at Rome, to keep an account of the number of years.

That part which lies to the south of the Ister, is the ancient Scythia, as far as the city of Carcinitis; the country which is contiguous, and extends to the same sea, and is also mountainous, and projects into the Euxine is inhabited by a Tauric nation as far as Chersonesus Trachea[f]; it terminates in the eastern sea[g]. Scythia is divided into two parts, both extending to the sea, one towards the south and the other towards the east, not unlike the region of Attica: for the Tauri are so placed in Scythia, as if any other people instead of the Athenians, possessed the corner of Sunium, which extends considerably out into the sea from the borough of Thoricus to that of Anaphlystus. Such is Tauris, if I may be permitted to compare small things with great. But to those who have never sailed by that part of Attica, I shall explain myself farther: suppose then that a nation distinct from the Japygians, should possess the promontory of Japygia, from the port of Brundusium to Tarentum, and by that means cut off from the other parts of the country. Many other instances of the same nature might be given; but I need add no more to illustrate the description of Tauris.

C. The Scythians inhabit the countries that lie beyond the Tauri, and those that extend to the eastern sea; together with the regions situate to the westward of the Cimmerian Bosphorus and the lake Mæotis, to the river Tanais, which flows into the inner part of that lake. So that those countries which, beginning at the Ister, advance upwards to the midland parts, are bordered first by the Agathyrsi, then by the Neuri, next by the Androphagi, and, in the last place, by the Melanchlæni.

CI. Two parts therefore of Scythia, which is quadrangular[h],

[f] Herodotus is not here talking of a peninsula, but of a Greek town, which had that name. Stephens of Byzantium positively affirms it, and also quotes this passage of Herodotus. *Larcher*. Schweighæuser and Holstein are of a contrary opinion.

[g] This description of Scythia is attended with great difficulties. 1st. It is not easy to get at the true meaning of Herodotus. 2ndly. I cannot believe that the description here given agrees in all points with the true position of the places. I am nevertheless astonished that it should be in general exact, when we consider the little knowledge that men had of this country. He must have made great researches, to have been able to speak with so much correctness as he does. Bellanger understands by *the eastern sea*, the Palus Mæotis. But I am fully persuaded that Herodotus, when he speaks in this description of the sea to the south, or to the east, means only different points of the Euxine. *Larcher*.

[h] Although the area and extent of Scythia were greatly under-rated by Herodotus, yet, by a misconception of the relative positions of the coasts of the Euxine and Palus Mæotis, he has overrated the extent of the *coast* of Scythia bordering on those seas. For, by the context it appears, that he supposed the coasts of the Euxine and Mæotis to form a right angle at their point of junction, at the peninsula of Taurica; (Krimea;) representing two sides which respectively faced the S. E. and S. W.; or perhaps more strictly the E. S.E. and S. S.W.

extend to the sea; each of which is equal to the other in every way, both the one which extends inland, and that which is along the coast. For from the Ister to the Borysthenes, is a journey of ten days; ten more from the Borysthenes to the lake Mæotis; and twenty from the sea, by the midland countries, to the Melanchlæni, who inhabit above the Scythians. I reckon two hundred stades[i] for every day's journey; so that thus the sides of Scythia must be four thousand stades in length; and the direct passage upwards, by the midland parts, the same number. Such is the extent of this country.

CII. The Scythians, after they had conferred together, and found they were not able with their own forces to repel the army of Darius in the open field, dispatched messengers to the adjoining nations; and when their kings were assembled, they consulted how to act, under the apprehensions of being invaded by so numerous an army. This assembly consisted of the kings of the Tauri, of the Agathyrsi, of the Neuri[k], of the Androphagi, of the Melanchlæni, of the Geloni, of the Budini, and of the Sauromatæ.

CIII. Of these, the Tauri[l] observe the following customs: all those who suffer shipwreck, and the Grecians they seize upon their coast, they sacrifice to a virgin in this manner. After the preparatory ceremonies, they strike the man on the head with a club, and, as some affirm, precipitate the body from a rock on which their temple is built, reserving only the head to be fixed on a pole; whilst others, acknowledging this to be the way they use in disposing of the head, yet pretend they never throw the body down from the hill, but bury it under ground. The Tauri themselves say, that the deity they worship with these sacrifices is Iphigenia[m] the daughter of

The truth is, that the coasts of the Euxine do not conjointly present any such form as he supposes, but, on the contrary, the maritime part of Scythia extends generally in an E. N. E. direction from the mouth of the Danube, to that of the Tanais; forming not *two* sides of a square, but in effect, *one* side only, of a parallegram of much greater dimensions; although that side be very crooked and indented. *Rennel*, p. 51. and seq. Major Rennel has also explained with great sagacity the causes of the errors of Herodotus.

[i] Authors are not at all agreed with each other, nor yet with themselves, about the length of a day's journey. In the 5th book, ch. 5. he gives only 150 stades.

[k] It would appear that some at least of these names were purely *Grecian*; and are therefore the *nicknames* given by that people, rather than the *proper* names of the nations. Or the Grecians may have given significant Greek names, which in sound resembled the proper ones. *Rennel*, p. 83.

[l] Their country was the same as the modern Krimea.

[m] On that inhospitable shore, Euripides, embellishing with exquisite art the tales of antiquity, has placed the scene of one of his most affecting tragedies. The bloody sacrifices of Diana, the arrival of Orestes and Pylades, and the triumph of virtue and religion over savage fierceness, serve to represent an historical truth, that the Tauri, the original inhabitants of the Peninsula, were, in some degree, reclaimed from their

Agamemnon. Those who fall into their hands in time of war, are treated in this manner: every one cuts off the head of an enemy, which he carries home, and fixes to a long pole, and erects it on the top of his house, and for the most part, over the chimney[n]; they say that these, thus loftily situated, are the guards of the whole house. This people live by war and rapine.

CIV. The Agathyrsi[o] are a most effeminate[p] people, and wear a very great number of golden ornaments. They have their women in common, to the end that they may be all brethren, and, being thus of one family, may never exercise any mutual envy and animosities. In other things they approach the manner of the Thracians.

CV. The Neuri[q] observe the customs of Scythia; and one generation, before the expedition of Darius, were driven out of their country by serpents. For besides those that were bred in their own territories, a much greater number came down from the deserts; until at length they were compelled to abandon their habitations, and retire among the Budini. These men seem to be[r] magicians[s]; for the Scythians, with the Greeks who inhabit in Scythia, say, that all the Neuri, once every year, are transformed into wolves[t] for a few days, and then resume their former shape. But I am not persuaded to believe this, though they affirm their assertion with oaths.

CVI. The Androphagi[u] live in a more savage manner than any other nation, having no public distribution of justice, nor established laws. They apply themselves to the breeding of cattle, clothe themselves like the Scythians, and speak a peculiar language. They are the only nation of these that I have mentioned who eat human flesh.

CVII. The Melanchlæni[x] wear no other garments than

brutal manners, by a gradual intercourse with the Grecian colonies, which settled along the maritime coast. Gibbon's Decline and Fall, ch. 10.

[n] The superstitious amongst us nail a horse-shoe on the threshold, or against the mast of a ship.

[o] These according to Rennel occupied the province of Transylvania generally; together with the N. E. part of Hungary. In M. D'Anville's ancient geography they are found on Rubo, or river of Riga.

[p] This does not agree with their vigorous conduct related in chapter 125.

[q] We must place the Neuri in the eastern part of the province of Gallicia, and in part of the adjoining country of Lutzk or Lusuc. *Rennel*, p. 86.

[r] Κινδυνεύουσιν εἶναι. This phrase does not occur again in Herodotus; it is very common in Plato and Xenophon.

[s] They were probably, says Rennel, an ingenious people, and exceeded their neighbours in arts, as well as in hospitality, p. 93.

[t] This is also related by Pomponius Mela, lib. ii. c. 1. Pellontier supposes that this opinion arose from their clothing themselves in the skins of wolves during the winter. This is rejected by Larcher.

[u] These must have occupied Polish Russia, and both banks of the river Prypetz, the western head of the Borysthenes. *Rennel*, p. 86.

[x] These should have possessed the present Russian governments, (either entirely or in part,) of Naugorod, Orel, Mohilow and Kursk; together with some

black[y], and have their name from that custom. These follow the usages of Scythia.

CVIII. The Budini[z] are a great and populous nation; they paint their bodies[a] entirely with blue and red. They have in their country a city called by the name of Gelonus, built with timber, and surrounded by a high wall of the same materials, each side of which is thirty stades in length. The buildings, as well sacred as private, are of timber likewise: and they have temples dedicated to the Gods of Greece, adorned after the Grecian manner with images, altars, and chapels of wood. They celebrate the triennial festivals[b] of Bacchus, and perform the bacchanalian ceremonies: for the Geloni were originally Grecians, who transplanted themselves from the trading ports of Greece, and settled among the Budini, where they use a language partly Scythian and partly Grecian.

CIX. But the Budini differ from the Geloni in language, and in their manner of living; for being original inhabitants of the country, they apply themselves to the keeping of cattle, and are the only people of these parts who eat lice; whereas the Geloni till the land, feed upon corn, cultivate gardens, and are utterly unlike the Budini both in form and complexion; though the Greeks, without ground, call these Budini by the name of Geloni. Their country abounds in trees of all kinds; and in that part where they grow in greatest numbers, lies a deep and spacious lake, surrounded by a morass covered with reeds. In this place otters, beavers, and other animals of a square visage, are frequently taken. Their skins are sown as borders to their cloaks, and their testicles are useful in hysteric diseases.

CX. Concerning the Sauromatæ[c] we have the following account. When the Grecians had fought a battle on the river Thermodon against the Amazons[d], who by the Scythians are

lesser tracts, towards the Tanais and the city of Moscow. *Rennel*, p. 86.

[y] Rennel relates in a note, that Tamerlane found in the mountains of Kawuck, (a part of the Indian Caucasus,) a tribe who are named by his historian Sherefeddin, *Sia-poshians*, or black-clothed. The Getæ beyond the Jaxartes had black ensigns. See Sherefeddin's Timur, book iii. ch. 6.

[z] The country of the Budini has been taken for Woronetz, and its neighbourhood, as well from description as position; it being, like the other, full of forests. *Rennel*, p. 93.

[a] Hence Virgil calls the Geloni, in his 2nd Georgic, v. 115, *Picti Geloni*.

[b] It is said that the Greeks celebrated the Trieterides, (or triennial festivals,) because Bacchus was absent three years in his expedition against the Indians. Diodorus Siculus, iii. 64. iv. 3.

[c] The Sauromatæ intended by Herodotus, (for his Scythia is the Sauromatia, or Sarmatia of later authors,) may be supposed to have extended along the eastern side of the Mæotis, and thence up the Tanais, to about the part where that river and the Wolga approach each other, to form the Isthmus at Zaritzyn: and on the probable supposition that the *lower part* of the *Donetz* was taken for the *Don*, they must have occupied *both* banks of that river to the same extent, that is 15 journeys of 3000 stadia. *Rennel*, p. 89.

[d] Since the story of the Amazons, in the way it is commonly told, is so justly

called *Aiorpata*, or, in our language, manslayers; *Aior* signifying a man, and *Pata* to kill; they departed after the victory they had obtained, and in three of their ships carried off all the Amazons they could take alive. Whilst they were out at sea, these Amazons conspired against the men, and killed all they found on board. But having no knowledge of navigation, nor any skill in the use of the rudder, sails, or oars, they were driven by wind and tide until they arrived at Cremni on the lake Mæotis, in the territories of the free Scythians. Here the Amazons went ashore, and, marching into the country, seized and mounted a herd of horses which they happened first to fall in with, and began to plunder the country.

CXI. The Scythians could not imagine the meaning of this incursion; and being utterly ignorant of their language, habit, and nation, wondered from whence they came. They first conjectured that they were men from the agreement of their height; but after they had skirmished with them, and taken some prisoners, they soon perceived they were women. The Scythians, therefore, consulting together, resolved not to kill them, but to send out a party consisting of a like number of young men, with orders to post themselves near their camp, and attend their motions. If the women should attack the party, they were commanded to fly, without making resistance; and when they should find themselves no longer pursued, to return again, and encamp near them. This resolution the Scythians took, out of a great desire to have children by these women.

CXII. The young men observed their instructions; and when the Amazons found they were not come with injurious intentions, they suffered them to continue there without molestation: they gradually drew their camps nearer each day, and as the young men had nothing except their arms and horses, they lived in the same manner, by hunting and pillage.

CXIII. About noon the Amazons usually separated themselves; and sometimes single, sometimes two together, went

exploded in these times, one is surprised how it came to be so universally believed, as that most of the writers of antiquity should speak of it as a fact. Nay, even our author has gone so far as to make (Calliop. 27.) the Athenians say that the Amazons had marched from the river Thermodon to attack Attica! That a community of women existed for a short time, is not improbable, since accidents may have deprived them of their husbands; but were there not in that, as in every community, males growing up to maturity? Justin, lib. ii. ch. 4. describes the origin of the Amazons to be this: a colony of *exiled* Scythians established themselves on the coast of the Euxine sea, in Cappadocia, near the river Thermodon; and being exceedingly troublesome to their neighbours, the men were all massacred. This accounts very rationally for the existence of a community of women; but who can believe that it continued. *Reinel*, p. 91.

out to comply with the necessities of nature; which when the Scythians perceived, they did so likewise. And thus one of them drew near one of the Amazons who was alone: she did not repel him, but suffered him to enjoy her person. She could not speak to him in words, because neither understood the language of the other, yet she made him understand, by certain motions of her hand, that if he would come the next day to the same place, accompanied by another Scythian, she would bring one of her companions with her. The young man, after this, departed; and having related his adventures to the rest, went the next day with another Scythian to the place of assignation, and found the Amazon waiting for him with a companion. Upon information of which success, the rest of the young men conciliated the remaining Amazons.

CXIV. The two camps were joined, and every one kept for his wife the person he first attached himself to. But because the men could not attain to speak the Amazonian tongue, the women learned the language of Scythia; and when they understood one another, the Scythians spoke to the Amazons in these terms: "We have our parents and "possessions, and being on that account unwilling to con- "tinue longer in this way of living, we would return and live "among our countrymen; always retaining you, and no other "persons, for our wives." To this the Amazons answered: "We shall never endure to live with the women of your "country, because we differ in manners. For we have "been accustomed to draw a bow, throw a javelin, and "mount a horse; and were never instructed in the usual "employments of other women. Whereas the Scythian "wives do none of the things we have mentioned, but are "employed in womanish labours, sitting still in their wag- "gons[f], unaccustomed to hunting or any other exercise; "and therefore we cannot comply with their manner of life. "Nevertheless, if you are desirous to keep us for your wives, "and to act like honest men, go to your parents; and after "you have received your part of their riches, return, and we "will live by ourselves."

CXV. The young men, consenting to go as they desired, obtained every one his portion; and at their return, the Amazons proposed another expedient in these words: "We feel "some alarm and fear[g] with regard to living in this country; "for we have deprived you of your parents, and have com-

[f] These waggons served them for houses; every one knows that in Greece the women went out but seldom, but I much fear that Herodotus attributes to the Scythian women the manners of those of Greece. *Larcher.*

[g] Φόβος signifies a sudden fright, Δέος a lasting fear of some future evil. *Ammonius.*

"mitted great depredations in these parts. Therefore, since "you have thought us worthy to be your wives, let us unanimously agree to pass the Tanais, and fix our habitations "on the other side of that river."

CXVI. The young men consenting to this also, they passed the Tanais; and after a march of three days from the river eastward, and three more from the lake Mæotis to the northward, they arrived and settled in the regions they now inhabit. Hence the wives of the Sauromatæ still continue their ancient way of living. They hunt on horseback in the company of their husbands, and sometimes alone; they march with their armies, and wear the same dress with the men.

CXVII. The Sauromatæ use the Scythian language; but corrupted from their commencement, because the Amazons never learned to speak correctly. Their marriages are attended with this circumstance: no virgin is permitted to marry, until she has killed an enemy in the field; so that some die from old age without being married, as they are not able to fulfil the conditions.

CXVIII. The messengers dispatched by the Scythians, informed the kings of the nations I have mentioned, in their assembly, that the Persians having subdued all the countries on the other continent, had thrown a bridge over the neck of the Bosphorus, and crossed to this side, where he had already reduced the Thracians, and laid another bridge upon the Ister, with design to make all these regions subject to him: "And therefore," said they, "do not you sit still at "home, and look upon our destruction with indifference; "but joining all our forces together, let us unanimously "march out, and meet the invader. If you refuse to take[h] "this resolution, we shall be compelled either to abandon the "country, or, if we stay there, we shall surrender on certain "conditions; for to what end should we suffer the last extremities, if you refuse to assist us? But it will not fall "more lightly on you on that account; for the Persian is "marching against you no less than against us; and, that he "will not content himself to destroy our country, and leave "you undisturbed, his own actions are the clearest demonstration: for if he had undertaken this expedition only "against us, in order to revenge former injuries, he ought to "have marched directly into our territories, without offering "violence to any other nation; and by that means he would "have convinced all, that he had no other enterprize in "his intentions, than the conquest of Scythia. Whereas, on

[h] The Greek is οὐκ ὦν ποιήσετε ταῦτα; which is for εἰ ὦν οὐ ποιήσετε ταῦτα. See Schæfer ad Bosii Ellips. Græc p. 758.

"the contrary, at his arrival on this continent, he immediately subdues all those places that lay in his way; and "holds in subjection the other Thracians, and more particularly the Getæ who are our neighbours."

CXIX. When the Scythians had finished these words, the kings who were present on the part of several nations, deliberated touching their proposal, and their opinions were divided. The kings of the Geloni, Budini, and Sauromatæ, unanimously determined to assist the Scythians; but the kings of the Agathyrsi, Neuri, Androphagi, Melanchlæni, and Tauri, made this answer to the messengers: "If you "had not been the first aggressors, and done the first injuries to the Persians, we should acknowledge the equity of "your present demands, and readily yielding to your desires, would concur with you in one common cause. But "as you invaded their territories without our participation, "and kept your acquisitions there, during all the time God "favoured your arms; so now by the instigation of the same "God, they return you the same measure: and therefore, "having had no part in that unjust invasion, we will not "now begin to injure the Persians. Yet if this man should "wrongfully attack us, and commence hostility against us, "we will not submit to it. Until we see that, we will remain quiet at home; because we think the Persians are not "come with hostile intentions against us, but against those "who were the authors of the first injuries."

CXX. When the Scythians had received an account of this negociation, they determined to fight no battle in the open field, because those nations had refused to assist them; but to withdraw themselves gradually from the frontiers, to fill up all the wells and springs they might pass by, and to destroy the herbage. Having divided their forces into two bodies, they resolved that the Sauromatæ should attach themselves to that division which Scopasis commanded, with directions, if the Persian should turn his march that way, to retire by the lake Mæotis to the river Tanais, and upon his retreat to follow him and harass his army. These orders were to be observed in relation to that part of the kingdom. The two other divisions of Royal Scythians, one of which being the greater, was under the government of Indathyrsus, and the other, commanded by Taxacis, were directed to act in conjunction, with the addition of the Geloni and Budini, to keep a day's march before the Persians, and gradually retreat as they had determined; and first of all to betake themselves towards the territories of those who had renounced their alliance; that since they refused to take part voluntarily in the war against the Persians, they might be compelled against their will to carry on war; and then they might return to their own country, and attack the enemy, if it should seem advantageous, after having consulted on the subject.

CXXI. When the Scythians had fixed these orders, they advanced towards the army of Darius, and commanded the best of their horse to advance before the rest; having already sent away their wives and children in the waggons they use instead of houses, with all their cattle, except so many as they thought necessary for their subsistence, ordering them to retire incessantly northward. These things therefore were being thus carried forward.

CXXII. The Scythian advanced troop, finding the Persians advanced about three days' march from the Ister, encamped about a day's march from them, and destroyed all the produce of the ground. The Persians, as soon as they saw this cavalry before them, followed their track, while they kept retiring; and then, as they directed their pursuit after one of the divisions, they advanced towards the east and the Tanais; and when they had crossed that river, the Persians also crossed after them, and pursued them until they had passed through the country of the Sauromatæ, and reached that of the Budini.

CXXIII. All the time the Persians were marching through the Scythian and Sauromatian regions, they found nothing to ravage, because those parts were dry and uncultivated. But when they had entered the country of the Budini, and had fallen in with their city, which was built with wood, and abandoned by the inhabitants after they had carried all away, they set fire to the place. After this they continued to follow the track of the enemy until they had traversed the whole region, and arrived in an uninhabited desert, situate above the Budini, and not to be passed in less than seven days. Beyond this desert the Thyssagetæ[1] inhabit; and four great rivers, known by the names of the Lycus, Oarus, Tanais, and Syrgis, rise within their country, and passing through the territories of the Mæotians, flow into the lake Mæotis.

CXXIV. Darius, as soon as he arrived at the desert, ceased his pursuit, and encamped with his army on the river Oarus. During his stay there he built eight large forts, equally distant, about sixty stades from each other, the ruins of which remain to this day; and whilst he was employed in

[1] The country of the Thyssagetæ may be readily conceived to extend along the *north* and *north-east* of the Budini, between the upper part of the Tanais, and the Wolga about Saratow. The Wolga may be taken for the *Oarus*; and perhaps the Medweditza and Choper for the *Lycus* and *Syrgis*, which seems to be the same as that intended by Hyrgis in ch. 57. *Rennel*, p. 90.

this work, the Scythians, marching about by the upper regions, returned into Scythia, and Darius perceiving they had entirely vanished, and appeared no more, left his forts half finished, and turned his march to the westward, supposing them to be all the Scythians, and that they had fled that way.

CXXV. He advanced with his army with all possible speed, and entering Scythia, fell in with the two Scythian divisions, and pursued them; but they kept a day's march before him. The Scythians, as had been determined, fled towards those nations that had refused to assist them, and entered first into the territories of the Melanchlæni; and when they and the Persians had put all things there into confusion, they drew the Persians after them into the country of the Androphagi, where, after they had committed the like disorders, the Scythians led the enemy among the Neuri; and having brought these also into the same circumstances, withdrew again towards the Agathyrsi. But before they entered the country, the Agathyrsi, seeing all their neighbours flying in confusion before the Scythians, dispatched a herald to forbid them to come within their limits, and at the same time to inform them, that if they should attempt to force their way, they must first fight with the Agathyrsi. This message was no sooner sent, than the Agathyrsi marched to the borders with a resolution to defend their territories against all invaders. Whereas the Melanchlæni, Androphagi, and Neuri, never thought of defending themselves against the invasion of the Scythians and Persians, but forgetting their former menaces, continued to fly in confusion to the northern deserts. The Scythians, upon the prohibition of the Agathyrsi, did not attempt to enter their country, but departing from Neuri retreated before the Persians into their own territories.

CXXVI. And after they had continued to withdraw themselves in this manner for a considerable time, Darius sent a horseman to Indathyrsus, king of Scythia, with the following message: "O ill-fated man, why dost thou incessantly betake "thyself to flight, when thou mayest choose one of these two "things? If thou art persuaded thy forces are able to en"counter my army in the field, cease your wanderings and "fight; but if you are conscious of your inferiority, on that "account also desist from flying, and bringing earth and "water[k] as presents to your master, come to a conference."

[k] The ancient nations of the west, when they surrendered, used to gather some grass and present it to the conqueror. Pliny says that the custom existed in his time among the Germans, (lib. xxii. cap. 4.) In the East and other countries, they gave earth and water. By this they acknowledged him their master without control, for earth and water involve every thing. *Larcher.*

CXXVII. To this message the Scythian king made answer in these words. "This is the state of my affairs. I never "fled from any man out of fear, neither have I declined to "give thee battle from that motive. For in all this I have "done nothing new, or different from our constant custom, "even in time of peace; but I will not conceal the reasons "that move us to this conduct. We have no towns nor cul-"tivated lands, and therefore, being under no apprehension "of depredation and ravage, we did not immediately offer you "battle. Yet if you are so desirous to constrain us to fight, "we have the sepulchres of our ancestors among us, which "if you find and attempt to violate, you will soon be con-"vinced whether we will fight on that account, or not. For "we are resolved not to come to a battle before, unless rea-"son urges us. But to leave this point; I am to tell you in "the next place, that I acknowledge no other lords than Ju-"piter my progenitor, and Vesta queen of the Scythians; "that instead of presenting you with earth and water, I shall "send you such presents as are becoming. And for having "said that you were my master, I bid you weep[l]." The herald departed to carry this answer to Darius.

CXXVIII. When the kings of Scythia had heard the name of servitude they were filled with indignation, and ordered the division of Scopasis, which had been joined by the Sauromatæ, to advance and confer with the Ionians, who guarded the bridge they had laid over the Ister. And after their departure the rest resolved to lead the Persians no longer about, but to attack them whenever they were taking their repast[m]; accordingly they observed those times and put their design in execution. In these encounters the Scythian horse always routed[n] the Persians, and drove them to their camp, where, finding they were succoured by their infantry, the Scythians were forced to retire out of fear of the Persian foot. Besides, they frequently attacked the enemy in the night, and alarmed their camp.

CXXIX. But that which was no less strange than prejudicial to the Scythians in the assaults they made, and very

[l] This was a proverbial expression; so Horace, Serm. lib. i. Sat. 10. v. 90.

———*Demetri, teque, Tigelli,*
Discipularum inter jubeo plorare cathedras.

[m] Some translate *Σῖτα ἀναιρεόμενοι' going out to forage*, &c.

[n] Like the modern Tartars, they fought mostly on horseback; like them also, daring and skilful skirmishers, but incapable of order, they defeated an enemy in detail, continually harassing and cutting off detached parties, without ever coming to a general engagement; to which, on account of their quick motion, and total disincumbrance from baggage and magazines, it was impossible to force them. Herodotus's account of this expedition exactly resembles what has been experienced in the same part of the world several times within the last century. Mitford's Greece, ch. vi. sect. 3.

advantageous to the Persians, was the braying of the asses[o] and form of the mules; for Scythia produces neither of those animals, as I have already observed, by reason of cold. The asses growing wanton, put the Scythian horse into confusion; and frequently, as they were advancing to fall upon the Persians, their horses no sooner heard the noise, than in a great fright they pricked up their ears[p] and turned short about, having never before heard such a voice, nor seen such a shape; and this accident was of some slight importance[q] in the war.

CXXX. But when the Scythians saw the Persians falling into great difficulties, they contrived this stratagem to detain them longer in Scythia, to the end that they might be reduced to the utmost straits, and to the want of all things necessary: they removed to a greater distance, leaving some of their cattle to the care of shepherds; and the Persians coming up, took the booty, and pleased themselves with their good fortune.

CXXXI. This they repeated several times, until at last the Scythian kings understanding that Darius was in great want and difficulty, sent a herald to present him on their part with a bird, a mouse, a frog, and five arrows. The Persians asked the meaning of this present; but the herald made answer, that he had no other orders than to deliver the things and return immediately; yet should advise that the Persians would consider, if they were men of any penetration, what such a gift might signify. The Persians having heard this answer, consulted together.

CXXXII. Darius declared his opinion to be, that the Scythians had by their present made a surrender of themselves, and given him possession of the land and water; "for," said he, "the mouse is bred in the earth, and subsists "by the same food as a man; a frog lives in the water; a "bird may be compared to a horse[r]; and with their arrows "they seem to deliver their whole force into my hands." This was the opinion of Darius. But the opinion of Gobryas, one of the seven who had deposed the magus, was opposed to it. He conjectured that the present intimated, "that un-"less the Persians could ascend into the air like a bird, or "conceal themselves in the earth like mice, or plunge into "the fens like frogs, they should inevitably perish by those

[o] Pindar (Pyth. Od. x. ver. 51.) says, that the Hyperboreans used to sacrifice whole hecatombs of asses to Apollo.

[p] This is nobly described by Soph. Elect. v. 25.

[q] Schweighæuser, in his Lexicon, explains the construction of this passage thus: οἱ Πέρσαι ἐφέροντο ταῦτα ἐπὶ σμικρόν τι τοῦ πολέμου: so that φερέσθαι is used in the sense of *reportare, percipere.*

[r] This can only be from the swiftness.

" arrows, and never return home;" to which interpretation the rest of the Persians concurred.

CXXXIII. In the mean time that part of the Scythians, which had been appointed to guard the lake Mæotis, and were then commanded to parley with the Ionians at the Ister, arrived in the place where the bridge was laid, and spoke to this effect: " Men of Ionia, if you will hearken to us, we are " come to make you an offer of your liberty. We have heard " that Darius commanded you to guard the bridge sixty days " only, and then to return into your own country, unless he " should arrive before the expiration of that time. Now there- " fore, since you have continued here till all those days are " elapsed, put his orders in execution, and make no difficulty " to depart, by which means you will avoid to give any just " occasion of offence either to Darius or to us." The Ionians promised to do as they desired, and the Scythians returned to their station with all expedition.

CXXXIV. The rest of the Scythians, after they had sent the present I have mentioned to Darius, drew themselves opposite the Persians with all their forces both of horse and foot, as if they intended to fight; and as they stood in order of battle, a hare ran through the space between the two armies. The Scythians immediately quitting their ranks, pursued the hare with loud outcries; and when Darius saw the confusion of the enemy, and understood that they followed a hare, he said to those he was accustomed to address on such occasions: " These men treat us with great contempt; and I " am convinced that Gobryas judged rightly concerning the " present of the Scythians. Therefore being now of the same " opinion, I think we stand in need of the best advice, to se- " cure our return into our own country." To this, Gobryas answered: " Fame had made me in some measure acquainted " with the indigence of these men; but I have learned much " more since I came hither, and observed in what manner " they deride us. My opinion therefore is, that immediately " upon the close of the day, we should light fires according to " custom, and having deceived those soldiers who are least " able to bear hardships, with all the asses tied up in the " usual manner, decamp and march away before the Scy- " thians go and break the bridge on the Ister, or the Ionians " take any resolution which may ruin us." This was the advice of Gobryas.

CXXXV. Afterwards, when night came, Darius put his counsel in execution; he left all the sick behind in his camp, with those whose loss would be of the least importance, and the asses ranged in order. He left the asses, that they might make a continual noise; and the men, evidently under pretence of attacking the enemy with the best part of the army, whilst they should remain for the security of the camp. Thus Darius imposing upon those he was preparing to abandon, and having caused the usual fires to be kindled, marched away in great haste towards the Ister. The asses being left alone, began to bray much louder than before[s]; so that the Scythians hearing the noise, firmly believed the Persians were still in their camp.

CXXXVI. But upon the appearance of day, the men that were abandoned, finding themselves betrayed by Darius, extended their hands, and acquainted the Scythians with the state of affairs, who presently drawing together the two Scythian divisions[t], and joining the other part, and the Sauromatæ, the Budini and Geloni, followed the Persians straight towards the Ister. But because the Persians had great numbers of foot in their army, and were altogether ignorant of the ways, as no roads were made, whereas the Scythians were all horse, and perfectly well acquainted with the shortest cuts, the two armies missed each other, by which means the Scythians arrived at the bridge much before the Persians, and having learnt that the enemy was not yet returned, they spoke to the Ionians, who were on board the ships, in these terms: "Since "the number of days appointed for your stay, O Ionians, is "already passed, you have not done as you ought in continuing here; and therefore, if fear has hitherto been the "cause of your delay, now take the bridge in pieces, depart "in full possession of your liberty, and give thanks to the "Gods and to the Scythians. As for the man who to this "time has been your master, we will take care to bring him "into such order, that he shall be no longer in a condition to "make war against any part of mankind." The Ionians met without delay to consult about the measures they should take in this conjuncture.

CXXXVII. Miltiades the Athenian, tyrant of the Chersonesites on the Hellespont, advised the assembly to comply with the demand of the Scythians, and to restore the liberty of Ionia. But Histiæus the Milesian, being of a contrary opinion, represented, that whereas every one there present was tyrant of his own country by the power of Darius; if that should be once abolished, he himself could no longer continue master of Miletus, nor any of the rest in the places they then possessed, because the people would undoubtedly choose to live under a popular government, rather than under the dominion of a single person. Histiæus had no sooner delivered

[s] The construction is *μᾶλλον ἴεσαν (φωνὴν) τῆς (εἰθισμένης) φωνῆς. Schw.*

[t] See ch. 120, 128, 133.

this opinion, than they all went over to his side, though they had before assented to the counsel of Miltiades.

CXXXVIII. The names of those who gave their votes[u] and were in high estimation with Darius, were, Daphnis tyrant of Abydos, Hippocles of Lampsacus[x], Erophantus of Parium[y], Metrodorus of Proconnesus[z], Aristagoras of Cyzicum, and Ariston of Byzantium; all these were from the Hellespont. Those of Ionia were, Strattis of Chios, Æacides of Samos, Laodamas of Phocæa, and Histiæus of Miletus, whose opinion was preferred before that of Miltiades. On the part of the Æolians no other person of consideration was present, except only Aristagoras of Cyme.

CXXXIX. When these men had approved the sentiment of Histiæus, they determined to add the following acts and words: they resolved to take away so much of the bridge on the Scythian side, as a bow-shot might reach, that they might not only seem to do something, when in effect they did nothing; but that they might prevent the Scythians from attempting by force to pass the Ister over their bridge; and whilst they should be employed in removing that part, which was on the Scythian side, they agreed to profess their readiness to do any thing that might be acceptable to the Scythians. When they had determined to make this addition to the opinion of Histiæus, and chosen him out of all the assembly to acquaint the Scythians with their answer, he spoke to this effect: "Men of Scythia, you have brought us good "advice, and seasonably pressed us to put it in execution; "you have pointed out the right way, and we readily obey "you. We are now cutting off the passage as you see, and "will finish the work with all diligence, because we resolve "to be free. In the mean time your part is to find out "the Persians, and having found them, to inflict proper ven-"geance on them, both on your own, and on our account."

CXL. The Scythians believing a second time that the Ionians were sincere, marched back to seek the Persians; but entirely missed the ways they had taken. Of this error the Scythians themselves were the cause, by destroying the pasture for the horse, and choking the springs, which if they had not done, they might without difficulty have found the

[u] Οἱ τὴν ψῆφον διαφέροντες. *Suffragia ultro citroque (pro suâ quisque sententiâ) ferentes.* Schweigh. Διαφέρειν is used in the same sense in the Orestes of Euripides, ver. 48.

[x] This town was situated on the Hellespont, north of Percotæ. It was anciently called Pityusa; and is now called Lampsaco or Lampsaki; and is at present very inconsiderable. Priapus was worshipped here more than in other places.

[y] Parium is to the N.W. of Lampsacus. It is now called Camanan.

[z] Proconnesus is an island in the Propontis. From the beautiful marble found there, it now bears the name of Marmara.

Persians. But now, that which they thought they had contrived to their great advantage, proved the very thing that misled them. For they sought the enemy in those parts of the country, where forage and water were to be found, imagining they would return by that way. But the Persians, repeating without deflexion the march they had made before, found the bridge with some difficulty. And as they arrived in the night, and perceived the bridge broken off, they fell into the utmost consternation, supposing they were abandoned by the Ionians.

CXLI. Darius had about his person an Egyptian, surpassing all other men in the strength of his voice. This man he commanded to stand on the bank of the Ister, and call Histiæus the Milesian. Which when he had done, Histiæus, who heard him at the first cry, brought all the vessels together, and joined the bridge immediately, that the army might pass. Thus the Persians escaped.

CXLII. The Scythians in their search missed them a second time. On this account they say, that the Ionians, considered as a free people, are the worst and basest of men; considered as slaves, they indeed love their master, and are not inclined to abandon his service. These reproaches the Scythians fling out against the Ionians.

CXLIII. Darius marched through Thrace to Sestos in the Chersonesus; and embarking there passed over into Asia, and left Megabyzus, a Persian, to be his general in Europe. He had already paid this man great honour, having expressed himself in this manner among the Persians; being one day about to eat some pomegranates, he had no sooner opened the first, than his brother Artabanus asked him, Of what thing he would wish to possess a number equal to the grains of that fruit; and received for answer, That he would rather choose so many men perfectly resembling Megabyzus, than the entire conquest of Greece. Thus he honoured him among the Persians, and now left him the command of an army consisting of eighty thousand men.

CXLIV. Megabyzus rendered his own name immortal among the Hellespontines, by the following expression: being informed, when he was at Byzantium, that the Chalcedonians[a] had inhabited in that country seventeen years before the arrival of the Byzantians; "Sure," said he, "the Chalcedonians were blind in those times; for if they could have seen, they would never have chosen so foul a situation, when they might have built their city in so beautiful a place." This same Megabyzus, being left in these parts to

[a] For a description of the situation of Chalcedon, see Gibbon's Decline and Fall, ch. 17. The saying of Megabyzus is alluded to by Tacitus, Annal. xii. 62.

command the army of Darius, subdued those nations who were not in the interest of the Medes.[b].

CXLV. About the same time another great expedition was undertaken into Lybia; the causes of which I shall relate, after having explained the following things by way of introduction. The descendants of the Argonauts being expelled Lemnos by those Pelasgians who seized the Athenian women at Brauron[c], set sail for Lacedæmon, and having stationed themselves on Taygetes, lighted fires, which the Lacedæmonians having seen, dispatched a messenger to demand who they were, and whence they came: their answer was, that they were Minyæ, descendants of those heroes who sailed in the Argo, who having touched at Lemnos, begot them. When the Lacedæmonians heard their extraction, they sent another messenger to inquire with what design they had landed, and lighed fires in their territories: they said, that being ejected by the Pelasgians, they might justly return to the country of their ancestors, and therefore desired to inhabit in Laconia, and to participate of their honours and lands. The Lacedæmonians received the Minyæ on such terms as they desired, for divers reasons; and especially because Castor and Pollux, the sons of Tyndarus, had sailed in the Argo. They allotted to every man a certain portion of land, and distributed the whole number among their tribes. On the other part, the Minyæ gave the wives they brought from Lemnos to other men, and took Spartan women in their place.

CXLVI. But not long after they became insolent, and demanded a share in the sovereignty, and committed other crimes. Upon which, the Lacedæmonians having determined to punish them with death, seized and imprisoned all the Minyæ. But because by the customs of the country all condemned persons are executed in the night, and not by day, the wives of the Minyæ[d], who were daughters to the principal persons of Sparta,

[b] Herodotus and the greater part of ancient writers almost always comprehend the Persians under the name of Medes. *Larcher.*

Probably the principal purposes of the Scythian expedition were accomplished. The ambitious spirits among the Persians had been diverted from domestic disturbance. If the army suffered in the Scythian wilds, yet a large extent of valuable country, inhabited by different nations, was nevertheless added to the empire. New honours and new appointments were thus brought within the monarch's disposal. And the acquisition was perhaps not the less valuable from the circumstance that both the people of the newly acquired territory, and the people still bordering on it, were in disposition restless and fierce; and therefore likely to furnish employment for those whom the prince (himself safe in his distant capital) might wish to employ. Mitford's Greece, ch. vi. sect. 3.

[c] See book vi. ch. 188. Plutarch (de Virtut. Mulier. p. 247.) relates this circumstance with some variation.

[d] The same story is told by Plutarch, Polyænus, and Valerius Maximus, who adds, (book iv. ch. 6.) that they were allowed to pass with their heads covered on account of their pretended sorrow. The escape of Lavalette will occur to every reader.

asked leave to speak with their husbands in the prison before the execution. The Lacedæmonians, not suspecting fraud, granted their request; and the women being admitted accordingly, gave their own garments to their husbands, and clothed themselves with those of the men. Upon which the Minyæ dressed like women went out of the prison, and fled in that disguise to Taygetus.

CXLVII. At the same time Theras the son of Austesion, and grandson to Tisamenus, whose father Thersander was the son of Polynices, went out with a colony[e] from Lacedæmon. He was of the Cadmæan race[f], uncle by the mother's side[g] to Eurysthenes and Procles, sons of Aristodemus, and regent of the kingdom during their minority. But after they came to be of age, and had taken the administration of affairs into their hands, Theras, who had tasted the pleasure of commanding, impatient to see himself reduced to obey, declared his resolution to depart from Sparta, in order to settle with those of his own blood. The island, now called Thera, and formerly known by the name of Callista, was then possessed by the posterity of Membliares, the son of Pæciles a Phœnician. For Cadmus the son of Agenor arriving there, in the search he made after Europa, either pleased with the beauty of the country, or moved by other reasons, left his kinsman Membliares with some Phœnicians in that island; and Callista had been in the possession of these Phœnicians eight generations before the arrival of Theras from Lacedæmon.

CXLVIII. To this place Theras went, accompanied by many persons drawn out of the Spartan tribes, not with design to expel the inhabitants, but to live among them in the closest friendship. And because the Lacedæmonians still persisted in their resolution to destroy the Minyæ, even after they had fled from the prison to Taygetus, he interceded for their lives, and promised he would transport them out of that country. Upon this assurance the Lacedæmonians conceded to his desires, and Theras departed with his company for Callista, in three galleys of thirty oars each, carrying some of the Minyæ with him, but not many; for the greater

[e] Ἔστελλε ἐς ἀποικίην: *ἑαυτὸν* is here understood, as also in ch. 148; another would have said *ἐστέλλετο*. *Reiske*. The Tragedians frequently use *στέλλειν* for *στέλλεσθαι*, *iter parare, proficisci*. You may also, both in this place and in ch. 148. suppose the construction to be *ἔστελλε λαὸν ἐς ἀποικίην*; but by the examples given by Brunck, in his Index to Sophocles, and Schneider in his Lexicon, the other interpretation is abundantly confirmed. In other writers the leader of the colony is said, *ἀποικίην στέλλειν, ἀποικίην ἄγειν*; the colonists, *ἐς ἀποικίην στέλλεσθαι* or *σταλῆναι*, as in ch. 159. *Schweigh.*

[f] He was the sixth descendant from Œdipus, and tenth from Cadmus. Callimach. Hymn. in Apoll. ver. 74.

[g] Argeia the mother of Eurysthenes, and Procles was sister to Theras.

part had already entered into the countries of the Paroreatæ and Caucones; where, after they had driven out the inhabitants, they distributed themselves into six divisions, and founded the cities of Leprium, Macistus, Phrixæ, Pyrgus, Epium, and Nudium; most of which have been destroyed in our time by the Eleans. Thera was given as a name to the island after the founder.

CXLIX. His son had refused to accompany him in his voyage, and he therefore said at his departure, that he would leave him as a sheep among wolves[h]: from which saying the young man was called Oiolycus, which name chanced to prevail. This Oiolycus was the father of Ægeus, from whom the Ægidæ, a principal tribe in Sparta, derive their name. The men of this tribe finding they had not the fortune to bring up their children, built a temple[i] by the admonition of an oracle, dedicated to the Furies of Laius and Œdipus; a similar thing afterwards occurred in Thera to those who were descended from these men.

CL. Thus far the Lacedæmonians and the Theræans agree; but of that part which remains, the Theræans only are the relaters. Grinus, say they, the son of Æsanius, one of the descendants of Theras, and king of the island Thera, went to Delphi in order to sacrifice a hecatomb. He was attended by divers citizens of the place, and among them by Battus son to Polymnestus, of the family of Euphemus, one of the Minyæ[k]; and whilst he consulted the oracle concerning other affairs, the Pythian admonished him to build a city in Lybia. But he answered, "I, O prince, am too old and too much "weighed down by years to move myself; therefore rather "command one of these young men to execute that order;" and as he said these words, he pointed to Battus. At that time so much passed. After their departure they slighted the oracle, because they had no knowledge of the situation of Lybia; nor durst adventure to send a colony upon so obscure an attempt.

CLI. For the space of seven years from this time, they had no rain[l] in Thera; during which period all the trees of the

h The saying of our Saviour in Matth. ch. x. ver. 16. may be here compared, "Behold, I send you forth as sheep in "the midst of wolves."

i The people of that tribe, since their children did not live, built for their own sake (this is the force of the middle verb) a temple, &c. The latter part of the chapter I conceive to be corrupt. *Schweigh.*

k Battus was not a descendant of Minyas; but Minyas having given his name to the people of Thessaly who followed Jason, all the Argonauts were called by that name. Jason himself was descended from Minyas by his mother Alcimede. So that Herodotus simply means that he was one of the Argonauts. *Larcher.*

l Οὐκ ὗε τὴν Θήρην. 'Ο θεὸς is here understood. *Schweigh.*

island, except one, had perished for want of moisture; the Theræans applied themselves again to the oracle, but the Pythian reproached them with not having sent a colony to Lybia. Thus seeing no remedy for their calamity, they dispatched certain persons to Crete, with orders to inquire, if any of the Cretans or of the strangers resident in that island had ever been in Lybia. These messengers, travelling from place to place, arrived in the city of Itanus; where having met with one Corobius, a dyer in purple, who assured them he had been driven by the winds to Lybia and to Platea[m], an island of Lybia, they persuaded him by the promise of a large recompence to go with them to Thera. At first the Theræans sent only a small number of men, under the conduct of Corobius, to this said island Platea; and they departed with all speed, to give an account of the place to the Theræans, leaving Corobius behind with provisions for about two months.

CLII. But these men staying away longer than the time appointed, Corobius was reduced to the last necessity; when a ship of Samos bound to Egypt, whose master was Colæus, arrived at the island, being driven thither by stress of weather; and after the Samians had been informed by Corobius of all things relating to this expedition, they left him subsistence for a year, and set sail from the island, wishing to recover the coast of Egypt; but on a sudden were carried away by an east wind, which never ceased, until they had passed the columns of Hercules, and arrived at Tartessus, under the conduct of some god. That port was at that time unfrequented[n]; so that at their return they gained from their cargo by far the most of any of the Grecians we know next to Sostratus the son of Laodamas of Ægina, for with him it is impossible for any one to contend. These Samians with the tenth part of their gain, amounting to six talents, made a bason of brass, resembling those of Argolis, and around it the heads of griffins project[o]. This they placed in the temple of Juno, supported by three colossal figures of brass, seven cubits in height, and resting on their knees. And on this occasion the Cyrenæans and Theræans contracted a great friendship with the Samians.

[m] This island is now called Bombe. *Rennel*, p. 609.

[n] This may appear to contradict book i. ch. 163. that the Phocæans were the first who caused Tartessus to be known to the Greeks. The Samians however were first acquainted with it, but did not discover it to other Greeks, and by that means kept to themselves the commerce of the place. *Larcher*.

[o] Πρόκροσσοί εἰσι. This word has given great trouble to interpreters; it occurs again in book vii. ch. 188. I have here followed the interpretation of Wesseling. Larcher translates it thus, "Des têtes de gryphons, l'une vis-a-vis "de l'autre." For a full explanation of the word, see the Ionic Lexicon of Portus.

CLIII. When those Theræans, who left Corobius in Platea, were returned home, with an account that they had taken possession of an island on the coast of Lybia, the Theræans resolved to send a colony thither, composed of men drawn out of all their districts, which were seven in number; and that every brother should cast lots with his brother to determine who should go; appointing Battus to be their king and leader, and commanding two galleys of fifty oars to be made ready for their transportation.

CLIV. These things are reported by the Theræans only: for what remains, we have the concurring testimony of the Cyrenæans; though they differ from the Theræans in the account of Battus, and relate the matter thus. Etearchus, say they, king of Axus, a city of Crete, after the death of his first wife, married another woman, who resolving to be effectually a stepmother to his daughter, whose name was Phronima, treated her in the most injurious manner; and besides an infinite number of other wicked contrivances, accused her at last of being unchase, and prevailed with her husband to believe the calumny. Etearchus, persuaded by his wife, formed a wicked design against his daughter; and sending for one Themison, a merchant of Thera, who was then at Axus, received him kindly, and compelled him to take an oath to serve him in any thing he should desire. When he had done this, he delivered his daughter to the merchant, and commanded him to drown her in the sea. Themison, grieved at the deceit of the oath he had been induced to swear, broke off the hospitality and acted in this manner. He received the king's daughter, and set sail: and when he was in the open sea, that he might satisfy the obligation of his oath, he let her down into the water with cords tied about her; and after he had drawn her up again, pursued his voyage to Thera.

CLV. Polymnestus, an eminent man in that island, took Phronima for his concubine, and after some time had a son by her, who, from his lisping and stammering voice[p], was named Battus, as the Theræans and Cyrenæans say; but I am of opinion he had another name[q], and that it was changed to Battus after his arrival in Lybia, pursuant to the answer of the Delphian oracle, and on account of the honour conferred upon him. For the Lybians call a king Battus; and therefore I conjecture that the Pythian prophetess, foreseeing he should be a king in Lybia, gave him that title in the Lybian lan-

[p] *Traulotes* consists in not being able to pronounce some particular letter. *Ischnophonia* in not being able to join quickly one syllable to another. Aristot. Problem. xi. 30.

[q] His proper name was Aristotle according to Callimachus (Hymn. in Apol. v. 76.) and his Scholiast. See also the Scholiast on Pindar Pyth. iv. ver. 10.

guage; having returned this answer, when, being grown a man, he came to consult the oracle concerning his speech;

> Battus! about thy voice inquire no more;
> Apollo sends thee to the Lybian shore,
> In wool abounding.

As if she had said in the language of Greece, *O king, about thy voice.* Battus answered, "I came to consult the oracle "about my voice, and the God requires things impossible, "commanding me to go to Lybia. I desire to know, with "what power, and with what numbers?" But when nothing could persuade the Pythian to give any other answer, and Battus found she repeated the same words again, he left the oracle, and returned to Thera.

CLVI. After this, fresh evils fell upon him and the other Theræans; and the people, not knowing whence their misfortunes came, sent again to Delphi to inquire concerning the cause, and received for answer, "That their affairs should "prosper better, if, with Battus, they would found Cyrene in "Lybia." Upon this admonition the Theræans dispatched Battus with two galleys of fifty oars each. These, since they had no other resource, sailed to Lybia, but afterwards returned home, where the Theræans having refused to receive them, or suffer the men to land, commanded them to resume their expedition. Thus compelled by necessity, they sailed again, and settled in an island of Lybia, called, as I said before, Platea, and reported to be of equal extent with the present city of Cyrene.

CLVII. After they had been two years in this place, and nothing turned out prosperously, they left one of their company behind, and the rest sailed to Delphi; and having approached the oracle, they addressed it, saying, that though they had settled in Lybia, yet the state of their affairs still continued the same; upon which they received the following answer from the Pythian:

> Strange! you should know wool-bearing Lybia's coast
> Better than I; you, who were never there.

When Battus and his companions heard this, and found they must return to Lybia, because the God would by no means permit them to abandon their enterprize, they departed, and arriving again in the island, took on board the man they had left there, and went to inhabit a country of Lybia, situate over against the island, and called Aziris, surrounded with most beautiful hills, and watered by two rivers running on each side.

CLVIII. Six years they continued in this region, and in

the seventh resolved to leave it, by the persuasion of the Lybians, who said they would shew them a better place. The Lybians conducted them from thence towards the west; and in order that they might not see the most beautiful country, as they passed through, they computed the hours of the day, so as to lead them through by night. The region is called by the name of Irasa: and when the Lybians had shewed them a fountain, accounted sacred[r] to Apollo, "Grecians," said they, "here you may inhabit conveniently, for here the heavens are open."

CLIX. Accordingly the Cyrenæans fixed their habitations in this place, and continued to be about the same number as at their arrival, during all the time of Battus, who reigned forty years, and that of his son Arcesilaus, who reigned sixteen. But under the reign of another Battus, their third king, surnamed the Happy, the Pythian encouraged all Grecians to undertake the voyage to Lybia, and join with the Cyrenæans, who invited them to an equal division of the country[s]. The words of the oracle were these;

Regret attends the man who comes too late
To share the lovely Lybia's fertile plains.

By these means a great multitude met together at Cyrene; the neighbouring Lybians with their king, whose name was Adicran, finding they were deprived of their possessions, and injuriously treated, sent an embassy to Egypt, with a tender of their submission to Apries king of that country; who, assembling a numerous army of Egyptians, sent them to attack Cyrene. But the Cyrenæans having drawn out their forces to the fountain Thetis in Irasa, fought and defeated the Egyptians, who not having before made trial of the Greeks, despised them, and were so destroyed, that few of them returned to Egypt; and the ill success of this expedition caused such discontent amongst that people, that they revolted against Apries.

CLX. Arcesilaus the son of Battus succeeded him; and in the beginning of his reign had so many contests with his

[r] This was probably the fountain Cyre, from which the town of Cyrene took its name. This may be the same fountain which Herodotus in the following chapter calls Thestis. Although this country is well watered, Cyre and Thestis may be two different names for the same stream. Thestis being the Lybian, Cyre the Greek name. *Larcher.*

[s] This province is named Pentapolis, from its having five towns of note in it, Cyrene, Barce, Ptolemais Bérenice and Tauchira; all of which not only exist at present under the form either of towns or villages, but it is remarkable that their names are scarcely changed from what we may suppose the pronunciation to have been among the Greeks. They are now called Kurin, Barca, Tollamata, Bernic and Taukera. *Rennel*, p. 611.

brothers[t], that they left the kingdom, and went to another place in Lybia; there with common counsel they founded the city of Barce, which bears the same name to this day; and whilst they were settling their new colony, persuaded the Lybians to revolt; but Arcesilaus led an army not only against the revolted Lybians, but also against those who had given them reception, which put them into such a consternation, that they fled to the eastern parts of Lybia. Arcesilaus pursued them till he arrived at Leucon; and there the Lybians, having resolved to attack him, fought the Cyrenæans successfully, and killed seven thousand heavy armed upon the spot. After this disaster Arcesilaus fell sick, and having taken a medicinal draught, was strangled by his brother Learchus. But his wife, whose name was Eryxo, revenged his death, and killed Learchus by stratagem[u].

CLXI. Battus the son of this Arcesilaus, a lame man, and not perfect in his feet, succeeding him in the kingdom, the Cyrenæans, on account of the disaster which had befallen them, sent to inquire of the Delphian oracle, under what form of government they might live most happily; and the Pythian in answer commanded them to take a man to settle their disturbances, from Mantinea[x] a city of Arcadia. The Cyrenæans did as they were instructed, and the Mantineans chose a man for that purpose, highly esteemed in their country, and known by the name of Demonax. This person arrived in Cyrene; and after he had fully informed himself of their affairs, divided the people into three tribes. The first consisted of the Theræans and their neighbours; the second of Peloponnesians and Cretans; and a third contained all the rest of the Islanders. And also, having selected for Battus certain sacred lands and priesthoods, he put all other things which had been peculiar to their kings, into the hands of the people.

CLXII. Things remained in this condition during the reign of Battus; but in the time of his son Arcesilaus great disorders arose about those honours. For Arcesilaus the son

[t] Perseus, Zacynthus, Aristomedon, and Lycus. Stephan. Byzant. voc. Βάρκη.

[u] According to Plutarch, (de Virtut. Mulier. p. 260.) Learchus was the friend, and not the brother of Arcesilaus, to whom he administered poison which caused a languor, and death ensued. He wished to marry Eryxo the widow. She shewed no repugnance, but said that she only wished to obtain the consent of her brothers. Her brothers designedly deferring to give an answer, she sent to invite him to come and enjoy her favours; since after that, her brothers could not oppose the marriage. Learchus came without any attendants. Eryxo had put in her bed her eldest brother Polyarchus, accompanied by two young men, armed with swords, who dispatched Learchus as soon as he appeared. *Larcher.*

[x] The Mantineans are said to have had excellent laws. Ælian, Hist. Var. ii. 22.

of the lame Battus and Pheretime, declaring he would not submit to the constitutions of Demonax, demanded back all the prerogatives his ancestors had enjoyed; and having raised a sedition on that occasion, he was defeated, and fled to Samos. His mother escaped to Salamis, a city of Cyprus, then in the possession of that Euelthon, who dedicated the curious censer at Delphi, which is deposited in the treasury of the Corinthians. Pheretime, after her arrival, desired Euelthon to assist her with an army, in order to re-establish her family in Cyrene; but he chose rather to present her with all other things, than to grant her the forces she demanded. Yet she accepted his presents; and said that this also was valuable, but that the giving her an army as she requested would be much more so. This she said at every present that was made. In the end, Euelthon gave her a golden spindle and distaff, with some wool attached; and finding she repeated her acknowledgment in the same terms, he told her, these were the most proper presents for women, and not armies.

CLXIII. In the mean time Arcesilaus continuing at Samos, was collecting men by a promise of a division of lands; and having by that means collected a numerous army, he sailed to Delphi, in order to consult the oracle concerning his return, and received the following answer from the Pythian: "Apollo grants you the dominion of Cyrene during "eight descents, down to the fourth Battus, and the fourth "Arcesilaus[y]; and exhorts you to aim at no more. Be contented therefore to live peaceably, when you return home: "and if you find a furnace full of amphoræ, do not cook "them, but let them float with the stream; but if you set "fire to the furnace, forbear to enter into a place bounded "with water on each side. Unless you observe this, you "shall certainly perish yourself, and the most beautiful bull[z]."

CLXIV. Arcesilaus, having received the answer of the

[y] The following are the eight generations of which the Pythia speaks:

	B. C.
Battus 1st. surnamed Οἰκιστής, the Founder, begun to reign	631
Arcesilaus 1st.	591
Battus 2nd. surnamed the Happy,	575
Arcesilaus 2nd. surnamed the Bad,	554
Battus 3rd. surnamed the Lame,	529
Arcesilaus 3rd	518
Battus 4th. surnamed the Beautiful,	464
Arcesilaus 4th	432

This last prince was killed B. C. 432. His son Battus endeavoured to ascend the throne, but was expelled by the Cyrenæans. *Larcher*.

[z] The Pythia seems to hint obscurely at Alazir, the father-in-law of Arcesilaus, who perished with him.

Pythian, took with him the forces he had collected in Samos; and returning to Cyrene, recovered the possession of his kingdom. But forgetting the counsel of the oracle, he demanded of the opposite party satisfaction for his expulsion: so that many were compelled to abandon their country; whilst others, falling into his hands, were sent to be executed in Cyprus. But these arriving in the port of Cnidus, were rescued by the people, and sent away safe to Thera. Several others who had fled into a large private tower belonging to Aglomachus, he surrounded with wood and burnt. Which he had no sooner done, than he understood the meaning of the oracle's command, *Not to cook the vessels he should find in the furnace;* and in that persuasion voluntarily departed from Cyrene, under violent apprehensions of his own death, predicted by the Pythian, as he supposed that Cyrene was the place bounded with water on all sides. He had a wife related to him in blood; and because she was daughter to Alazir king of the Barcæans, he retired to Barca, where some of the inhabitants, in conjunction with others of the exiled Cyrenæans, having seen him walking in the public place, killed both him and his father-in-law. Thus Arcesilaus disobeying the oracle, whether wilfully or otherwise, accomplished his own destiny.

CLXV. While Arcesilaus was living at Barce, and had worked out his own destruction, his mother Pheretime was enjoying at Cyrene all the honours of her son, exercising the same functions, and taking her seat in the council; but when she heard that he had been put to death at Barce, she fled to Egypt, because her son Arcesilaus had conferred some benefits on Cambyses the son of Cyrus, by putting Cyrene into his protection, and settling a tribute to be paid for an acknowledgment of their submission. When she arrived in Egypt, she approached Aryandes as a suppliant, and besought him to revenge the death of her son, who, she pretended had been killed, because he was a partizan of the Medes.

CLXVI. Aryandes had been constituted governor of Egypt under Cambyses, and in succeeding time was put to death by Darius for attempting to make himself equal to him. He had seen that Darius exceedingly desired to leave such a monument of himself as no king had done before; and he imitated him until he received the reward of his presumption. For after Darius had coined pieces of gold[a], refined to the utmost

[a] These pieces were called Darics. The Daric was equivalent to 20 drachmas. Harpocration and Suidas pretend that they did not derive their name from Darius, the father of Xerxes, but from another king of that name. *Larcher.*

perfection, Aryandes, governor of Egypt, caused the same to be imitated in the purest silver; and this Aryandian money is in high esteem to this day. But when Darius knew what he had done, he charged him with a design to rebel, and under that colour put him to death.

CLXVII. This Aryandes, in compassion to Pheretime, assisted her with all the forces of Egypt, both by land and sea; appointing Amasis, one of the Maraphian blood, to lead the land army, and Badres of Passargadian extraction to command the fleet. But before he gave orders for the departure of these forces, he sent a herald to Barce, to demand who they were that had assassinated Arcesilaus. All the Barcæans took it upon themselves; "for," they said, "they had suffered many injuries at his hands." And when Aryandes received their answer, he caused the army to march away with Pheretime. This was the pretended reason[b] for the war. But in my opinion he sent these forces to conquer the Lybians. For of the Lybian nations, which are many and different, few were subject to Darius, and the far greater part thought nothing about him.

CLXVIII. Beginning from Egypt the Lybians dwell as follows; the Adrymachidæ are the first people we find, and for the most part observe the usages of Egypt, only they clothe in the Lybian habit. Their wives wear a chain of brass[c] on each leg; when they comb their hair, if they happen to find a louse[d], they kill it with their teeth, in revenge of the bite they received, and then throw it away. In the observation of one custom they are singular; being the only people of all Lybia, who bring their virgins before marriage into the king's presence, that if he like any one above the rest, he lies with her[e]. These Adrymachidæ extend from the borders of Egypt to the port of Plynus.

CLXIX. The Giligammæ are next to these, and occupy the country towards the west as far as the island Aphrodisias[f].

See also Prideaux's Connections, part i. book 2.

[b] Πρόσχημα τοῦ λόγου; *velamentum et color sermonis, quo veritatem dissimulabant Persæ. Wesseling.*

[c] This custom is still observed among the greater part of the African nations. In the kingdom of Angola, (Historie des Voyages, tom. v.) the women wear below their knees circles of brass, which reach as far as the calf. *Larcher.*

[d] The Hottentots abound with all sorts of vermin, and especially lice of an immense size. These they eat, and argue that it is not at all wrong to eat those animals who eat them. Hist. des Voyages, tom. v.

[e] It is singular that a custom should have been introduced here, (in Britain,) which was too barbarous to obtain amongst more than one of the African tribes; and that a privilege reserved for the king *alone, there,* should be extended to every superior lord, *here,* in the quarter where the custom prevailed. *Rennel,* p 608.

[f] Now as this island was situated *beyond* the part of Cyrene, westward, there must needs be a mistake *here,* because a great part of the fertile and cultivated district of Cyrenaica, would otherwise be allotted to a Nomadic tribe. Possibly

In the midst of their coast the island of Platea is situate, which was colonized by the Cyrenæans; and the harbour of Menelaus, with the city of Aziris, built likewise by the same people, are on the continent. At this place the plant Silphium[g] is first found, and extends from the island of Platea, to the mouth of the Syrtis[h]. This people in their customs resemble the rest of the Lybians.

CLXX. The Asbystæ[i] are next adjoining to the Giligammæ, and inhabit a country lying to the westward above Cyrene. They possess no part of the coast, because the Cyrenæans are masters of the maritime places. They ride in four-horsed chariots[k] most of all the Lybians; and for the most part endeavour to imitate the manners of the Cyrenæans.

CLXXI. The Auschisæ are seated to the westward of the Asbystæ in a region situate above Barce, and extending to the sea by the country of Euesperides[l]. In the midst of the Auschisæ, the Cabales[m], a small nation, dwell and extend to Tauchira, a maritime city of Barce. Both these observe the same customs with those who dwell above Cyrene.

CLXXII. The next country to the westward of the Auschisæ is possessed by the Nasamones[n], a very numerous people. In summer they leave their cattle on the coast, and go up to the plains of Augila[o], in order to gather the fruit of the palm-trees, which abound in that place, and are all bearers without exception. There they take locusts[p], which, having

the island of *Drepanum*, near Derna, might be meant. *Rennel*, p. 609.

[g] This is generally considered to be a kind of laserpitium or assafœtida; a full description of it is given in the 36th vol. of the Memoires de l'Academ. des Belles Lettres, Hist. p. 18. Others suppose it to be a country, which takes its name from the plant which abounds in it.

[h] The Great Syrtis must be here meant, which is in the neighbourhood of Barce, and nearer Egypt than the Less Syrtis. *Larcher*.

For an account of the two Syrtis see Rennel's 23rd sect.

[i] Pliny places the Asbystæ, as well as the Masæ or Macæ, to the west of the Nasamones, and of course he is at variance with our author; but Strabo, with more probability, says, after the Nasamones, who are situated at the Greater Syrtis, and beyond Cyrene, are the Psylli, Gætuli and Garamantes. *Rennel*, p. 609.

[k] The custom of harnessing four horses to a chariot was borrowed by the Greeks from the Africans. See ch. 189.

[l] This country was very fertile, and Edrisi, p. 93, informs us there is a wood there, which, from his mentioning it, we may conclude is something remarkable. The history of the gardens, &c. are too well known to be repeated here; the town was afterwards called Berenice, in honor of the wife of Ptolemy. It is now called Bernic. *Larcher*; and *Rennel*, p. 611.

[m] Wesseling doubts whether this word ought to be Bacales. Rennel asks, whether they are the *Kabyles* of Shaw. See Shaw's Travels in Barbary, &c. ch. vi. p. 36, and Preface, p. 8.

[n] See book ii. ch. 32. As in later times, the boundaries of Carthagi and Cyrene met at the Philenian altars, situated at the innermost recesses of the Syrtis, it is evident that the Nasamones must have been dispossessed in their turn. Accordingly, in Ptolemy, we find them removed to the inland tract of Augela itself; in which Diodorus Siculus agrees. Lib. iii. ch. 3. *Rennel*, p. 613.

[o] The name of this place has not undergone the least change, for the exact situation of it see Rennel, p. 568.

[p] These animals are accurately described by Shaw, p. 187, &c.

dried in the sun, they reduce to powder, and infusing them in milk, compose a liquor for their drink. Every man, by the custom of the country, has divers wives, which they use, like the Massagetæ[q], in public, after they have set up a staff for a mark; when one of them marries for the first time, it is the custom that the bride on the first night should lay with all the guests in order, and that each should at the time give her whatever he may have brought from home. In their solemn oaths and divinations, they observe the following manner: when they swear, they lay their hands on the sepulchres of those who are generally esteemed to have been the most just and excellent persons among them: and when they would divine, they go to the tombs of their ancestors, and after certain prayers, they lie down to sleep, and ground their predictions upon the dreams they have at those times. In pledging their faith they drink out of each other's hand[r]; and if they have no liquid, the parties take up some dust from the ground and lick it.

CLXXIII. The Psylli[s] are the next adjacent people to the Nasamones, and were destroyed in this manner: all their country lies within the Syrtis, and is destitute of springs; and when the south wind had dried up all their reserves of water, they consulted together, and determined to make war against that wind; (I only repeat what the Lybians say;) and after they were arrived at the sands, the south wind blowing hard, buried them alive, and the Nasamoues took possession of their habitations.

CLXXIV. Above these, in a country abounding with wild beasts, live the Garamantes[t], who avoid the sight and society of all other men; they possess no warlike weapon, nor do they know how to defend themselves.

CLXXV. In the maritime places, situate to the westward, they have the Macæ[u] for their neighbours, who shave

q See book i. ch. 216.

r The ancient ceremony of the Nasamones to drink from each other's hands, in pledging their faith, is at present the only ceremony observed in the marriages of the Algerines. *Shaw*, p. 303.

s Pliny (Hist. Nat. vii. 2.) says that they were destroyed by the Nasamones. And it hence appears probable that the Nasamones circulated this story among their neighbours. The reputation which the Psylli had for charming serpents and curing their stings, is mentioned by several ancient authors. In India there are people who completely subdue the most venomous serpents, and have them entirely at command. See Rennel, p. 614.

t These people may clearly be made out to be the people of Fezzan; a considerable tract of inland country, between Tunis and Egypt. Its capital was Germa, or Garama. See Rennel, p. 615, and seq.

u Pliny confirms this situation generally, by placing the Masæ (as he writes the name) on the west of the Nasamones. According to the ideas of Herodotus, the Masæ ought to extend westward to the neighbourhood of the present Tripoly. *Rennel*, p. 621.

their heads so as to leave a tuft[x] of hair on the top; they suffer the middle hair to grow, but shave quite close on both sides: when they make war, they wear the skins of ostriches[y] for defensive armour. The river Cinyps runs through their country, rising in an eminence, called the Hill of the Graces, which is covered with trees, (though all the other parts I have mentioned are bare,) and distant two hundred stades from the sea.

CLXXVI. Next in situation are the Gindanes[z], whose wives, it is said, wear as many bands round their ancles as they have known men; and she who has the most of those bands is most esteemed, because she has had the greatest number of lovers.

CLXXVII. The promontory that advances from this country to the sea is possessed by the Lotophagi[a], who live altogether upon the fruit of the lotus, which is of equal bigness with that of the lentiscus, but exceedingly sweet, like the date. The inhabitants make wine of this fruit.

CLXXVIII. Next adjoining to the Lotophagi are the Machlyes, on that side which descends to the sea. They eat the fruit of the lotus[b]; but make less use of it than those I

[x] The prohibition in Levit. xix. 27. against the Israelites rounding *the corners of their heads, and marring the corner of their beards*, evidently refers to customs which must have existed among the Egyptians during their residence among that people; though it is now difficult to determine what those customs were. Herodotus informs us, (iii. 8.) that the Arabians shave or *cut their hair round* in honour of Bacchus, and (iv. 175.) that the Macians, a people of Lybia, cut their hair *round*, so as to leave a tuft on the top of the head: in this manner the Chinese cut their hair to the present day. This might have been in honour of some idol, and therefore forbidden to the Israelites. Horne's Introd. Crit. Study, vol. iii. p. 356.

[y] The Ethiopians use the same kind of skins as a defence. See book vii. ch. 70.

[z] It is not very clear what nation or people Herodotus intended by the Gindanes, but from very strong circumstances we conceive those of Gadamis to be meant. Gadamis (the Gadzamis of Reiske) is a well-known city and territory, situated in the road from Tunis to Agadez and Kasseena. *Rennel*, p. 623.

[a] It appears that the sea-coast between the two Syrtis was divided between the Macæ and Lotophagi, the latter of whom also possessed the island of Menix, (or Meninx,) now Jerba, and the coast beyond it, as far as the lake and river Tritonis, to the Machlyes, who touched on the inner part of the Lesser Syrtis. *Rennel*, p. 624.

[b] The tree or shrub that bears the lotus fruit is disseminated over the edge of the Great Desert, from the coast of Cyrene, round by Tripoly and Africa proper, to the borders of the Atlantic, to Senegal and the Niger. See Rennel's Enquiry on the subject of the Lotus, p. 626, and seq.

The lotos is very common in all the kingdoms which I visited, but is found in the greatest plenty on the sandy soil of Kaarta, Ludamor, and the northern parts of Bombarra; where it is one of the most common shrubs of the country. I had observed the same species at Gambia, and had an opportunity to make a drawing of a branch in flower. It bears small farinaceous berries, of a yellow colour, and delicious taste. The natives convert them into a sort of bread, by exposing them some days to the sun, and afterwards pounding them gently in a wooden mortar, until the farinaceous part of the berry is separated from the stone. The stones are afterwards put into a vessel of water and shaken about, so as to separate the meal which may

mentioned before. The Triton, a considerable river, runs along the borders of this country, and falls into the great lake Tritonis, in which the island of Phla[c] is situate. It is reported that an oracle was delivered to the Lacedæmonians to colonize this island.

CLXXIX. The following story is also related; when Jason had built the Argos at the foot of mount Pelion, and put a hecatomb on board, with a tripod of brass, he sailed round the coast of Peloponnesus, in order to go to Delphi. But endeavouring to double the cape of Malea, he was surprised by a violent storm blowing from the north, and driven to the coast of Lybia; where, before he could discern the shore, he found his ship engaged in the shallows of the lake Tritonis[d]. It is said, that while he was in great anxiety and doubts about getting out, a Triton appeared to him, and bid Jason give him the tripod, promising that he would both shew them the passage, and dismiss them safe and sound. Jason accepted the condition, and then the triton shewed him a passage out of the shallows, and placed the tripod in his own temple; which he had no sooner done, than he delivered an oracle from thence, declaring to Jason[e] and his companions, that when any of the descendants of those who were on board the Argos should be possessed of that tripod, fate had determined that a hundred Grecian cities should be built about the lake Tritonis: and when the neighbouring nations of Lybia were informed of this prediction, they concealed the tripod.

CLXXX. Next to these is the seat of the Ausenses[f],

still adhere to them; this communicates a sweet and agreeable taste to the water, and with the addition of a little pounded millet, forms a pleasant gruel, called *fondi*, which is the common breakfast in many parts of Ludamor, during the months of February and March. This fruit is collected by spreading a cloth upon the ground, and beating the branches with a stick. Park's Travels, p. 99.

An army may very well have been fed with the bread I have tasted, made of the meal of the fruit, as is said by Pliny to have been done in Lybia; and as the taste of the bread is sweet and agreeable, it is not likely the soldiers would complain of it. Ibid. p. 100. See Pliny, xiii. c. 17. Shaw's Travels, p. 226, &c. The descriptions of Shaw, Park, and Desfountaines perfectly agree amongst themselves, and also with those of the ancients.

c An island of the lake Tritonis is described by Diodorus Siculus (lib. iii. 67, and seq.) as abounding in gardens, &c. Shaw (p. 127. ed. 4to.) describes several islands, but one large one in particular, which he supposes to be the same as the Phla of our author, and that described by the Sicilian historian.

d Herodotus only knew the Greater Syrtis by the name of Syrtis, the less by that of the Lake Tritonis. We must, however, regard the lake Tritonis of Herodotus to be made up of the Lesser Syrtis and the lake of Lowdeah, or lake of Marks, united. See Shaw's Travels, p. 126. ed. 4to. See also Rennel's learned Inquiry, sect. 23.

e Apollonius Rhodius has made some alterations in this story. See book iv. from v. 1551 to v. 1617.

f We find no traces of this name in modern geography. Of the Machlyes and Maxyes, we meet with several that have some similarity. The Machryes of Ptolemy occupy a space between Gephes (perhaps the Gaffsa of Shaw) and Jovis Mons, i. e. a mountain to the N. N.E.

whose territories, together with those of the Machlyes, encompass the whole lake of Tritonis, and are separated by the river Triton. They let their hair grow on the fore part of their head, and the Machlyes behind. The Ausenses celebrate an annual festival to Minerva, in which the virgins, dividing themselves into two companies, engage in a combat with sticks and stones. This, they say, is done pursuant to ancient custom, in honour of a national goddess, called Minerva, and maintain, that all those who die of the wounds they receive in these combats, were not virgins. But before they leave off fighting, they with common consent adorn the most distinguished virgin with a Corinthian helmet, and a whole suit of Grecian armour, and place her in a chariot, and conduct her in triumph round the lake[g]. What decoration these virgins used before the Grecians dwelt near them I cannot affirm; but I conjecture they were such as the Egyptians use, and I am of opinion, that the shield and helmet were brought from Egypt into Greece. They say, Minerva was born of Neptune and the lake Tritonis; and that being discontented with her father on some occasion, she gave herself to Jupiter, who made her his daughter by adoption[h]. The men of his country have no wives appropriated to particular persons, but accompany with all women indifferently, after the manner of other animals. The men meet every third month, and if any boy has arrived at manhood, he is considered to be the son of that man whom he most resembles.

CLXXXI. Those then of the Lybian Nomades who live on the sea coast have been mentioned. Above these the inland parts abound in wild beasts; beyond which is a ridge of sand, stretching from the Egyptian Thebes to the columns of Hercules. After a journey of ten days in this brow pieces of salt are found in large lumps on hills, and at the top of each hill, from the midst of the salt, a cool and sweet water shoots out. Those who inhabit the parts adjacent to these springs are the last of all the Lybians on this side the deserts, and beyond the beasts of prey. Ten days' journey from Thebes the territories of the Ammonians[i] begin, who have a

of the lake Tritonis. His Machyni are placed towards the gulf of Adrumentum. These may possibly be meant for the Machlyes and Maxyes of Herodotus. The Machres of Leo, and Makaress of Shaw, at the northern part of the Lesser Syrtis, certainly agree with the supposed position of a part of the Maxyes. *Rennel*, p. 637.

[g] Τὴν λίμνην κύκλῳ. Κύκλῳ and πέριξ are put with an accusative case. So also in ch. 72. l. 23. *Schweighæuser*.

[h] This probably gave rise to the fable of her coming armed from the head of Jupiter.

[i] For a learned and accurate investigation on this subject, see Major Rennel's 21st section. He determines that Seewa, lately visited by Mr. Browne, answers decidedly to the Oasis of Ammon; and the remains found there appear to be those of the temple.

temple resembling that of Theban Jupiter. För, as I said before[i], the image of Jupiter, which is placed in the temple of Thebes, has the head of a ram. They have likewise a fountain, which in the morning is tepid; and growing cool about the time of full forum, becomes very cold about noon, and is then used in watering their gardens. As the day declines this cold gradually diminishes, till about the setting of the sun the water becomes tepid again, and continuing to increase in heat, boils at midnight, and bubbles up; and from that time to the morning cools by degrees. This fountain is called, *The Fountain of the Sun*[m].

CLXXXII. At the end of another journey of ten days, along the ridge of sand, there is a hill of salt[n], like that of the Ammonians, spouting out water in the same manner, and surrounded with habitations. The region goes by the name of Augila[o]; to this place the Nasamones go to gather the dates.

CLXXXIII. Ten days more bring a man to another hill of salt, with an eruption of water, and palm trees covering the adjacent lands, as in the places above mentioned. The country is inhabited by a very large nation, known by the name of Garamantes[p], who, after they have laid fresh earth upon the salt, sow their corn in that ground. From these to the Lotophagi the way is very short, being about thirty days journey. In that country there are oxen which are called *opisthonomi, or feeding backwards*. The horns of these animals are bent forward, and compel them to draw back as they feed. For they could not possibly go forward, because their horns must stick in the ground. In every thing else they are like other oxen, except only that their hide is harder and thicker[q]. These Garamantes are accustomed to sit in chariots, and hunt

[k] See book ii. ch. 54.

[l] This is described nearly in the same words by Diodorus Siculus, xvii. 50. See also Pliny, Hist. Nat. ii. 103. Quint. Curt. iv. 7. *Larcher*.

[n] Although it is improbable that either mountains, or beds of salt, should be placed in such order, yet we learn from Dr. Shaw that both hills and beds, or lakes of salt, do exist in the country between Tripoly and Mauretania; also that the soil is generally impregnated with it; and that it sends forth a great number of copious salt springs. Shaw, p. 228, and seq. We learn also from authorities, that there are vast lakes of salt in other parts of the country; and it would appear, that scarcely any country whatsoever contains so much salt, on its surface, as that region of Africa, which borders on the Mediterranean. Dr. Shaw enumerates three mountains of salt only; but Herodotus five. The Doctor went no farther eastward than the Lesser Syrtis; otherwise it is possible that he might have told us of more. We cannot refer either of the mountains of Shaw to any particular one of Herodotus. *Rennel*, p. 641.

[o] See chapter 172.

[p] Herodotus spoke before (ch. 174.) of those Garamantes who had a fixed abode, he here speaks of the Garamantes Nomandes. *Larcher*. Others are of opinion that some other name ought to be read either in this passage, or in the former.

[q] Larcher translates τριψις, *suppleness*. Schweighæuser and Schneider, *hardness*.

the Ethiopian Troglodytes[r]; who are reported to be swifter of foot than any other nation of which we have heard any stories related. The Troglodytes feed upon serpents and lizards, with many other kinds of reptiles: they speak a language which bears no resemblance to that of any other nation; but they screech like bats.

CLXXXIV. At the distance of about ten days' journey from the Garamantes, is seen another mound of salt, with a fountain issuing out of the summit. The adjacent parts are inhabited by the Atarantes, who are the only people, we know, destitute of names for each individual. For that of Atarantes[s] is the common appellation of all the people in conjunction; but there is no name to each individual. This people curse the sun as he passes over their heads; pursuing him with the vilest reproaches, because he consumes both the men and the country with his scorching heat. After a journey of ten days more, another hill of salt appears, with a spring like the former, and habitations of men in the adjoining region. In the neighbourhood of this place mount Atlas is situate; circular in form, and slender in circumference; but of so great a height, that his head is always invisible, being ever surrounded with clouds, both in summer and winter; and therefore by the inhabitants called, *The Pillar of Heaven*. From hence these men derive their name, and are called Atlantes[t]. They neither eat the flesh of any animal, nor ever have dreams.

CLXXXV. Thus far I have been able to set down the names of those nations that inhabit this ridge of sand; but cannot proceed farther, though they reach as far as, and even beyond, the columns of Hercules. In that ridge a mine of salt is found, after regular intervals of ten days' journey; and those parts are inhabited by men, who build their houses with lumps of this salt[u]. In these parts of Lybia no rain falls[x]; for

[r] These people derive their name from τρώγλη, *a cave*, and δύνω, *to go under, to enter*.

[s] There are great doubts about the reading of this word. The greater number of manuscripts have Atlantes. Mela, i. 8. refers what is here related of two different nations, to one only whom he calls Atlantes. See also Pliny, Hist. Nat. v. 8.

[t] Leo (Description of Africa, vii. p. 255.) relates that in the kingdom of Bornou, there is a country, in which the people profess no religion, but live like beasts, that their women and children are common, and each individual has no peculiar name. I am aware that Lybia is very far from Bornou, but since both people are African, it makes what is related by Herodotus probable. *Larch.*

[u] These appear to be the same with the Hummanians, or Hammanientes of Pliny, (v. 5.) and the Ammantes of Solinus. *Rennel*, p. 643.

[v] Gerrha, a town on the Persian gulf, (Strab. xvi.) inhabited by the exiled Chaldeans, was built of salt; the salt of the mountain Had-deffa, near lake Marks (Shaw, p. 229.) in Africa, is hard and white like stone. *Larcher.*

[x] In effect, Herodotus has spoken truly with respect to the houses of *salt*.

walls of salt could not stand long, if any rain should fall there. The salt which is dug out of these mines is of two colours, white and purple[y]. All above this ridge, tending to the south, and midland parts of Lybia, is utterly desert, without spring or beast, wood, rain, or any kind of moisture.

CLXXXVI. From Egypt to the lake Tritonis, the Lybians are breeders of cattle; they eat flesh, and drink milk; but abstain from the flesh of cows, for the same reason as the Egyptians, and will not keep swine. Nay, among the women of Cyrene, to taste the flesh of a heifer is accounted a crime, because they celebrate the fasts and festivals of the Egyptian Isis: neither will the Barcæan women taste the flesh either of swine in addition to that of heifers. And this is the state of things in those parts.

CLXXXVII. The Lybians who inhabit to the westward of the lake Tritonis[z] are not keepers of cattle, and do not observe the same customs, nor yet do to their children what the Nomades do. For many of the shepherds, though I cannot affirm the same of all, are accustomed, when their children attain to the age of four years, to burn their veins either on the crown or temples, with uncleaned sheep's wool; to the end that, during all the time of their lives, they may never be offended by pituitous defluxions[a] from the head. This, they say, is the cause of the perfect health they enjoy: and indeed the Lybians, of all the nations we know, are the most healthy; but whether from this or any other cause, I am unable to affirm with certainty. If convulsions seize the children, when they burn them, there is a remedy discovered; for by sprinkling goats' urine[b] they cure them. I repeat what the Lybians say.

CLXXXVIII. In their sacrifices, these Lybian Nomades use the following ceremonies. They cut off the ear of the victim, which they throw over the top of the building, as the

He also fixes the scene, in a tract where, says he, "it never rains." This remark is true of the country, generally, along the Mediterranean, between Africa *proper* (which ends at the Lesser Syrtis) and the Red sea; and more particularly in the *Jereed*, which is the tract bordering on the Syrtis, where the purple mountain stands. See also Shaw, p. 219. *Rennel*, p. 642.

[y] The salt of the mountain Had-deffa is as hard and solid as stone, and of a reddish and purple colour. Yet what is washed down from these precipices by the *dews*, attaineth another colour, becoming as white as snow, and losing that share of bitterness which is in the parent rock salt. Shaw, p. 229. See a farther account of the salt mountains and salines in pages 35, 116, and 230.

[z] Herodotus is here speaking generally, for the nearest people, (ch. 191.) the Ausenses, are Nomades. *Larcher*.

[a] The Scythians (Hippocrat. de Æribus, &c. p. 355.) apply fire to their shoulders, arms, stomachs, &c. on account of the moisture and relaxed state of their temperament; this operation dries up the excess of moisture in the joints, and renders them more free. *Larcher*.

[b] This remedy is excellent, and has the same effect as spirits of hartshorn which we use. *Larcher*.

first-fruits; and after that, they twist its neck. They sacrifice to no other deities than the sun and moon, which are universally worshipped by all the Lybians; but those who inhabit about the lake Tritonis, sacrifice also to Triton and Neptune[c], and principally to Minerva.

CLXXXIX. From these the Grecians received the apparel and ægis of Minerva's statues; except only, that in Lybia her habit is made of skins, and the fringes that hang below the ægis are thongs of leather, and not serpents. In all other respects it is adorned in the same manner; and even the name declares that the robe of the Palladion came from Lybia. For the Lybian women wear goats' skins[d] without the hair, fringed and stained with red around their garments. From these skins the Grecians gave the name of Ægis[e] to Minerva's shield; and I am inclined to think that the loud howlings which are uttered in the sacred rites, had the same original, because they are commonly used by the women of Lybia, and gracefully performed. The Grecians likewise learned from the Lybians the manner of harnessing four horses to their chariots.

CXC. All the Nomades inter the dead like the Grecians, except the Nasamones, who observe the time when the sick person is ready to expire, and then place him in a sitting posture, that he may not die with his face upward. Their houses are compactly made of the asphodel shrub, interwoven with rushes, and are portable. Such are the customs of these people.

CXCI. To the west of the river Triton, certain Lybians, who plough the earth, and are accustomed to live in houses, called Maxyes, border on the Ausenses. They wear long hair on the right side of the head, and shave the left. They paint the body with vermilion, and pretend to be of Trojan extraction. Their country, with all the rest of the western parts of Lybia, abounds more in woods and wild beasts than that of the Nomades; for the regions of Lybia that lie to the eastward, and are inhabited by herdsmen, are low and sandy, as far the river Triton: whereas, those that are possessed by

[c] Neptune was originally a Lybian God, and the Greeks derived him from that country, (Herodot. ii, 50.) The horse was consecrated to him, and the Mythologists assert that it was named by him. It appears to me very probable that the Phoenicians formerly landed in Africa, and were the first who managed horses: and the savage inhabitants of that part of the world, seeing them master that terrible element, and the most spirited of animals, regarded them as divinities. Perhaps also the Greeks have enveloped the same story in their fables. *Larcher.*

[d] Apollonius Rhodius, (iv. ver. 1347.) describes three Lybian women as clothed in those skins.

[e] From *αἴξ αἰγός, a goat,* the Greeks made *αἰγὶς αἰγίδος*, which signifies *a goat's skin,* and *the ægis of Minerva. Larcher.*

husbandmen, and situate beyond the river to the westward, are very mountainous, and abound in woods and beasts of prey. Serpents of incredible bigness are seen in this country, with lions, elephants, bears[f], aspics, and asses with horns; and the cynocephali, and the acephali[g], which, as the Lybians say, have eyes placed on their breasts, together with savages, both men and women, and many other wild beasts which are not fabulous[h].

CXCII. None of these things are seen among the Nomades; but others of the following kind: pygargi[i], goats, buffaloes, and asses, not of that kind which have horns but others that do not drink. They have likewise the orys[k], which is a wild beast, equal in bigness to a cow; and from the horns of this animal the Phœnicians make the frames of their citheræ. There are also bassaria[l], hyænas, porcupines, wild rams, dictyes[m], thoes[n], panthers, the boryes[o], and land

[f] Pliny (Hist. Nat. viii. 36.) pretends that Africa does not produce bears, although he gives us the annals of Rome, testifying that in the consulship of M. Piso and M. Messala, Domitius Ænobarbus gave, during his ædileship, public games, in which were an hundred Numidian bears. Lipsius (Elect. ii. ch. 1.) pretends, that these beasts were lions, and that this is the animal meant by the *Libystis ursa* of Virgil. Virgil mentions lions by their proper names in a hundred places. Shaw (p. 249.) enumerates bears among the animals he found in Africa. *Larcher.*

[g] Herodotus merely relates what the Lybians said. These cynocephali, whom the Africans considered as men with the heads of dogs, were a species of apes, remarkable for their boldness and ferocity. Mr. Bryant imagining that these people called themselves acephali, decomposes the word, which is purely Greek, and makes it come from the Egyptian *Ac-Caph-El*, which he interprets "the sacred rock of the sun." The same author (Analysis of Ancient Mythology, p. 340.) pretends with as much reason that cynocephali comes from *Cahen-Caph-El*, to which he assigns a similar interpretation. Here there seems to me a great deal of erudition thrown away. *Larcher.*

[h] These are opposed to the cynocephali, &c. above mentioned, whose existence he did not believe.

[i] Aristotle (Hist. Anim. vi. 6.) ranks this animal among the birds of prey. But as Herodotus here speaks only of quadrupeds, it is probable that this is one. Pliny also, (Hist. Nat. viii. 53.) mentions it among quadrupeds. Hardouin makes it a species of goat. See also Deuteronomy, ch. xiv. ver. 5. "The "hart, and the roebuck, and the fallow "deer, and the wild goat, and the pygarg, and the wild ox, and the chamois." *Larcher.*

Besides the common *gazell or antelope*, this country produces another species of the same shape and colour, though of the bigness of a roebuck, with horns sometimes two feet long. This, which the Africans call *lidmee*, may be the same with the strepsiceros and addace of the ancients. Bochart, from the supposed whiteness of the buttocks, finds great affinity between addace and dison, which, in Deut. xiv. 5. our translation, agreeably to the Septuagint and Vulgate versions, renders the pygarg. *Shaw*, p. 171.

[k] Pliny (Hist. Nat. xi. 44.) describes this as, "animal unicorne et bisulcum "oryx." Oppian, who had seen it, says the contrary. Aristotle (de Part. Anim. iii. 2.) classes it with the animals that have but one horn. Bochart latterly coincided with Damis an Arabian author, and supposed it to be a species of gazell. *Larcher.*

[l] This Larcher translates foxes. For Hesychius says the Cyrenæans called that animal Bassaris.

[m] It is not known what animal this is.

[n] This appears to be the Jackall. This name is derived from the Arabian name *Chathal*. See Shaw, p. 174, and seq.

[o] We are quite unacquainted with this animal.

crocodiles of about three cubits in length, very closely resembling lizards in shape, ostriches, and small serpents with one horn. These and all kinds of animals that live in other countries, except the stag and the wild boar[p], abound in the regions of the Nomades; but neither of those two are ever seen in any part of Lybia. They have three sorts of mice, some of which are called by the name of dipodes[q], or two-footed; some by that of zegeries[r], which is a Lybian name and means the same as the word signifying hills in Greek; and others are named echines. There are also weasels which breed in the Silphium, perfectly like those of Tartessus. So many are the wild beasts produced in the countries of the Lybian Nomades, according to the best information I could attain by the strictest and most diligent enquiry.

CXCIII. Next adjoining to the Maxyes, the Zaveces[s] are situate, whose wives drive their chariots in war.

CXCIV. Next to these are the Gyzantes[t], where abundance of honey is made by bees; and, they say, a much greater quantity by the artifice of men[u]. All these paint themselves with vermilion, and eat monkies, which are bred there in great numbers in the hills.

CXCV. The Carthaginians say, that an island called Cyraunis[x] lies near this people, inconsiderable in breadth, but comprehending two hundred stades in length, of easy access from the continent, and abounding in olive trees and vines. They add, that there is a lake in this island, from the mud of which the virgins of the country draw up gold dust with

[p] Aristotle (Hist. Anim. viii. 28.) agrees with Herodotus. Shaw (p. 176.) assures us that they abound there, and his testimony is confirmed by Sir James Bruce, (Travels to discover the Source of the Nile, vol. 4. p. 306.) *Larcher*.

[q] That remarkable disproportion betwixt the fore and the hinder legs of the jerboa, or δίπους, (though I never saw them run, but only stand or rest themselves upon the latter,) may induce us to take it for one of the δίποδες, or two-footed γάλαι, or rats which Herodotus and other authors describe as inhabitants of these countries. *Shaw*, p. 177.

Bruce has also described this animal, vol. v. p. 121.

[r] This rat burrows and throws up the earth, which presents the appearance of a hill. Hence its name. Beckmann on Arist. Mirab. Auscult. 26.

[s] There are no traces of this name in modern geography as far as we can learn. We must suppose them to have occupied the space between the Lesser Syrtis and the gulf of Adrumetum, since the Zygantes were next beyond them; and these are clearly the Zeugitanians of Pliny, being the inhabitants of the province which contained Carthage; and whose boundary began on the west, at the river Tusca, where Numidia ended. How far this province extended southward, we know not. *Rennel*, p. 637.

[t] This is in some editions Zygantes. Dr. Shaw, with much plausibility, conjectures that the name Zygantes or Zugantes, may have been derived from that of the town and mountain of Zow-aan or Zagwan, situated about 406 miles S.W. of Carthage. See p. 97, and seq.

[u] This is explained by Shaw, as it is in Algiers, and Tunis occasionally made of the palm tree, p. 143. See also 337, and seq.

[x] We can only suppose the islands of Querkyness or Kerkiness, the Cercina and Circinitis of the ancients to be meant. *Rennel*, p. 639.

feathers covered with pitch. I cannot affirm the fact to be true, but I write no more than they say; yet it is not impossible; for I have seen pitch drawn up out of a lake in the island of Zacynthus[y], which contains several lakes, the largest of which is seventy feet every way, and two fathoms in depth. They let down a pole into this lake, with a myrtle branch fastened to the end, and draw out pitch hanging about the myrtle, which has the smell of asphaltus, but is in other respects better than that of Pieria[z]. This they put into a pit prepared for that purpose near the lake, and when they have collected a great quantity, they pour it off into vessels. All that falls into the water passes under ground, and appears again upon the surface of the sea, which is about four stades distant from the lake. These things being so, the account given of the Lybian lake resembles the truth.

CXCVI. The Carthaginians farther say, that beyond the columns of Hercules there is a region of Lybia well inhabited; where, when they arrive, they unload their merchandize, and when they have set it in order on the shore they return to their ships, and make a great smoke: that the inhabitants, seeing the smoke, come down to the coast, and, leaving gold in exchange for the goods, depart again to some distance from the place: that the Carthaginians then going ashore, view the gold, and if the quantity seem sufficient for the goods, they take it up and sail away; but if it is not equivalent, they return to their ships and continue there: that the Lybians upon this come again, and lay down more gold to the former, until they have satisfied the merchants: that no wrong is done on either part[a], the Carthaginians never touching the gold before it is made adequate to the value of the merchandize, nor the inhabitants the merchandize before the other party have taken the gold.

[y] They still obtain pitch from a spring in this island which is now called Zante. See Chandler's Travels, ch. 79. and Spon. vol. i. p. 89.

[z] This was highly esteemed. Pliny (Hist. Nat. xiv. 20.) says, "Asia picem "Idæam maxime probat, Græcia Pei-"riam." So also Didymus. *Larcher*.

[a] At a certain time of the year (in the winter, if I am not mistaken,) they (the western Moors) make a journey in a numerous caravan, carrying with them coral and glass beads, bracelets of horn, knives and such like trinkets. When they arrive at the place appointed, which is on such a day of the moon, they find in the evening several different heaps of gold-dust lying at a small distance from each other, against which the Moors place so many of their trinkets as they judge will be taken in exchange for them. If the Nigritians the next morning approve of the bargain, they take up the trinkets and leave the gold-dust, or else make some deductions from the latter. In this manner they transact their exchange without seeing one another, or without the least instance of dishonesty or perfidiousness on either side. *Shaw*, p. 239.

Wadstrom relates the same of certain people, on the windward coast of Guinea. Cada Mosto (Hist. Voyages, v. 2.) relates that the people of Melli exchange in the same way salt for gold. *Larcher*.

CXCVII. And thus I have named all the people of Lybia I can; the greater part of which have paid no regard to the king of the Medes, either at that time or since. But I must add, that this country is inhabited by four several sorts of people, and no more, that we know: two of these are original inhabitants, and the other two are strangers. The Lybians and Æthiopians are indigenous, one of whom inhabits the northern, the other the southern parts of Lybia; but the Phoenicians and Greeks are strangers.

CXCVIII. Nevertheless in my opinion Lybia is not comparable to Asia or Europe in fertility, except the territories of Cinyps, which lies upon a river of the same name, and is equal to any other land in the production of corn, and altogether unlike the rest of Lybia; for the soil is black, and well watered with springs, secure from immoderate dryness, and never hurt by excessive wet, though some rain falls in that region. The measure of the produce of this land is the same as that of Babylon. The country of the Euesperides is likewise fruitful, yielding, when it is most fruitful, a hundred for one; but that of Cinyps about three hundred.

CXCIX. The territories of Cyrene are in situation higher than any other part of the country that belongs to the Nomades, and have three seasons worthy of admiration; for first the maritime places abound with fruits ready[b] for the harvest and vintage; and when these are gathered in, the fruits of the second region, which they call the hills, attain to maturity; and when these are collected, those of the highest part become ripe. So that when they have eaten and drank the first crop, the last is ready. Thus the Cyrenæans are eight months employed in collecting the productions of the land; and this may be sufficient to say concerning these things.

CC. The Persians, who were sent by Aryandes from Egypt to revenge the quarrel of Pheretime, arriving before Barce, laid siege to the city, demanding the surrender of those persons who had been concerned in the death of Arcesilaus; but the inhabitants having universally consented to the fact, refused to hearken to the message. Upon this they besieged Barce for nine months, during which they dug mines to the walls and made violent assaults. A worker of brass discovered their mines in this manner. He carried a shield of that metal round the city within the wall, and applying it to the ground, it made no noise where the earth was solid; but when he came to the parts that were undermined, the brass rung.

[b] Ὀργᾷ. This word indicates that the fruits were become mature. See Ruhnken on this word in the Lexicon of Timæus. *Larcher*.

Upon which discovery some of the Barcæans fell to countermining, and killed all the Persians who were employed in the mines. All assaults they repulsed.

CCI. Much time had been spent in the siege, many of the Barcæans were killed, and the loss of the Persians was no less considerable, when Amasis, general of the army, finding he could not succeed by force, resolved to reduce the city by fraud; and to that end contrived this stratagem. He opened a broad trench in the night, which he covered with slight planks of wood, and by spreading a surface of earth upon the timber, rendered that part even with the adjoining ground. Early the next morning he demanded a conference with the Barcæans, which they readily listened to, till at last they were willing to come to an accommodation; and accordingly a treaty was concluded on both sides, and confirmed by oath on that spot of ground which was undermined, importing, "That the "agreement should continue in force as long as the earth on "which they stood should remain in the present condition: "that the Barcæans should pay a competent tribute to the "king, and that the Persians should innovate nothing in "Barce." Under the faith of this treaty the Barcæans opening their gates, went frequently out of the city, and received all the Persians who desired to be admitted. The Persians hastily entered the walls after they had broken down the covering of the trench they had made; which they did, to free themselves from the obligation of the oath they had taken to the Barcæans, "That the treaty should subsist so long as the "earth on which they stood should continue in the same con"dition;" and supposed, that upon the alteration they had made in that place, they had likewise dissolved the force of their engagement.

CCII. When the Persians had put the power into the hands of Pheretime, she caused those who had been principally concerned in the death of Arcesilaus, to be empaled round the walls; and having cut off the breasts of their wives, affixed them[c] about the same places. She gave the pillage of the other inhabitants to the Persians, excepting only the Battiadæ, and those who had not participated in the murder; to these she entrusted the city.

CCIII. The Persians, after they had reduced the rest to servitude, marched away; and when they arrived in the territories of Cyrene, the Cyrenæans, in obedience to some oracle, permitted them to pass through the city. But as they passed, Bares, who commanded the naval forces, endeavoured

[c] The word περιέστιξε is most significant. It shews that the walls were studded with the breasts of the women. See ch. 2. note. *Wesseling.*

to persuade them to take the city; to which Amasis, general of the land army, would not consent, saying, he was sent against no other Grecian city than that of Barce. Nevertheless when they had marched through, and had arrived at the hill of the Lycæan Jupiter, they began to repent that they had not possessed themselves of Cyrene, and attempted to pass through a second time. But the Cyrenæans would not suffer them; and although no one attacked them, the Persians were struck with a panic[d]; and having retired in great haste as far as sixty stades from the place, they pitched their camp. In this camp they received an order of Aryandes for their return; and having desired a supply of provisions from the Cyrenæans, they obtained their request, and marched away towards Egypt. In their march they were continually harassed by the Lybians, who, to get their clothes and baggage, killed all they found left behind or straggling, until the army arrived in Egypt.

CCIV. The farthest point of Africa to which this Persian army penetrated was the country of the Euesperides. The Barcæan captives were sent from Egypt to king Darius, and by his command settled in a district of Bactria, which they afterwards called by the name of Barce; and the place is inhabited at this time.

CCV. Pheretime, however, did not close her life happily; for soon after she had taken revenge against the Barcæans, and had returned to Egypt from Lybia, she perished miserably; for while alive she was destroyed by worms[e] which issued from her body. So odious to the Gods are the excesses of human vengeance. Such and so exhorbitant was the cruelty exercised against the Barcæans by Pheretime the wife of Battus.

[d] The Greeks applied this term to all alarms which came upon men, without their being able to assign any cause. Eratosthenes (Catast. p. 10.) says, that the name was given, because Pan, in the war of the Titans, armed his allies with marine shells, the noise of which so frightened the Titans, that they fled. Plutarch (de Is. et Osirid. p. 356.) says, that the Pans and the Satyrs who dwelt near Chemmis, gave the first tidings of the death of Osiris, which spread terror over all the country. *Larcher.*

[e] Viva vermibus ebullivit.

This passage cannot fail to bring to mind the end of Herod the Great. Acts, ch. xii. v. 21, 22, 23.

END OF VOL. I.

Ingram Content Group UK Ltd.
Milton Keynes UK
UKHW022114200723
425532UK00005B/167